Basic St

Busines   omics

Douglas A. Lind

Coastal Carolina University and The University of Toledo

William G. Marchal

The University of Toledo

Samuel A. Wathen

Coastal Carolina University

McGraw-Hill

The McGraw-Hill Companies

McGraw-Hill
Irwin

BASIC STATISTICS FOR BUSINESS AND ECONOMICS

Published by McGraw-Hill/Irwin, a business unit of The McGraw-Hill Companies, Inc., 1221 Avenue of the Americas, New York, NY, 10020. Copyright © 2013, 2011, 2008, 2006, 2003, 2000, 1997, 1994 by The McGraw-Hill Companies, Inc. All rights reserved. Printed in the United States of America. No part of this publication may be reproduced or distributed in any form or by any means, or stored in a database or retrieval system, without the prior written consent of The McGraw-Hill Companies, Inc., including, but not limited to, in any network or other electronic storage or transmission, or broadcast for distance learning.

Some ancillaries, including electronic and print components, may not be available to customers outside the United States.

This book is printed on acid-free paper.

1 2 3 4 5 6 7 8 9 0 DOW/DOW 1 0 9 8 7 6 5 4 3 2

ISBN   978-0-07-131807-5
MHID   0-07-131807-0

Dedication

To Jane, my wife and best friend, and our sons, their wives, and our grandchildren: Mike and Sue (Steve and Courtney), Steve and Kathryn (Kennedy, Jake, and Brady), and Mark and Sarah (Jared, Drew, and Nate).

Douglas A. Lind

To Thalika and the Oum family. Welcome to our family.

William G. Marchal

To my wife, Barb.

Samuel A. Wathen

Over the years, we have received many compliments on this text and understand that it's a favorite among students. We accept that as the highest compliment and continue to work very hard to maintain that status.

The objective of *Basic Statistics for Business and Economics* is to provide students majoring in management, marketing, finance, accounting, economics, and other fields of business administration with an introductory survey of the many applications of descriptive and inferential statistics. We focus on business applications, but we also use many exercises and examples that relate to the current world of the college student. A previous course in statistics is not necessary, and the mathematical requirement is first-year algebra.

In this text, we show beginning students every step needed to be successful in a basic statistics course. This step-by-step approach enhances performance, accelerates preparedness, and significantly improves motivation. Understanding the concepts, seeing and doing plenty of examples and exercises, and comprehending the application of statistical methods in business and economics are the focus of this book.

The first edition of *Basic Statistics for Business and Economics* was published in 1994. In 1994, locating relevant business data was difficult. That has changed! Today, locating data is not a problem. The number of items you purchase at the grocery store is automatically recorded at the checkout counter. Phone companies track the time of our calls, the length of calls, and the identity of the person called. Credit card companies maintain information on the number, time and date, and amount of our purchases. Medical devices automatically monitor our heart rate, blood pressure, and temperature from remote locations. A large amount of business information is recorded and reported almost instantly. CNN, USA Today, and MSNBC, for example, all have websites that track stock prices with a delay of less than 20 minutes.

Today, skills are needed to deal with a large volume of numerical information. First, we need to be critical consumers of information presented by others. Second, we need to be able to reduce large amounts of information into a concise and meaningful form to enable us to make effective interpretations, judgments, and decisions. All students have calculators and most have either personal computers or access to personal computers in a campus lab. Statistical software, such as Microsoft Excel and Minitab, is available on these computers. The commands necessary to achieve the software results are available in a special section at the end of each chapter. We use screen captures within the chapters, so the student becomes familiar with the nature of the software output.

Because of the availability of computers and software, it is no longer necessary to dwell on calculations. We have replaced many of the calculation examples with interpretative ones, to assist the student in understanding and interpreting the statistical results. In addition, we now place more emphasis on the conceptual nature of the statistical topics. While making these changes, we still continue to present, as best we can, the key concepts, along with supporting interesting and relevant examples.

What's New in This Eighth Edition?

We have made changes to this edition that we think you and your students will find useful and timely.

- We have revised the learning objectives so they are more specific, added new ones, identified them in the margin, and keyed them directly to sections within the chapter.
- We have replaced the key example in Chapters 1 to 4. The new example includes more variables and more observations. It presents a realistic business situation. It is also used later in the text in Chapters 13 and 15.
- We have added or revised several new sections in various chapters:
  - Chapter 9 has been reorganized to make it more teachable and improve the flow of the topics.
  - Chapter 13 has been reorganized and includes a test of hypothesis for the slope of the regression equation.
  - Chapter 15 now includes a graphic test for normality and the chi-square test for normality.
- New exercises and examples use Excel 2010 screenshots and the latest version of Minitab. We have also increased the size and clarity of these screenshots.
- There are new Excel 2010 software commands and updated Minitab commands at the ends of chapters.
- We have carefully reviewed the exercises and added many new or revised exercises throughout. You can still find and assign your favorites that have worked well, or you can introduce fresh examples.
- Section numbers have been added to more clearly identify topics and more easily reference them.
- The exercises that contain data files are identified by an icon for easy identification.
- The Data Exercises at the end of each chapter have been revised. The baseball data has been updated to the most current completed season, 2010. A new business application has been added that refers to the use and maintenance of the school bus fleet of the Buena School District.
- There are many new photos throughout, with updated exercises in the chapter openers.

Chapter Learning Objectives

Each chapter begins with a set of learning objectives designed to provide focus for the chapter and motivate student learning. These objectives, located in the margins next to the topic, indicate what the student should be able to do after completing the chapter.

Chapter Opening Exercise

A representative exercise opens the chapter and shows how the chapter content can be applied to a real-world situation.

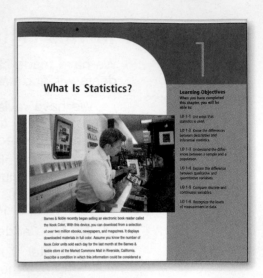

What Is Statistics?

Barnes & Noble recently began selling an electronic book reader called the Nook Color. With this device, you can download from a selection of over two million ebooks, newspapers, and magazines. It displays downloaded materials in full color. Assume you know the number of Nook Color units sold each day for the last month at the Barnes & Noble store at the Market Commons Mall in Riverside, California. Describe a condition in which this information could be considered a

Introduction to the Topic

Each chapter starts with a review of the important concepts of the previous chapter and provides a link to the material in the current chapter. This step-by-step approach increases comprehension by providing continuity across the concepts.

2.1 Introduction

The highly competitive automobile retailing industry in the United States has changed dramatically in recent years. These changes spurred events such as the:

- bankruptcies of General Motors and Chrysler in 2009.
- elimination of well-known brands like Pontiac and Saturn.
- closing of over 1,500 local dealerships.
- collapse of consumer credit availability.
- consolidation of dealership groups.

Traditionally, a local family owned and operated the community dealership, which might have included one or two manufacturers or brands, like Pontiac and GMC Trucks or Chrysler and the popular Jeep line. Recently, however, skillfully managed and well-financed companies have been acquiring local dealerships in large regions of the country. As these groups acquire the

Example/Solution

After important concepts are introduced, a solved example is given to provide a how-to illustration for students and to show a relevant business or economics-based application that helps answer the question, "What will I use this for?" All examples provide a realistic scenario or application and make the math size and scale reasonable for introductory students.

Example

Layton Tire and Rubber Company wishes to set a minimum mileage guarantee on its new MX100 tire. Tests reveal the mean mileage is 67,900 with a standard deviation of 2,050 miles and that the distribution of miles follows the normal probability distribution. Layton wants to set the minimum guaranteed mileage so that no more than 4% of the tires will have to be replaced. What minimum guaranteed mileage should Layton announce?

Solution

The facets of this case are shown in the following diagram, where X represents the minimum guaranteed mileage.

Self-Reviews

Self-Reviews are interspersed throughout each chapter and closely patterned after the preceding Examples. They reinforce important topics and provide students with immediate feedback regarding their comprehension of the topics.

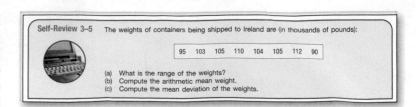

Self-Review 3–5 The weights of containers being shipped to Ireland are (in thousands of pounds):

| 95 | 103 | 105 | 110 | 104 | 105 | 112 | 90 |

(a) What is the range of the weights?
(b) Compute the arithmetic mean weight.
(c) Compute the mean deviation of the weights.

Statistics in Action

Statistics in Action articles are scattered throughout the text, usually about two per chapter. They provide unique and interesting applications and historical insights in the field of statistics.

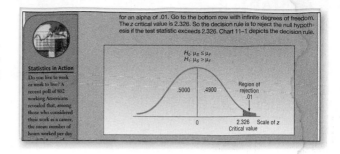

Margin Notes

There are more than 300 concise notes in the margin. Each is aimed at reemphasizing the key concepts presented immediately adjacent to it.

Definitions

Definitions of new terms or terms unique to the study of statistics are set apart from the text and highlighted for easy reference and review.

The variance is non-negative and is zero only if all observations are the same.

STANDARD DEVIATION The square root of the variance.

Variance and standard deviation are based on squared deviations from the mean.

Population Variance The formulas for the population variance and the sample variance are slightly different. The population variance is considered first. (Recall that a population is the totality of all observations being studied.) The **population variance** is found by:

Formulas

Formulas that are used for the first time are boxed and numbered for reference. In addition, a formula card is bound into the back of the text, which lists all the key formulas.

POPULATION VARIANCE	$\sigma^2 = \dfrac{\Sigma(X - \mu)^2}{N}$	[3–6]

Exercises

Exercises are included after sections within the chapter and at the end of the chapter. Section exercises cover the material studied in the section.

Exercises

connect

For Exercises 27–30, calculate the (a) range, (b) arithmetic mean, and (c) mean deviation and (d) interpret the values.

27. There were five customer service representatives on duty at the Electronic Super Store during last weekend's sale. The numbers of HDTVs these representatives sold are: 5, 8, 4, 10, and 3.

28. The Department of Statistics at Western State University offers eight sections of basic statistics. Following are the numbers of students enrolled in these sections: 34, 46, 52, 29, 41, 38, 36, and 28.

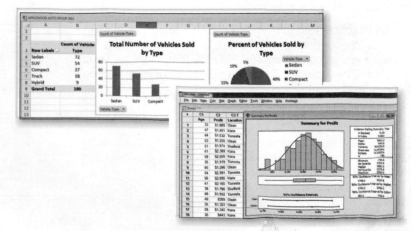

Computer Output

The text includes many software examples, using Excel, MegaStat®, and Minitab.

BY CHAPTER

Chapter Summary

Each chapter contains a brief summary of the chapter material, including the vocabulary and the critical formulas.

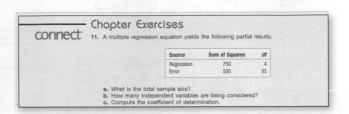

Chapter Summary

I. There are many reasons for sampling a population.
   A. The results of a sample may adequately estimate the value of the population parameter, thus saving time and money.
   B. It may be too time consuming to contact all members of the population.
   C. It may be impossible to check or locate all the members of the population.
   D. The cost of studying all the items in the population may be prohibitive.
   E. Often testing destroys the sampled item and it cannot be returned to the population.
II. In an unbiased or probability sample, all members of the population have a chance of being

Pronunciation Key

This tool lists the mathematical symbol, its meaning, and how to pronounce it. We believe this will help the student retain the meaning of the symbol and generally enhance course communications.

Pronunciation Key

SYMBOL	MEANING	PRONUNCIATION
μ	Population mean	mu
Σ	Operation of adding	sigma
ΣX	Adding a group of values	sigma X
$\bar{X}$	Sample mean	X bar

Chapter Exercises

Generally, the end-of-chapter exercises are the most challenging and integrate the chapter concepts. The answers and worked-out solutions for all odd-numbered exercises appear at the end of the text. For exercises with more than 20 observations, the data can be found on the text's website. These files are formatted so that they can be opened in Excel and Minitab.

connect

Chapter Exercises

11. A multiple regression equation yields the following partial results.

Source	Sum of Squares	df
Regression	750	4
Error	500	35

a. What is the total sample size?
b. How many independent variables are being considered?
c. Compute the coefficient of determination.

Data Set Exercises

The last several exercises at the end of each chapter are based on three large data sets. These data sets are printed in Appendix A in the text and are also on the text's website. These data sets present the students with real-world and more complex applications.

Data Set Exercises

49. Refer to the Real Estate data, which report information on the homes sold in Goodyear, Arizona, last year.
   a. At the .05 significance level, can we conclude that there is a difference in the mean selling price of homes with a pool and homes without a pool?
   b. At the .05 significance level, can we conclude that there is a difference in the mean selling price of homes with an attached garage and homes without an attached garage?
   c. At the .05 significance level, can we conclude that there is a difference in the mean selling price of homes in Township 1 and Township 2?
   d. Find the median selling price of the homes. Divide the homes into two groups, those that sold for more than (or equal to) the median price and those that sold for less. Is there a difference in the proportion of homes with a pool for those that sold at or above the median price versus those that sold for less than the median price? Use the .05 significance level.
   e. Write a summary report on your findings to parts (a), (b), (c), and (d). Address the report to all real estate agents who sell property in Goodyear.
50. Refer to the Baseball 2010 data, which report information on the 30 Major League Baseball teams for the 2010 season.
   a. At the .05 significance level, can we conclude that there is a difference in the mean payroll of teams in the American League versus teams in the National League?

Practice Test

The Practice Test that appears at the end of each chapter is intended to give students an idea of content that might appear on a test and how the test might be structured. The Practice Test includes both objective questions and problems covering the material studied in the chapter.

Part 1—Objective
1. A listing of the possible outcomes of an experiment and the probability associated with each outcome is called a _____.
2. The essential difference between a discrete random variable and a discrete probability distribution is that a discrete probability distribution includes the _____.
3. In a discrete probability distribution, the sum of the possible probabilities is always equal to _____.
4. The expected value of a probability distribution is also called the _____.
5. How many outcomes are there in a particular binomial trial? _____.
6. Under what
7. In a Poisson
8. The Poisson small.
9. Suppose taking the
10. The mean will be no

Part II—Problems
1. IRS data show that 15% of personal tax returns reporting an adjusted gross income more than $1,000,000 will be subject to a computer audit. This year a CPA completed 16 returns with adjusted gross incomes more than $1,000,000. The CPA wants to know the likelihoods that the returns will be audited.
   a. What probability distribution applies to this situation?
   b. What is the probability exactly one of these returns is audited?
   c. What is the probability at least one of these returns is audited?
2. For certain personal tax returns, the IRS will compute the amount to refund a taxpayer. Suppose the Cincinnati office of the IRS processes an average of three returns per hour that require a refund calculation.
   a. What probability distribution applies to this situation?
   b. What is the probability the IRS processes exactly three returns in a particular hour that require a refund calculation?
   c. What is the probability the IRS does not compute a refund on any return in an hour?
   d. What is the probability the IRS processes at least one return in a particular hour that requires a refund calculation?
3. A CPA studied the number of exemptions claimed on tax returns. The data are summarized in the following table.

Exemptions	Percent
1	20
2	50
3	20
4	10

a. What is the mean number of exemptions claimed?
b. What is the variance of the number of exemptions claimed?

Software Commands

Software examples using Excel, MegaStat®, and Minitab are included throughout the text, but the explanations of the computer input commands for each program are placed at the end of the chapter. This allows students to focus on the statistical techniques rather than on how to input data.

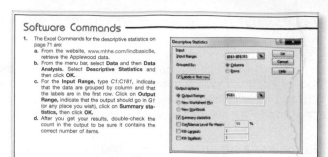

Answers to Self-Review

The worked-out solutions to the Self-Reviews are provided at the end of each chapter.

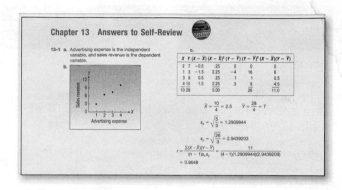

McGraw-Hill *Connect® Business Statistics*

McGraw-Hill *Connect Business Statistics* is an online assignment and assessment solution that connects students with the tools and resources they'll need to achieve success through faster learning, higher retention, and more efficient studying. It provides instructors with tools to quickly select content for assignments according to the topics and learning objectives they want to emphasize.

Online Assignments. *Connect Business Statistics* helps students learn more efficiently by providing practice material and feedback when they are needed. *Connect* grades homework automatically and provides instant feedback on any problems that students are challenged to solve.

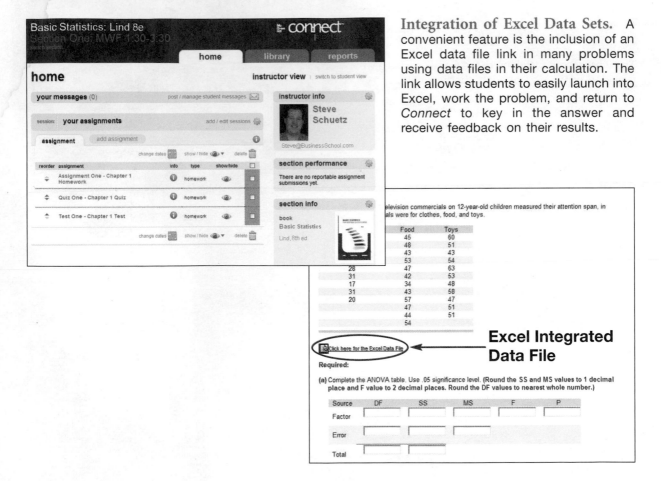

Integration of Excel Data Sets. A convenient feature is the inclusion of an Excel data file link in many problems using data files in their calculation. The link allows students to easily launch into Excel, work the problem, and return to *Connect* to key in the answer and receive feedback on their results.

Student Resource Library. The *Connect Business Statistics* Student Library is the place for students to access additional resources. The Student Library provides quick access to recorded lectures, practice materials, the eBooks, data files, PowerPoint files, and more.

Guided Examples.   These narrated video walkthroughs provide students with step-by-step guidelines for solving selected exercises similar to those contained in the text. The student is given personalized instruction on how to solve a problem by applying the concepts presented in the chapter. The narrated voiceover shows the steps to take to work through an exercise. Students can go through each example multiple times if needed.

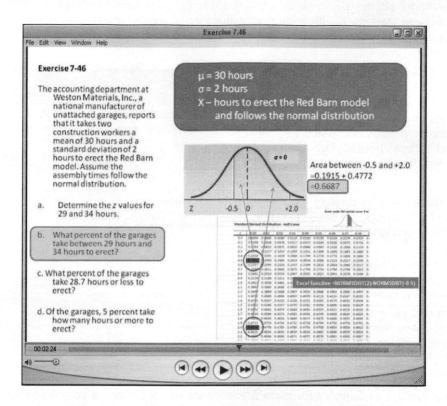

Simple Assignment Management and Smart Grading. When it comes to studying, time is precious. *Connect Business Statistics* helps students learn more efficiently by providing feedback and practice material when they need it, where they need it. When it comes to teaching, your time also is precious. The grading function enables you to:

- Have assignments scored automatically, giving students immediate feedback on their work and the ability to compare their work with correct answers.
- Access and review each response; manually change grades or leave comments for students to review.

Student Reporting. *Connect Business Statistics* keeps instructors informed about how each student, section, and class is performing, allowing for more productive use of lecture and office hours. The progress-tracking function enables you to:

- View scored work immediately and track individual or group performance with assignment and grade reports.
- Access an instant view of student or class performance relative to topic and learning objectives.
- Collect data and generate reports required by many accreditation organizations, such as AACSB.

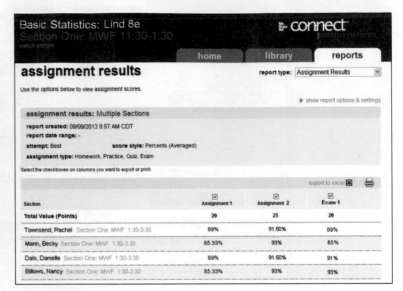

Instructor Library. The *Connect Business Statistics* Instructor Library is your repository for additional resources to improve student engagement in and out of class. You can select and use any asset that enhances your lecture. The *Connect Business Statistics* Instructor Library includes:

- eBook
- PowerPoint presentations
- Test Bank
- Instructor's Solutions Manual
- Digital Image Library

McGraw-Hill *Connect® Plus Business Statistics*

Connect Plus Business Statistics includes a seamless integration of an eBook and *Connect Business Statistics,* with rich functionality integrated into the product.

Integrated Media-Rich eBook. An integrated media-rich eBook allows students to access media in context with each chapter. Students can highlight, take notes, and access shared instructor highlights/notes to learn the course material.

Dynamic Links. Dynamic links provide a connection between the problems or questions you assign to your students and the location in the eBook where that problem or question is covered.

Powerful Search Function. A powerful search function pinpoints and connects key concepts in a snap. This state-of-the-art, thoroughly tested system supports you in preparing students for the world that awaits. For more information about *Connect,* go to www.mcgrawhillconnect.com or contact your local McGraw-Hill sales representative.

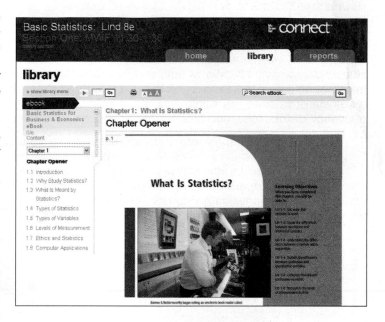

Tegrity Campus: Lectures 24/7

Tegrity Campus is integrated in *Connect* to help make your class time available 24/7. With Tegrity, you can capture your every lecture in a searchable format for students to review when they study and complete assignments using *Connect*. With a simple one-click start-and-stop process, you can capture everything that is presented to students during your lecture from your computer, including audio. Students can replay any part of any class with easy-to-use browser-based viewing on a PC or Mac.

Educators know that the more students can see, hear, and experience class resources, the better they learn. In fact, studies prove it. With *Tegrity Campus,* students quickly recall key moments by using *Tegrity Campus's* unique search feature. This search helps students efficiently find what they need, when they need it, across an entire semester of class recordings. Help turn all your students' study time into learning moments immediately supported by your lecture. To learn more about *Tegrity,* watch a two-minute Flash demo at http://tegritycampus.mhhe.com.

MegaStat® for Microsoft Excel®
2003, 2007, and 2010 (and Excel: Mac 2011)

CD ISBN: 0077496442
Note: The CD-ROM is for Windows users only.
Access Card ISBN: 0077426274
Note: Best option for both Windows and Mac users.

MegaStat® by J. B. Orris of Butler University is a full-featured Excel add-in that is available on CD and on the *MegaStat* website at www.mhhe.com/megastat. It works with Excel 2003, 2007, and 2010. On the website, students have 10 days to successfully download and install *MegaStat* on their local computer. Once installed, *MegaStat* will remain active in Excel with no expiration date or time limitations. The software performs statistical analyses within an Excel workbook. It does basic functions, such as descriptive statistics, frequency distributions, and probability calculations, as well as hypothesis testing, ANOVA, and regression.

MegaStat output is carefully formatted and ease-of-use features include Auto Expand for quick data selection and Auto Label detect. Since *MegaStat* is easy to use, students can focus on learning statistics without being distracted by the software. *MegaStat* is always available from Excel's main menu. Selecting a menu item pops up a dialog box. *MegaStat* works with all recent versions of Excel, including Excel 2007 and Excel 2010. Screencam tutorials are included that provide a walkthrough of major business statistics topics. Help files are built in, and an introductory user's manual is also included.

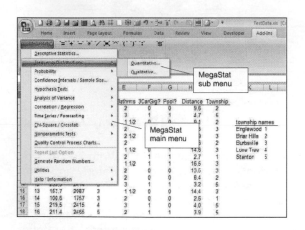

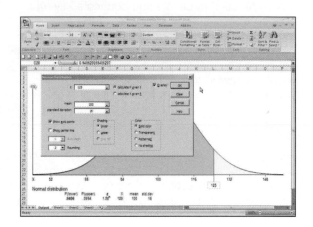

Minitab® (ISBN: 007305237X)
SPSS® (ISBN: 0077327144)
JMP® (ISBN: 007739030X)

Minitab® Student Version 14, SPSS® Student Version 18.0, and JMP® Student Edition Version 8 are software tools that are available to help students solve the business statistics exercises in the text. Each can be packaged with any McGraw-Hill business statistics text.

Instructor's Resources CD-ROM
(ISBN: 0077416759)

This resource allows instructors to conveniently access the Instructor's Solutions Manual, Test Bank in Word and EZ Test formats, Instructor PowerPoint slides, data files, and data sets.

Online Learning Center:
www.mhhe.com/lindbasic8e

The Online Learning Center (OLC) provides the instructor with a complete Instructor's Solutions Manual in Word format, the complete Test Bank in both Word files and computerized EZ Test format, Instructor PowerPoint slides, text art files, an introduction to ALEKS®, an introduction to McGraw-Hill *Connect Business Statistics*, access to Visual Statistics, and more.

All test bank questions are available in an EZ Test electronic format. Included are a number of multiple-choice, true/false, and short-answer questions and problems. The answers to all questions are given, along with a rating of the level of difficulty, the chapter goal that the question tests, Bloom's taxonomy question type, and the AACSB knowledge category.

McGraw-Hill Customer Experience Information

For Customer Support, call **800-331-5094** or visit www.mhhe.com/support. One of our Customer Experience Team members will be able to assist you in a timely fashion.

Online Course Management

McGraw-Hill Higher Education and Blackboard have teamed up. What does this mean for you?

1. **Single sign-on.** Now you and your students can access McGraw-Hill's *Connect*® and Create™ right from within your Blackboard course—all with one single sign-on.

2. **Deep integration of content and tools.** You get a single sign-on with *Connect* and Create, and you also get integration of McGraw-Hill content and content engines right into Blackboard. Whether you're choosing a book for your course or building *Connect* assignments, all the tools you need are right where you want them—inside of Blackboard.

3. **One grade book.** Keeping several grade books and manually synchronizing grades into Blackboard is no longer necessary. When a student completes an integrated *Connect* assignment, the grade for that assignment automatically (and instantly) feeds your Blackboard grade center.

4. **A solution for everyone.** Whether your institution is already using Blackboard of you just want to try Blackboard on your own, we have a solution for you. McGraw-Hill and Blackboard can now offer you easy access to industry-leading technology and content, whether your campus hosts it, or we do. Be sure to ask your local McGraw-Hill representative for details.

CourseSmart

CourseSmart is a convenient way to find and buy eTextbooks. CourseSmart has the largest selection of eTextbooks available anywhere, offering thousands of the most commonly adopted textbooks from a wide variety of higher-education publishers. CourseSmart eTextbooks are available in one standard online reader with full text search, notes and highlighting, and e-mail tools for sharing notes between classmates. Visit www.CourseSmart.com for more information on ordering.

ALEKS®

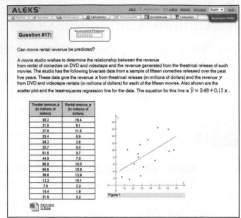

ALEKS is an assessment and learning program that provides individualized instruction in Business Statistics, Business Math, and Accounting. Available online in partnership with McGraw-Hill/Irwin, ALEKS interacts with students much like a skilled human tutor, with the ability to assess precisely a student's knowledge and provide instruction on the exact topics the student is most ready to learn. By providing topics to meet individual students' needs, allowing students to move between explanation and practice, correcting and analyzing errors, and defining terms, ALEKS helps students to master course content quickly and easily.

ALEKS also includes a new instructor module with powerful, assignment-driven features and extensive content flexibility. ALEKS simplifies course management and allows instructors to spend less time with administrative tasks and more time directing student learning. To learn more about ALEKS, visit www.aleks.com.

Online Learning Center:
www.mhhe.com/lindbasic8e

The Online Learning Center (OLC) provides students with the following content:

- Quizzes
- PowerPoint
- *Narrated PowerPoint
- *Screencam tutorials

- *Guided Examples
- Data sets/files
- Appendixes

*Available through *Connect*

Basic Statistics Using Excel 2010 (ISBN: 0077416821)

Connect®: One Semester Access Card (ISBN: 0077416716)

Connect Plus®: One Semester Access Card (ISBN: 0077416813)

This workbook introduces students to Excel and shows how to apply it to introductory statistics. It presumes no prior familiarity with Excel or statistics and provides step-by-step directions in a how-to style using Excel 2007 with text examples and problems.

Acknowledgments

This edition of *Basic Statistics for Business and Economics* is the product of many people: students, colleagues, reviewers, and the staff at McGraw-Hill/Irwin. We thank them all. We wish to express our sincere gratitude to the survey and focus group participants, and the reviewers:

Reviewers

Robert F. Abbey, Jr.
Troy University

Ram Acharya
New Mexico State University

Larry Ammann
University of Texas—Dallas

Hope Baker
Kennesaw State University

Doug Barrett
University of North Alabama

Doris Bennett
Jacksonville State University

Pam Boger
Ohio University

Kathy Broneck
Pima Community College

Derek Burnett
Loras College

Nancy Burnett
University of Wisconsin—Oshkosh

Stephanie Campbell
Mineral Area College

Deborah Carter
Coahoma Community College

Susan Carter
Doane College

Juan Castro
LeTourneau University

Gary Cummings
Walsh College

Robert Cutshall
Texas A&M University–Corpus Christi

Jeremy DalleTezze
Grove City College

Linda Dawson
University of Washington—Tacoma

Susanne Delaney
University of Arizona

Carol B. Diminnie
Angelo State University

Joe Easton
Pueblo Community College

Ronald Elkins
Central Washington University

Kathryn Ernstberger
Indiana University Southeast

Joseph Fuhr
Widener University

Marcel Fulop
Kean University

Edward Gallo
Sinclair Community College

Kemit Grafton
Oklahoma State University—Oklahoma City

Mary Gray
American University

Don Gren
Salt Lake Community College

Frank T. Griggs
Grand Valley State University

M. Ryan Haley
University of Wisconsin—Oshkosh

Janice Harder
Motlow State Community College

Richard Herschel
Saint Joseph's University

Lisa G. Jackson
Black River Technical College

Stacey Jones
Seattle University

Felix Kamuche
Morehouse College

Bruce Ketler
Grove City College

Melody Kiang
California State University—Long Beach

Bharat R. Kolluri
University of Hartford

Susan Lenker
Central Michigan University

Carel Ligeon
Auburn University—Montgomery

Constance Lightner
Fayetteville State University

Michael McLain
Hampton University

Stephen McMillion
Midlands Technical College

Kristen Monaco
California State University—Long Beach

Steve Montreal
Concordia University

Madhu Motha
Butler County Community College

Mihail Motzev
Walla Walla College

Alan W. Neebe
University of North Carolina

Pin Ng
Northern Arizona University

Joe Nowakowski
Muskingum College

John O'Neill
Siena College

Kevin Palmateer
Yakima Valley Community College

Kameliia Petrova
State University of New York—Plattsburgh

Darlene Riedemann
Eastern Illinois University

Yvonne Sandoval
Pima Community College, West

Otto B. Schacht
Wayland Baptist University

Xuguang Sheng
SUNY–Fredonia

Bongsik Shin
San Diego State University

Teresa Speck
Saint Mary's University of Minnesota

Courtenay C. Stone
Ball State University

Leonie Stone
State University of New York—Genneseo

Scott Stroher
Glendale Community College

Debbie Tesch
Xavier University

Jesus M. Valencia
Slippery Rock University

Samme Wallace-Ormiston
Otero Junior College

John W. Yarber, Jr.
Northeast Mississippi Community College

Survey and Focus Group Participants

Larry Ammann
University of Texas—Dallas

Scott Bailey
Troy University

Doug Barrett
University of North Alabama

Acknowledgments

Quidong Cao
Winthrop University

James Carden
University of Mississippi

Juan Castro
LeTourneau University

Joan Donahue
University of South Carolina

Chia-Shin Chung
Cleveland State University

Gary Cummings
Walsh College

Linda Dawson
University of Washington— Tacoma

Kathryn Ernstberger
Indiana University Southeast

Joseph Fuhr
Widener University

Alison Kelly Hawke
Suffolk University

Fred Hulme
Baylor University

L. Allison Jones-Farmer
Auburn University

John Landry
Metropolitan State College of Denver

Carel Ligeon
Auburn University—Montgomery

Ed Melnick
New York University

Carol Monroe
Baylor University

Khosrow Moshirvaziri
California State University—Long Beach

Maureen O'Brien
University of Minnesota— Duluth

J. Burdeane Orris
Butler University

Priya Rajagopalan
Purdue University

Mary Anne Rothermel
University of Akron

Paul Sen
University of North Florida

Murali Shanker
Kent State University

Debra Stiver
University of Nevada—Reno

Jesus Valencia
Slippery Rock University

Kathleen Whitcomb
University of South Carolina

Blake Whitten
University of Iowa

Bill Younkin
University of Miami

Xiaolong (Jonathan) Zhang
Georgia Southern University

Zhiwei (Henry) Zhu
University of Louisiana

Their suggestions and thorough reviews of the previous edition and the manuscript of this edition make this a better text.

Special thanks go to a number of people. Julia Norton of California State University–Hayward, Christopher Rogers of Miami Dade College, Carol Diminnie of Angelo State University, and Ed Pappanastos, Troy University, reviewed the manuscript and page proofs, checking exercises for accuracy. Samuel Wathen of Coastal Carolina University prepared the quizzes and the Test Bank. René Ordonez of Southern Oregon University prepared the PowerPoint presentation, screencam tutorials, and guided examples. Denise Heban and the authors prepared the Instructor's Solutions Manual.

We also wish to thank the staff at McGraw-Hill. This includes Steve Schuetz, Executive Editor; Wanda Zeman, Senior Development Editor; Diane Nowaczyk, Senior Project Manager; and others we do not know personally, but who have made valuable contributions.

Enhancements to *Basic Statistics for Business and Economics*, 8e

Changes Made in All Chapters and Major Changes to Individual Chapters:

- Changed Goals to Learning Objectives and identified the location in the chapter where the learning objective is discussed.
- Added section numbering to each main heading.
- Identified exercises where the data file is included on the text website.
- Revised the Major League Baseball data set to reflect the latest complete season, 2010.
- Revised the Real Estate data to ensure the outcomes are more realistic to the current economy.
- Added a new data set regarding school buses in a public school system.
- Updated screens for Excel 2010, Minitab, and MegaStat.
- Revised the core example in Chapters 1–4 to reflect the current economic conditions as it relates to automobile dealers. This example is also discussed in Chapter 13 and 15.
- Added a new section in Chapter 13 describing a test to determine whether the slope of the regression line differs from zero.
- Added updates and clarifications throughout.

Chapter 1 What Is Statistics?

- New photo and chapter opening exercise on the "Nook Color" sold by Barnes & Noble.
- New ordinal scale example based on rankings of states based on business climate.
- Census updates on U.S. population, sales of Boeing aircraft, and *Forbes* data in "Statistics in Action" feature.
- New chapter exercises 17 (data on 2010 vehicle sales) and 19 (ExxonMobil sales prior to the Deepwater Horizon, Gulf of Mexico oil spill.).

Chapter 2 Describing Data: Frequency Tables, Frequency Distributions, and Graphic Presentation

- New featured data set, Applewood Auto Group.
- New presentation of frequency tables, bar charts, and pie charts using the Applewood Auto Group data set.
- New presentation of Excel's PivotTable application, with emphasis on creating frequency and relative frequency tables and distributions, and bar charts, pie charts, and histograms.
- New self-review with data set (Barry Bonds's home runs).
- New exercises 45 (brides picking their wedding site) and 46 (revenue in the state of Georgia).

Chapter 3 Describing Data: Numerical Measures

- New data on averages in the introduction: average number of TV sets per home, average spending on a wedding, and the average price of a theater ticket.
- A new description of the calculation and interpretation of the population mean using the distance between exits on I-75 through Kentucky.
- A new description of the median using the time managing Facebook accounts.
- Updated example/solution on the population in Las Vegas.
- Update "Statistics in Action" on the highest batting average in Major League Baseball for 2010. It was Josh Hamilton of the Texas Rangers, with an average of .359.
- New chapter exercises 22 (real estate commissions), 53 (laundry habits), 58 (blood sugar numbers), 60 (public universities in Ohio), and 64 (Kentucky Derby payoffs).

Chapter 4 Describing Data: Displaying and Exploring Data

- New exercise 14 with 2010 salary data for the New York Yankees.
- New chapter exercise 26 (American Society of Peri-Anesthesia nurses component membership).

Chapter 5 A Survey of Probability Concepts

- New exercises 31 (number of successful field goal attempts), 52 (number of hits in a Major League Baseball game), 53 (winning a tournament), and 54 (winning *Jeopardy*).

Chapter 6 Discrete Probability Distributions

- New Self-Review 6–4.
- New exercises 34 (raffle ticket), 45 (scented body wash), and 50 (home foreclosures).

Chapter 7 Continuous Probability Distributions

- New Self-Review 7–2 (water consumption).
- New Self-Reviews 7–4 and 7–5 involving coffee temperature.
- New exercise 26 (SAT Reasoning Test).
- New exercise 29 (Hurdle Rate for economic investment).
- Several glossary updates and clarifications.

Enhancements to *Basic Statistics for Business and Economics, 8e*

Chapter 8   Sampling Methods and the Central Limit Theorem

- New exercise 44 (price of milk).

Chapter 9   Estimation and Confidence Intervals

- A new "Statistics in Action" describing EPA fuel economy.
- New separate section on point estimates.
- Integration and application of the central limit theorem.
- A revised simulation demonstrating the interpretation of confidence level.
- New presentation on using the *t* table to find *z* values.
- A revised discussion of determining the confidence interval for the population mean.
- Expanded section on calculating sample size.
- New exercises 12 (milk consumption), 29 (cost of apartments in Milwaukee), 43 (drug testing in the fashion industry), and 44 (survey of small-business owners regarding health care).

Chapter 10   One-Sample Tests of Hypothesis

- New Example/Solution involving airport parking.
- Revised Software Solution and explanation of *p*-values.
- New exercises 17 (daily water consumption), 19 (number of text messages by teenagers), 33 (household size in the United States), 47 (Super Bowl coin flip results), 52 (failure of gaming industry slot machines), 55 (study of the percentage of Americans that do not eat breakfast), and 58 (daily water usage).

Chapter 11   Two-Sample Tests of Hypothesis

- New exercises 15 (2011 New York Yankee salaries), 33 (consumer confidence survey), 35 (pets as listeners), 49 (business volume), and 50 (childrens' allowance).

Chapter 12   Analysis of Variance

- Revised the names of airlines in the one-way ANOVA example.
- New exercise 22 (flight times between Los Angeles and San Francisco), and 31 (investing).

Chapter 13   Correlation and Linear Regression

- Rewrote the introduction section to the chapter.
- Added a new section using the Applewood Auto Group data from Chapters 1 to 4.
- Added a section on testing the slope of a regression line.
- Added discussion of the regression ANOVA table with Excel examples.
- Rewrote and relocated the section on the coefficient of determination.
- Revised section on Transforming Data using the economic relationship between price and demand.
- New exercises 35 (transforming data), 36 (Masters prizes and scores), 43 (2010 NFL points scored versus points allowed), 44 (store size and sales), and 61 (airline distance and fare).

Chapter 14   Multiple Regression Analysis

- Rewrote the section on evaluating the multiple regression equation.
- More emphasis on the regression ANOVA table.
- Enhanced the discussion of the *p*-value in decision making.
- Added a separate section on qualitative variables in regression analysis.
- Added "Stepwise Regression."
- Added a summary problem at the end of the chapter to review the major concepts.

Chapter 15   Nonparametric Methods: Goodness-of-Fit Tests

- Reworked the Example/Solution on the chi-square goodness-of-fit test with equal cell frequencies (favorite meals of adults).
- Added a section and corresponding examples describing the goodness-of-fit test for testing whether sample data are from a normal population.
- Added a section and corresponding examples using graphical methods for testing whether sample data are from a normal population.

Brief Contents

Contents

Chapter

7 Continuous Probability Distributions   196

Chapter

8 Sampling Methods and the Central Limit Theorem   223

Chapter

9 Estimation and Confidence Intervals   256

Chapter

14 Multiple Regression Analysis   443

Chapter

15 Nonparametric Methods: Goodness-of-Fit Tests   497

What Is Statistics?

Barnes & Noble recently began selling an electronic book reader called the Nook Color. With this device, you can download from a selection of over two million ebooks, newspapers, and magazines. It displays downloaded materials in full color. Assume you know the number of Nook Color units sold each day for the last month at the Barnes & Noble store at the Market Commons Mall in Riverside, California. Describe a condition in which this information could be considered a sample. Illustrate a second situation in which the same data would be regarded as a population. (See Exercise 11 and LO 1-3.)

1.1 Introduction

More than 100 years ago, H. G. Wells, an English author and historian, suggested that one day quantitative reasoning will be as necessary for effective citizenship as the ability to read. He made no mention of business because the Industrial Revolution was just beginning. Mr. Wells could not have been more correct. While "business experience," some "thoughtful guesswork," and "intuition" are key attributes of successful managers, today's business problems tend to be too complex for this type of decision making alone.

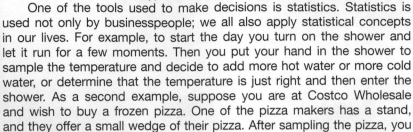

One of the tools used to make decisions is statistics. Statistics is used not only by businesspeople; we all also apply statistical concepts in our lives. For example, to start the day you turn on the shower and let it run for a few moments. Then you put your hand in the shower to sample the temperature and decide to add more hot water or more cold water, or determine that the temperature is just right and then enter the shower. As a second example, suppose you are at Costco Wholesale and wish to buy a frozen pizza. One of the pizza makers has a stand, and they offer a small wedge of their pizza. After sampling the pizza, you decide whether to purchase the pizza or not. In both the shower and pizza examples, you make a decision and select a course of action based on a sample.

Businesses face similar situations. The Kellogg Company must ensure that the mean amount of Raisin Bran in the 25.5-gram box meets label specifications. To do so, it sets a "target" weight somewhat higher than the amount specified on the label. Each box is then weighed after it is filled. The weighing machine reports a distribution of the content weights for each hour as well as the number "kicked-out" for being under the label specification during the hour. The Quality Inspection Department also randomly selects samples from the production line and checks the quality of the product and the weight of the contents of the box. If the mean product weight differs significantly from the target weight or the percent of kick-outs is too large, the process is adjusted.

As a student of business or economics, you will need basic knowledge and skills to organize, analyze, and transform data and to present the information. In this text, we will show you basic statistical techniques and methods that will develop your ability to make good personal and business decisions.

LO 1-1 List ways that statistics is used.

1.2 Why Study Statistics?

If you look through your university catalog, you will find that statistics is required for many college programs. Why is this so? What are the differences in the statistics courses taught in the Engineering College, the Psychology or Sociology Departments in the Liberal Arts College, and the College of Business? The biggest difference is the examples used. The course content is basically the same. In the College of Business we are interested in such things as profits, hours worked, and wages. Psychologists are interested in test scores, and engineers are interested in how many units are manufactured on a particular machine. However, all three are interested in what is a typical value and how much variation there is in the data. There may also be a difference in the level of mathematics required. An engineering statistics course usually requires calculus. Statistics courses in colleges of business and education usually teach the course at a more applied level. You should be able to handle the mathematics in this text if you have completed high school algebra.

So why is statistics required in so many majors? The first reason is that numerical information is everywhere. Look in the newspapers (*USA Today*), news magazines (*Time, Newsweek, U.S. News and World Report*), business magazines (*Bloomberg Businessweek, Forbes*), general interest magazines (*People*), women's

Examples of why we study statistics

magazines *(Ladies Home Journal* or *Elle),* or sports magazines *(Sports Illustrated, ESPN The Magazine),* and you will be bombarded with numerical information.
Here are some examples:

- Adjusting for inflation, the average hourly wage in May 2011 decreased $0.17 to $10.22 from the May 2010 average of $10.39.
- The average credit card debt per household is $9,858. The Federal Reserve Board estimates that 75% of Americans own at least one credit card.
- The following table summarizes the number of commercial aircraft ordered by Boeing Inc. customers between 2006 and 2010.

Orders for Boeing Aircraft						
Type of Aircraft						
Year	737	747	767	777	787	Total
2006	733	72	8	77	160	1,050
2007	850	25	36	143	369	1,423
2008	488	4	29	54	94	669
2009	197	5	7	30	24	263
2010	508	1	3	76	37	625

- **Go to the following website:** www.youtube.com/watch?v=pMcfrLYDm2U. It provides interesting numerical information about countries, business, geography, and politics.
- *USA Today* (www.usatoday.com) prints "Snapshots" that are the result of surveys conducted by various research organizations, foundations, and the federal government. The following chart summarizes what recruiters look for in hiring seasonal employees.

USA TODAY Snapshot

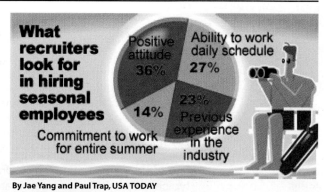

Recruiters look for positive attitude the most when hiring seasonal workers.

What recruiters look for in hiring seasonal employees

Positive attitude 36%
Ability to work daily schedule 27%
Previous experience in the industry 23%
Commitment to work for entire summer 14%

By Jae Yang and Paul Trap, USA TODAY
Source: SnagAJob.com
Reprinted with permission (April 29, 2010) USA TODAY.

A second reason for taking a statistics course is that statistical techniques are used to make decisions that affect our daily lives. That is, they affect our personal welfare. Here are a few examples:

- Insurance companies use statistical analysis to set rates for home, automobile, life, and health insurance. Tables are available showing estimates that a 20-year-old female has 60.25 years of life remaining, an 87-year-old woman 4.56 years remaining, and a 50-year-old man 27.85 years remaining. Life insurance premiums are established based on these estimates of life expectancy. These tables are available at www.ssa.gov/OACT/STATS/table4cb.html. [This site is sensitive to capital letters.]

- The Environmental Protection Agency is interested in the water quality of Lake Erie as well as other lakes. They periodically take water samples to establish the level of contamination and maintain the level of quality.
- Medical researchers study the cure rates for diseases using different drugs and different forms of treatment. For example, what is the effect of treating a certain type of knee injury surgically or with physical therapy? If you take an aspirin each day, does that reduce your risk of a heart attack?

A third reason for taking a statistics course is that the knowledge of statistical methods will help you understand how decisions are made and give you a better understanding of how they affect you.

No matter what career you select, you will find yourself faced with decisions where an understanding of statistics is helpful. In order to make an informed decision, you will need to:

1. Determine whether the existing information is adequate or additional information is required.
2. Gather additional information, if it is needed, in such a way that it does not provide misleading results.
3. Summarize the information in a useful and informative manner.
4. Analyze the available information.
5. Draw conclusions and make inferences while assessing the risk of an incorrect conclusion.

The statistical methods presented in the text will provide you with a framework for the decision-making process.

In summary, there are at least three reasons for studying statistics: (1) data are everywhere, (2) statistical techniques are used to make many decisions that affect our lives, and (3) no matter what your career, you will make professional decisions that involve data. An understanding of statistical methods will help you make these decisions more effectively.

1.3 What Is Meant by Statistics?

How do we define the word *statistics*? We encounter it frequently in our everyday language. It really has two meanings. In the more common usage, statistics refers to numerical information. Examples include the average starting salary of college graduates, the number of missed working days per year due to illness, the change in the Dow Jones Industrial Average from yesterday to today, and the number of home runs hit by the Chicago Cubs during the 2011 season. In these examples, statistics are a value or a percentage. Other examples include:

- The typical automobile in the United States travels 11,099 miles per year, the typical bus 9,353 miles per year, and the typical truck 13,942 miles per year. In Canada, the corresponding information is 10,371 miles for automobiles, 19,823 miles for buses, and 7,001 miles for trucks.
- The mean time waiting for technical support is 17 minutes.
- The unemployment rate for June 2011 is 9.2%.

These are all examples of **statistics.** A collection of numerical information is called **statistics** (plural).

We frequently present statistical information in a graphical form. A graph is often useful for capturing reader attention and to portray a large amount of information. For example, Chart 1–1 shows Frito-Lay volume and market share for the major snack and potato chip categories in supermarkets in the United States. It requires only a quick glance to discover there were nearly 800 million pounds of potato chips sold and that Frito-Lay sold 64% of that total. Also note that Frito-Lay has 82% of the corn chip market.

Statistics in Action

We call your attention to a feature title—*Statistics in Action*. Read each one carefully to get an appreciation of the wide application of statistics in management, economics, nursing, law enforcement, sports, and other disciplines.

- In 2010, *Forbes* published a list of the richest Americans. William Gates, founder of Microsoft Corporation, is the richest. His net worth is estimated at $54.0 billion. (www.forbes.com)

- In 2010, the four largest American companies, ranked by revenue, were Wal-Mart Stores, ExxonMobil, Chevron, and General Electric. (www.forbes.com)

- In the United States, a typical high school graduate earns $626 per week, a typical college graduate with a bachelor's degree earns $1,025 per week, and a typical college graduate with a master's degree earns $1,257. (www.bls.gov/emp/ep_chart_001.htm)

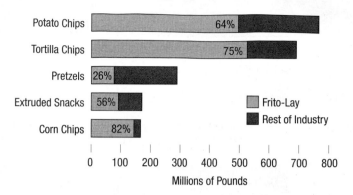

CHART 1–1 Frito-Lay Volume and Share of Major Snack Chip Categories in U.S. Supermarkets

The subject of statistics, as we will explore it in this text, has a much broader meaning than just collecting and publishing numerical information. We define statistics as:

> **STATISTICS** The science of collecting, organizing, presenting, analyzing, and interpreting data to assist in making more effective decisions.

As the definition suggests, the first step in using statistics is to collect relevant data. Only after the data have been organized and presented, such as in Chart 1–1, can we start to analyze and interpret them. Here are some examples of using statistics to support business decisions.

- Research analysts for Merrill Lynch evaluate many facets of a particular stock before making a "buy" or "sell" recommendation. They collect the past sales data of the company and estimate future earnings. Other factors, such as the projected worldwide demand for the company's products, the strength of the competition, and the effect of the new union–management contract, are also considered before making a recommendation.
- The marketing department at Colgate-Palmolive Co., a manufacturer of soap products, has the responsibility of making recommendations regarding the potential profitability of a newly developed group of face soaps having fruit smells, such as grape, orange, and pineapple. Before making a final decision, the marketers will test it in several markets. That is, they may advertise and sell it in Topeka, Kansas, and Tampa, Florida. On the basis of test marketing in these two regions, Colgate-Palmolive will make a decision whether to market the soaps in the entire country.
- Managers must make decisions about the quality of their product or service. For example, customers call software companies for technical advice when they are not able to resolve an issue regarding the software. One measure of the quality of customer service is the time a customer must wait for a technical consultant to answer the call. A software company might set a target of one minute as the typical response time. The company would then collect and analyze data on the response time. Does the typical response time differ by day of the week or time of day? If the response times are increasing, managers might decide to increase the number of technical consultants at particular times of the day or week.

1.4 Types of Statistics

The study of statistics is usually divided into two categories: descriptive statistics and inferential statistics.

LO 1-2 Know the differences between descriptive and inferential statistics.

Descriptive Statistics

The definition of statistics given earlier referred to "organizing, presenting, analyzing . . . data." This facet of statistics is usually referred to as **descriptive statistics.**

> **DESCRIPTIVE STATISTICS** Methods of organizing, summarizing, and presenting data in an informative way.

For instance, the United States government reports the population of the United States was 179,323,000 in 1960; 203,302,000 in 1970; 226,542,000 in 1980; 248,709,000 in 1990; 265,000,000 in 2000; and 308,400,000 in 2010. This information is descriptive statistics. It is descriptive statistics if we calculate the percentage growth from one decade to the next. However, it would *not* be descriptive statistics if we used these to estimate the population of the United States in the year 2020 or the percentage growth from 2010 to 2020. Why? The reason is these statistics are not being used to summarize past populations but to estimate future populations. The following are some other examples of descriptive statistics.

- There are a total of 46,837 miles of interstate highways in the United States. The interstate system represents only 1% of the nation's total roads but carries more than 20% of the traffic. The longest is I-90, which stretches from Boston to Seattle, a distance of 3,099 miles. The shortest is I-878 in New York City, which is 0.70 of a mile in length. Alaska does not have any interstate highways, Texas has the most interstate miles at 3,232, and New York has the most interstate routes with 28.
- The average person spent $103.00 on traditional Valentine's Day merchandise in 2010. This is an increase of $0.50 from 2009. As in previous years, men will spend nearly twice the amount women spend on the holiday. The average man spent $135.35 to impress the people in his life while women only spent $72.28. Family pets will also feel the love, the average person spending $3.27 on their furry friends, up from $2.17 last year.

Masses of unorganized data—such as the census of population, the weekly earnings of thousands of computer programmers, and the individual responses of 2,000 registered voters regarding their choice for president of the United States—are of little value as is. However, statistical techniques are available to organize this type of data into a meaningful form. Data can be organized into a **frequency distribution.** (This procedure is covered in Chapter 2.) Various **charts** may be used to describe data; several basic chart forms are also presented in Chapter 4.

Specific measures of central location, such as the mean, describe the central value of a group of numerical data. A number of statistical measures are used to describe how closely the data cluster about an average. These measures of central tendency and dispersion are discussed in Chapter 3.

Inferential Statistics

The second type of statistics is **inferential statistics**—also called **statistical inference.** Our main concern regarding inferential statistics is finding something about a population from a sample taken from that population. For example, a recent survey showed only 46% of high school seniors can solve problems involving fractions, decimals, and percentages; and only 77% of high school seniors correctly totaled the cost of a salad, burger, fries, and a cola on a restaurant menu. Since these are inferences about a population (all high school seniors) based on sample data, we refer to them as inferential statistics. You might think of inferential statistics as a "best guess" of a population value based on sample information.

> **INFERENTIAL STATISTICS** The methods used to estimate a property of a population on the basis of a sample.

Note the words *population* and *sample* in the definition of inferential statistics. We often make reference to the population of 308.8 million people living in the United States or the 1,336.1 million people living in China. However, in statistics the word *population* has a broader meaning. A **population** may consist of *individuals*—such as all the students enrolled at Utah State University, all the students in Accounting 201, or all the CEOs from the Fortune 500 companies. A population may also consist of *objects,* such as all the Cobra G/T tires produced at Cooper Tire and Rubber Company in the Findlay, Ohio, plant; the accounts receivable at the end of October for Lorrange Plastics, Inc.; or auto claims filed in the first quarter of 2010 at the Northeast Regional Office of State Farm Insurance. The *measurement* of interest might be the scores on the first examination of all students in Accounting 201, the tread wear of the Cooper Tires, the dollar amount of Lorrange Plastics's accounts receivable, or the amount of auto insurance claims at State Farm. Thus, a population in the statistical sense does not always refer to people.

> **POPULATION** The entire set of individuals or objects of interest or the measurements obtained from all individuals or objects of interest.

LO 1-3 Understand the differences between a sample and a population.

To infer something about a population, we usually take a **sample** from the population.

> **SAMPLE** A portion, or part, of the population of interest.

Reasons for sampling

Why take a sample instead of studying every member of the population? There are several reasons illustrated by the following examples. A sample of registered voters is necessary because of the prohibitive cost of contacting millions of voters before an election. Testing wheat for moisture content destroys the wheat, thus making a sample imperative. If the wine tasters tested all the wine, none would be available for sale. It would be physically impossible for a few marine biologists to capture and tag all the seals in the ocean. (These and other reasons for sampling are discussed in Chapter 8.)

As noted, using a sample to learn something about a population is done extensively in business, agriculture, politics, and government, as cited in the following examples:

- Television networks constantly monitor the popularity of their programs by hiring Nielsen and other organizations to sample the preferences of TV viewers. For example, in a sample of 800 prime-time viewers, 320, or 40%, indicated they watched *American Idol* on Fox last week. These program ratings are used to set advertising rates or to cancel programs.
- Gamous and Associates, a public accounting firm, is conducting an audit of Pronto Printing Company. To begin, the accounting firm selects a random sample of 100 invoices and checks each invoice for accuracy. There is at least one error on five of the invoices; hence, the accounting firm estimates that 5% of the population of invoices contain at least one error.

• A random sample of 1,260 marketing graduates from four-year schools showed their mean starting salary was $42,694. We therefore estimate the mean starting salary for all marketing graduates of four-year institutions to be $42,694.

The relationship between a sample and a population is portrayed below. For example, we wish to estimate the mean miles per gallon of SUVs. Six SUVs are selected from the population. The mean MPG of the six is used to estimate MPG for the population.

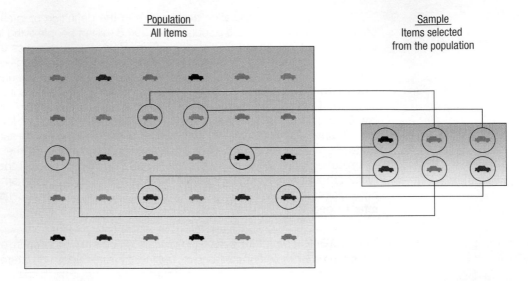

Population
All items

Sample
Items selected
from the population

We strongly suggest you do the Self-Review exercise.

Following is a self-review problem. There are a number of them interspersed throughout each chapter. They test your comprehension of the preceding material. The answer and method of solution are given at the end of the chapter. You can find the answer to the following Self-Review on page 20. We recommend that you solve each one and then check your answer.

Self-Review 1–1

The answers are at the end of the chapter.
The Atlanta-based advertising firm Brandon and Associates asked a sample of 1,960 consumers to try a newly developed chicken dinner by Boston Market. Of the 1,960 sampled, 1,176 said they would purchase the dinner if it is marketed.
(a) What could Brandon and Associates report to Boston Market regarding acceptance of the chicken dinner in the population?
(b) Is this an example of descriptive statistics or inferential statistics? Explain.

1.5 Types of Variables

Qualitative variable

LO 1-4 Explain the difference between qualitative and quantitative variables.

There are two basic types of variables: (1) qualitative and (2) quantitative (see Chart 1–2). When the characteristic being studied is nonnumeric, it is called a **qualitative variable** or an **attribute.** Examples of qualitative variables are gender, religious affiliation, type of automobile owned, state of birth, and eye color. When the data are qualitative, we are usually interested in how many or what percent fall in each category. For example, what percent of the population has blue eyes? What percent of the total number of cars sold last month were SUVs? Qualitative data are often summarized in charts and bar graphs (Chapter 2).

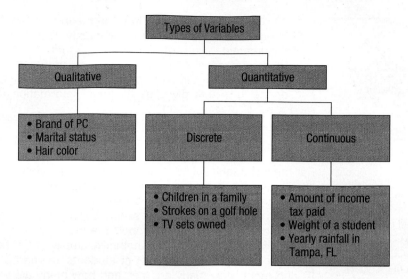

CHART 1–2 Summary of the Types of Variables

Quantitative variable

When the variable studied can be reported numerically, the variable is called a **quantitative variable.** Examples of quantitative variables are the balance in your checking account, the ages of company presidents, the life of an automobile battery (such as 42 months), and the number of children in a family.

LO 1-5 Compare discrete and continuous variables.

Quantitative variables are either discrete or continuous. **Discrete variables** can assume only certain values, and there are "gaps" between the values. Examples of discrete variables are the number of bedrooms in a house (1, 2, 3, 4, etc.), the number of cars arriving at Exit 25 on I-4 in Florida near Walt Disney World in an hour (326, 421, etc.), and the number of students in each section of a statistics course (25 in section A, 42 in section B, and 18 in section C). We count, for example, the number of cars arriving at Exit 25 on I-4, and we count the number of statistics students in each section. Notice that a home can have 3 or 4 bedrooms, but it cannot have 3.56 bedrooms. Thus, there is a "gap" between possible values. Typically, discrete variables result from counting.

Observations of a **continuous variable** can assume any value within a specific range. Examples of continuous variables are the air pressure in a tire and the weight of a shipment of tomatoes. Other examples are the amount of raisin bran in a box and the duration of flights from Orlando to San Diego. Grade point average (GPA) is a continuous variable. We could report the GPA of a particular student as 3.2576952. The usual practice is to round to 3 places—3.258. Typically, continuous variables result from measuring.

LO 1-6 Recognize the levels of measurement in data.

1.6 Levels of Measurement

Data can be classified according to levels of measurement. The level of measurement of the data dictates the calculations that can be done to summarize and present the data. It will also determine the statistical tests that should be performed. For example, there are six colors of candies in a bag of M&M's. Suppose we assign brown a value of 1, yellow 2, blue 3, orange 4, green 5, and red 6. For the bag of candies, we add the assigned color values and divide by the number of candies and report that the mean color is 3.56. Does this mean that the average color is blue or orange? Of course not! As a second example, in a high school track meet there are eight competitors in the 400-meter run. We report the order of finish and that the mean finish is 4.5. What does the mean finish tell us? Nothing! In both of these instances, we have not properly used the level of measurement.

There are actually four levels of measurement: nominal, ordinal, interval, and ratio. The lowest, or the most primitive, measurement is the nominal level. The highest, or the level that gives us the most information about the observation, is the ratio level of measurement.

Nominal-Level Data

For the **nominal level** of measurement, observations of a qualitative variable can only be classified and counted. There is no particular order to the labels. The classification of the six colors of M&M's milk chocolate candies is an example of the nominal level of measurement. We simply classify the candies by color. There is no natural order. That is, we could report the brown candies first, the orange first, or any of the colors first. Gender is another example of the nominal level of measurement. Suppose we count the number of students entering a football game with a student ID and report how many are men and how many are women. We could report either the men or the women first. For the nominal level, the only measurement involved consists of counts. Sometimes, for better reader understanding, we convert these counts to percentages. The following "Snapshot" from *USA Today* shows the results from a survey of workers. The variable of interest is "Perks" and there are five possible outcomes: "More money," "Better healthcare," "Better retirement," "Work/family balance," and, we will assume, "Other." The outcome "Other" is not shown on the chart, but is necessary to make the percent of respondents total 100%. There is no natural order to the outcomes. We could have put "Better healthcare" first instead of "More money."

To process the data, such as the information regarding worker perks, or information on gender, employment by industry, or state of birth of a student, we often numerically code the information. That is, we assign students from Alabama a code of 1, Alaska a code of 2, Arizona as 3, and so on. Using this procedure, Wisconsin is coded 49 and Wyoming 50. This coding facilitates counting by a computer. However, because we have assigned numbers to the various categories, this does not give us license to manipulate the numbers. To explain, 1 + 2 does not equal 3; that is, Alabama + Alaska does *not* yield Arizona.

To summarize, the nominal level has the following properties:

1. The variable of interest is divided into categories or outcomes.
2. There is no natural order to the outcomes.

USA TODAY Snapshot

03/15/2007-updated 11:51 PM ET

Workers say they prefer higher salaries to any other perks.

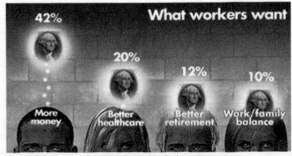

By Anne R. Carey and Chad Palmer, USA Today
Source: hudson-index.com
Reprinted with permission (March 15, 2007) USA TODAY.

Ordinal-Level Data

The next higher level of data is the **ordinal level.** Table 1–1 lists the student ratings of Professor James Brunner in an Introduction to Finance course. Each student in the class answered the question "Overall, how did you rate the instructor in this class?" The variable rating illustrates the use of the ordinal scale of measurement. One classification is "higher" or "better" than the next one. That is, "Superior" is better than "Good," "Good" is better than "Average," and so on. However, we are not able to distinguish the magnitude of the differences between groups. Is the difference between "Superior" and "Good" the same as the difference between "Poor" and "Inferior"? We cannot tell. If we substitute a 5 for "Superior" and a 4 for "Good," we can conclude that the rating of "Superior" is better than the rating of "Good," but we cannot add a ranking of "Superior" and a ranking of "Good," with the result being meaningful. Further, we cannot conclude that a rating of "Good" (rating is 4) is necessarily twice as high as a "Poor" (rating is 2). We can only conclude that a rating of "Good" is better than a rating of "Poor." We cannot conclude how much better the rating is.

TABLE 1–1 Rating of a Finance Professor

Rating	Frequency
Superior	6
Good	28
Average	25
Poor	12
Inferior	3

Best Business Climate

1. TEXAS
2. VIRGINIA
3. UTAH
4. SOUTH CAROLINA
5. TENNESSEE
6. NORTH CAROLINA
7. FLORIDA
8. LOUISIANA
9. SOUTH DAKOTA
10. WYOMING

Ordinal level data is also used to rank items in a list. For example, many businesses make decisions about where to locate their facilities, in other words, where is the best place for their business? Businesses rely on both qualitative and quantitative economic data to support these decisions. In fact, Business Facilities (www.businessfacilities.com) publishes a list of the top 10 states for the "best business climate." The 2010 rankings are shown to the left. It is based on their evaluation of 20 different factors, including the cost of labor, business tax climate, quality of life, transportation infrastructure, educated workforce, and economic growth potential.

This is an example of an ordinal scale, because we know the relative order of the states. For example, in 2010 Texas had the best business climate. Tennessee was fifth, and that was better than Florida but not as good as Utah. Notice that we cannot say that Texas's business climate is five times better than Tennessee's business climate, because the magnitude of the differences between the states is not known.

In summary, the properties of an ordinal level of measurement are:

1. Data are represented by an attribute. A student's rating of a professor and a state's "business climate" are examples.
2. The data can only be ranked or ordered, because the ordinal level of measurement assigns relative values such as high, medium, or low; or good, better, or best.

Interval-Level Data

The **interval level** of measurement is the next highest level. It includes all the characteristics of the ordinal level, but in addition, the difference between values is a constant size. The Fahrenheit temperature scale is an example of the interval level of measurement. Suppose the high temperatures on three consecutive winter days in Boston are 28, 31, and 20 degrees Fahrenheit. These temperatures can be easily ranked, but we can also determine the difference between temperatures. This is possible because 1 degree Fahrenheit represents a constant unit of measurement. Equal differences between two temperatures are the same, regardless of their position on the scale. That is, the difference between 10 degrees Fahrenheit and

15 degrees is 5, the difference between 50 and 55 degrees is also 5 degrees. It is also important to note that 0 is just a point on the scale. It does not represent the absence of the condition. Zero degrees Fahrenheit does not represent the absence of heat, just that it is cold! In fact 0 degrees Fahrenheit is about -18 degrees on the Celsius scale.

Another example of the interval scale of measurement is women's dress sizes. Listed below is information on several dimensions of a standard U.S. women's dress.

Size	Bust (in)	Waist (in)	Hips (in)
8	32	24	35
10	34	26	37
12	36	28	39
14	38	30	41
16	40	32	43
18	42	34	45
20	44	36	47
22	46	38	49
24	48	40	51
26	50	42	53
28	52	44	55

Why is the "size" scale an interval measurement? Observe as the size changes by 2 units (say from size 10 to size 12 or from size 24 to size 26) each of the measurements increases by 2 inches. To put it another way, the intervals are the same.

There is no natural zero point for dress size. A "size 0" dress does not have "zero" material. Instead, it would have a 24-inch bust, 16-inch waist, and 27-inch hips. Moreover, the ratios are not reasonable. If you divide a size 28 by a size 14, you do not get the same answer as dividing a size 20 by 10. Neither ratio is equal to two as the "size" number would suggest. In short, if the distances between the numbers make sense, but the ratios do not, then you have an interval scale of measurement.

The properties of the interval-level data are:

1. Data classifications are ordered according to the amount of the characteristic they possess.
2. Equal differences in the characteristic are represented by equal differences in the measurements.

Ratio-Level Data

Practically all quantitative data are recorded on the ratio level of measurement. The **ratio level** is the "highest" level of measurement. It has all the characteristics of the interval level, but in addition, the 0 point is meaningful and the ratio between two numbers is meaningful. Examples of the ratio scale of measurement include wages, units of production, weight, changes in stock prices, distance between branch offices, and height. Money is a good illustration. If you have zero dollars, then you have no money. Weight is another example. If the dial on the scale of a correctly calibrated device is at 0, then there is a complete absence of weight. The ratio of two numbers is also meaningful. If Jim earns $40,000 per year selling insurance and Rob earns $80,000 per year selling cars, then Rob earns twice as much as Jim.

Table 1–2 illustrates the use of the ratio scale of measurement. It shows the incomes of four father-and-son combinations.

TABLE 1–2 Father–Son Income Combinations

Name	Father	Son
Lahey	$80,000	$ 40,000
Nale	90,000	30,000
Rho	60,000	120,000
Steele	75,000	130,000

Observe that the senior Lahey earns twice as much as his son. In the Rho family, the son makes twice as much as the father.

In summary, the properties of the ratio-level data are:

1. Data classifications are ordered according to the amount of the characteristics they possess.
2. Equal differences in the characteristic are represented by equal differences in the numbers assigned to the classifications.
3. The zero point is the absence of the characteristic and the ratio between two numbers is meaningful.

Chart 1–3 summarizes the major characteristics of the various levels of measurement.

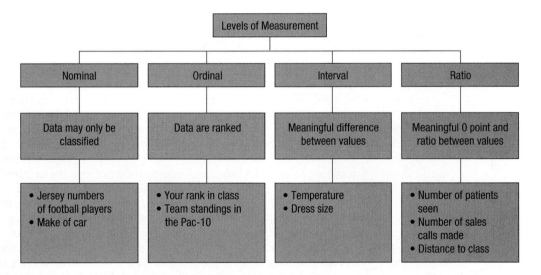

CHART 1–3 Summary of the Characteristics for Levels of Measurement

Self-Review 1–2

What is the level of measurement reflected by the following data?

(a) The age of each person in a sample of 50 adults who listen to one of the 1,230 talk radio stations in the United States is:

35	29	41	34	44	46	42	42	37	47
30	36	41	39	44	39	43	43	44	40
47	37	41	27	33	33	39	38	43	22
44	39	35	35	41	42	37	42	38	43
35	37	38	43	40	48	42	31	51	34

(b) In a survey of 200 luxury-car owners, 100 were from California, 50 from New York, 30 from Illinois, and 20 from Ohio.

Exercises

The answers to the odd-numbered exercises are at the end of the book.

1. What is the level of measurement for each of the following variables?
   a. Student IQ ratings.
   b. Distance students travel to class.
   c. The jersey numbers of a sorority soccer team.
   d. A student's state of birth.
   e. A student's academic class—that is, freshman, sophomore, junior, or senior.
   f. Number of hours students study per week.
2. The *San Francisco Chronicle* is a large newspaper published daily. What is the level of measurement for each of the following variables?
   a. The number of papers sold each Sunday during 2011.
   b. The departments, such as editorial, advertising, sports, etc.
   c. The number of papers sold by county.
   d. The number of years with the paper for each employee.
3. Look in the latest edition of *USA Today* or your local newspaper and find examples of each level of measurement. Write a brief memo summarizing your findings.
4. For each of the following, determine whether the group is a sample or a population.
   a. The participants in a study of a new cholesterol drug.
   b. The drivers who received a speeding ticket in Kansas City last month.
   c. Those on welfare in Cook County (Chicago), Illinois.
   d. The 30 stocks that make up the Dow Jones Industrial Average.

1.7 Ethics and Statistics

Following events such as Wall Street money manager Bernie Madoff's Ponzi scheme, which swindled billions from investors, and financial misrepresentations by Enron and Tyco, business students need to understand that these events were based on the misrepresentation of business and financial data. In each case, people within each organization reported financial information to investors that indicated the companies were performing much better than the actual situation. When the true financial information was reported, the companies were worth much less than advertised. The result was many investors lost all or nearly all of the money they put into these companies.

The article "Statistics and Ethics: Some Advice for Young Statisticians," in *The American Statistician* 57, no. 1 (2003), offers guidance. The authors advise us to practice statistics with integrity and honesty, and urge us to "do the right thing" when collecting, organizing, summarizing, analyzing, and interpreting numerical information. The real contribution of statistics to society is a moral one. Financial analysts need to provide information that truly reflects a company's performance so as not to mislead individual investors. Information regarding product defects that may be harmful to people must be analyzed and reported with integrity and honesty. The authors of *The American Statistician* article further indicate that when we practice statistics, we need to maintain "an independent and principled point-of-view."

As you progress through this text, we will highlight ethical issues in the collection, analysis, presentation, and interpretation of statistical information. We also hope that, as you learn about using statistics, you will become a more informed consumer of information. For example, you will question a report based on data that do not fairly represent the population, a report that does not include all relevant statistics, one that includes an incorrect choice of statistical measures, or a presentation that introduces the writer's bias in a deliberate attempt to mislead or misrepresent.

1.8 Computer Applications

Computers are now available to students at most colleges and universities. Spreadsheets, such as Microsoft Excel, and statistical software packages, such as Minitab, are available in most computer labs. The Microsoft Excel package is bundled with many home computers. In this text, we use both Excel and Minitab for the applications. We also use an Excel add-in called MegaStat. This add-in gives Excel the capability to produce additional statistical reports.

The following example shows the application of computers in statistical analysis. In Chapters 2, 3, and 4, we illustrate methods for summarizing and describing data. An example used in these chapters refers to profit, as well as other variables, on each of the 180 vehicles sold last month by the Applewood Auto Group. The following Excel output reveals, among other things, (1) there were 180 vehicles sold, the mean (average) profit per vehicle was $1,843.17, and the amount of profit ranged from $294 to $3,292.

APPLEWOOD AUTO GROUP 2011							
	A	B	C	D	E	F	G	H
1	Age	Profit	Location	Vehicle-Type	Previous		*Profit*	
2	33	$1,889	Olean	SUV	1			
3	47	$1,461	Kane	Sedan	0		Mean	1843.17
4	44	$1,532	Tionesta	SUV	3		Standard Error	47.97
5	53	$1,220	Olean	Sedan	0		Median	1882.50
6	51	$1,674	Sheffield	Sedan	1		Mode	1915.00
7	41	$2,389	Kane	Truck	1		Standard Deviation	643.63
8	58	$2,058	Kane	SUV	1		Sample Variance	414256.61
9	35	$1,919	Tionesta	SUV	1		Kurtosis	-0.22
10	45	$1,266	Olean	Sedan	0		Skewness	-0.24
11	54	$2,991	Tionesta	Sedan	0		Range	2998
12	56	$2,695	Kane	Sedan	2		Minimum	294
13	41	$2,165	Tionesta	SUV	0		Maximum	3292
14	38	$1,766	Sheffield	SUV	0		Sum	331770
15	48	$1,952	Tionesta	Compact	1		Count	180

The following output is from the Minitab system. It contains much of the same information.

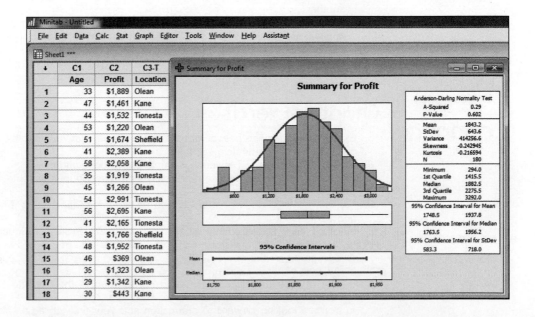

Had we used a calculator to arrive at these measures and others needed to fully analyze the selling prices, hours of calculation would have been required. The likelihood of an error in arithmetic is high when a large number of values are concerned. On the other hand, statistical software packages and spreadsheets can provide accurate information in seconds.

At the option of your instructor, and depending on the software system available, we urge you to apply a computer package to the exercises in the **Data Set Exercises** section in each chapter. It will relieve you of the tedious calculations and allow you to concentrate on data analysis.

Chapter Summary

I. Statistics is the science of collecting, organizing, presenting, analyzing, and interpreting data to assist in making more effective decisions.
II. There are two types of statistics.
   A. Descriptive statistics are procedures used to organize and summarize data.
   B. Inferential statistics involve taking a sample from a population and making estimates about a population based on the sample results.
      1. A population is an entire set of individuals or objects of interest or the measurements obtained from all individuals or objects of interest.
      2. A sample is a part of the population.
III. There are two types of variables.
   A. A qualitative variable is nonnumeric.
      1. Usually we are interested in the number or percent of the observations in each category.
      2. Qualitative data are usually summarized in graphs and bar charts.
   B. There are two types of quantitative variables and they are usually reported numerically.
      1. Discrete variables can assume only certain values, and there are usually gaps between values.
      2. A continuous variable can assume any value within a specified range.
IV. There are four levels of measurement.
   A. With the nominal level, the data are sorted into categories with no particular order to the categories.
   B. The ordinal level of measurement presumes that one classification is ranked higher than another.
   C. The interval level of measurement has the ranking characteristic of the ordinal level of measurement plus the characteristic that the distance between values is a constant size.
   D. The ratio level of measurement has all the characteristics of the interval level, plus there is a 0 point and the ratio of two values is meaningful.

Chapter Exercises

connect

5. Explain the difference between qualitative and quantitative variables. Give an example of qualitative and quantitative variables.
6. Explain the difference between a sample and a population.
7. Explain the difference between a discrete and a continuous variable. Give an example of each not included in the text.
8. For the following questions, would you collect information using a sample or a population? Why?
   a. Statistics 201 is a course taught at a university. Professor Rauch has taught nearly 1,500 students in the course over the past 5 years. You would like to know the average grade for the course.
   b. As part of a research project, you need to report the average profit as a percentage of revenue for the #1-ranked corporation in the Fortune 500 for each of the last 10 years.
   c. You are looking forward to graduation and your first job as a salesperson for one of five large pharmaceutical corporations. Planning for your interviews, you will need to know about each company's mission, profitability, products, and markets.

d. You are shopping for a new MP3 music player such as the Apple iPod. The manufacturers advertise the number of music tracks that can be stored in the memory. Usually, the advertisers assume relatively short, popular songs to estimate the number of tracks that can be stored. You, however, like Broadway musical tunes and they are much longer. You would like to estimate how many Broadway tunes will fit on your MP3 player.

9. Exits along interstate highways were formerly numbered successively from the western or southern border of a state. However, the Department of Transportation has recently changed most of them to agree with the numbers on the mile markers along the highway.
   a. What level of measurement were data on the consecutive exit numbers?
   b. What level of measurement are data on the milepost numbers?
   c. Discuss the advantages of the newer system.

10. A poll solicits a large number of college undergraduates for information on the following variables: the name of their cell phone provider (AT&T, Verizon, and so on), the numbers of minutes used last month (200, 400, for example), and their satisfaction with the service (Terrible, Adequate, Excellent, and so forth). What is the data scale for each of these three variables?

11. Barnes & Noble recently began selling an electronic book reader called the Nook Color. With this device, you can download over two million ebooks and newpapers and magazines. It displays downloaded materials in full color. Assume you know the number of Nook Color units sold each day for the last month at the Barnes & Noble store at the Market Commons Mall in Riverside, California. Describe a condition in which this information could be considered a sample. Illustrate a second situation in which the same data would be regarded as a population.

12. Utilize the concepts of sample and population to describe how a presidential election is unlike an "exit" poll of the electorate.

13. Place these variables in the following classification tables. For each table, summarize your observations and evaluate if the results are generally true. For example, salary is reported as a continuous quantitative variable. It is also a continuous ratio-scaled variable.
   a. Salary
   b. Gender
   c. Sales volume of MP3 players
   d. Soft drink preference
   e. Temperature
   f. SAT scores
   g. Student rank in class
   h. Rating of a finance professor
   i. Number of home computers

	Discrete Variable	**Continuous Variable**
Qualitative		
Quantitative		a. Salary

	Discrete	**Continuous**
Nominal		
Ordinal		
Interval		
Ratio		a. Salary

14. Using data from such publications as the *Statistical Abstract of the United States, The World Almanac, Forbes,* or your local newspaper, give examples of the nominal, ordinal, interval, and ratio levels of measurement.

15. The Struthers Wells Corporation employs more than 10,000 white collar workers in its sales offices and manufacturing facilities in the United States, Europe, and Asia. A sample of 300 United States workers revealed 120 would accept a transfer to a location outside the United States. On the basis of these findings, write a brief memo to Ms. Wanda Carter, Vice President of Human Services, regarding all white collar workers in the firm and their willingness to relocate.

16. AVX Stereo Equipment, Inc., recently began a "no-hassles" return policy. A sample of 500 customers who recently returned items showed 400 thought the policy was fair, 32 thought it took too long to complete the transaction, and the rest had no opinion. On the basis of this information, make an inference about customer reaction to the new policy.

17. The following table reports the number of cars and light duty trucks sold by the eight largest automakers in the first two months of 2010 compared to the first two months of 2009.

| | Year-to-Date Sales | |
Manufacturer	Through February 2010	Through February 2009
General Motors Corp.	287,242	252,701
Ford Motor Company	249,514	185,825
Chrysler LLC	141,592	146,207
Toyota Motor Sales USA Inc.	198,823	226,870
American Honda Motor Co. Inc.	148,150	142,606
Nissan North America Inc.	132,761	108,133
Hyundai Motor America	64,507	55,133
Mazda Motor of America Inc.	32,748	31,821

a. Compare the total sales for the eight automakers. Has there been an increase or a decrease in sales for 2010 compared to the same period in 2009?

b. Compute the market share for each of the companies. Has there been a large change in the market share for any of the companies?

c. Compute the percentage change in sales for each of the eight companies. Which companies had a significant change in sales?

18. The following chart depicts the average amounts spent by consumers on holiday gifts.

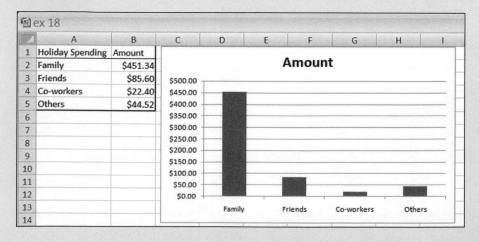

Write a brief report summarizing the amounts spent during the holidays. Be sure to include the total amount spent, and the percent spent by each group.

19. The following chart depicts the earnings in billions of dollars for ExxonMobil for the period 2003 until 2010. Write a brief report discussing the earnings at ExxonMobil during the period. Was one year higher than the others? Did the earnings increase, decrease, or stay the same over the period?

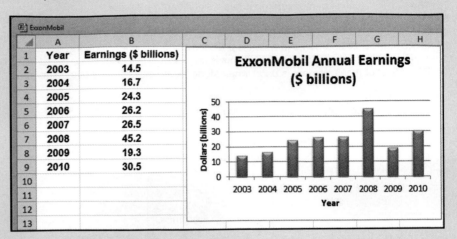

Data Set Exercises

(The data for these exercises are available at the text website www.mhhe.com/lindbasic8e).

20. Refer to the Real Estate data which report information on homes sold in the Goodyear, Arizona, area last year. Consider the following variables: selling price, number of bedrooms, township, and distance from the center of the city.
    a. Which of the variables are qualitative and which are quantitative?
    b. Determine the level of measurement for each of the variables.
21. Refer to the Baseball 2010 data, which report information on the 30 Major League Baseball teams for the 2010 season. Consider the following variables: number of wins, payroll, season attendance, whether the team is in the American or National League, and the number of home runs hit.
    a. Which of these variables are quantitative and which are qualitative?
    b. Determine the level of measurement for each of the variables.
22. Refer to the Buena School District bus data, which report information on the school district's bus fleet.
    a. Which of the variables are qualitative and which are quantitative?
    b. Determine the level of measurement for each variable.

Practice Test

There is a practice test at the end of each chapter. The tests are in two parts. The first part includes 10 to 15 objective questions, usually in a fill-in-the-blank format. The second part includes problems. In most cases, it should take 30 to 45 minutes to complete the test. The problems will require a calculator. Check your answers against those provided in Appendix C in the back of the book.

Part 1—Objective
1. The science of collecting, organizing, presenting, analyzing, and interpreting data to assist in making more effective decisions is referred to as _____.
2. Methods of organizing, summarizing, and presenting data in an enlightening way are called _____.
3. The methods used to estimate a value of a population on the basis of a sample are called _____.
4. A portion, or part, of the group of interest is referred to as a _____.

5. The entire set of individuals or objects of interest or the measurements obtained from all individuals or objects of interest is known as a _____.
6. With the _____ level of measurement, the data are sorted into categories with no particular order to the categories.
7. The _____ level of measurement has a significant zero point.
8. The _____ level of measurement presumes that one classification is ranked higher than another.
9. The _____ level of measurement has the characteristic that the distance between values is a constant size.
10. Is the number of bedrooms in a house a discrete or continuous variable? _____.
11. The jersey numbers on baseball uniforms is an example of the level _____ of measurement.
12. What level of measurement is used when students are classified by eye color? _____.

Part 2—Problems

1. Thirty million pounds of snack food were eaten during a recent Super Bowl Sunday. The chart below describes this information.

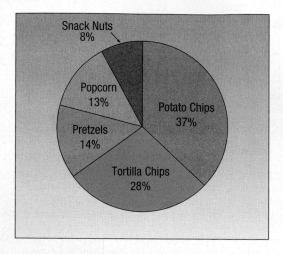

   a. Estimate, in millions of pounds, the amount of potato chips eaten during the game.
   b. Calculate approximately the ratio of potato chips consumed to popcorn consumed (twice as much, half as much, three times as much, etc.).
   c. What percent of the total consists of potato chips and tortilla chips?
2. There are 14 freshmen, 18 sophomores, 10 juniors, and 6 seniors enrolled in an introductory finance class. Answer the following questions.
   a. What is the level of measurement for this student data?
   b. What percent of the students are either freshmen or sophomores?

Chapter 1   Answers to Self-Review

1–1 a. On the basis of the sample of 1,960 consumers, we estimate that, if it is marketed, 60% of all consumers will purchase the chicken dinner $(1,176/1,960) \times 100 = 60\%$.
   b. Inferential statistics, because a sample was used to draw a conclusion about how all consumers in the population would react if the chicken dinner was marketed.

1–2 a. Age is a ratio-scale variable. A 40-year-old is twice as old as someone 20 years old.
   b. Nominal scale. We could arrange the states in any order.

Describing Data:

Frequency Tables, Frequency Distributions, and Graphic Presentation

Where We Stand

Global Markets & Investment Banking | Global Research | Global Wealth Management   🐻 **Merrill Lynch**

Merrill Lynch recently completed a study of online investment portfolios for a sample of clients. For the 70 participants in the study, organize these data into a frequency distribution. (See Exercise 43 and LO 2-4.)

Learning Objectives

When you have completed this chapter, you will be able to:

LO 2-1 Make a frequency table for a set of data.

LO 2-2 Organize data into a bar chart.

LO 2-3 Present a set of data using a pie chart.

LO 2-4 Create a frequency distribution for a data set.

LO 2-5 Understand a relative frequency distribution.

LO 2-6 Present data from a frequency distribution in a histogram or frequency polygon.

LO 2-7 Construct and interpret a cumulative frequency distribution.

2.1 Introduction

The highly competitive automobile retailing industry in the United States has changed dramatically in recent years. These changes spurred events such as the:

- bankruptcies of General Motors and Chrysler in 2009.
- elimination of well-known brands like Pontiac and Saturn.
- closing of over 1,500 local dealerships.
- collapse of consumer credit availability.
- consolidation of dealership groups.

Traditionally, a local family owned and operated the community dealership, which might have included one or two manufacturers or brands, like Pontiac and GMC Trucks or Chrysler and the popular Jeep line. Recently, however, skillfully managed and well-financed companies have been acquiring local dealerships in large regions of the country. As these groups acquire the local dealerships, they often bring standardized selling practices, common software and hardware technology platforms, and management reporting techniques. The goal of these new organizations is to provide an improved buying experience for the consumer, while increasing profitability. Megadealerships often employ over 10,000 people, generate several billion dollars in annual sales, own more than 50 franchises, and are traded on the New York Stock Exchange or NASDAQ. Today, the largest megadealership is AutoNation (ticker symbol AN). Others include Penske Auto Group (PAG and second largest), Asbury Automotive Group (ABG), and Hendrick Auto Group (which is privately held).

The Applewood Auto Group is an ownership group that includes four dealerships. The group sells a wide range of vehicles, including the inexpensive but popular Korean brands Kia and Hyundai, BMW and Volvo sedans and luxury SUVs, and a full line of Ford and Chevrolet cars and trucks.

Ms. Kathryn Ball is a member of the senior management team at Applewood Auto Group, which has its corporate offices adjacent to Kane Motors. She is responsible for tracking and analyzing vehicle sales and the profitability of those vehicles. Kathryn would like to summarize the profit earned on the vehicles sold with tables, charts, and graphs that she would review monthly. She wants to know the profit per vehicle sold, as well as the lowest and highest amount of profit. She is also interested in describing the demographics of the buyers. What are their ages? How many vehicles have they previously purchased from one of the Applewood dealerships? What type of vehicle did they purchase?

	A	B	C	D	E
1	Age	Profit	Location	Vehicle-Type	Previous
2	33	$1,889	Olean	SUV	1
3	47	$1,461	Kane	Sedan	0
4	44	$1,532	Tionesta	SUV	3
5	53	$1,220	Olean	Sedan	0
6	51	$1,674	Sheffield	Sedan	1
7	41	$2,389	Kane	Truck	1
8	58	$2,058	Kane	SUV	1
9	35	$1,919	Tionesta	SUV	1
10	45	$1,266	Olean	Sedan	0
11	54	$2,991	Tionesta	Sedan	0
12	56	$2,695	Kane	Sedan	2
13	41	$2,165	Tionesta	SUV	0
14	38	$1,766	Sheffield	SUV	0
15	48	$1,952	Tionesta	Compact	1

APPLEWOOD AUTO GROUP 2011

The Applewood Auto Group operates four dealerships:

- **_Tionesta Ford Lincoln Mercury_** sells the Ford, Lincoln, and Mercury cars and trucks.
- **_Olean Automotive Inc._** has the Nissan franchise as well as the General Motors brands of Chevrolet, Cadillac, and GMC Trucks.
- **_Sheffield Motors Inc._** sells Buick, GMC trucks, Hyundai, and Kia.
- **_Kane Motors_** offers the Chrysler, Dodge, and Jeep line as well as BMW and Volvo.

Every month, Ms. Ball collects data from each of the four dealerships and enters it into an Excel spreadsheet. Last month the Applewood Auto Group sold 180 vehicles at the four dealerships. A copy of the first few observations appears at the bottom of the previous page. The variables collected include:

- **Age**—the age of the buyer at the time of the purchase.
- **Profit**—the amount earned by the dealership on the sale of each vehicle.
- **Location**—the dealership where the vehicle was purchased.
- **Vehicle type**—SUV, sedan, compact, hybrid, or truck.
- **Previous**—the number of vehicles previously purchased at any of the four Applewood dealerships by the consumer.

The entire data set is available on the McGraw-Hill website at www.mhhe.com/lindbasic8e and in Appendix A.4 at the end of the text.

2.2 Constructing a Frequency Table

Recall from Chapter 1 that techniques used to describe a set of data are called descriptive statistics. Descriptive statistics organize data to show the general pattern of the data, to identify where values tend to concentrate, and to expose extreme or unusual data values. The first technique we discuss is a frequency table.

> **FREQUENCY TABLE** A grouping of qualitative data into mutually exclusive classes showing the number of observations in each class.

LO 2-1 Make a frequency table for a set of data.

In Chapter 1, we distinguished between qualitative and quantitative variables. To review, a qualitative variable is nonnumeric, that is, it can only be classified into distinct categories. Examples of qualitative data include political affiliation (Republican, Democrat, Independent), state of birth (Alabama, . . . , Wyoming), and method of payment for a purchase at Barnes & Noble (cash, check, debit, or credit). On the other hand, quantitative variables are numerical in nature. Examples of quantitative data relating to college students include the price of their textbooks, their age, and the number of credit hours they are registered for this semester.

In the Applewood Auto Group data set, there are five variables for each vehicle sale: age of the buyer, amount of profit, dealer that made the sale, type of vehicle sold, and number of previous purchases by the buyer. The dealer and the type of vehicle are *qualitative* variables. The amount of profit, the age of the buyer, and the number of previous purchases are *quantitative* variables.

Suppose Ms. Ball wanted to summarize last month's sales by location. To summarize this qualitative data, we classify the vehicles sold last month according to their location: Tionesta, Olean, Sheffield, or Kane. We use location to develop a frequency table with four mutually exclusive (distinctive) classes. This means that a particular vehicle cannot belong to more than one class. Each vehicle is uniquely classified into one of the four mutually exclusive locations. This frequency table is shown in Table 2–1. The number of observations, representing the sales at each location, is called the class frequency. So the class frequency for vehicles sold at the Kane location is 52.

Relative Class Frequencies

You can convert class frequencies to relative class frequencies to show the fraction of the total number of observations in each class. A relative frequency captures the relationship between a class total and the total number of observations. In the

TABLE 2–1 Frequency Table for Vehicles Sold Last Month at Applewood Auto Group by Location

Location	Number of Cars
Kane	52
Olean	40
Sheffield	45
Tionesta	43
Total	180

vehicle sales example, we may want to know the percentage of total cars sold at each of the four locations. To convert a frequency distribution to a relative frequency distribution, each of the class frequencies is divided by the total number of observations. For example, the fraction of vehicles sold last month at the Kane location is 0.289, found by 52 divided by 180. The relative frequency for each location is shown in Table 2–2.

TABLE 2–2 Relative Frequency Table of Vehicles Sold by Type Last Month at Applewood Auto Group

Location	Number of Cars	Relative Frequency
Kane	52	.289
Olean	40	.222
Sheffield	45	.250
Tionesta	43	.239
Total	180	1.000

Graphic Presentation of Qualitative Data

LO 2-2 Organize data into a bar chart.

The most common graphic form to present a qualitative variable is a **bar chart.** In most cases, the horizontal axis shows the variable of interest. The vertical axis shows the frequency or fraction of each of the possible outcomes. A distinguishing feature of a bar chart is there is distance or a gap between the bars. That is, because the variable of interest is qualitative, the bars are not adjacent to each other. Thus, a bar chart graphically describes a frequency table using a series of uniformly wide rectangles, where the height of each rectangle is the class frequency.

> **BAR CHART** A graph that shows qualitative classes on the horizontal axis and the class frequencies on the vertical axis. The class frequencies are proportional to the heights of the bars.

We use the Applewood Auto Group data as an example (Chart 2–1). The variable of interest is the location where the vehicle was sold and the number of vehicles sold at each location is the class frequency. We label the horizontal axis with the four locations and scale the vertical axis with the number sold. The height of the bars, or rectangles, corresponds to the number of vehicles at each location. There were 52 vehicles sold last month at the Kane location, so the height of the Kane bar is 52; the height of the bar for the Olean location is 40. The variable

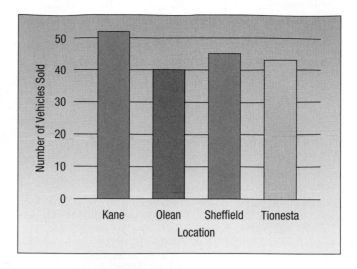

CHART 2–1 Number of Vehicles Sold by Location

location is of nominal scale, so the order of the locations on the horizontal axis does not matter. Listing this variable alphabetically, as shown in Chart 2–1, or in order of decreasing frequencies is also appropriate.

Another useful type of chart for depicting qualitative information is a **pie chart.**

> **PIE CHART** A chart that shows the proportion or percentage that each class represents of the total number of frequencies.

We explain the details of constructing a pie chart using the information in Table 2–3, which shows the frequency and percent of cars sold by the Applewood Auto Group for each vehicle type.

TABLE 2–3 Vehicle Sales by Type at Applewood Auto Group

Vehicle Type	Number Sold	Percent Sold
Sedan	72	40
SUV	54	30
Compact	27	15
Truck	18	10
Hybrid	9	5
Total	180	100

LO 2-3 Present a set of data using a pie chart.

The first step to develop a pie chart is to mark the percentages 0, 5, 10, 15, and so on evenly around the circumference of a circle (see Chart 2–2). To plot the 40% of total sales represented by sedans, draw a line from the center of the circle to 0 and another line from the center of the circle to 40%. The area in this "slice" represents the number of sedans sold as a percentage of the total sales. Next, add the SUV's percentage of total sales, 30%, to the sedan's percentage of total sales, 40. The result is 70%. Draw a line from the center of the circle to 70%, so the area between 40 and 70 shows the sales of SUVs as a percentage of total sales.

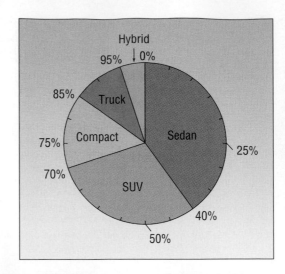

CHART 2–2 Pie Chart of Vehicles by Type

Continuing, add the 15% of total sales for compact vehicles, which gives us a total of 85%. Draw a line from the center of the circle to 85, so the "slice" between 70% and 85% represents the number of compact vehicles sold as a percentage of the total sales. The remaining 10% for truck sales and 5% for hybrid sales are added to the chart using the same method.

Because each slice of the pie represents the relative frequency of each vehicle type as a percentage of the total sales, we can easily compare them:

- The largest percentage of sales is for sedans.
- Sedans and SUVs together account for 70% of vehicle sales.
- Hybrids account for 5% of vehicle sales, in spite of being on the market for only a few years.

We can use Excel software to quickly count the number of cars for each vehicle type and create the frequency table, bar chart, and pie chart below. The Excel tool is called a Pivot Table. The instructions to produce these descriptive statistics and charts are given at the end of the chapter.

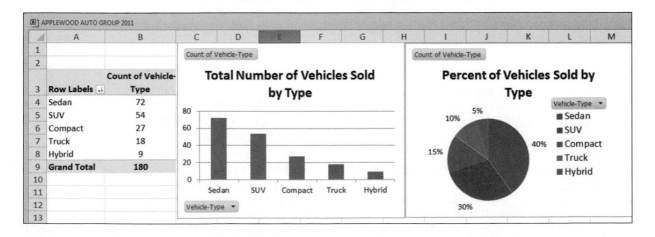

Pie and bar charts both serve to illustrate descriptive statistics. When is a pie chart preferred to a bar chart? In most cases, pie charts are used to show and compare the relative differences in the percentage of observations for each value or class of a qualitative variable. Bar charts are preferred when the goal is to compare the number or frequency of observations for each value or class of a qualitative variable.

Example

SkiLodges.com is test marketing its new website and is interested in how easy its website design is to navigate. It randomly selected 200 regular Internet users and asked them to perform a search task on the website. Each person was asked to rate the relative ease of navigation as poor, good, excellent, or awesome. The results are shown in the following table:

Awesome	102
Excellent	58
Good	30
Poor	10

1. What type of measurement scale is used for ease of navigation?
2. Draw a bar chart for the survey results.
3. Draw a pie chart for the survey results.

Solution

The data are measured on an ordinal scale. That is, the scale is ranked in relative ease when moving from "poor" to "awesome." Also, the interval between each rating is unknown so it is impossible, for example, to conclude that a rating of good is twice the value of a poor rating.

We can use a bar chart to graph the data. The vertical scale shows the relative frequency and the horizontal scale shows the values of the ease of navigation variable.

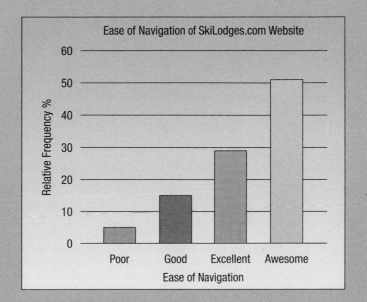

A pie chart can also be used to graph this data. The pie chart emphasizes that more than half of the respondents rate the relative ease of using the website awesome.

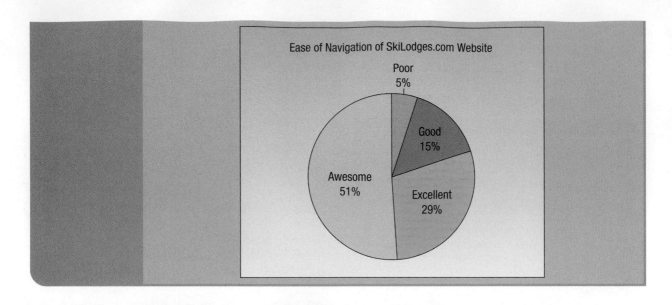

Ease of Navigation of SkiLodges.com Website

Self-Review 2–1   *The answers are at the end of the chapter.*

DeCenzo Specialty Food and Beverage Company has been serving a cola drink with an additional flavoring, Cola-Plus, that is very popular among its customers. The company is interested in customer preferences for Cola-Plus versus Coca-Cola, Pepsi, and a lemon-lime beverage. They ask 100 randomly sampled customers to take a taste test and select the beverage they preferred most. The results are shown in the following table:

Beverage	Number
Cola-Plus	40
Coca-Cola	25
Pepsi	20
Lemon-Lime	15
Total	100

(a) Is the data qualitative or quantitative? Why?
(b) What is the table called? What does it show?
(c) Develop a bar chart to depict the information.
(d) Develop a pie chart using the relative frequencies.

Exercises

connect™   *The answers to the odd-numbered exercises are at the end of the book.*

1. A pie chart shows the relative market share of cola products. The "slice" for Pepsi-Cola has a central angle of 90 degrees. What is its market share?
2. In a marketing study, 100 consumers were asked to select the best digital music player from the iPod, the iRiver, and the Magic Star MP3. To summarize the consumer responses with a frequency table, how many classes would the frequency table have?
3. A total of 1,000 residents in Minnesota were asked which season they preferred. One hundred liked winter best, 300 liked spring, 400 liked summer, and 200 liked fall. Develop a frequency table and a relative frequency table to summarize this information.
4. Two thousand frequent business travelers are asked which midwestern city they prefer: Indianapolis, Saint Louis, Chicago, or Milwaukee. One hundred liked Indianapolis best, 450 liked Saint Louis, 1,300 liked Chicago, and the remainder preferred Milwaukee. Develop a frequency table and a relative frequency table to summarize this information.

5. Wellstone Inc. produces and markets replacement covers for cell phones in a variety of colors. The company would like to allocate its production plans to five different colors: bright white, metallic black, magnetic lime, tangerine orange, and fusion red. The company set up a kiosk in the Mall of America for several hours and asked randomly selected people which cover color was their favorite. The results follow:

Bright white	130
Metallic black	104
Magnetic lime	325
Tangerine orange	455
Fusion red	286

   a. What is the table called?
   b. Draw a bar chart for the table.
   c. Draw a pie chart.
   d. If Wellstone Inc. plans to produce 1 million cell phone covers, how many of each color should it produce?

6. A small business consultant is investigating the performance of several companies. The fourth-quarter sales for last year (in thousands of dollars) for the selected companies were:

Corporation	Fourth-Quarter Sales ($ thousands)
Hoden Building Products	$ 1,645.2
J & R Printing Inc.	4,757.0
Long Bay Concrete Construction	8,913.0
Mancell Electric and Plumbing	627.1
Maxwell Heating and Air Conditioning	24,612.0
Mizelle Roofing & Sheet Metals	191.9

The consultant wants to include a chart in his report comparing the sales of the six companies. Use a bar chart to compare the fourth-quarter sales of these corporations and write a brief report summarizing the bar chart.

2.3 Constructing Frequency Distributions: Quantitative Data

LO 2-4 Create a frequency distribution for a data set.

In Chapter 1 and earlier in this chapter, we distinguished between qualitative and quantitative data. In the previous section, using the Applewood Automotive Group data, we summarized two qualitative variables, the location of the sale and the type of vehicle sold. We created frequency and relative frequency tables and depicted the results in bar and pie charts.

The Applewood Auto Group data also includes several quantitative variables: the age of the buyer, the profit earned on the sale of the vehicle, and the number of previous purchases. Suppose Ms. Ball wants to summarize last month's sales by profit earned. We can describe profit using a **frequency distribution.**

> **FREQUENCY DISTRIBUTION** A grouping of data into mutually exclusive classes showing the number of observations in each class.

How do we develop a frequency distribution? The first step is to tally the data into a table that shows the classes and the number of observations in each class. The steps in constructing a frequency distribution are best described by an example. Remember, our goal is to construct tables, charts, and graphs that will quickly reveal the concentration, extreme values, and shape of the data.

Example

We return to the situation where Ms. Kathryn Ball of the Applewood Auto Group wants to develop tables, charts, and graphs to show the typical profit for each sale. Table 2–4 reports the profit on each of the 180 vehicles sold last month at the four Applewood locations. What is the *typical* profit on each sale? What is the *largest or maximum* profit on any sale? What is the *smallest* or *minimum* profit on any sale? Around what value did the profits tend to cluster?

TABLE 2–4 Profit on Vehicles Sold Last Month by the Applewood Auto Group

Maximum

$1,387	$2,148	$2,201	$ 963	$ 820	$2,230	$3,043	$2,584	$2,370
1,754	2,207	996	1,298	1,266	2,341	1,059	2,666	2,637
1,817	2,252	2,813	1,410	1,741	3,292	1,674	2,991	1,426
1,040	1,428	323	1,553	1,772	1,108	1,807	934	2,944
1,273	1,889	352	1,648	1,932	1,295	2,056	2,063	2,147
1,529	1,166	482	2,071	2,350	1,344	2,236	2,083	1,973
3,082	1,320	1,144	2,116	2,422	1,906	2,928	2,856	2,502
1,951	2,265	1,485	1,500	2,446	1,952	1,269	2,989	783
2,692	1,323	1,509	1,549	369	2,070	1,717	910	1,538
1,206	1,760	1,638	2,348	978	2,454	1,797	1,536	2,339
1,342	1,919	1,961	2,498	1,238	1,606	1,955	1,957	2,700
443	2,357	2,127	294	1,818	1,680	2,199	2,240	2,222
754	2,866	2,430	1,115	1,824	1,827	2,482	2,695	2,597
1,621	732	1,704	1,124	1,907	1,915	2,701	1,325	2,742
870	1,464	1,876	1,532	1,938	2,084	3,210	2,250	1,837
1,174	1,626	2,010	1,688	1,940	2,639	377	2,279	2,842
1,412	1,762	2,165	1,822	2,197	842	1,220	2,626	2,434
1,809	1,915	2,231	1,897	2,646	1,963	1,401	1,501	1,640
2,415	2,119	2,389	2,445	1,461	2,059	2,175	1,752	1,821
1,546	1,766	335	2,886	1,731	2,338	1,118	2,058	2,487

Minimum

Solution

Table 2–4 shows the profits from the 180 sales. We refer to this unorganized information as **raw data** or **ungrouped data.** With a little searching, we can find the smallest profit ($294) and the largest or maximum profit ($3,292), but that is about all. It is difficult to determine a typical profit. It is also difficult to visualize where the profits tend to cluster. The raw data are more easily interpreted if organized into a frequency distribution.

The steps for organizing data into a frequency distribution.

Step 1: Decide on the number of classes. The goal is to use just enough groupings or **classes** to reveal the shape of the set of observations. Some judgment is needed here. Too many classes or too few classes might not reveal the basic shape of the data set. In the vehicle profit example, three classes would not give much insight into the pattern of the data (see Table 2–5).

TABLE 2–5 An Example of Too Few Classes

Vehicle Profit ($)	Number of Vehicles
$ 200 up to $1,400	42
1,400 up to 2,600	115
2,600 up to 3,800	23
Total	180

A useful recipe to determine the number of classes (k) is the "2 to the k rule." This guide suggests you select the smallest number (k) for the number of classes such that 2^k (in words, 2 raised to the power of k) is greater than the number of observations (n). In the Applewood Auto Group

example, there were 180 vehicles sold. So $n = 180$. If we try $k = 7$, which means we would use 7 classes, $2^7 = 128$, which is less than 180. Hence, 7 is too few classes. If we let $k = 8$, then $2^8 = 256$, which is greater than 180. So the recommended number of classes is 8.

Step 2: Determine the class interval or class width. Generally the **class interval** or **class width** is the same for all classes. The classes all taken together must cover at least the distance from the minimum value in the data up to the maximum value. Expressing these words in a formula:

$$i \geq \frac{Maximum\ value - Minimum\ value}{k}$$

where i is the class interval, and k is the number of classes.

For the Applewood Auto Group, the minimum value is $294 and the maximum value is $3,292. If we need 8 classes, the interval should be:

$$i \geq \frac{Maximum\ value - Minimum\ value}{k} = \frac{\$3,292 - \$294}{8} = \$374.75$$

In practice, this interval size is usually rounded up to some convenient number, such as a multiple of 10 or 100. The value of $400 is a reasonable choice.

In frequency distributions, equal class intervals are preferred. However, unequal class intervals may be necessary in certain situations to avoid a large number of empty, or almost empty, classes. Such is the case in Table 2–6. The Internal Revenue Service used unequal-sized class intervals to report the adjusted gross income on individual tax returns. Had they used an equal-sized interval of, say, $1,000, more than 1,000 classes would have been required to describe all the incomes. A frequency distribution with 1,000 classes would be difficult to interpret. In this case, the distribution is easier to understand in spite of the unequal class intervals. Note also that the number of income tax returns or "frequencies" is reported in thousands in this particular table. This also makes the information easier to understand.

TABLE 2–6 Adjusted Gross Income for Individuals Filing Income Tax Returns

Adjusted Gross Income	Number of Returns (in thousands)
No adjusted gross income	178.2
$ 1 up to 5,000	1,204.6
5,000 up to 10,000	2,595.5
10,000 up to 15,000	3,142.0
15,000 up to 20,000	3,191.7
20,000 up to 25,000	2,501.4
25,000 up to 30,000	1,901.6
30,000 up to 40,000	2,502.3
40,000 up to 50,000	1,426.8
50,000 up to 75,000	1,476.3
75,000 up to 100,000	338.8
100,000 up to 200,000	223.3
200,000 up to 500,000	55.2
500,000 up to 1,000,000	12.0
1,000,000 up to 2,000,000	5.1
2,000,000 up to 10,000,000	3.4
10,000,000 or more	0.6

Step 3: Set the individual class limits. State clear class limits so you can put each observation into only one category. This means you must avoid overlapping or unclear class limits. For example, classes such as "$1,300–$1,400" and "$1,400–$1,500" should not be used, because it is not clear whether the value $1,400 is in the first or second class. Classes stated as "$1,300–$1,400" and "$1,500–$1,600" are frequently used, but may also be confusing without the additional common convention of rounding all data at or above $1,450 up to the second class and data below $1,450 down to the first class. In this text, we will generally use the format $1,300 **up to** $1,400 and $1,400 **up to** $1,500 and so on. With this format, it is clear that $1,399 goes into the first class and $1,400 in the second.

Because we round the class interval up to get a convenient class size, we cover a larger than necessary range. For example, using 8 classes with a width of $400 in the Applewood Auto Group example results in a range of 8($400) = $3,200. The actual range is $2,998, found by ($3,292 − $294). Comparing that value to $3,200, we have an excess of $202. Because we need to cover only the range *(Maximum − Minimum)*, it is natural to put approximately equal amounts of the excess in each of the two tails. Of course, we should also select convenient class limits. A guideline is to make the lower limit of the first class a multiple of the class interval. Sometimes this is not possible, but the lower limit should at least be rounded. So here are the classes we could use for this data.

Classes
$ 200 up to $ 600
600 up to 1,000
1,000 up to 1,400
1,400 up to 1,800
1,800 up to 2,200
2,200 up to 2,600
2,600 up to 3,000
3,000 up to 3,400

Step 4: Tally the vehicle profit into the classes. To begin, the profit from the sale of the first vehicle in Table 2–4 is $1,387. It is tallied in the $1,000 up to $1,400 class. The second profit in the first row of Table 2–4 is $2,148. It is tallied in the $1,800 up to $2,200 class. The other profits are tallied in a similar manner. When all the profits are tallied, the table would appear as:

Profit	Frequency
$ 200 up to $ 600	JHT III
600 up to 1,000	JHT JHT I
1,000 up to 1,400	JHT JHT JHT JHT III
1,400 up to 1,800	JHT JHT JHT JHT JHT JHT JHT III
1,800 up to 2,200	JHT JHT JHT JHT JHT JHT JHT JHT JHT
2,200 up to 2,600	JHT JHT JHT JHT JHT JHT II
2,600 up to 3,000	JHT JHT JHT IIII
3,000 up to 3,400	IIII
Total	

Step 5: Count the number of items in each class. The number of observations in each class is called the **class frequency.** In the $200 up to $600 class there are 8 observations, and in the $600 up to $1,000 class there are 11 observations. Therefore, the class frequency in the first class is 8 and the class frequency in the second class is 11. There are a total of

180 observations or frequencies in the entire set of data. So the sum of all the frequencies should be equal to 180.

TABLE 2–7 Frequency Distribution of Profit for Vehicles Sold Last Month at Applewood Auto Group

Profit	Frequency
$ 200 up to $ 600	8
600 up to 1,000	11
1,000 up to 1,400	23
1,400 up to 1,800	38
1,800 up to 2,200	45
2,200 up to 2,600	32
2,600 up to 3,000	19
3,000 up to 3,400	4
Total	180

Now that we have organized the data into a frequency distribution, we can summarize the pattern in the profits of the vehicles for the Applewood Auto Group. Observe the following:

1. The profit from a vehicle ranged between $200 and $3,400.
2. The profits are concentrated between $1,000 and $3,000. The profit on 157 vehicles, or 87%, was within this range.
3. The largest concentration, or highest frequency, is in the $1,800 up to $2,200 class. There are 45 observations. The middle of this class is $2,000. So we say that the typical profit on selling a vehicle is $2,000.

By presenting this information to Ms. Ball, we give her a clear picture of the distribution of the vehicle profits for last month.

We admit that arranging the information on profits into a frequency distribution does result in the loss of some detailed information. That is, by organizing the data into a frequency distribution, we cannot pinpoint the exact profit on any vehicle, such as $1,387, $2,148, or $2,201. Further, we cannot tell that the actual minimum amount of profit for any vehicle sold is $294 or that the most profit was $3,292. However, the lower limit of the first class and the upper limit of the last class convey essentially the same meaning. Likely, Ms. Ball will make the same judgment if she knows the smallest profit is about $200 that she will if she knows the exact profit is $292. The advantages of condensing the data into a more understandable and organized form more than offset this disadvantage.

Self-Review 2–2

The commissions earned for the first quarter of last year by the 11 members of the sales staff at Master Chemical Company are:

$1,650 $1,475 $1,510 $1,670 $1,595 $1,760 $1,540 $1,495 $1,590 $1,625 $1,510

(a) What are the values such as $1,650 and $1,475 called?
(b) Using $1,400 up to $1,500 as the first class, $1,500 up to $1,600 as the second class, and so forth, organize the quarterly commissions into a frequency distribution.
(c) What are the numbers in the right column of your frequency distribution called?
(d) Describe the distribution of quarterly commissions, based on the frequency distribution. What is the largest concentration of commissions earned? What is the smallest, and the largest? What is the typical amount earned?

We will use two other terms frequently: **class midpoint** and **class interval.** The midpoint is halfway between the lower limits of two consecutive classes. It is computed by adding the lower limits of consecutive classes and dividing the result by 2. Referring to Table 2–7, the lower class limit of the first class is $200 and the next class limit is $600. The class midpoint is $400, found by ($600 + $200)/2. The midpoint of $400 best represents, or is typical of, the profits of the vehicles in that class.

To determine the class interval, subtract the lower limit of the class from the lower limit of the next class. The class interval of the Applewood data is $400, which we find by subtracting the lower limit of the first class, $200, from the lower limit of the next class; that is, $600. ($600 − $200 = $400.) You can also determine the class interval by finding the difference between consecutive midpoints. The midpoint of the first class is $400 and the midpoint of the second class is $800. The difference is $400.

2.4 Relative Frequency Distribution

LO 2-5 Understand a relative frequency distribution.

A relative frequency converts the frequency to a percentage.

It may be desirable, as we did earlier with qualitative data, to convert class frequencies to relative class frequencies to show the proportion of the total number of observations in each class. In our vehicle profits, we may want to know what percentage of the vehicle profits are in the $1,000 up to $1,400 class. In another study, we may want to know what percentage of the employees used 5 up to 10 personal leave days last year. To convert a frequency distribution to a *relative* frequency distribution, each of the class frequencies is divided by the total number of observations. From the distribution of vehicle profits, Table 2–7, the relative frequency for the $1,000 up to $1,400 class is 0.128, found by dividing 23 by 180. That is, profit on 12.8% of the vehicles sold is between $1,000 and $1,400. The relative frequencies for the remaining classes are shown in Table 2–8.

TABLE 2–8 Relative Frequency Distribution of Profit for Vehicles Sold Last Month at Applewood Auto Group

Profit	Frequency	Relative Frequency	Found by
$ 200 up to $ 600	8	.044	8/180
600 up to 1,000	11	.061	11/180
1,000 up to 1,400	23	.128	23/180
1,400 up to 1,800	38	.211	38/180
1,800 up to 2,200	45	.250	45/180
2,200 up to 2,600	32	.178	32/180
2,600 up to 3,000	19	.106	19/180
3,000 up to 3,400	4	.022	4/180
Total	180	1.000	

As we mentioned in Chapter 1, there are many software packages that perform statistical calculations. Throughout this text, we will show the output from Microsoft Excel, MegaStat (a Microsoft Excel add-in), and Minitab (a statistical software package).

On page 26 of this chapter we used the PivotTable tool in Excel to create a frequency table. We use the same Excel tool to create frequency and relative frequency distributions for the profit variable in the Applewood Auto Group data. The necessary steps for the table to the left are given in the Software Commands section at the end of the chapter.

APPLEWOOD AUTO GROUP 2011

	A	B	C
1	Profit Class	Frequency	Relative Frequency
2	200-600	8	4.44%
3	600-1000	11	6.11%
4	1000-1400	23	12.78%
5	1400-1800	38	21.11%
6	1800-2200	45	25.00%
7	2200-2600	32	17.78%
8	2600-3000	19	10.56%
9	3000-3400	4	2.22%
10	Grand Total	180	100.00%

Self-Review 2–3

Barry Bonds of the San Francisco Giants established a new single-season Major League Baseball home run record by hitting 73 home runs during the 2001 season. Listed below is the sorted distance of each of the 73 home runs.

320	320	347	350	360	360	360	361	365	370
370	375	375	375	375	380	380	380	380	380
380	390	390	391	394	396	400	400	400	400
405	410	410	410	410	410	410	410	410	410
410	410	411	415	415	416	417	417	420	420
420	420	420	420	420	420	429	430	430	430
430	430	435	435	436	440	440	440	440	440
450	480	488							

(a) Show that seven classes would be used to create a frequency distribution for these data.
(b) Show that a class interval of 30 would summarize the data in seven classes.
(c) Construct frequency and relative frequency distributions for the data with seven classes and a class interval of 30. Start the first class with a lower limit of 300.
(d) How many home runs traveled a distance of 360 up to 390 feet?
(e) What percentage of the home runs traveled a distance of 360 up to 390 feet?
(f) What percentage of the home runs traveled a distance of 390 feet or more?

Exercises

connect

7. A set of data consists of 38 observations. How many classes would you recommend for the frequency distribution?
8. A set of data consists of 45 observations between $0 and $29. What size would you recommend for the class interval?
9. A set of data consists of 230 observations between $235 and $567. What class interval would you recommend?
10. A set of data contains 53 observations. The minimum value is 42 and the maximum value is 129. The data are to be organized into a frequency distribution.
   a. How many classes would you suggest?
   b. What would you suggest as the lower limit of the first class?
11. Wachesaw Manufacturing Inc. produced the following number of units in the last 16 days. (df) This icon indicates that the data is available at the text website: www.mhhe.com/lindbasic8e. You will be able to download the data directly into Excel or Minitab from this site.

27	27	27	28	27	25	25	28
26	28	26	28	31	30	26	26

The information is to be organized into a frequency distribution.
   a. How many classes would you recommend?
   b. What class interval would you suggest?
   c. What lower limit would you recommend for the first class?
   d. Organize the information into a frequency distribution and determine the relative frequency distribution.
   e. Comment on the shape of the distribution.
12. The Quick Change Oil Company has a number of outlets in the metropolitan Seattle area. The daily number of oil changes at the Oak Street outlet in the past 20 days are: (df)

65	98	55	62	79	59	51	90	72	56
70	62	66	80	94	79	63	73	71	85

The data are to be organized into a frequency distribution.
   a. How many classes would you recommend?
   b. What class interval would you suggest?

c. What lower limit would you recommend for the first class?

d. Organize the number of oil changes into a frequency distribution.

e. Comment on the shape of the frequency distribution. Also determine the relative frequency distribution.

13. The manager of the BiLo Supermarket in Mt. Pleasant, Rhode Island, gathered the following information on the number of times a customer visits the store during a month. The responses of 51 customers were: 🄳

5	3	3	1	4	4	5	6	4	2	6	6	6	7	1
1	14	1	2	4	4	4	5	6	3	5	3	4	5	6
8	4	7	6	5	9	11	3	12	4	7	6	5	15	1
1	10	8	9	2	12									

a. Starting with 0 as the lower limit of the first class and using a class interval of 3, organize the data into a frequency distribution.

b. Describe the distribution. Where do the data tend to cluster?

c. Convert the distribution to a relative frequency distribution.

14. The food services division of Cedar River Amusement Park Inc. is studying the amount that families who visit the amusement park spend per day on food and drink. A sample of 40 families who visited the park yesterday revealed they spent the following amounts: 🄳

$77	$18	$63	$84	$38	$54	$50	$59	$54	$56	$36	$26	$50	$34	$44
41	58	58	53	51	62	43	52	53	63	62	62	65	61	52
60	60	45	66	83	71	63	58	61	71					

a. Organize the data into a frequency distribution, using seven classes and 15 as the lower limit of the first class. What class interval did you select?

b. Where do the data tend to cluster?

c. Describe the distribution.

d. Determine the relative frequency distribution.

2.5 Graphic Presentation of a Frequency Distribution

LO 2-6 Present data from a frequency distribution in a histogram or a frequency polygon.

Sales managers, stock analysts, hospital administrators, and other busy executives often need a quick picture of the distributions of sales, stock prices, or hospital costs. These distributions can often be depicted by the use of charts and graphs. Three charts that will help portray a frequency distribution graphically are the histogram, the frequency polygon, and the cumulative frequency polygon.

Histogram

A **histogram** for a frequency distribution based on quantitative data is similar to the bar chart showing the distribution of qualitative data. The classes are marked on the horizontal axis and the class frequencies on the vertical axis. The class frequencies are represented by the heights of the bars. However, there is one important difference based on the nature of the data. Quantitative data are usually measured using scales that are continuous, not discrete. Therefore, the horizontal axis represents all possible values, and the bars are drawn adjacent to each other to show the continuous nature of the data.

HISTOGRAM A graph in which the classes are marked on the horizontal axis and the class frequencies on the vertical axis. The class frequencies are represented by the heights of the bars, and the bars are drawn adjacent to each other.

Example

Below is the frequency distribution of the profits on vehicle sales last month at the Applewood Auto Group.

Profit	Frequency
$ 200 up to $ 600	8
600 up to 1,000	11
1,000 up to 1,400	23
1,400 up to 1,800	38
1,800 up to 2,200	45
2,200 up to 2,600	32
2,600 up to 3,000	19
3,000 up to 3,400	4
Total	180

Construct a histogram. What observations can you reach based on the information presented in the histogram?

Solution

The class frequencies are scaled along the vertical axis (Y-axis) and either the class limits or the class midpoints along the horizontal axis. To illustrate the construction of the histogram, the first three classes are shown in Chart 2–3.

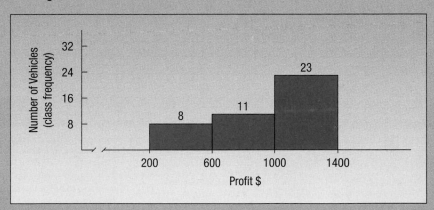

CHART 2–3 Construction of a Histogram

From Chart 2–3 we note the profit on eight vehicles was $200 up to $600. Therefore, the height of the column for that class is 8. There are 11 vehicle sales where the profit was $600 up to $1,000. So, logically, the height of that column is 11. The height of the bar represents the number of observations in the class.

This procedure is continued for all classes. The complete histogram is shown in Chart 2–4. Note that there is no space between the bars. This is a feature of the histogram. Why is this so? Because the variable plotted on the horizontal axis is a continuous variable. In a bar chart, the scale of measurement is often nominal and the vertical bars are separated. This is an important distinction between the histogram and the bar chart.

From Chart 2–4 we can make the following statement:

1. The profit from a vehicle ranged from about $200 up to about $3,400.
2. The profits are concentrated between $1,000 and $3,000. The profit on 157 vehicles, or 87%, was within this range.
3. The largest concentration, or highest frequency, is in the $1,800 up to $2,200 class. The middle of this class is $2,000. So we say that the typical profit on selling a vehicle is $2,000.

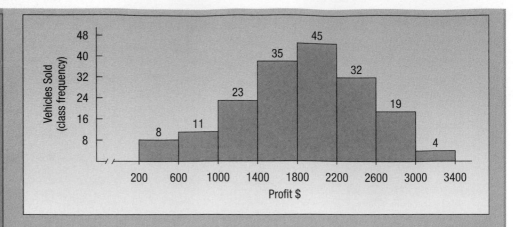

CHART 2–4 Histogram of the Profit on 180 Vehicles Sold at the Applewood Auto Group

Thus, the histogram provides an easily interpreted visual representation of a frequency distribution. We should also point out that we would have made the same observations and the shape of the histogram would have been the same had we used a relative frequency distribution instead of the actual frequencies. That is, if we had used the relative frequencies of Table 2–8, we would have had a histogram of the same shape as Chart 2–4. The only difference is that the vertical axis would have been reported in percentage of vehicles instead of the number of vehicles.

We use the Microsoft Excel system to produce the histogram for the Applewood Auto Group vehicle sales data. The software commands to create this output are given in the **Software Commands** section at the end of the chapter.

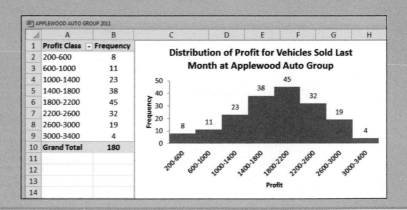

Frequency Polygon

A **frequency polygon** also shows the shape of a distribution and is similar to a histogram. It consists of line segments connecting the points formed by the intersections of the class midpoints and the class frequencies. The construction of a frequency polygon is illustrated in Chart 2–5 on the following page. We use the profits from the cars sold last month at the Applewood Auto Group. The midpoint of each class is scaled on the X-axis and the class frequencies on the Y-axis. Recall that the class midpoint is the value at the center of a class and represents the typical values in that class. The class frequency is the number of observations in a particular class. The profit earned on the vehicles sold last month by the Applewood Auto Group is repeated below.

Profit	Midpoint	Frequency
$ 200 up to $ 600	$ 400	8
600 up to 1,000	800	11
1,000 up to 1,400	1,200	23
1,400 up to 1,800	1,600	38
1,800 up to 2,200	2,000	45
2,200 up to 2,600	2,400	32
2,600 up to 3,000	2,800	19
3,000 up to 3,400	3,200	4
Total		180

As noted previously, the $200 up to $600 class is represented by the midpoint $400. To construct a frequency polygon, move horizontally on the graph to the midpoint, $400, and then vertically to 8, the class frequency, and place a dot. The X and the Y values of this point are called the *coordinates.* The coordinates of the next point are X = 800 and Y = 11. The process is continued for all classes. Then the points are connected in order. That is, the point representing the lowest class is joined to the one representing the second class and so on. Note in Chart 2–5 that, to complete the frequency polygon, midpoints of $0 and $3,600 are added to the X-axis to "anchor" the polygon at zero frequencies. These two values, $0 and $3,600, were derived by subtracting the class interval of $400 from the lowest midpoint ($400) and by adding $400 to the highest midpoint ($3,200) in the frequency distribution.

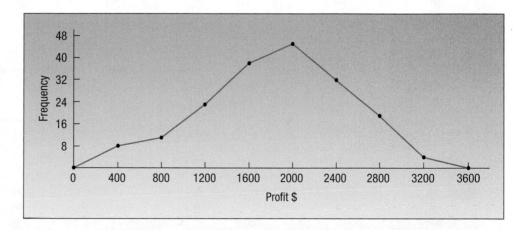

CHART 2–5 Frequency Polygon of Profit on 180 Vehicles Sold at Applewood Auto Group

Both the histogram and the frequency polygon allow us to get a quick picture of the main characteristics of the data (highs, lows, points of concentration, etc.). Although the two representations are similar in purpose, the histogram has the advantage of depicting each class as a rectangle, with the height of the rectangular bar representing the number in each class. The frequency polygon, in turn, has an advantage over the histogram. It allows us to compare directly two or more frequency distributions. Suppose Ms. Ball wants to compare the profit per vehicle sold at Applewood Auto Group with a similar auto group, Fowler Auto in Grayling, Michigan. To do this, two frequency polygons are constructed, one on top of the other, as in Chart 2–6. Two things are clear from the chart:

- The typical vehicle profit is larger at Fowler Motors—about $2,000 for Applewood and about $2,400 for Fowler.
- There is less dispersion in the profits at Fowler Motors than at Applewood. The lower limit of the first class for Applewood is $0 and the upper limit is $3,600. For Fowler Motors, the lower limit is $800 and the upper limit is the same: $3,600.

The total number of cars sold at the two dealerships is about the same, so a direct comparison is possible. If the difference in the total number of cars sold is large, then converting the frequencies to relative frequencies and then plotting the two distributions would allow a clearer comparison.

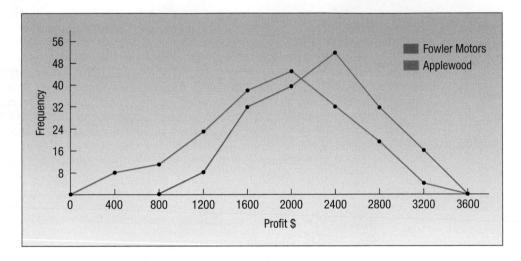

CHART 2–6 Distribution of Profit at Applewood Auto Group and Fowler Motors

Self-Review 2–4

The annual imports of a selected group of electronic suppliers are shown in the following frequency distribution.

Imports ($ millions)	Number of Suppliers	Imports ($ millions)	Number of Suppliers
2 up to 5	6	11 up to 14	10
5 up to 8	13	14 up to 17	1
8 up to 11	20		

(a) Portray the imports as a histogram.
(b) Portray the imports as a relative frequency polygon.
(c) Summarize the important facets of the distribution (such as classes with the highest and lowest frequencies).

Exercises

connect™

15. Molly's Candle Shop has several retail stores in the coastal areas of North and South Carolina. Many of Molly's customers ask her to ship their purchases. The following chart shows the number of packages shipped per day for the last 100 days.

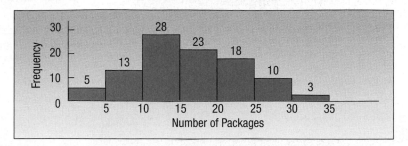

a. What is this chart called?
b. What is the total number of frequencies?
c. What is the class interval?
d. What is the class frequency for the 10 up to 15 class?
e. What is the relative frequency of the 10 up to 15 class?
f. What is the midpoint of the 10 up to 15 class?
g. On how many days were there 25 or more packages shipped?

16. The following chart shows the number of patients admitted daily to Memorial Hospital through the emergency room.

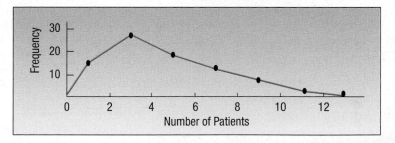

a. What is the midpoint of the 2 up to 4 class?
b. How many days were 2 up to 4 patients admitted?
c. What is the class interval?
d. What is this chart called?

17. The following frequency distribution reports the number of frequent flier miles, reported in thousands, for employees of Brumley Statistical Consulting Inc. during the most recent quarter.

Frequent Flier Miles (000)	Number of Employees
0 up to 3	5
3 up to 6	12
6 up to 9	23
9 up to 12	8
12 up to 15	2
Total	50

a. How many employees were studied?
b. What is the midpoint of the first class?
c. Construct a histogram.

  d. A frequency polygon is to be drawn. What are the coordinates of the plot for the first class?
  e. Construct a frequency polygon.
  f. Interpret the frequent flier miles accumulated using the two charts.
18. Ecommerce.com, a large Internet retailer, is studying the lead time (elapsed time between when an order is placed and when it is filled) for a sample of recent orders. The lead times are reported in days.

Lead Time (days)	Frequency
0 up to 5	6
5 up to 10	7
10 up to 15	12
15 up to 20	8
20 up to 25	7
Total	40

  a. How many orders were studied?
  b. What is the midpoint of the first class?
  c. What are the coordinates of the first class for a frequency polygon?
  d. Draw a histogram.
  e. Draw a frequency polygon.
  f. Interpret the lead times using the two charts.

Cumulative Frequency Distributions

LO 2-7 Construct and interpret a cumulative frequency distribution.

Consider once again the distribution of the profits on vehicles sold by the Applewood Auto Group. Suppose we were interested in the number of vehicles that sold for a profit of less than $1,400 or the profit earned on the lowest selling 40% of the vehicles. These values can be approximated by developing a **cumulative frequency distribution** and portraying it graphically in a **cumulative frequency polygon**.

Example

The frequency distribution of the profits earned at Applewood Auto Group is repeated from Table 2–7.

Profit	Frequency
$ 200 up to $ 600	8
600 up to 1,000	11
1,000 up to 1,400	23
1,400 up to 1,800	38
1,800 up to 2,200	45
2,200 up to 2,600	32
2,600 up to 3,000	19
3,000 up to 3,400	4
Total	180

Construct a cumulative frequency polygon. Seventy-five percent of the vehicles sold earned a profit of less than what amount? Sixty of the vehicles earned a profit of less than what amount?

Solution

As the names imply, a cumulative frequency distribution and a cumulative frequency polygon require *cumulative frequencies*. To construct a cumulative frequency distribution, refer to the preceding table and note that there were eight vehicles in which the profit earned was less than $600. Those 8 vehicles, plus the 11 in the next higher class, for a total of 19, earned a profit of less than $1,000. The cumulative frequency for the next higher class is 42, found by 8 + 11 + 23. This process is continued for all the classes. All the vehicles earned a profit of less than $3,400. (See Table 2–9.)

TABLE 2–9 Cumulative Frequency Distribution for Profit on Vehicles Sold Last Month at Applewood Auto Group

Profit	Frequency	Cumulative Frequency	Found by
$ 200 up to $ 600	8	8	8
600 up to 1,000	11	19	8 + 11
1,000 up to 1,400	23	42	8 + 11 + 23
1,400 up to 1,800	38	80	8 + 11 + 23 + 38
1,800 up to 2,200	45	125	8 + 11 + 23 + 38 + 45
2,200 up to 2,600	32	157	8 + 11 + 23 + 38 + 45 + 32
2,600 up to 3,000	19	176	8 + 11 + 23 + 38 + 45 + 32 + 19
3,000 up to 3,400	4	180	8 + 11 + 23 + 38 + 45 + 32 + 19 + 4
Total	180		

To plot a cumulative frequency distribution, scale the upper limit of each class along the X-axis and the corresponding cumulative frequencies along the Y-axis. To provide additional information, you can label the vertical axis on the left in units and the vertical axis on the right in percent. In the Applewood Auto Group, the vertical axis on the left is labeled from 0 to 180 and on the right from 0% to 100%. The value of 50% corresponds to 90 vehicles.

To begin, the first plot is at $X = 200$ and $Y = 0$. None of the vehicles sold for a profit of less than $200. The profit on 8 vehicles was less than $600, so the next plot is at $X = 600$ and $Y = 8$. Continuing, the next plot is $X = 1,000$ and $Y = 19$. There were 19 vehicles that sold for a profit of less than $1,000. The rest of the points are plotted and then the dots connected to form Chart 2–7 below.

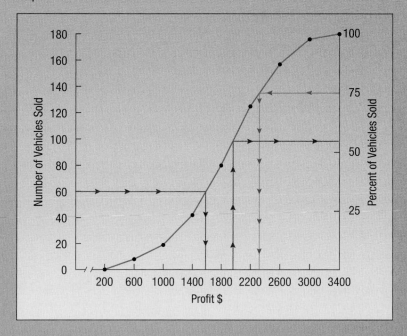

CHART 2–7 Cumulative Frequency Polygon for Profit on Vehicles Sold Last Month at Applewood Auto Group

Using Chart 2–7 to find the amount of profit earned on 75% of the cars sold, draw a horizontal line from the 75% mark on the right-hand vertical axis over to the polygon, then drop down to the *X*-axis and read the amount of profit. The value on the *X*-axis is about $2,300, so we estimate that 75% of the vehicles sold earned a profit for the Applewood group of less than $2,230.

To find the profit that separates the 60 vehicles with the lowest profit from the rest, use Chart 2–7 to locate the value of 60 on the left-hand vertical axis. Next, we draw a horizontal line from the value of 60 to the polygon and then drop down to the *X*-axis and read the profit. It is about $1,600, so we estimate that 60 of the vehicles sold for a profit of less than $1,600. We can also make estimates of the percentage of vehicles that sold for less than a particular amount. To explain, suppose we want to estimate the percentage of vehicles that sold for a profit of less than $2,000. We begin by locating the value of $2,000 on the *X*-axis, move vertically to the polygon, and then horizontally to the vertical axis on the right. The value is about 56%, so we conclude that 56% of the vehicles sold for a profit of less than $2,000.

Self-Review 2–5   A sample of the hourly wages of 15 employees at Home Depot in Brunswick, Georgia, was organized into the following table.

Hourly Wages	Number of Employees
$ 8 up to $10	3
10 up to 12	7
12 up to 14	4
14 up to 16	1

(a) What is the table called?
(b) Develop a cumulative frequency distribution and portray the distribution in a cumulative frequency polygon.
(c) On the basis of the cumulative frequency polygon, how many employees earn less than $10 per hour? Ten employees earn less than what amount?

Exercises

connect

19. The following chart shows the hourly wages of a sample of certified welders in the Atlanta, Georgia, area.

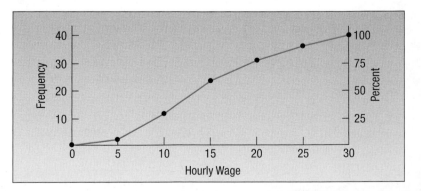

a. How many welders were studied?
b. What is the class interval?

  c. About how many welders earn less than $10.00 per hour?
  d. About 75% of the welders make less than what amount?
  e. Ten of the welders studied made less than what amount?
  f. What percentage of the welders make less than $20.00 per hour?
20. The following chart shows the selling price ($000) of houses sold in the Billings, Montana, area.

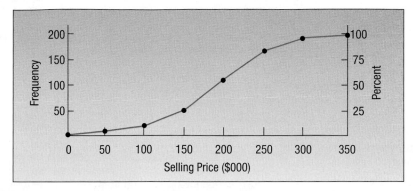

  a. How many homes were studied?
  b. What is the class interval?
  c. One hundred homes sold for less than what amount?
  d. About 75% of the homes sold for less than what amount?
  e. Estimate the number of homes in the $150,000 up to $200,000 class.
  f. About how many homes sold for less than $225,000?
21. The frequency distribution representing the number of frequent flier miles accumulated by employees at Brumley Statistical Consulting Company is repeated from Exercise 17.

Frequent Flier Miles (000)	Frequency
0 up to 3	5
3 up to 6	12
6 up to 9	23
9 up to 12	8
12 up to 15	2
Total	50

  a. How many employees accumulated less than 3,000 miles?
  b. Convert the frequency distribution to a cumulative frequency distribution.
  c. Portray the cumulative distribution in the form of a cumulative frequency polygon.
  d. Based on the cumulative frequency polygon, about 75% of the employees accumulated how many miles or less?
22. The frequency distribution of order lead time at Ecommerce.com from Exercise 18 is repeated below.

Lead Time (days)	Frequency
0 up to 5	6
5 up to 10	7
10 up to 15	12
15 up to 20	8
20 up to 25	7
Total	40

  a. How many orders were filled in less than 10 days? In less than 15 days?
  b. Convert the frequency distribution to a cumulative frequency distribution.
  c. Develop a cumulative frequency polygon.
  d. About 60% of the orders were filled in less than how many days?

Chapter Summary

I. A frequency table is a grouping of qualitative data into mutually exclusive classes showing the number of observations in each class.

II. A relative frequency table shows the fraction of the number of frequencies in each class.

III. A bar chart is a graphic representation of a frequency table.

IV. A pie chart shows the proportion each distinct class represents of the total number of observations.

V. A frequency distribution is a grouping of data into mutually exclusive classes showing the number of observations in each class.
   A. The steps in constructing a frequency distribution are:
      1. Decide on the number of classes.
      2. Determine the class interval.
      3. Set the individual class limits.
      4. Tally the raw data into classes.
      5. Count the number of tallies in each class.
   B. The class frequency is the number of observations in each class.
   C. The class interval is the difference between the limits of two consecutive classes.
   D. The class midpoint is halfway between the limits of consecutive classes.

VI. A relative frequency distribution shows the percent of observations in each class.

VII. There are three methods for graphically portraying a frequency distribution.
   A. A histogram portrays the number of frequencies in each class in the form of a rectangle.
   B. A frequency polygon consists of line segments connecting the points formed by the intersection of the class midpoint and the class frequency.
   C. A cumulative frequency distribution shows the number or percent of observations below given values.

Chapter Exercises

connect

23. Describe the similarities and differences of qualitative and quantitative variables. Be sure to include:
    a. What level of measurement is required for each variable type?
    b. Can both types be used to describe both samples and populations?

24. Describe the similarities and differences between a frequency table and a frequency distribution. Be sure to include which requires qualitative data and which requires quantitative data.

25. Alexandra Damonte will be building a new resort in Myrtle Beach, South Carolina. She must decide how to design the resort based on the type of activities that the resort will offer to its customers. A recent poll of 300 potential customers showed the following results about customers' preferences for planned resort activities:

Like planned activities	63
Do not like planned activities	135
Not sure	78
No answer	24

    a. What is the table called?
    b. Draw a bar chart to portray the survey results.
    c. Draw a pie chart for the survey results.
    d. If you are preparing to present the results to Ms. Damonte as part of a report, which graph would you prefer to show? Why?

26. Speedy Swift is a package delivery service that serves the greater Atlanta, Georgia, metropolitan area. To maintain customer loyalty, one of Speedy Swift's performance objectives is on-time delivery. To monitor its performance, each delivery is measured on the following scale: early (package delivered before the promised time), on-time (package delivered within 5 minutes of the promised time), late (package delivered more than 5 minutes past the promised time), lost (package never delivered). Speedy Swift's objective

is to deliver 99% of all packages either early or on-time. Another objective is to never lose a package. (df)

Speedy collected the following data for last month's performance:

On-time	On-time	Early	Late	On-time	On-time	On-time	On-time	Late	On-time
Early	On-time	On-time	Early	On-time	On-time	On-time	On-time	On-time	On-time
Early	On-time	Early	On-time	On-time	On-time	Early	On-time	On-time	On-time
Early	On-time	On-time	Late	Early	Early	On-time	On-time	On-time	Early
On-time	Late	Late	On-time	On-time	On-time	On-time	On-time	On-time	On-time
On-time	Late	Early	On-time	Early	On-time	Lost	On-time	On-time	On-time
Early	Early	On-time	On-time	Late	Early	Lost	On-time	On-time	On-time
On-time	On-time	Early	On-time	Early	On-time	Early	On-time	Late	On-time
On-time	Early	On-time	On-time	On-time	Late	On-time	Early	On-time	On-time
On-time	On-time	On-time	On-time	On-time	Early	Early	On-time	On-time	On-time

    a. What scale is used to measure delivery performance? What kind of variable is delivery performance?
    b. Construct a frequency table for delivery performance for last month.
    c. Construct a relative frequency table for delivery performance last month.
    d. Construct a bar chart of the frequency table for delivery performance for last month.
    e. Construct a pie chart of on-time delivery performance for last month.
    f. Analyze the data summaries and write an evaluation of last month's delivery performance as it relates to Speedy Swift's performance objectives. Write a general recommendation for further analysis.
27. A data set consists of 83 observations. How many classes would you recommend for a frequency distribution?
28. A data set consists of 145 observations that range from 56 to 490. What size class interval would you recommend?
29. The following is the number of minutes to commute from home to work for a group of automobile executives. (df)

28	25	48	37	41	19	32	26	16	23	23	29	36
31	26	21	32	25	31	43	35	42	38	33	28	

    a. How many classes would you recommend?
    b. What class interval would you suggest?
    c. What would you recommend as the lower limit of the first class?
    d. Organize the data into a frequency distribution.
    e. Comment on the shape of the frequency distribution.
30. The following data give the weekly amounts spent on groceries for a sample of households. (df)

$271	$363	$159	$ 76	$227	$337	$295	$319	$250
279	205	279	266	199	177	162	232	303
192	181	321	309	246	278	50	41	335
116	100	151	240	474	297	170	188	320
429	294	570	342	279	235	434	123	325

    a. How many classes would you recommend?
    b. What class interval would you suggest?
    c. What would you recommend as the lower limit of the first class?
    d. Organize the data into a frequency distribution.

31. A social scientist is studying the use of iPods by college students. A sample of 45 students revealed they played the following number of songs yesterday. df

4	6	8	7	9	6	3	7	7	6	7	1	4	7	7
4	6	4	10	2	4	6	3	4	6	8	4	3	3	6
8	8	4	6	4	6	5	5	9	6	8	8	6	5	10

Organize the above information into a frequency distribution.
  a. How many classes would you suggest?
  b. What is the most suitable class interval?
  c. What is the lower limit of the initial class?
  d. Create the frequency distribution.
  e. Describe the profile of the distribution.

32. David Wise handles his own investment portfolio, and has done so for many years. Listed below is the holding time (recorded to the nearest whole year) between purchase and sale for his collection of stocks. df

8	8	6	11	11	9	8	5	11	4	8	5	14	7	12	8	6	11	9	7
9	15	8	8	12	5	9	8	5	9	10	11	3	9	8	6				

  a. How many classes would you propose?
  b. What class interval would you suggest?
  c. What quantity would you use for the lower limit of the initial class?
  d. Using your responses to parts (a), (b), and (c), create a frequency distribution.
  e. Identify the appearance of the frequency distribution.

33. You are exploring the music in your iTunes library. The total play counts over the past year for the songs on your "smart playlist" are shown below. Make a frequency distribution of the counts and describe its shape. It is often claimed that a small fraction of a person's songs will account for most of their total plays. Does this seem to be the case here? df

128	56	54	91	190	23	160	298	445	50
578	494	37	677	18	74	70	868	108	71
466	23	84	38	26	814	17			

34. The monthly issues of the *Journal of Finance* are available on the Internet. The table below shows the number of times an issue was downloaded over the last 33 months. Suppose you wish to summarize the number of downloads with a frequency distribution. df

312	2,753	2,595	6,057	7,624	6,624	6,362	6,575	7,760	7,085	7,272
5,967	5,256	6,160	6,238	6,709	7,193	5,631	6,490	6,682	7,829	7,091
6,871	6,230	7,253	5,507	5,676	6,974	6,915	4,999	5,689	6,143	7,086

  a. How many classes would you propose?
  b. What class interval would you suggest?
  c. What quantity would you use for the lower limit of the initial class?
  d. Using your responses to parts (a), (b), and (c), create a frequency distribution.
  e. Identify the appearance of the frequency distribution.

35. The following histogram shows the scores on the first exam for a statistics class.

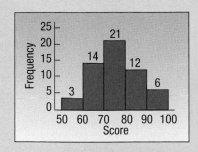

    a. How many students took the exam?
    b. What is the class interval?
    c. What is the class midpoint for the first class?
    d. How many students earned a score of less than 70?
36. The following chart summarizes the selling price of homes sold last month in the Sarasota, Florida, area.

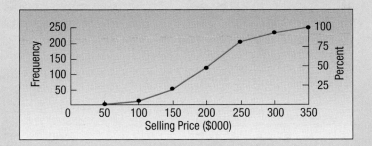

    a. What is the chart called?
    b. How many homes were sold during the last month?
    c. What is the class interval?
    d. About 75% of the houses sold for less than what amount?
    e. One hundred and seventy-five of the homes sold for less than what amount?
37. A chain of sport shops catering to beginning skiers, headquartered in Aspen, Colorado, plans to conduct a study of how much a beginning skier spends on his or her initial purchase of equipment and supplies. Based on these figures, it wants to explore the possibility of offering combinations, such as a pair of boots and a pair of skis, to induce customers to buy more. A sample of cash register receipts revealed these initial purchases: (df)

$140	$ 82	$265	$168	$ 90	$114	$172	$230	$142
86	125	235	212	171	149	156	162	118
139	149	132	105	162	126	216	195	127
161	135	172	220	229	129	87	128	126
175	127	149	126	121	118	172	126	

    a. Arrive at a suggested class interval.
    b. Organize the data into a frequency distribution using a lower limit of $70.
    c. Interpret your findings.

38. Following is the number of shareholders for a selected group of large companies (in thousands):

Company	Number of Shareholders (thousands)	Company	Number of Shareholders (thousands)
Southwest Airlines	144	Standard Oil (Indiana)	173
General Public Utilities	177	Home Depot	195
Occidental Petroleum	266	Detroit Edison	220
Middle South Utilities	133	Eastman Kodak	251
Chrysler	209	Dow Chemical	137
Standard Oil of California	264	Pennsylvania Power	150
Bethlehem Steel	160	American Electric Power	262
Long Island Lighting	143	Ohio Edison	158
RCA	246	Transamerica Corporation	162
Greyhound Corporation	151	Columbia Gas System	165
Pacific Gas & Electric	239	International Telephone & Telegraph	223
Niagara Mohawk Power	204	Union Electric	158
E. I. du Pont de Nemours	204	Virginia Electric and Power	162
Westinghouse Electric	195	Public Service Electric & Gas	225
Union Carbide	176	Consumers Power	161
Bank of America	175		
Northeast Utilities	200		

The shareholder numbers are to be organized into a frequency distribution and several graphs drawn to portray the distribution.

a. Using seven classes and a lower limit of 130, construct a frequency distribution.
b. Portray the distribution as a frequency polygon.
c. Portray the distribution in a cumulative frequency polygon.
d. According to the polygon, three out of four (75%) of the companies have how many shareholders or less?
e. Write a brief analysis of the number of shareholders based on the frequency distribution and graphs.

39. A recent survey showed that the typical American car owner spends $2,950 per year on operating expenses. Below is a breakdown of the various expenditure items. Draw an appropriate chart to portray the data and summarize your findings in a brief report.

Expenditure Item	Amount
Fuel	$ 603
Interest on car loan	279
Repairs	930
Insurance and license	646
Depreciation	492
Total	$2,950

40. Midland National Bank selected a sample of 40 student checking accounts. Below are their end-of-the-month balances.

$404	$ 74	$234	$149	$279	$215	$123	$ 55	$ 43	$321
87	234	68	489	57	185	141	758	72	863
703	125	350	440	37	252	27	521	302	127
968	712	503	489	327	608	358	425	303	203

  a. Tally the data into a frequency distribution using $100 as a class interval and $0 as the starting point.

  b. Draw a cumulative frequency polygon.

  c. The bank considers any student with an ending balance of $400 or more a "preferred customer." Estimate the percentage of preferred customers.

  d. The bank is also considering a service charge to the lowest 10% of the ending balances. What would you recommend as the cutoff point between those who have to pay a service charge and those who do not?

41. Residents of the state of South Carolina earned a total of $69.5 billion in adjusted gross income. Seventy-three percent of the total was in wages and salaries; 11% in dividends, interest, and capital gains; 8% in IRAs and taxable pensions; 3% in business income pensions; 2% in Social Security, and the remaining 3% from other sources. Develop a pie chart depicting the breakdown of adjusted gross income. Write a paragraph summarizing the information.

42. A recent study of home technologies reported the number of hours of personal computer usage per week for a sample of 60 persons. Excluded from the study were people who worked out of their home and used the computer as a part of their work.

9.3	5.3	6.3	8.8	6.5	0.6	5.2	6.6	9.3	4.3
6.3	2.1	2.7	0.4	3.7	3.3	1.1	2.7	6.7	6.5
4.3	9.7	7.7	5.2	1.7	8.5	4.2	5.5	5.1	5.6
5.4	4.8	2.1	10.1	1.3	5.6	2.4	2.4	4.7	1.7
2.0	6.7	1.1	6.7	2.2	2.6	9.8	6.4	4.9	5.2
4.5	9.3	7.9	4.6	4.3	4.5	9.2	8.5	6.0	8.1

  a. Organize the data into a frequency distribution. How many classes would you suggest? What value would you suggest for a class interval?

  b. Draw a histogram. Interpret your result.

43. Merrill Lynch recently completed a study regarding the size of online investment portfolios (stocks, bonds, mutual funds, and certificates of deposit) for a sample of clients in the 40- to 50-year-old age group. Listed following is the value of all the investments in thousands of dollars for the 70 participants in the study.

$669.9	$ 7.5	$ 77.2	$ 7.5	$125.7	$516.9	$ 219.9	$645.2
301.9	235.4	716.4	145.3	26.6	187.2	315.5	89.2
136.4	616.9	440.6	408.2	34.4	296.1	185.4	526.3
380.7	3.3	363.2	51.9	52.2	107.5	82.9	63.0
228.6	308.7	126.7	430.3	82.0	227.0	321.1	403.4
39.5	124.3	118.1	23.9	352.8	156.7	276.3	23.5
31.3	301.2	35.7	154.9	174.3	100.6	236.7	171.9
221.1	43.4	212.3	243.3	315.4	5.9	1,002.2	171.7
295.7	437.0	87.8	302.1	268.1	899.5		

  a. Organize the data into a frequency distribution. How many classes would you suggest? What value would you suggest for a class interval?

  b. Draw a histogram. Interpret your result.

44. A total of 5.9% of the prime time viewing audience watched shows on ABC, 7.6% watched shows on CBS, 5.5% on Fox, 6.0% on NBC, 2.0% on Warner Brothers, and 2.2% on UPN. A total of 70.8% of the audience watched shows on other cable networks, such as CNN and ESPN. You can find the latest information on TV viewing from the following website: http://tv.zap2it.com/news/ratings. Develop a pie chart or a bar chart to depict this information. Write a paragraph summarizing your findings.

45. Refer to the following chart, which appeared recently in the Snapshot section of *USA Today.*

a. What is the name given to this type of chart?
b. If you studied 500 weddings, how many would you expect to take place in a house of worship?
c. Would it be reasonable to conclude that about 80% of weddings take place in either a house of worship or outdoors? Cite evidence.

46. The following chart depicts the annual revenues, by type of tax, for the state of Georgia. The chart was developed using Kids Zone, a NCES project. Their website is: nces.ed.gov/nceskids/createagraph/.

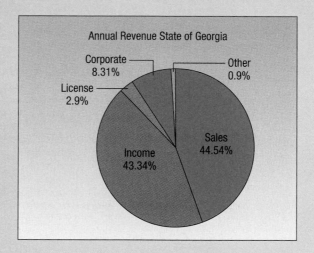

a. What percentage of the state revenue is accounted for by sales tax and individual income tax?
b. Which category will generate more revenue, corporate taxes, or license fees?
c. The total annual revenue for the state of Georgia is $6.3 billion. Estimate the amount of revenue in billions of dollars for sales taxes and for individual taxes.

47. In 2009, Canada exported $224.9 billion worth of products to the United States. The five largest were:

Product	Amount
Mineral fuel and oil	$63.9 billion
Vehicles	31.6
Machinery	15.7
Plastic electric machinery	8.1
Paper and paperboard	7.7

   a. Use a software package to develop a bar chart.

   b. What percentage of Canada's *total* exports to the United States is represented by the two categories "Mineral fuel and oil" and "Vehicles"?

   c. Of the top five exported products, what percentage of the total do "Mineral fuel and oil" and "Vehicles" represent?

48. Farming has changed from the early 1900s. In the early 20th century, machinery gradually replaced animal power. For example, in 1910, U.S. farms used 24.2 million horses and mules and only about 1,000 tractors. By 1960, 4.6 million tractors were used and only 3.2 million horses and mules. In 1920, there were over 6 million farms in the United States. Today there are fewer than 2 million. Listed below is the number of farms, in thousands, for each of the 50 states. Write a paragraph summarizing your findings. (df)

47	1	8	46	76	26	4	3	39	45
4	21	80	63	100	65	91	29	7	15
7	52	87	39	106	25	55	2	3	8
14	38	59	33	76	71	37	51	1	24
35	86	185	13	7	43	36	20	79	9

49. One of the most popular candies in the United States is M&M's, which are produced by the Mars Company. In the beginning M&M's were all brown; more recently they were produced in red, green, blue, orange, brown, and yellow. You can read about the history of the product, find ideas for baking, purchase the candies in the colors of your school or favorite team, and learn the percent of each color in the standard bags at www.m-ms.com. Recently, the purchase of a 14-ounce bag of M&M's Plain had 444 candies with the following breakdown by color: 130 brown, 98 yellow, 96 red, 35 orange, 52 blue, and 33 green. Develop a chart depicting this information and write a paragraph summarizing the results.

50. The number of families who used the Minneapolis YWCA day care service was recorded during a 30-day period. The results are as follows: (df)

31	49	19	62	24	45	23	51	55	60
40	35	54	26	57	37	43	65	18	41
50	56	4	54	39	52	35	51	63	42

   a. Construct a cumulative frequency distribution.

   b. Sketch a graph of the cumulative frequency polygon.

   c. How many days saw fewer than 30 families utilize the day care center?

   d. How busy were the highest 80% of the days?

Data Set Exercises

(The data for these exercises are available at the text website www.mhhe.com/lindbasic8e).

51. Refer to the Real Estate data, which reports information on homes sold in the Goodyear, Arizona, area during the last year. Select an appropriate class interval and organize the selling prices into a frequency distribution. Write a brief report summarizing your finding. Be sure to answer the following questions in your report.

   a. Around what values do the data tend to cluster?

   b. Based on the frequency distribution, what is the typical selling price in the first class? What is the typical selling price in the last class?

   c. Draw a cumulative frequency distribution. How many homes sold for less than $200,000? Estimate the percent of the homes that sold for more than $220,000. What percent of the homes sold for less than $125,000?

   d. Refer to the variable regarding the townships. Draw a bar chart showing the number of homes sold in each township. Are there any differences or is the number of homes sold about the same in each township?

52. Refer to the 2010 Baseball data that reports information on the 30 Major League Baseball teams for the 2010 season. Create a frequency distribution for the team payroll variable and answer the following questions.
   a. What is the typical payroll for a team? What is the range of the payrolls?
   b. Comment on the shape of the distribution. Does it appear that any of the teams have a payroll that is out of line with the others?
   c. Draw a cumulative frequency distribution. Thirty percent of the teams have a payroll of less than what amount? About how many teams have total payroll of less than $100,000,000?

53. Refer to the Buena School District bus data. Select the variable referring to the number of miles traveled last month, and then organize these data into a frequency distribution.
   a. What is a typical amount of miles traveled? What is the range?
   b. Comment on the shape of the distribution. Are there any outliers in terms of miles driven?
   c. Draw a cumulative frequency distribution. Forty percent of the buses were driven fewer than how many miles? How many buses were driven less than 850 miles?
   d. Refer to the variables regarding the bus type and the number of seats in each bus. Draw a pie chart of each variable and comment on your findings.

Practice Test

Part 1—Objective

1. A grouping of *qualitative data* into mutually exclusive classes showing the number of observations in each class is known as a _____ .
2. A grouping of *quantitative data* into mutually exclusive classes showing the number of observations in each class is known as a _____ .
3. A graph in which the classes for qualitative data are reported on the horizontal axis and the class frequencies (proportional to the heights of the bars) on the vertical axis is called a _____ .
4. A circular chart that shows the proportion or percentage that each class represents of the total is called a _____ .
5. A graph in which the classes of a quantitative variable are marked on the horizontal axis and the class frequencies on the vertical axis is called a _____ .
6. A set of data included 70 observations. How many classes would you suggest to construct a frequency distribution? _____
7. The distance between successive lower class limits is called the _____ .
8. The average of the respective class limits of two consecutive classes is the class _____ .
9. In a relative frequency distribution, the class frequencies are divided by the _____ .
10. A cumulative frequency polygon is created by line segments connecting the class _____ and the corresponding cumulative frequencies.

Part 2—Problems
1. Consider these data on the selling prices ($000) of homes in the city of Warren, Pennsylvania, last year.

Selling Price ($000)	Frequency
120 up to 150	4
150 up to 180	18
180 up to 210	30
210 up to 240	20
240 up to 270	17
270 up to 300	10
300 up to 330	6

   a. What is the class interval?
   b. How many homes were sold last year?
   c. How many homes sold for less than $210,000?
   d. What is the relative frequency for the $210 up to $240 class?
   e. What is the midpoint of the $150 up to $180 class?
   f. What were the maximum and minimum selling prices?
   g. Construct a histogram of these data.
   h. Make a frequency polygon of these data.

Software Commands

1. The Excel commands to use the PivotTable Wizard to create the frequency table, bar chart, and pie chart on page 26 are:
   a. Open the Applewood Auto Group data file.
   b. Click on a cell somewhere in the data set, such as cell *C5*.
   c. Click on the *Insert* menu on the toolbar. Then click *PivotTable* on the far left of the *Ribbon*.

   d. The following screen will appear. Click on "*Select a table or range,*" to select the data range as shown in the *Table/Range* row. Next, click on "*Existing Worksheet*" and select a cell location, such a *N1* and click *OK*.

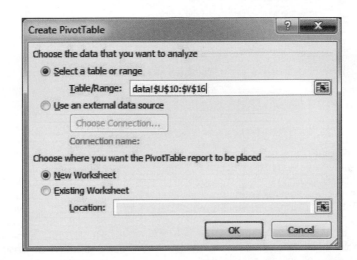

   e. On the right-hand side of the spreadsheet, a *PivotTable Field List* will appear with a list of the data set variables. To summarize the "Vehicle-Type" variable, click on the "Vehicle-Type" variable and it will appear in the lower left box called *Row Label*. You will note that the frequency table is started in cell *N1* with the rows labeled with the values of the variable "Vehicle-Type." Next, return to the top box, and select and drag the "Vehicle-Type" variable to the "Σ Values" box. A column of frequencies will be added to the table. Note that you can format the table to center the values and also relabel the column headings as needed.
   f. To create the bar chart, select any cell in the PivotTable. Next, select the *Insert* menu from the tool bar and within the *Charts* group, select a bar chart from the *Column* drop-down menu. A bar chart appears. Click on the chart heading and label the chart as needed.
   g. To create the pie chart, the frequencies should be converted to relative frequencies. Click in the body of the PivotTable and the *PivotTable Field List* will appear to the right. In the "Σ Values" box, click on the pull-down menu for "Count of Vehicle Type" and select the *Value Field Settings* option. You will see a number of different selections that can be used to summarize the variables in a PivotTable. Click on the tab "*Show Values As*" and, in the pull-down menu, select

"*% of Grand Total*." The frequencies will be converted to relative frequencies.

To create the pie chart, select any cell in the PivotTable. Next, select the *Insert* menu from the tool bar, and within the *Charts* group, select a pie chart from the *Column* drop-down menu. A pie chart appears. Click on the chart heading and label the chart as needed. To add the percentages, click on the pie chart and a menu will appear. Click on "Add Data Labels."

2. The Excel commands to use the PivotTable Wizard to create the frequency and relative frequency distributions on page 34 and the histogram on page 38 follow.
   a. Open the Applewood Auto Group data file.
   b. Click on a cell somewhere in the data set, such as cell *C5*.
   c. Click on the *Insert* menu on the toolbar. Then click on *PivotTable* on the far left of the *Ribbon*.
   d. The following screen will appear. Click on "*Select a table or range,*" to select the data range as shown in the *Table/Range* row. Next, click on "*New Worksheet*" and the PivotTable will be created in a new worksheet.
   e. On the right-hand side of the spreadsheet, a *PivotTable Field List* will appear with a list of the data set variables. To summarize the "Profit" variable, click on the "Profit" variable and drag it to the "Row Labels" box. Then return to the top box, click on "Profits" again and drag it to

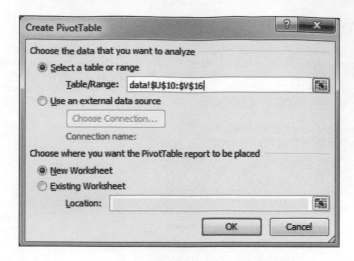

the "Σ Values" box. Staying in this box, click on the pull-down menu for "Sum of Profit." You will see a number of different selections that can be used to summarize the variables in a PivotTable. In the "*Summarize Values As*" tab, select "Count" to create frequencies for the variable "Profit." A PivotTable will appear in the new worksheet.

f. In the PivotTable, the left column shows each value of the variable "Profit." To create classes for "Profit," select any cell in the column and right click. A menu appears. Select "Group" from the menu to create the classes. First, uncheck both boxes. Then, in the dialogue box, enter the lower limit of the first class as the "Starting at" value. Enter the upper limit of the last class as the "Ending at" value. Then enter the class interval as the "By" value. Click OK. A frequency distribution appears.

g. To create a relative frequency distribution, point and click on one of the cells in the PivotTable and the "PivotTable Field List" appears to the right. Click and drag the variable "Profits" to the "Σ Values" box. A second "Counts of Profit" appears. In the "Σ Values," click on the second "Counts of Profit" and select the "Value Fields Setting." You will see a number of different

selections that can be used to summarize the variables in a PivotTable. Click on the tab "*Show Values As*" and, in the pull-down menu, select "*% of Grand Total.*" The relative frequencies will be added to the table. You can format the table by relabeling the column headings such as "Frequency" and "Relative Frequency."

h. To create a histogram, select a cell in the PivotTable, choose the *Insert* menu from the tool bar, and within the *Charts* group, select a *column* chart from the *Column* drop-down menu. A histogram appears with both "Count of Profit" and "Count of Profit2." On the "Count of Profit2" bubble at the top of the chart, right click and select "Remove Field." Then the chart and PivotTable only report the frequencies. To eliminate the space between the bars, select the entire chart area, and "PivotChart Tools" will appear at the top. Select "Design." In the "Chart Layouts" choices, select the option that shows no spaces between the bars. The option is illustrated in the figure to the right. To add data labels, select the histogram, right click, and select "Add Data Labels." Relabel the chart and axes as needed.

Chapter 2   Answers to Self-Review

2–1 **a.** Qualitative data, because the customers' response to the taste test is the name of a beverage.

b. Frequency table. It shows the number of people who prefer each beverage.

c.

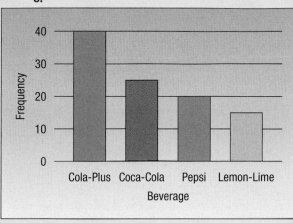

d.

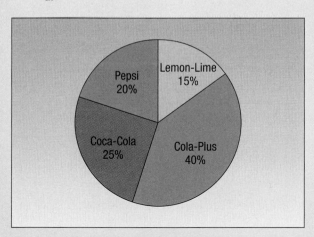

2–2 **a.** The raw data or ungrouped data.

b.

Commission	Number of Salespeople
$1,400 up to $1,500	2
1,500 up to 1,600	5
1,600 up to 1,700	3
1,700 up to 1,800	1
Total	11

c. Class frequencies.

d. The largest concentration of commissions is $1,500 up to $1,600. The smallest commission is about $1,400 and the largest is about $1,800. The typical amount earned is $1,550.

2–3 **a.** $2^6 = 64 < 73 < 128 = 2^7$. So seven classes are recommended.

b. The range of the data is the (maximum − minimum) values, or $(488 - 320) = 168$. The number of classes (seven) multiplied by the class interval (30) should be at least the range of the data (168) or $7 \times 30 = 210$, which is greater than 168. A class interval of 30 is appropriate.

c.

Distance Classes	Frequency	Percent
300 up to 330	2	2.7%
330 up to 360	2	2.7%
360 up to 390	17	23.3%
390 up to 420	27	37.0%
420 up to 450	22	30.1%
450 up to 480	1	1.4%
480 up to 510	2	2.7%
Total	**73**	**100.00%**

d. 17

e. 23.3%, found by 17/73

f. 71.2%, found by $(27 + 22 + 1 + 2)/73$

2–4 **a.**

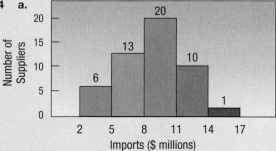

b.

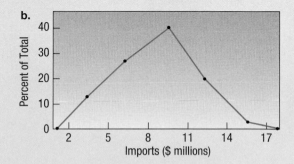

The plots are: (3.5, 12), (6.5, 26), (9.5, 40), (12.5, 20), and (15.5, 2).

c. The smallest annual volume of imports by a supplier is about $2 million, the largest about $17 million. The highest frequency is between $8 million and $11 million.

2–5 a. A frequency distribution.

b.

Hourly Wages	Cumulative Number
Less than $8	0
Less than $10	3
Less than $12	10
Less than $14	14
Less than $16	15

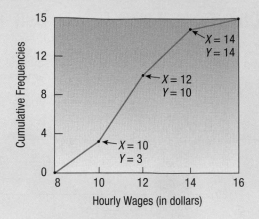

c. Three employees earn less than $10. Ten employees earn less than $12.

Describing Data:

Numerical Measures

Learning Objectives
When you have completed this chapter, you will be able to:

LO 3-1 Explain the concept of central tendency.

LO 3-2 Identify and compute the arithmetic mean.

LO 3-3 Compute and interpret the weighted mean.

LO 3-4 Determine the median.

LO 3-5 Identify the mode.

LO 3-6 Explain and apply measures of dispersion.

LO 3-7 Compute and explain the variance and the standard deviation.

LO 3-8 Explain Chebyshev's Theorem and the Empirical Rule.

The Kentucky Derby is held the first Saturday in May at Churchill Downs in Louisville, Kentucky. The race track is one and one-quarter miles. The table in Exercise 64 shows the winners since 1990, their margin of victory, the winning time, and the payoff on a $2 bet. Determine the mean and median for the variables winning time and payoff on a $2 bet. (See Exercise 64 and LO 3-2 and LO 3-4.)

LO 3-1 Explain the concept of central tendency.

Statistics in Action

Did you ever meet the "average" American man? Well, his name is Robert (that is the nominal level of measurement), he is 31 years old (that is the ratio level), he is 69.5 inches tall (again the ratio level of measurement), weighs 172 pounds, wears a size 9½ shoe, has a 34-inch waist, and wears a size 40 suit. In addition, the average man eats 4 pounds of potato chips, watches 1,456 hours of TV, and eats 26 pounds of bananas each year and also sleeps 7.7 hours per night.

The average American woman is 5' 4" tall and weighs 140 pounds, while the average American model is 5' 11" tall and weighs 117 pounds. On any given day, almost half of the women in the United States are on a diet. Idolized in the 1950s, Marilyn Monroe would be considered overweight by today's standards. She fluctuated between a size 14 and 18 dress, and was a healthy and attractive woman.

3.1 Introduction

Chapter 2 began our study of descriptive statistics. To summarize raw data into a meaningful form, we organized qualitative data into a frequency table and portrayed the results in a bar chart. In a similar fashion, we organized quantitative data into a frequency distribution and portrayed the results in a histogram. We also looked at other graphical techniques such as pie charts to portray qualitative data and frequency polygons to portray quantitative data.

This chapter is concerned with two numerical ways of describing quantitative variables, namely, **measures of location** and **measures of dispersion.** Measures of location are often referred to as averages. The purpose of a measure of location is to pinpoint the center of a distribution of data. An average is a measure of location that shows the central value of the data. Averages appear daily on TV, on various websites, in the newspaper, and in other journals. Here are some examples:

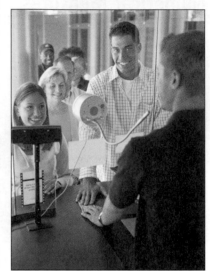

- The average U.S. home changes ownership every 11.8 years.
- An American receives an average of 568 pieces of mail per year.
- The average American home has more TV sets than people. There are 2.73 TV sets and 2.55 people in the typical home.
- The average American couple spends $20,398 for their wedding, while their budget is 50% less. This does not include the cost of a honeymoon or engagement ring.
- The average price of a theater ticket in the United States is $7.50, according to the National Association of Theatre Owners.

If we consider only measures of location in a set of data, or if we compare several sets of data using central values, we may draw an erroneous conclusion. In addition to measures of location, we should consider the **dispersion**—often called the *variation* or the *spread*—in the data. As an illustration, suppose the average annual income of executives for Internet-related companies is $80,000, and the average income for executives in pharmaceutical firms is also $80,000. If we looked only at the average incomes, we might wrongly conclude that the distributions of the two salaries are the same. However, we need to examine the dispersion or spread of the distributions of salary. A look at the salary ranges indicates that this conclusion of equal distributions is not correct. The salaries for the executives in the Internet firms range from $70,000 to $90,000, but salaries for the marketing executives in pharmaceuticals range from $40,000 to $120,000. Thus, we conclude that although the average salaries are the same for the two industries, there is much more spread or dispersion in salaries for the pharmaceutical executives. To describe the dispersion, we will consider the range, the mean deviation, the variance, and the standard deviation.

We begin by discussing measures of location. There is not just one measure of location; in fact, there are many. We will consider four: the arithmetic mean, the weighted mean, the median, and the mode. The arithmetic mean is the most widely used and widely reported measure of location. We study the mean as both a population parameter and a sample statistic.

3.2 The Population Mean

Many studies involve all the values in a population. For example, there are 12 sales associates employed at the Reynolds Road Carpet Outlet. The mean amount of commission they earned last month was $1,345. This is a population value, because we considered the commission of *all* the sales associates. Other examples of a population mean would be:

- The mean closing price for Johnson & Johnson stock for the last 5 days is $64.75.
- The mean number of hours of overtime worked last week by the six welders in the welding department of Butts Welding Inc. is 6.45 hours.
- Caryn Tirsch began a website last month devoted to organic gardening. The mean number of hits on her site for the 31 days in July was 84.36.

For raw data—that is, data that have not been grouped in a frequency distribution—the population mean is the sum of all the values in the population divided by the number of values in the population. To find the population mean, we use the following formula.

$$\text{Population mean} = \frac{\text{Sum of all the values in the population}}{\text{Number of values in the population}}$$

LO 3-2 Identify and compute the arithmetic mean.

Instead of writing out in words the full directions for computing the population mean (or any other measure), it is more convenient to use the shorthand symbols of mathematics. The mean of the population using mathematical symbols is:

POPULATION MEAN	$\mu = \dfrac{\Sigma X}{N}$	[3–1]

where:

μ represents the population mean. It is the Greek lowercase letter "mu."
N is the number of values in the population.
X represents any particular value.
Σ is the Greek capital letter "sigma" and indicates the operation of adding.
ΣX is the sum of the X values in the population.

Any measurable characteristic of a population is called a **parameter.** The mean of a population is an example of a parameter.

PARAMETER A characteristic of a population.

Example

There are 42 exits on I-75 through the state of Kentucky. Listed below are the distances between exits (in miles).

11	4	10	4	9	3	8	10	3	14	1	10	3	5
2	2	5	6	1	2	2	3	7	1	3	7	8	10
1	4	7	5	2	2	5	1	1	3	3	1	2	1

Why is this information a population? What is the mean number of miles between exits?

Solution

This is a population because we are considering all the exits in Kentucky on I-75. We add the distances between each of the 42 exits. The total distance is 192 miles. To find the arithmetic mean, we divide this total by 42. So the arithmetic mean is 4.57 miles, found by 192/42. From formula (3–1):

$$\mu = \frac{\Sigma X}{N} = \frac{11 + 4 + 10 + \cdots + 1}{42} = \frac{192}{42} = 4.57$$

How do we interpret the value of 4.57? It is the typical number of miles between exits. Because we considered all the exits in Kentucky on I-75, this value is a population parameter.

3.3 The Sample Mean

As explained in Chapter 1, we often select a sample from the population to estimate a specific characteristic of the population. Smucker's quality assurance department needs to be assured that the amount of strawberry jam in the jar labeled as containing 12 ounces actually contains that amount. It would be very expensive and time-consuming to check the weight of each jar. Therefore, a sample of 20 jars is selected, the mean of the sample is determined, and that value is used to estimate the amount of jam in each jar.

For raw data—that is, ungrouped data—*the mean is the sum of all the sampled values divided by the total number of sampled values.* To find the mean for a sample:

Sample mean of ungrouped data.

$$\text{Sample mean} = \frac{\text{Sum of all the values in the sample}}{\text{Number of values in the sample}}$$

The mean of a sample and the mean of a population are computed in the same way, but the shorthand notation used is different. The formula for the mean of a *sample* is:

| SAMPLE MEAN | $\bar{X} = \dfrac{\Sigma X}{n}$ | [3–2] |

where:
$\bar{X}$ represents the sample mean. It is read "X bar."
n is the number of values in the sample.
X represents any particular value.
Σ is the Greek capital letter "sigma" and indicates the operation of adding.
ΣX is the sum of the X values in the sample.

The mean of a sample, or any other measure based on sample data, is called a **statistic.** If the mean weight of a sample of 10 jars of Smucker's strawberry jam is 11.5 ounces, this is an example of a statistic.

> **STATISTIC** A characteristic of a sample.

Example

Verizon is studying the number of minutes used by clients in a particular cell phone rate plan. A random sample of 12 clients showed the following number of minutes used last month.

90	77	94	89	119	112
91	110	92	100	113	83

What is the arithmetic mean number of minutes used?

Solution

Using formula (3–2), the sample mean is:

$$\text{Sample mean} = \frac{\text{Sum of all values in the sample}}{\text{Number of values in the sample}}$$

$$\bar{X} = \frac{\Sigma X}{n} = \frac{90 + 77 + \cdots + 83}{12} = \frac{1170}{12} = 97.5$$

The arithmetic mean number of minutes used last month by the sample of cell phone users is 97.5 minutes.

3.4 Properties of the Arithmetic Mean

The arithmetic mean is a widely used measure of location. It has several important properties:

1. **Every set of interval- or ratio-level data has a mean.** Recall from Chapter 1 that ratio-level data include such data as ages, incomes, and weights, with the distance between numbers being constant.
2. **All the values are included in computing the mean.**
3. **The mean is unique.** That is, there is only one mean in a set of data. Later in the chapter, we will discover a measure of location that might appear twice, or more than twice, in a set of data.
4. **The sum of the deviations of each value from the mean is zero.** Expressed symbolically:

$$\Sigma(X - \overline{X}) = 0$$

As an example, the mean of 3, 8, and 4 is 5. Then:

$$\Sigma(X - \overline{X}) = (3 - 5) + (8 - 5) + (4 - 5)$$
$$= -2 + 3 - 1$$
$$= 0$$

Mean as a balance point

Thus, we can consider the mean as a balance point for a set of data. To illustrate, we have a long board with the numbers 1, 2, 3, . . . , 9 evenly spaced on it. Suppose three bars of equal weight were placed on the board at numbers 3, 4, and 8, and the balance point was set at 5, the mean of the three numbers. We would find that the board is balanced perfectly! The deviations below the mean (−3) are equal to the deviations above the mean (+3). Shown schematically:

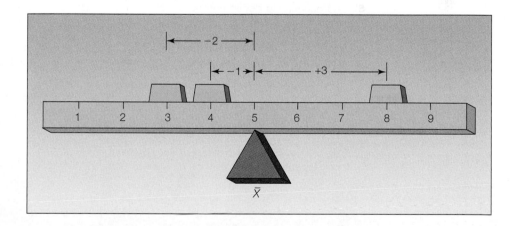

Mean unduly affected by unusually large or small values

The mean does have a weakness. Recall that the mean uses the value of every item in a sample, or population, in its computation. If one or two of these values are either extremely large or extremely small compared to the majority of data, the mean might not be an appropriate average to represent the data. For example, suppose the annual incomes of a small group of stockbrokers at Merrill Lynch are $62,900, $61,600, $62,500, $60,800, and $1,200,000. The mean income is $289,560. Obviously, it is not representative of this group, because all but one broker has an income in the $60,000 to $63,000 range. One income ($1.2 million) is unduly affecting the mean.

Self-Review 3–1

1. The annual incomes of a sample of middle-management employees at Westinghouse are: $62,900, $69,100, $58,300, and $76,800.
   (a) Give the formula for the sample mean.
   (b) Find the sample mean.
   (c) Is the mean you computed in (b) a statistic or a parameter? Why?
   (d) What is your best estimate of the population mean?
2. All the students in advanced Computer Science 411 are a population. Their course grades are 92, 96, 61, 86, 79, and 84.
   (a) Give the formula for the population mean.
   (b) Compute the mean course grade.
   (c) Is the mean you computed in (b) a statistic or a parameter? Why?

Exercises

connect™   *The answers to the odd-numbered exercises are at the end of the book.*

1. Compute the mean of the following population values: 6, 3, 5, 7, 6.
2. Compute the mean of the following population values: 7, 5, 7, 3, 7, 4.
3. **a.** Compute the mean of the following sample values: 5, 9, 4, 10.
   b. Show that $\Sigma(X - \bar{X}) = 0$.
4. **a.** Compute the mean of the following sample values: 1.3, 7.0, 3.6, 4.1, 5.0.
   b. Show that $\Sigma(X - \bar{X}) = 0$.
5. Compute the mean of the following sample values: 16.25, 12.91, 14.58.
6. Suppose you go to the grocery store and spend $61.85 for the purchase of 14 items. What is the mean price per item?

For Exercises 7–10, (a) compute the arithmetic mean and (b) indicate whether it is a statistic or a parameter.

7. There are 10 salespeople employed by Midtown Ford. The number of new cars sold last month by the respective salespeople were: 15, 23, 4, 19, 18, 10, 10, 8, 28, 19.
8. The accounting department at a mail-order company counted the following numbers of incoming calls per day to the company's toll-free number during the first 7 days in May: 14, 24, 19, 31, 36, 26, 17.
9. The Cambridge Power and Light Company selected a random sample of 20 residential customers. Following are the amounts, to the nearest dollar, the customers were charged for electrical service last month:

54	48	58	50	25	47	75	46	60	70
67	68	39	35	56	66	33	62	65	67

10. The Human Relations Director at Ford began a study of the overtime hours in the Inspection Department. A sample of 15 workers showed they worked the following number of overtime hours last month.

13	13	12	15	7	15	5	12
6	7	12	10	9	13	12	

11. AAA Heating and Air Conditioning completed 30 jobs last month with a mean revenue of $5,430 per job. The president wants to know the total revenue for the month. Based on the limited information, can you compute the total revenue? What is it?
12. A large pharmaceutical company hires business administration graduates to sell its products. The company is growing rapidly and dedicates only one day of sales training for new salespeople. The company's goal for new salespeople is $10,000 per month. The goal is based on the current mean sales for the entire company, which is $10,000 per month. After reviewing the retention rates of new employees, the company finds that only 1 in 10 new employees stays longer than three months. Comment on using the current mean sales per month as a sales goal for new employees. Why do new employees leave the company?

3.5 The Weighted Mean

LO 3-3 Compute and interpret the weighted mean.

The weighted mean is used when there are several observations of the same value. To explain, suppose the nearby Wendy's Restaurant sold medium, large, and Biggie-sized soft drinks for $.90, $1.25, and $1.50, respectively. Of the last 10 drinks sold, 3 were medium, 4 were large, and 3 were Biggie-sized. To find the mean price of the last 10 drinks sold, we could use formula (3–2).

$$\overline{X} = \frac{\$.90 + \$.90 + \$.90 + \$1.25 + \$1.25 + \$1.25 + \$1.25 + \$1.50 + \$1.50 + \$1.50}{10}$$

$$\overline{X} = \frac{\$12.20}{10} = \$1.22$$

The mean selling price of the last 10 drinks is $1.22.

An easier way to find the mean selling price is to determine the weighted mean. That is, we multiply each observation by the number of times it happens. We will refer to the weighted mean as $\overline{X}_w$. This is read "X bar sub w."

$$\overline{X}_w = \frac{3(\$0.90) + 4(\$1.25) + 3(\$1.50)}{10} = \frac{\$12.20}{10} = \$1.22$$

In this case, the weights are frequency counts. However, any measure of importance could be used as a weight. In general, the weighted mean of a set of numbers designated $X_1, X_2, X_3, \ldots, X_n$ with the corresponding weights $w_1, w_2, w_3, \ldots, w_n$ is computed by:

WEIGHTED MEAN	$\overline{X}_w = \dfrac{w_1X_1 + w_2X_2 + w_3X_3 + \cdots + w_nX_n}{w_1 + w_2 + w_3 + \cdots + w_n}$	[3–3]

This may be shortened to:

$$\overline{X}_w = \frac{\Sigma(wX)}{\Sigma w}$$

Note that the denominator of a weighted mean is always the sum of the weights.

Example

The Carter Construction Company pays its hourly employees $16.50, $19.00, or $25.00 per hour. There are 26 hourly employees, 14 of which are paid at the $16.50 rate, 10 at the $19.00 rate, and 2 at the $25.00 rate. What is the mean hourly rate paid the 26 employees?

Solution

To find the mean hourly rate, we multiply each of the hourly rates by the number of employees earning that rate. From formula (3–3), the mean hourly rate is

$$\overline{X}_w = \frac{14(\$16.50) + 10(\$19.00) + 2(\$25.00)}{14 + 10 + 2} = \frac{\$471.00}{26} = \$18.1154$$

The weighted mean hourly wage is rounded to $18.12.

Self-Review 3–2

Springers sold 95 Antonelli men's suits for the regular price of $400. For the spring sale, the suits were reduced to $200 and 126 were sold. At the final clearance, the price was reduced to $100 and the remaining 79 suits were sold.
(a) What was the weighted mean price of an Antonelli suit?
(b) Springers paid $200 a suit for the 300 suits. Comment on the store's profit per suit if a salesperson receives a $25 commission for each one sold.

Exercises

connect

13. In June, an investor purchased 300 shares of Oracle (an information technology company) stock at $20 per share. In August, she purchased an additional 400 shares at $25 per share. In November, she purchased an additional 400 shares, but the stock declined to $23 per share. What is the weighted mean price per share?

14. The Bookstall Inc. is a specialty bookstore concentrating on used books sold via the Internet. Paperbacks are $1.00 each, and hardcover books are $3.50. Of the 50 books sold last Tuesday morning, 40 were paperback and the rest were hardcover. What was the weighted mean price of a book?

15. The Loris Healthcare System employs 200 persons on the nursing staff. Fifty are nurse's aides, 50 are practical nurses, and 100 are registered nurses. Nurse's aides receive $8 an hour, practical nurses $15 an hour, and registered nurses $24 an hour. What is the weighted mean hourly wage?

16. Andrews and Associates specialize in corporate law. They charge $100 an hour for researching a case, $75 an hour for consultations, and $200 an hour for writing a brief. Last week one of the associates spent 10 hours consulting with her client, 10 hours researching the case, and 20 hours writing the brief. What was the weighted mean hourly charge for her legal services?

3.6 The Median

LO 3-4 Determine the median.

We have stressed that, for data containing one or two very large or very small values, the arithmetic mean may not be representative. The center for such data can be better described by a measure of location called the **median.**

To illustrate the need for a measure of location other than the arithmetic mean, suppose you are seeking to buy a condominium in Palm Aire. Your real estate agent says that the typical price of the units currently available is $110,000. Would you still want to look? If you had budgeted your maximum purchase price at $75,000, you might think they are out of your price range. However, checking the prices of the individual units might change your mind. They are $60,000, $65,000, $70,000, and $80,000, and a superdeluxe penthouse costs $275,000. The arithmetic mean price is $110,000, as the real estate agent reported, but one price ($275,000) is pulling the arithmetic mean upward, causing it to be an unrepresentative average. It does seem that a price around $70,000 is a more typical or representative average, and it is. In cases such as this, the median provides a more valid measure of location.

> **MEDIAN** The midpoint of the values after they have been ordered from the minimum to the maximum, or the maximum to the minimum values.

The median price of the units available is $70,000. To determine this, we order the prices from minimum value ($60,000) to maximum value ($275,000) and select the middle value ($70,000). For the median, the data must be at least an ordinal level of measurement.

Prices Ordered from Minimum to Maximum		Prices Ordered from Maximum to Minimum
$ 60,000		$275,000
65,000		80,000
70,000	← Median→	70,000
80,000		65,000
275,000		60,000

Median less affected by extreme values

Note that there is the same number of prices below the median of $70,000 as above it. The median is, therefore, unaffected by extremely low or high prices. Had the highest price been $90,000, or $300,000, or even $1 million, the median price would still be $70,000. Likewise, had the lowest price been $20,000 or $50,000, the median price would still be $70,000.

In the previous illustration, there is an *odd* number of observations (five). How is the median determined for an *even* number of observations? As before, the observations are ordered. Then by convention we calculate the mean of the two middle observations. So for an even number of observations, the median may not be one of the given values.

Example

Facebook is a popular social networking website. Users can add friends and send them messages, and update their personal profiles to notify friends about themselves and their activities. A sample of 10 adults revealed they spent the following number of hours last month using Facebook.

| 3 | 5 | 7 | 5 | 9 | 1 | 3 | 9 | 17 | 10 |

Find the median number of hours.

Solution

Note that the number of adults sampled is even (10). The first step, as before, is to order the hours using Facebook from the minimum value to the maximum value. Then identify the two middle values. The arithmetic mean of the two middle values gives us the median hours. Arranging the values from minimum to maximum:

| 1 | 3 | 3 | 5 | 5 | 7 | 9 | 9 | 10 | 17 |

The median is found by averaging the two middle values. The middle values are 5 hours and 7 hours, and the mean of these two values is 6. We conclude that the typical Facebook user spends 6 hours per month at the website. Notice that the median is not one of the values. Also, half of the times are below the median and half are above it.

The major properties of the median are:

The median can be determined for all levels of data but the nominal.

1. **It is not affected by extremely large or small values.** Therefore, the median is a valuable measure of location when such values do occur.
2. **It can be computed for ordinal-level data or higher.** Recall from Chapter 1 that ordinal-level data can be ranked from low to high.

3.7 The Mode

The **mode** is another measure of location.

LO 3-5 Identify the mode.

> **MODE** The value of the observation that appears most frequently.

The mode is especially useful in summarizing nominal-level data. As an example of its use for nominal-level data, a company has developed five bath oils. The bar chart in Chart 3–1 shows the results of a marketing survey designed to find which bath oil consumers prefer. The largest number of respondents favored Lamoure, as evidenced by the highest bar. Thus, Lamoure is the mode.

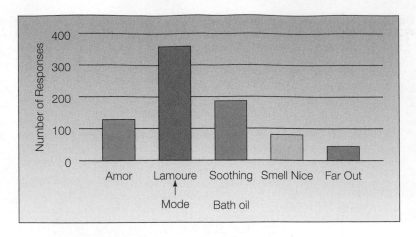

CHART 3–1 Number of Respondents Favoring Various Bath Oils

Example

Recall the data regarding the distance in miles between exits on I-75 through Kentucky. The information is repeated below.

11	4	10	4	9	3	8	10	3	14	1	10	3	5
2	2	5	6	1	2	2	3	7	1	3	7	8	10
1	4	7	5	2	2	5	1	1	3	3	1	2	1

What is the modal distance?

Solution

The first step is to organize the distances into a frequency table. This will help us determine the distance that occurs most frequently.

Distance in Miles between Exits	Frequency
1	8
2	7
3	7
4	3
5	4
6	1
7	3
8	2
9	1
10	4
11	1
14	1
Total	42

The distance that occurs most often is one mile. This happens eight times—that is, there are eight exits that are one mile apart. So the modal distance between exits is one mile.

Which of the three measures of location (mean, median, or mode) best represents the central location of this data? Is the mode the best measure of location to represent the Kentucky data? No. The mode assumes only the nominal scale of measurement and the variable miles is measured using the ratio scale. We calculated the mean to be 4.57 miles. See page 61. Is the mean the best measure of location to represent this data? Probably not. There are several cases in which the distance between exits is large. These values are affecting the mean, making it too large and not representative of the distances between exits. What about the median? The median distance is 3 miles. That is, half of the distances between exits are 3 miles or less. In this case, the median of 3 miles between exits is probably a more representative measure of the distance between exits.

In summary, we can determine the mode for all levels of data—nominal, ordinal, interval, and ratio. The mode also has the advantage of not being affected by extremely high or low values.

Disadvantages of the mode

The mode does have disadvantages, however, that cause it to be used less frequently than the mean or median. For many sets of data, there is no mode because no value appears more than once. For example, there is no mode for this set of price data: $19, $21, $23, $20, and $18. Since every value is different, however, it could be argued that every value is the mode. Conversely, for some data sets there is more than one mode. Suppose the ages of the individuals in a stock investment club are 22, 26, 27, 27, 31, 35, and 35. Both the ages 27 and 35 are modes. Thus, this grouping of ages is referred to as *bimodal* (having two modes). One would question the use of two modes to represent the location of this set of age data.

Self-Review 3–3

1. A sample of single persons in Towson, Texas, receiving Social Security payments revealed these monthly benefits: $852, $598, $580, $1,374, $960, $878, and $1,130.
   (a) What is the median monthly benefit?
   (b) How many observations are below the median? Above it?
2. The number of work stoppages in the automobile industry for selected months are 6, 0, 10, 14, 8, and 0.
   (a) What is the median number of stoppages?
   (b) How many observations are below the median? Above it?
   (c) What is the modal number of work stoppages?

Exercises

connect™

17. What would you report as the modal value for a set of observations if there were a total of:
    a. 10 observations and no two values were the same?
    b. 6 observations and they were all the same?
    c. 6 observations and the values were 1, 2, 3, 3, 4, and 4?

For Exercises 18–20, determine the (a) mean, (b) median, and (c) mode.

18. The following is the number of oil changes for the last 7 days at the Jiffy Lube located at the corner of Elm Street and Pennsylvania Avenue.

41	15	39	54	31	15	33

19. The following is the percent change in net income from last year to this year for a sample of 12 construction companies in Denver.

5	1	−10	−6	5	12	7	8	2	6	−1	11

20. The following are the ages of the 10 people in the video arcade at the Southwyck Shopping Mall at 10 A.M.

12	8	17	6	11	14	8	17	10	8

21. Several indicators of long-term economic growth in the United States are listed below.

Economic Indicator	Percent Change	Economic Indicator	Percent Change
Inflation	4.5%	Real GNP	2.9%
Exports	4.7	Investment (residential)	3.6
Imports	2.3	Investment (nonresidential)	2.1
Real disposable income	2.9	Productivity (total)	1.4
Consumption	2.7	Productivity (manufacturing)	5.2

  a. What is the median percent change?
  b. What is the modal percent change?

22. Sally Reynolds sells real estate along the coastal area of Northern California. Below is the total amount of her commissions earned since 2000. Find the mean, median, and mode of the commissions she earned for the 11 years.

Year	Amount (thousands)
2000	$237.51
2001	233.80
2002	206.97
2003	248.14
2004	164.69
2005	292.16
2006	269.11
2007	225.57
2008	255.33
2009	202.67
2010	206.53

23. The accounting firm of Rowatti and Koppel specializes in income tax returns for self-employed professionals, such as physicians, dentists, architects, and lawyers. The firm employs 11 accountants who prepare the returns. For last year, the number of returns prepared by each accountant was:

58	75	31	58	46	65	60	71	45	58	80

  Find the mean, median, and mode for the number of returns prepared by each accountant. If you could report only one, which measure of location would you recommend reporting?

24. The demand for the video games provided by Mid-Tech Video Games Inc. has exploded in the last several years. Hence, the owner needs to hire several new technical people to keep up with the demand. Mid-Tech gives each applicant a special test that Dr. McGraw, the designer of the test, believes is closely related to the ability to create video games. For the general population, the mean on this test is 100. Below are the scores on this test for the applicants.

95	105	120	81	90	115	99	100	130	10

  The president is interested in the overall quality of the job applicants based on this test. Compute the mean and the median score for the ten applicants. What would you report to the president? Does it seem that the applicants are better than the general population?

3.8 Software Solution

We can use a statistical software package to find many measures of location.

Example

Table 2–4 on page 30 shows the profit on the sales of 180 vehicles at Applewood Auto Group. Determine the mean and the median selling price.

Solution

The mean, median, and modal amounts of profit are reported in the following Excel output (highlighted in the screen shot). (Reminder: The instructions to create the output appear in the **Software Commands** section at the end of the chapter.) There are 180 vehicles in the study, so using a calculator would be tedious and prone to error.

APPLEWOOD AUTO GROUP 2011

	A	B	C	D	E	F	G	H
1	Age	Profit	Location	Vehicle-Type	Previous		*Profit*	
2	33	$1,889	Olean	SUV	1			
3	47	$1,461	Kane	Sedan	0		Mean	1843.17
4	44	$1,532	Tionesta	SUV	3		Standard Error	47.97
5	53	$1,220	Olean	Sedan	0		Median	1882.50
6	51	$1,674	Sheffield	Sedan	1		Mode	1915.00
7	41	$2,389	Kane	Truck	1		Standard Deviation	643.63
8	58	$2,058	Kane	SUV	1		Sample Variance	414256.61
9	35	$1,919	Tionesta	SUV	1		Kurtosis	-0.22
10	45	$1,266	Olean	Sedan	0		Skewness	-0.24
11	54	$2,991	Tionesta	Sedan	0		Range	2998
12	56	$2,695	Kane	Sedan	2		Minimum	294
13	41	$2,165	Tionesta	SUV	0		Maximum	3292
14	38	$1,766	Sheffield	SUV	0		Sum	331770
15	48	$1,952	Tionesta	Compact	1		Count	180

The mean profit is $1,843.17 and the median is $1,882.50. These two values are less than $40 apart, so either value is reasonable. We can also see from the Excel output that there were 180 vehicles sold and their total profit was $331,770.00. We will describe the meaning of standard error, standard deviation, and other measures reported on the output later in this chapter and in later chapters.

What can we conclude? The typical profit on a vehicle is about $1,850. Management at Applewood might use this value for revenue projections. For example, if the dealership could increase the number sold in a month from 180 to 200, this would result in an additional estimated $37,000 of revenue, found by 20($1,850).

3.9 The Relative Positions of the Mean, Median, and Mode

For a symmetric, mound-shaped distribution, mean, median, and mode are equal.

Refer to the histogram in Chart 3–2 at the top of the following page. It is a symmetric distribution, which is also mound-shaped. This distribution *has the same shape on either side of the center*. If the histogram were folded in half, the two halves would be identical. For any symmetric distribution, the mode, median, and mean are located at the center and are always equal. They are all equal to 20 years in Chart 3–2. We should point out that there are symmetric distributions that are not mound-shaped.

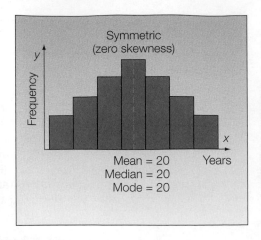

CHART 3–2 A Symmetric Distribution

The number of years corresponding to the highest point of the curve is the *mode* (20 years). Because the distribution is symmetrical, the *median* corresponds to the point where the distribution is cut in half (20 years). Also, because the arithmetic mean is the balance point of a distribution (as shown on page 63), and the distribution is symmetric, the arithmetic mean is 20. Logically, any of the three measures would be appropriate to represent the distribution's center.

A skewed distribution is not symmetrical.

If a distribution is nonsymmetrical, or **skewed,** the relationship among the three measures changes. In a **positively skewed distribution,** such as the distribution of weekly income in Chart 3–3, the arithmetic mean is the largest of the three measures. Why? Because the mean is influenced more than the median or mode by a few extremely high values. The median is generally the next largest measure in a positively skewed frequency distribution. The mode is the smallest of the three measures.

If the distribution is highly skewed, such as the weekly incomes in Chart 3–3, the mean would not be a good measure to use. The median and mode would be more representative.

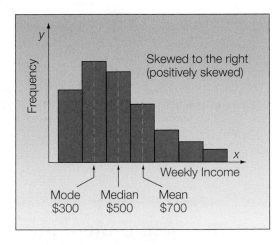

CHART 3–3 A Positively Skewed Distribution

Conversely, if a distribution is **negatively skewed,** such as the distribution of tensile strength in Chart 3–4, the mean is the lowest of the three measures. The mean is, of course, influenced by a few extremely low observations. The median is greater than the arithmetic mean, and the modal value is the largest of the three measures. Again, if the distribution is highly skewed, the mean should not be used to represent the data.

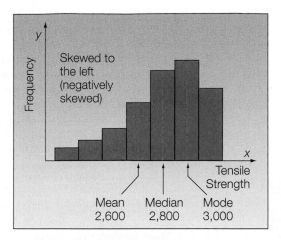

CHART 3–4 A Negatively Skewed Distribution

Self-Review 3–4

The weekly sales from a sample of Hi-Tec electronic supply stores were organized into a frequency distribution. The mean of weekly sales was computed to be $105,900, the median $105,000, and the mode $104,500.
(a) Sketch the sales in the form of a smoothed frequency polygon. Note the location of the mean, median, and mode on the X-axis.
(b) Is the distribution symmetrical, positively skewed, or negatively skewed? Explain.

Exercises

connect

25. The unemployment rate in the state of Alaska by month is given in the table below:

Jan	Feb	Mar	Apr	May	Jun	Jul	Aug	Sep	Oct	Nov	Dec
8.7	8.8	8.7	7.8	7.3	7.8	6.6	6.5	6.5	6.8	7.3	7.6

    a. What is the arithmetic mean of the Alaska unemployment rates?
    b. Find the median and the mode for the unemployment rates.
    c. Compute the arithmetic mean and median for just the winter (Dec–Mar) months. Is it much different?

26. Big Orange Trucking is designing an information system for use in "in-cab" communications. It must summarize data from eight sites throughout a region to describe typical conditions. Compute an appropriate measure of central location for the variables wind direction, temperature, and pavement.

City	Wind Direction	Temperature	Pavement
Anniston, AL	West	89	Dry
Atlanta, GA	Northwest	86	Wet
Augusta, GA	Southwest	92	Wet
Birmingham, AL	South	91	Dry
Jackson, MS	Southwest	92	Dry
Meridian, MS	South	92	Trace
Monroe, LA	Southwest	93	Wet
Tuscaloosa, AL	Southwest	93	Trace

3.10 Why Study Dispersion?

A measure of dispersion can be used to evaluate the reliability of two or more measures of location.

Statistics in Action

The United States Postal Service has tried to become more "user friendly" in the last several years. A recent survey showed that customers were interested in more *consistency* in the time it takes to make a delivery. Under the old conditions, a local letter might take only one day to deliver, or it might take several. "Just tell me how many days ahead I need to mail the birthday card to Mom so it gets there on her birthday, not early, not late," was a common complaint. The level of consistency is measured by the standard deviation of the delivery times.

A measure of location, such as the mean or the median, only describes the center of the data. It is valuable from that standpoint, but it does not tell us anything about the spread of the data. For example, if your nature guide told you that the river ahead averaged 3 feet in depth, would you want to wade across on foot without additional information? Probably not. You would want to know something about the variation in the depth. Is the maximum depth of the river 3.25 feet and the minimum 2.75 feet? If that is the case, you would probably agree to cross. What if you learned the river depth ranged from 0.50 feet to 5.5 feet? Your decision would probably be not to cross. Before making a decision about crossing the river, you want information on both the typical depth and the dispersion in the depth of the river.

A small value for a measure of dispersion indicates that the data are clustered closely, say, around the arithmetic mean. The mean is therefore considered representative of the data. Conversely, a large measure of dispersion indicates that the mean is not reliable. Refer to Chart 3–5. The 100 employees of Hammond Iron Works Inc. a steel fabricating company, are organized into a histogram based on the number of years of employment with the company. The mean is 4.9 years, but the spread of the data is from 6 months to 16.8 years. The mean of 4.9 years is not very representative of all the employees.

A second reason for studying the dispersion in a set of data is to compare the spread in two or more distributions. Suppose, for example, that the new Vision Quest LCD computer monitor is assembled in Baton Rouge and also in Tucson. The arithmetic mean hourly output in both the Baton Rouge plant and the Tucson plant is 50. Based on the two means, you might conclude that the distributions of the hourly outputs are identical. Production records for 9 hours at the two plants, however, reveal that this conclusion is not correct (see Chart 3–6). Baton Rouge production varies from 48 to 52 assemblies per hour. Production at the Tucson plant is more erratic, ranging from 40 to 60 per hour. Therefore, the hourly output for Baton Rouge is clustered near the mean of 50; the hourly output for Tucson is more dispersed.

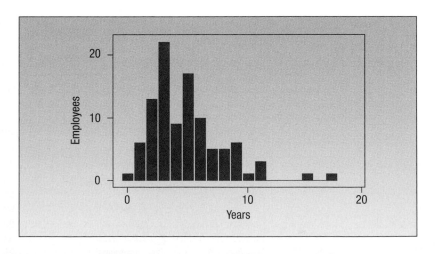

CHART 3–5 Histogram of Years of Employment at Hammond Iron Works Inc.

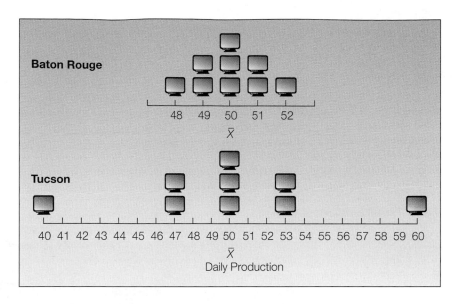

CHART 3–6 Hourly Production of Computer Monitors at the Baton Rouge and Tucson Plants

3.11 Measures of Dispersion

LO 3-6 Explain and apply measures of dispersion.

We will consider several measures of dispersion. The range is based on the maximum and the minimum values in the data set, that is, only two values are considered. The mean deviation, the variance, and the standard deviation use all the values in a data set and are all based on deviations from the arithmetic mean.

Range

The simplest measure of dispersion is the **range.** It is the difference between the maximum and the minimum values in a data set. In the form of an equation:

| RANGE | Range = Maximum value − Minimum value | [3–4] |

The range is widely used in statistical process control (SPC) applications because it is very easy to calculate and understand.

| **Example** | Refer to Chart 3–6 above. Find the range in the number of computer monitors produced per hour for the Baton Rouge and the Tucson plants. Interpret the two ranges. |
| **Solution** | The range of the hourly production of computer monitors at the Baton Rouge plant is 4, found by the difference between the maximum hourly production of 52 and the minimum of 48. The range in the hourly production for the Tucson plant is 20 computer monitors, found by 60 − 40. We therefore conclude that (1) there is less dispersion in the hourly production in the Baton Rouge plant than in the Tucson plant because the range of 4 computer monitors is less than a range of 20 computer monitors, and (2) the production is clustered more closely around the mean of 50 at the Baton Rouge plant than at the Tucson plant (because a range of 4 is less than a range of 20). Thus, the mean production in the Baton Rouge plant (50 computer monitors) is a more representative measure of location than the mean of 50 computer monitors for the Tucson plant. |

Mean Deviation

A shortcoming of the range is that it is based on only two values, the maximum and the minimum; it does not take into consideration all of the values. The **mean deviation** does. For a number of observations, it is the mean of the absolute differences between each value and the mean of the values. It is a measure of the average distance between an observation and the mean of the observations.

> **MEAN DEVIATION** The arithmetic mean of the absolute values of the deviations from the arithmetic mean.

The formula to compute the mean deviation, designated *MD,* is:

MEAN DEVIATION	$MD = \dfrac{\Sigma\lvert X - \bar{X}\rvert}{n}$	[3–5]

where:
   X is the value of each observation.
   $\bar{X}$ is the arithmetic mean of the values.
   n is the number of observations in the sample.
   $\lvert\ \rvert$ indicates the absolute value.

Why do we ignore the signs of the deviations from the mean? If we didn't, the positive and negative deviations from the mean would exactly offset each other, and the mean deviation would always be zero. Such a measure (zero) would be a useless statistic.

Example

The chart below shows the number of cappuccinos sold at the Starbucks in the Orange County airport and the Ontario, California, airport between 4 and 5 P.M. for a sample of five days last month.

California Airports	
Orange County	Ontario
20	20
40	49
50	50
60	51
80	80

Determine the mean, median, range, and mean deviation for each location. Comment on the similarities and differences in these measures.

Solution

The mean, median, and range for each of the airport locations are reported below as part of an Excel spreadsheet.

	A	B	C
1		**California Airports**	
2		Orange County	Ontario
3		20	20
4		40	49
5		50	50
6		60	51
7		80	80
8			
9	**Mean**	50	50
10	**Median**	50	50
11	**Range**	60	60

Notice that all three of the measures are exactly the same. Does this indicate that there is no difference in the two sets of data? We get a clearer picture if we calculate the mean deviations. First, for Orange County:

	A	B	C
1	**Calculation of Mean Deviation Orange County**		
2	**Number Sold**	**Each Value – Mean**	**Absolute Deviation**
3	20	20 – 50 = -30	30
4	40	40 – 50 = -10	10
5	50	50 – 50 = 0	0
6	60	60 – 50 = 10	10
7	80	80 – 50 = 30	30
8			
9		**Total**	**80**

$$MD = \frac{\Sigma |X - \bar{X}|}{n} = \frac{30 + 10 + 0 + 10 + 30}{5} = \frac{80}{5} = 16$$

The mean deviation is 16 cappuccinos. That is, the number of cappuccinos sold deviates, on average, by 16 from the mean of 50 cappuccinos.

The following shows the detail of determining the mean deviation for the number of cappuccinos sold at the Ontario Airport.

	A	B	C
1	**Calculation of Mean Deviation Ontario**		
2	**Number Sold**	**Each Value – Mean**	**Absolute Deviation**
3	20	20 – 50 = -30	30
4	49	49 – 50 = -1	1
5	50	50 – 50 = 0	0
6	51	51 – 50 = 1	1
7	80	80 – 50 = 30	30
8			
9		**Total**	**62**

$$MD = \frac{\Sigma|X - \bar{X}|}{n} = \frac{30 + 1 + 0 + 1 + 30}{5} = \frac{62}{5} = 12.4$$

So the mean, median, and range of the cappuccinos sold are the same at the two airports, but the mean deviations are different. The mean deviation at Orange County is 16, but it is 12.4 at Ontario.

Let's interpret and compare the results of our measures for the two Starbucks airport locations. The mean and median of the two locations are exactly the same, 50 cappuccinos sold. These measures of location indicate the two distributions are the same. The range for both locations is also the same, 60. However, recall that the range provides limited information about the dispersion, because it is based on only two of the observations.

The mean deviations are not the same for the two airports. The mean deviation is based on the differences between each observation and the arithmetic mean. It shows the closeness or clustering of the data relative to the mean or center of the distribution. Compare the mean deviation for Orange County of 16 to the mean deviation for Ontario of 12.4. Based on the mean deviation, we conclude that the dispersion for the sales distribution of the Ontario Starbucks is more concentrated—that is, nearer the mean of 50—than the Orange County location.

Advantages of the mean deviation

The mean deviation has two advantages. First, it uses all the values in the computation. Recall that the range uses only the maximum and minimum values. Second, it is easy to understand—it is the average amount by which values deviate from the mean. However, its drawback is the use of absolute values. Generally, absolute values are difficult to work with and to explain, so the mean deviation is not used as frequently as other measures of dispersion, such as the standard deviation.

Self-Review 3–5

The weights of containers being shipped to Ireland are (in thousands of pounds):

| 95 | 103 | 105 | 110 | 104 | 105 | 112 | 90 |

(a) What is the range of the weights?
(b) Compute the arithmetic mean weight.
(c) Compute the mean deviation of the weights.

Exercises

connect

For Exercises 27–30, calculate the (a) range, (b) arithmetic mean, and (c) mean deviation, and (d) interpret these statistics.

27. There were five customer service representatives on duty at the Electronic Super Store during last weekend's sale. The numbers of HDTVs these representatives sold are: 5, 8, 4, 10, and 3.

28. The Department of Statistics at Western State University offers eight sections of basic statistics. Following are the numbers of students enrolled in these sections: 34, 46, 52, 29, 41, 38, 36, and 28.

29. Dave's Automatic Door installs automatic garage door openers. The following list indicates the number of minutes needed to install a sample of 10 door openers: 28, 32, 24, 46, 44, 40, 54, 38, 32, and 42.

30. A sample of eight companies in the aerospace industry was surveyed as to their return on investment last year. The results are (in percent): 10.6, 12.6, 14.8, 18.2, 12.0, 14.8, 12.2, and 15.6.

31. Ten randomly selected young adults living in California rated the taste of a newly developed sushi pizza topped with tuna, rice, and kelp on a scale of 1 to 50, with 1 indicating they did not like the taste and 50 that they did. The ratings were:

| 34 | 39 | 40 | 46 | 33 | 31 | 34 | 14 | 15 | 45 |

In a parallel study, 10 randomly selected young adults in Iowa rated the taste of the same pizza. The ratings were:

| 28 | 25 | 35 | 16 | 25 | 29 | 24 | 26 | 17 | 20 |

As a market researcher, compare the potential markets for sushi pizza.

32. A sample of the personnel files of eight employees at the Pawnee location of Acme Carpet Cleaners Inc. revealed that during the last six-month period they lost the following number of days due to illness:

| 2 | 0 | 6 | 3 | 10 | 4 | 1 | 2 |

A sample of eight employees during the same period at the Chickpee location of Acme Carpets revealed they lost the following number of days due to illness.

| 2 | 0 | 1 | 0 | 5 | 0 | 1 | 0 |

As the director of human relations, compare the two locations. What would you recommend?

Variance and Standard Deviation

LO 3-7 Compute and explain the variance and the standard deviation.

The **variance** and **standard deviation** are also based on the deviations from the mean. However, instead of using the absolute value of the deviations, the variance and the standard deviation square the deviations.

> **VARIANCE** The arithmetic mean of the squared deviations from the mean.

The variance is non-negative and is zero only if all observations are the same.

> **STANDARD DEVIATION** The square root of the variance.

Variance and standard deviation are based on squared deviations from the mean.

Population Variance The formulas for the population variance and the sample variance are slightly different. The population variance is considered first. (Recall that a population is the totality of all observations being studied.) The **population variance** is found by:

| POPULATION VARIANCE | $$\sigma^2 = \frac{\Sigma(X - \mu)^2}{N}$$ | [3–6] |

where:

σ^2 is the population variance (σ is the lowercase Greek letter sigma). It is read as "sigma squared."

X is the value of an observation in the population.

μ is the arithmetic mean of the population.

N is the number of observations in the population.

Note the process of computing the variance.

1. Begin by finding the mean.
2. Find the difference between each observation and the mean, and square that difference.
3. Sum all the squared differences.
4. Divide the sum of the squared differences by the number of items in the population.

So you might think of the population variance as the mean of the squared difference between each value and the mean. For populations whose values are near the mean, the variance will be small. For populations whose values are dispersed from the mean, the population variance will be large.

The variance overcomes the weakness of the range by using all the values in the population, whereas the range uses only the maximum and minimum. We overcome the issue where $\Sigma(X - \mu) = 0$ by squaring the differences. Squaring the differences will always result in non-negative values.

Example

The number of traffic citations issued last year by month in Beaufort County, South Carolina, is reported below.

Citations by Month

January	February	March	April	May	June	July	August	September	October	November	December
19	17	22	18	28	34	45	39	38	44	34	10

Determine the population variance.

Solution

Because we are studying all the citations for a year, the data comprise a population. To determine the population variance, we use formula (3–6). The table below details the calculations.

Month	Citations (X)	$X - \mu$	$(X - \mu)^2$
January	19	−10	100
February	17	−12	144
March	22	−7	49
April	18	−11	121
May	28	−1	1
June	34	5	25
July	45	16	256
August	39	10	100
September	38	9	81
October	44	15	225
November	34	5	25
December	10	−19	361
Total	348	0	1,488

1. We begin by determining the arithmetic mean of the population. The total number of citations issued for the year is 348, so the mean number issued per month is 29.

$$\mu = \frac{\Sigma X}{N} = \frac{19 + 17 + \cdots + 10}{12} = \frac{348}{12} = 29$$

2. Next we find the difference between each observation and the mean. This is shown in the third column of the table. Recall that earlier in the chapter (page 63) we indicated that the sum of the differences between each value and the mean is 0. From the spreadsheet, the sum of the differences between the mean and the number of citations each month is 0.

3. The next step is to square the difference between each monthly value. That is shown in the fourth column of the table. All of the squared differences will be positive. Note that squaring a negative value, multiplying a negative value by itself, results in a value.

4. The squared differences are totaled. The total of the fourth column is 1,488. That is the term $\Sigma(X - \mu)^2$.

5. Finally, we divide the squared differences by N, the number of observations in the population.

$$\sigma^2 = \frac{\Sigma(X - \mu)^2}{N} = \frac{1488}{12} = 124$$

So, the population variance for the number of citations is 124.

Like the range and the mean deviation, the variance can be used to compare dispersion in two or more sets of observations. For example, the variance for the number of citations issued in Beaufort County was just computed to be 124. If the variance in the number of citations issued in Marlboro County, South Carolina, is 342.9, we conclude that (1) there is less dispersion in the distribution of the number of citations issued in Beaufort County than in Marlboro County (because 124 is less than 342.9); and (2) the number of citations in Beaufort County is more closely clustered around the mean of 29 than for the number of citations issued in Marlboro County. Thus the mean number of citations issued in Beaufort County is a more representative measure of location than the mean number of citations in Marlboro County.

Population Standard Deviation Both the range and the mean deviation are easy to interpret. The range is the difference between the maximum and minimum values of a set of data, and the mean deviation is the mean of the absolute deviations from the mean. However, the variance is difficult to interpret for a single set of observations. The variance of 124 for the number of citations issued is not in terms of citations, but citations squared.

Variance is difficult to interpret because the units are squared.

There is a way out of this difficulty. By taking the square root of the population variance, we can transform it to the same unit of measurement used for the original data. The square root of 124 citations-squared is 11.14 citations. The units are now simply citations. The square root of the population variance is the **population standard deviation.**

Standard deviation is in the same units as the data.

POPULATION STANDARD DEVIATION	$\sigma = \sqrt{\dfrac{\Sigma(X - \mu)^2}{N}}$	[3–7]

Self-Review 3–6 The Philadelphia office of PricewaterhouseCoopers LLP hired five accounting trainees this year. Their monthly starting salaries were: $3,536; $3,173; $3,448; $3,121; and $3,622.
(a) Compute the population mean.
(b) Compute the population variance.
(c) Compute the population standard deviation.
(d) The Pittsburgh office hired six trainees. Their mean monthly salary was $3,550, and the standard deviation was $250. Compare the two groups.

Exercises

connect

33. Consider these five values a population: 8, 3, 7, 3, and 4.
   a. Determine the mean of the population.
   b. Determine the variance.
34. Consider these six values a population: 13, 3, 8, 10, 8, and 6.
   a. Determine the mean of the population.
   b. Determine the variance.
35. The annual report of Dennis Industries cited these primary earnings per common share for the past 5 years: $2.68, $1.03, $2.26, $4.30, and $3.58. If we assume these are population values, what is:
   a. The arithmetic mean primary earnings per share of common stock?
   b. The variance?
36. Referring to Exercise 35, the annual report of Dennis Industries also gave these returns on stockholder equity for the same five-year period (in percent): 13.2, 5.0, 10.2, 17.5, and 12.9.
   a. What is the arithmetic mean return?
   b. What is the variance?
37. Plywood Inc. reported these returns on stockholder equity for the past 5 years: 4.3, 4.9, 7.2, 6.7, and 11.6. Consider these as population values.
   a. Compute the range, the arithmetic mean, the variance, and the standard deviation.
   b. Compare the return on stockholder equity for Plywood Inc. with that for Dennis Industries cited in Exercise 36.
38. The annual incomes of the five vice presidents of TMV Industries are: $125,000; $128,000; $122,000; $133,000; and $140,000. Consider this a population.
   a. What is the range?
   b. What is the arithmetic mean income?
   c. What is the population variance? The standard deviation?
   d. The annual incomes of officers of another firm similar to TMV Industries were also studied. The mean was $129,000 and the standard deviation $8,612. Compare the means and dispersions in the two firms.

Sample Variance The formula for the population mean is $\mu = \Sigma X/N$. We just changed the symbols for the sample mean; that is, $\overline{X} = \Sigma X/n$. Unfortunately, the conversion from the population variance to the sample variance is not as direct. It requires a change in the denominator. Instead of substituting n (number in the sample) for N (number in the population), the denominator is $n - 1$. Thus the formula for the **sample variance** is:

SAMPLE VARIANCE	$s^2 = \dfrac{\Sigma(X - \overline{X})^2}{n - 1}$	[3–8]

where:
   s^2 is the sample variance.
   X is the value of each observation in the sample.
   $\overline{X}$ is the mean of the sample.
   n is the number of observations in the sample.

Why is this change made in the denominator? Although the use of n is logical since $\overline{X}$ is used to estimate μ, it tends to underestimate the population variance, σ^2. The use of $(n - 1)$ in the denominator provides the appropriate correction for this tendency. Because the primary use of sample statistics like s^2 is to estimate population parameters like σ^2, $(n - 1)$ is preferred to n in defining the sample variance. We will also use this convention when computing the sample standard deviation.

Example	The hourly wages for a sample of part-time employees at Home Depot are: $12, $20, $16, $18, and $19. What is the sample variance?
Solution	The sample variance is computed by using formula (3–8).

$$\overline{X} = \frac{\Sigma X}{n} = \frac{\$85}{5} = \$17$$

Hourly Wage (X)	X − X̄	(X − X̄)²
$12	−$5	25
20	3	9
16	−1	1
18	1	1
19	2	4
$85	0	40

$$s^2 = \frac{\Sigma(X - \overline{X})^2}{n - 1} = \frac{40}{5 - 1}$$

$$= 10 \text{ in dollars squared}$$

Sample Standard Deviation   The sample standard deviation is used as an estimator of the population standard deviation. As noted previously, the population standard deviation is the square root of the population variance. Likewise, the *sample standard deviation is the square root of the sample variance*. The sample standard deviation is determined by:

SAMPLE STANDARD DEVIATION	$$s = \sqrt{\frac{\Sigma(X - \overline{X})^2}{n - 1}}$$	[3–9]

Example	The sample variance in the previous example involving hourly wages was computed to be 10. What is the sample standard deviation?
Solution	The sample standard deviation is $3.16, found by $\sqrt{10}$. Note again that the sample variance is in terms of dollars squared, but taking the square root of 10 gives us $3.16, which is in the same units (dollars) as the original data.

3.12 Software Solution

On page 71, we used Excel to determine the mean and median of the Applewood Auto Group data. You will also note that it lists the sample standard deviation. Excel, like most other statistical software, assumes the data are from a sample.

Another software package that we will use in this text is Minitab. This package uses a spreadsheet format, much like Excel, but produces a wider variety of statistical information. The information for the profit on the sales of 180 vehicles last month at Applewood Auto Group follows.

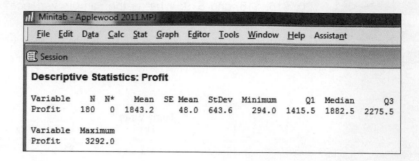

```
Minitab - Applewood 2011.MPJ

File  Edit  Data  Calc  Stat  Graph  Editor  Tools  Window  Help  Assistant

Session

Descriptive Statistics: Profit

Variable    N   N*    Mean  SE Mean  StDev  Minimum      Q1  Median      Q3
Profit    180    0  1843.2     48.0  643.6    294.0  1415.5  1882.5  2275.5

Variable  Maximum
Profit     3292.0
```

Self-Review 3–7 The years of service for a sample of seven employees at a State Farm Insurance claims office in Cleveland, Ohio, are: 4, 2, 5, 4, 5, 2, and 6. What is the sample variance? Compute the sample standard deviation.

Exercises

For Exercises 39–44, do the following:

  a. Compute the sample variance.
  b. Determine the sample standard deviation.

39. Consider these values a sample: 7, 2, 6, 2, and 3.
40. The following five values are a sample: 11, 6, 10, 6, and 7.
41. Dave's Automatic Door, referred to in Exercise 29, installs automatic garage door openers. Based on a sample, following are the times, in minutes, required to install 10 door openers: 28, 32, 24, 46, 44, 40, 54, 38, 32, and 42.
42. The sample of eight companies in the aerospace industry, referred to in Exercise 30, was surveyed as to their return on investment last year. The results are: 10.6, 12.6, 14.8, 18.2, 12.0, 14.8, 12.2, and 15.6.
43. The Houston, Texas, Motel Owner Association conducted a survey regarding weekday motel rates in the area. Listed below is the room rate for business-class guests for a sample of 10 motels.

$101	$97	$103	$110	$78	$87	$101	$80	$106	$88

44. A consumer watchdog organization is concerned about credit card debt. A survey of 10 young adults with credit card debt of more than $2,000 showed they paid an average of just over $100 per month against their balances. Listed below are the amounts each young adult paid last month.

| $110 | $126 | $103 | $93 | $99 | $113 | $87 | $101 | $109 | $100 |

3.13 Interpretation and Uses of the Standard Deviation

Statistics in Action

Most colleges report the "average class size." This information can be misleading because average class size can be found in several ways. If we find the number of students *in each class* at a particular university, the result is the mean number of students per class. If we compile a list of the class sizes for each student and find the mean class size, we might find the mean to be quite

(continued)

The standard deviation is commonly used as a measure to compare the spread in two or more sets of observations. For example, the standard deviation of the biweekly amounts invested in the Dupree Paint Company profit-sharing plan is computed to be $7.51. Suppose these employees are located in Georgia. If the standard deviation for a group of employees in Texas is $10.47, and the means are about the same, it indicates that the amounts invested by the Georgia employees are not dispersed as much as those in Texas (because $7.51 < $10.47). Since the amounts invested by the Georgia employees are clustered more closely about the mean, the mean for the Georgia employees is a more reliable measure than the mean for the Texas group.

Chebyshev's Theorem

We have stressed that a small standard deviation for a set of values indicates that these values are located close to the mean. Conversely, a large standard deviation reveals that the observations are widely scattered about the mean. The Russian mathematician P. L. Chebyshev (1821–1894) developed a theorem that allows us to determine the minimum proportion of the values that lie within a specified number of standard deviations of the mean. For example, according to **Chebyshev's theorem,** at least three out of every four, or 75%, of the values, must lie between the mean plus two standard deviations and the mean minus two standard deviations. This relationship applies regardless of the shape of the distribution. Further, at least eight of nine values, or 88.9%, will lie between plus three standard deviations and minus three standard deviations of the mean. At least 24 of 25 values, or 96%, will lie between plus and minus five standard deviations of the mean.

LO 3-8 Explain Chebyshev's Theorem and the Empirical Rule.

Chebyshev's theorem states:

> **CHEBYSHEV'S THEOREM** For any set of observations (sample or population), the proportion of the values that lie within k standard deviations of the mean is at least $1 - 1/k^2$, where k is any value greater than 1.

Example

The arithmetic mean biweekly amount contributed by the Dupree Paint employees to the company's profit-sharing plan is $51.54, and the standard deviation is $7.51. At least what percent of the contributions lie within plus 3.5 standard deviations and minus 3.5 standard deviations of the mean?

Solution

About 92%, found by

$$1 - \frac{1}{k^2} = 1 - \frac{1}{(3.5)^2} = 1 - \frac{1}{12.25} = 0.92$$

The Empirical Rule

The Empirical Rule applies only to symmetrical, bell-shaped distributions.

Chebyshev's theorem applies to any set of values; that is, the distribution of values can have any shape. However, for a symmetrical, bell-shaped distribution such as the one in Chart 3–7, we can be more precise in explaining the dispersion about the mean. These relationships involving the standard deviation and the mean are described by the **Empirical Rule,** sometimes called the **Normal Rule.**

> **EMPIRICAL RULE** For a symmetrical, bell-shaped frequency distribution, approximately 68% of the observations will lie within plus and minus one standard deviation of the mean; about 95% of the observations will lie within plus and minus two standard deviations of the mean; and practically all (99.7%) will lie within plus and minus three standard deviations of the mean.

These relationships are portrayed graphically in Chart 3–7 for a bell-shaped distribution with a mean of 100 and a standard deviation of 10.

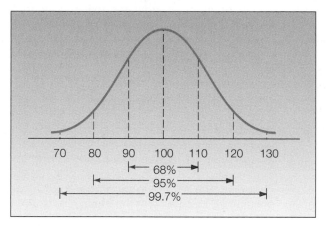

CHART 3–7 A Symmetrical, Bell-Shaped Curve Showing the Relationships between the Standard Deviation and the Percentage of Observations

Applying the Empirical Rule, if a distribution is symmetrical and bell-shaped, practically all of the observations lie between the mean plus and minus three standard deviations. Thus, if $\overline{X} = 100$ and $s = 10$, practically all the observations lie between $100 + 3(10)$ and $100 - 3(10)$, or 70 and 130. The estimated range is therefore 60, found by $130 - 70$.

Conversely, if we know that the range is 60 and the distribution is bell-shaped, we can approximate the standard deviation by dividing the range by 6. For this illustration: range $\div 6 = 60 \div 6 = 10$, the standard deviation.

(continued from p. 85) different. One school found the mean number of students in each of its 747 classes to be 40. But when it found the mean from a list of the class sizes of each student, it was 147. Why the disparity? Because there are few students in the small classes and a larger number of students in the larger classes, which has the effect of increasing the mean class size when it is calculated this way. A school could reduce this mean class size for each student by reducing the number of students in each class. That is, cut out the large freshman lecture classes.

Example	A sample of the rental rates at University Park Apartments approximates a symmetrical, bell-shaped distribution. The sample mean is $500; the standard deviation is $20. Using the Empirical Rule, answer these questions:
	1. About 68% of the monthly rentals are between what two amounts?
	2. About 95% of the monthly rentals are between what two amounts?
	3. Almost all of the monthly rentals are between what two amounts?
Solution	1. About 68% are between $480 and $520, found by $\overline{X} \pm 1s = \$500 \pm 1(\$20)$.
	2. About 95% are between $460 and $540, found by $\overline{X} \pm 2s = \$500 \pm 2(\$20)$.
	3. Almost all (99.7%) are between $440 and $560, found by $\overline{X} \pm 3s = \$500 \pm 3(\$20)$.

Self-Review 3–8

The Pitney Pipe Company is one of several domestic manufacturers of PVC pipe. The quality control department sampled 600 10-foot lengths. At a point 1 foot from the end of the pipe, they measured the outside diameter. The mean was 14.0 inches and the standard deviation 0.1 inches.
(a) If the shape of the distribution is not known, at least what percent of the observations will be between 13.85 inches and 14.15 inches?
(b) If we assume that the distribution of diameters is symmetrical and bell-shaped, about 95% of the observations will be between what two values?

Exercises

connect

45. According to Chebyshev's theorem, at least what percent of any set of observations will be within 1.8 standard deviations of the mean?
46. The mean income of a group of sample observations is $500; the standard deviation is $40. According to Chebyshev's theorem, at least what percent of the incomes will lie between $400 and $600?
47. The distribution of the weights of a sample of 1,400 cargo containers is symmetric and bell-shaped. According to the Empirical Rule, what percent of the weights will lie:
   a. Between $\overline{X} - 2s$ and $\overline{X} + 2s$?
   b. Between $\overline{X}$ and $\overline{X} + 2s$? Below $\overline{X} - 2s$?
48. The following graph portrays the distribution of the number of Biggie-sized soft drinks sold at a nearby Wendy's for the last 141 days. The mean number of drinks sold per day is 91.9 and the standard deviation is 4.67.

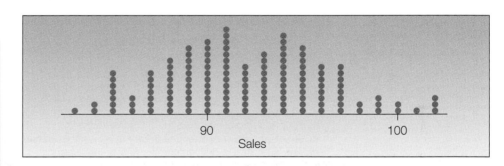

Sales

If we use the Empirical Rule, sales will be between what two values on 68% of the days? Sales will be between what two values on 95% of the days?

3.14 Ethics and Reporting Results

In Chapter 1, we discussed the ethical and unbiased reporting of statistical results. While you are learning about how to organize, summarize, and interpret data using statistics, it is also important to understand statistics so that you can be an intelligent consumer of information.

In this chapter, we learned how to compute numerical descriptive statistics. Specifically, we showed how to compute and interpret measures of location for a data set: the mean, median, and mode. We also discussed the advantages and disadvantages for each statistic. For example, if a real estate developer tells a client that the average home in a particular subdivision sold for $150,000, we assume that $150,000 is a representative selling price for all the homes. But suppose that the client also asks what the median sales price is, and the median is $60,000. Why was the developer only reporting the mean price? This information is extremely important to a person's decision making when buying a home.

Statistics in Action

Miguel Cabrera of the Detroit Tigers had the highest batting average, at .344, during the 2011 Major League Baseball season. Tony Gwynn hit .394 in the strike-shortened season of 1994, and Ted Williams hit .406 in 1941. No one has hit over .400 since 1941. The mean batting average has remained constant at about .260 for more than 100 years, but the
(continued)

standard deviation declined from .049 to .031. This indicates less dispersion in the batting averages today and helps explain the lack of any .400 hitters in recent times.

Knowing the advantages and disadvantages of the mean, median, and mode is important as we report statistics and as we use statistical information to make decisions.

We also learned how to compute measures of dispersion: range, mean deviation, and standard deviation. Each of these statistics also has advantages and disadvantages. Remember that the range provides information about the overall spread of a distribution. However, it does not provide any information about how the data is clustered or concentrated around the center of the distribution. As we learn more about statistics, we need to remember that when we use statistics we must maintain an independent and principled point of view. Any statistical report requires objective and honest communication of the results.

Chapter Summary

I. A measure of location is a value used to describe the center of a set of data.
  A. The arithmetic mean is the most widely reported measure of location.
    1. It is calculated by adding the values of the observations and dividing by the total number of observations.
      a. The formula for a population mean of ungrouped or raw data is

$$\mu = \frac{\Sigma X}{N} \qquad \text{[3–1]}$$

      b. The formula for the mean of a sample is

$$\overline{X} = \frac{\Sigma X}{n} \qquad \text{[3–2]}$$

    2. The major characteristics of the arithmetic mean are:
      a. At least the interval scale of measurement is required.
      b. All the data values are used in the calculation.
      c. A set of data has only one mean. That is, it is unique.
      d. The sum of the deviations from the mean equals 0.
  B. The weighted mean is found by multiplying each observation by its corresponding weight.
    1. The formula for determining the weighted mean is

$$\overline{X}_w = \frac{w_1X_1 + w_2X_2 + w_3X_3 + \cdots + w_nX_n}{w_1 + w_2 + w_3 + \cdots + w_n} \qquad \text{[3–3]}$$

  C. The median is the value in the middle of a set of ordered data.
    1. To find the median, sort the observations from minimum to maximum and identify the middle value.
    2. The major characteristics of the median are:
      a. At least the ordinal scale of measurement is required.
      b. It is not influenced by extreme values.
      c. Fifty percent of the observations are larger than the median.
      d. It is unique to a set of data.
  D. The mode is the value that occurs most often in a set of data.
    1. The mode can be found for nominal-level data.
    2. A set of data can have more than one mode.
II. The dispersion is the variation or spread in a set of data.
  A. The range is the difference between the maximum and minimum values in a set of data.
    1. The formula for the range is

$$\text{Range} = \text{Maximum value} - \text{Minimum value} \qquad \text{[3–4]}$$

2. The major characteristics of the range are:
    a. Only two values are used in its calculation.
    b. It is influenced by extreme values.
    c. It is easy to compute and to understand.
B. The mean absolute deviation is the sum of the absolute values of the deviations from the mean divided by the number of observations.
    1. The formula for computing the mean absolute deviation is

$$MD = \frac{\Sigma |X - \overline{X}|}{n} \qquad \text{[3–5]}$$

    2. The major characteristics of the mean absolute deviation are:
        a. It is not unduly influenced by large or small values.
        b. All observations are used in the calculation.
        c. The absolute values are somewhat difficult to work with.
C. The variance is the mean of the squared deviations from the arithmetic mean.
    1. The formula for the population variance is

$$\sigma^2 = \frac{\Sigma (X - \mu)^2}{N} \qquad \text{[3–6]}$$

    2. The formula for the sample variance is

$$s^2 = \frac{\Sigma (X - \overline{X})^2}{n - 1} \qquad \text{[3–8]}$$

    3. The major characteristics of the variance are:
        a. All observations are used in the calculation.
        b. It is not unduly influenced by extreme observations.
        c. The units are somewhat difficult to work with; they are the original units squared.
D. The standard deviation is the square root of the variance.
    1. The major characteristics of the standard deviation are:
        a. It is in the same units as the original data.
        b. It is the square root of the average squared distance from the mean.
        c. It cannot be negative.
        d. It is the most widely reported measure of dispersion.
    2. The formula for the sample standard deviation is

$$s = \sqrt{\frac{\Sigma (X - \overline{X})^2}{n - 1}} \qquad \text{[3–9]}$$

III. We interpret the standard deviation using two measures.
    A. Chebyshev's theorem states that regardless of the shape of the distribution, at least $1 - 1/k^2$ of the observations will be within k standard deviations of the mean, where k is greater than 1.
    B. The Empirical Rule states that for a bell-shaped distribution about 68% of the values will be within one standard deviation of the mean, 95% within two, and virtually all within three.

Pronunciation Key

SYMBOL	MEANING	PRONUNCIATION
μ	Population mean	*mu*
Σ	Operation of adding	*sigma*
ΣX	Adding a group of values	*sigma X*
$\overline{X}$	Sample mean	*X bar*
$\overline{X}_w$	Weighted mean	*X bar sub w*
σ^2	Population variance	*sigma squared*
σ	Population standard deviation	*sigma*

Chapter Exercises

49. The accounting firm of Crawford and Associates has five senior partners. Yesterday the senior partners saw six, four, three, seven, and five clients, respectively.
   a. Compute the mean and median number of clients seen by the partners.
   b. Is the mean a sample mean or a population mean?
   c. Verify that $\Sigma(X - \mu) = 0$.

50. Owens Orchards sells apples in a large bag by weight. A sample of seven bags contained the following numbers of apples: 23, 19, 26, 17, 21, 24, 22.
   a. Compute the mean and median number of apples in a bag.
   b. Verify that $\Sigma(X - \overline{X}) = 0$.

51. A sample of households that subscribe to United Bell Phone Company for landline phone service revealed the following number of calls received per household last week. Determine the mean and the median number of calls received. (df)

52	43	30	38	30	42	12	46	39	37
34	46	32	18	41	5				

52. The Citizens Banking Company is studying the number of times the ATM located in a Loblaws Supermarket at the foot of Market Street is used per day. Following are the number of times the machine was used daily over each of the last 30 days. Determine the mean number of times the machine was used per day. (df)

83	64	84	76	84	54	75	59	70	61
63	80	84	73	68	52	65	90	52	77
95	36	78	61	59	84	95	47	87	60

53. A recent study of the laundry habits of Americans included the time in minutes of the wash cycle. A sample of 40 observations follows. Determine the mean and the median of a typical wash cycle. (df)

35	37	28	37	33	38	37	32	28	29
39	33	32	37	33	35	36	44	36	34
40	38	46	39	37	39	34	39	31	33
37	35	39	38	37	32	43	31	31	35

54. Trudy Green works for the True-Green Lawn Company. Her job is to solicit lawn-care business via the telephone. Listed below is the number of appointments she made in each of the last 25 hours of calling. What is the arithmetic mean number of appointments she made per hour? What is the median number of appointments per hour? Write a brief report summarizing the findings. (df)

9	5	2	6	5	6	4	4	7	2	3	6	3
4	4	7	8	4	4	5	5	4	8	3	3	

55. The Split-A-Rail Fence Company sells three types of fence to homeowners in suburban Seattle, Washington. Grade A costs $5.00 per running foot to install, Grade B costs $6.50 per running foot, and Grade C, the premium quality, costs $8.00 per running foot. Yesterday, Split-A-Rail installed 270 feet of Grade A, 300 feet of Grade B, and 100 feet of Grade C. What was the mean cost per foot of fence installed?

56. Rolland Poust is a sophomore in the College of Business at Scandia Tech. Last semester he took courses in statistics and accounting, 3 hours each, and earned an A in both. He earned a B in a five-hour history course and a B in a two-hour history of jazz course. In addition, he took a one-hour course dealing with the rules of basketball so he could get his license to officiate high school basketball games. He got an A in this course. What was his GPA for the semester? Assume that he receives 4 points for an A, 3 for a B, and so on. What measure of location did you just calculate?

57. The table below shows the percent of the labor force that is unemployed and the size of the labor force for three counties in Northwest Ohio. Jon Elsas is the Regional Director of Economic Development. He must present a report to several companies that are considering locating in Northwest Ohio. What would be an appropriate unemployment rate to show for the entire region?

County	Percent Unemployed	Size of Workforce
Wood	4.5	15,300
Ottawa	3.0	10,400
Lucas	10.2	150,600

58. The American Diabetes Association recommends a blood glucose reading of less than 130 for those with Type 2 diabetes. Blood glucose measures the amount of sugar in the blood. Below are the readings for February for a person recently diagnosed with Type 2 diabetes.

112	122	116	103	112	96	115	98	106	111
106	124	116	127	116	108	112	112	121	115
124	116	107	118	123	109	109	106		

   a. What is the arithmetic mean glucose reading?
   b. What is the median glucose reading?
   c. What is the modal glucose reading?

59. The ages of a sample of Canadian tourists flying from Toronto to Hong Kong were: 32, 21, 60, 47, 54, 17, 72, 55, 33, and 41.

   a. Compute the range.
   b. Compute the mean deviation.
   c. Compute the standard deviation.

60. The enrollments of the 13 public universities in the state of Ohio are listed below.

College	Enrollment
University of Akron	25,942
Bowling Green State University	18,989
Central State University	1,820
University of Cincinnati	36,415
Cleveland State University	15,664
Kent State University	34,056
Miami University	17,161
Ohio State University	59,091
Ohio University	20,437
Shawnee State University	4,300
University of Toledo	20,775
Wright State University	18,786
Youngstown State University	14,682

   a. Is this a sample or a population?
   b. What is the mean enrollment?
   c. What is the median enrollment?
   d. What is the range of the enrollments?
   e. Compute the standard deviation.

61. The Apollo space program lasted from 1967 until 1972 and included 13 missions. The missions lasted from as little as 7 hours to as long as 301 hours. The duration of each flight is listed below.

9	195	241	301	216	260	7	244	192	147
10	295	142							

  a. Explain why the flight times are a population.
  b. Find the mean and median of the flight times.
  c. Find the range and the standard deviation of the flight times.

62. Creek Ratz is a very popular restaurant located along the coast of northern Florida. They serve a variety of steak and seafood dinners. During the summer beach season, they do not take reservations or accept "call ahead" seating. Management of the restaurant is concerned with the time a patron must wait before being seated for dinner. Listed below is the wait time, in minutes, for the 25 tables seated last Saturday night.

28	39	23	67	37	28	56	40	28	50
51	45	44	65	61	27	24	61	34	44
64	25	24	27	29					

  a. Explain why the times are a population.
  b. Find the mean and median of the times.
  c. Find the range and the standard deviation of the times.

63. A sample of 25 undergraduates reported the following dollar amounts of entertainment expenses last year:

684	710	688	711	722	698	723	743	738	722	696	721	685
763	681	731	736	771	693	701	737	717	752	710	697	

  a. Find the mean, median, and mode of this information.
  b. What are the range and standard deviation?
  c. Use the Empirical Rule to establish an interval which includes about 95% of the observations.

64. The Kentucky Derby is held the first Saturday in May at Churchill Downs in Louisville, Kentucky. The race track is one and one-quarter miles. The following table shows the winners since 1990, their margin of victory, the winning time, and the payoff on a $2 bet.

Year	Winner	Winning Margin (lengths)	Winning Time (minutes)	Payoff on a $2 Win Bet
1990	Unbridled	3.5	2.03333	10.80
1991	Strike the Gold	1.75	2.05000	4.80
1992	Lil E. Tee	1	2.05000	16.80
1993	Sea Hero	2.5	2.04000	12.90
1994	Go For Gin	2	2.06000	9.10
1995	Thunder Gulch	2.25	2.02000	24.50
1996	Grindstone	nose	2.01667	5.90
1997	Silver Charm	head	2.04000	4.00
1998	Real Quiet	0.5	2.03667	8.40
1999	Charismatic	neck	2.05333	31.30
2000	Fusaichi Pegasus	1.5	2.02000	2.30

(continued)

Year	Winner	Winning Margin (lengths)	Winning Time (minutes)	Payoff on a $2 Win Bet
2001	Monarchos	4.75	1.99950	10.50
2002	War Emblem	4	2.01883	20.50
2003	Funny Cide	1.75	2.01983	12.80
2004	Smarty Jones	2.75	2.06767	4.10
2005	Giacomo	0.5	2.04583	50.30
2006	Barbaro	6.5	2.02267	6.10
2007	Street Sense	2.25	2.03617	4.90
2008	Big Brown	4.75	2.03033	6.80
2009	Mine That Bird	6.75	2.04433	103.20
2010	Super Saver	2.50	2.07417	18.00
2011	Animal Kingdom	2.75	2.034	43.80

a. Determine the mean and median for the variables winning time and payoff on a $2 bet.
b. Determine the range and standard deviation of the variables winning time and payoff.
c. Refer to the variable winning margin. What is the level of measurement? What measure of location would be most appropriate?

65. The manager of the local Walmart Supercenter is studying the number of items purchased by customers in the evening hours. Listed below is the number of items for a sample of 30 customers.

15	8	6	9	9	4	18	10	10	12
12	4	7	8	12	10	10	11	9	13
5	6	11	14	5	6	6	5	13	5

a. Find the mean and the median of the number of items.
b. Find the range and the standard deviation of the number of items.

Data Set Exercises

(The data for these exercises are available at the text website www.mhhe.com/lindbasic8e).

66. Refer to the Real Estate data, which reports information on homes sold in the Goodyear, Arizona, area during the last year. Prepare a report on the selling prices of the homes. Be sure to answer the following questions in your report.
   a. Around what values do the data tend to cluster? What is the mean selling price? What is the median selling price? Is one measure more representative of the typical selling prices than the others?
   b. What is the range of selling prices? What is the standard deviation? About 95% of the selling prices are between what two values?
67. Refer to the Baseball 2010 data, which reports information on the 30 Major League Baseball teams for the 2010 season. Prepare a report on the variable team payroll that specifically addresses each of the following questions.
   a. Around what values do the payrolls tend to cluster? What are the mean and median of payroll? Is one measure of location for payroll more representative than the other?
   b. What is the range of team payroll? What is the standard deviation? Based on Chebyshev's Theorem, at least 75% of the payrolls are between what two values?
   c. Find the mean and standard deviation of team payroll for the 14 American League and the 16 National League teams. Does there appear to be a difference in the means? Is there a difference in the dispersion for team payroll between the two leagues?
68. Refer to the Buena School District bus data. Prepare a report on the maintenance cost for last month. Be sure to answer the following questions in your report.
   a. Around what values do the data tend to cluster? Specifically what was the mean maintenance cost last month? What is the median cost? Is one measure more representative of the typical cost than the others?
   b. What is the range of maintenance costs? What is the standard deviation? About 95% of the maintenance costs are between what two values?

Practice Test

Part 1—Objective

1. An observable characteristic of a population is called a _____ .
2. A measure, such as the mean, based on sample data is called a _____ .
3. The sum of the differences between each value and the mean is always equal to _____ .
4. The midpoint of a set of values after they have been ordered from the minimum to the maximum values is called the _____ .
5. What percentage of the values in every data set is larger than the median? _____
6. The value of the observation that appears most frequently in a data set is called the _____ .
7. The _____ is the difference between the maximum and minimum values in a data set.
8. The _____ is the arithmetic mean of the squared deviations from the mean.
9. The square of the standard deviation is the _____ .
10. The standard deviation assumes a negative value when (all the values are negative, at least half the values are negative, or never—pick one) _____ .
11. Which of the following is least affected by an outlier? (mean, median, or range—pick one) _____ .
12. The _____ states that for any symmetrical, bell-shaped frequency distribution, approximately 68% of the observations will lie within plus and minus one standard deviation of the mean.

Part 2—Problems

1. A sample of college students reported they owned the following number of CDs.

| 52 | 76 | 64 | 79 | 80 | 74 | 66 | 69 |

   a. What is the mean number of CDs owned?
   b. What is the median number of CDs owned?
   c. What is the range of the number of CDs owned?
   d. What is the standard deviation of the number of CDs owned?
2. An investor purchased 200 shares of the Blair Company for $36 each in July 2008, 300 shares at $40 each in September 2008, and 500 shares at $50 each in January 2009. What is the investor's weighted mean price per share?
3. *The Wall Street Journal* regularly surveys a group of about 50 economists. Their forecasts for the change in the domestic gross national product (GNP) are normally distributed with a mean change of −0.88%. That indicates a predicted decline in GNP of almost nine tenths of a percent. If the standard deviation is 1.41%, use the Empirical Rule to estimate the range that includes 95% of the forecast changes in GNP.

Software Commands

1. The Excel Commands for the descriptive statistics on page 71 are:
   a. From the website, www.mhhe.com/lindbasic8e, retrieve the Applewood data.
   b. From the menu bar, select **Data** and then **Data Analysis.** Select **Descriptive Statistics** and then click **OK.**
   c. For the **Input Range,** type *C1:C181,* indicate that the data are grouped by column and that the labels are in the first row. Click on **Output Range,** indicate that the output should go in *G1* (or any place you wish), click on **Summary statistics,** then click **OK.**
   d. After you get your results, double-check the count in the output to be sure it contains the correct number of items.

Descriptive Statistics

Input
Input Range: $B$1:$B$181
Grouped By: ⦿ Columns
                                ◯ Rows
☑ Labels in first row

Output options
⦿ Output Range: $G$1
◯ New Worksheet Ply:
◯ New Workbook
☑ Summary statistics
☐ Confidence Level for Mean: 95   %
☐ Kth Largest: 1
☐ Kth Smallest: 1

OK
Cancel
Help

2. The Minitab commands for the descriptive summary on page 84 are:
   a. From the website, www.mhhe.com/lindbasic8e, retrieve the Applewood data.
   b. Select **Stat, Basic Statistics,** and then **Display Descriptive Statistics.** In the dialog box, select *Profit* as the variable and then click **OK.**

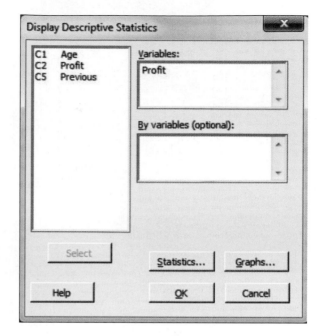

Chapter 3   Answers to Self-Review

3–1 1. a. $\bar{X} = \dfrac{\Sigma X}{n}$

   b. $\bar{X} = \dfrac{\$267,100}{4} = \$66,775$

   c. Statistic, because it is a sample value.
   d. $66,775. The sample mean is our best estimate of the population mean.

   2. a. $\mu = \dfrac{\Sigma X}{N}$

   b. $\mu = \dfrac{498}{6} = 83$

   c. Parameter, because it was computed using all the population values.

3–2 a. $237, found by:

$$\frac{(95 \times \$400) + (126 \times \$200) + (79 \times \$100)}{95 + 126 + 79} = \$237.00$$

   b. The profit per suit is $12, found by $237 − $200 cost − $25 commission. The total profit for the 300 suits is $3,600, found by 300 × $12.

3–3 1. a. $878
   b. 3, 3

2. a. 7, found by (6 + 8)/2 = 7
   b. 3, 3
   c. 0

3–4 a.

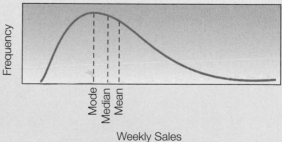

   b. Positively skewed, because the mean is the largest average and the mode is the smallest.

3–5 a. 22 thousands of pounds, found by 112 − 90

   b. $\bar{X} = \dfrac{824}{8} = 103$ thousands of pounds

c.

X	$\|X - \bar{X}\|$	Absolute Deviation
95	$\|-8\|$	8
103	$\|0\|$	0
105	$\|+2\|$	2
110	$\|+7\|$	7
104	$\|+1\|$	1
105	$\|+2\|$	2
112	$\|+9\|$	9
90	$\|-13\|$	13
		Total 42

$$MD = \frac{42}{8} = 5.25 \text{ thousands of pounds}$$

3–6 **a.** $\mu = \dfrac{\$16,900}{5} = \$3,380$

b. $\sigma^2 = \dfrac{(3536 - 3380)^2 + \cdots + (3622 - 3380)^2}{5}$

$= \dfrac{\begin{array}{c}(156)^2 + (-207)^2 + (68)^2 \\ + (-259)^2 + (242)^2\end{array}}{5}$

$= \dfrac{197,454}{5} = 39,490.8$

c. $\sigma = \sqrt{39,490.8} = 198.72$

d. There is more variation in the Pittsburgh office because the standard deviation is larger. The mean is also larger in the Pittsburgh office.

3–7 2.33, found by:

$$\bar{X} = \frac{\Sigma X}{n} = \frac{28}{7} = 4$$

X	$X - \bar{X}$	$(X - \bar{X})^2$
4	0	0
2	-2	4
5	1	1
4	0	0
5	1	1
2	-2	4
6	2	4
28	0	14

$$s^2 = \frac{\Sigma(X - \bar{X})^2}{n - 1}$$

$$= \frac{14}{7 - 1}$$

$$= 2.33$$

$$s = \sqrt{2.33} = 1.53$$

3–8 **a.** $k = \dfrac{14.15 - 14.00}{.10} = 1.5$

$k = \dfrac{13.85 - 14.0}{.10} = -1.5$

$1 - \dfrac{1}{(1.5)^2} = 1 - .44 = .56$

b. 13.8 and 14.2

Describing Data:

Displaying and Exploring Data

McGivern Jewelers recently ran an advertisement in the local newspaper reporting the shape, size, price, and cut grade for 33 of its diamonds in stock. Develop a box plot of the variable price and comment on the result. (See Exercise 27 and LO 4-3.)

4

4.1 Introduction

Chapter 2 began our study of descriptive statistics. In order to transform raw or ungrouped data into a meaningful form, we organize the data into a frequency distribution. We present the frequency distribution in graphic form as a histogram or a frequency polygon. This allows us to visualize where the data tends to cluster, the largest and the smallest values, and the general shape of the data.

In Chapter 3, we first computed several measures of location, such as the mean and the median. These measures of location allow us to report a typical value in the set of observations. We also computed several measures of dispersion, such as the range and the standard deviation. These measures of dispersion allow us to describe the variation or the spread in a set of observations.

We continue our study of descriptive statistics in this chapter. We study (1) dot plots, (2) percentiles, and (3) box plots. These charts and statistics give us additional insight into where the values are concentrated as well as the general shape of the data. Then we consider bivariate data. In bivariate data, we observe two variables for each individual or observation selected. Examples include: the number of hours a student studied and the points earned on an examination; whether a sampled product is acceptable or not and the shift on which it is manufactured; and the amount of electricity used in a month by a homeowner and the mean daily high temperature in the region for the month.

4.2 Dot Plots

LO 4-1 Construct and interpret a dot plot.

Recall for the Applewood Auto Group data, we summarized the profit earned on the 180 vehicles sold into eight classes. When we organized the data into the eight classes, we lost the exact value of the observations. A **dot plot,** on the other hand, groups the data as little as possible, and we do not lose the identity of an individual observation. To develop a dot plot, we display a dot for each observation along a horizontal number line indicating the possible values of the data. If there are identical observations or the observations are too close to be shown individually, the dots are "piled" on top of each other. This allows us to see the shape of the distribution, the value about which the data tend to cluster, and the largest and smallest observations. Dot plots are most useful for smaller data sets, whereas histograms tend to be most useful for large data sets. An example will show how to construct and interpret dot plots.

Dot plots give a visual idea of the spread and concentration of the data.

Example

The service departments at Tionesta Ford Lincoln Mercury and Sheffield Motors Inc., two of the four Applewood Auto Group dealerships, were both open 24 working days last month. Listed below is the number of vehicles serviced last month at the two dealerships. Construct dot plots and report summary statistics to compare the two dealerships.

Tionesta Ford Lincoln Mercury					
Monday	Tuesday	Wednesday	Thursday	Friday	Saturday
23	33	27	28	39	26
30	32	28	33	35	32
29	25	36	31	32	27
35	32	35	37	36	30

Sheffield Motors Inc.					
Monday	Tuesday	Wednesday	Thursday	Friday	Saturday
31	35	44	36	34	37
30	37	43	31	40	31
32	44	36	34	43	36
26	38	37	30	42	33

Solution

The Minitab system provides a dot plot and outputs the mean, median, maximum, and minimum values, and the standard deviation for the number of cars serviced at both of the dealerships over the last 24 working days.

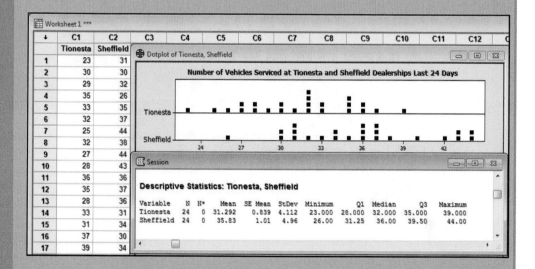

The dot plots, shown in the center of the software output, graphically illustrate the distributions for both dealerships. The plots show the difference in the location and dispersion of the observations. By looking at the dot plots, we can see that the number of vehicles serviced at the Sheffield dealership is more widely dispersed and has a larger mean than at the Tionesta dealership. Several other features of the number of vehicles serviced are:

- Tionesta serviced the fewest cars in any day, 23.
- Sheffield serviced 26 cars during their slowest day, which is 4 cars less than the next lowest day.
- Tionesta serviced exactly 32 cars on four different days.
- The numbers of cars serviced cluster around 36 for Sheffield and 32 for Tionesta.

From the descriptive statistics, we see that Sheffield serviced a mean of 35.83 vehicles per day. Tionesta serviced a mean of 31.292 vehicles per day during the same period. So Sheffield typically services 4.54 more vehicles per day. There is also more dispersion, or variation, in the daily number of vehicles serviced at Sheffield than at Tionesta. How do we know this? The standard deviation is larger at Sheffield (4.96 vehicles per day) than at Tionesta (4.112 cars per day).

Self-Review 4–1

The number of employees at each of the 142 Home Depot Stores in the Southeast region is shown in the following dot plot.

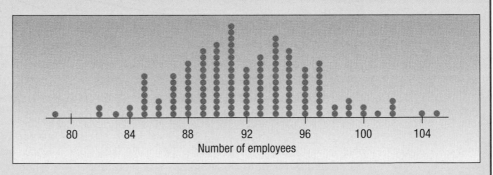

Number of employees

(a)   What are the maximum and minimum numbers of employees per store?
(b)   How many stores employ 91 people?
(c)   Around what values does the number of employees per store tend to cluster?

Exercises

connect

1. Consider the following chart.

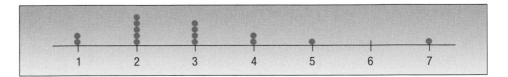

  a. What is this chart called?
  b. How many observations are in the study?

  c. What are the maximum and the minimum values?
  d. Around what values do the observations tend to cluster?
2. The following chart reports the number of cell phones sold at RadioShack for the last 26 days.

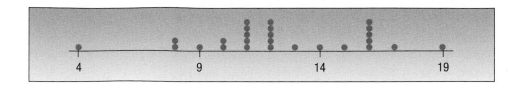

  a. What are the maximum and the minimum number of cell phones sold in a day?
  b. What is a typical number of cell phones sold?

4.3 Measures of Position

LO 4-2 Identify and compute measures of position.

Quartiles divide a set of data into four parts.

The standard deviation is the most widely used measure of dispersion. However, there are other ways of describing the variation or spread in a set of data. One method is to determine the *location* of values that divide a set of observations into equal parts. These measures include **quartiles, deciles,** and **percentiles.**

Quartiles divide a set of observations into four equal parts. To explain further, think of any set of values arranged from the minimum to the maximum. In Chapter 3, we called the middle value of a set of data arranged from the minimum to the maximum the median. That is, 50% of the observations are larger than the median and 50% are smaller. The median is a measure of location because it pinpoints the center of the data. In a similar fashion, **quartiles** divide a set of observations into four equal parts. The first quartile, usually labeled Q_1, is the value below which 25% of the observations occur, and the third quartile, usually labeled Q_3, is the value below which 75% of the observations occur.

Similarly, **deciles** divide a set of observations into 10 equal parts and **percentiles** into 100 equal parts. So if you found that your GPA was in the 8th decile at your university, you could conclude that 80% of the students had a GPA lower than yours and 20% had a higher GPA. If your GPA was in the 92nd percentile, then 92% of students had a GPA less than your GPA and only 8% of students had a GPA greater than your GPA. Percentile scores are frequently used to report results on such national standardized tests as the SAT, ACT, GMAT (used to judge entry into many master of business administration programs), and LSAT (used to judge entry into law school).

Quartiles, Deciles, and Percentiles

To formalize the computational procedure, let L_p refer to the location of a desired percentile. So if we want to find the 92nd percentile we would use L_{92}, and if we wanted the median, the 50th percentile, then L_{50}. For a number of observations, *n*, the location of the *Pth* percentile, can be found using the formula:

LOCATION OF A PERCENTILE	$L_p = (n + 1)\dfrac{P}{100}$	[4–1]

An example will help to explain further.

Example

Listed below are the commissions earned last month by a sample of 15 brokers at Morgan Stanley Smith Barney's Oakland, California, office. Morgan Stanley Smith Barney is an investment company with offices located throughout the United States.

$2,038	$1,758	$1,721	$1,637	$2,097	$2,047	$2,205	$1,787	$2,287
1,940	2,311	2,054	2,406	1,471	1,460			

Locate the median, the first quartile, and the third quartile for the commissions earned.

Solution

The first step is to sort the data from the smallest commission to the largest.

$1,460	$1,471	$1,637	$1,721	$1,758	$1,787	$1,940	$2,038
2,047	2,054	2,097	2,205	2,287	2,311	2,406	

The median value is the observation in the center and is the same as the 50th percentile, so P equals 50. So the median or L_{50} is located at $(n + 1)(50/100)$, where n is the number of observations. In this case, that is position number 8, found by $(15 + 1)(50/100)$. The eighth-largest commission is $2,038. So we con-

clude this is the median and that half the brokers earned commissions more than $2,038 and half earned less than $2,038. The result using formula (4–1) to find the median is the same as the method presented in Chapter 3.

Recall the definition of a quartile. Quartiles divide a set of observations into four equal parts. Hence 25% of the observations will be less than the first quartile. Seventy-five percent of the observations will be less than the third quartile. To locate the first quartile, we use formula (4–1), where $n = 15$ and $P = 25$:

$$L_{25} = (n + 1)\frac{P}{100} = (15 + 1)\frac{25}{100} = 4$$

and to locate the third quartile, $n = 15$ and $P = 75$:

$$L_{75} = (n + 1)\frac{P}{100} = (15 + 1)\frac{75}{100} = 12$$

Therefore, the first and third quartile values are located at positions 4 and 12, respectively. The fourth value in the ordered array is $1,721 and the twelfth is $2,205. These are the first and third quartiles.

In the above example, the location formula yielded a whole number. That is, we wanted to find the first quartile and there were 15 observations, so the location formula indicated we should find the fourth ordered value. What if there were 20 observations in the sample, that is $n = 20$, and we wanted to locate the first quartile? From the location formula (4–1):

$$L_{25} = (n + 1)\frac{P}{100} = (20 + 1)\frac{25}{100} = 5.25$$

We would locate the fifth value in the ordered array and then move .25 of the distance between the fifth and sixth values and report that as the first quartile. Like the median, the quartile does not need to be one of the actual values in the data set.

Statistics in Action

John W. Tukey (1915–2000) received a PhD in mathematics from Princeton in 1939. However, when he joined the Fire Control Research Office during World War II, his interest in abstract mathematics shifted to applied statistics. He developed effective numerical and graphical methods for studying patterns in data. Among the graphics he developed are the stem-and-leaf diagram and the box-and-whisker plot or box plot. From 1960 to 1980, Tukey headed the statistical division of NBC's election night vote projection team. He became renowned in 1960 for preventing an early call of victory for Richard Nixon in the presidential election won by John F. Kennedy.

To explain further, suppose a data set contained the six values: 91, 75, 61, 101, 43, and 104. We want to locate the first quartile. We order the values from the minimum to the maximum: 43, 61, 75, 91, 101, and 104. The first quartile is located at

$$L_{25} = (n + 1) \frac{P}{100} = (6 + 1) \frac{25}{100} = 1.75$$

The position formula tells us that the first quartile is located between the first and the second value and that it is .75 of the distance between the first and the second values. The first value is 43 and the second is 61. So the distance between these two values is 18. To locate the first quartile, we need to move .75 of the distance between the first and second values, so .75(18) = 13.5. To complete the procedure, we add 13.5 to the first value, 43, and report that the first quartile is 56.5.

We can extend the idea to include both deciles and percentiles. To locate the 23rd percentile in a sample of 80 observations, we would look for the 18.63 position.

$$L_{23} = (n + 1) \frac{P}{100} = (80 + 1) \frac{23}{100} = 18.63$$

To find the value corresponding to the 23rd percentile, we would locate the 18th value and the 19th value and determine the distance between the two values. Next, we would multiply this difference by 0.63 and add the result to the smaller value. The result would be the 23rd percentile.

Statistical software is very helpful when describing and summarizing data. Excel, Minitab, and MegaStat, a statistical analysis Excel add-in, all provide summary statistics that include quartiles. For example, Minitab's summary of the Smith Barney commission data, shown below, includes the first and third quartiles, and other statistics. Based on the reported quartiles, 25% of the commissions earned were less than $1,721 and 75% were less then $2,205. These are the same values that we calculated using formula (4–1).

	Sheet1 ***			Session										
↓	**C1**		**Descriptive Statistics: Commissions**											
	Commissions													
1	1460		Variable	N	N*	Mean	SE Mean	StDev	Minimum	Q1	Median	Q3	Maximum	
2	1471		Commissions	15	0	1947.9	77.1	298.8	1460.0	1721.0	2038.0	2205.0	2406.0	
3	1637													
4	1721													

There are ways other than formula (4–1) to locate quartile values. For example, another method uses $0.25n + 0.75$ to locate the position of the first quartile and

	SmithBarney			
	A	**B**	**C**	**D**
1	Commissions			
2	1460			
3	1471		Equation 4-1	
4	1637		Quartile 1	1721
5	1721			
6	1758		Quartile 3	2205
7	1787			
8	1940		Excel Method	
9	2038		Quartile 1	1739.5
10	2047			
11	2054		Quartile 3	2151
12	2097			

$0.75n + 0.25$ to locate the position of the third quartile. We will call this the *Excel Method.* In the Smith Barney data, this method would place the first quartile at position 4.5 (.25 × 15 + .75) and the third quartile at position 11.5 (.75 × 15 + .25). The first quartile would be interpolated as 0.5, or one-half the difference between the fourth- and the fifth-ranked values. Based on this method, the first quartile is $1739.5, found by ($1,721 + 0.5[$1,758 − $1,721]). The third quartile, at position 11.5, would be $2,151 or one-half the distance between the eleventh- and the twelfth-ranked values, found by ($2,097 + 0.5[$2,205 − $2,097]). Excel, as shown in the Smith Barney

☒ APPLEWOOD AUTO GROUP 2011				
⧄	A	B	C	D	E
1	Age	Profit			
2	33	$1,889			
3	47	$1,461		Equation 4-1	
4	44	$1,532		1st Quartile	1415.5
5	53	$1,220			
6	51	$1,674		3rd Quartile	2275.5
7	41	$2,389			
8	58	$2,058			
9	35	$1,919		Excel Method	
10	45	$1,266		1st Quartile	1422.5
11	54	$2,991			
12	56	$2,695		3rd Quartile	2268.5
13	41	$2,165			

and Applewood examples, can compute quartiles using either of the two methods. **Please note the text uses formula (4–1) to calculate quartiles.**

Is the difference between the two methods important? No. Usually it is just a nuisance. In general, both methods calculate values that will support the statement that approximately 25% of the values are less than the value of the first quartile, and approximately 75% of the data values are less than the value of the third quartile. When the sample is large, the difference in the results from the two methods is small. For example, in the Applewood Auto Group data there are 180 vehicles. The quartiles computed using both methods are shown to the left. Based on the variable profit, 45 of the 180 values (25%) are less than both values of the first quartile, and 135 of the 180 values (75%) are less than both values of the third quartile.

When using Excel, be careful to understand the method used to calculate quartiles. In Excel 2007, quartiles are calculated using the *Excel Method*. Excel 2010 provides both methods to calculate quartiles. The Excel 2010 commands to compute the quartiles are shown in the **Software Commands** section at the end of the chapter.

Self-Review 4–2

The Quality Control department of Plainsville Peanut Company is responsible for checking the weight of the 8-ounce jar of peanut butter. The weights of a sample of nine jars produced last hour are:

7.69	7.72	7.8	7.86	7.90	7.94	7.97	8.06	8.09

(a) What is the median weight?
(b) Determine the weights corresponding to the first and third quartiles.

Exercises

connect™

3. Determine the median and the values corresponding to the first and third quartiles in the following data. ⓓⓕ

46	47	49	49	51	53	54	54	55	55	59

4. Determine the median and the values corresponding to the first and third quartiles in the following data. ⓓⓕ

5.24	6.02	6.67	7.30	7.59	7.99	8.03	8.35	8.81	9.45
9.61	10.37	10.39	11.86	12.22	12.71	13.07	13.59	13.89	15.42

5. The Thomas Supply Company Inc. is a distributor of gas-powered generators. As with any business, the length of time customers take to pay their invoices is important. Listed

below, arranged from smallest to largest, is the time, in days, for a sample of The Thomas Supply Company Inc. invoices.

13	13	13	20	26	27	31	34	34	34	35	35	36	37	38
41	41	41	45	47	47	47	50	51	53	54	56	62	67	82

a. Determine the first and third quartiles.
b. Determine the second decile and the eighth decile.
c. Determine the 67th percentile.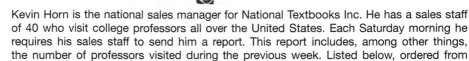

6. Kevin Horn is the national sales manager for National Textbooks Inc. He has a sales staff of 40 who visit college professors all over the United States. Each Saturday morning he requires his sales staff to send him a report. This report includes, among other things, the number of professors visited during the previous week. Listed below, ordered from smallest to largest, are the number of visits last week.

38	40	41	45	48	48	50	50	51	51	52	52	53	54	55	55	55	56	56	57
59	59	59	62	62	62	63	64	65	66	66	67	67	69	69	71	77	78	79	79

a. Determine the median number of calls.
b. Determine the first and third quartiles.
c. Determine the first decile and the ninth decile.
d. Determine the 33rd percentile.

Box Plots

LO 4-3 Construct and analyze a box plot.

A **box plot** is a graphical display, based on quartiles, that helps us picture a set of data. To construct a box plot, we need only five statistics: the minimum value, Q_1 (the first quartile), the median, Q_3 (the third quartile), and the maximum value. An example will help to explain.

Example

Alexander's Pizza offers free delivery of its pizza within 15 miles. Alex, the owner, wants some information on the time it takes for delivery. How long does a typical delivery take? Within what range of times will most deliveries be completed? For a sample of 20 deliveries, he determined the following information:

Minimum value = 13 minutes

Q_1 = 15 minutes

Median = 18 minutes

Q_3 = 22 minutes

Maximum value = 30 minutes

Develop a box plot for the delivery times. What conclusions can you make about the delivery times?

Solution

The first step in drawing a box plot is to create an appropriate scale along the horizontal axis. Next, we draw a box that starts at Q_1 (15 minutes) and ends at Q_3 (22 minutes). Inside the box we place a vertical line to represent the median (18 minutes). Finally, we extend horizontal lines from the box out to the minimum value (13 minutes) and the maximum value (30 minutes). These horizontal lines outside of the box are sometimes called "whiskers" because they look a bit like a cat's whiskers.

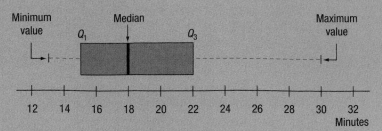

The box plot shows that the middle 50% of the deliveries take between 15 minutes and 22 minutes. The distance between the ends of the box, 7 minutes, is the **interquartile range.** The interquartile range is the distance between the first and the third quartile. It shows the spread or dispersion of the middle 50% of the deliveries.

The box plot also reveals that the distribution of delivery times is positively skewed. Recall from page 72 in Chapter 3 that we defined skewness as the lack of symmetry in a set of data. How do we know this distribution is positively skewed? In this case, there are actually two pieces of information that suggest this. First, the dashed line to the right of the box from 22 minutes (Q_3) to the maximum time of 30 minutes is longer than the dashed line from the left of 15 minutes (Q_1) to the minimum value of 13 minutes. To put it another way, the 25% of the data larger than the third quartile is more spread out than the 25% less than the first quartile. A second indication of positive skewness is that the median is not in the center of the box. The distance from the first quartile to the median is smaller than the distance from the median to the third quartile. We know that the number of delivery times between 15 minutes and 18 minutes is the same as the number of delivery times between 18 minutes and 22 minutes.

Example

Refer to the Applewood Auto Group data. Develop a box plot for the variable age of the buyer. What can we conclude about the distribution of the age of the buyer?

Solution

The Minitab statistical software system was used to develop the following chart and summary statistics.

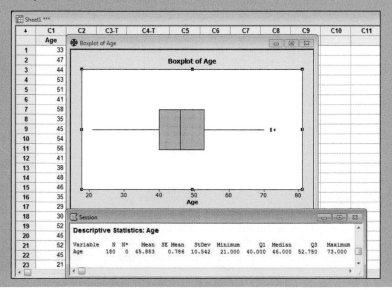

The median age of the purchaser was 46 years, 25% of the purchasers were less than 40 years of age, and 25% were more than 52.75 years of age. Based on the summary information and the box plot, we conclude:

- Fifty percent of the purchasers were between the ages of 40 and 52.75 years.
- The distribution of ages is symmetric. There are two reasons for this conclusion. The length of the whisker above 52.75 years (Q_3) is about the same length as the whisker below 40 years (Q_1). Also, the area in the box between 40 years and the median of 46 years is about the same as the area between the median and 52.75.

There are three asterisks (*) above 70 years. What do they indicate? In a box plot, an asterisk identifies an **outlier**. An outlier is a value that is inconsistent with the rest of the data. It is defined as a value that is more than 1.5 times the interquartile range smaller than Q_1 or larger than Q_3. In this example, an outlier would be a value larger than 71.875 years, found by:

$$Outlier > Q_3 + 1.5(Q_3 - Q_1) = 52.75 + 1.5(52.75 - 40) = 71.875$$

An outlier would also be a value less than 20.875 years.

$$Outlier < Q_1 - 1.5(Q_3 - Q_1) = 40 - 1.5(52.75 - 40) = 20.875$$

From the box plot, we conclude that there are three purchasers 72 years of age or older and none less than 21 years of age. Technical note: In some cases, a single asterisk may represent more than one observation, because of the limitations of the software and space available. It is a good idea to check the actual data. In this instance, there are three purchasers 72 years old or older; two are 72 and one is 73.

Self-Review 4–3

The following box plot shows the assets in millions of dollars for credit unions in Seattle, Washington.

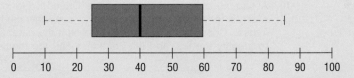

What are the smallest and largest values, the first and third quartiles, and the median? Would you agree that the distribution is symmetrical? Are there any outliers?

Exercises

connect

7. The box plot below shows the amount spent for books and supplies per year by students at four-year public colleges.

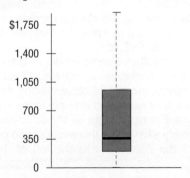

  a. Estimate the median amount spent.
  b. Estimate the first and third quartiles for the amount spent.
  c. Estimate the interquartile range for the amount spent.
  d. Beyond what point is a value considered an outlier?
  e. Identify any outliers and estimate their value.
  f. Is the distribution symmetrical or positively or negatively skewed?
8. The box plot shows the undergraduate in-state charge per credit hour at four-year public colleges.

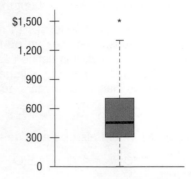

  a. Estimate the median.
  b. Estimate the first and third quartiles.
  c. Determine the interquartile range.
  d. Beyond what point is a value considered an outlier?
  e. Identify any outliers and estimate their value.
  f. Is the distribution symmetrical or positively or negatively skewed?
9. In a study of the gasoline mileage of model year 2011 automobiles, the mean miles per gallon was 27.5 and the median was 26.8. The smallest value in the study was 12.70 miles per gallon, and the largest was 50.20. The first and third quartiles were 17.95 and 35.45 miles per gallon, respectively. Develop a box plot and comment on the distribution. Is it a symmetric distribution?
10. A sample of 28 timeshares in the Orlando, Florida, area revealed the following daily charges for a one-bedroom suite. For convenience, the data are ordered from smallest to largest. Construct a box plot to represent the data. Comment on the distribution. Be sure to identify the first and third quartiles and the median.

$116	$121	$157	$192	$207	$209	$209
229	232	236	236	239	243	246
260	264	276	281	283	289	296
307	309	312	317	324	341	353

4.4 Skewness

In Chapter 3, we described measures of central location for a set of observations by reporting the mean, median, and mode. We also described measures that show the amount of spread or variation in a set of data, such as the range and the standard deviation.

Another characteristic of a set of data is the shape. There are four shapes commonly observed: symmetric, positively skewed, negatively skewed, and bimodal. In a **symmetric** set of observations the mean and median are equal and the data values are evenly spread around these values. The data values below the mean and median are a mirror image of those above. A set of values is **skewed to the right** or **positively skewed** if there is a single peak and the values extend much further to the right of the peak than to the left of the peak. In this case, the mean is larger than the

LO 4-4 Compute and describe the coefficient of skewness.

median. In a **negatively skewed** distribution there is a single peak, but the observations extend further to the left in the negative direction than to the right. In a negatively skewed distribution, the mean is smaller than the median. Positively skewed distributions are more common. Salaries often follow this pattern. Think of the salaries of those employed in a small company of about 100 people. The president and a few top executives would have very large salaries relative to the other workers and hence the distribution of salaries would exhibit positive skewness. A **bimodal distribution** will have two or more peaks. This is often the case when the values are from two or more populations. This information is summarized in Chart 4–1.

Skewness shows the lack of symmetry in a set of observations.

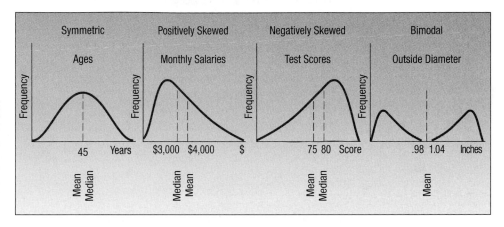

CHART 4–1 Shapes of Frequency Polygons

There are several formulas in the statistical literature used to calculate skewness. The simplest, developed by Professor Karl Pearson (1857–1936), is based on the difference between the mean and the median.

PEARSON'S COEFFICIENT OF SKEWNESS
$$sk = \frac{3(\overline{X} - \text{Median})}{s}$$
[4–2]

Using this relationship, the coefficient of skewness can range from −3 up to 3. A value near −3, such as −2.57, indicates considerable negative skewness. A value such as 1.63 indicates moderate positive skewness. A value of 0, which will occur when the mean and median are equal, indicates the distribution is symmetrical and that there is no skewness present.

In this text, we present output from the statistical software packages Minitab and Excel. Both of these software packages compute a value for the coefficient of skewness that is based on the cubed deviations from the mean. The formula is:

SOFTWARE COEFFICIENT OF SKEWNESS
$$sk = \frac{n}{(n-1)(n-2)}\left[\sum\left(\frac{X - \overline{X}}{s}\right)^3\right]$$
[4–3]

Formula (4–3) offers an insight into skewness. The right-hand side of the formula is the difference between each value and the mean, divided by the standard deviation. That is the portion $(X - \overline{X})/s$ of the formula. This idea is called **standardizing.** We will discuss the idea of standardizing a value in more detail in Chapter 7 when we describe the normal probability distribution. At this point, observe that the result is to report the difference between each value and the mean in units

Statistics in Action

The late Stephen Jay Gould (1941–2002) was a professor of zoology and professor of geology at Harvard University. In 1982, he was diagnosed with cancer and had an expected survival time of eight months. However, never to be discouraged, his research showed that the distribution of survival time is dramatically skewed to the right and showed that not only do 50% of similar cancer patients survive more than 8 months, but that the survival time could be years rather than months! In fact, Dr. Gould lived another 20 years. Based on his experience, he wrote a widely published essay titled, "The Median Is not the Message."

of the standard deviation. If this difference is positive, the particular value is larger than the mean; if the value is negative, the standardized quantity is smaller than the mean. When we cube these values, we retain the information on the direction of the difference. Recall that in the formula for the standard deviation [see formula (3–9)] we squared the difference between each value and the mean, so that the result was all non-negative values.

If the set of data values under consideration is symmetric, when we cube the standardized values and sum over all the values, the result would be near zero. If there are several large values, clearly separate from the others, the sum of the cubed differences would be a large positive value. If there are several small values clearly separate from the others, the sum of the cubed differences will be negative.

An example will illustrate the idea of skewness.

Example

Following are the earnings per share for a sample of 15 software companies for the year 2010. The earnings per share are arranged from smallest to largest.

$0.09	$0.13	$0.41	$0.51	$ 1.12	$ 1.20	$ 1.49	$3.18
3.50	6.36	7.83	8.92	10.13	12.99	16.40	

Compute the mean, median, and standard deviation. Find the coefficient of skewness using Pearson's estimate and the software methods. What is your conclusion regarding the shape of the distribution?

Solution

These are sample data, so we use formula (3–2) to determine the mean

$$\bar{X} = \frac{\Sigma X}{n} = \frac{\$74.26}{15} = \$4.95$$

The median is the middle value in a set of data, arranged from smallest to largest. In this case, the middle value is $3.18, so the median earnings per share is $3.18.

We use formula (3–9) on page 83 to determine the sample standard deviation.

$$s = \sqrt{\frac{\Sigma(X - \bar{X})^2}{n - 1}} = \sqrt{\frac{(\$0.09 - \$4.95)^2 + \cdots + (\$16.40 - \$4.95)^2}{15 - 1}} = \$5.22$$

Pearson's coefficient of skewness is 1.017, found by

$$sk = \frac{3(\bar{X} - \text{Median})}{s} = \frac{3(\$4.95 - \$3.18)}{\$5.22} = 1.017$$

This indicates there is moderate positive skewness in the earnings per share data.

We obtain a similar, but not exactly the same, value from the software method. The details of the calculations are shown in Table 4–1. To begin, we find the difference between each earnings per share value and the mean and divide this result by the standard deviation. Recall that we referred to this as standardizing. Next, we cube, that is, raise to the third power, the result of the first step. Finally, we sum the cubed values. The details for the first company, that is, the company with an earnings per share of $0.09, are:

$$\left(\frac{X - \bar{X}}{s}\right)^3 = \left(\frac{0.09 - 4.95}{5.22}\right)^3 = (-0.9310)^3 = -0.8070$$

TABLE 4–1 Calculation of the Coefficient of Skewness

Earnings per Share	$\dfrac{(X - \bar{X})}{s}$	$\left(\dfrac{X - \bar{X}}{s}\right)^3$
0.09	−0.9310	−0.8070
0.13	−0.9234	−0.7873
0.41	−0.8697	−0.6579
0.51	−0.8506	−0.6154
1.12	−0.7337	−0.3950
1.20	−0.7184	−0.3708
1.49	−0.6628	−0.2912
3.18	−0.3391	−0.0390
3.50	−0.2778	−0.0214
6.36	0.2701	0.0197
7.83	0.5517	0.1679
8.92	0.7605	0.4399
10.13	0.9923	0.9772
12.99	1.5402	3.6539
16.40	2.1935	10.5537
		11.8274

When we sum the 15 cubed values, the result is 11.8274. That is, the term $\sum[(X - \bar{X})/s]^3 = 11.8274$. To find the coefficient of skewness, we use formula (4–3), with $n = 15$.

$$sk = \frac{n}{(n - 1)(n - 2)} \sum\left(\frac{X - \bar{X}}{s}\right)^3 = \frac{15}{(15 - 1)(15 - 2)}(11.8274) = 0.975$$

We conclude that the earnings per share values are somewhat positively skewed. The following summary, from Minitab, reports the descriptive measures, such as the mean, median, and standard deviation of the earnings per share data. Also included are the coefficient of skewness and a histogram with a bell-shaped curve superimposed.

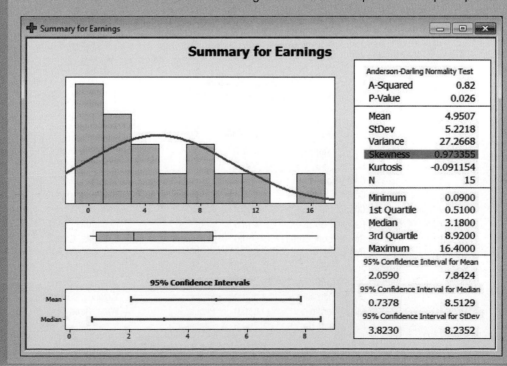

Self-Review 4–4

A sample of five data entry clerks employed in the Horry County Tax Office revised the following number of tax records last hour: 73, 98, 60, 92, and 84.
(a) Find the mean, median, and the standard deviation.
(b) Compute the coefficient of skewness using Pearson's method.
(c) Calculate the coefficient of skewness using the software method.
(d) What is your conclusion regarding the skewness of the data?

Exercises

connect™

For Exercises 11–14:

a. Determine the mean, median, and the standard deviation.
b. Determine the coefficient of skewness using Pearson's method.
c. Determine the coefficient of skewness using the software method.

11. The following values are the starting salaries, in $000, for a sample of five accounting graduates who accepted positions in public accounting last year.

36.0	26.0	33.0	28.0	31.0

12. Listed below are the salaries, in $000, for a sample of 15 chief financial officers in the electronics industry.

$516.0	$548.0	$566.0	$534.0	$586.0	$529.0
546.0	523.0	538.0	523.0	551.0	552.0
486.0	558.0	574.0			

13. Listed below are the commissions earned ($000) last year by the sales representatives at Furniture Patch Inc.

$ 3.9	$ 5.7	$ 7.3	$10.6	$13.0	$13.6	$15.1	$15.8	$17.1
17.4	17.6	22.3	38.6	43.2	87.7			

14. Listed below are the salaries in $000 of the 25 players on the opening day roster of the 2010 New York Yankees Major League Baseball team.

Player	Salary ($000)	Position	Player	Salary ($000)	Position
Aceves, Alfredo	435.7	Pitcher	Pena, Ramiro	412.1	Infielder
Burnett, A.J.	16,500.0	Pitcher	Pettitte, Andy	11,750.0	Pitcher
Cano, Robinson	9,000.0	Second Baseman	Posada, Jorge	13,100.0	Catcher
Cervelli, Francisco	410.8	Catcher	Rivera, Mariano	15,000.0	Pitcher
Chamberlain, Joba	488.0	Pitcher	Robertson, David	426.7	Pitcher
Gardner, Brett	452.5	Outfielder	Rodriguez, Alex	33,000.0	Third Baseman
Granderson, Curtis	5,500.0	Outfielder	Sabathia, CC	24,285.7	Pitcher
Hughes, Phil	447.0	Pitcher	Swisher, Nick	6,850.0	Outfielder
Jeter, Derek	22,600.0	Shortstop	Teixeira, Mark	20,625.0	First Baseman
Johnson, Nick	5,500.0	First Baseman	Thames, Marcus	900.0	Outfielder
Marte, Damaso	4,000.0	Pitcher	Vazquez, Javier	11,500.0	Pitcher
Mitre, Sergio	850.0	Pitcher	Winn, Randy	1,100.0	Outfielder
Park, Chan Ho	1,200.0	Pitcher			

4.5 Describing the Relationship between Two Variables

In Chapter 2 and the first section of this chapter, we presented graphical techniques to summarize the distribution of a single variable. We used a histogram in Chapter 2 to summarize the profit on vehicles sold by the Applewood Auto Group. Earlier in this chapter, we used dot plots to visually summarize a set of data. Because we are studying a single variable, we refer to this as **univariate** data.

There are situations where we wish to study and visually portray the relationship between two variables. When we study the relationship between two variables, we refer to the data as **bivariate.** Data analysts frequently wish to understand the relationship between two variables. Here are some examples:

- Tybo and Associates is a law firm that advertises extensively on local TV. The partners are considering increasing their advertising budget. Before doing so, they would like to know the relationship between the amount spent per month on advertising and the total amount of billings for that month. To put it another way, will increasing the amount spent on advertising result in an increase in billings?
- Coastal Realty is studying the selling prices of homes. What variables seem to be related to the selling price of homes? For example, do larger homes sell for more than smaller ones? Probably. So Coastal might study the relationship between the area in square feet and the selling price.
- Dr. Stephen Givens is an expert in human development. He is studying the relationship between the height of fathers and the height of their sons. That is, do tall fathers tend to have tall children? Would you expect Dwight Howard, the 6′ 11″, 265-pound professional basketball player, to have relatively tall sons?

LO 4-5 Create and interpret a scatter diagram.

One graphical technique we use to show the relationship between variables is called a **scatter diagram.**

To draw a scatter diagram, we need two variables. We scale one variable along the horizontal axis (*X*-axis) of a graph and the other variable along the vertical axis (*Y*-axis). Usually one variable depends to some degree on the other. In the third example above, the height of the son *depends* on the height of the father. So we scale the height of the father on the horizontal axis and that of the son on the vertical axis.

We can use statistical software, such as Excel, to perform the plotting function for us. *Caution:* You should always be careful of the scale. By changing the scale of either the vertical or the horizontal axis, you can affect the apparent visual strength of the relationship.

A scatter diagram is used as a way to understand the relationship between two variables.

Following are three scatter diagrams (Chart 4–2). The one on the left shows a rather strong positive relationship between the age in years and the maintenance cost last year for a sample of 10 buses owned by the city of Cleveland, Ohio. Note that as the age of the bus increases, the yearly maintenance cost also increases. The example in the center, for a sample of 20 vehicles, shows a rather strong indirect relationship between the odometer reading and the auction price. That is, as the number of miles driven increases, the auction price decreases. The example on the right depicts the relationship between the height and yearly salary for a sample of 15 shift supervisors. This graph indicates there is little relationship between their height and yearly salary.

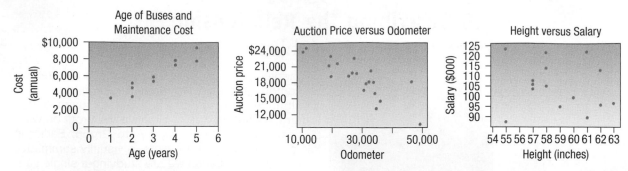

CHART 4–2 Three Examples of Scatter Diagrams.

Example

In the introduction to Chapter 2, we presented data from the Applewood Auto Group. We gathered information concerning several variables, including the profit earned from the sale of 180 vehicles sold last month. In addition to the amount of profit on each sale, one of the other variables is the age of the purchaser. Is there a relationship between the profit earned on a vehicle sale and the age of the purchaser? Would it be reasonable to conclude that more profit is made on vehicles purchased by older buyers?

Solution

We can investigate the relationship between vehicle profit and the age of the buyer with a scatter diagram. We scale age on the horizontal, or X-axis, and the profit on the vertical, or Y-axis. We use Microsoft Excel to develop the scatter diagram. The Excel commands necessary for the output are shown in the **Software Commands** section at the end of the chapter.

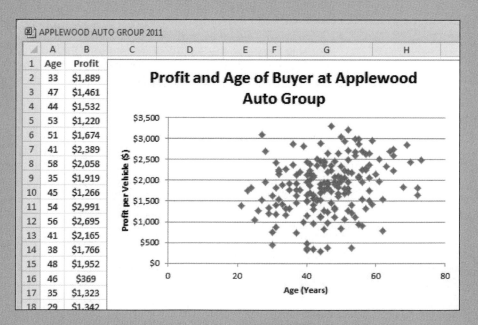

The scatter diagram shows a rather weak positive relationship between the two variables. It does not appear there is much relationship between the vehicle profit and the age of the buyer. In Chapter 13, we will study the relationship between variables more extensively, even calculating several numerical measures to express the relationship between variables.

In the preceding example, there is a weak positive, or direct, relationship between the variables. There are, however, many instances where there is a relationship between the variables, but that relationship is inverse or negative. For example:

- The value of a vehicle and the number of miles driven. As the number of miles increases, the value of the vehicle decreases.
- The premium for auto insurance and the age of the driver. Auto rates tend to be the highest for younger drivers and less for older drivers.
- For many law enforcement personnel, as the number of years on the job increases, the number of traffic citations decreases. This may be because personnel become more liberal in their interpretations or they may be in supervisor positions and not in a position to issue as many citations. But in any event, as age increases, the number of citations decreases.

A scatter diagram requires that both of the variables be at least interval scale. In the Applewood Auto Group example, both age and vehicle profit are ratio scale variables. Height is also ratio scale as used in the discussion of the relationship between the height of fathers and the height of their sons. What if we wish to study the relationship between two variables when one or both are nominal or ordinal scale? In this case, we tally the results in a **contingency table.**

LO 4-6 Develop and explain a contingency table.

CONTINGENCY TABLE A table used to classify observations according to two identifiable characteristics.

A contingency table is a cross-tabulation that simultaneously summarizes two variables of interest. For example:

- Students at a university are classified by gender and class (freshman, sophomore, junior, or senior).
- A product is classified as acceptable or unacceptable and by the shift (day, afternoon, or night) on which it is manufactured.
- A voter in a school bond referendum is classified as to party affiliation (Democrat, Republican, other) and the number of children that voter has attending school in the district (0, 1, 2, etc.).

Example

There are four dealerships in the Applewood Auto Group. Suppose we want to compare the profit earned on each vehicle sold by the particular dealership. To put it another way, is there a relationship between the amount of profit earned and the dealership?

Solution

In a contingency table, the variables should be nominal or ordinal. In this example, the variable dealership is a nominal variable and the variable profit is a ratio variable. To convert profit to an ordinal variable, we classify the variable profit into two categories, those cases where the profit earned is more than the median and those cases where it is less. On page 71, we calculated the median profit for all sales last month at Applewood Auto Group to be $1,882.50.

Contingency Table Showing the Relationship between Profit and Dealership					
Above/Below Median Profit	Kane	Olean	Sheffield	Tionesta	Total
Above	25	20	19	26	90
Below	27	20	26	17	90
Total	52	40	45	43	180

By organizing the information into a contingency table, we can compare the profit at the four dealerships. We observe the following:

- From the Total column on the right, 90 of the 180 cars sold had a profit above the median and half below. From the definition of the median, this is expected.
- For the Kane dealership, 25 out of the 52, or 48%, of the cars sold were sold for a profit more than the median.
- The percentage of profits above the median for the other dealerships are 50% for Olean, 42% for Sheffield, and 60% for Tionesta.

We will return to the study of contingency tables in Chapter 5 during the study of probability and in Chapter 15 during the study of nonparametric methods of analysis.

Self-Review 4–5

The rock group Blue String Beans is touring the United States. The following chart shows the relationship between concert seating capacity and revenue in $000 for a sample of concerts.

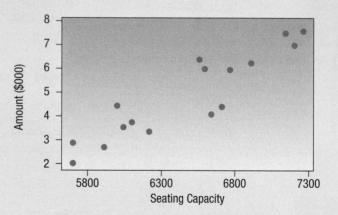

(a) What is the diagram called?
(b) How many concerts were studied?
(c) Estimate the revenue for the concert with the largest seating capacity.
(d) How would you characterize the relationship between revenue and seating capacity? Is it strong or weak, direct or inverse?

Exercises

connect™

15. Develop a scatter diagram for the following sample data. How would you describe the relationship between the values?

X-Value	Y-Value	X-Value	Y-Value
10	6	11	6
8	2	10	5
9	6	7	2
11	5	7	3
13	7	11	7

16. Silver Springs Moving and Storage Inc. is studying the relationship between the number of rooms in a move and the number of labor hours required for the move. As part of the analysis, the CFO of Silver Springs developed the following scatter diagram.

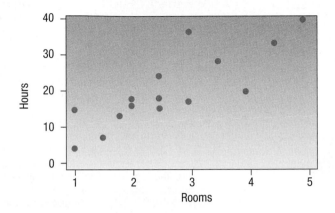

a. How many moves are in the sample?
b. Does it appear that more labor hours are required as the number of rooms increases, or do labor hours decrease as the number of rooms increases?

17. The Director of Planning for Devine Dining Inc. wishes to study the relationship between the gender of a guest and whether the guest orders dessert. To investigate the relationship, the manager collected the following information on 200 recent customers.

	Gender		
Dessert Ordered	**Male**	**Female**	**Total**
Yes	32	15	47
No	68	85	153
Total	100	100	200

a. What is the level of measurement of the two variables?
b. What is the above table called?
c. Does the evidence in the table suggest men are more likely to order dessert than women? Explain why.

18. Ski Resorts of Vermont Inc. is considering a merger with Gulf Shores Beach Resorts Inc. of Alabama. The board of directors surveyed 50 stockholders concerning their position on the merger. The results are reported below.

	Opinion			
Number of Shares Held	**Favor**	**Oppose**	**Undecided**	**Total**
Under 200	8	6	2	16
200 up to 1,000	6	8	1	15
Over 1,000	6	12	1	19
Total	20	26	4	50

a. What level of measurement is used in this table?
b. What is this table called?
c. What group seems most strongly opposed to the merger?

Chapter Summary

I. A dot plot shows the range of values on the horizontal axis and the number of observations for each value on the vertical axis.
   A. Dot plots report the details of each observation.
   B. They are useful for comparing two or more data sets.
II. Measures of location also describe the shape of a set of observations.
   A. Quartiles divide a set of observations into four equal parts.
      1. Twenty-five percent of the observations are less than the first quartile, 50% are less than the second quartile, and 75% are less than the third quartile.
      2. The interquartile range is the difference between the third quartile and the first quartile.
   B. Deciles divide a set of observations into 10 equal parts and percentiles into 100 equal parts.
   C. A box plot is a graphic display of a set of data.
      1. A box is drawn enclosing the regions between the first quartile and the third quartile.
         a. A line is drawn inside the box at the median value.
         b. Dotted line segments are drawn from the third quartile to the largest value to show the highest 25% of the values and from the first quartile to the smallest value to show the lowest 25% of the values.
      2. A box plot is based on five statistics: the maximum and minimum values, the first and third quartiles, and the median.
III. The coefficient of skewness is a measure of the symmetry of a distribution.
   A. There are two formulas for the coefficient of skewness.
      1. The formula developed by Pearson is:

$$sk = \frac{3(\bar{X} - \text{Median})}{s} \qquad [4\text{--}2]$$

      2. The coefficient of skewness computed by statistical software is:

$$sk = \frac{n}{(n-1)(n-2)}\left[\sum\left(\frac{X - \bar{X}}{s}\right)^3 \right] \qquad [4\text{--}3]$$

IV. A scatter diagram is a graphic tool to portray the relationship between two variables.
   A. Both variables are measured with interval or ratio scales.
   B. If the scatter of points moves from the lower left to the upper right, the variables under consideration are directly or positively related.
   C. If the scatter of points moves from the upper left to the lower right, the variables are inversely or negatively related.
V. A contingency table is used to classify nominal-scale observations according to two characteristics.

Pronunciation Key

SYMBOL	MEANING	PRONUNCIATION
L_p	Location of percentile	L sub p
Q_1	First quartile	Q sub 1
Q_3	Third quartile	Q sub 3

Chapter Exercises

connect

19. A sample of students attending Southeast Florida University is asked the number of social activities in which they participated last week. The chart below was prepared from the sample data.

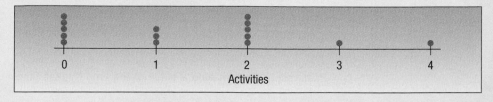

  a. What is the name given to this chart?
  b. How many students were in the study?
  c. How many students reported attending no social activities?
20. Doctor's Care is a walk-in clinic, with locations in Georgetown, Monks Corners, and Aynor, at which patients may receive treatment for minor injuries, colds, and flu, as well as physical examinations. The following charts report the number of patients treated in each of the three locations last month.

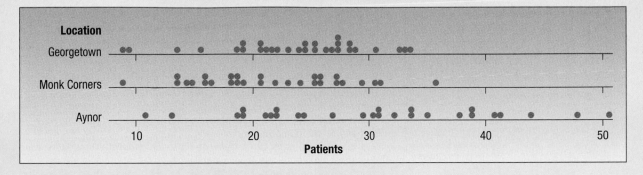

Describe the number of patients served at the three locations each day. What are the maximum and minimum numbers of patients served at each of the locations?

21. In recent years, due to low interest rates, many homeowners refinanced their home mortgages. Linda Lahey is a mortgage officer at Down River Federal Savings and Loan. Below is the amount refinanced for 20 loans she processed last week. The data are reported in thousands of dollars and arranged from smallest to largest.

59.2	59.5	61.6	65.5	66.6	72.9	74.8	77.3	79.2
83.7	85.6	85.8	86.6	87.0	87.1	90.2	93.3	98.6
100.2	100.7							

  a. Find the median, first quartile, and third quartile.
  b. Find the 26th and 83rd percentiles.
  c. Draw a box plot of the data.
22. A study is made by the recording industry in the United States of the number of music CDs owned by senior citizens and young adults. The information is reported below.

Seniors									
28	35	41	48	52	81	97	98	98	99
118	132	133	140	145	147	153	158	162	174
177	180	180	187	188					

Young Adults									
81	107	113	147	147	175	183	192	202	209
233	251	254	266	283	284	284	316	372	401
417	423	490	500	507	518	550	557	590	594

  a. Find the median and the first and third quartiles for the number of CDs owned by senior citizens. Develop a box plot for the information.
  b. Find the median and the first and third quartiles for the number of CDs owned by young adults. Develop a box plot for the information.
  c. Compare the number of CDs owned by the two groups.
23. The corporate headquarters of *Bank.com,* a new Internet company that performs all banking transactions via the Internet, is located in downtown Philadelphia. The director of human resources is making a study of the time it takes employees to get to work. The city is planning to offer incentives to each downtown employer if they will encourage their

employees to use public transportation. Below is a listing of the time to get to work this morning according to whether the employee used public transportation or drove a car.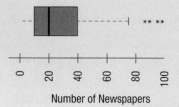

Public Transportation									
23	25	25	30	31	31	32	33	35	36
37	42								

Private									
32	32	33	34	37	37	38	38	38	39
40	44								

a. Find the median and the first and third quartiles for the time it took employees using public transportation. Develop a box plot for the information.

b. Find the median and the first and third quartiles for the time it took employees who drove their own vehicle. Develop a box plot for the information.

c. Compare the times of the two groups.

24. The following box plot shows the number of daily newspapers published in each state and the District of Columbia. Write a brief report summarizing the number published. Be sure to include information on the values of the first and third quartiles, the median, and whether there is any skewness. If there are any outliers, estimate their value.

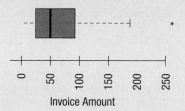

Number of Newspapers

25. Walter Gogel Company is an industrial supplier of fasteners, tools, and springs. The amounts of its invoices vary widely, from less than $20.00 to more than $400.00. During the month of January, the company sent out 80 invoices. Here is a box plot of these invoices. Write a brief report summarizing the invoice amounts. Be sure to include information on the values of the first and third quartiles, the median, and whether there is any skewness. If there are any outliers, approximate the value of these invoices.

Invoice Amount

26. The American Society of PeriAnesthesia Nurses (ASPAN; www.aspan.org) is a national organization serving nurses practicing in ambulatory surgery, preanesthesia, and postanesthesia care. The organization consists of 40 components listed below.

State/Region	Membership	State/Region	Membership
Alabama	95	Illinois	562
Arizona	399	Indiana	270
Maryland, Delaware, DC	531	Iowa	117
Connecticut	239	Kentucky	197
Florida	631	Louisiana	258
Georgia	384	Michigan	411
Hawaii	73	Massachusetts	480
			(continued)

State/Region	Membership	State/Region	Membership
Maine	97	California	1,165
Minnesota, Dakotas	289	New Mexico	79
Missouri, Kansas	282	Pennsylvania	575
Mississippi	90	Rhode Island	53
Nebraska	115	Colorado	409
North Carolina	542	South Carolina	237
Nevada	106	Texas	1,026
New Jersey, Bermuda	517	Tennessee	167
Alaska, Idaho, Montana,		Utah	67
Oregon, Washington	708	Virginia	414
New York	891	Vermont,	
Ohio	708	New Hampshire	144
Oklahoma	171	Wisconsin	311
Arkansas	68	West Virginia	62

Use statistical software to answer the following questions.

a. Find the mean, median, and standard deviation of the number of members per component.

b. Find the coefficient of skewness, using the software. What do you conclude about the shape of the distribution of component size?

c. Compute the first and third quartiles using formula (4–1).

d. Develop a box plot. Are there any outliers? Which components are outliers? What are the limits for outliers?

27. McGivern Jewelers is located in the Levis Square Mall just south of Toledo, Ohio. Recently it ran an advertisement in the local newspaper reporting the shape, size, price, and cut grade for 33 of its diamonds currently in stock. The information is reported below.

Shape	Size (carats)	Price	Cut Grade	Shape	Size (carats)	Price	Cut Grade
Princess	5.03	$44,312	Ideal cut	Round	0.77	$2,828	Ultra ideal cut
Round	2.35	20,413	Premium cut	Oval	0.76	3,808	Premium cut
Round	2.03	13,080	Ideal cut	Princess	0.71	2,327	Premium cut
Round	1.56	13,925	Ideal cut	Marquise	0.71	2,732	Good cut
Round	1.21	7,382	Ultra ideal cut	Round	0.70	1,915	Premium cut
Round	1.21	5,154	Average cut	Round	0.66	1,885	Premium cut
Round	1.19	5,339	Premium cut	Round	0.62	1,397	Good cut
Emerald	1.16	5,161	Ideal cut	Round	0.52	2,555	Premium cut
Round	1.08	8,775	Ultra ideal cut	Princess	0.51	1,337	Ideal cut
Round	1.02	4,282	Premium cut	Round	0.51	1,558	Premium cut
Round	1.02	6,943	Ideal cut	Round	0.45	1,191	Premium cut
Marquise	1.01	7,038	Good cut	Princess	0.44	1,319	Average cut
Princess	1.00	4,868	Premium cut	Marquise	0.44	1,319	Premium cut
Round	0.91	5,106	Premium cut	Round	0.40	1,133	Premium cut
Round	0.90	3,921	Good cut	Round	0.35	1,354	Good cut
Round	0.90	3,733	Premium cut	Round	0.32	896	Premium cut
Round	0.84	2,621	Premium cut				

a. Develop a box plot of the variable price and comment on the result. Are there any outliers? What is the median price? What is the value of the first and the third quartile?

b. Develop a box plot of the variable size and comment on the result. Are there any outliers? What is the median price? What is the value of the first and the third quartile?

c. Develop a scatter diagram between the variables price and size. Be sure to put price on the vertical axis and size on the horizontal axis. Does there seem to be an association between the two variables? Is the association direct or indirect? Does any point seem to be different from the others?

d. Develop a contingency table for the variables shape and cut grade. What is the most common cut grade? What is the most common shape? What is the most common combination of cut grade and shape? 🔵

28. Listed below is the amount of commissions earned last month for the eight members of the sales staff at Best Electronics. Calculate the coefficient of skewness using both methods. *Hint:* Use of a spreadsheet will expedite the calculations.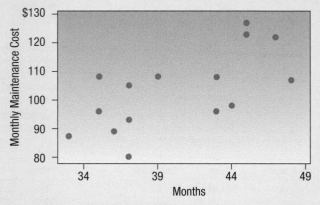

980.9	1,036.5	1,099.5	1,153.9	1,409.0	1,456.4	1,718.4	1,721.2

29. Listed below is the number of car thefts in a large city over the last week. Calculate the coefficient of skewness using both methods. *Hint:* Use of a spreadsheet will expedite the calculations.

3	12	13	7	8	3	8

30. The manager of Information Services at Wilkin Investigations, a private investigation firm, is studying the relationship between the age (in months) of a combination printer, copy, and fax machine and its monthly maintenance cost. For a sample of 15 machines, the manager developed the following chart. What can the manager conclude about the relationship between the variables?

31. An auto insurance company reported the following information regarding the age of a driver and the number of accidents reported last year. Develop a scatter diagram for the data and write a brief summary.

Age	Accidents	Age	Accidents
16	4	23	0
24	2	27	1
18	5	32	1
17	4	22	3

32. Wendy's offers eight different condiments (mustard, catsup, onion, mayonnaise, pickle, lettuce, tomato, and relish) on hamburgers. A store manager collected the following information on the number of condiments ordered and the age group of the customer. What can you conclude regarding the information? Who tends to order the most or least number of condiments?

	Age			
Number of Condiments	**Under 18**	**18 up to 40**	**40 up to 60**	**60 or older**
0	12	18	24	52
1	21	76	50	30
2	39	52	40	12
3 or more	71	87	47	28

33. Listed at the top of the next page is a table showing the number of employed and unemployed workers 20 years or older by gender in the United States.

Gender	Number of Workers (000)	
	Employed	Unemployed
Men	70,415	4,209
Women	61,402	3,314

a. How many workers were studied?
b. What percent of the workers were unemployed?
c. Compare the percent unemployed for the men and the women.

Data Set Exercises

(The data for these exercises are available at the text website www.mhhe.com/lindbasic8e).

34. Refer to the Real Estate data, which reports information on homes sold in the Goodyear, Arizona, area during the last year. Prepare a report on the selling prices of the homes. Be sure to answer the following questions in your report.
   a. Develop a box plot. Estimate the first and the third quartiles. Are there any outliers?
   b. Develop a scatter diagram with price on the vertical axis and the size of the home on the horizontal. Does there seem to be a relationship between these variables? Is the relationship direct or inverse?
   c. Develop a scatter diagram with price on the vertical axis and distance from the center of the city on the horizontal axis. Does there seem to be a relationship between these variables? Is the relationship direct or inverse?

35. Refer to the Baseball 2010 data that reports information on the 30 Major League Baseball teams for the 2010 season.
   a. In the data set, the variable Built is the year that a stadium was constructed. Using this variable, create a new variable, Age, by subtracting the value of the variable Built from the current year for each team. Develop a box plot with the new variable, Age. Are there any outliers? If so, which of the stadiums are outliers?
   b. Using the variable Payroll, create a box plot. Are there any outliers? What are the quartiles? How does the New York Yankees' payroll compare to other team payrolls? Write a brief summary of your analysis.
   c. Draw a scatter diagram with the variable Wins on the vertical axis and Payroll on the horizontal axis. What are your conclusions?
   d. Using the variable Wins, draw a dot plot. What can you conclude from this plot?

36. Refer to the Buena School District bus data.
   a. Refer to the maintenance cost variable. Develop a box plot. What are the first and third quartiles? Are there any outliers?
   b. Determine the median maintenance cost. Based on the median, develop a contingency table with bus manufacturer as one variable and whether the maintenance cost was above or below the median as the other variable. What are your conclusions?

Practice Test

Part 1—Objective
1. A graph for displaying data in which each individual value is represented along a number line is called a _____.
2. A _____ is a graphical display based on five statistics: the maximum and minimum values, the first and third quartiles, and the median.
3. A _____ is a graphical technique used to show the relationship between two interval- or ratio-scaled variables.
4. A _____ table is used to classify observations according to two identifiable characteristics.
5. _____ divide a set of observations into four equal parts.
6. _____ divide a set of observations into 100 equal parts.
7. The coefficient of _____ measures the symmetry of a distribution.
8. The _____ is the point below which one-fourth of the ranked values lie.
9. The _____ is the difference between the first and third quartiles.

Part 2—Problems

1. Eleven insurance companies reported their market capitalization (in millions of dollars) for the most recent fiscal year as:

15	17	23	26	27	35	72	88	91	98	102

   a. Draw a dot plot of the data.
   b. Determine the median market capitalization.
   c. Compute the first quartile of market capitalization.
   d. Find the 75th percentile of market capitalization.
   e. Make a box plot of the data.

2. A Texas farm co-op sponsored a health screening for its members. Part of the process included a blood pressure screen. The results of the blood pressure screen are summarized by age groups in the following table:

Blood Pressure	Age			Total
	Under 30	30 up to 60	Over 60	
Low	21	29	37	87
Medium	45	82	91	218
High	23	46	75	144
Total	89	157	203	449

   a. What fraction of the members have high blood pressure?
   b. What fraction of the "Under 30" members have low blood pressure?
   c. Is there a relationship between age and blood pressure? Describe it.

Software Commands

1. The Minitab commands for the dot plot on page 99 are:
   a. Enter the number of vehicles serviced at Tionesta Ford Lincoln Mercury in column *C1* and Sheffield Motors in *C2*. Name the variables accordingly.
   b. Select **Graph** and **Dotplot.** In the first dialog box, select **Multiple Y's, Simple** in the lower left corner, and click **OK.** In the next dialog box, select **Tionesta** and **Sheffield** as the variables to **Graph,** click on **Labels,** and write an appropriate title. Then click **OK.**
   c. To calculate the descriptive statistics shown in the output, select **Stat, Basic statistics,** and then **Display Descriptive statistics.** In the dialog box, select **Tionesta** and **Sheffield** as the Variables, click on **Statistics,** select the desired statistics to be output, and finally click **OK** twice.

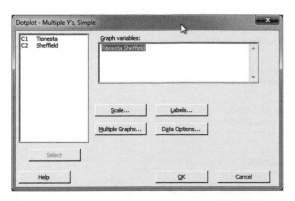

2. The Minitab commands for the descriptive summary on page 103 are:
   a. Input the data on the Smith Barney commissions from the Example on page 102.
   b. From the toolbar, select **Stat, Basic Statistics,** and **Display Descriptive Statistics.** In the dialog box, select **Commissions** as the **Variable,** and then click **OK.**

3. The Excel commands for the quartiles on pages 103–104 follow.
   a. Input the data on the Smith Barney commissions from the Example on page 102 in column A.
   If you are using Excel 2010 and wish to compute quartiles using formula (4–1), the steps are:
   b. In cell *C3* type **Formula (4–1),** in *C4* write **Quartile 1,** and in *C6* type **Quartile 3.**
   c. In cell *D4* type **"=QUARTILE.EXC(A2:A16,1)"** and hit **Enter.** In cell *D6* type **"=QUARTILE.EXC (A2:A16,3)"** and hit **Enter.**
   If you are using either Excel 2007 or 2010 and wish to compute quartiles using the Excel Method:
   b. In cell *C8* type **Excel Method,** in *C9* write **Quartile 1,** and in *11* type **Quartile 3.**
   c. In cell *D8* type **"=QUARTILE(A2:A16,1)"** and hit **Enter.** In cell *D11* type **"=QUARTILE(A2:A16,3)"** and hit **Enter.**

4. The Minitab commands for the box plot on page 106 are:
   a. Import the Applewood Auto Group data.

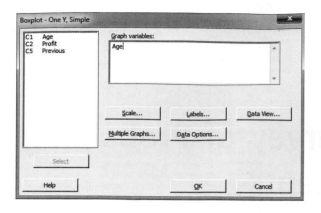

b. Select **Graph** and then **Boxplot.** In the dialog box, select **Simple** in the upper left corner and click **OK.** Select **Age** as the **Graph Variable,** click on **Labels** and include an appropriate heading, and then click **OK.**

5. The Minitab commands for the descriptive summary on page 111 are:
   a. Enter the data in the first column. In the cell below *C1,* enter the variable *Earnings.*

b. Select **Stat, Basic Statistics,** and then click on **Graphical Summary.** Select **Earnings** as the variable, and then click **OK.**

6. The Excel commands for the scatter diagram on page 114 are:
   a. Retrieve the Applewood Auto data.
   b. Using the mouse, highlight the column of age and profit. Include the first row.
   c. Select the **Insert** tab. Select **Scatter** from the **Chart** options. Select the top left option. The scatter plot will appear.
   d. With **Chart Tools** displayed at the top, select the **Layout** tab. Select **Chart Title** and type in a title for the plot. Next, under the same **Layout** tab, select **AxisTitles.** Using **Primary Vertical Axis Title,** name the vertical axis *Profit.* Using the **Primary Horizontal Axis Title,** name the horizontal axis *Age.* Next, select **Legend** and select **None.**

Chapter 4   Answers to Self-Review

4–1 a. 79, 105
   b. 15
   c. From 88 to 97; 75% of the stores are in this range.

4–2 a. 7.9
   b. $Q_1 = 7.76$, $Q_3 = 8.015$

4–3 The smallest value is 10 and the largest 85; the first quartile is 25 and the third 60. About 50% of the values are between 25 and 60. The median value is 40. The distribution is positively skewed. There are no outliers.

4–4 a. $\bar{X} = \dfrac{407}{5} = 81.4$, Median = 84

$$s = \sqrt{\dfrac{923.2}{5-1}} = 15.19$$

   b. $sk = \dfrac{3(81.4 - 84.0)}{15.19} = -0.51$

c.

X	$\dfrac{X - \bar{X}}{s}$	$\left[\dfrac{X - \bar{X}}{s}\right]^3$
73	−0.5530	−0.1691
98	1.0928	1.3051
60	−1.4088	−2.7962
92	0.6978	0.3398
84	0.1712	0.0050
		−1.3154

$$sk = \dfrac{5}{(4)(3)}[-1.3154]$$

$$= -0.5481$$

   d. The distribution is somewhat negatively skewed.

4–5 a. Scatter diagram
   b. 16
   c. $7,500
   d. Strong and direct

5

A Survey of Probability Concepts

It was found that 60% of the tourists to China visited the Forbidden City, the Temple of Heaven, the Great Wall, and other historical sites in or near Beijing. Forty percent visited Xi'an and its magnificent terracotta soldiers, horses, and chariots, which lay buried for over 2,000 years. Thirty percent of the tourists went to both Beijing and Xi'an. What is the probability that a tourist visited at least one of these places? (See Exercise 68 and LO 5-3.)

5.1 Introduction

The emphasis in Chapters 2, 3, and 4 is on descriptive statistics. In Chapter 2, we organize the profits on 180 vehicles sold by the Applewood Auto Group into a frequency distribution. This frequency distribution shows the smallest and the largest profits and where the largest concentration of data occurs. In Chapter 3, we use numerical measures of location and dispersion to locate a typical profit on vehicle sales and to examine the variation in the profit of a sale. We describe the variation in the profits with such measures of dispersion as the range and the standard deviation. In Chapter 4, we develop charts and graphs, such as a scatter diagram, to further describe the data graphically.

Descriptive statistics is concerned with summarizing data collected from past events. We now turn to the second facet of statistics, namely, *computing the chance that something will occur in the future*. This facet of statistics is called **statistical inference** or **inferential statistics.**

Seldom does a decision maker have complete information to make a decision. For example:

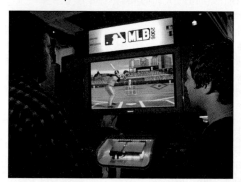

- Toys and Things, a toy and puzzle manufacturer, recently developed a new game based on sports trivia. It wants to know whether sports buffs will purchase the game. "Slam Dunk" and "Home Run" are two of the names under consideration. One way to minimize the risk of making an incorrect decision is to hire a market research firm to select a sample of 2,000 consumers from the population and ask each respondent for a reaction to the new game and its proposed titles. Using the sample results, the company can estimate the proportion of the population that will purchase the game.
- The quality assurance department of a United States Steel Corporation mill must assure management that the quarter-inch wire being produced has an acceptable tensile strength. Obviously, not all the wire produced can be tested for tensile strength because testing requires the wire to be stretched until it breaks—thus destroying it. So a random sample of 10 pieces is selected and tested. Based on the test results, all the wire produced is deemed to be either acceptable or unacceptable.
- Other questions involving uncertainty are: Should the daytime drama *Days of Our Lives* be discontinued immediately? Will a newly developed mint-flavored cereal be profitable if marketed? Will Charles Linden be elected to county auditor in Batavia County?

Statistical inference deals with conclusions about a population based on a sample taken from that population. (The populations for the preceding illustrations are: all consumers who like sports trivia games, all the quarter-inch steel wire produced, all television viewers who watch soaps, all who purchase breakfast cereal, and so on.)

Because there is uncertainty in decision making, it is important that all the known risks involved be scientifically evaluated. Helpful in this evaluation is *probability theory,* which has often been referred to as the science of uncertainty. Probability theory allows a manager to assess the risks and benefits associated with a set of decision alternatives. For example, a marketing executive who is responsible for the development of new products will use probability theory to assess the likelihood that a new product will be successful in the marketplace. A purchasing manager who is responsible for the quality of purchased materials will use probability theory to evaluate the quality standards of purchased materials and the risk of accepting an incoming shipment.

Because probability concepts are so important in the field of statistical inference (to be discussed starting with Chapter 8), this chapter introduces the basic language of probability, including such terms as *experiment, event, subjective probability,* and *addition* and *multiplication rules.*

5.2 What Is a Probability?

No doubt you are familiar with terms such as *probability, chance,* and *likelihood.* They are often used interchangeably. The weather forecaster announces that there is a 70% chance of rain for Super Bowl Sunday. Based on a survey of consumers who tested a newly developed pickle with a banana taste, the probability is .03 that, if marketed, it will be a financial success. (This means that the chance of the banana-flavor pickle being accepted by the public is rather remote.) What is a probability? In general, it is a number that describes the chance that something will happen.

> **PROBABILITY** A value between zero and one, inclusive, describing the relative possibility (chance or likelihood) an event will occur.

A probability is frequently expressed as a decimal, such as .70, .27, or .50. However, it may be given as a fraction such as 7/10, 27/100, or 1/2. It can assume any number from 0 to 1, inclusive. If a company has only five sales regions, and each region's name or number is written on a slip of paper and the slips put in a hat, the probability of selecting one of the five regions is 1. The probability of selecting from the hat a slip of paper that reads "Pittsburgh Steelers" is 0. Thus, the probability of 1 represents something that is certain to happen, and the probability of 0 represents something that cannot happen.

The closer a probability is to 0, the more improbable it is the event will happen. The closer the probability is to 1, the more sure we are it will happen. The relationship is shown in the following diagram along with a few of our personal beliefs. You might, however, select a different probability for Slo Poke's chances to win the Kentucky Derby or for an increase in federal taxes.

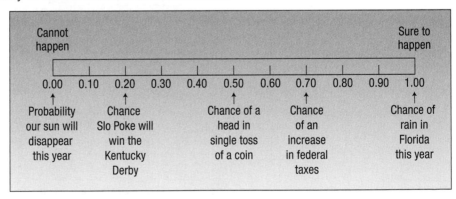

Sometimes, the likelihood of an event is expressed using the term, *odds.* For example, someone says the odds are "five to two" that an event will occur. This means that in a total of seven trials (5 + 2), the event will occur five times and not occur two times. Using odds, we can compute the probability that the event occurs as 5/(5 + 2) or 5/7. So, if the odds in favor of an event are x to y, the probability of the event is $x/(x + y)$.

Three keywords are used in the study of probability: **experiment, outcome,** and **event.** These terms are used in our everyday language, but in statistics they have specific meanings.

> **EXPERIMENT** A process that leads to the occurrence of one and only one of several possible results.

LO 5-1 Explain the terms *experiment, event,* and *outcome.*

This definition is more general than the one used in the physical sciences, where we picture someone manipulating test tubes or microscopes. In reference to probability, an experiment has two or more possible results, and it is uncertain which will occur.

> **OUTCOME** A particular result of an experiment.

For example, the tossing of a coin is an experiment. You may observe the toss of the coin, but you are unsure whether it will come up "heads" or "tails." If the coin is tossed, one particular outcome is a "head." The alternative outcome is a "tail." Similarly, asking 500 college students if they would plan to travel more than 100 miles to attend a Foo Fighters concert is an experiment. In this experiment, one possible outcome is that 273 students indicate they would travel more than 100 miles to attend the concert. Another outcome is that 317 students would travel more than 100 miles to attend the concert. Still another outcome is that 423 students indicate that they would travel more than 100 miles to attend the concert. When one or more of the experiment's outcomes are observed, we call this an event.

> **EVENT** A collection of one or more outcomes of an experiment.

Examples to clarify the definitions of the terms *experiment, outcome,* and *event* are presented in the following figure.

In the die-rolling experiment, there are six possible outcomes, but there are many possible events. When counting the number of members of the board of directors for Fortune 500 companies over 60 years of age, the number of possible outcomes can be anywhere from zero to the total number of members. There are an even larger number of possible events in this experiment.

Experiment	Roll a die	Count the number of members of the board of directors for Fortune 500 companies who are over 60 years of age
All possible outcomes	Observe a 1 Observe a 2 Observe a 3 Observe a 4 Observe a 5 Observe a 6	None are over 60 One is over 60 Two are over 60 ... 29 are over 60 ... ... 48 are over 60 ...
Some possible events	Observe an even number Observe a number greater than 4 Observe a number 3 or less	More than 13 are over 60 Fewer than 20 are over 60

Video Games Inc. recently developed a new video game. Its playability is to be tested by 80 veteran game players.
(a) What is the experiment?
(b) What is one possible outcome?
(c) Suppose 65 players tried the new game and said they liked it. Is 65 a probability?
(d) The probability that the new game will be a success is computed to be −1.0. Comment.
(e) Specify one possible event.

5.3 Approaches to Assigning Probabilities

In this section, we discuss two approaches to assigning a probability to an event: the objective approach and the subjective approach. **Objective probability** is subdivided into (1) *classical probability* and (2) *empirical probability*.

Classical Probability

LO 5-2 Identify and apply the appropriate approach to assigning probabilities.

Classical probability is based on the assumption that the outcomes of an experiment are *equally likely*. Using the classical viewpoint, the probability of an event happening is computed by dividing the number of favorable outcomes by the number of possible outcomes:

$$\text{CLASSICAL PROBABILITY} \qquad \begin{array}{l}\text{Probability} \\ \text{of an event}\end{array} = \frac{\text{Number of favorable outcomes}}{\text{Total number of possible outcomes}} \qquad \textbf{[5–1]}$$

Example

Consider an experiment of rolling a six-sided die. What is the probability of the event "an even number of spots appear face up"?

Solution

The possible outcomes are:

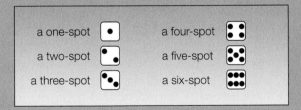

There are three "favorable" outcomes (a two, a four, and a six) in the collection of six equally likely possible outcomes. Therefore:

$$\text{Probability of an even number} = \frac{3}{6} \begin{array}{l}\leftarrow \\ \leftarrow\end{array} \boxed{\begin{array}{l}\text{Number of favorable outcomes} \\ \text{Total number of possible outcomes}\end{array}}$$

$$= .5$$

The mutually exclusive concept appeared earlier in our study of frequency distributions in Chapter 2. Recall that we create classes so that a particular value is included in only one of the classes and there is no overlap between classes. Thus, only one of several events can occur at a particular time.

MUTUALLY EXCLUSIVE The occurrence of one event means that none of the other events can occur at the same time.

The variable "gender" presents mutually exclusive outcomes, male and female. An employee selected at random is either male or female but cannot be both. A manufactured part is acceptable or unacceptable. The part cannot be both acceptable and unacceptable at the same time. In a sample of manufactured parts, the event of selecting an unacceptable part and the event of selecting an acceptable part are mutually exclusive.

If an experiment has a set of events that includes every possible outcome, such as the events "an even number" and "an odd number" in the die-tossing experiment, then the set of events is **collectively exhaustive.** For the die-tossing experiment, every outcome will be either even or odd. So the set is collectively exhaustive.

> **COLLECTIVELY EXHAUSTIVE** At least one of the events must occur when an experiment is conducted.

If the set of events is collectively exhaustive and the events are mutually exclusive, the sum of the probabilities is 1. Historically, the classical approach to probability was developed and applied in the 17th and 18th centuries to games of chance, such as cards and dice. It is unnecessary to do an experiment to determine the probability of an event occurring using the classical approach because the total number of outcomes is known before the experiment. The flip of a coin has two possible outcomes; the roll of a die has six possible outcomes. We can logically arrive at the probability of getting a tail on the toss of one coin or three heads on the toss of three coins.

The classical approach to probability can also be applied to lotteries. In South Carolina, one of the games of the Education Lottery is "Pick 3." A person buys a lottery ticket and selects three numbers between 0 and 9. Once per week, the three numbers are randomly selected from a machine that tumbles three containers each with balls numbered 0 through 9. One way to win is to match the numbers and the order of the numbers. Given that 1,000 possible outcomes exist (000 through 999), the probability of winning with any three-digit number is 0.001, or 1 in 1,000.

Empirical Probability

Empirical or **relative frequency** is the second type of objective probability. It is based on the number of times an event occurs as a proportion of a known number of trials.

> **EMPIRICAL PROBABILITY** The probability of an event happening is the fraction of the time similar events happened in the past.

In terms of a formula:

$$\text{Empirical probability} = \frac{\text{Number of times the event occurs}}{\text{Total number of observations}}$$

The empirical approach to probability is based on what is called the law of large numbers. The key to establishing probabilities empirically is that more observations will provide a more accurate estimate of the probability.

> **LAW OF LARGE NUMBERS** Over a large number of trials, the empirical probability of an event will approach its true probability.

To explain the law of large numbers, suppose we toss a fair coin. The result of each toss is either a head or a tail. With just one toss of the coin the empirical probability for heads is either zero or one. If we toss the coin a great number of times, the probability of the outcome of heads will approach .5. The following table reports the results of seven different experiments flipping a fair coin 1, 10, 50, 100, 500, 1,000, and 10,000 times and then computing the relative frequency of heads. Note as we increase the number of trials the empirical probability of a head appearing approaches .5, which is its value based on the classical approach to probability.

Number of Trials	Number of Heads	Relative Frequency of Heads
1	0	.00
10	3	.30
50	26	.52
100	52	.52
500	236	.472
1,000	494	.494
10,000	5,027	.5027

What have we demonstrated? Based on the classical definition of probability, the likelihood of obtaining a head in a single toss of a fair coin is .5. Based on the empirical or relative frequency approach to probability, the probability of the event happening approaches the same value based on the classical definition of probability.

This reasoning allows us to use the empirical or relative frequency approach to finding a probability. Here are some examples.

- Last semester, 80 students registered for Business Statistics 101 at Scandia University. Twelve students earned an A. Based on this information and the empirical approach to assigning a probability, we estimate the likelihood a student will earn an A is .15.
- During the 2010–2011 NBA season, Stephen Curry of the Golden State Warriors made 212 out of 227 free throw attempts. Using the empirical approach to probability, the likelihood that he makes his next free throw attempt is .934.

Life insurance companies rely on past data to determine the acceptability of an applicant as well as the premium to be charged. Mortality tables list the likelihood a person of a particular age will die within the upcoming year. For example, the likelihood a 20-year-old female will die within the next year is .00105.

The empirical concept is illustrated with the following example.

Example

On February 1, 2003, the Space Shuttle Columbia exploded. This was the second disaster in 113 space missions for NASA. On the basis of this information, what is the probability that a future mission is successfully completed?

Solution

To simplify, letters or numbers may be used. P stands for probability, and in this case $P(A)$ stands for the probability a future mission is successfully completed.

$$\text{Probability of a successful flight} = \frac{\text{Number of successful flights}}{\text{Total number of flights}}$$

$$P(A) = \frac{111}{113} = .98$$

We can use this as an estimate of probability. In other words, based on past experience, the probability is .98 that a future space shuttle mission will be safely completed.

Subjective Probability

If there is little or no experience or information on which to base a probability, it may be estimated subjectively. Essentially, this means an individual evaluates the available opinions and information and then estimates or assigns the probability. This probability is aptly called a **subjective probability.**

> **SUBJECTIVE CONCEPT OF PROBABILITY** The likelihood (probability) of a particular event happening that is assigned by an individual based on whatever information is available.

Illustrations of subjective probability are:

1. Estimating the likelihood the New England Patriots will play in the Super Bowl next year.
2. Estimating the likelihood you will be involved in an automobile accident in the next year.
3. Estimating the likelihood the U.S. budget deficit will be reduced by half in the next 10 years.

The types of probability are summarized in Chart 5–1. A probability statement always assigns a likelihood to an event that has not yet occurred. There is, of course, a considerable latitude in the degree of uncertainty that surrounds this probability, based primarily on the knowledge possessed by the individual concerning the underlying process. The individual possesses a great deal of knowledge about the toss of a die and can state that the probability that a one-spot will appear face up on the toss of a true die is one-sixth. But we know very little concerning the acceptance in the marketplace of a new and untested product. For example, even though a market research director tests a newly developed product in 40 retail stores and states that there is a 70% chance that the product will have sales of more than 1 million units, she has limited knowledge of how consumers will react when it is marketed nationally. In both cases (the case of the person rolling a die and the testing of a new product), the individual is assigning a probability value to an event of interest, and a difference exists only in the predictor's confidence in the precision of the estimate. However, regardless of the viewpoint, the same laws of probability (presented in the following sections) will be applied.

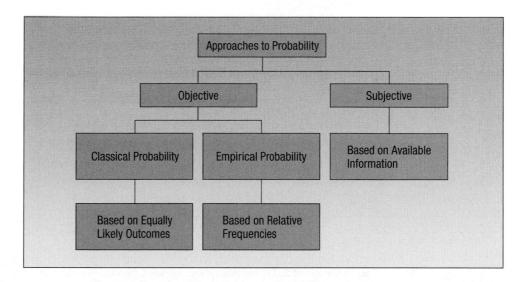

CHART 5–1 Summary of Approaches to Probability

Self-Review 5–2

1. One card will be randomly selected from a standard 52-card deck. What is the probability the card will be a queen? Which approach to probability did you use to answer this question?
2. The Center for Child Care reports on 539 children and the marital status of their parents. There are 333 married, 182 divorced, and 24 widowed parents. What is the probability a particular child chosen at random will have a parent who is divorced? Which approach did you use?
3. What is the probability that you will save one million dollars by the time you retire? Which approach to probability did you use to answer this question?

Exercises

connect

1. Some people are in favor of reducing federal taxes to increase consumer spending and others are against it. Two persons are selected and their opinions are recorded. Assuming no one is undecided, list the possible outcomes.

2. A quality control inspector selects a part to be tested. The part is then declared acceptable, repairable, or scrapped. Then another part is tested. List the possible outcomes of this experiment regarding two parts.

3. A survey of 34 students at the Wall College of Business showed the following majors:

Accounting	10
Finance	5
Economics	3
Management	6
Marketing	10

Suppose you select a student and observe his or her major.
   a. What is the probability he or she is a management major?
   b. Which concept of probability did you use to make this estimate?

4. A large company that must hire a new president prepares a final list of five candidates, all of whom are equally qualified. Two of these candidates are members of a minority group. To avoid bias in the selection of the candidate, the company decides to select the president by lottery.
   a. What is the probability one of the minority candidates is hired?
   b. Which concept of probability did you use to make this estimate?

5. In each of the following cases, indicate whether classical, empirical, or subjective probability is used.
   a. A baseball player gets a hit in 30 out of 100 times at bat. The probability is .3 that he gets a hit in his next at bat.
   b. A seven-member committee of students is formed to study environmental issues. What is the likelihood that any one of the seven is chosen as the spokesperson?
   c. You purchase one of 5 million tickets sold for Lotto Canada. What is the likelihood you will win the $1 million jackpot?
   d. The probability of an earthquake in northern California in the next 10 years above 5.0 on the Richter Scale is .80.

6. A firm will promote two employees out of a group of six men and three women.
   a. List the chances of this experiment if there is particular concern about gender equity.
   b. Which concept of probability would you use to estimate these probabilities?

7. A sample of 40 oil industry executives was selected to test a questionnaire. One question about environmental issues required a yes or no answer.
   a. What is the experiment?
   b. List one possible event.
   c. Ten of the 40 executives responded yes. Based on these sample responses, what is the probability that an oil industry executive will respond yes?
   d. What concept of probability does this illustrate?
   e. Are each of the possible outcomes equally likely and mutually exclusive?

8. A sample of 2,000 licensed drivers revealed the following number of speeding violations.

Number of Violations	Number of Drivers
0	1,910
1	46
2	18
3	12
4	9
5 or more	5
Total	2,000

   a. What is the experiment?
   b. List one possible event.

    c. What is the probability that a particular driver had exactly two speeding violations?

    d. What concept of probability does this illustrate?

9. Bank of America customers select their own three-digit personal identification number (PIN) for use at ATMs.

    a. Think of this as an experiment and list four possible outcomes.

    b. What is the probability Mr. Jones and Mrs. Smith select the same PIN?

    c. Which concept of probability did you use to answer (b)?

10. An investor buys 100 shares of AT&T stock and records its price change daily.

    a. List several possible events for this experiment.

    b. Estimate the probability for each event you described in (a).

    c. Which concept of probability did you use in (b)?

5.4 Some Rules for Computing Probabilities

Now that we have defined probability and described the different approaches to probability, we turn our attention to computing the probability of two or more events by applying rules of addition and multiplication.

Rules of Addition

There are two rules of addition, the special rule of addition and the general rule of addition. We begin with the special rule of addition.

LO 5-3 Calculate probabilities using the rules of addition.

Special Rule of Addition   To apply the **special rule of addition,** the events must be *mutually exclusive*. Recall that mutually exclusive means that when one event occurs, none of the other events can occur at the same time. An illustration of mutually exclusive events in the die-tossing experiment is the events "a number 4 or larger" and "a number 2 or smaller." If the outcome is in the first group {4, 5, and 6}, then it cannot also be in the second group {1 and 2}. Another illustration is a product coming off the assembly line cannot be defective and satisfactory at the same time.

    If two events *A* and *B* are mutually exclusive, the special rule of addition states that the probability of one *or* the other event's occurring equals the sum of their probabilities. This rule is expressed in the following formula:

SPECIAL RULE OF ADDITION	$P(A \text{ or } B) = P(A) + P(B)$	[5–2]

For three mutually exclusive events designated *A*, *B*, and *C*, the rule is written:

$$P(A \text{ or } B \text{ or } C) = P(A) + P(B) + P(C)$$

An example will help to show the details.

Example

A machine fills plastic bags with a mixture of beans, broccoli, and other vegetables. Most of the bags contain the correct weight, but because of the variation in the size of the beans and other vegetables, a package might be underweight or overweight. A check of 4,000 packages filled in the past month revealed:

Weight	Event	Number of Packages	Probability of Occurrence	
Underweight	A	100	.025	← $\dfrac{100}{4,000}$
Satisfactory	B	3,600	.900	
Overweight	C	300	.075	
		4,000	1.000	

Solution

What is the probability that a particular package will be either underweight or overweight?

The outcome "underweight" is the event A. The outcome "overweight" is the event C. Applying the special rule of addition:

$$P(A \text{ or } C) = P(A) + P(C) = .025 + .075 = .10$$

Note that the events are mutually exclusive, meaning that a package of mixed vegetables cannot be underweight, satisfactory, and overweight at the same time. They are also collectively exhaustive; that is, a selected package must be either underweight, satisfactory, or overweight.

English logician J. Venn (1834–1923) developed a diagram to portray graphically the outcome of an experiment. The *mutually exclusive* concept and various other rules for combining probabilities can be illustrated using this device. To construct a Venn diagram, a space is first enclosed representing the total of all possible outcomes. This space is usually in the form of a rectangle. An event is then represented by a circular area which is drawn inside the rectangle proportional to the probability of the event. The following Venn diagram shows the mutually exclusive concept. Events A, B, and C do not overlap, so the events are mutually exclusive. The diagram also shows that the three events are equally likely because the areas of the circles are the same.

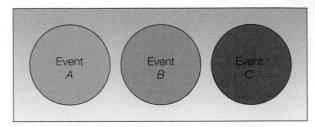

Complement Rule   The probability that a bag of mixed vegetables selected is underweight, $P(A)$, plus the probability that it is not an underweight bag, written $P(\sim A)$ and read "not A," must logically equal 1. This is written:

$$P(A) + P(\sim A) = 1$$

This can be revised to read:

COMPLEMENT RULE	$P(A) = 1 - P(\sim A)$	[5–3]

This is the **complement rule.** It is used to determine the probability of an event occurring by subtracting the probability of the event not occurring from 1. This rule is useful because sometimes it is easier to calculate the probability of an event happening by determining the probability of it not happening and subtracting the result from 1. Notice that the events A and $\sim A$ are mutually exclusive and collectively exhaustive. Therefore, the probabilities of A and $\sim A$ sum to 1. A Venn diagram illustrating the complement rule is shown as:

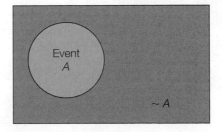

Example

Recall the probability a bag of mixed vegetables is underweight is .025 and the probability of an overweight bag is .075. Use the complement rule to show the probability of a satisfactory bag is .900. Show the solution using a Venn diagram.

Solution

The probability the bag is unsatisfactory equals the probability the bag is overweight plus the probability it is underweight. That is, $P(A \text{ or } C) = P(A) + P(C) = .025 + .075 = .100$. The bag is satisfactory if it is not underweight or overweight, so $P(B) = 1 - [P(A) + P(C)] = 1 - [.025 + .075] = 0.900$. The Venn diagram portraying this situation is:

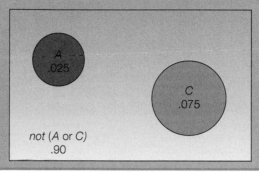

A
.025

C
.075

not (A or C)
.90

Self-Review 5–3

A sample of employees of Worldwide Enterprises is to be surveyed about a new health care plan. The employees are classified as follows:

Classification	Event	Number of Employees
Supervisors	*A*	120
Maintenance	*B*	50
Production	*C*	1,460
Management	*D*	302
Secretarial	*E*	68

(a) What is the probability that the first person selected is:
   (i)   either in maintenance or a secretary?
   (ii)   not in management?
(b) Draw a Venn diagram illustrating your answers to part (a).
(c) Are the events in part (a)(i) complementary or mutually exclusive or both?

The General Rule of Addition The outcomes of an experiment may not be mutually exclusive. For example, the Florida Tourist Commission selected a sample of 200 tourists who visited the state during the year. The survey revealed that 120 tourists went to Disney World and 100 went to Busch Gardens near Tampa. What is the probability that a person selected visited either Disney World or Busch Gardens? If the special rule of addition is used, the probability of selecting a tourist who went to Disney World is .60, found by 120/200. Similarly, the probability of a tourist going to Busch Gardens is .50. The sum of these probabilities is 1.10. We know, however, that this probability cannot be greater than 1. The explanation is that many tourists visited both attractions and are being counted twice! A check of the survey responses revealed that 60 out of 200 sampled did, in fact, visit both attractions.

To answer our question, "What is the probability a selected person visited either Disney World or Busch Gardens?" (1) add the probability that a tourist visited Disney

Statistics in Action

If you wish to get some attention at the next gathering you attend, announce that you believe that at least two people present were born on the same date—that is, the same day of the year but not necessarily the same year. If there are 30 people in the room, the probability of a duplicate is .706. If there are 60 people in the room, the probability is .994 that at least two people share the same birthday. With as few as 23 people the chances are even, that is .50, that at least two people share the same birthday. Hint: To compute this, find the probability everyone was born on a different day and use the complement rule. Try this in your class.

World and the probability he or she visited Busch Gardens, and (2) subtract the probability of visiting both. Thus:

$$P(\text{Disney or Busch}) = P(\text{Disney}) + P(\text{Busch}) - P(\text{both Disney and Busch})$$

$$= .60 + .50 - .30 = .80$$

When two events both occur, the probability is called a **joint probability.** The probability that a tourist visits both attractions (.30) is an example of a joint probability.

The following Venn diagram shows two events that are not mutually exclusive. The two events overlap to illustrate the joint event that some people have visited both attractions.

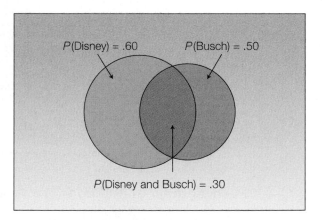

LO 5-4 Define the term *joint probability*.

> **JOINT PROBABILITY** A probability that measures the likelihood two or more events will happen concurrently.

The general rule of addition to compute the probability of two events, *A* and *B*, that are not mutually exclusive is:

> **GENERAL RULE OF ADDITION** $P(A \text{ or } B) = P(A) + P(B) - P(A \text{ and } B)$ [5–4]

For the expression *P*(*A* or *B*), the word *or* suggests that *A* may occur or *B* may occur. This also includes the possibility that *A* and *B* may occur. The use of *or* is called an **inclusive.** You could also write *P*(*A* or *B* or both) to emphasize that the union of the events includes the intersection of *A* and *B*.

If we compare the general and special rules of addition, the important difference is determining if the events are mutually exclusive. If the events *are* mutually exclusive, then the joint probability *P*(*A* and *B*) is 0 and we could use the special rule of addition. Otherwise, we must account for the joint probability and use the general rule of addition.

Example	What is the probability that a card chosen at random from a standard deck of cards will be either a king or a heart?
Solution	We may be inclined to add the probability of a king and the probability of a heart. But this creates a problem. If we do that, the king of hearts is counted with the kings and also with the hearts. So, if we simply add the probability of a king (there are 4 in a deck of 52 cards) to the probability of a heart (there are 13 in a deck of 52 cards) and report that 17 out of 52 cards meet the requirement, we have counted the king of hearts twice. We need to subtract 1 card from the 17 so the king of hearts is counted only once. Thus, there are 16 cards that are either hearts or kings. So the probability is 16/52 = .3077.

Card	Probability		Explanation
King	*P*(*A*)	= 4/52	4 kings in a deck of 52 cards
Heart	*P*(*B*)	= 13/52	13 hearts in a deck of 52 cards
King of Hearts	*P*(*A* and *B*) =	1/52	1 king of hearts in a deck of 52 cards

From formula (5–4):

$$P(A \text{ or } B) = P(A) + P(B) - P(A \text{ and } B)$$

$$= 4/52 + 13/52 - 1/52$$

$$= 16/52, \text{ or } .3077$$

A Venn diagram portrays these outcomes, which are not mutually exclusive.

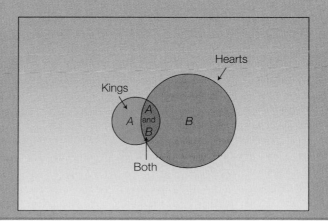

Self-Review 5–4   Routine physical examinations are conducted annually as part of a health service program for General Concrete Inc. employees. It was discovered that 8% of the employees need corrective shoes, 15% need major dental work, and 3% need both corrective shoes and major dental work.
(a)   What is the probability that an employee selected at random will need either corrective shoes or major dental work?
(b)   Show this situation in the form of a Venn diagram.

Exercises

connect

11. The events A and B are mutually exclusive. Suppose $P(A) = .30$ and $P(B) = .20$. What is the probability of either A or B occurring? What is the probability that neither A nor B will happen?

12. The events X and Y are mutually exclusive. Suppose $P(X) = .05$ and $P(Y) = .02$. What is the probability of either X or Y occurring? What is the probability that neither X nor Y will happen?

13. A study of 200 advertising firms revealed their income after taxes:

Income after Taxes	Number of Firms
Under $1 million	102
$1 million to $20 million	61
$20 million or more	37

  a. What is the probability an advertising firm selected at random has under $1 million in income after taxes?

  b. What is the probability an advertising firm selected at random has either an income between $1 million and $20 million, or an income of $20 million or more? What rule of probability was applied?

14. The chair of the board of directors says, "There is a 50% chance this company will earn a profit, a 30% chance it will break even, and a 20% chance it will lose money next quarter."

  a. Use an addition rule to find the probability the company will not lose money next quarter.

  b. Use the complement rule to find the probability it will not lose money next quarter.

15. Suppose the probability you will get an A in this class is .25 and the probability you will get a B is .50. What is the probability your grade will be above a C?

16. Two coins are tossed. If A is the event "two heads" and B is the event "two tails," are A and B mutually exclusive? Are they complements?

17. The probabilities of the events A and B are .20 and .30, respectively. The probability that both A and B occur is .15. What is the probability of either A or B occurring?

18. Let $P(X) = .55$ and $P(Y) = .35$. Assume the probability that they both occur is .20. What is the probability of either X or Y occurring?

19. Suppose the two events A and B are mutually exclusive. What is the probability of their joint occurrence?

20. A student is taking two courses, history and math. The probability the student will pass the history course is .60, and the probability of passing the math course is .70. The probability of passing both is .50. What is the probability of passing at least one?

21. A survey of grocery stores in the Southeast revealed 40% had a pharmacy, 50% had a floral shop, and 70% had a deli. Suppose 10% of the stores have all three departments, 30% have both a pharmacy and a deli, 25% have both a floral shop and deli, and 20% have both a pharmacy and floral shop.

  a. What is the probability of selecting a store at random and finding it has both a pharmacy and a floral shop?

  b. What is the probability of selecting a store at random and finding it has both a pharmacy and a deli?

  c. Are the events "select a store with a deli" and "select a store with a pharmacy" mutually exclusive?

  d. What is the name given to the event of "selecting a store with a pharmacy, a floral shop, and a deli?"

  e. What is the probability of selecting a store that does *not* have all three departments?

22. A study by the National Park Service revealed that 50% of vacationers going to the Rocky Mountain region visit Yellowstone Park, 40% visit the Tetons, and 35% visit both.

  a. What is the probability a vacationer will visit at least one of these attractions?

  b. What is the probability .35 called?

  c. Are the events mutually exclusive? Explain.

Rules of Multiplication

In this section, we discuss rules for computing the likelihood that two events both happen or joint probability. For example,16% of tax returns in 2011 were prepared by H&R Block, and 75% of those returns showed a refund. What is the likelihood a person's taxes were prepared by H&R Block and received a refund? Venn diagrams illustrate this as the intersection of two events. To find the likelihood of two events happening, we use the rules of multiplication. There are two rules of multiplication, the special rule and the general rule.

Special Rule of Multiplication The special rule of multiplication requires that two events *A* and *B* are independent. Two events are independent if the occurrence of one event does not alter the probability of the occurrence of the other event.

> **INDEPENDENCE** The occurrence of one event has no effect on the probability of the occurrence of another event.

One way to think about independence is to assume that events *A* and *B* occur at different times. For example, when event *B* occurs after event *A* occurs, does *A* have any effect on the likelihood that event *B* occurs? If the answer is no, then *A* and *B* are independent events. To illustrate independence, suppose two coins are tossed. The outcome of a coin toss (head or tail) is unaffected by the outcome of any other prior coin toss (head or tail).

For two independent events *A* and *B*, the probability that *A* and *B* will both occur is found by multiplying the two probabilities. This is the **special rule of multiplication** and is written symbolically as:

LO 5-5 Calculate probabilities using the rules of multiplication.

> **SPECIAL RULE OF MULTIPLICATION** $P(A \text{ and } B) = P(A)P(B)$ **[5–5]**

For three independent events, *A*, *B*, and *C*, the special rule of multiplication used to determine the probability that all three events will occur is:

$$P(A \text{ and } B \text{ and } C) = P(A)P(B)P(C)$$

Example A survey by the American Automobile Association (AAA) revealed 60% of its members made airline reservations last year. Two members are selected at random. What is the probability both made airline reservations last year?

Solution The probability the first member made an airline reservation last year is .60, written $P(R_1) = .60$, where R_1 refers to the fact that the first member made a reservation.

The probability that the second member selected made a reservation is also .60, so $P(R_2) = .60$. Because the number of AAA members is very large, you may assume that R_1 and R_2 are independent. Consequently, using formula (5–5), the probability they both make a reservation is .36, found by:

$$P(R_1 \text{ and } R_2) = P(R_1)P(R_2) = (.60)(.60) = .36$$

All possible outcomes can be shown as follows. R means a reservation is made, and $\sim R$ means no reservation was made.

  With the probabilities and the complement rule, we can compute the joint probability of each outcome. For example, the probability that neither member makes a reservation is .16. Further, the probability of the first or the second member (special addition rule) making a reservation is .48 (.24 + .24). You can also observe that the outcomes are mutually exclusive and collectively exhaustive. Therefore, the probabilities sum to 1.00.

Outcomes		Joint Probability	
R_1	R_2	(.60)(.60) =	.36
R_1	$\sim R_2$	(.60)(.40) =	.24
$\sim R_1$	R_2	(.40)(.60) =	.24
$\sim R_1$	$\sim R_2$	(.40)(.40) =	.16
Total			1.00

Self-Review 5–5

From experience, Teton Tire knows the probability is .95 that a particular XB-70 tire will last 60,000 miles before it becomes bald or fails. An adjustment is made on any tire that does not last 60,000 miles. You purchase four XB-70s. What is the probability all four tires will last at least 60,000 miles?

General Rule of Multiplication   If two events are not independent, they are referred to as **dependent.** To illustrate dependency, suppose there are 10 cans of soda in a cooler, 7 are regular and 3 are diet. A can is selected from the cooler. The probability of selecting a can of diet soda is 3/10, and the probability of selecting a can of regular soda is 7/10. Then, a second can is selected from the cooler, without returning the first. The probability the second is diet depends on whether the first one selected was diet or not. The probability that the second is diet is:

  2/9, if the first can is diet. (Only two cans of diet soda remain in the cooler.)
  3/9, if the first can selected is regular. (All three diet sodas are still in the cooler.)

The fraction 2/9 (or 3/9) is aptly called a **conditional probability** because its value is conditional on (dependent on) whether a diet or regular soda was the first selection from the cooler.

LO 5-6 Define the term *conditional probability.*

CONDITIONAL PROBABILITY The probability of a particular event occurring, given that another event has occurred.

In the general rule of multiplication, the conditional probability is required to compute the joint probability of two events that are not independent. The conditional probability for two events, A and B, that are not independent is written $P(A|B)$. The "|" is a mathematical symbol for the expression "given that." So $P(A|B)$ is the probability of event A happening given that B has already happened. We refer to $P(A|B)$ as a conditional probability because the probability of the event A is conditional on the outcome of event B. Symbolically, the general rule of multiplication for two events that are not independent is:

GENERAL RULE OF MULTIPLICATION	$P(A \text{ and } B) = P(A)P(B|A)$	[5–6]

Example

A golfer has 12 golf shirts in his closet. Suppose nine of these shirts are white and the others blue. He gets dressed in the dark, so he just grabs a shirt and puts it on. He plays golf two days in a row and does not launder and return the used shirts to the closet. What is the likelihood both shirts selected are white?

Solution

The event that the first shirt selected is white is W_1. The probability is $P(W_1) = 9/12$ because 9 of the 12 shirts are white. The event that the second shirt selected is also white is identified as W_2. The conditional probability that the second shirt selected is white, given that the first shirt selected is also white, is $P(W_2|W_1) = 8/11$. Why is this so? Because after the first shirt is selected there are only 11 shirts remaining in the closet and 8 of these are white. To determine the probability of two white shirts being selected, we use formula (5–6).

$$P(W_1 \text{ and } W_2) = P(W_1)P(W_2|W_1) = \left(\frac{9}{12}\right)\left(\frac{8}{11}\right) = .55$$

So the likelihood of selecting two shirts and finding them both to be white is .55.

We can extend the general rule of multiplication to more than two events. For three events A, B, and C, the formula is:

$$P(A \text{ and } B \text{ and } C) = P(A)P(B|A)P(C|A \text{ and } B)$$

In the case of the golf shirt example, the probability of selecting three white shirts without replacement is:

$$P(W_1 \text{ and } W_2 \text{ and } W_3) = P(W_1)P(W_2|W_1)P(W_3|W_1 \text{ and } W_2) = \left(\frac{9}{12}\right)\left(\frac{8}{11}\right)\left(\frac{7}{10}\right) = .38$$

So the likelihood of selecting three shirts without replacement and all being white is .38.

Self-Review 5–6

The board of directors of Tarbell Industries consists of eight men and four women. A four-member search committee is to be chosen at random to conduct a nationwide search for a new company president.
(a) What is the probability all four members of the search committee will be women?
(b) What is the probability all four members will be men?
(c) Does the sum of the probabilities for the events described in parts (a) and (b) equal 1? Explain.

Statistics in Action

In 2000, George W. Bush won the U.S. presidency by the slimmest of margins. Many election stories resulted, some involving voting irregularities, others raising interesting election questions. In a local Michigan election, there was a tie between two candidates for an elected position. To break the tie, the candidates drew a slip of paper from a box that contained two slips of paper, one marked "Winner" and the other unmarked. To determine which candidate drew first, election officials flipped a coin. The winner of the coin flip also drew the winning slip of paper. But was the coin flip really necessary? No, because the two events are independent. Winning the coin flip did not alter the probability of either candidate drawing the winning slip of paper.

5.5 Contingency Tables

Often we tally the results of a survey in a two-way table and use the results of this tally to determine various probabilities. We described this idea beginning on page 115 in Chapter 4. To review, we refer to a two-way table as a contingency table.

> **CONTINGENCY TABLE** A table used to classify sample observations according to two or more identifiable categories or classes.

A contingency table is a cross-tabulation that simultaneously summarizes two variables of interest and their relationship. Here are several examples.

- A survey of 150 adults classified each as to gender and the number of movies attended last month. Each respondent is classified according to two criteria—the number of movies attended and gender.

Movies Attended	Gender		Total
	Men	Women	
0	20	40	60
1	40	30	70
2 or more	10	10	20
Total	70	80	150

- The American Coffee Producers Association reports the following information on age and the amount of coffee consumed in a month.

Age (Years)	Coffee Consumption			Total
	Low	Moderate	High	
Under 30	36	32	24	92
30 up to 40	18	30	27	75
40 up to 50	10	24	20	54
50 and over	26	24	29	79
Total	90	110	100	300

According to this table, each of the 300 respondents is classified according to two criteria: (1) age and (2) the amount of coffee consumed.

LO 5-7 Compute probabilities using a contingency table.

The following example shows how the rules of addition and multiplication are used when we employ contingency tables.

Example

A sample of executives were surveyed about loyalty to their company. One of the questions was, "If you were given an offer by another company equal to or slightly better than your present position, would you remain with the company or take the other position?" The responses of the 200 executives in the survey were cross-classified with their length of service with the company. (See Table 5–1.)

TABLE 5–1 Loyalty of Executives and Length of Service with Company

	Length of Service				
Loyalty	Less than 1 Year, B_1	1–5 Years, B_2	6–10 Years, B_3	More than 10 Years, B_4	Total
Would remain, A_1	10	30	5	75	120
Would not remain, A_2	25	15	10	30	80
	35	45	15	105	200

What is the probability of randomly selecting an executive who is loyal to the company (would remain) and who has more than 10 years of service?

Solution

Note that two events occur at the same time—the executive would remain with the company, and he or she has more than 10 years of service.

1. Event A_1 happens if a randomly selected executive will remain with the company despite an equal or slightly better offer from another company. To find the probability that event A_1 will happen, refer to Table 5–1. Note there are 120 executives out of the 200 in the survey who would remain with the company, so $P(A_1) = 120/200$, or .60.
2. Event B_4 happens if a randomly selected executive has more than 10 years of service with the company. Thus, $P(B_4|A_1)$ is the conditional probability that an executive with more than 10 years of service would remain with the company despite an equal or slightly better offer from another company. Referring to the contingency table, Table 5–1, 75 of the 120 executives who would remain have more than 10 years of service, so $P(B_4|A_1) = 75/120$.

Solving for the probability that an executive randomly selected will be one who would remain with the company and who has more than 10 years of service with the company, using the general rule of multiplication in formula (5–6), gives:

$$P(A_1 \text{ and } B_4) = P(A_1)P(B_4|A_1) = \left(\frac{120}{200}\right)\left(\frac{75}{120}\right) = \frac{9,000}{24,000} = .375$$

To find the probability of selecting an executive who would remain with the company *or* has less than 1 year of experience, we use the general rule of addition, formula (5–4).

1. Event A_1 refers to executives that would remain with the company. So $P(A_1) = 120/200 = .60$.
2. Event B_1 refers to executives that have been with the company less than 1 year. The probability of B_1 is $P(B_1) = 35/200 = .175$.
3. The events A_1 and B_1 are not mutually exclusive. That is, an executive can both be willing to remain with the company and have less than 1 year of experience.

We write this probability, which is called the joint probability, as $P(A_1$ and $B_1)$. There are 10 executives who would both stay with the company and have less than one year of service, so $P(A_1$ and $B_1) = 10/200 = .05$. These 10 people are in both groups, those who would remain with the company and those with less than one year with the company. They are actually being counted twice, so we need to subtract out this value.

4. We insert these values in formula (5–4) and the result is as follows.

$$P(A_1 \text{ or } B_1) = P(A_1) + P(B_1) - P(A_1 \text{ and } B_1)$$
$$= .60 + .175 - .05 = .725$$

So the likelihood that a selected executive would either remain with the company or has been with the company less than one year is .725.

Self-Review 5–7

Refer to Table 5–1 on page 145 to find the following probabilities.
(a) What is the probability of selecting an executive with more than 10 years of service?
(b) What is the probability of selecting an executive who would not remain with the company, given that he or she has more than 10 years of service?
(c) What is the probability of selecting an executive with more than 10 years of service or one who would not remain with the company?

5.6 Tree Diagrams

The **tree diagram** is a graph that is helpful in organizing calculations that involve several stages. Each segment in the tree is one stage of the problem. The branches of a tree diagram are weighted by probabilities. We will use the data in Table 5–1 to show the construction of a tree diagram.

1. To construct a tree diagram, we begin by drawing a heavy dot on the left to represent the root of the tree (see Chart 5–2).
2. For this problem, two main branches go out from the root, the upper one representing "would remain" and the lower one "would not remain." Their probabilities are written on the branches, namely, 120/200 and 80/200. These probabilities could also be denoted $P(A_1)$ and $P(A_2)$.
3. Four branches "grow" out of each of the two main branches. These branches represent the length of service—less than 1 year, 1–5 years, 6–10 years, and more than 10 years. The conditional probabilities for the upper branch of the tree, 10/120, 30/120, 5/120, and so on are written on the appropriate branches. These are $P(B_1|A_1)$, $P(B_2|A_1)$, $P(B_3|A_1)$, and $P(B_4|A_1)$, where B_1 refers to less than 1 year of service, B_2 1 to 5 years, B_3 6 to 10 years, and B_4 more than 10 years. Next, write the conditional probabilities for the lower branch.
4. Finally, joint probabilities, that the events A_1 and B_i or the events A_2 and B_i will occur together, are shown on the right side. For example, the joint probability of randomly selecting an executive who would remain with the company and who has less than one year of service, from formula (5–6), is:

$$P(A_1 \text{ and } B_1) = P(A_1)P(B_1|A_1) = \left(\frac{120}{200}\right)\left(\frac{10}{120}\right) = .05$$

In Chart 5–2, the joint probabilities for all possible combinations of loyalty ("would remain" and "would not remain") and service (less than 1 year, 1–5 years, 6–10 years, and over 10 years) are computed. Because all possible outcomes are listed, the sum of the joint probabilities must equal 1.00.

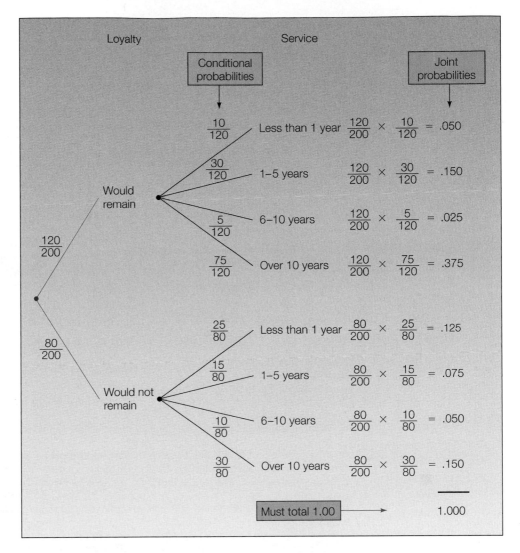

CHART 5–2 Tree Diagram Showing Loyalty and Length of Service

Self-Review 5–8

Consumers were surveyed on the number of visits to a Sears store (often, occasional, and never) and if the store was located in an enclosed mall (yes and no). The results are summarized in a contingency table.

	Enclosed Mall		
Visits	**Yes**	**No**	**Total**
Often	60	20	80
Occasional	25	35	60
Never	5	50	55
	90	105	195

(a) Are the number of visits and enclosed mall variables independent? Why? Interpret your conclusion.

(b) Draw a tree diagram and determine the joint probabilities.

Exercises

connect™

23. Suppose $P(A) = .40$ and $P(B|A) = .30$. What is the joint probability of A and B?
24. Suppose $P(X_1) = .75$ and $P(Y_2|X_1) = .40$. What is the joint probability of X_1 and Y_2?
25. A local bank reports that 80% of its customers maintain a checking account, 60% have a savings account, and 50% have both. If a customer is chosen at random, what is the probability the customer has either a checking or a savings account? What is the probability the customer does not have either a checking or a savings account?
26. All Seasons Plumbing has two service trucks that frequently need repair. If the probability the first truck is available is .75, the probability the second truck is available is .50, and the probability that both trucks are available is .30, what is the probability neither truck is available?
27. Refer to the following table. (df)

| | First Event | | | |
Second Event	A_1	A_2	A_3	Total
B_1	2	1	3	6
B_2	1	2	1	4
Total	3	3	4	10

   a. Determine $P(A_1)$.
   b. Determine $P(B_1|A_2)$.
   c. Determine $P(B_2$ and $A_3)$.
28. Three defective electric toothbrushes were accidentally shipped to a drugstore by Cleanbrush Products along with 17 nondefective ones.
   a. What is the probability the first two electric toothbrushes sold will be returned to the drugstore because they are defective?
   b. What is the probability the first two electric toothbrushes sold will not be defective?
29. Each salesperson at Puchett, Sheets, and Hogan Insurance Agency is rated either below average, average, or above average with respect to sales ability. Each salesperson is also rated with respect to his or her potential for advancement—either fair, good, or excellent. These traits for the 500 salespeople were cross-classified into the following table. (df)

| Sales Ability | Potential for Advancement | | |
	Fair	Good	Excellent
Below average	16	12	22
Average	45	60	45
Above average	93	72	135

   a. What is this table called?
   b. What is the probability a salesperson selected at random will have above average sales ability and excellent potential for advancement?
   c. Construct a tree diagram showing all the probabilities, conditional probabilities, and joint probabilities.
30. An investor owns three common stocks. Each stock, independent of the others, has equally likely chances of (1) increasing in value, (2) decreasing in value, or (3) remaining the same value. List the possible outcomes of this experiment. Estimate the probability at least two of the stocks increase in value.
31. David Akers is the field goal kicker for the Philadelphia Eagles of the National Football League. During the 2010 season, he attempted 38 field goals and made 32 of the attempts. A summary of his field goal outcomes by distance is shown on the next page.

Distance (yards)	Made	Missed	Total
20 up to 30	12	0	12
30 up to 40	10	2	12
40 up to 50	9	2	11
50 or more	1	2	3
Total	32	6	38

    a. What is the name given to this table?
    b. Overall, what is the probability of a successful field goal attempt?
    c. Is the distance of the attempt independent of success?
    d. If we were to study the attempts of the 2010 season, what is the likelihood of selecting an attempt that was between 30 and 40 yards or an attempt that was successful?
    e. What is the likelihood of selecting an attempt for study that was successful and over 50 yards?
32. If you ask three strangers about their birthdays, what is the probability: (a) All were born on Wednesday? (b) All were born on different days of the week? (c) None were born on Saturday?

LO 5-8 Determine the number of outcomes using the appropriate principle of counting.

5.7 Principles of Counting

If the number of possible outcomes in an experiment is small, it is relatively easy to count them. There are six possible outcomes, for example, resulting from the roll of a die, namely:

If, however, there are a large number of possible outcomes, such as the number of heads and tails for an experiment with 10 tosses, it would be tedious to count all the possibilities. They could have all heads, one head and nine tails, two heads and eight tails, and so on. To facilitate counting, we discuss three formulas: the **multiplication formula** (not to be confused with the multiplication *rule* described earlier in the chapter), the **permutation formula,** and the **combination formula.**

The Multiplication Formula

We begin with the multiplication formula.

> **MULTIPLICATION FORMULA** If there are m ways of doing one thing and n ways of doing another thing, there are $m \times n$ ways of doing both.

In terms of a formula:

> **MULTIPLICATION FORMULA**   Total number of outcomes $= (m)(n)$ **[5–7]**

This can be extended to more than two events. For three events m, n, and o:

$$\text{Total number of outcomes} = (m)(n)(o)$$

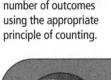

Example

An automobile dealer wants to advertise that for $29,999 you can buy a convertible, a two-door or a four-door model with your choice of either wire wheel covers or solid wheel covers. Based on the number of possible models and wheel covers, how many different cars can the dealer offer?

Solution

Of course the dealer could determine the total number of different cars by picturing and counting them. There are six.

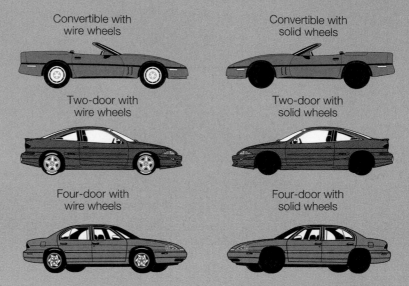

Convertible with wire wheels   Convertible with solid wheels

Two-door with wire wheels   Two-door with solid wheels

Four-door with wire wheels   Four-door with solid wheels

We can employ the multiplication formula as a check (where m is the number of models and n the wheel cover type). From formula (5–7):

$$\text{Total possible outcomes} = (m)(n) = (3)(2) = 6$$

(continued from p. 149)

2. The odds of a high school senior playing college basketball as a senior in college are about 1 in 60.

3. If you play basketball as a senior in college, the odds of making a professional team are about 1 in 37.5.

It was not difficult to count all the possible model and wheel cover combinations in this example. Suppose, however, that the dealer decided to offer eight models and six types of wheel covers. It would be tedious to picture and count all the possible alternatives. Instead, the multiplication formula can be used. In this case, there are $(m)(n) = (8)(6) = 48$ possible outcomes.

Note in the preceding applications of the multiplication formula that there were *two or more groupings from which you made selections*. The automobile dealer, for example, offered a choice of models and a choice of wheel covers. If a home builder offered you four different exterior styles of a home to choose from and three interior floor plans, the multiplication formula would be used to find how many different outcomes were possible. There are 12 possibilities.

Self-Review 5–9

1. The Women's Shopping Network on cable TV offers sweaters and slacks for women. The sweaters and slacks are offered in coordinating colors. If sweaters are available in five colors and the slacks are available in four colors, how many different outfits can be advertised?

2. Pioneer manufactures three models of stereo receivers, two MP3 docking stations, four speakers, and three CD carousels. When the four types of components are sold together, they form a "system." How many different systems can the electronics firm offer?

The Permutation Formula

As noted, the multiplication formula is applied to find the number of possible outcomes for two or more groups. The **permutation formula** is applied to find the possible number of outcomes when there is only *one* group of objects. Illustrations of this type of problem are:

- Three electronic parts are to be assembled into a plug-in unit for a television set. The parts can be assembled in any order. How many different ways can the three parts be assembled?
- A machine operator must make four safety checks before starting his machine. It does not matter in which order the checks are made. In how many different ways can the operator make the checks?

One order for the first illustration might be: the transistor first, the LEDs second, and the synthesizer third. This arrangement is called a **permutation.**

> **PERMUTATION** Any arrangement of *r* objects selected from a single group of *n* possible objects.

Note that the arrangements *a b c* and *b a c* are different permutations. The formula to count the total number of different permutations is:

> **PERMUTATION FORMULA** $$_nP_r = \frac{n!}{(n-r)!}$$ **[5–8]**

where:
> *n* is the total number of objects.
> *r* is the number of objects selected.

Before we solve the two problems illustrated, note that permutations and combinations (to be discussed shortly) use a notation called *n factorial*. It is written *n*! and means the product of $n(n-1)(n-2)(n-3)\cdots(1)$. For instance, $5! = 5 \cdot 4 \cdot 3 \cdot 2 \cdot 1 = 120$.

Many of your calculators have a button with *x*! that will perform this calculation for you. It will save you a great deal of time. For example, the Texas Instruments TI-36X calculator has the following key:

$x!$

10^x
LOG

It is the "third function," so check your users' manual or the Internet for instructions.

The factorial notation can also be canceled when the same number appears in both the numerator and the denominator, as shown below.

$$\frac{6!}{4!} = \frac{6 \cdot 5 \cdot 4 \cdot 3 \cdot 2 \cdot 1}{4 \cdot 3 \cdot 2 \cdot 1} = 30$$

By definition, zero factorial, written 0!, is 1. That is, 0! = 1.

Example

Referring to the group of three electronic parts that are to be assembled in any order, in how many different ways can they be assembled?

Solution

There are three electronic parts to be assembled, so $n = 3$. Because all three are to be inserted in the plug-in unit, $r = 3$. Solving using formula (5–8) gives:

$$_nP_r = \frac{n!}{(n-r)!} = \frac{3!}{(3-3)!} = \frac{3!}{0!} = \frac{3!}{1} = 6$$

We can check the number of permutations arrived at by using the permutation formula. We determine how many "spaces" have to be filled and the possibilities for each "space." In the problem involving three electronic parts, there are three locations in the plug-in unit for the three parts. There are three possibilities for the first place, two for the second (one has been used up), and one for the third, as follows:

$$(3)(2)(1) = 6 \text{ permutations}$$

The six ways in which the three electronic parts, lettered A, B, C, can be arranged are:

ABC	BAC	CAB	ACB	BCA	CBA

In the previous example, we selected and arranged all the objects, that is $n = r$. In many cases, only some objects are selected and arranged from the n possible objects. We explain the details of this application in the following example.

Example

Betts Machine Shop Inc. has eight screw machines but only three spaces available in the production area for the machines. In how many different ways can the eight machines be arranged in the three spaces available?

Solution

There are eight possibilities for the first available space in the production area, seven for the second space (one has been used up), and six for the third space. Thus:

$$(8)(7)(6) = 336$$

that is, there are a total of 336 different possible outcomes. This could also be found by using formula (5–8). If $n = 8$ machines, and $r = 3$ spaces available, the formula leads to

$$_nP_r = \frac{n!}{(n-r)!} = \frac{8!}{(8-3)!} = \frac{8!}{5!} = \frac{(8)(7)(6)\cancel{5!}}{\cancel{5!}} = 336$$

The Combination Formula

If the order of the selected objects is *not* important, any selection is called a **combination.** The formula to count the number of r object combinations from a set of n objects is:

COMBINATION FORMULA	$_nC_r = \dfrac{n!}{r!(n-r)!}$	[5–9]

For example, if executives Able, Baker, and Chauncy are to be chosen as a committee to negotiate a merger, there is only one possible combination of these three; the committee of Able, Baker, and Chauncy is the same as the committee of Baker, Chauncy, and Able. Using the combination formula:

$$_nC_r = \frac{n!}{r!(n-r)!} = \frac{3 \cdot 2 \cdot 1}{3 \cdot 2 \cdot 1(1)} = 1$$

Example

The Grand 16 movie theater uses teams of three employees to work the concession stand each evening. There are seven employees available to work each evening. How many different teams can be scheduled to staff the concession stand?

Solution

According to formula (5–9), there are 35 combinations, found by

$$_7C_3 = \frac{n!}{r!(n-r)!} = \frac{7!}{3!(7-3)!} = \frac{7!}{3!4!} = 35$$

The seven employees taken three at a time would create 35 different teams.

When the number of permutations or combinations is large, the calculations are tedious. Computer software and handheld calculators have "functions" to compute these numbers. The Excel output for the location of the eight screw machines in the production area of Betts Machine Shop Inc. is shown below. There are a total of 336 arrangements.

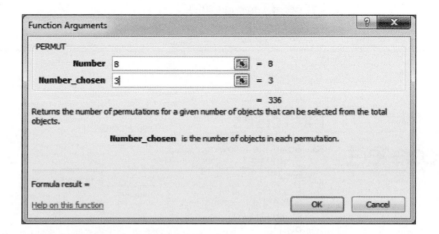

The output for the number of teams at the Grand 16 movie theater is shown next. Three employees are chosen from the seven possible. The number of combinations possible is 35.

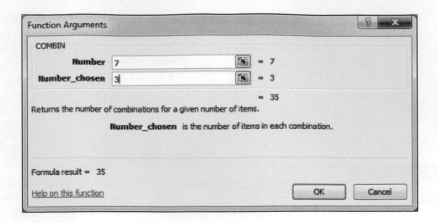

Self-Review 5–10

1. A musician wants to write a score based on only five chords: B-flat, C, D, E, and G. However, only three chords out of the five will be used in succession, such as C, B-flat, and E. Repetitions, such as B-flat, B-flat, and E, will not be permitted.
   (a) How many permutations of the five chords, taken three at a time, are possible?
   (b) Using formula (5–8), how many permutations are possible?
2. The 10 numbers 0 through 9 are to be used in code groups of four to identify an item of clothing. Code 1083 might identify a blue blouse, size medium; the code group 2031 might identify a pair of pants, size 18; and so on. Repetitions of numbers are not permitted. That is, the same number cannot be used twice (or more) in a total sequence. For example, 2256, 2562, or 5559 would not be permitted. How many different code groups can be designed?
3. In the preceding example involving the Grand 16 movie theater, we said that there are 35 possible teams of three taken from seven employees.
   (a) Use formula (5–9) to show this is true.
   (b) The manager of the theater wants to plan for staffing the concession stand with teams of five on the weekends to serve more people. From the 7 employees, how many teams of five employees are possible?
4. In a lottery game, three numbers are randomly selected from a tumbler of balls numbered 1 through 50.
   (a) How many permutations are possible?
   (b) How many combinations are possible?

Exercises

connect

33. Solve the following:
    a. 40!/35!
    b. $_7P_4$
    c. $_5C_2$
34. Solve the following:
    a. 20!/17!
    b. $_9P_3$
    c. $_7C_2$
35. A pollster randomly selected 4 of 10 available people. How many different groups of four are possible?
36. A telephone number consists of seven digits, the first three representing the exchange. How many different telephone numbers are possible within the 537 exchange?
37. An overnight express company must include five cities on its route. How many different routes are possible, assuming that it does not matter in which order the cities are included in the routing?

38. A representative of the Environmental Protection Agency (EPA) wants to select samples from 10 landfills. The director has 15 landfills from which she can collect samples. How many different samples are possible?

39. A national pollster has developed 15 questions designed to rate the performance of the president of the United States. The pollster will select 10 of these questions. How many different arrangements are there for the order of the 10 selected questions?

40. A company is creating three new divisions and seven managers are eligible to be appointed head of a division. How many different ways could the three new heads be appointed? Hint: Assume the division assignment makes a difference.

Chapter Summary

Statistics in Action

Government statistics show there are about 1.7 automobile-caused fatalities for every 100,000,000 vehicle-miles. If you drive 1 mile to the store to buy your lottery ticket and then return home, you have driven 2 miles. Thus the probability that you will join this statistical group on your next 2-mile round trip is $2 \times 1.7/100,000,000 = 0.000000034$. This can also be stated as "One in 29,411,765." Thus, if you drive to the store to buy your Powerball ticket, your chance of being killed (or killing someone else) is more than 4 times greater than the chance that you will win the Powerball Jackpot, one chance in 120,526,770. http://www.durangobill.com/Powerball Odds.html

I. A probability is a value between 0 and 1 inclusive that represents the likelihood a particular event will happen.
   A. An experiment is the observation of some activity or the act of taking some measurement.
   B. An outcome is a particular result of an experiment.
   C. An event is the collection of one or more outcomes of an experiment.

II. There are three definitions of probability.
   A. The classical definition applies when there are n equally likely outcomes to an experiment.
   B. The empirical definition occurs when the number of times an event happens is divided by the number of observations.
   C. A subjective probability is based on whatever information is available.

III. Two events are mutually exclusive if by virtue of one event happening the other cannot happen.

IV. Events are independent if the occurrence of one event does not affect the occurrence of another event.

V. The rules of addition refer to the union of events.
   A. The special rule of addition is used when events are mutually exclusive.

$$P(A \text{ or } B) = P(A) + P(B) \qquad \text{[5–2]}$$

   B. The general rule of addition is used when the events are not mutually exclusive.

$$P(A \text{ or } B) = P(A) + P(B) - P(A \text{ and } B) \qquad \text{[5–4]}$$

   C. The complement rule is used to determine the probability of an event happening by subtracting the probability of the event not happening from 1.

$$P(A) = 1 - P(\sim A) \qquad \text{[5–3]}$$

VI. The rules of multiplication refer to the product of events.
   A. The special rule of multiplication refers to events that are independent.

$$P(A \text{ and } B) = P(A)P(B) \qquad \text{[5–5]}$$

   B. The general rule of multiplication refers to events that are not independent.

$$P(A \text{ and } B) = P(A)P(B|A) \qquad \text{[5–6]}$$

   C. A joint probability is the likelihood that two or more events will happen at the same time.
   D. A conditional probability is the likelihood that an event will happen, given that another event has already happened.

VII. There are three counting rules that are useful in determining the number of outcomes in an experiment.
   A. The multiplication rule states that if there are m ways one event can happen and n ways another event can happen, then there are mn ways the two events can happen.

$$\text{Number of outcomes} = (m)(n) \qquad \text{[5–7]}$$

B. A permutation is an arrangement in which the order of the objects selected from a specific pool of objects is important.

$$_nP_r = \frac{n!}{(n-r)!}$$ **[5–8]**

C. A combination is an arrangement where the order of the objects selected from a specific pool of objects is not important.

$$_nC_r = \frac{n!}{r!(n-r)!}$$ **[5–9]**

Pronunciation Key

SYMBOL	MEANING	PRONUNCIATION
$P(A)$	Probability of A	P of A
$P(\sim A)$	Probability of not A	P of not A
$P(A$ and $B)$	Probability of A and B	P of A and B
$P(A$ or $B)$	Probability of A or B	P of A or B
$P(A\|B)$	Probability of A given B has happened	P of A given B
$_nP_r$	Permutation of n items selected r at a time	Pnr
$_nC_r$	Combination of n items selected r at a time	Cnr

Chapter Exercises

connect

41. The marketing research department at Pepsico plans to survey teenagers about a newly developed soft drink. Each will be asked to compare it with his or her favorite soft drink.
  a. What is the experiment?
  b. What is one possible event?
42. The number of times a particular event occurred in the past is divided by the number of occurrences. What is this approach to probability called?
43. The probability that the cause and the cure for all cancers will be discovered before the year 2020 is .20. What viewpoint of probability does this statement illustrate?
44. Berdine's Chicken Factory has several stores in the Hilton Head, South Carolina, area. When interviewing applicants for server positions, the owner would like to include information on the amount of tip a server can expect to earn per check (or bill). A study of 500 recent checks indicated the server earned the following amounts in tips per 8-hour shift.

Amount of Tip	Number
$0 up to $ 20	200
20 up to 50	100
50 up to 100	75
100 up to 200	75
200 or more	50
Total	500

  a. What is the probability of a tip of $200 or more?
  b. Are the categories "$0 up to $20," "$20 up to $50," and so on considered mutually exclusive?
  c. If the probabilities associated with each outcome were totaled, what would that total be?
  d. What is the probability of a tip of up to $50?
  e. What is the probability of a tip of less than $200?
45. Winning all three "Triple Crown" races is considered the greatest feat of a pedigree racehorse. After a successful Kentucky Derby, Big Brown is a 1-to-2 favorite to win the Preakness Stakes.

    a. If he is a 1-to-2 favorite to win the Belmont Stakes as well, what is his probability of winning the Triple Crown?

    b. What do his chances for the Preakness Stakes have to be in order for him to be "even money" to earn the Triple Crown?

46. The first card selected from a standard 52-card deck is a king.

    a. If it is returned to the deck, what is the probability that a king will be drawn on the second selection?

    b. If the king is not replaced, what is the probability that a king will be drawn on the second selection?

    c. What is the probability that a king will be selected on the first draw from the deck and another king on the second draw (assuming that the first king was not replaced)?

47. Armco, a manufacturer of traffic light systems, found that under accelerated-life tests, 95% of the newly developed systems lasted three years before failing to change signals properly.

    a. If a city purchased four of these systems, what is the probability all four systems would operate properly for at least three years?

    b. Which rule of probability does this illustrate?

    c. Using letters to represent the four systems, write an equation to show how you arrived at the answer to part (a).

48. Refer to the following picture.

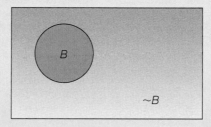

    a. What is the picture called?

    b. What rule of probability is illustrated?

    c. B represents the event of choosing a family that receives welfare payments. What does $P(B) + P(\sim B)$ equal?

49. In a management trainee program at Claremont Enterprises, 80% of the trainees are female and 20% male. Ninety percent of the females attended college, and 78% of the males attended college.

    a. A management trainee is selected at random. What is the probability that the person selected is a female who did not attend college?

    b. Are gender and attending college independent? Why?

    c. Construct a tree diagram showing all the probabilities, conditional probabilities, and joint probabilities.

    d. Do the joint probabilities total 1.00? Why?

50. Assume the likelihood that any flight on Delta Airlines arrives within 15 minutes of the scheduled time is .90. We select four flights from yesterday for study.

    a. What is the likelihood all four of the selected flights arrived within 15 minutes of the scheduled time?

    b. What is the likelihood that none of the selected flights arrived within 15 minutes of the scheduled time?

    c. What is the likelihood at least one of the selected flights did not arrive within 15 minutes of the scheduled time?

51. There are 100 employees at Kiddie Carts International. Fifty-seven of the employees are production workers, 40 are supervisors, 2 are secretaries, and the remaining employee is the president. Suppose an employee is selected:

    a. What is the probability the selected employee is a production worker?

    b. What is the probability the selected employee is either a production worker or a supervisor?

    c. Refer to part (b). Are these events mutually exclusive?

    d. What is the probability the selected employee is neither a production worker nor a supervisor?

52. Josh Hamilton of the Texas Rangers had the highest batting average in the 2010 Major League Baseball season. His average was .359. So assume the probability of getting a hit is .359 for each time he batted. In a particular game, assume he batted three times.
   a. This is an example of what type of probability?
   b. What is the probability of getting three hits in a particular game?
   c. What is the probability of not getting any hits in a game?
   d. What is the probability of getting at least one hit?

53. Four sports teams remain in a single-elimination playoff competition. If one team is favored in its semi-final match by odds of 2 to 1 and another squad is favored in its contest by odds of 3 to 1, what is the probability that:
   a. Both favored teams win their games?
   b. Neither favored team wins its game?
   c. At least one of the favored teams wins its game?

54. There are three clues labeled "daily double" on the game show *Jeopardy.* If three equally matched contenders play, what is the probability that:
   a. A single contestant finds all three "daily doubles"?
   b. The returning champion gets all three of the "daily doubles"?
   c. Each of the players selects precisely one of the "daily doubles"?

55. Brooks Insurance Inc. wishes to offer life insurance to men age 60 via the Internet. Mortality tables indicate the likelihood of a 60-year-old man surviving another year is .98. If the policy is offered to five men age 60:
   a. What is the probability all five men survive the year?
   b. What is the probability at least one does not survive?

56. Forty percent of the homes constructed in the Quail Creek area include a security system. Three homes are selected at random:
   a. What is the probability all three of the selected homes have a security system?
   b. What is the probability none of the three selected homes have a security system?
   c. What is the probability at least one of the selected homes has a security system?
   d. Did you assume the events to be dependent or independent?

57. Refer to Exercise 56, but assume there are 10 homes in the Quail Creek area and 4 of them have a security system. Three homes are selected at random:
   a. What is the probability all three of the selected homes have a security system?
   b. What is the probability none of the three selected homes have a security system?
   c. What is the probability at least one of the selected homes has a security system?
   d. Did you assume the events to be dependent or independent?

58. There are 20 families living in the Willbrook Farms Development. Of these families, 10 prepared their own federal income taxes for last year, 7 had their taxes prepared by a local professional, and the remaining 3 by H&R Block.
   a. What is the probability of selecting a family that prepared their own taxes?
   b. What is the probability of selecting two families, both of which prepared their own taxes?
   c. What is the probability of selecting three families, all of which prepared their own taxes?
   d. What is the probability of selecting two families, neither of which had their taxes prepared by H&R Block?

59. The board of directors of Saner Automatic Door Company consists of 12 members, 3 of whom are women. A new policy and procedures manual is to be written for the company. A committee of 3 is randomly selected from the board to do the writing.
   a. What is the probability that all members of the committee are men?
   b. What is the probability that at least 1 member of the committee is a woman?

60. A recent survey reported in *BusinessWeek* dealt with the salaries of CEOs at large corporations and whether company shareholders made money or lost money. df

	CEO Paid More Than $1 Million	CEO Paid Less Than $1 Million	Total
Shareholders made money	2	11	13
Shareholders lost money	4	3	7
Total	6	14	20

If a company is randomly selected from the list of 20 studied, what is the probability:
   a. The CEO made more than $1 million?
   b. The CEO made more than $1 million or the shareholders lost money?
   c. The CEO made more than $1 million given the shareholders lost money?
   d. Of selecting two CEOs and finding they both made more than $1 million?

61. Althoff and Roll, an investment firm in Augusta, Georgia, advertises extensively in the *Augusta Morning Gazette,* the newspaper serving the region. The *Gazette* marketing staff estimates that 60% of Althoff and Roll's potential market read the newspaper. It is further estimated that 85% of those who read the *Gazette* remember the Althoff and Roll advertisement.
  a. What percentage of the investment firm's potential market sees and remembers the advertisement?
  b. What percentage of the investment firm's potential market sees, but does not remember, the advertisement?

62. An Internet company located in Southern California has season tickets to the Los Angeles Lakers basketball games. The company president always invites one of the four vice presidents to attend games with him, and claims he selects the person to attend at random. One of the four vice presidents has not been invited to attend any of the last five Lakers home games. What is the likelihood this could be due to chance?

63. A computer-supply retailer purchased a batch of 1,000 CD-R disks and attempted to format them for a particular application. There were 857 perfect CDs, 112 CDs were usable but had bad sectors, and the remainder could not be used at all.
  a. What is the probability a randomly chosen CD is not perfect?
  b. If the disk is not perfect, what is the probability it cannot be used at all?

64. An investor purchased 100 shares of Fifth Third Bank stock and 100 shares of Santee Electric Cooperative stock. The probability the bank stock will appreciate over a year is .70. The probability the electric utility will increase over the same period is .60.
  a. What is the probability both stocks appreciate during the period?
  b. What is the probability the bank stock appreciates but the utility does not?
  c. What is the probability at least one of the stocks appreciates?

65. With each purchase of a large pizza at Tony's Pizza, the customer receives a coupon that can be scratched to see if a prize will be awarded. The odds of winning a free soft drink are 1 in 10, and the odds of winning a free large pizza are 1 in 50. You plan to eat lunch tomorrow at Tony's. What is the probablilty:
  a. That you will win either a large pizza or a soft drink?
  b. That you will not win a prize?
  c. That you will not win a prize on three consecutive visits to Tony's?
  d. That you will win at least one prize on one of your next three visits to Tony's?

66. For the daily lottery game in Illinois, participants select three numbers between 0 and 9. A number cannot be selected more than once, so a winning ticket could be, say, 307 but not 337. Purchasing one ticket allows you to select one set of numbers. The winning numbers are announced on TV each night.
  a. How many different outcomes (three-digit numbers) are possible?
  b. If you purchase a ticket for the game tonight, what is the likelihood you will win?
  c. Suppose you purchase three tickets for tonight's drawing and select a different number for each ticket. What is the probability that you will not win with any of the tickets?

67. Several years ago, Wendy's Hamburgers advertised that there are 256 different ways to order your hamburger. You may choose to have, or omit, any combination of the following on your hamburger: mustard, ketchup, onion, pickle, tomato, relish, mayonnaise, and lettuce. Is the advertisement correct? Show how you arrive at your answer.

68. It was found that 60% of the tourists to China visited the Forbidden City, the Temple of Heaven, the Great Wall, and other historical sites in or near Beijing. Forty percent visited Xi'an with its magnificent terracotta soldiers, horses, and chariots, which lay buried for over 2,000 years. Thirty percent of the tourists went to both Beijing and Xi'an. What is the probability that a tourist visited at least one of these places?

69. A new chewing gum has been developed that is helpful to those who want to stop smoking. If 60% of those people chewing the gum are successful in stopping smoking, what is the probability that in a group of four smokers using the gum at least one quits smoking?

70. Reynolds Construction Company has agreed not to erect all "look-alike" homes in a new subdivision. Five exterior designs are offered to potential home buyers. The builder has standardized three interior plans that can be incorporated in any of the five exteriors. How many different ways can the exterior and interior plans be offered to potential home buyers?

71. A new sports car model has defective brakes 15% of the time and a defective steering mechanism 5% of the time. Let's assume (and hope) that these problems occur independently. If one or the other of these problems is present, the car is called a "lemon." If both of these problems are present, the car is a "hazard." Your instructor purchased one of these cars yesterday. What is the probability it is:
  a. A lemon?
  b. A hazard?

72. The state of Maryland has license plates with three numbers followed by three letters. How many different license plates are possible?

73. There are four people being considered for the position of chief executive officer of Dalton Enterprises. Three of the applicants are over 60 years of age. Two are female, of which only one is over 60.
   a. What is the probability that a candidate is over 60 and female?
   b. Given that the candidate is male, what is the probability he is less than 60?
   c. Given that the person is over 60, what is the probability the person is female?

74. Tim Bleckie is the owner of Bleckie Investment and Real Estate Company. The company recently purchased four tracts of land in Holly Farms Estates and six tracts in Newburg Woods. The tracts are all equally desirable and sell for about the same amount.
   a. What is the probability that the next two tracts sold will be in Newburg Woods?
   b. What is the probability that of the next four sold at least one will be in Holly Farms?
   c. Are these events independent or dependent?

75. A computer password consists of four characters. The characters can be one of the 26 letters of the alphabet. Each character may be used more than once. How many different passwords are possible?

76. A case of 24 cans contains 1 can that is contaminated. Three cans are to be chosen randomly for testing.
   a. How many different combinations of 3 cans could be selected?
   b. What is the probability that the contaminated can is selected for testing?

77. You take a trip by air that involves three independent flights. If there is an 80% chance each specific leg of the trip is on time, what is the probability all three flights arrive on time?

78. The probability an HP network server is down is .05. If you have three independent servers, what is the probability that at least one of them is operational?

79. Twenty-two percent of all liquid crystal displays (LCDs) are manufactured by Samsung. What is the probability that in a collection of three independent LCD purchases, at least one is a Samsung?

Data Set Exercises

(The data for these exercises are available at the text website www.mhhe.com/lindbasic8e).

80. Refer to the Real Estate data, which reports information on homes sold in the Goodyear, Arizona, area during the last year.
   a. Sort the data into a table that shows the number of homes that have a pool versus the number that don't have a pool in each of the five townships. If a home is selected at random, compute the following probabilities.
      1. The home is in Township 1 or has a pool.
      2. Given that it is in Township 3, that it has a pool.
      3. The home has a pool and is in Township 3.
   b. Sort the data into a table that shows the number of homes that have a garage attached versus those that don't in each of the five townships. If a home is selected at random, compute the following probabilities:
      1. The home has a garage attached.
      2. The home does not have a garage attached, given that it is in Township 5.
      3. The home has a garage attached and is in Township 3.
      4. The home does not have a garage attached or is in Township 2.

81. Refer to the Baseball 2010 data, which reports information on the 30 Major League Baseball teams for the 2010 season. Set up three variables:
   • Divide the teams into two groups, those that had a winning season and those that did not. That is, create a variable to count the teams that won 81 games or more, and those that won 80 or less.
   • Create a new variable for attendance, using three categories: attendance less than 2.0 million, attendance of 2.0 million up to 3.0 million, and attendance of 3.0 million or more.
   • Create a variable that shows the teams that play in a stadium less than 15 years old versus one that is 15 years old or more.

a. Create a table that shows the number of teams with a winning season versus those with a losing season by the three categories of attendance. If a team is selected at random, compute the following probabilities:
  1. The team had a winning season.
  2. The team had a winning season or attendance of more than 3.0 million.
  3. The team had a winning season given attendance was more than 3.0 million.
  4. The team had a winning season and attracted fewer than 2.0 million fans.

b. Create a table that shows the number of teams with a winning season versus those that play in new or old stadiums. If a team is selected at random, compute the following probabilities:
  1. Selecting a team with a winning season.
  2. The likelihood of selecting a team with a winning record and playing in a new stadium.
  3. The team had a winning record or played in a new stadium.

82. Refer to the data on the school buses in the Buena School District. Set up a variable that divides the age of the buses into three groups: new (less than 5 year old), medium (5 but less than 10 years), and old (10 or more years). The median maintenance cost is $456. Based on this value, create a variable for those less than the median (low maintenance) and those more than the median (high maintenance). Finally, develop a table to show the relationship between maintenance cost and the age of the bus.

a. What percentage of the buses are new?
b. What percentage of the new buses have low maintenance?
c. What percentage of the old buses have high maintenance?
d. Does maintenance cost seem to be related to the age of the bus? Hint: Compare the maintenance cost of the old buses with the cost of the new buses? Would you conclude maintenance cost is independent of the age?

Practice Test

Part 1—Objective

1. A _____ is a value between zero and one, inclusive, describing the relative chance or likelihood an event will occur.
2. An _____ is a process that leads to the occurrence of one and only one of several possible outcomes.
3. An _____ is a collection of one or more outcomes of an experiment.
4. Using the _____ viewpoint, the probability of an event happening is the fraction of the time similar events happened in the past.
5. Using the _____ viewpoint, an individual evaluates the available opinions and information and then estimates or assigns the probability.
6. Using the _____ viewpoint, the probability of an event happening is computed by dividing the number of favorable outcomes by the number of possible outcomes.
7. If several events are described as _____, then the occurrence of one event means that none of the other events can occur at the same time.
8. If an experiment has a set of events that includes every possible outcome, then the set of events is described as _____ .
9. If two events A and B are _____, the special rule of addition states that the probability of one or the other events occurring equals the sum of their probabilities.
10. The _____ is used to determine the probability of an event occurring by subtracting the probability of the event not occurring from 1.
11. A probability that measures the likelihood two or more events will happen concurrently is called a _____ .
12. The special rule of multiplication requires that two events A and B are _____ .

Part 2—Problems

1. Fred Friendly, CPA, has a stack of 20 tax returns to complete before the April 15th deadline. Of the 20 tax returns, 12 are from individuals, 5 are from businesses, and 3 are from charitable organizations. He randomly selects two returns. What is the probability that:
   a. Both are businesses?
   b. At least one is a business?

2. Fred exercises regularly. His fitness log for the last 12 months shows that he jogged 30% of the days, rode his bike 20% of the days, and did both on 12% of the days. What is the probability that Fred would do at least one of these two types of exercises on any given day?

3. Fred works in a tax office with four other CPAs. There are five parking spots beside the office. If they all drive to work, how many different ways can the cars belonging to the CPAs be arranged in the five spots?

Software Commands

1. The Excel Commands to determine the number of permutations shown on page 153 are:

a. Click on the **Formulas** tab in the top menu, then, on the far left, select **Insert Function** *fx*.

b. In the **Insert Function** box, select **Statistical** as the category, then scroll down to **PERMUT** in the **Select a function list.** Click **OK.**

c. In the **PERM** box after **Number**, enter *8* and in the **Number_chosen** box enter *3*. The correct answer of *336* appears twice in the box.

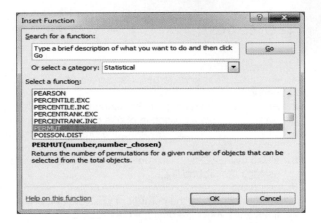

2. The Excel Commands to determine the number of combinations shown on page 154 are:

a. Click on the **Formulas** tab in the top menu, then, on the far left, select **Insert Function** *fx*.

b. In the **Insert Function** box, select **Math & Trig** as the category, then scroll down to **COMBIN** in the **Select a function list**. Click **OK.**

c. In the **COMBIN** box after **Number**, enter *7,* and in the **Number_chosen** box enter *3.* The correct answer of *35* appears twice in the box.

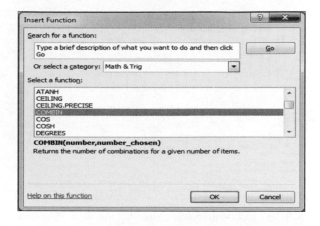

Chapter 5   Answers to Self-Review

5–1 **a.** Count the number who think the new game is playable.

b. Seventy-three players found the game playable. Many other answers are possible.

c. No. Probability cannot be greater than 1. The probability that the game, if put on the market, will be successful is 65/80, or .8125.

d. Cannot be less than 0. Perhaps a mistake in arithmetic.

e. More than half of the players testing the game liked it. (Of course, other answers are possible.)

5–2 **1.** $\dfrac{4 \text{ queens in deck}}{52 \text{ cards total}} = \dfrac{4}{52} = .0769$
Classical.

2. $\dfrac{182}{539} = .338$ Empirical.

3. Your assigned probability must be from 0.0 to 1.0, inclusive. Answers will vary with the person assigning the probability. This problem applies the subjective approach.

5–3 **a.** **i.** $\dfrac{(50 + 68)}{2,000} = .059$

ii. $1 - \dfrac{302}{2,000} = .849$

b.

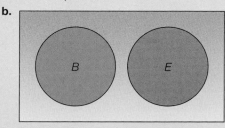

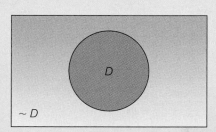

c. They are not complementary, but are mutually exclusive.

5–4 **a.** Need for corrective shoes is event *A*. Need for major dental work is event *B*.

$$P(A \text{ or } B) = P(A) + P(B) - P(A \text{ and } B)$$
$$= .08 + .15 - .03$$
$$= .20$$

b. One possibility is:

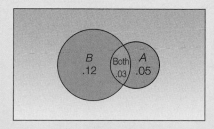

5–5 $(.95)(.95)(.95)(.95) = .8145$

5–6 **a.** .002, found by:

$$\left(\dfrac{4}{12}\right)\left(\dfrac{3}{11}\right)\left(\dfrac{2}{10}\right)\left(\dfrac{1}{9}\right) = \dfrac{24}{11,880} = .002$$

b. .14, found by:

$$\left(\frac{8}{12}\right)\left(\frac{7}{11}\right)\left(\frac{6}{10}\right)\left(\frac{5}{9}\right) = \frac{1,680}{11,880} = .1414$$

c. No, because there are other possibilities, such as three women and one man.

5–7 a. $P(B_4) = \dfrac{105}{200} = .525$

b. $P(A_2|B_4) = \dfrac{30}{105} = .286$

c. $P(A_2 \text{ or } B_4) = \dfrac{80}{200} + \dfrac{105}{200} - \dfrac{30}{200} = \dfrac{155}{200} = .775$

5–8 a. Independence requires that $P(A|B) = P(A)$. One possibility is:

$$P(\text{visit often}|\text{yes enclosed mall}) = P(\text{visit often})$$

Does 60/90 = 80/195? No, the two variables are *not* independent.

Therefore, any joint probability in the table must be computed by using the general rule of multiplication.

b.

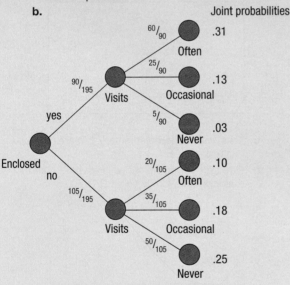

5–9 1. (5)(4) = 20

2. (3)(2)(4)(3) = 72

5–10 1. a. 60, found by (5)(4)(3).

b. 60, found by:

$$\frac{5!}{(5-3)!} = \frac{5\cdot4\cdot3\cdot2\cdot\cancel{1}}{2\cdot\cancel{1}}$$

2. 5,040, found by:

$$\frac{10!}{(10-4)!} = \frac{10\cdot9\cdot8\cdot7\cdot\cancel{6\cdot5\cdot4\cdot3\cdot2\cdot1}}{\cancel{6\cdot5\cdot4\cdot3\cdot2\cdot1}}$$

3. a. 35, found by:

$$\frac{7!}{3!(7-3)!} = \frac{7\cdot6\cdot5\cdot\cancel{4\cdot3\cdot2\cdot1}}{(3\cdot2\cdot1)\cdot(\cancel{4\cdot3\cdot2\cdot1})}$$

b. 21, found by:

$$\frac{7!}{5!(7-5)!} = \frac{7\cdot6\cdot\cancel{5\cdot4\cdot3\cdot2\cdot1}}{(\cancel{5\cdot4\cdot3\cdot2\cdot1})\cdot(2\cdot1)}$$

4. a. $_{50}P_3 = \dfrac{50!}{(50-3)!} = 117{,}600$

b. $_{50}C_3 = \dfrac{50!}{3!\,(50-3)!} = 19{,}600$

Discrete Probability Distributions

Learning Objectives

When you have completed this chapter, you will be able to:

LO 6-1 Identify the characteristics of a probability distribution.

LO 6-2 Distinguish between a discrete and a continuous random variable.

LO 6-3 Compute the mean of a probability distribution.

LO 6-4 Compute the variance and standard deviation of a probability distribution.

LO 6-5 Describe and compute probabilities for a binomial distribution.

LO 6-6 Describe and compute probabilities for a Poisson distribution.

Recent statistics suggest that 15% of those who visit a retail site on the Web make a purchase. A retailer wished to verify this claim. To do so, she selected a sample of 16 "hits" to her site and found that 4 had actually made a purchase. What is the likelihood of exactly four purchases? How many purchases should she expect? What is the likelihood that four or more "hits" result in a purchase? (See Exercise 43 and LO 6-5.)

6.1 Introduction

Chapters 2 through 4 are devoted to descriptive statistics. We describe raw data by organizing it into a frequency distribution and portraying the distribution in tables, graphs, and charts. Also, we compute a measure of location—such as the arithmetic mean, median, or mode—to locate a typical value near the center of the distribution. The range and the standard deviation are used to describe the spread in the data. These chapters focus on describing *something that has already happened.*

Starting with Chapter 5, the emphasis changes—we begin examining *something that could happen.* We note that this facet of statistics is called *statistical inference.* The objective is to make inferences (statements) about a population based on a number of observations, called a sample, selected from the population. In Chapter 5, we state that a probability is a value between 0 and 1 inclusive, and we examine how probabilities can be combined using rules of addition and multiplication.

This chapter will begin the study of **probability distributions.** A probability distribution gives the entire range of values that can occur based on an experiment. A probability distribution is similar to a relative frequency distribution. However, instead of describing the past, it describes a likely future event. For example, a drug manufacturer may claim a treatment will cause weight loss for 80% of the population. A consumer protection agency may test the treatment on a sample of six people. If the manufacturer's claim is true, it is *almost impossible* to have an outcome where no one in the sample loses weight and it is *most likely* that five out of the six do lose weight.

In this chapter, we discuss the mean, variance, and standard deviation of a probability distribution. We also describe two frequently occurring probability distributions: the binomial and the Poisson.

6.2 What Is a Probability Distribution?

A probability distribution shows the possible outcomes of an experiment and the probability of each of these outcomes.

LO 6-1 Identify the characteristics of a probability distribution.

> **PROBABILITY DISTRIBUTION** A listing of all the outcomes of an experiment and the probability associated with each outcome.

Below are the major characteristics of a probability distribution.

> **CHARACTERISTICS OF A PROBABILITY DISTRIBUTION**
> 1. The probability of a particular outcome is between 0 and 1 inclusive.
> 2. The outcomes are mutually exclusive events.
> 3. The list is exhaustive. So the sum of the probabilities of the various events is equal to 1.

How can we generate a probability distribution? The following example will explain.

Example

Suppose we are interested in the number of heads showing face up on three tosses of a coin. This is the experiment. The possible results are: zero heads, one head, two heads, and three heads. What is the probability distribution for the number of heads?

Solution

There are eight possible outcomes. A tail might appear face up on the first toss, another tail on the second toss, and another tail on the third toss of the coin. Or we might get a tail, tail, and head, in that order. We use the multiplication formula for counting outcomes (5–7). There are (2)(2)(2) or 8 possible results. These results are shown on the next page.

Possible Result	Coin Toss			Number of Heads
	First	Second	Third	
1	T	T	T	0
2	T	T	H	1
3	T	H	T	1
4	T	H	H	2
5	H	T	T	1
6	H	T	H	2
7	H	H	T	2
8	H	H	H	3

Note that the outcome "zero heads" occurred only once, "one head" occurred three times, "two heads" occurred three times, and the outcome "three heads" occurred only once. That is, "zero heads" happened one out of eight times. Thus, the probability of zero heads is one-eighth, the probability of one head is three-eighths, and so on. The probability distribution is shown in Table 6–1. Because one of these outcomes must happen, the total of the probabilities of all possible events is 1.000. This is always true. The same information is shown in Chart 6–1.

TABLE 6–1 Probability Distribution for the Events of Zero, One, Two, and Three Heads Showing Face Up on Three Tosses of a Coin

Number of Heads, x	Probability of Outcome, $P(x)$
0	$\frac{1}{8} = .125$
1	$\frac{3}{8} = .375$
2	$\frac{3}{8} = .375$
3	$\frac{1}{8} = .125$
Total	$\frac{8}{8} = 1.000$

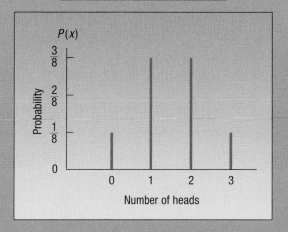

CHART 6–1 Graphical Presentation of the Number of Heads Resulting from Three Tosses of a Coin and the Corresponding Probability

Refer to the coin-tossing example in Table 6–1. We write the probability of *x* as *P(x)*. So the probability of zero heads is *P*(0 heads) = .125, and the probability of one head is *P*(1 head) = .375, and so forth. The sum of these mutually exclusive probabilities is 1; that is, from Table 6–1, 0.125 + 0.375 + 0.375 + 0.125 = 1.00.

Self-Review 6–1   The possible outcomes of an experiment involving the roll of a six-sided die are a one-spot, a two-spot, a three-spot, a four-spot, a five-spot, and a six-spot.
(a) Develop a probability distribution for the number of possible spots.
(b) Portray the probability distribution graphically.
(c) What is the sum of the probabilities?

6.3 Random Variables

In any experiment of chance, the outcomes occur randomly. So it is often called a *random variable.* For example, rolling a single die is an experiment: any one of six possible outcomes can occur. Some experiments result in outcomes that are quantitative (such as dollars, weight, or number of children), and others result in qualitative outcomes (such as color or religious preference). In a probability distribution, each value of the random variable is associated with a probability to indicate the chance of a particular outcome. A few examples will further illustrate what is meant by a **random variable.**

- If we count the number of employees absent from the day shift on Monday, the number might be 0, 1, 2, 3, . . . The number absent is the random variable.
- If we weigh four steel beams, the weights might be 2,492 pounds, 2,497 pounds, 2,506 pounds, and so on. The weight is the random variable.
- If we toss two coins and count the number of heads, there could be zero, one, or two heads. Because the number of heads resulting from this experiment is due to chance, the number of heads appearing is the random variable.
- Other random variables might be the number of defective lightbulbs produced in an hour at the Cleveland Company Inc., the grade level (9, 10, 11, or 12) of the members of the St. James girls' basketball team, the number of runners in the 2011 Boston Marathon, and the number of drivers charged with driving under the influence of alcohol in Brazoria County, Texas, last month.

RANDOM VARIABLE A quantity resulting from an experiment that, by chance, can assume different values.

The following diagram illustrates the terms *experiment, outcome, event,* and *random variable.* First, for the experiment where a coin is tossed three times, there are eight possible outcomes. In this experiment, we are interested in the event that one head occurs in the three tosses. The random variable is the number of heads. In terms of probability, we want to know the probability of the event that the random variable equals 1. The result is *P*(1 head in 3 tosses) = 0.375.

Possible *outcomes* for three coin tosses

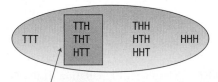

The *event* {one head} occurs and the *random variable x* = 1.

A random variable may be either *discrete* or *continuous.*

Discrete Random Variable

A discrete random variable can assume only a certain number of separated values. If there are 100 employees, then the count of the number absent on Monday can only be 0, 1, 2, 3, . . . , 100. A discrete random variable is usually the result of counting something.

LO 6-2 Distinguish between a discrete and a continuous random variable.

> **DISCRETE RANDOM VARIABLE** A random variable that can assume only certain clearly separated values.

A discrete random variable can, in some cases, assume fractional or decimal values. These values must be separated—that is, have distance between them. As an example, the scores awarded by judges for technical competence and artistic form in figure skating are decimal values, such as 7.2, 8.9, and 9.7. Such values are discrete because there is distance between scores of, say, 8.3 and 8.4. A score cannot be 8.34 or 8.347, for example.

Continuous Random Variable

On the other hand, a random variable can be continuous. If we measure something such as the width of a room, the height of a person, or the pressure in an automobile tire, the variable is a *continuous random variable.* It can assume one of an infinitely large number of values, within certain limitations. As examples:

- The times of commercial flights between Atlanta and Los Angeles are 4.67 hours, 5.13 hours, and so on. The random variable is the time in hours.
- Tire pressure, measured in pounds per square inch (psi), for a new Chevy Trailblazer might be 32.78 psi, 31.62 psi, 33.07 psi, and so on. In other words, any values between 28 and 35 could reasonably occur. The random variable is the tire pressure.

As with discrete random variables, the likelihood of a continuous random variable can be summarized with a **probability distribution.** So what is the difference between a probability distribution and a random variable? A random variable reports the particular outcome of an experiment. A probability distribution reports all the possible outcomes as well as the corresponding probability.

The tools used, as well as the probability interpretations, are different for discrete and continuous probability distributions. This chapter is limited to the discussion and interpretation of discrete distributions. In the next chapter, we discuss continuous distributions. How do you tell the difference between the two types of distributions? Usually a discrete distribution is the result of counting something, such as:

- The number of heads appearing when a coin is tossed 3 times.
- The number of students earning an A in this class.
- The number of production employees absent from the second shift today.
- The number of 30-second commercials on NBC from 8 to 11 P.M. tonight.

Continuous distributions are usually the result of some type of measurement, such as:

- The length of each song on the latest Linkin Park CD.
- The weight of each student in this class.

- The temperature outside as you are reading this book.
- The age of Facebook employees.

6.4 The Mean, Variance, and Standard Deviation of a Discrete Probability Distribution

In Chapter 3, we discussed measures of location and variation for a frequency distribution. The mean reports the central location of the data, and the variance describes the spread in the data. In a similar fashion, a probability distribution is summarized by its mean and variance. We identify the mean of a probability distribution by the lowercase Greek letter mu (μ) and the standard deviation by the lowercase Greek letter sigma (σ).

Mean

The mean is a typical value used to represent the central location of a probability distribution. It also is the long-run average value of the random variable. The mean of a probability distribution is also referred to as its **expected value.** It is a weighted average where the possible values of a random variable are weighted by their corresponding probabilities of occurrence.

The mean of a discrete probability distribution is computed by the formula:

LO 6-3 Compute the mean of a probability distribution.

MEAN OF A PROBABILITY DISTRIBUTION	$\mu = \Sigma[xP(x)]$	**[6–1]**

where $P(x)$ is the probability of a particular value x. In other words, multiply each x value by its probability of occurrence, and then add these products.

Variance and Standard Deviation

As noted, the mean is a typical value used to summarize a discrete probability distribution. However, it does not describe the amount of spread (variation) in a distribution. The variance does this. The formula for the variance of a probability distribution is:

LO 6-4 Compute the variance and standard deviation of a probability distribution.

VARIANCE OF A PROBABILITY DISTRIBUTION	$\sigma^2 = \Sigma[(x - \mu)^2 P(x)]$	**[6–2]**

The computational steps are

1. Subtract the mean from each value of the random variable, and square this difference.
2. Multiply each squared difference by its probability.
3. Sum the resulting products to arrive at the variance.

The standard deviation, σ, is found by taking the positive square root of σ^2; that is, $\sigma = \sqrt{\sigma^2}$.

An example will help explain the details of the calculation and interpretation of the mean and standard deviation of a probability distribution.

Example

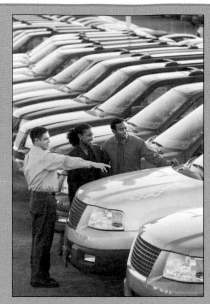

John Ragsdale sells new cars for Pelican Ford. John usually sells the largest number of cars on Saturday. He has developed the following probability distribution for the number of cars he expects to sell on a particular Saturday.

Number of Cars Sold, x	Probability, P(x)
0	.10
1	.20
2	.30
3	.30
4	.10
Total	1.00

1. What type of distribution is this?
2. On a typical Saturday, how many cars does John expect to sell?
3. What is the variance of the distribution?

Solution

1. This is a discrete probability distribution for the random variable called "number of cars sold." Note that John expects to sell only within a certain range of cars; he does not expect to sell 5 cars or 50 cars. Further, he cannot sell half a car. He can sell only 0, 1, 2, 3, or 4 cars. Also, the outcomes are mutually exclusive—he cannot sell a total of both 3 and 4 cars on the same Saturday. The sum of the possible outcomes total 1. Hence, these circumstance qualify as a probability distribution.

2. The mean number of cars sold is computed by weighting the number of cars sold by the probability of selling that number and adding or summing the products, using formula (6–1):

$$\mu = \Sigma[xP(x)]$$
$$= 0(.10) + 1(.20) + 2(.30) + 3(.30) + 4(.10)$$
$$= 2.1$$

These calculations are summarized in the following table.

Number of Cars Sold, x	Probability, P(x)	x · P(x)
0	.10	0.00
1	.20	0.20
2	.30	0.60
3	.30	0.90
4	.10	0.40
Total	1.00	$\mu = 2.10$

How do we interpret a mean of 2.1? This value indicates that, over a large number of Saturdays, John Ragsdale expects to sell a mean of 2.1 cars a day. Of course, it is not possible for him to sell *exactly* 2.1 cars on any particular Saturday. However, the expected value can be used to predict the arithmetic mean number of cars sold on Saturdays in the long run. For example, if John works 50 Saturdays during a year, he can expect to sell (50)(2.1) or 105 cars just on Saturdays. Thus, the mean is sometimes called the expected value.

3. The following table illustrates the steps to calculate the variance using formula (6-2). The first two columns show the probability distribution. The third column shows that the mean is subtracted from each value of the random variable x. The fourth column shows that each difference in column three is squared. In the last column, each value in column four is multiplied by the corresponding probability in column two. The variance is the sum of the values in the last column.

Number of Cars Sold, x	Probability, $P(x)$	$(x - \mu)$	$(x - \mu)^2$	$(x - \mu)^2 P(x)$
0	.10	0 − 2.1	4.41	0.441
1	.20	1 − 2.1	1.21	0.242
2	.30	2 − 2.1	0.01	0.003
3	.30	3 − 2.1	0.81	0.243
4	.10	4 − 2.1	3.61	0.361
				$\sigma^2 = 1.290$

Recall that the standard deviation, σ, is the positive square root of the variance. In this example, $\sqrt{\sigma^2} = \sqrt{1.290} = 1.136$ cars. How do we interpret a standard deviation of 1.136 cars? If salesperson Rita Kirsch also sold a mean of 2.1 cars on Saturdays, and the standard deviation in her sales was 1.91 cars, we would conclude that there is more variability in the Saturday sales of Ms. Kirsch than in those of Mr. Ragsdale (because 1.91 > 1.136).

Self-Review 6–2

The Pizza Palace sells three sizes of cola. The price of the small size is $0.80, the price of the medium is $0.90, and the price of the large size is $1.20. Thirty percent of the colas ordered are small, 50% are medium, and 20% are large. Summarize the random variable, price, with a probability distribution.

(a) Is this a discrete probability distribution? Indicate why or why not.

(b) Compute the mean amount charged for a cola.

(c) What is the variance in the amount charged for a cola? The standard deviation?

Exercises

connect

1. Compute the mean and variance of the following discrete probability distribution.

x	$P(x)$
0	.2
1	.4
2	.3
3	.1

2. Compute the mean and variance of the following discrete probability distribution.

x	$P(x)$
2	.5
8	.3
10	.2

3. Compute the mean and variance of the following probability distribution.

x	P(x)
5	.1
10	.3
15	.2
20	.4

4. Which of these variables are discrete and which are continuous random variables?
   a. The number of new accounts established by a salesperson in a year.
   b. The time between customer arrivals to a bank ATM.
   c. The number of customers in Big Nick's barber shop.
   d. The amount of fuel in your car's gas tank.
   e. The number of minorities on a jury.
   f. The outside temperature today.

5. The information below is the number of daily emergency service calls made by the volunteer ambulance service of Walterboro, South Carolina, for the last 50 days. To explain, there were 22 days on which there were 2 emergency calls, and 9 days on which there were 3 emergency calls.

Number of Calls	Frequency
0	8
1	10
2	22
3	9
4	1
Total	50

   a. Convert this information on the number of calls to a probability distribution.
   b. Is this an example of a discrete or continuous probability distribution?
   c. What is the mean number of emergency calls per day?
   d. What is the standard deviation of the number of calls made daily?

6. The director of admissions at Kinzua University in Nova Scotia estimated the distribution of student admissions for the fall semester on the basis of past experience. What is the expected number of admissions for the fall semester? Compute the variance and the standard deviation of the number of admissions.

Admissions	Probability
1,000	.6
1,200	.3
1,500	.1

7. Belk Department Store is having a special sale this weekend. Customers charging purchases of more than $50 to their Belk credit card will be given a special Belk Lottery card. The customer will scratch off the card, which will indicate the amount to be taken off the total amount of the purchase. Listed below are the amount of the prize and the percent of the time that amount will be deducted from the total amount of the purchase.

Prize Amount	Probability
$ 10	.50
25	.40
50	.08
100	.02

   a. What is the mean amount deducted from the total purchase amount?
   b. What is the standard deviation of the amount deducted from the total purchase?

8. The Downtown Parking Authority of Tampa, Florida, reported the following information for a sample of 250 customers on the number of hours cars are parked and the amount they are charged.

Number of Hours	Frequency	Amount Charged
1	20	$ 3.00
2	38	6.00
3	53	9.00
4	45	12.00
5	40	14.00
6	13	16.00
7	5	18.00
8	36	20.00
	250	

    a. Convert the information on the number of hours parked to a probability distribution. Is this a discrete or a continuous probability distribution?
    b. Find the mean and the standard deviation of the number of hours parked. How would you answer the question: How long is a typical customer parked?
    c. Find the mean and the standard deviation of the amount charged.

6.5 Binomial Probability Distribution

LO 6-5 Describe and compute probabilities for a binomial distribution.

The **binomial probability distribution** is a widely occurring discrete probability distribution. One characteristic of a binomial distribution is that there are only two possible outcomes on a particular trial of an experiment. For example, the statement in a true/false question is either true or false. The outcomes are mutually exclusive, meaning that the answer to a true/false question cannot be both true and false at the same time. As other examples, a product is classified as either acceptable or not acceptable by the quality control department, a person is classified as employed or unemployed, and a sales call results in the customer either purchasing the product or not purchasing the product. Frequently, we classify the two possible outcomes as "success" and "failure." However, this classification does *not* imply that one outcome is good and the other is bad.

Another characteristic of the binomial distribution is the number of successes is counted for a fixed and known number of trials. For example, we decide to flip a coin five times and count the number of times a head appears in the five flips, or we decide to randomly select 10 employees and count the number who are older than 50 years of age, or we decide to randomly select 20 boxes of Kellogg's Raisin Bran and count the number of boxes that weigh more than the amount indicated on the package. In each example, the number of trials is fixed and known before we count the number of successes.

A third characteristic of a binomial distribution is that the probability of a success is the same for each trial. In addition, we need to know this probability. Two examples are:

- For a test with 10 true/false questions, we know that the probability of correctly guessing the answer for each of the 10 trials is 1/2. For a test with 20 multiple choice questions with four options, the probability of randomly guessing the correct answer for each of the 20 trials is 1/4.
- If past experience revealed the swing bridge over the Intracoastal Waterway in Socastee was raised one out of every 20 times you approach it, then the

probability is one-twentieth that it will be raised (a "success") the next time you approach it, one-twentieth the following time, and so on.

The final characteristic of a binomial probability distribution is that each trial is *independent* of any other trial. Independent means that there is no pattern to the trials. The outcome of a particular trial does not affect the outcome of any other trial. Two examples are:

- A young family has two children, both boys. The probability of a third birth being a boy is still .50. That is, the gender of the third child is independent of the other two.
- Suppose 20% of the patients served in the emergency room at Waccamaw Hospital do not have insurance. If the second patient served on the afternoon shift today did not have insurance, that does not affect the probability the third, the tenth, or any of the other patients will or will not have insurance.

BINOMIAL PROBABILITY EXPERIMENT
1. An outcome on each trial of an experiment is classified into one of two mutually exclusive categories—a success or a failure.
2. The random variable counts the number of successes in a fixed number of trials.
3. The probability of success and failure stay the same for each trial.
4. The trials are independent, meaning that the outcome of one trial does not affect the outcome of any other trial.

How Is a Binomial Probability Computed?

To construct a particular binomial probability, we use (1) the number of trials and (2) the probability of success on each trial. For example, if the Hannah Landscaping Company plants 10 trees today and we know that 90% of the trees survive, we can compute a binomial probability that exactly 8 trees survive. In this case, the number of trials is the 10 trees, the probability of success is .90, and the number of successes is eight. In fact, we can compute a binomial probability for any number of successes from 0 to 10 surviving trees.

A binomial probability is computed by the formula:

BINOMIAL PROBABILITY FORMULA $P(x) = {}_nC_x\, \pi^x(1 - \pi)^{n-x}$ **[6–3]**

where:
   C denotes a combination.
   n is the number of trials.
   x is the random variable defined as the number of successes.
   π is the probability of a success on each trial.

We use the Greek letter π (pi) to denote a binomial population parameter. Do not confuse it with the mathematical constant 3.1416.

Example There are five flights daily from Pittsburgh via US Airways into the Bradford Regional Airport in Bradford, Pennsylvania. Suppose the probability that any flight arrives late is .20. What is the probability that none of the flights are late today? What is the probability that exactly one of the flights is late today?

Solution We can use formula (6–3). The probability that a particular flight is late is .20, so let $\pi = .20$. There are five flights, so $n = 5$, and x, the random variable, refers to the number of successes. In this case, a "success" is a flight that arrives late. Because there are no late arrivals, $x = 0$.

$$P(0) = {}_nC_x(\pi)^x(1 - \pi)^{n-x}$$
$$= {}_5C_0(.20)^0(1 - .20)^{5-0} = (1)(1)(.3277) = .3277$$

The probability that exactly one of the five flights will arrive late today is .4096, found by

$$P(1) = {}_nC_x(\pi)^x(1 - \pi)^{n-x}$$
$$= {}_5C_1(.20)^1(1 - .20)^{5-1} = (5)(.20)(.4096) = .4096$$

The entire binomial probability distribution with $\pi = .20$ and $n = 5$ is shown in the following bar chart. We observe that the probability of exactly 3 late flights is .0512 and from the bar chart that the distribution of the number of late arrivals is positively skewed.

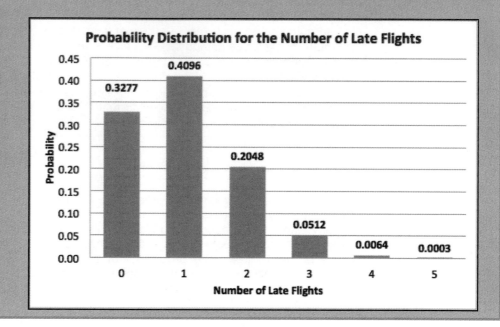

The mean (μ) and the variance (σ^2) of a binomial distribution are computed in a "shortcut" fashion by:

MEAN OF A BINOMIAL DISTRIBUTION	$\mu = n\pi$	[6–4]

VARIANCE OF A BINOMIAL DISTRIBUTION	$\sigma^2 = n\pi(1 - \pi)$	[6–5]

For the example regarding the number of late flights, recall that $\pi = .20$ and $n = 5$. Hence:

$$\mu = n\pi = (5)(.20) = 1.0$$
$$\sigma^2 = n\pi(1 - \pi) = 5(.20)(1 - .20) = .80$$

The mean of 1.0 and the variance of .80 can be verified from formulas (6–1) and (6–2). The probability distribution from the Excel output on the previous page and the details of the calculations are shown below.

Number of Late Flights, x	P(x)	xP(x)	x − μ	(x − μ)²	(x − μ)²P(x)
0	0.3277	0.0000	−1	1	0.3277
1	0.4096	0.4096	0	0	0
2	0.2048	0.4096	1	1	0.2048
3	0.0512	0.1536	2	4	0.2048
4	0.0064	0.0256	3	9	0.0576
5	0.0003	0.0015	4	16	0.0048
		μ = 1.0000			σ² = 0.7997

Binomial Probability Tables

Formula (6–3) can be used to build a binomial probability distribution for any value of n and π. However, for a larger n, the calculations take more time. For convenience, the tables in Appendix B.9 show the result of using the formula for various values of n and π. Table 6–2 shows part of Appendix B.9 for $n = 6$ and various values of π.

TABLE 6–2 Binomial Probabilities for $n = 6$ and Selected Values of π

						n = 6 Probability					
x\π	.05	.1	.2	.3	.4	.5	.6	.7	.8	.9	.95
0	.735	.531	.262	.118	.047	.016	.004	.001	.000	.000	.000
1	.232	.354	.393	.303	.187	.094	.037	.010	.002	.000	.000
2	.031	.098	.246	.324	.311	.234	.138	.060	.015	.001	.000
3	.002	.015	.082	.185	.276	.313	.276	.185	.082	.015	.002
4	.000	.001	.015	.060	.138	.234	.311	.324	.246	.098	.031
5	.000	.000	.002	.010	.037	.094	.187	.303	.393	.354	.232
6	.000	.000	.000	.001	.004	.016	.047	.118	.262	.531	.735

Example

In a region of a country, five percent of all cell phone calls are dropped. What is the probability that out of six randomly selected calls, none were dropped? Exactly one? Exactly two? Exactly three? Exactly four? Exactly five? Exactly six out of six?

Solution

The binomial conditions are met: (a) there are only two possible outcomes (a particular call is either dropped or not dropped), (b) there is a fixed number of trials (6), (c) there is a constant probability of success (.05), and (d) the trials are independent.

Refer to Table 6–2 above for the probability of exactly zero dropped calls. Go down the left margin to an x of 0. Now move horizontally to the column headed by a π of .05 to find the probability. It is .735. The values in Table 6–2 are rounded to three decimal places.

The probability of exactly one dropped call in a random sample of six calls is .232. The complete binomial probability distribution for $n = 6$ and $\pi = .05$ is:

Number of Dropped Calls x	Probability of Occurrence, $P(x)$	Number of Dropped Calls x	Probability of Occurrence, $P(x)$
0	.735	4	.000
1	.232	5	.000
2	.031	6	.000
3	.002		

Of course, there is a slight chance of getting exactly five dropped calls out of six random selections. It is .00000178, found by inserting the appropriate values in the binomial formula:

$$P(5) = {}_6C_5(.05)^5(.95)^1 = (6)(.05)^5(.95) = .00000178$$

For six out of the six, the exact probability is .000000016. Thus, the probability is very small that five or six dropped calls will occur in a sample of six.

We can compute the mean or expected value of the distribution of the number defective:

$$\mu = n\pi = (6)(.05) = 0.30$$
$$\sigma^2 = n\pi(1 - \pi) = 6(.05)(.95) = 0.285$$

Self-Review 6–3

Ninety-five percent of the employees at the J. M. Smucker Company plant on Laskey Road have their bimonthly wages sent directly to their bank by electronic funds transfer. This is called direct deposit. Suppose we select a random sample of seven employees.
(a) Does this situation fit the assumptions of the binomial distribution?
(b) What is the probability that all seven employees use direct deposit?
(c) Use formula (6–3) to determine the exact probability that four of the seven sampled employees use direct deposit.

	A	B
1	**Success**	**Probability**
2	0	0.0230
3	1	0.0910
4	2	0.1754
5	3	0.2198
6	4	0.2011
7	5	0.1432
8	6	0.0826
9	7	0.0397
10	8	0.0162
11	9	0.0057
12	10	0.0017
13	11	0.0005
14	12	0.0001
15	13	0.0000
16	14	0.0000
17	15	0.0000

Appendix B.9 is limited. It gives probabilities for n values from 1 to 15 and π values of .05, .10, ..., .90, and .95. A software program can generate the probabilities for a specified number of successes, given n and π. The Excel output to the left shows the probability when $n = 40$ and $\pi = .09$. Note that the number of successes stops at 15 because the probabilities for 16 to 40 are very close to 0. The instructions are detailed in the Software Commands section on page 193.

Several additional points should be made regarding the binomial probability distribution.

1. If n remains the same but π increases from .05 to .95, the shape of the distribution changes. Look at Table 6–3 and Chart 6–2. The distribution for a π of

.05 is positively skewed. As π approaches .50, the distribution becomes symmetrical. As π goes beyond .50 and moves toward .95, the probability distribution becomes negatively skewed. Table 6–3 highlights probabilities for $n = 10$ and a π of .05, .10, .20, .50, and .70. The graphs of these probability distributions are shown in Chart 6–2.

TABLE 6–3 Probability of 0, 1, 2, . . . Successes for a π of .05, .10, .20, .50, and .70, and an n of 10

$x\backslash\pi$	.05	.1	.2	.3	.4	.5	.6	.7	.8	.9	.95
0	.599	.349	.107	.028	.006	.001	.000	.000	.000	.000	.000
1	.315	.387	.268	.121	.040	.010	.002	.000	.000	.000	.000
2	.075	.194	.302	.233	.121	.044	.011	.001	.000	.000	.000
3	.010	.057	.201	.267	.215	.117	.042	.009	.001	.000	.000
4	.001	.011	.088	.200	.251	.205	.111	.037	.006	.000	.000
5	.000	.001	.026	.103	.201	.246	.201	.103	.026	.001	.000
6	.000	.000	.006	.037	.111	.205	.251	.200	.088	.011	.001
7	.000	.000	.001	.009	.042	.117	.215	.267	.201	.057	.010
8	.000	.000	.000	.001	.011	.044	.121	.233	.302	.194	.075
9	.000	.000	.000	.000	.002	.010	.040	.121	.268	.387	.315
10	.000	.000	.000	.000	.000	.001	.006	.028	.107	.349	.599

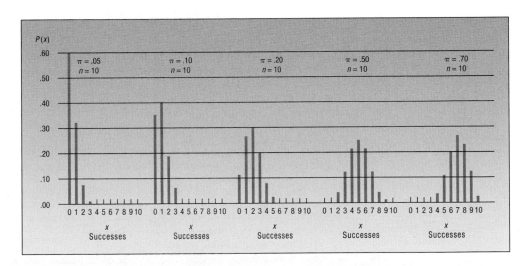

CHART 6–2 Graphing the Binomial Probability Distribution for a π of .05, .10, .20, .50, and .70, and an n of 10

2. If π, the probability of success, remains the same but n becomes larger, the shape of the binomial distribution becomes more symmetrical. Chart 6–3 shows a situation where π remains constant at .10 but n increases from 7 to 40.

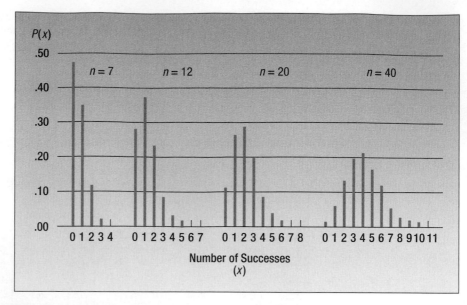

CHART 6–3 Chart Representing the Binomial Probability Distribution for a π of .10 and an n of 7, 12, 20, and 40

Exercises

connect™

9. In a binomial situation, $n = 4$ and $\pi = .25$. Determine the probabilities of the following events using the binomial formula.
   a. $x = 2$
   b. $x = 3$

10. In a binomial situation, $n = 5$ and $\pi = .40$. Determine the probabilities of the following events using the binomial formula.
   a. $x = 1$
   b. $x = 2$

11. Assume a binomial distribution where $n = 3$ and $\pi = .60$.
   a. Refer to Appendix B.9 and list the probabilities for values of x from 0 to 3.
   b. Determine the mean and standard deviation of the distribution from the general definitions given in formulas (6–1) and (6–2).

12. Assume a binomial distribution where $n = 5$ and $\pi = .30$.
   a. Refer to Appendix B.9 and list the probabilities for values of x from 0 to 5.
   b. Determine the mean and standard deviation of the distribution from the general definitions given in formulas (6–1) and (6–2).

13. An American Society of Investors survey found 30% of individual investors have used a discount broker. In a random sample of nine individuals, what is the probability:
   a. Exactly two of the sampled individuals have used a discount broker?
   b. Exactly four of them have used a discount broker?
   c. None of them have used a discount broker?

14. The United States Postal Service reports 95% of first-class mail within the same city is delivered within two days of the time of mailing. Six letters are randomly sent to different locations. 🔵
   a. What is the probability that all six arrive within two days?
   b. What is the probability that exactly five arrive within two days?
   c. Find the mean number of letters that will arrive within two days.
   d. Compute the variance and standard deviation of the number that will arrive within two days.

15. Industry standards suggest that 10% of new vehicles require warranty service within the first year. Jones Nissan in Sumter, South Carolina, sold 12 Nissans yesterday. 🔵
   a. What is the probability that none of these vehicles requires warranty service?
   b. What is the probability exactly one of these vehicles requires warranty service?

    c. Determine the probability that exactly two of these vehicles require warranty service.

    d. Compute the mean and standard deviation of this probability distribution.

16. A telemarketer makes six phone calls per hour and is able to make a sale on 30% of these contacts. During the next two hours, find: (df)

    a. The probability of making exactly four sales.

    b. The probability of making no sales.

    c. The probability of making exactly two sales.

    d. The mean number of sales in the two-hour period.

17. A recent survey by the American Accounting Association revealed 23% of students graduating with a major in accounting select public accounting. Suppose we select a sample of 15 recent graduates. (df)

    a. What is the probability two select public accounting?

    b. What is the probability five select public accounting?

    c. How many graduates would you expect to select public accounting?

18. It is reported that 16% of American households use a cell phone exclusively for their telephone service. In a sample of eight households, find the probability that: (df)

    a. None use a cell phone as their exclusive service.

    b. At least one uses the cell exclusively.

    c. At least five use the cell phone.

Cumulative Binomial Probability Distributions

We may wish to know the probability of correctly guessing the answers to 6 *or more* true/false questions out of 10. Or we may be interested in the probability of *selecting less than two* defectives at random from production during the previous hour. In these cases, we need cumulative frequency distributions similar to the ones developed in Chapter 2. See page 42. The following example will illustrate.

Example

A study by the Illinois Department of Transportation concluded that 76.2% of front seat occupants used seat belts. That means that both occupants of the front seat were using their seat belts. Suppose we decide to compare that information with current usage. We select a sample of 12 vehicles.

1.   What is the probability the front seat occupants in exactly 7 of the 12 vehicles selected are wearing seat belts?

2.   What is the probability the front seat occupants in at least 7 of the 12 vehicles are wearing seat belts?

Solution

This situation meets the binomial requirements.

- In a particular vehicle, both the front seat occupants are either wearing seat belts or they are not. There are only two possible outcomes.
- There are a fixed number of trials, 12 in this case, because 12 vehicles are checked.
- The probability of a "success" (occupants wearing seat belts) is the same from one vehicle to the next: 76.2%.
- The trials are independent. If the fourth vehicle selected in the sample has all the occupants wearing their seat belts, this does not have any effect on the results for the fifth or tenth vehicle.

To find the likelihood the occupants of *exactly* 7 of the sampled vehicles are wearing seat belts, we use formula 6-3. In this case, $n = 12$ and $\pi = .762$.

$$P(x = 7 \mid n = 12 \text{ and } \pi = .762)$$
$$= {}_{12}C_7(.762)^7(1 - .762)^{12-7} = 792(.149171)(.000764) = .0902$$

So we conclude the likelihood that the occupants of exactly 7 of the 12 sampled vehicles will be wearing their seat belts is about 9%. We often use, as we did in this equation, a bar "|" to mean "given that." So in this equation we want to know the probability that x is equal to 7 "given that the number of trials is 12 and the probability of a success is .762."

To find the probability that the occupants in 7 or more of the vehicles will be wearing seat belts, we use formula (6–3) from this chapter as well as the special rule of addition from the previous chapter. See formula (5–2) on page 135.

Because the events are mutually exclusive (meaning that a particular sample of 12 vehicles cannot have both a *total* of 7 and a *total* of 8 vehicles where the occupants are wearing seat belts), we find the probability of 7 vehicles where the occupants are wearing seat belts, the probability of 8, and so on up to the probability that occupants of all 12 sample vehicles are wearing seat belts. The probability of each of these outcomes is then totaled.

$$P(x \geq 7 \mid n = 12 \text{ and } \pi = .762)$$

$$= P(x = 7) + P(x = 8) + P(x = 9) + P(x = 10) + P(x = 11) + P(x = 12)$$

$$= .0902 + .1805 + .2569 + .2467 + .1436 + .0383$$

$$= .9562$$

So the probability of selecting 12 cars and finding that the occupants of 7 or more vehicles were wearing seat belts is .9562. This information is shown on the following Excel spreadsheet. There is a slight difference in the software answer due to rounding. The Excel commands are similar to those detailed in the Software Commands section on page 193, number 1.

Cumulative binomial

	A	B	C	D	E
1	**Success**	**Probability**			
2	0	0.0000			
3	1	0.0000			
4	2	0.0000			
5	3	0.0002			
6	4	0.0017			
7	5	0.0088			
8	6	0.0329			
9	7	0.0902			
10	8	0.1805	Sum of Probabilities		
11	9	0.2569	for 7 or more		
12	10	0.2467	successes		
13	11	0.1436			
14	12	0.0383			
15		0.9563			

Self-Review 6–4

A recent study revealed that 40% of women in the San Diego metropolitan area who work full time also volunteer in the community. Suppose we randomly select eight women in the San Diego area.
(a) What are the values for n and π?
(b) What is the probability that exactly three of the women volunteer in the community?
(c) What is the probability that at least one of the women volunteers in the community?

Exercises

connect

19. In a binomial distribution, $n = 8$ and $\pi = .30$. Find the probabilities of the following events.
    a. $x = 2$.
    b. $x \leq 2$ (the probability that x is equal to or less than 2).
    c. $x \geq 3$ (the probability that x is equal to or greater than 3).

20. In a binomial distribution, $n = 12$ and $\pi = .60$. Find the following probabilities.
    a. $x = 5$.
    b. $x \leq 5$.
    c. $x \geq 6$.

21. In a recent study, 90% of the homes in the United States were found to have large-screen TVs. In a sample of nine homes, what is the probability that: df

    a. All nine have large-screen TVs?
    b. Less than five have large-screen TVs?
    c. More than five have large-screen TVs?
    d. At least seven homes have large-screen TVs?

22. A manufacturer of window frames knows from long experience that 5% of the production will have some type of minor defect that will require an adjustment. What is the probability that in a sample of 20 window frames: df

    a. None will need adjustment?
    b. At least one will need adjustment?
    c. More than two will need adjustment?

23. The speed with which utility companies can resolve problems is very important. GTC, the Georgetown Telephone Company, reports it can resolve customer problems the same day they are reported in 70% of the cases. Suppose the 15 cases reported today are representative of all complaints. df

    a. How many of the problems would you expect to be resolved today? What is the standard deviation?
    b. What is the probability 10 of the problems can be resolved today?
    c. What is the probability 10 or 11 of the problems can be resolved today?
    d. What is the probability more than 10 of the problems can be resolved today?

24. It is asserted that 80% of the cars approaching an individual toll both in New Jersey are equipped with an E-ZPass transponder. Find the probability that in a sample of six cars: df

    a. All six will have the transponder.
    b. At least three will have the transponder.
    c. None will have a transponder.

LO 6-6 Describe and compute probabilities for a Poisson distribution.

Statistics in Action

Near the end of World War II, the Germans developed *(continued)*

6.6 Poisson Probability Distribution

The **Poisson probability distribution** describes the number of times some event occurs during a specified interval. The interval may be time, distance, area, or volume.

The distribution is based on two assumptions. The first assumption is that the probability is proportional to the length of the interval. The second assumption is that the intervals are independent. To put it another way, the longer the interval, the larger the probability, and the number of occurrences in one interval does not affect the other intervals. This distribution is also a limiting form of the binomial distribution when the probability of a success is very small and n is large. It is often referred to as the "law of improbable events," meaning that the probability, π, of a particular event's happening is quite small. The Poisson distribution is a discrete probability distribution because it is formed by counting.

184   **Chapter 6**

The Poisson distribution has these characteristics:

> **POISSON PROBABILITY EXPERIMENT**
> 1. The random variable is the number of times some event occurs during a defined interval.
> 2. The probability of the event is proportional to the size of the interval.
> 3. The intervals do not overlap and are independent.

This probability distribution has many applications. It is used as a model to describe the distribution of errors in data entry, the number of scratches and other imperfections in newly painted car panels, the number of defective parts in outgoing shipments, the number of customers waiting to be served at a restaurant or waiting to get into an attraction at Disney World, and the number of accidents on I–75 during a three-month period.

The Poisson distribution can be described mathematically by the formula:

POISSON DISTRIBUTION $$P(x) = \frac{\mu^x e^{-\mu}}{x!}$$ [6–6]

where:

μ (mu) is the mean number of occurrences (successes) in a particular interval.
e is the constant 2.71828 (base of the Napierian logarithmic system).
x is the number of occurrences (successes).
$P(x)$ is the probability for a specified value of x.

The mean number of successes, μ, is determined by $n\pi$, where n is the total number of trials and π the probability of success.

MEAN OF A POISSON DISTRIBUTION $\mu = n\pi$ [6–7]

The variance of the Poisson is also equal to its mean. If, for example, the probability that a check cashed by a bank will bounce is .0003, and 10,000 checks are cashed, the mean and the variance for the number of bad checks is 3.0, found by $\mu = n\pi = 10,000(.0003) = 3.0$.

Recall that for a binomial distribution there is a fixed number of trials. For example, for a four-question multiple-choice test there can only be zero, one, two, three, or four successes (correct answers). The random variable, x, for a Poisson distribution, however, can assume an *infinite number of values*—that is, 0, 1, 2, 3, 4, 5, . . . However, *the probabilities become very small after the first few occurrences* (successes).

To illustrate the Poisson probability computation, assume baggage is rarely lost by Northeast Airlines. Most flights do not experience any mishandled bags; some have one bag lost; a few have two bags lost; rarely a flight will have three lost bags; and so on. Suppose a random sample of 1,000 flights shows a total of 300 bags were lost. Thus, the arithmetic mean number of lost bags per flight is 0.3, found by 300/1,000. If the number of lost bags per flight follows a Poisson distribution with $\mu = 0.3$, we can compute the various probabilities using formula (6–6):

$$P(x) = \frac{\mu^x e^{-\mu}}{x!}$$

For example, the probability of not losing any bags is:

$$P(0) = \frac{(0.3)^0 (e^{-0.3})}{0!} = 0.7408$$

rocket bombs, which were fired at the city of London. The Allied military command didn't know whether these bombs were fired at random or whether they had an aiming device. To investigate, the city of London was divided into 586 square regions. The distribution of hits in each square was recorded as follows:

Hits	0	1	2	3	4	5
Regions	229	221	93	35	7	1

To interpret, the above chart indicates that 229 regions were not hit with one of the bombs. Seven regions were hit four times. Using the Poisson distribution, with a mean of 0.93 hits per region, the expected number of hits is as follows:

Hits	0	1	2	3	4	5 or more
Regions	231.2	215.0	100.0	31.0	7.2	1.6

Because the actual number of hits was close to the expected number of hits, the military command concluded that the bombs were falling at random. The Germans had not developed a bomb with an aiming device.

In other words, 74% of the flights will have no lost baggage. The probability of exactly one lost bag is:

$$P(1) = \frac{(0.3)^1(e^{-0.3})}{1!} = 0.2222$$

Thus, we would expect to find exactly one lost bag on 22% of the flights.
Poisson probabilities can also be found in the table in Appendix B.5.

Example

Recall from the previous illustration that the number of lost bags follows a Poisson distribution with a mean of 0.3. Use Appendix B.5 to find the probability that no bags will be lost on a particular flight. What is the probability exactly one bag will be lost on a particular flight? When should the supervisor become suspicious that a flight is having too many lost bags?

Solution

Part of Appendix B.5 is repeated as Table 6–4. To find the probability of no lost bags, locate the column headed "0.3" and read down that column to the row labeled "0." The probability is .7408. That is the probability of no lost bags. The probability of one lost bag is .2222, which is in the next row of the table, in the same column. The probability of two lost bags is .0333, in the row below; for three lost bags, it is .0033; and for four lost bags, it is .0003. Thus, a supervisor should not be surprised to find one lost bag but should expect to see more than one lost bag infrequently.

TABLE 6–4 Poisson Table for Various Values of μ (from Appendix B.5)

x	0.1	0.2	0.3	0.4	0.5	0.6	0.7	0.8	0.9
0	0.9048	0.8187	0.7408	0.6703	0.6065	0.5488	0.4966	0.4493	0.4066
1	0.0905	0.1637	0.2222	0.2681	0.3033	0.3293	0.3476	0.3595	0.3659
2	0.0045	0.0164	0.0333	0.0536	0.0758	0.0988	0.1217	0.1438	0.1647
3	0.0002	0.0011	0.0033	0.0072	0.0126	0.0198	0.0284	0.0383	0.0494
4	0.0000	0.0001	0.0003	0.0007	0.0016	0.0030	0.0050	0.0077	0.0111
5	0.0000	0.0000	0.0000	0.0001	0.0002	0.0004	0.0007	0.0012	0.0020
6	0.0000	0.0000	0.0000	0.0000	0.0000	0.0000	0.0001	0.0002	0.0003
7	0.0000	0.0000	0.0000	0.0000	0.0000	0.0000	0.0000	0.0000	0.0000

These probabilities can also be found using Excel. The commands necessary are reported at the end of the chapter.

	A	B	C	D
1				
2		Success	Probability	
3		0	0.740818	
4		1	0.222245	
5		2	0.033337	
6		3	0.003334	
7		4	0.000250	
8		5	0.000015	
9				

Earlier in this section, we mentioned that the Poisson probability distribution is a limiting form of the binomial. That is, we could estimate a binomial probability using the Poisson.

The Poisson probability distribution is characterized by the number of times an event happens during some interval or continuum. Examples include:

- The number of misspelled words per page in a newspaper.
- The number of calls per hour received by Dyson Vacuum Cleaner Company.
- The number of vehicles sold per day at Hyatt Buick GMC in Durham, North Carolina.
- The number of goals scored in a college soccer game.

In each of these examples, there is some type of continuum—misspelled words per page, calls per hour, vehicles per day, or goals per game.

In the previous example, we investigated the number of bags lost per flight, so the continuum was a "flight." We knew the mean number of bags of luggage lost per flight, but we did not know the number of passengers or the probability of a bag being lost. We suspected the number of passengers was fairly large and the probability of a passenger losing his or her bag of luggage was small. In the following example, we use the Poisson distribution to estimate a binomial probability when *n,* the number of trials, is large and π, the probability of a success, small.

Example

Coastal Insurance Company underwrites insurance for beachfront properties along the Virginia, North and South Carolina, and Georgia coasts. It uses the estimate that the probability of a named Category III hurricane (sustained winds of more than 110 miles per hour) or higher striking a particular region of the coast (for example, St. Simons Island, Georgia) in any one year is .05. If a homeowner takes a 30-year mortgage on a recently purchased property in St. Simons, what is the likelihood that the owner will experience at least one hurricane during the mortgage period?

Solution

To use the Poisson probability distribution, we begin by determining the mean or expected number of storms meeting the criterion hitting St. Simons during the 30-year period. That is:

$$\mu = n\pi = 30(.05) = 1.5$$

where:
n is the number of years, 30 in this case.
π is the probability a hurricane meeting the strength criteria comes ashore.
μ is the mean or expected number of storms in a 30-year period.

To find the probability of at least one storm hitting St. Simons Island, Georgia, we first find the probability of no storms hitting the coast and subtract that value from 1.

$$P(x \geq 1) = 1 - P(x = 0) = 1 - \frac{\mu^0 e^{-1.5}}{0!} = 1 - .2231 = .7769$$

We conclude that the likelihood a hurricane meeting the strength criteria will strike the beachfront property at St. Simons during the 30-year period when the mortgage is in effect is .7769. To put it another way, the probability St. Simons will be hit by a Category III or higher hurricane during the 30-year period is a little more than 75%.

We should emphasize that the continuum, as previously described, still exists. That is, there are expected to be 1.5 storms hitting the coast per 30-year period. The continuum is the 30-year period.

In the preceding case, we are actually using the Poisson distribution as an estimate of the binomial. Note that we've met the binomial conditions outlined on page 175.

- There are only two possible outcomes: a hurricane hits the St. Simons area or it does not.

- There is a fixed number of trials, in this case 30 years.
- There is a constant probability of success; that is, the probability of a hurricane hitting the area is .05 each year.
- The years are independent. That means if a named storm strikes in the fifth year, that has no effect on any other year.

To find the probability of at least one storm striking the area in a 30-year period using the binomial distribution:

$$P(x \geq 1) = 1 - P(x = 0) = 1 - {}_{30}C_0(.05)^0(.95)^{30} = 1 - (1)(1)(.2146) = .7854$$

The probability of at least one hurricane hitting the St. Simons area during the 30-year period using the binomial distribution is .7854.

Which answer is correct? Why should we look at the problem both ways? The binomial is the more "technically correct" solution. The Poisson can be thought of as an approximation for the binomial, when n, the number of trials is large, and π, the probability of a success, is small. We look at the problem using both distributions to emphasize the convergence of the two discrete distributions. In some instances, using the Poisson may be the quicker solution, and as you see there is little practical difference in the answers. In fact, as n gets larger and π smaller, the differences between the two distributions gets smaller.

The Poisson probability distribution is always positively skewed and the random variable has no specific upper limit. The Poisson distribution for the lost bags illustration, where $\mu = 0.3$, is highly skewed. As μ becomes larger, the Poisson distribution becomes more symmetrical. For example, Chart 6–4 shows the distributions of the number of transmission services, muffler replacements, and oil changes per day at Avellino's Auto Shop. They follow Poisson distributions with means of 0.7, 2.0, and 6.0, respectively.

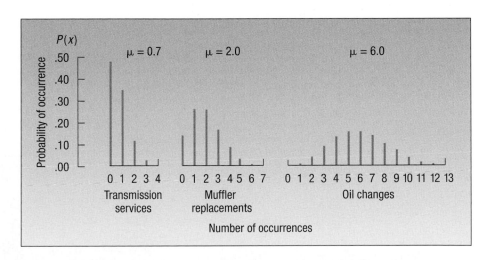

CHART 6–4 Poisson Probability Distributions for Means of 0.7, 2.0, and 6.0

Only μ needed to construct Poisson distribution

In summary, the Poisson distribution is actually a family of discrete distributions. All that is needed to construct a Poisson probability distribution is the mean number of defects, errors, and so on—designated as μ.

Self-Review 6–5   From actuary tables, Washington Insurance Company determined the likelihood that a man age 25 will die within the next year is .0002. If Washington Insurance sells 4,000 policies to 25-year-old men this year, what is the probability they will pay on exactly one policy?

Exercises

connect

25. In a Poisson distribution $\mu = 0.4$.
   a. What is the probability that $x = 0$?
   b. What is the probability that $x > 0$?
26. In a Poisson distribution $\mu = 4$.
   a. What is the probability that $x = 2$?
   b. What is the probability that $x \leq 2$?
   c. What is the probability that $x > 2$?
27. Ms. Bergen is a loan officer at Coast Bank and Trust. From her years of experience, she estimates that the probability is .025 that an applicant will not be able to repay his or her installment loan. Last month she made 40 loans.
   a. What is the probability that three loans will be defaulted?
   b. What is the probability that at least three loans will be defaulted?
28. Automobiles arrive at the Elkhart exit of the Indiana Toll Road at the rate of two per minute. The distribution of arrivals approximates a Poisson distribution.
   a. What is the probability that no automobiles arrive in a particular minute?
   b. What is the probability that at least one automobile arrives during a particular minute?
29. It is estimated that 0.5% of the callers to the Customer Service department of Dell Inc. will receive a busy signal. What is the probability that of today's 1,200 callers at least 5 received a busy signal?
30. In the past, schools in Los Angeles County have closed an average of three days each year for weather emergencies. What is the probability that schools in Los Angeles County will close for four days next year?

Chapter Summary

I. A random variable is a numerical value determined by the outcome of an experiment.
II. A probability distribution is a listing of all possible outcomes of an experiment and the probability associated with each outcome.
   A. A discrete probability distribution can assume only certain values. The main features are:
      1. The sum of the probabilities is 1.00.
      2. The probability of a particular outcome is between 0.00 and 1.00.
      3. The outcomes are mutually exclusive.
   B. A continuous distribution can assume an infinite number of values within a specific range.
III. The mean and variance of a probability distribution are computed as follows.
   A. The mean is equal to:

$$\mu = \Sigma[xP(x)] \qquad\qquad \textbf{[6–1]}$$

   B. The variance is equal to:

$$\sigma^2 = \Sigma[(x - \mu)^2 P(x)] \qquad\qquad \textbf{[6–2]}$$

IV. The binomial distribution has the following characteristics.
   A. Each outcome is classified into one of two mutually exclusive categories.
   B. The distribution results from a count of the number of successes in a fixed number of trials.
   C. The probability of a success remains the same from trial to trial.

D. Each trial is independent.
E. A binomial probability is determined as follows:

$$P(x) = {}_nC_x \pi^x (1 - \pi)^{n-x}$$ **[6–3]**

F. The mean is computed as:

$$\mu = n\pi$$ **[6–4]**

G. The variance is

$$\sigma^2 = n\pi(1 - \pi)$$ **[6–5]**

V. The Poisson distribution has the following characteristics.
   A. It describes the number of times some event occurs during a specified interval.
   B. The probability of a "success" is proportional to the length of the interval.
   C. Nonoverlapping intervals are independent.
   D. It is a limiting form of the binomial distribution when n is large and π is small.
   E. A Poisson probability is determined from the following equation:

$$P(x) = \frac{\mu^x e^{-\mu}}{x!}$$ **[6–6]**

   F. The mean and the variance are:

$$\mu = n\pi$$ **[6–7]**
$$\sigma^2 = n\pi$$

Chapter Exercises

connect

31. What is the difference between a random variable and a probability distribution?
32. For each of the following, indicate whether the random variable is discrete or continuous.
   a. The length of time to get a haircut.
   b. The number of cars a jogger passes each morning while running.
   c. The number of hits for a team in a high school girls' softball game.
   d. The number of patients treated at the South Strand Medical Center between 6 and 10 P.M. each night.
   e. The distance your car traveled on the last fill-up.
   f. The number of customers at the Oak Street Wendy's who used the drive-through facility.
   g. The distance between Gainesville, Florida, and all Florida cities with a population of at least 50,000.
33. An investment will be worth $1,000, $2,000, or $5,000 at the end of the year. The probabilities of these values are .25, .60, and .15, respectively. Determine the mean and variance of the worth of the investment. (df)
34. The following notice appeared in the golf shop at a Myrtle Beach, South Carolina, area golf course.

> Blackmoor Golf Club Members
> The golf shop is holding a raffle to win a
> TaylorMade R9 10.5° Regular Flex Driver ($300 value).
> Tickets are $5.00 each.
> Only 80 tickets will be sold.
> Please see the golf shop to get your ticket!

John Underpar buys a ticket.
   a. What are Mr. Underpar's possible monetary outcomes?
   b. What are the probabilities of the possible outcomes?
   c. Summarize Mr. Underpar's "experiment" in a probability distribution.
   d. What is the mean or expected value of the probability distribution? Explain your result.
   e. If all 80 tickets are sold, what is the expected return to the Club?

35. Croissant Bakery Inc. offers special decorated cakes for birthdays, weddings, and other occasions. It also has regular cakes available in its bakery. The following table gives the total number of cakes sold per day and the corresponding probability. Compute the mean, variance, and standard deviation of the number of cakes sold per day.

Number of Cakes Sold in a Day	Probability
12	.25
13	.40
14	.25
15	.10

36. The payouts for the Powerball lottery and their corresponding odds and probabilities of occurrence are shown below. The price of a ticket is $1.00. Find the mean and standard deviation of the payout. Hint: Don't forget to include the cost of the ticket and its corresponding probability.

Divisions	Payout	Odds	Probability
Five plus Powerball	$50,000,000	146,107,962	0.000000006844
Match 5	200,000	3,563,609	0.000000280614
Four plus Powerball	10,000	584,432	0.000001711060
Match 4	100	14,255	0.000070145903
Three plus Powerball	100	11,927	0.000083836351
Match 3	7	291	0.003424657534
Two plus Powerball	7	745	0.001340482574
One plus Powerball	4	127	0.007812500000
Zero plus Powerball	3	69	0.014285714286

37. In a recent survey, 35% indicated chocolate was their favorite flavor of ice cream. Suppose we select a sample of 10 people and ask them to name their favorite flavor of ice cream.
   a. How many of those in the sample would you expect to name chocolate?
   b. What is the probability exactly four of those in the sample name chocolate?
   c. What is the probability four or more name chocolate?

38. Thirty percent of the population in a southwestern community are Spanish-speaking Americans. A Spanish-speaking person is accused of killing a non-Spanish-speaking American and goes to trial. Of the first 12 potential jurors, only 2 are Spanish-speaking Americans, and 10 are not. The defendant's lawyer challenges the jury selection, claiming bias against her client. The government lawyer disagrees, saying that the probability of this particular jury composition is common. Compute the probability and discuss the assumptions.

39. An auditor for Health Maintenance Services of Georgia reports 40% of policyholders 55 years or older submit a claim during the year. Fifteen policyholders are randomly selected for company records.
   a. How many of the policyholders would you expect to have filed a claim within the last year?
   b. What is the probability that 10 of the selected policyholders submitted a claim last year?
   c. What is the probability that 10 or more of the selected policyholders submitted a claim last year?
   d. What is the probability that more than 10 of the selected policyholders submitted a claim last year?

40. Tire and Auto Supply is considering a 2-for-1 stock split. Before the transaction is finalized, at least two-thirds of the 1,200 company stockholders must approve the proposal. To evaluate the likelihood the proposal will be approved, the CFO selected a sample of 18 stockholders. He contacted each and found 14 approved of the proposed split. What is the likelihood of this event, assuming two-thirds of the stockholders approve?

41. A federal study reported that 7.5% of the U.S. workforce has a drug problem. A drug enforcement official for the State of Indiana wished to investigate this statement. In her sample of 20 employed workers:
   a. How many would you expect to have a drug problem? What is the standard deviation?
   b. What is the likelihood that *none* of the workers sampled has a drug problem?
   c. What is the likelihood *at least one* has a drug problem?

42. The Bank of Hawaii reports that 7% of its credit card holders will default at some time in their life. The Hilo branch just mailed out 12 new cards today.
   a. How many of these new cardholders would you expect to default? What is the standard deviation?
   b. What is the likelihood that *none* of the cardholders will default?
   c. What is the likelihood *at least one* will default?

43. Recent statistics suggest that 15% of those who visit a retail site on the World Wide Web make a purchase. A retailer wished to verify this claim. To do so, she selected a sample of 16 "hits" to her site and found that 4 had actually made a purchase.
   a. What is the likelihood of exactly four purchases?
   b. How many purchases should she expect?
   c. What is the likelihood that four or more "hits" result in a purchase?

44. Acceptance sampling is a statistical method used to monitor the quality of purchased parts and components. To ensure the quality of incoming parts, a purchaser or manufacturer normally samples 20 parts and allows 1 defect.
   a. What is the likelihood of accepting a lot that is 1% defective?
   b. If the quality of the incoming lot was actually 2%, what is the likelihood of accepting it?
   c. If the quality of the incoming lot was actually 5%, what is the likelihood of accepting it?

45. Unilever Inc. recently developed a new body wash with a scent of ginger. Their research indicates that 30% of men like the new scent. To further investigate, Unilever's marketing research group randomly selected 15 people and asked them whether they liked the scent. What is the probability that 6 or more people like the ginger scent in the body wash?

46. Suppose 1.5% of the antennas on new Nokia cell phones are defective. For a random sample of 200 antennas, find the probability that:
   a. None of the antennas is defective.
   b. Three or more of the antennas are defective.

47. A study of the checkout lines at the Safeway Supermarket in the South Strand area revealed that between 4 and 7 P.M. on weekdays there is an average of four customers waiting in line. What is the probability that you visit Safeway today during this period and find:
   a. No customers are waiting?
   b. Four customers are waiting?
   c. Four or fewer are waiting?
   d. Four or more are waiting?

48. An internal study by the Technology Services department at Lahey Electronics revealed company employees receive an average of two emails per hour. Assume the arrival of these emails is approximated by the Poisson distribution.
   a. What is the probability Linda Lahey, company president, received exactly 1 email between 4 P.M. and 5 P.M. yesterday?
   b. What is the probability she received 5 or more emails during the same period?
   c. What is the probability she did not receive any emails during the period?

49. Recent crime reports indicate that 3.1 motor vehicle thefts occur each minute in the United States. Assume that the distribution of thefts per minute can be approximated by the Poisson probability distribution.
   a. Calculate the probability exactly *four* thefts occur in a minute.
   b. What is the probability there are *no* thefts in a minute?
   c. What is the probability there is *at least one* theft in a minute?

50. Recent difficult economic times have caused an increase in the foreclosure rate of home mortgages. Statistics from the Penn Bank and Trust Company show their monthly foreclosure rate is now one loan out of every 136 loans. Last month the bank approved 300 loans.
   a. How many foreclosures would you expect the bank to have last month?
   b. What is the probability of exactly two foreclosures?
   c. What is the probability of at least one foreclosure?

51. The National Aeronautics and Space Administration (NASA) has experienced two disasters. The Challenger exploded over the Atlantic Ocean in 1986, and the Columbia disintegrated on reentry over East Texas in 2003. Based on the first 113 missions, and assuming failures occur at the same rate, consider the next 23 missions. What is the probability of exactly two failures? What is the probability of no failures?

52. Suppose the National Hurricane Center forecasts that hurricanes will hit the strike area with a .95 probability.
a. What probability distribution does this follow?
b. What is the probability that 10 hurricanes reach landfall in the strike area?
c. What is the probability at least one of 10 hurricanes reaches land outside the strike area?

STORM CONTINUES NORTHWEST
Position : **27.8 N, 71.4 W**
Movement: **NNW at 8 mph**
Sustained winds: **105 mph**
As of 11 p.m. EDT Tuesday

—— Hurricane watch
—— Tropical storm watch

53. A recent CBS News survey reported that 67% of adults felt the U.S. Treasury should continue making pennies.

Suppose we select a sample of 15 adults.
a. How many of the 15 would we expect to indicate that the Treasury should continue making pennies? What is the standard deviation?
b. What is the likelihood that exactly 8 adults would indicate the Treasury should continue making pennies?
c. What is the likelihood at least 8 adults would indicate the Treasury should continue making pennies?

Data Set Exercises

(The data for these exercises are available at the text website www.mhhe.com/lindbasic8e).

54. Refer to the Real Estate data, which report information on homes sold in the Goodyear, Arizona, area last year.
a. Create a probability distribution for the number of bedrooms. Compute the mean and the standard deviation of this distribution.
b. Create a probability distribution for the number of bathrooms. Compute the mean and the standard deviation of this distribution.

55. Refer to the Baseball 2010 data. Compute the mean number of home runs per game. To do this, first find the mean number of home runs per team for 2010. Next, divide this value by 162 (a season comprises 162 games). Then multiply by 2, because there are two teams in each game. Use the Poisson distribution to estimate the number of home runs that will be hit in a game. Find the probability that:
  a. There are no home runs in a game.
  b. There are two home runs in a game.
  c. There are at least four home runs in a game.

Practice Test

Part 1—Objective
  1. A listing of the possible outcomes of an experiment and the probability associated with each outcome is called a _____ .
  2. The essential difference between a discrete random variable and a discrete probability distribution is that a discrete probability distribution includes the _____ .
  3. In a discrete probability distribution, the sum of the possible probabilities is always equal to _____ .
  4. The expected value of a probability distribution is also called the _____ .
  5. How many outcomes are there in a particular binomial trial? _____ .
  6. Under what conditions will the probability of a success change from trial to trial in a binomial experiment? _____ .
  7. In a Poisson experiment, the mean and variance are _____ .
  8. The Poisson distribution is a limiting case of the binomial probability distribution when n is large and _____ is small.
  9. Suppose 5% of patients who take a certain drug suffer undesirable side effects. If we select 10 patients currently taking the drug, what is the probability exactly two suffer undesirable side effects? _____ .
  10. The mean number of work-related accidents per month in a manufacturing plant is 1.70. What is the probability there will be no work-related accidents in a particular month? _____ .

Part 2—Problems
  1. IRS data show that 15% of personal tax returns reporting an adjusted gross income more than $1,000,000 will be subject to a computer audit. This year a CPA completed 16 returns with adjusted gross incomes more than $1,000,000. The CPA wants to know the likelihoods that the returns will be audited.
    a. What probability distribution applies to this situation?
    b. What is the probability exactly one of these returns is audited?
    c. What is the probability at least one of these returns is audited?
  2. For certain personal tax returns, the IRS will compute the amount to refund a taxpayer. Suppose the Cincinnati office of the IRS processes an average of three returns per hour that require a refund calculation.
    a. What probability distribution applies to this situation?
    b. What is the probability the IRS processes exactly three returns in a particular hour that require a refund calculation?
    c. What is the probability the IRS does not compute a refund on any return in an hour?
    d. What is the probability the IRS processes at least one return in a particular hour that requires a refund calculation?
  3. A CPA studied the number of exemptions claimed on tax returns. The data are summarized in the following table.

Exemptions	Percent
1	20
2	50
3	20
4	10

    a. What is the mean number of exemptions claimed?
    b. What is the variance of the number of exemptions claimed?

Software Commands

1. The Excel commands necessary to determine the binomial probability distribution on page 178 are:
   a. On a blank Excel worksheet, write the word *Success* in cell A1 and the word *Probability* in B1. In cells A2 through A17, write the integers *0* to *15*. Click on *B2* as the active cell.
   b. Click on the **Formulas** tab in the top menu, then, on the far left, select **Insert Function fx.**
   c. In the first dialog box, select **Statistical** in the function category. For Excel 2007, select **BINOMDIST;** for Excel 2010, select **BINOM.DIST** in the function name category. Then click **OK.**
   d. In the second dialog box, enter the four items necessary to compute a binomial probability.
      1. Enter *0* for the number of successes.
      2. Enter *40* for the number of trials.
      3. Enter *.09* for the probability of a success.
   4. Enter the word *false* or the number *0* for the individual probabilities and click on **OK.**
   5. Excel will compute the probability of 0 successes in 40 trials, with a .09 probability of success. The result, .02299618, is stored in cell B2.
   e. To complete the probability distribution for successes of 1 through 15, double-click on cell **B2.** The binomial function should appear. Replace the **0** to the right of the open parentheses with the cell reference **A2.**
   f. Move the mouse to the lower right corner of cell B2 till a solid black + symbol appears, then click and hold and highlight the B column to cell B17. The probability of a success for the various values of the random variable will appear.

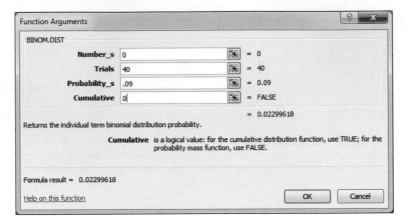

2. The Excel commands necessary to determine the Poisson probability distribution on page 185 are:
   a. On a blank Excel worksheet, write the word *Success* in cell B2 and the word *Probability* in C2. In cells B3 through B8, enter the integers *0* to *5*.
   b. Click on the **Formulas** tab in the top menu. Then, on the far left, select **Insert Function fx.**
   c. In the first dialog box, select **Statistical** in the function category. For Excel 2007, select **POISSONDIST;** for Excel 2010, select **POISSON.DIST** in the function name category. Then click **OK.**
   d. In the second dialog box, enter the four items necessary to compute a Poisson probability.
      1. Enter *0* for **X.**
      2. Enter *0.3* for the **mean** of the distribution.
      3. Enter the word *false* or the number *0* for the **Cumulative** entry and click on **OK.**
   4. Excel will compute the probability of 0 successes for a Poisson Distribution with a mean of 0.3. The result, 0.740818, is stored in B3.

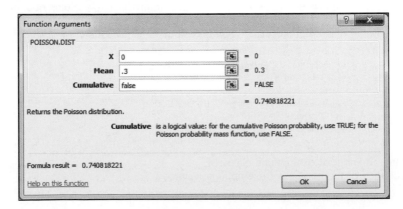

Chapter 6   Answers to Self-Review

6–1 a.

Number of Spots	Probability
1	$\frac{1}{6}$
2	$\frac{1}{6}$
3	$\frac{1}{6}$
4	$\frac{1}{6}$
5	$\frac{1}{6}$
6	$\frac{1}{6}$
Total	$\frac{6}{6}$ = 1.00

b.

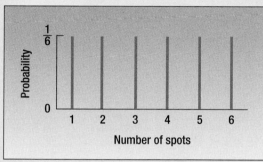

c. $\frac{6}{6}$ or 1.

6–2 a. It is discrete, because the values $0.80, $0.90, and $1.20 are clearly separated from each other. Also the sum of the probabilities is

1.00, and the outcomes are mutually exclusive.

b.

x	P(x)	xP(x)
$ .80	.30	0.24
.90	.50	0.45
1.20	.20	0.24
		0.93

The mean is 93 cents.

c.

x	P(x)	(x − μ)	(x − μ)²P(x)
$0.80	.30	−0.13	.00507
0.90	.50	−0.03	.00045
1.20	.20	0.27	.01458
			.02010

The variance is .02010, and the standard deviation is 14 cents.

6–3 a. It is reasonable because each employee either uses direct deposit or does not; employees are independent; the probability of using direct deposit is .95 for all; and we count the number using the service out of 7.

b. $P(7) = {}_7C_7(.95)^7(.05)^0 = .6983$

c. $P(4) = {}_7C_4(.95)^4(.05)^3 = .0036$

6–4 a. $n = 8; \pi = .4$

Using the Binomial Probability Distribution Tables with $n = 8$ and a probability of success equal to 0.40:

b. $P(x = 3) = .279$ or $P(x = 3) = {}_8C_3(.4)^3(.6)^5$
$= .2787$

c. $P(x \geqslant 1) = .983$ or $P(x \geqslant 1) = 1 - {}_8C_0(.4)^0(.6)^8$
$= .9832$

6–5 $\mu = 4,000(.0002) = 0.8$

$$P(1) = \frac{0.8^1 e^{-0.8}}{1!} = .3595$$

7

Continuous Probability Distributions

Most four-year automobile leases allow up to 60,000 miles. If the lessee goes beyond this amount, a penalty of 20 cents per mile is added to the lease cost. Suppose the distribution of miles driven on four-year leases follows the normal distribution. The mean is 52,000 miles, and the standard deviation is 5,000 miles. What percent of the leases will yield a penalty because of excess mileage? (See Exercise 49 and LO 7-5).

7.1 Introduction

Chapter 6 began our study of probability distributions. We studied two discrete probability distributions, namely, the binomial and the Poisson. These distributions are based on discrete random variables, which can assume only clearly separated values. For example, we select for study 10 small businesses that began operations during the year 2000. The number still operating in 2011 can be 0, 1, 2, . . . , 10. There cannot be 3.7, 12, or −7 still operating in 2011. In this example, only certain outcomes are possible and these outcomes are represented by clearly separated values. In addition, the result is usually found by counting the number of successes. We count the number of the businesses in the study that are still in operation in 2011.

We continue our study of probability distributions by examining *continuous* probability distributions. A continuous probability distribution usually results from measuring something, such as the distance from the dormitory to the classroom, the weight of an individual, or the amount of bonus earned by CEOs. Suppose we select five students and find the distance, in miles, they travel to attend class as 12.2, 8.9, 6.7, 3.6, and 14.6. When examining a continuous distribution we are usually interested in information such as the percent of students who travel less than 10 miles or the percent who travel more than 8 miles. In other words, for a continuous distribution we may wish to know the percent of observations that occur within a certain range. It is important to realize that a continuous random variable has an infinite number of values within a particular range. So you think of the probability a variable will have a value within a specified range, rather than the probability for a specific value.

This chapter presents and shows how to use two continuous probability distributions: the uniform probability distribution and the normal probability distribution.

7.2 The Family of Uniform Probability Distributions

The uniform probability distribution is perhaps the simplest distribution for a continuous random variable. This distribution is rectangular in shape and is defined by minimum and maximum values. Here are some examples that follow a uniform distribution.

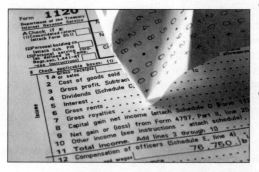

- The time to fly via a commercial airliner from Orlando, Florida, to Atlanta, Georgia, is uniformly distributed and ranges from 60 minutes to 120 minutes. The random variable is the flight time within this interval. The variable of interest, flight time in minutes, is continuous in the interval from 60 minutes to 120 minutes.
- Volunteers at the Grand Strand Public Library prepare federal income tax forms. The time to prepare form 1040-EZ follows a uniform distribution over the interval between 10 minutes and 30 minutes. The random variable is the number of minutes to complete the form, and it can assume any value between 10 and 30.

A uniform distribution is shown in Chart 7–1. The distribution's shape is rectangular and has a minimum value of *a* and a maximum of *b*. Also notice in Chart 7–1 the height of the distribution is constant or uniform for all values between *a* and *b*.

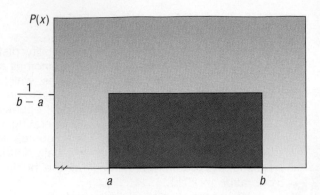

CHART 7–1 A Continuous Uniform Distribution

The mean of a uniform distribution is located in the middle of the interval between the minimum and maximum values. It is computed as:

$$\text{MEAN OF THE UNIFORM DISTRIBUTION} \qquad \mu = \frac{a+b}{2} \qquad \text{[7–1]}$$

LO 7-1 List the characteristics of the uniform distribution.

The standard deviation describes the dispersion of a distribution. In the uniform distribution, the standard deviation is also related to the interval between the maximum and minimum values.

$$\text{STANDARD DEVIATION OF THE UNIFORM DISTRIBUTION} \qquad \sigma = \sqrt{\frac{(b-a)^2}{12}} \qquad \text{[7–2]}$$

The equation for the uniform probability distribution is:

$$\text{UNIFORM DISTRIBUTION} \qquad P(x) = \frac{1}{b-a} \qquad \text{if } a \le x \le b \text{ and 0 elsewhere} \qquad \text{[7–3]}$$

As described in Chapter 6, probability distributions are useful for making probability statements concerning the values of a random variable. For distributions describing a continuous random variable, areas within the distribution represent probabilities. In the uniform distribution, its rectangular shape allows us to apply the area formula for a rectangle. Recall that we find the area of a rectangle by multiplying its length by its height. For the uniform distribution, the height of the rectangle is $P(x)$, which is $1/(b-a)$. The length or base of the distribution is $b-a$. So if we multiply the height of the distribution by its entire range to find the area, the result is always 1.00. To put it another way, the total area within a continuous probability distribution is equal to 1.00. In general

The total area under the curve is always 1.

$$\text{Area} = (\text{height})(\text{base}) = \frac{1}{(b-a)}(b-a) = 1.00$$

So if a uniform distribution ranges from 10 to 15, the height is 0.20, found by $1/(15-10)$. The base is 5, found by $15-10$. The total area is:

$$\text{Area} = (\text{height})(\text{base}) = \frac{1}{(15-10)}(15-10) = 1.00$$

An example will illustrate the features of a uniform distribution and how we calculate probabilities using it.

Example

Southwest Arizona State University provides bus service to students while they are on campus. A bus arrives at the North Main Street and College Drive stop every 30 minutes between 6 A.M. and 11 P.M. during weekdays. Students arrive at the bus stop at random times. The time that a student waits is uniformly distributed from 0 to 30 minutes.

1. Draw a graph of this distribution.
2. Show that the area of this uniform distribution is 1.00.
3. How long will a student "typically" have to wait for a bus? In other words, what is the mean waiting time? What is the standard deviation of the waiting times?
4. What is the probability a student will wait more than 25 minutes?
5. What is the probability a student will wait between 10 and 20 minutes?

Solution

In this case, the random variable is the length of time a student must wait. Time is measured on a continuous scale, and the wait times may range from 0 minutes up to 30 minutes.

1. The graph of the uniform distribution is shown in Chart 7–2. The horizontal line is drawn at a height of .0333, found by 1/(30 − 0). The range of this distribution is 30 minutes.

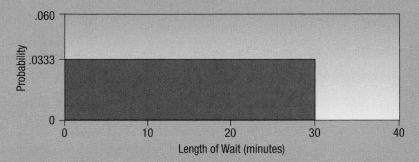

CHART 7–2 Uniform Probability Distribution of Student Waiting Times

2. The times students must wait for the bus is uniform over the interval from 0 minutes to 30 minutes, so in this case *a* is 0 and *b* is 30.

$$\text{Area} = (\text{height})(\text{base}) = \frac{1}{(30 - 0)}(30 - 0) = 1.00$$

3. To find the mean, we use formula (7–1).

$$\mu = \frac{a + b}{2} = \frac{0 + 30}{2} = 15$$

The mean of the distribution is 15 minutes, so the typical wait time for bus service is 15 minutes.

To find the standard deviation of the wait times, we use formula (7–2).

$$\sigma = \sqrt{\frac{(b - a)^2}{12}} = \sqrt{\frac{(30 - 0)^2}{12}} = 8.66$$

The standard deviation of the distribution is 8.66 minutes. This measures the variation in the student wait times.

4. The area within the distribution for the interval 25 to 30 represents this particular probability. From the area formula:

LO 7-2 Compute probabilities using the uniform distribution.

$$P(25 < \text{wait time} < 30) = (\text{height})(\text{base}) = \frac{1}{(30 - 0)}(5) = .1667$$

So the probability a student waits between 25 and 30 minutes is .1667. This conclusion is illustrated by the following graph.

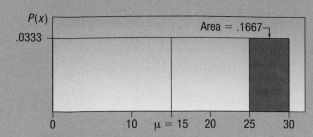

5. The area within the distribution for the interval 10 to 20 represents the probability.

$$P(10 < \text{wait time} < 20) = (\text{height})(\text{base}) = \frac{1}{(30 - 0)}(10) = .3333$$

We can illustrate this probability as follows.

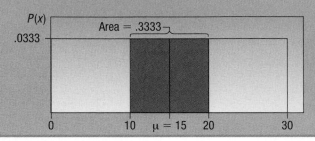

Self-Review 7–1 Australian sheepdogs have a relatively short life. The length of their life follows a uniform distribution between 8 and 14 years.
(a) Draw this uniform distribution. What are the height and base values?
(b) Show the total area under the curve is 1.00.
(c) Calculate the mean and the standard deviation of this distribution.
(d) What is the probability a particular dog lives between 10 and 14 years?
(e) What is the probability a dog will live less than 9 years?

Exercises

connect

1. A uniform distribution is defined over the interval from 6 to 10.
    a. What are the values for *a* and *b*?
    b. What is the mean of this uniform distribution?
    c. What is the standard deviation?
    d. Show that the total area is 1.00.
    e. Find the probability of a value more than 7.
    f. Find the probability of a value between 7 and 9.
2. A uniform distribution is defined over the interval from 2 to 5.
    a. What are the values for *a* and *b*?
    b. What is the mean of this uniform distribution?
    c. What is the standard deviation?
    d. Show that the total area is 1.00.
    e. Find the probability of a value more than 2.6.
    f. Find the probability of a value between 2.9 and 3.7.
3. The closing price of Schnur Sporting Goods Inc. common stock is uniformly distributed between $20 and $30 per share. What is the probability that the stock price will be:
    a. More than $27?
    b. Less than or equal to $24?

4. According to the Insurance Institute of America, a family of four spends between $400 and $3,800 per year on all types of insurance. Suppose the money spent is uniformly distributed between these amounts.
   a. What is the mean amount spent on insurance?
   b. What is the standard deviation of the amount spent?
   c. If we select a family at random, what is the probability they spend less than $2,000 per year on insurance?
   d. What is the probability a family spends more than $3,000 per year?
5. The April rainfall in Flagstaff, Arizona, follows a uniform distribution between 0.5 and 3.00 inches.
   a. What are the values for a and b?
   b. What is the mean amount of rainfall for the month? What is the standard deviation?
   c. What is the probability of less than an inch of rain for the month?
   d. What is the probability of *exactly* 1.00 inch of rain?
   e. What is the probability of more than 1.50 inches of rain for the month?
6. Customers experiencing technical difficulty with their Internet cable hookup may call an 800 number for technical support. It takes the technician between 30 seconds to 10 minutes to resolve the problem. The distribution of this support time follows the uniform distribution.
   a. What are the values for a and b in minutes?
   b. What is the mean time to resolve the problem? What is the standard deviation of the time?
   c. What percent of the problems take more than 5 minutes to resolve?
   d. Suppose we wish to find the middle 50% of the problem-solving times. What are the end points of these two times?

7.3 The Family of Normal Probability Distributions

Next, we consider the normal probability distribution. Unlike the uniform distribution [see formula (7–3)] the normal probability distribution has a very complex formula.

NORMAL PROBABILITY DISTRIBUTION
$$P(x) = \frac{1}{\sigma\sqrt{2\pi}} e^{-\left[\frac{(X-\mu)^2}{2\sigma^2}\right]}$$
[7–4]

However, do not be bothered by how complex this formula looks. You are already familiar with many of the values. The symbols μ and σ refer to the mean and the standard deviation, as usual. The Greek symbol π is a constant and its value is approximately 22/7 or 3.1416. The letter e is also a mathematical constant. It is the base of the natural log system and is approximately equal to 2.718. X is the value of a continuous random variable. So a normal distribution is based on—that is, it is defined by—its mean and standard deviation.

You will not need to make any calculations using formula (7–4). Instead, you will use a table, given in Appendix B.1, to find various probabilities. These probabilities can also be calculated using Excel functions and statistical software.

The normal probability distribution has the following major characteristics:

LO 7-3 List the characteristics of the normal distribution.

- It is **bell-shaped** and has a single peak at the center of the distribution. The arithmetic mean, median, and mode are equal and located in the center of the distribution. The total area under the curve is 1.00. Half the area under the normal curve is to the right of this center point and the other half to the left of it.
- It is **symmetrical** about the mean. If we cut the normal curve vertically at the center value, the two halves will be mirror images.
- It falls off smoothly in either direction from the central value. That is, the distribution is **asymptotic:** The curve gets closer and closer to the X-axis but never actually touches it. To put it another way, the tails of the curve extend indefinitely in both directions.
- The location of a normal distribution is determined by the mean, μ. The dispersion or spread of the distribution is determined by the standard deviation, σ.

These characteristics are shown graphically in Chart 7–3.

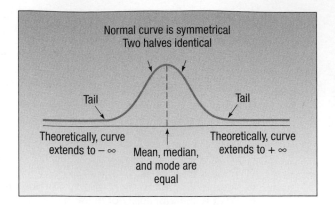

CHART 7–3 Characteristics of a Normal Distribution

There is not just one normal probability distribution, but rather a "family" of them. For example, in Chart 7–4 the probability distributions of length of employee service in three different plants are compared. In the Camden plant, the mean is 20 years and the standard deviation is 3.1 years. There is another normal probability distribution for the length of service in the Dunkirk plant, where $\mu = 20$ years and $\sigma = 3.9$ years. In the Elmira plant, $\mu = 20$ years and $\sigma = 5.0$ years. Note that the means are the same but the standard deviations are different.

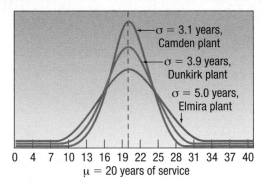

Equal means, unequal standard deviations

CHART 7–4 Normal Probability Distributions with Equal Means but Different Standard Deviations

Chart 7–5 shows the distribution of box weights of three different cereals. The weights follow a normal distribution with different means but identical standard deviations.

Unequal means, equal standard deviations

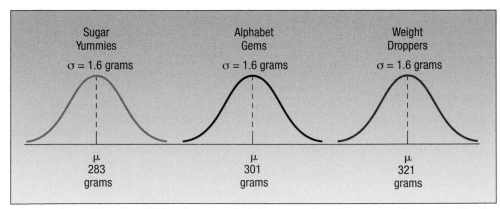

CHART 7–5 Normal Probability Distributions Having Different Means but Equal Standard Deviations

Unequal means, unequal standard deviations

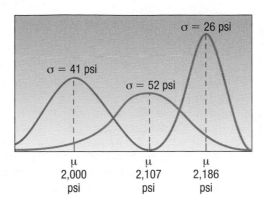

CHART 7–6 Normal Probability Distributions with Different Means and Standard Deviations

are between 60.0 inches (5 feet) and 76.4 inches (6 feet 4 inches). Shaquille O'Neal, a recently retired professional basketball player, is 86 inches or 7 feet 2 inches, which is clearly beyond 3 standard deviations from the mean. The height of a standard doorway is 6 feet 8 inches, and should be high enough for almost all adult males, except for a rare person like Shaquille O'Neal.

As another example, the driver's seat in most vehicles is set to comfortably fit a person who is at least 159 cm (62.5 inches) tall. The distribution of heights of adult women is approximately a normal distribution with a mean of 161.5 cm and a standard deviation of 6.3 cm. Thus about 35% of adult women will not fit comfortably in the driver's seat.

Finally, Chart 7–6 shows three normal distributions having different means and standard deviations. They show the distribution of tensile strengths, measured in pounds per square inch (psi), for three types of cables.

In Chapter 6, recall that discrete probability distributions show the specific likelihood a discrete value will occur. For example, in Section 6.5 on page 175, the binomial distribution is used to calculate the probability that none of the five flights arriving at the Bradford Pennsylvania Regional Airport would be late.

With a continuous probability distribution, areas below the curve define probabilities. The total area under the normal curve is 1.0. This accounts for all possible outcomes. Because a normal probability distribution is symmetric, the area under the curve to the left of the mean is 0.5, and the area under the curve to the right of the mean is 0.5. Apply this to the distribution of Sugar Yummies in Chart 7–5. It is normally distributed with a mean of 283 grams. Therefore, the probability of filling a box with more than 283 grams is 0.5 and the probability of filling a box with less than 283 grams is 0.5. We can also determine the probability that a box weighs between 280 and 286 grams. However, to determine this probability we need to know about the standard normal probability distribution.

7.4 The Standard Normal Probability Distribution

The number of normal distributions is unlimited, each having a different mean (μ), standard deviation (σ), or both. While it is possible to provide a limited number of probability tables for discrete distributions such as the binomial and the Poisson, providing tables for the infinite number of normal distributions is impractical. Fortunately, one member of the family can be used to determine the probabilities for all normal probability distributions. It is called the **standard normal probability distribution,** and it is unique because it has a mean of 0 and a standard deviation of 1.

Any *normal probability distribution* can be converted into a *standard normal probability distribution* by subtracting the mean from each observation and dividing this difference by the standard deviation. The results are called **z values** or **z scores.**

There is only one standard normal distribution. It has a mean of 0 and a standard deviation of 1.

> **z VALUE** The signed distance between a selected value, designated X, and the mean, μ, divided by the standard deviation, σ.

So, a z value is the distance from the mean, measured in units of the standard deviation.

In terms of a formula:

LO 7-4 Convert a normal distribution to the standard normal distribution.

> **STANDARD NORMAL VALUE** $$z = \frac{X - \mu}{\sigma}$$ [7–5]

LO 7-5 Find probabilities for a normally distributed random variable.

where:

X is the value of any particular observation or measurement.

μ is the mean of the distribution.

σ is the standard deviation of the distribution.

As noted in the preceding definition, a z value expresses the distance or difference between a particular value of X and the arithmetic mean in units of the standard deviation. Once the normally distributed observations are standardized, the z values are normally distributed with a mean of 0 and a standard deviation of 1. So the z distribution has all the characteristics of any normal probability distribution. These characteristics are listed on page 201. The table in Appendix B.1 (also on the inside back cover) lists the probabilities for the standard normal probability distribution. A small portion of this table follows.

TABLE 7–1 Areas under the Normal Curve

z	0.00	0.01	0.02	0.03	0.04	0.05	...
1.3	0.4032	0.4049	0.4066	0.4082	0.4099	0.4115	
1.4	0.4192	0.4207	0.4222	0.4236	0.4251	0.4265	
1.5	0.4332	0.4345	0.4357	0.4370	0.4382	0.4394	
1.6	0.4452	0.4463	0.4474	0.4484	0.4495	0.4505	
1.7	0.4554	0.4564	0.4573	0.4582	0.4591	0.4599	
1.8	0.4641	0.4649	0.4656	0.4664	0.4671	0.4678	
1.9	0.4713	0.4719	0.4726	0.4732	0.4738	0.4744	
.							
.							
.							

To explain, suppose we wish to compute the probability that boxes of Sugar Yummies weigh between 283 and 285.4 grams. From Chart 7–5, we know that the box weight of Sugar Yummies follows the normal distribution with a mean of 283 grams and a standard deviation of 1.6 grams. We want to know the probability or area under the curve between the mean, 283 grams, and 285.4 grams. We can also express this problem using probability notation, similar to the style used in the previous chapter: $P(283 < \text{weight} < 285.4)$. To find the probability, it is necessary to convert both 283 grams and 285.4 grams to z values using formula (7–5). The z value corresponding to 283 is 0, found by $(283 - 283)/1.6$. The z value corresponding to 285.4 is 1.50 found by $(285.4 - 283)/1.6$. Next, we go to the table in Appendix B.1. A portion of the table is repeated as Table 7–1. Go down the column of the table headed by the letter z to 1.5. Then, move horizontally to the right and read the probability under the column headed 0.00. It is 0.4332. This means the area under the curve between 0.00 and 1.50 is 0.4332. This is the probability that a randomly selected box of Sugar Yummies will weigh between 283 and 285.4 grams. This is illustrated in the following graph.

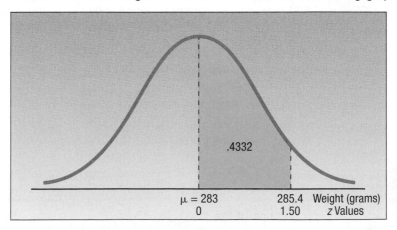

Applications of the Standard Normal Distribution

What is the area under the curve between the mean and X for the z values in Table 7–2 below? Check your answers against those given. You will need to use Appendix B.1 or the table located on the inside back cover of the text.

TABLE 7–2 Areas for Selected Values of z

Selected z Values	Area
2.84	.4977
1.00	.3413
0.49	.1879

Now we will compute the z value given the population mean, μ, the population standard deviation, σ, and a selected X.

Example

The weekly incomes of shift foremen in the glass industry follow the normal probability distribution with a mean of $1,000 and a standard deviation of $100. What is the z value for the income, let's call it X, of a foreman who earns $1,100 per week? For a foreman who earns $900 per week?

Solution

Using formula (7–5), the z values for the two X values ($1,100 and $900) are:

For $X = \$1,100$:

$$z = \frac{X - \mu}{\sigma}$$

$$= \frac{\$1,100 - \$1,000}{\$100}$$

$$= 1.00$$

For $X = \$900$:

$$z = \frac{X - \mu}{\sigma}$$

$$= \frac{\$900 - \$1,000}{\$100}$$

$$= -1.00$$

The z of 1.00 indicates that a weekly income of $1,100 is one standard deviation above the mean, and a z of -1.00 shows that a $900 income is one standard deviation below the mean. Note that both incomes ($1,100 and $900) are the same distance ($100) from the mean.

Self-Review 7–2

A recent national survey reported that the average person consumes 48 ounces of water per day. Assume the standard deviation of water consumption is 12.8 ounces per day and the consumption rate follows a normal probability distribution.
(a) What is the z value for a person who drinks 64 ounces of water per day? Based on the z value, how does this person compare to the national average?
(b) What is the z value for a person who drinks 32 ounces of water per day? Based on the z value, how does this person compare to the national average?

The Empirical Rule

Before examining further applications of the standard normal probability distribution, we will consider three areas under the normal curve that will be used extensively in the following chapters. These facts were called the Empirical Rule in Chapter 3 (see page 86).

LO 7-6 Find probabilities using the Empirical Rule.

1. About 68% of the area under the normal curve is within one standard deviation of the mean. This can be written as $\mu \pm 1\sigma$.
2. About 95% of the area under the normal curve is within two standard deviations of the mean, written as $\mu \pm 2\sigma$.
3. Practically all of the area under the normal curve is within three standard deviations of the mean, written as $\mu \pm 3\sigma$.

This information is summarized in the following graph.

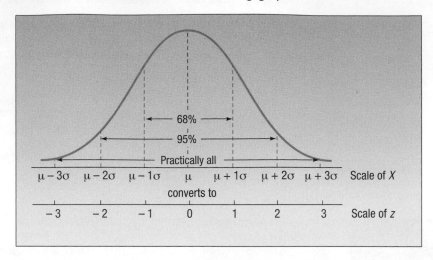

Transforming measurements to standard normal deviates changes the scale. The conversions are also shown in the graph. For example, $\mu + 1\sigma$ is converted to a z value of 1.00. Likewise, $\mu - 2\sigma$ is transformed to a z value of -2.00. Note that the center of the z distribution is zero, indicating no deviation from the mean, μ.

Example

As part of its quality assurance program, the Autolite Battery Company conducts tests on battery life. For a particular D-cell alkaline battery, the mean life is 19 hours. The useful life of the battery follows a normal distribution with a standard deviation of 1.2 hours. Answer the following questions.

1. About 68% of the batteries failed between what two values?
2. About 95% of the batteries failed between what two values?
3. Virtually all of the batteries failed between what two values?

Solution

We can use the results of the Empirical Rule to answer these questions.

1. About 68% of the batteries will fail between 17.8 and 20.2 hours, found by $19.0 \pm 1(1.2)$ hours.
2. About 95% of the batteries will fail between 16.6 and 21.4 hours, found by $19.0 \pm 2(1.2)$ hours.
3. Practically all failed between 15.4 and 22.6 hours, found by $19.0 \pm 3(1.2)$ hours.

This information is summarized on the following chart.

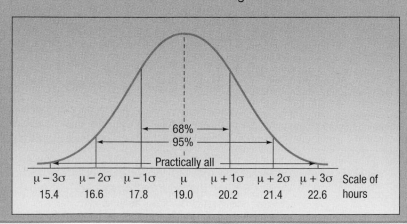

Self-Review 7–3

The distribution of the annual incomes of a group of middle-management employees at Compton Plastics approximates a normal distribution with a mean of $47,200 and a standard deviation of $800.
(a) About 68% of the incomes lie between what two amounts?
(b) About 95% of the incomes lie between what two amounts?
(c) Virtually all of the incomes lie between what two amounts?
(d) What are the median and the modal incomes?
(e) Is the distribution of incomes symmetrical?

Exercises

connect

7. Explain what is meant by this statement: "There is not just one normal probability distribution but a 'family' of them."
8. List the major characteristics of a normal probability distribution.
9. The mean of a normal probability distribution is 500; the standard deviation is 10.
   a. About 68% of the observations lie between what two values?
   b. About 95% of the observations lie between what two values?
   c. Practically all of the observations lie between what two values?
10. The mean of a normal probability distribution is 60; the standard deviation is 5.
    a. About what percent of the observations lie between 55 and 65?
    b. About what percent of the observations lie between 50 and 70?
    c. About what percent of the observations lie between 45 and 75?
11. The Kamp family has twins, Rob and Rachel. Both Rob and Rachel graduated from college two years ago, and each is now earning $50,000 per year. Rachel works in the retail industry, where the mean salary for executives with less than five years' experience is $35,000 with a standard deviation of $8,000. Rob is an engineer. The mean salary for engineers with less than five years' experience is $60,000 with a standard deviation of $5,000. Compute the z values for both Rob and Rachel and comment on your findings.
12. A recent article in *The Cincinnati Enquirer* reported that the mean labor cost to repair a heat pump is $90 with a standard deviation of $22. Monte's Plumbing and Heating Service completed repairs on two heat pumps this morning. The labor cost for the first was $75 and it was $100 for the second. Assume the distribution of labor costs follows the normal probability distribution. Compute z values for each and comment on your findings.

Finding Areas under the Normal Curve

The next application of the standard normal distribution involves finding the area in a normal distribution between the mean and a selected value, which we identify as X. The following example will illustrate the details.

Example

Recall in an earlier example (see page 205) we reported that the mean weekly income of a shift foreman in the glass industry is normally distributed with a mean of $1,000 and a standard deviation of $100. That is, $\mu = \$1,000$ and $\sigma = \$100$. What is the likelihood of selecting a foreman whose weekly income is between $1,000 and $1,100? We write this question in probability notation as: $P(\$1,000 < $ weekly income $< \$1,100)$.

Solution

We have already converted $1,100 to a z value of 1.00 using formula (7–5). To repeat:

$$z = \frac{X - \mu}{\sigma} = \frac{\$1,100 - \$1,000}{\$100} = 1.00$$

The probability associated with a *z* of 1.00 is available in Appendix B.1. A portion of Appendix B.1 follows. To locate the probability, go down the left column to 1.0, and then move horizontally to the column headed .00. The value is .3413.

z	0.00	0.01	0.02
.	.	.	.
.	.	.	.
.	.	.	.
0.7	.2580	.2611	.2642
0.8	.2881	.2910	.2939
0.9	.3159	.3186	.3212
1.0	.3413	.3438	.3461
1.1	.3643	.3665	.3686
.	.	.	.
.	.	.	.
.	.	.	.

The area under the normal curve between $1,000 and $1,100 is .3413. We could also say 34.13% of the shift foremen in the glass industry earn between $1,000 and $1,100 weekly, or the likelihood of selecting a foreman and finding his or her income is between $1,000 and $1,100 is .3413.

This information is summarized in the following diagram.

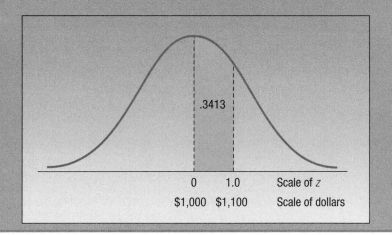

In the example just completed, we are interested in the probability between the mean and a given value. Let's change the question. Instead of wanting to know the probability of selecting at random a foreman who earned between $1,000 and $1,100, suppose we wanted the probability of selecting a foreman who earned less than $1,100. In probability notation, we write this statement as *P*(weekly income < $1,100). The method of solution is the same. We find the probability of selecting a foreman who earns between $1,000, the mean, and $1,100. This probability is .3413. Next, recall that half the area, or probability, is above the mean and half is below. So the probability of selecting a foreman earning less than $1,000 is .5000. Finally, we add the two probabilities, so .3413 + .5000 = .8413. About 84% of the foremen in the glass industry earn less than $1,100 per week. See the following diagram.

Statistics in Action

Many processes, such as filling soda bottles and canning fruit, are normally distributed. Manufacturers must guard against both over- and underfilling. If they put too much in the can or bottle, they are giving away their product. If they put too little in, the customer may feel cheated and the government may question the label description. "Control charts," with limits drawn three standard deviations above and below the mean, are routinely used to monitor this type of production process.

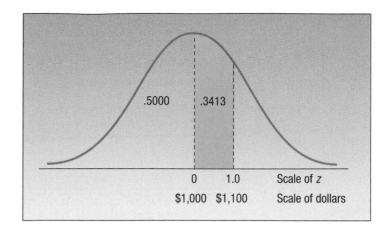

Excel will calculate this probability. The necessary commands are in the **Software Commands** section at the end of the chapter. The answer is .8413, the same as we calculated.

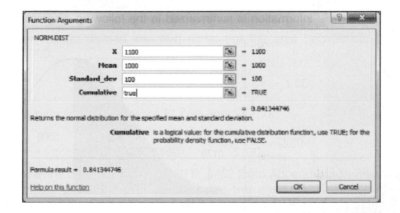

Example	Refer to the information regarding the weekly income of shift foremen in the glass industry. The distribution of weekly incomes follows the normal probability distribution, with a mean of $1,000 and a standard deviation of $100. What is the probability of selecting a shift foreman in the glass industry whose income is: 1. Between $790 and $1,000? 2. Less than $790?
Solution	We begin by finding the z value corresponding to a weekly income of $790. From formula (7–5): $$z = \frac{X - \mu}{s} = \frac{\$790 - \$1{,}000}{\$100} = -2.10$$ See Appendix B.1. Move down the left margin to the row 2.1 and across that row to the column headed 0.00. The value is .4821. So the area under the standard normal curve corresponding to a z value of 2.10 is .4821. However, because the normal distribution Is symmetric, the area between 0 and a negative z value is the same as that between 0 and the corresponding positive z value. The likelihood of finding a foreman earning between $790 and $1,000 is .4821. In probability notation, we write P($790 < weekly income < $1000) = .4821.

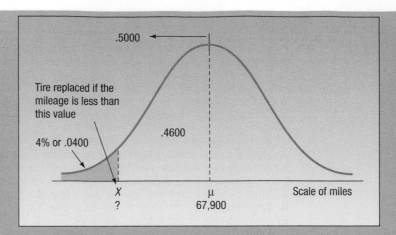

Inserting these values in formula (7–5) for z gives:

$$z = \frac{X - \mu}{\sigma} = \frac{X - 67{,}900}{2{,}050}$$

Notice that there are two unknowns, z and X. To find X, we first find z, and then solve for X. Notice the area under the normal curve to the left of μ is .5000. The area between μ and X is .4600, found by .5000 − .0400. Now refer to Appendix B.1. Search the body of the table for the area closest to .4600. The closest area is .4599. Move to the margins from this value and read the z value of 1.75. Because the value is to the left of the mean, it is actually −1.75. These steps are illustrated in Table 7–3.

TABLE 7–3 Selected Areas under the Normal Curve

z ...	.03	.04	.05	.06
.	.	.	.	.
.	.	.	.	.
.	.	.	.	.
1.5	.4370	.4382	.4394	.4406
1.6	.4484	.4495	.4505	.4515
1.7	.4582	.4591	.4599	.4608
1.8	.4664	.4671	.4678	.4686

Knowing that the distance between μ and X is -1.75σ or $z = -1.75$, we can now solve for X (the minimum guaranteed mileage):

$$z = \frac{X - 67{,}900}{2{,}050}$$

$$-1.75 = \frac{X - 67{,}900}{2{,}050}$$

$$-1.75(2{,}050) = X - 67{,}900$$

$$X = 67{,}900 - 1.75(2{,}050) = 64{,}312$$

So Layton can advertise that it will replace for free any tire that wears out before it reaches 64,312 miles, and the company will know that only 4% of the tires will be replaced under this plan.

Excel will also find the mileage value. See the following output. The necessary commands are given in the **Software Commands** section at the end of the chapter.

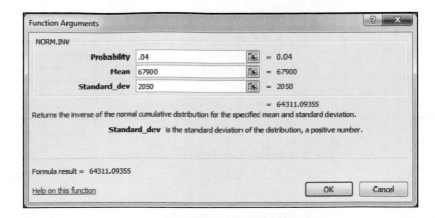

Self-Review 7–6

An analysis of the final test scores for Introduction to Business reveals the scores follow the normal probability distribution. The mean of the distribution is 75 and the standard deviation is 8. The professor wants to award an A to students whose score is in the highest 10%. What is the dividing point for those students who earn an A and those earning a B?

Exercises

connect™

23. A normal distribution has a mean of 50 and a standard deviation of 4. Determine the value below which 95% of the observations will occur.

24. A normal distribution has a mean of 80 and a standard deviation of 14. Determine the value above which 80% of the values will occur.

25. Assume that the mean hourly cost to operate a commercial airplane follows the normal distribution with a mean of $2,100 per hour and a standard deviation of $250. What is the operating cost for the lowest 3% of the airplanes?

26. The SAT Reasoning Test is perhaps the most widely used standardized test for college admissions in the United States. Scores are based on a normal distribution with a mean of 1,500 and a standard deviation of 300. Clinton College would like to offer an honors scholarship to students who score in the top 10% of this test. What is the minimum score that qualifies for the scholarship?

27. According to media research, the typical American listened to 195 hours of music in the last year. This is down from 290 hours four years earlier. Dick Trythall is a big country and western music fan. He listens to music while working around the house, reading, and riding in his truck. Assume the number of hours spent listening to music follows a normal probability distribution with a standard deviation of 8.5 hours.
   a. If Dick is in the top 1% in terms of listening time, how many hours does he listen per year?
   b. Assume that the distribution of times four years earlier also follows the normal probability distribution with a standard deviation of 8.5 hours. How many hours did the 1% who listen to the *least* music actually listen?

28. For the most recent year available, the mean annual cost to attend a private university in the United States was $26,889. Assume the distribution of annual costs follows the normal probability distribution and the standard deviation is $4,500. Ninety-five percent of all students at private universities pay less than what amount?

29. In economic theory, a "hurdle rate" is the minimum return that a person requires before they will make an investment. A research report says that annual returns from a specific class of common equities are distributed according to a normal distribution with a mean of 12% and a standard deviation of 18%. A stock screener would like to identify a hurdle rate such that only 1 in 20 equities is above that value. Where should the hurdle rate be set?

30. The manufacturer of a laser printer reports the mean number of pages a cartridge will print before it needs replacing is 12,200. The distribution of pages printed per cartridge closely follows the normal probability distribution and the standard deviation is 820 pages. The manufacturer wants to provide guidelines to potential customers as to how long they can expect a cartridge to last. How many pages should the manufacturer advertise for each cartridge if it wants to be correct 99% of the time?

Chapter Summary

I. The uniform distribution is a continuous probability distribution with the following characteristics.

  A. It is rectangular in shape.

  B. The mean and the median are equal.

  C. It is completely described by its minimum value a and its maximum value b.

  D. It is described by the following equation for the region from a to b:

$$P(x) = \frac{1}{b-a} \qquad \text{[7–3]}$$

  E. The mean and standard deviation of a uniform distribution are computed as follows:

$$\mu = \frac{(a+b)}{2} \qquad \text{[7–1]}$$

$$\sigma = \sqrt{\frac{(b-a)^2}{12}} \qquad \text{[7–2]}$$

II. The normal probability distribution is a continuous distribution with the following characteristics.

  A. It is bell-shaped and has a single peak at the center of the distribution.

  B. The distribution is symmetric.

  C. It is asymptotic, meaning the curve approaches but never touches the X-axis.

  D. It is completely described by its mean and standard deviation.

  E. There is a family of normal probability distributions.

  1. Another normal probability distribution is created when either the mean or the standard deviation changes.

  2. The normal probability distribution is described by the following formula:

$$P(x) = \frac{1}{\sigma\sqrt{2\pi}} e^{-\left[\frac{(x-\mu)^2}{2\sigma^2}\right]} \qquad \text{[7–4]}$$

III. The standard normal probability distribution is a particular normal distribution.

  A. It has a mean of 0 and a standard deviation of 1.

  B. Any normal probability distribution can be converted to the standard normal probability distribution by the following formula.

$$z = \frac{X - \mu}{\sigma} \qquad \text{[7–5]}$$

  C. By standardizing a normal probability distribution, we can report the distance of a value from the mean in units of the standard deviation.

Chapter Exercises

connect™

31. The amount of cola in a 12-ounce can is uniformly distributed between 11.96 ounces and 12.05 ounces.

  a. What is the mean amount per can?

  b. What is the standard deviation amount per can?

  c. What is the probability of selecting a can of cola and finding it has less than 12 ounces?

   d. What is the probability of selecting a can of cola and finding it has more than 11.98 ounces?

   e. What is the probability of selecting a can of cola and finding it has more than 11.00 ounces?

32. A tube of Listerine Tartar Control toothpaste contains 4.2 ounces. As people use the toothpaste, the amount remaining in any tube is random. Assume the amount of toothpaste remaining in the tube follows a uniform distribution. From this information, we can determine the following information about the amount remaining in a toothpaste tube without invading anyone's privacy.

   a. How much toothpaste would you expect to be remaining in the tube?

   b. What is the standard deviation of the amount remaining in the tube?

   c. What is the likelihood there is less than 3.0 ounces remaining in the tube?

   d. What is the probability there is more than 1.5 ounces remaining in the tube?

33. Many retail stores offer their own credit cards. At the time of the credit application, the customer is given a 10% discount on the purchase. The time required for the credit application process follows a uniform distribution with the times ranging from 4 minutes to 10 minutes.

   a. What is the mean time for the application process?

   b. What is the standard deviation of the process time?

   c. What is the likelihood a particular application will take less than 6 minutes?

   d. What is the likelihood an application will take more than 5 minutes?

34. The time patrons at the Grande Dunes Hotel in the Bahamas spend waiting for an elevator follows a uniform distribution between 0 and 3.5 minutes.

   a. Show that the area under the curve is 1.00.

   b. How long does the typical patron wait for elevator service?

   c. What is the standard deviation of the waiting time?

   d. What percent of the patrons wait for less than a minute?

   e. What percent of the patrons wait more than 2 minutes?

35. The net sales and the number of employees for aluminum fabricators with similar characteristics are organized into frequency distributions. Both are normally distributed. For the net sales, the mean is $180 million and the standard deviation is $25 million. For the number of employees, the mean is 1,500 and the standard deviation is 120. Clarion Fabricators had sales of $170 million and 1,850 employees.

   a. Convert Clarion's sales and number of employees to z values.

   b. Locate the two z values.

   c. Compare Clarion's sales and number of employees with those of the other fabricators.

36. The accounting department at Weston Materials Inc., a national manufacturer of unattached garages, reports that it takes two construction workers a mean of 32 hours and a standard deviation of 2 hours to erect the Red Barn model. Assume the assembly times follow the normal distribution.

   a. Determine the z values for 29 and 34 hours. What percent of the garages take between 32 hours and 34 hours to erect?

   b. What percent of the garages take between 29 hours and 34 hours to erect?

   c. What percent of the garages take 28.7 hours or less to erect?

   d. Of the garages, 5% take how many hours or more to erect?

37. A recent report in *USA Today* indicated a typical family of four spends $490 per month on food. Assume the distribution of food expenditures for a family of four follows the normal distribution, with a standard deviation of $90 per month.

   a. What percent of the families spend more than $30 but less than $490 per month on food?

   b. What percent of the families spend less than $430 per month on food?

   c. What percent spend between $430 and $600 per month on food?

   d. What percent spend between $500 and $600 per month on food?

38. A study of long-distance phone calls made from General Electric's corporate headquarters in Fairfield, Connecticut, revealed the length of the calls, in minutes, follows the normal probability distribution. The mean length of time per call was 4.2 minutes and the standard deviation was 0.60 minutes.

   a. What fraction of the calls last between 4.2 and 5 minutes?

   b. What fraction of the calls last more than 5 minutes?

   c. What fraction of the calls last between 5 and 6 minutes?

   d. What fraction of the calls last between 4 and 6 minutes?

   e. As part of her report to the president, the director of communications would like to report the length of the longest (in duration) 4% of the calls. What is this time?

39. Shaver Manufacturing Inc. offers dental insurance to its employees. A recent study by the human resource director shows the annual cost per employee per year followed the normal probability distribution, with a mean of $1,280 and a standard deviation of $420 per year.
   a. What fraction of the employees cost more than $1,500 per year for dental expenses?
   b. What fraction of the employees cost between $1,500 and $2,000 per year?
   c. Estimate the percent that did not have any dental expense.
   d. What was the cost for the 10% of employees who incurred the highest dental expense?

40. The annual commissions earned by sales representatives of Machine Products Inc., a manufacturer of light machinery, follow the normal probability distribution. The mean yearly amount earned is $40,000 and the standard deviation is $5,000.
   a. What percent of the sales representatives earn more than $42,000 per year?
   b. What percent of the sales representatives earn between $32,000 and $42,000?
   c. What percent of the sales representatives earn between $32,000 and $35,000?
   d. The sales manager wants to award the sales representatives who earn the largest commissions a bonus of $1,000. He can award a bonus to 20% of the representatives. What is the cutoff point between those who earn a bonus and those who do not?

41. According to the South Dakota Department of Health, the mean number of hours of TV viewing per week is higher among adult women than men. A recent study showed women spent an average of 34 hours per week watching TV and men 29 hours per week. Assume that the distribution of hours watched follows the normal distribution for both groups, and that the standard deviation among the women is 4.5 hours and is 5.1 hours for the men.
   a. What percent of the women watch TV less than 40 hours per week?
   b. What percent of the men watch TV more than 25 hours per week?
   c. How many hours of TV do the 1% of women who watch the most TV per week watch? Find the comparable value for the men.

42. According to a government study among adults in the 25- to 34-year age group, the mean amount spent per year on reading and entertainment is $1,994. Assume that the distribution of the amounts spent follows the normal distribution with a standard deviation of $450.
   a. What percent of the adults spend more than $2,500 per year on reading and entertainment?
   b. What percent spend between $2,500 and $3,000 per year on reading and entertainment?
   c. What percent spend less than $1,000 per year on reading and entertainment?

43. Management at Gordon Electronics is considering adopting a bonus system to increase production. One suggestion is to pay a bonus on the highest 5% of production based on past experience. Past records indicate weekly production follows the normal distribution. The mean of this distribution is 4,000 units per week and the standard deviation is 60 units per week. If the bonus is paid on the upper 5% of production, the bonus will be paid on how many units or more?

44. Fast Service Truck Lines uses the Ford Super Duty F-750 exclusively. Management made a study of the maintenance costs and determined the number of miles traveled during the year followed the normal distribution. The mean of the distribution was 60,000 miles and the standard deviation 2,000 miles.
   a. What percent of the Ford Super Duty F-750s logged 65,200 miles or more?
   b. What percent of the trucks logged more than 57,060 but less than 58,280 miles?
   c. What percent of the Fords traveled 62,000 miles or less during the year?
   d. Is it reasonable to conclude that any of the trucks were driven more than 70,000 miles? Explain.

45. Best Electronics Inc. offers a "no hassle" returns policy. The number of items returned per day follows the normal distribution. The mean number of customer returns is 10.3 per day and the standard deviation is 2.25 per day.
   a. In what percent of the days are there 8 or fewer customers returning items?
   b. In what percent of the days are between 12 and 14 customers returning items?
   c. Is there any chance of a day with no returns?

46. The funds dispensed at the ATM machine located near the checkout line at the Kroger's in Union, Kentucky, follows a normal probability distribution with a mean of $4,200 per day and a standard deviation of $720 per day. The machine is programmed to notify the nearby bank if the amount dispensed is very low (less than $2,500) or very high (more than $6,000).
  a. What percent of the days will the bank be notified because the amount dispensed is very low?
  b. What percent of the time will the bank be notified because the amount dispensed is high?
  c. What percent of the time will the bank not be notified regarding the amount of funds dispersed?

47. The weights of canned hams processed at Henline Ham Company follow the normal distribution, with a mean of 9.20 pounds and a standard deviation of 0.25 pounds. The label weight is given as 9.00 pounds.
  a. What proportion of the hams actually weigh less than the amount claimed on the label?
  b. The owner, Glen Henline, is considering two proposals to reduce the proportion of hams below label weight. He can increase the mean weight to 9.25 and leave the standard deviation the same, or he can leave the mean weight at 9.20 and reduce the standard deviation from 0.25 pounds to 0.15. Which change would you recommend?

48. *The Cincinnati Enquirer,* in its Sunday business supplement, reported that the mean number of hours worked per week by those employed full time is 43.9. The article further indicated that about one-third of those employed full time work less than 40 hours per week.
  a. Given this information and assuming that number of hours worked follows the normal distribution, what is the standard deviation of the number of hours worked?
  b. The article also indicated that 20% of those working full time work more than 49 hours per week. Determine the standard deviation with this information. Are the two estimates of the standard deviation similar? What would you conclude?

49. Most four-year automobile leases allow up to 60,000 miles. If the lessee goes beyond this amount, a penalty of 20 cents per mile is added to the lease cost. Suppose the distribution of miles driven on four-year leases follows the normal distribution. The mean is 52,000 miles and the standard deviation is 5,000 miles.
  a. What percent of the leases will yield a penalty because of excess mileage?
  b. If the automobile company wanted to change the terms of the lease so that 25% of the leases went over the limit, where should the new upper limit be set?
  c. One definition of a low-mileage car is one that is 4 years old and has been driven less than 45,000 miles. What percent of the cars returned are considered low-mileage?

50. The price of shares of Bank of Florida at the end of trading each day for the last year followed the normal distribution. Assume there were 240 trading days in the year. The mean price was $42.00 per share and the standard deviation was $2.25 per share.
  a. What percent of the days was the price over $45.00? How many days would you estimate?
  b. What percent of the days was the price between $38.00 and $40.00?
  c. What was the stock's price on the *highest* 15% of days?

51. The annual sales of romance novels follow the normal distribution. However, the mean and the standard deviation are unknown. Forty percent of the time sales are more than 470,000, and 10% of the time sales are more than 500,000. What are the mean and the standard deviation?

52. In establishing warranties on HDTV sets, the manufacturer wants to set the limits so that few will need repair at the manufacturer's expense. On the other hand, the warranty period must be long enough to make the purchase attractive to the buyer. For a new LCD HDTV, the mean number of months until repairs are needed is 36.84 with a standard deviation of 3.34 months. Where should the warranty limits be set so that only 10% of the LCD HDTVs need repairs at the manufacturer's expense?

53. A goal of U.S. airports handling international flights is to clear these flights within 45 minutes. Let's interpret this to mean that 95% of the flights are cleared in 45 minutes, so

5% of the flights take longer to clear. Let's also assume that the distribution is approximately normal.

a. If the standard deviation of the time to clear an international flight is 5 minutes, what is the mean time to clear a flight?

b. Suppose the standard deviation is 10 minutes, not the 5 minutes suggested in part (a). What is the new mean?

c. A customer has 30 minutes from the time her flight lands to catch her limousine. Assuming a standard deviation of 10 minutes, what is the likelihood that she will be cleared in time?

Data Set Exercises

(The data for these exercises are available at the text website www.mhhe.com/lindbasic8e).

54. Refer to the Real Estate data, which report information on homes sold in the Goodyear, Arizona, area during the last year.

a. The mean selling price (in $ thousands) of the homes was computed earlier to be $221.10, with a standard deviation of $47.11. Use the normal distribution to estimate the percentage of homes selling for more than $280.00. Compare this to the actual results. Does the normal distribution yield a good approximation of the actual results?

b. The mean distance from the center of the city is 14.629 miles, with a standard deviation of 4.874 miles. Use the normal distribution to estimate the number of homes 18 or more miles but less than 22 miles from the center of the city. Compare this to the actual results. Does the normal distribution yield a good approximation of the actual results?

55. Refer to the Baseball 2010 data that report information on the 30 Major League Baseball teams for the 2010 season.

a. The mean attendance per team for the season was 2.436 million, with a standard deviation of 0.713 million. Use the normal distribution to estimate the number of teams with attendance of more than 3.5 million. Compare that estimate with the actual number. Comment on the accuracy of your estimate.

b. The mean team payroll was $91.020 million, with a standard deviation of $38.258 million. Use the normal distribution to estimate the number of teams with a team salary of more than $50 million. Compare that estimate with the actual number. Comment on the accuracy of the estimate.

56. Refer to the Buena School District bus data.

a. Refer to the maintenance cost variable. The mean maintenance cost for last year is $450.29, with a standard deviation of 53.69. Estimate the number of buses with a cost of more than $500. Compare that with the actual number.

b. Refer to the variable on the number of miles driven. The mean is 830.11 and the standard deviation is 42.19 miles. Estimate the number of buses traveling more than 900 miles. Compare that number with the actual value.

Practice Test

Part 1—Objective

1. For a continuous probability distribution, the total area under the curve is equal to _____ .
2. For a uniform distribution that ranges from 10 to 20, how many values can be in that range? (1, 10, 100, infinite—pick one) _____ .
3. Which of the following is NOT a characteristic of the normal distribution? (bell-shaped, symmetrical, discrete, asymptotic—pick one) _____ .
4. For a normal distribution, what is true about the mean and median? (always equal, the mean is twice the median, the mean and median are equal to the standard deviation, none of these is true—pick one) _____ .
5. How many normal distributions are there? (1, 10, 30, infinite—pick one) _____ .
6. How many standard normal distributions are there? (1, 10, 30, infinite—pick one) _____ .
7. The signed difference between a selected value and the mean divided by the standard deviation is called a _____ . (z score, z value, standardized value, all of these—pick one)
8. What is the probability of a z value between 0 and -0.76? _____ .

9. What is the probability of a *z* value between −2.03 and 1.76? _____.
10. What is the probability of a *z* value between −1.86 and −1.43? _____.

Part 2—Problem

1. The IRS reports that the mean refund for a particular group of taxpayers was $1,600. The distribution of tax refunds follows a normal distribution with a standard deviation of $850.
   a. What percentage of the refunds are between $1,600 and $2,000?
   b. What percentage of the refunds are between $900 and $2,000?
   c. What percentage of the refunds are between $1,800 and $2,000?
   d. Ninety-five percent of the refunds are for less than what amount?

Software Commands

1. The Excel commands necessary to produce the output on page 209 are:
   a. Click on the **Formulas** tab in the top menu, then, on the far left, select **Insert Function fx.** Then, from the category box, select **Statistical** and below that **NORM.DIST,** and click **OK.**
   b. In the dialog box, put *1100* in the box for **X,** *1000* for the **Mean,** *100* for the **Standard_dev,** *True* in the **Cumulative** box, and click **OK.**
   c. The result will appear in the dialog box. If you click **OK,** the answer appears in your spreadsheet.
2. The Excel Commands necessary to produce the output on page 215 are:
   a. Click the **Formulas** tab in the top menu, then, on the far left, select **Insert Function fx.** Then, from the category box, select **Statistical** and below that **NORM.INV,** and click **OK.**
   b. In the dialog box, set the **Probability** to *.04*, the **Mean** to *67900*, and the **Standard_dev** to *2050*.
   c. The results will appear in the dialog box. Note that the answer is different from page 214 because of rounding error. If you click **OK,** the answer also appears in your spreadsheet.
   d. Try entering a **Probability** of *.04*, a **Mean** of *0*, and a **Standard_dev** of *1*. The *z* value will be computed.

Chapter 7   Answers to Self-Review

7–1 **a.**

$P(x)$

.167 —

8   14

b. $P(x)$ = (height)(base)

$$= \left(\frac{1}{14 - 8}\right)(14 - 8)$$

$$= \left(\frac{1}{6}\right)(6) = 1.00$$

c. $\mu = \dfrac{a + b}{2} = \dfrac{14 + 8}{2} = \dfrac{22}{2} = 11$

$$\sigma = \sqrt{\frac{(b - a)^2}{12}} = \sqrt{\frac{(14 - 8)^2}{12}} = \sqrt{\frac{36}{12}} = \sqrt{3}$$

$$= 1.73$$

d. $P(10 < x < 14)$ = (height)(base)

$$= \left(\frac{1}{14 - 8}\right)(14 - 10)$$

$$= \frac{1}{6}(4)$$

$$= .667$$

e. $P(x < 9)$ = (height)(base)

$$= \left(\frac{1}{14 - 8}\right)(9 - 8)$$

$$= 0.167$$

7–2 **a.** $z = (64 - 48)/12.8 = 1.25$. This person's difference of 16 ounces more than average is 1.25 standard deviations above the average.

b. $z = (32 - 48)/12.8 = -1.25$. This person's difference of 16 ounces less than average is 1.25 standard deviations below the average.

7–3 **a.** $46,400 and $48,000, found by $47,200 ± 1($800).

b. $45,600 and $48,800, found by $47,200 ± 2($800).

c. $44,800 and $49,600, found by $47,200 ± 3($800).

d. $47,200. The mean, median, and mode are equal for a normal distribution.

e. Yes, a normal distribution is symmetrical.

7–4 **a.** Computing *z*:

$$z = \frac{154 - 150}{5} = 0.80$$

Referring to Appendix B.1, the area is .2881. So $P(150 < \text{temp} < 154) = .2881$.

b. Computing z:

$$z = \frac{164 - 150}{5} = 2.80$$

Referring to Appendix B.1, the area is .4974. So $P(164 > \text{temp}) = .5000 - .4974 = .0026$.

7–5　a. Computing the z-values:

$$z = \frac{146 - 150}{5} = -0.80 \quad \text{and} \quad z = \frac{156 - 150}{5} = 1.20$$

$$P(146 < \text{temp} < 156) = P(-0.80 < z < 1.20) = .2881 + .3849 = .6730$$

b. Computing the z-values:

$$z = \frac{162 - 150}{5} = 2.40 \quad \text{and} \quad z = \frac{156 - 150}{5} = 1.20$$

$$P(156 < \text{temp} < 162) = P(1.20 < z < 2.40)$$
$$= .4918 - .3849 = .1069$$

7–6　85.24 (the instructor would no doubt make it 85). The closest area to .4000 is .3997; z is 1.28. Then:

$$1.28 = \frac{X - 75}{8}$$

$$10.24 = X - 75$$

$$X = 85.24$$

Sampling Methods and the Central Limit Theorem

Learning Objectives

When you have completed this chapter, you will be able to:

LO 8-1 Explain why a sample is often the only feasible way to learn something about a population.

LO 8-2 Describe methods to select a sample.

LO 8-3 Define sampling error.

LO 8-4 Describe the sampling distribution of the sample mean.

LO 8-5 Explain the central limit theorem.

LO 8-6 Define the standard error of the mean.

LO 8-7 Apply the central limit theorem to find probabilities of selecting possible sample means from a specified population.

The Nike annual report says that the average American buys 6.5 pairs of sports shoes per year. Suppose the population standard deviation is 2.1 and that a sample of 81 customers will be examined next year. What is the standard error of the mean in this experiment? (See Exercise 45 and LO 8-6.)

Statistics in Action

With the significant role played by inferential statistics in all branches of science, the availability of large sources of random numbers has become a necessity. The first book of random numbers, containing 41,600 random digits generated by L. Tippett, was published in 1927. In 1938, R. A. Fisher and F. Yates published 15,000 random digits generated using two decks of cards. In 1955, RAND Corporation published a million random digits, generated by the random frequency pulses of an electronic roulette wheel. By 1970, applications of sampling required billions of random numbers. Methods have since been developed for generating, using a computer, digits that are "almost" random and hence are called *pseudo-random*. The question of whether a computer program can be used to generate numbers that are truly random remains a debatable issue.

8.1 Introduction

Chapters 2 through 4 emphasize techniques to describe data. To illustrate these techniques, we organize the profits for the sale of 180 vehicles by the four dealers included in the Applewood Auto Group into a frequency distribution and compute various measures of location and dispersion. Such measures as the mean and the standard deviation describe the typical profit and the spread in the profits. In these chapters, the emphasis is on describing the condition of the data. That is, we describe something that has already happened.

In Chapter 5, we begin to lay the foundation for statistical inference with the study of probability. Recall that in statistical inference our goal is to determine something about a *population* based only on the *sample*. The population is the entire group of individuals or objects under consideration, and the sample is a part or subset of that population. Chapter 6 extends the probability concepts by describing two discrete probability distributions: the binomial and Poisson. Chapter 7 describes two continuous probability distributions: the uniform and normal. Probability distributions encompass all possible outcomes of an experiment and the probability associated with each outcome. We use probability distributions to evaluate the likelihood something occurs in the future.

This chapter begins our study of sampling. Sampling is a process of selecting items from a population so that we can use this information to make judgments or inferences about the population. We begin this chapter by discussing methods of selecting a sample from a population. Next, we construct a distribution of the sample mean to understand how the sample means tend to cluster around the population mean. Finally, we show that for any population the shape of this sampling distribution tends to follow the normal probability distribution.

8.2 Sampling Methods

In Chapter 1, we said the purpose of inferential statistics is to find something about a population based on a sample. A sample is a portion or part of the population of interest. In many cases, sampling is more feasible than studying the entire population. In this section, we discuss the major reasons for sampling, and then several methods for selecting a sample.

Reasons to Sample

When studying characteristics of a population, there are many practical reasons why we prefer to select portions or samples of a population to observe and measure. Here are some of the reasons for sampling:

1. **To contact the whole population would be time consuming.** A candidate for a national office may wish to determine her chances for election. A sample poll using the regular staff and field interviews of a professional polling firm would take only one or two days. Using the same staff and interviewers and working seven days a week, it would take nearly 200 years to contact all the voting population! Even if a large staff of interviewers could be assembled, the benefit of contacting all of the voters would probably not be worth the time.

2. **The cost of studying all the items in a population may be prohibitive.** Public opinion polls and consumer testing organizations, such as Harris International, CBS News Polls, and Zogby International, usually contact fewer than 2,000 of the nearly 60 million families in the United States. One consumer panel–type organization charges about $40,000 to mail samples and tabulate responses in order to test a product (such as breakfast cereal, cat food, or perfume). The same product test using all 60 million families would cost about $1 billion.

LO 8-1 Explain why a sample is often the only feasible way to learn something about a population.

3. **The physical impossibility of checking all items in the population.** Some populations are infinite. It would be impossible to check all the water in Lake Erie for bacterial levels, so we select samples at various locations. The populations of fish, birds, snakes, mosquitoes, and the like are large and are constantly moving, being born, and dying. Instead of even attempting to count all the ducks in Canada or all the fish in Lake Pontchartrain, we make estimates using various techniques—such as counting all the ducks on a pond picked at random, tracking fish catches, or netting fish at predetermined places in the lake.

4. **The destructive nature of some tests.** If the wine tasters at the Sutter Home Winery in California drank all the wine to evaluate the vintage, they would consume the entire crop, and none would be available for sale. In the area of industrial production, steel plates, wires, and similar products must have a certain minimum tensile strength. To ensure that the product meets the minimum standard, the Quality Assurance Department selects a sample from the current production. Each piece is stretched until it breaks and the breaking point (usually measured in pounds per square inch) recorded. Obviously, if all the wire or all the plates were tested for tensile strength, none would be available for sale or use. For the same reason, only a few seeds are tested for germination by Burpee Seeds Inc. prior to the planting season.

5. **The sample results are adequate.** Even if funds were available, it is doubtful the additional accuracy of a 100% sample—that is, studying the entire population—is essential in most problems. For example, the federal government uses a sample of grocery stores scattered throughout the United States to determine the monthly index of food prices. The prices of bread, beans, milk, and other major food items are included in the index. It is unlikely that the inclusion of all grocery stores in the United States would significantly affect the index, since the prices of milk, bread, and other major foods usually do not vary by more than a few cents from one chain store to another.

Simple Random Sampling

The most widely used type of sampling is a **simple random sample.**

LO 8-2 Describe methods to select a sample.

> **SIMPLE RANDOM SAMPLE** A sample selected so that each item or person in the population has the same chance of being included.

A table of random numbers is an efficient way to select members of the sample.

To illustrate simple random sampling and selection, suppose a population consists of 845 employees of Nitra Industries. A sample of 52 employees is to be selected from that population. One way of ensuring that every employee in the population has the same chance of being chosen is to first write the name of each employee on a small slip of paper and deposit all of the slips in a box. After they have been thoroughly mixed, the first selection is made by drawing a slip out of the box without looking at it. This process is repeated until the sample of 52 employees is chosen.

A more convenient method of selecting a random sample is to use the identification number of each employee and a **table of random numbers** such as the one in Appendix B.6. As the name implies, these numbers have been generated by a random process (in this case, by a computer). For each digit of a number, the probability of 0, 1, 2, . . . , 9 is the same. Thus, the probability that employee number 011 will be selected is the same as for employee 722 or employee 382. By using random numbers to select employees, bias is eliminated from the selection process.

A portion of a table of random numbers is shown in the following illustration. To select a sample of employees, you first choose a starting point in the table. Any starting point will do. Suppose the time is 3:04. You might look at the third column and then move down to the fourth set of numbers. The number is 03759. Since there are only 845 employees, we will use the first three digits of a five-digit random number. Thus, 037 is the number of the first employee to be a member of the sample. Another way of selecting the starting point is to close your eyes and point at a number in the table. To continue selecting employees, you could move in any direction. Suppose you move right. The first three digits of the number to the right of 03759 are 447—the number of the employee selected to be the second member of the sample. The next three-digit number to the right is 961. You skip 961 because there are only 845 employees. You continue to the right and select employee 784, then 189, and so on.

5 0 5 2 5	5 7 4 5 4	2 8 4 5 5	6 8 2 2 6	3 4 6 5 6	3 8 8 8 4	3 9 0 1 8
7 2 5 0 7	5 3 3 8 0	5 3 8 2 7	4 2 4 8 6	5 4 4 6 5	7 1 8 1 9	9 1 1 9 9
3 4 9 8 6	7 4 2 9 7	0 0 1 4 4	3 8 6 7 6	8 9 9 6 7	9 8 8 6 9	3 9 7 4 4
6 8 8 5 1	2 7 3 0 5	0 3 7 5 9	4 4 7 2 3	9 6 1 0 8	7 8 4 8 9	1 8 9 1 0
0 6 7 3 8	6 2 8 7 9	0 3 9 1 0	1 7 3 5 0	4 9 1 6 9	0 3 8 5 0	1 8 9 1 0
1 1 4 4 8	1 0 7 3 4	0 5 8 3 7	2 4 3 9 7	1 0 4 2 0	1 6 7 1 2	9 4 4 9 6

		Starting point	Second employee		Third employee	Fourth employee

Statistical packages, such as Minitab, and spreadsheet packages, such as Excel, have software that will select a simple random sample. The following example uses the Excel system to select a random sample.

Example

Jane and Joe Miley operate the Foxtrot Inn, a bed and breakfast in Tryon, North Carolina. There are eight rooms available for rent at this B&B. Listed below is the number of these eight rooms rented each day during June 2011. Use Excel to select a sample of five nights during the month of June.

June	Rentals	June	Rentals	June	Rentals
1	0	11	3	21	3
2	2	12	4	22	2
3	3	13	4	23	3
4	2	14	4	24	6
5	3	15	7	25	0
6	4	16	0	26	4
7	2	17	5	27	1
8	3	18	3	28	1
9	4	19	6	29	3
10	7	20	2	30	3

Solution

Excel will select the random sample and report the results. On the first sampled date, four of the eight rooms were rented. On the second sampled date in June, seven of the eight rooms were rented. The information is reported in column D of the Excel spreadsheet. The Excel steps are listed in the **Software Commands** section at the end of the chapter. The Excel system performs the sampling *with* replacement. This means it is possible for the same day to appear more than once in a sample.

	A	B	C	D	E
	Num 1 one sample				
1	June	Rentals		Sample	
2	1	0		4	
3	2	2		7	
4	3	3		4	
5	4	2		3	
6	5	3		1	
7	6	4			
8	7	2			
9	8	3			
10	9	4			
11	10	7			
12	11	3			
13	12	4			
14	13	4			
15	14	4			

Self-Review 8–1

The following class roster lists the students enrolling in an introductory course in business statistics. Three students are to be randomly selected and asked various questions regarding course content and method of instruction.

(a) The numbers 00 through 45 are handwritten on slips of paper and placed in a bowl. The three numbers selected are 31, 7, and 25. Which students would be included in the sample?

(b) Now use the table of random digits, Appendix B.6, to select your own sample.

(c) What would you do if you encountered the number 59 in the table of random digits?

```
              CSPM 264 01 BUSINESS & ECONOMIC STAT
                8:00 AM 9:40 AM MW ST 118 LIND D
```

RANDOM NUMBER	NAME	CLASS RANK	RANDOM NUMBER	NAME	CLASS RANK
00	ANDERSON, RAYMOND	SO	23	MEDLEY, CHERYL ANN	SO
01	ANGER, CHERYL RENEE	SO	24	MITCHELL, GREG R	FR
02	BALL, CLAIRE JEANETTE	FR	25	MOLTER, KRISTI MARIE	SO
03	BERRY, CHRISTOPHER G	FR	26	MULCAHY, STEPHEN ROBERT	SO
04	BOBAK, JAMES PATRICK	SO	27	NICHOLAS, ROBERT CHARLES	JR
05	BRIGHT, M. STARR	JR	28	NICKENS, VIRGINIA	SO
06	CHONTOS, PAUL JOSEPH	SO	29	PENNYWITT, SEAN PATRICK	SO
07	DETLEY, BRIAN HANS	JR	30	POTEAU, KRIS E	JR
08	DUDAS, VIOLA	SO	31	PRICE, MARY LYNETTE	SO
09	DULBS, RICHARD ZALFA	JR	32	RISTAS, JAMES	SR
10	EDINGER, SUSAN KEE	SR	33	SAGER, ANNE MARIE	SO
11	FINK, FRANK JAMES	SR	34	SMILLIE, HEATHER MICHELLE	SO
12	FRANCIS, JAMES P	JR	35	SNYDER, LEISHA KAY	SR
13	GAGHEN, PAMELA LYNN	JR	36	STAHL, MARIA TASHERY	SO
14	GOULD, ROBYN KAY	SO	37	ST. JOHN, AMY J	SO
15	GROSENBACHER, SCOTT ALAN	SO	38	STURDEVANT, RICHARD K	SO
16	HEETFIELD, DIANE MARIE	SO	39	SWETYE, LYNN MICHELE	SO
17	KABAT, JAMES DAVID	JR	40	WALASINSKI, MICHAEL	SO
18	KEMP, LISA ADRIANE	FR	41	WALKER, DIANE ELAINE	SO
19	KILLION, MICHELLE A	SO	42	WARNOCK, JENNIFER MARY	SO
20	KOPERSKI, MARY ELLEN	SO	43	WILLIAMS, WENDY A	SO
21	KOPP, BRIDGETTE ANN	SO	44	YAP, HOCK BAN	SO
22	LEHMANN, KRISTINA MARIE	JR	45	YODER, ARLAN JAY	JR

Systematic Random Sampling

The simple random sampling procedure may be awkward in some research situations. For example, suppose the sales division of Computer Graphic Inc. needs to quickly estimate the mean dollar revenue per sale during the past month. It finds that 2,000 sales invoices were recorded and stored in file drawers, and decides to select 100 invoices to estimate the mean dollar revenue. Simple random sampling requires the numbering of each invoice before using the random number table to select the 100 invoices. The numbering process would be a very time-consuming task. Instead, we use **systematic random sampling.**

> **SYSTEMATIC RANDOM SAMPLE** A random starting point is selected, and then every kth member of the population is selected.

First, k is calculated as the population size divided by the sample size. For Computer Graphic Inc., we would select every 20th (2,000/100) invoice from the file drawers; in so doing, the numbering process is avoided. If k is not a whole number, then round down.

Random sampling is used in the selection of the first invoice. For example, a number from a random number table between 1 and k, or 20, would be selected. Say the random number was 18. Then, starting with the 18th invoice, every 20th invoice (18, 38, 58, etc.) would be selected as the sample.

Before using systematic random sampling, we should carefully observe the physical order of the population. When the physical order is related to the population characteristic, then systematic random sampling should not be used. For example, if the invoices in the example were filed in order of increasing sales, systematic random sampling would not guarantee a random sample. Other sampling methods should be used.

Stratified Random Sampling

When a population can be clearly divided into groups based on some characteristic, we may use **stratified random sampling.** It guarantees each group is represented in the sample. The groups are also called **strata.** For example, college students can be grouped as full time or part time, male or female, or traditional or nontraditional. Once the strata are defined, we can apply simple random sampling within each group or stratum to collect the sample.

> **STRATIFIED RANDOM SAMPLE** A population is divided into subgroups, called strata, and a sample is randomly selected from each stratum.

For instance, we might study the advertising expenditures for the 352 largest companies in the United States. Suppose the objective of the study is to determine whether firms with high returns on equity (a measure of profitability) spent more of each sales dollar on advertising than firms with a low return or deficit. To make sure that the sample is a fair representation of the 352 companies, the companies are grouped on percent return on equity. Table 8–1 shows the strata and the relative frequencies. If simple random sampling was used, observe that firms in the 3rd and 4th strata have a high chance of selection (probability of 0.87) while firms in the other strata have a low chance of selection (probability of 0.13). We might not select any firms in stratum 1 or 5 *simply by chance.* However, stratified random sampling will guarantee that at least one firm in strata 1 and 5 are represented in the sample. Let's say that 50 firms are selected for intensive study. Then one (0.02 × 50) firm from stratum 1 would be randomly selected, five (0.10 × 50) firms from stratum 2 would be randomly selected, and so on. In this case, the number of firms sampled from each stratum is proportional to the stratum's relative frequency in the population. Stratified sampling has the advantage, in

Statistics in Action

Random and unbiased sampling methods are extremely important to make valid statistical inferences. In 1936, a straw vote to predict the outcome of the presidential race between Franklin Roosevelt and Alfred Landon was done. Ten million ballots in the form of returnable postcards were sent to addresses taken from telephone directories and automobile registrations. A high proportion of the ballots were returned, with 59% in favor of Landon and 41% favoring Roosevelt. On Election Day, Roosevelt won with 61% of the vote. Landon had 39%. In the mid-1930s people who had telephones and drove automobiles clearly did not represent American voters!

some cases, of more accurately reflecting the characteristics of the population than does simple random or systematic random sampling.

TABLE 8–1 Number Selected for a Proportional Stratified Random Sample

Stratum	Profitability (return on equity)	Number of Firms	Relative Frequency	Number Sampled
1	30% and over	8	0.02	1*
2	20 up to 30%	35	0.10	5*
3	10 up to 20%	189	0.54	27
4	0 up to 10%	115	0.33	16
5	Deficit	5	0.01	1
Total		352	1.00	50

*0.02 of 50 = 1, 0.10 of 50 = 5, etc.

Cluster Sampling

Another common type of sampling is **cluster sampling.** It is often employed to reduce the cost of sampling a population scattered over a large geographic area.

> **CLUSTER SAMPLE** A population is divided into clusters using naturally occurring geographic or other boundaries. Then, clusters are randomly selected and a sample is collected by randomly selecting from each cluster.

Suppose you want to determine the views of residents in Oregon about state and federal environmental protection policies. Selecting a random sample of residents in Oregon and personally contacting each one would be time consuming and very expensive. Instead, you could employ cluster sampling by subdividing the state into small units—either counties or regions. These are often called *primary units*.

Suppose you divided the state into 12 primary units, then selected at random four regions—2, 7, 4, and 12—and concentrated your efforts in these primary units. You could take a random sample of the residents in each of these regions and interview them. (Note that this is a combination of cluster sampling and simple random sampling.)

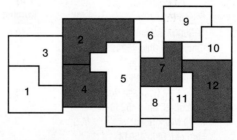

Many other sampling methods

The discussion of sampling methods in the preceding sections did not include all the sampling methods available to a researcher. Should you become involved in a major research project in marketing, finance, accounting, or other areas, you would need to consult books devoted solely to sample theory and sample design.

Self-Review 8–2

Refer to Self-Review 8–1 and the class roster on page 227. Suppose a systematic random sample will select every ninth student enrolled in the class. Initially, the fourth student on the list was selected at random. That student is numbered 03. Remembering that the random numbers start with 00, which students will be chosen to be members of the sample?

Exercises

connect™

1. The following is a list of Marco's Pizza stores in Lucas County. Also noted is whether the store is corporate-owned (C) or manager-owned (M). A sample of four locations is to be selected and inspected for customer convenience, safety, cleanliness, and other features.

ID No.	Address	Type	ID No.	Address	Type
00	2607 Starr Av	C	12	2040 Ottawa River Rd	C
01	309 W Alexis Rd	C	13	2116 N Reynolds Rd	C
02	2652 W Central Av	C	14	3678 Rugby Dr	C
03	630 Dixie Hwy	M	15	1419 South Av	C
04	3510 Dorr St	C	16	1234 W Sylvania Av	C
05	5055 Glendale Av	C	17	4624 Woodville Rd	M
06	3382 Lagrange St	M	18	5155 S Main	M
07	2525 W Laskey Rd	C	19	106 E Airport Hwy	C
08	303 Louisiana Av	C	20	6725 W Central	M
09	149 Main St	C	21	4252 Monroe	C
10	835 S McCord Rd	M	22	2036 Woodville Rd	C
11	3501 Monroe St	M	23	1316 Michigan Av	M

a. The random numbers selected are 08, 18, 11, 54, 02, 41, and 54. Which stores are selected?

b. Use the table of random numbers to select your own sample of locations.

c. A sample is to consist of every seventh location. The number 03 is the starting point. Which locations will be included in the sample?

d. Suppose a sample is to consist of three locations, of which two are corporate-owned and one is manager-owned. Select a sample accordingly.

2. The following is a list of hospitals in the Cincinnati (Ohio) and Northern Kentucky Region. Also included is whether the hospital is a general medical/surgical hospital (M/S) or a specialty hospital (S). We are interested in estimating the average number of full- and part-time nurses employed in the area hospitals.

a. A sample of five hospitals is to be randomly selected. The random numbers are 09, 16, 00, 49, 54, 12, and 04. Which hospitals are included in the sample?

b. Use a table of random numbers to develop your own sample of five hospitals.

ID Number	Name	Address	Type	ID Number	Name	Address	Type
00	Bethesda North	10500 Montgomery Cincinnati, Ohio 45242	M/S	10	Christ Hospital	2139 Auburn Avenue Cincinnati, Ohio 45219	M/S
01	Ft. Hamilton-Hughes	630 Eaton Avenue Hamilton, Ohio 45013	M/S	11	Deaconess Hospital	311 Straight Street Cincinnati, Ohio 45219	M/S
02	Jewish Hospital-Kenwood	4700 East Galbraith Rd. Cincinnati, Ohio 45236	M/S	12	Good Samaritan Hospital	375 Dixmyth Avenue Cincinnati, Ohio 45220	M/S
03	Mercy Hospital-Fairfield	3000 Mack Road Fairfield, Ohio 45014	M/S	13	Jewish Hospital	3200 Burnet Avenue Cincinnati, Ohio 45229	M/S
04	Mercy Hospital-Hamilton	100 Riverfront Plaza Hamilton, Ohio 45011	M/S	14	University Hospital	234 Goodman Street Cincinnati, Ohio 45267	M/S
05	Middletown Regional	105 McKnight Drive Middletown, Ohio 45044	M/S	15	Providence Hospital	2446 Kipling Avenue Cincinnati, Ohio 45239	M/S
06	Clermont Mercy Hospital	3000 Hospital Drive Batavia, Ohio 45103	M/S	16	St. Francis-St. George Hospital	3131 Queen City Avenue Cincinnati, Ohio 45238	M/S
07	Mercy Hospital-Anderson	7500 State Road Cincinnati, Ohio 45255	M/S	17	St. Elizabeth Medical Center, North Unit	401 E. 20th Street Covington, Kentucky 41014	M/S
08	Bethesda Oak Hospital	619 Oak Street Cincinnati, Ohio 45206	M/S	18	St. Elizabeth Medical Center, South Unit	One Medical Village Edgewood, Kentucky 41017	M/S
09	Children's Hospital Medical Center	3333 Burnet Avenue Cincinnati, Ohio 45229	M/S	19	St. Luke's Hospital West	7380 Turfway Drive Florence, Kentucky 41075	M/S

ID Number	Name	Address	Type	ID Number	Name	Address	Type
20	St. Luke's Hospital East	85 North Grand Avenue Ft. Thomas, Kentucky 41042	M/S	25	Drake Center Rehab— Long Term	151 W. Galbraith Road Cincinnati, Ohio 45216	S
21	Care Unit Hospital	3156 Glenmore Avenue Cincinnati, Ohio 45211	S	26	No. Kentucky Rehab Hospital—Short Term	201 Medical Village Edgewood, Kentucky	S
22	Emerson Behavioral Science	2446 Kipling Avenue Cincinnati, Ohio 45239	S	27	Shriners Burns Institute	3229 Burnet Avenue Cincinnati, Ohio 45229	S
23	Pauline Warfield Lewis Center for Psychiatric Treat.	1101 Summit Road Cincinnati, Ohio 45237	S	28	VA Medical Center	3200 Vine Cincinnati, Ohio 45220	S
24	Children's Psychiatric No. Kentucky	502 Farrell Drive Covington, Kentucky 41011	S				

      c. A sample is to consist of every fifth location. We select 02 as the starting point. Which hospitals will be included in the sample?

      d. A sample is to consist of four medical and surgical hospitals and one specialty hospital. Select an appropriate sample.

3. Listed below are the 35 members of the Metro Toledo Automobile Dealers Association. We would like to estimate the mean revenue from dealer service departments.

ID Number	Dealer	ID Number	Dealer	ID Number	Dealer
00	Dave White Acura	11	Thayer Chevrolet/Toyota	23	Kistler Ford, Inc.
01	Autofair Nissan	12	Spurgeon Chevrolet Motor Sales, Inc.	24	Lexus of Toledo
02	Autofair Toyota-Suzuki	13	Dunn Chevrolet	25	Mathews Ford Oregon, Inc.
03	George Ball's Buick GMC Truck	14	Don Scott Chevrolet	26	Northtowne Chevrolet
04	Yark Automotive Group	15	Dave White Chevrolet Co.	27	Quality Ford Sales, Inc.
05	Bob Schmidt Chevrolet	16	Dick Wilson Hyundai	28	Rouen Chrysler Jeep Eagle
06	Bowling Green Lincoln Mercury Jeep Eagle	17	Doyle Pontiac Buick	29	Saturn of Toledo
		18	Franklin Park Lincoln Mercury	30	Ed Schmidt Jeep Eagle
07	Brondes Ford	19	Genoa Motors	31	Southside Lincoln Mercury
08	Brown Honda	20	Great Lakes Ford Nissan	32	Valiton Chrysler
09	Brown Mazda	21	Grogan Towne Chrysler	33	Vin Divers
10	Charlie's Dodge	22	Hatfield Motor Sales	34	Whitman Ford

      a. We want to select a random sample of five dealers. The random numbers are: 05, 20, 59, 21, 31, 28, 49, 38, 66, 08, 29, and 02. Which dealers would be included in the sample?

      b. Use the table of random numbers to select your own sample of five dealers.

      c. A sample is to consist of every seventh dealer. The number 04 is selected as the starting point. Which dealers are included in the sample?

4. Listed below are the 27 Nationwide Insurance agents in the Toledo, Ohio, metropolitan area. We would like to estimate the mean number of years employed with Nationwide.

ID Number	Agent	ID Number	Agent	ID Number	Agent
00	**Bly Scott** 3332 W Laskey Rd	10	**Heini Bernie** 7110 W Centra	19	**Riker Craig** 2621 N Reynolds Rd
01	**Coyle Mike** 5432 W Central Av	11	**Hinckley Dave** 14 N Holland Sylvania Rd	20	**Schwab Dave** 572 W Dussel Dr
02	**Denker Brett** 7445 Airport Hwy			21	**Seibert John H** 201 S Main
03	**Denker Rollie** 7445 Airport Hwy	12	**Joehlin Bob** 3358 Navarre Av	22	**Smithers Bob** 229 Superior St
04	**Farley Ron** 1837 W Alexis Rd	13	**Keisser David** 3030 W Sylvania Av	23	**Smithers Jerry** 229 Superior St
05	**George Mark** 7247 W Central Av	14	**Keisser Keith** 5902 Sylvania Av	24	**Wright Steve** 105 S Third St
06	**Gibellato Carlo** 6616 Monroe St	15	**Lawrence Grant** 342 W Dussel Dr	25	**Wood Tom** 112 Louisiana Av
07	**Glemser Cathy** 5602 Woodville Rd	16	**Miller Ken** 2427 Woodville Rd	26	**Yoder Scott** 6 Willoughby Av
08	**Green Mike** 4149 Holland Sylvania Rd	17	**O'Donnell Jim** 7247 W Central Av		
09	**Harris Ev** 2026 Albon Rd	18	**Priest Harvey** 5113 N Summit St		

a. We want to select a random sample of four agents. The random numbers are: 02, 59, 51, 25, 14, 29, 77, 69, and 18. Which dealers would be included in the sample?

b. Use the table of random numbers to select your own sample of four agents.

c. A sample is to consist of every seventh dealer. The number 04 is selected as the starting point. Which agents will be included in the sample?

8.3 Sampling "Error"

In the previous section, we discussed sampling methods that are used to select a sample that is a fair and unbiased representation of the population. In each method, the selection of every possible sample of a specified size from a population has a known chance or probability. This is another way to describe an unbiased sampling method.

Samples are used to estimate population characteristics. For example, the mean of a sample is used to estimate the population mean. However, because the sample is a part or portion of the population, it is unlikely that the sample mean would be *exactly equal* to the population mean. Similarly, it is unlikely that the sample standard deviation would be *exactly equal* to the population standard deviation. We can therefore expect a difference between a *sample statistic* and its corresponding *population parameter*. This difference is called **sampling error.**

LO 8-3 Define sampling error.

> **SAMPLING ERROR** The difference between a sample statistic and its corresponding population parameter.

The following example clarifies the idea of sampling error.

Example	Refer to the Example/Solution on page 226, where we studied the number of rooms rented at the Foxtrot Inn bed and breakfast in Tryon, North Carolina. The variable of interest is the number of rooms rented each of the 30 nights in June 2011. Find the mean of the population. Use Excel or other statistical software to select three random samples of five nights. Calculate the mean of each sample and compare it to the population mean. What is the sampling error in each case?
Solution	During the month, there were a total of 94 rentals. So the mean number of units rented per night is 3.13. This is the population mean. Hence we designate this value with the Greek letter μ.

$$\mu = \frac{\Sigma X}{N} = \frac{0 + 2 + 3 + \cdots + 3}{30} = \frac{94}{30} = 3.13$$

The first random sample of five nights resulted in the following number of rooms rented: 4, 7, 4, 3, and 1. The mean of this sample of five nights is 3.8 rooms, which we designate as $\overline{X}_1$. The bar over the X reminds us that it is a sample mean and the subscript 1 indicates it is the mean of the first sample.

$$\overline{X}_1 = \frac{\Sigma X}{n} = \frac{4 + 7 + 4 + 3 + 1}{5} = \frac{19}{5} = 3.80$$

The sampling error for the first sample is the difference between the first sample mean (3.80) and the population mean (3.13). Hence, the sampling error is ($\overline{X}_1 - \mu = 3.80 - 3.13 = 0.67$). The second random sample of five nights from the population of all 30 nights in June revealed the following number of rooms rented: 3, 3, 2, 3, and 6. The mean of these five values is 3.4, found by

$$\overline{X}_2 = \frac{\Sigma X}{n} = \frac{3 + 3 + 2 + 3 + 6}{5} = 3.4$$

The sampling error is ($\overline{X}_2 - \mu = 3.4 - 3.13 = 0.27$).

In the third random sample, the mean was 1.8 and the sampling error was −1.33.

Each of these differences, 0.67, 0.27, and −1.33, is the sampling error made in estimating the population mean. Sometimes these errors are positive values, indicating that the sample mean overestimated the population mean; other times they are negative values, indicating the sample mean was less than the population mean.

Random Samples

	A	B	C	D	E	F	G	H
1	June	Rentals			Sample 1	Sample 2	Sample 3	
2	1	0			4	3	0	
3	2	2			7	3	0	
4	3	3			4	2	3	
5	4	2			3	3	3	
6	5	3			1	6	3	
7	6	4		Totals	19	17	9	
8	7	2		Sample means	3.8	3.4	1.8	
9	8	3						
10	9	4						
11	10	7						
12	11	3						
13	12	4						
14	13	4						
15	14	4						
16	15	7						

In this case, where we have a population of 30 values and samples of 5 values, there is a very large number of possible samples—142,506 to be exact! To find this value, use the combination formula (5–9) in Section 5.7 on page 152. Each of the 142,506 different samples has the same chance of being selected. Each sample may have a different sample mean and therefore a different sampling error. The value of the sampling error is based on the particular one of the 142,506 different possible samples selected. Therefore, the sampling errors are random and occur by chance. If you were to determine the sum of these sampling errors over a large number of samples, the result would be very close to zero. This is true because the sample mean is an *unbiased estimator* of the population mean.

A sample mean is an unbiased estimate of the population mean.

8.4 Sampling Distribution of the Sample Mean

LO 8-4 Describe the sampling distribution of the sample mean.

Now that we have discovered the possibility of a sampling error when sample results are used to estimate a population parameter, how can we make an accurate prediction about the possible success of a newly developed toothpaste or other product, based only on sample results? How can the quality-assurance department in a mass-production firm release a shipment of microchips based only on a sample of 10 chips? How can the CNN/*USA Today* or ABC News/*Washington Post* polling organizations make an accurate prediction about a presidential race based on a sample of 1,200 registered voters out of a voting population of nearly 90 million? To answer these questions, we first develop a *sampling distribution of the sample mean*.

Sample means vary from sample to sample.

The sample means in the previous Example/Solution varied from one sample to the next. The mean of the first sample of five days was 3.80 rooms, and the second sample mean was 3.40 rooms. The population mean was 3.13 rooms. If we organized the means of all possible samples of five days into a probability distribution, the result is called the **sampling distribution of the sample mean.**

> **SAMPLING DISTRIBUTION OF THE SAMPLE MEAN** A probability distribution of all possible sample means of a given sample size.

The following example illustrates the construction of a sampling distribution of the sample mean.

Example

Tartus Industries has seven production employees (considered the population). The hourly earnings of each employee are given in Table 8–2.

TABLE 8–2 Hourly Earnings of the Production Employees of Tartus Industries

Employee	Hourly Earnings	Employee	Hourly Earnings
Joe	$7	Jan	$7
Sam	7	Art	8
Sue	8	Ted	9
Bob	8		

1. What is the population mean?
2. What is the sampling distribution of the sample mean for samples of size 2?
3. What is the mean of the sampling distribution?
4. What observations can be made about the population and the sampling distribution?

Solution

Here are the solutions to the questions.

1. The population mean is $7.71, found by:

$$\mu = \frac{\Sigma X}{N} = \frac{\$7 + \$7 + \$8 + \$8 + \$7 + \$8 + \$9}{7} = \$7.71$$

We identify the population mean with the Greek letter μ. Our policy, stated in Chapters 1, 3, and 4, is to identify population parameters with Greek letters.

2. To arrive at the sampling distribution of the sample mean, we need to select all possible samples of 2 without replacement from the population, then compute the mean of each sample. There are 21 possible samples, found by using formula (5–9) in Section 5.7 on page 152.

$$_NC_n = \frac{N!}{n!(N - n)!} = \frac{7!}{2!(7 - 2)!} = 21$$

where $N = 7$ is the number of items in the population and $n = 2$ is the number of items in the sample.

The 21 sample means from all possible samples of 2 that can be drawn from the population are shown in Table 8–3. These 21 sample means are used to construct a probability distribution. This is the sampling distribution of the sample mean, and it is summarized in Table 8–4.

TABLE 8–3 Sample Means for All Possible Samples of Two Employees

Sample	Employees	Hourly Earnings	Sum	Mean	Sample	Employees	Hourly Earnings	Sum	Mean
1	Joe, Sam	$7, $7	$14	$7.00	12	Sue, Bob	$8, $8	$16	$8.00
2	Joe, Sue	7, 8	15	7.50	13	Sue, Jan	8, 7	15	7.50
3	Joe, Bob	7, 8	15	7.50	14	Sue, Art	8, 8	16	8.00
4	Joe, Jan	7, 7	14	7.00	15	Sue, Ted	8, 9	17	8.50
5	Joe, Art	7, 8	15	7.50	16	Bob, Jan	8, 7	15	7.50
6	Joe, Ted	7, 9	16	8.00	17	Bob, Art	8, 8	16	8.00
7	Sam, Sue	7, 8	15	7.50	18	Bob, Ted	8, 9	17	8.50
8	Sam, Bob	7, 8	15	7.50	19	Jan, Art	7, 8	15	7.50
9	Sam, Jan	7, 7	14	7.00	20	Jan, Ted	7, 9	16	8.00
10	Sam, Art	7, 8	15	7.50	21	Art, Ted	8, 9	17	8.50
11	Sam, Ted	7, 9	16	8.00					

TABLE 8–4 Sampling Distribution of the Sample Mean for $n = 2$

Sample Mean	Number of Means	Probability
$7.00	3	.1429
7.50	9	.4285
8.00	6	.2857
8.50	3	.1429
	21	1.0000

3. Using the data in Table 8–3 on the previous page, the mean of the sampling distribution of the sample mean is obtained by summing all sample means and dividing the sum by the number of samples. The mean of all the sample means is usually written $\mu_{\bar{X}}$. The μ reminds us that it is a population value because we have considered all possible samples. The subscript $\bar{X}$ indicates that it is the sampling distribution of the sample mean.

$$\mu_{\bar{X}} = \frac{\text{Sum of all sample means}}{\text{Total number of samples}} = \frac{\$7.00 + \$7.50 + \$7.50 + \cdots + \$8.00 + \$8.50}{21}$$

$$= \frac{\$162}{21} = \$7.71$$

Population mean is equal to the mean of the sample means.

4. Refer to Chart 8–1, which shows both the population distribution and the distribution of the sample mean. These observations can be made:
    a. The mean of the distribution of the sample mean ($7.71) is equal to the mean of the population: $\mu = \mu_{\bar{X}}$.
    b. The spread in the distribution of the sample mean is less than the spread in the population values. The sample mean ranges from $7.00 to $8.50, while the population values vary from $7.00 up to $9.00. Notice, as we increase the size of the sample, the spread of the distribution of the sample mean becomes smaller.
    c. The shape of the sampling distribution of the sample mean and the shape of the frequency distribution of the population values are different. The distribution of the sample mean tends to be more bell-shaped and to approximate the normal probability distribution.

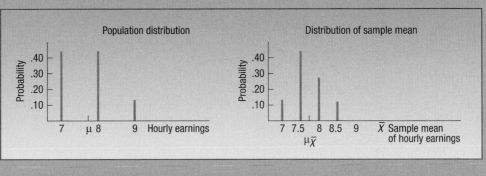

CHART 8–1 Distributions of Population Values and Sample Mean

In summary, we took all possible random samples from a population and for each sample calculated a sample statistic (the mean amount earned). This example illustrates important relationships between the population distribution and the sampling distribution of the sample mean:

1. The mean of the sample means is exactly equal to the population mean.
2. The dispersion of the sampling distribution of sample means is narrower than the population distribution.
3. The sampling distribution of sample means tends to become bell-shaped and to approximate the normal probability distribution.

Given a bell-shaped or normal probability distribution, we will be able to apply concepts from Chapter 7 to determine the probability of selecting a sample with a specified sample mean. In the next section, we will show the importance of sample size as it relates to the sampling distribution of sample means.

Self-Review 8–3

The years of service of all the executives employed by Standard Chemicals are:

Name	Years
Mr. Snow	20
Ms. Tolson	22
Mr. Kraft	26
Ms. Irwin	24
Mr. Jones	28

(a) Using the combination formula, how many samples of size 2 are possible?
(b) List all possible samples of 2 executives from the population and compute their means.
(c) Organize the means into a sampling distribution.
(d) Compare the population mean and the mean of the sample means.
(e) Compare the dispersion in the population with that in the distribution of the sample mean.
(f) A chart portraying the population values follows. Is the distribution of population values normally distributed (bell-shaped)?

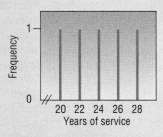

(g) Is the distribution of the sample mean computed in part (c) starting to show some tendency toward being bell-shaped?

Exercises

5. A population consists of the following four values: 12, 12, 14, and 16.
   a. List all samples of size 2, and compute the mean of each sample.
   b. Compute the mean of the distribution of the sample mean and the population mean. Compare the two values.
   c. Compare the dispersion in the population with that of the sample mean.

6. A population consists of the following five values: 2, 2, 4, 4, and 8.
   a. List all samples of size 2, and compute the mean of each sample.
   b. Compute the mean of the distribution of sample means and the population mean. Compare the two values.
   c. Compare the dispersion in the population with that of the sample means.

7. A population consists of the following five values: 12, 12, 14, 15, and 20.
   a. List all samples of size 3, and compute the mean of each sample.
   b. Compute the mean of the distribution of sample means and the population mean. Compare the two values.
   c. Compare the dispersion in the population with that of the sample means.

8. A population consists of the following five values: 0, 0, 1, 3, 6.
   a. List all samples of size 3, and compute the mean of each sample.
   b. Compute the mean of the distribution of sample means and the population mean. Compare the two values.
   c. Compare the dispersion in the population with that of the sample means.

9. In the law firm Tybo and Associates, there are six partners. Listed next is the number of cases each associate actually tried in court last month.

Associate	Number of Cases
Ruud	3
Wu	6
Sass	3
Flores	3
Wilhelms	0
Schueller	1

  a. How many different samples of 3 are possible?
  b. List all possible samples of size 3, and compute the mean number of cases in each sample.
  c. Compare the mean of the distribution of sample means to the population mean.
  d. On a chart similar to Chart 8–1, compare the dispersion in the population with that of the sample means.

10. There are five sales associates at Mid-Motors Ford. The five representatives and the number of cars they sold last week are:

Sales Representative	Cars Sold
Peter Hankish	8
Connie Stallter	6
Juan Lopez	4
Ted Barnes	10
Peggy Chu	6

  a. How many different samples of size 2 are possible?
  b. List all possible samples of size 2, and compute the mean of each sample.
  c. Compare the mean of the sampling distribution of sample means with that of the population.
  d. On a chart similar to Chart 8–1, compare the dispersion in sample means with that of the population.

8.5 The Central Limit Theorem

LO 8-5 Explain the central limit theorem.

In this section, we examine the **central limit theorem.** Its application to the sampling distribution of the sample mean, introduced in the previous section, allows us to use the normal probability distribution to create confidence intervals for the population mean (described in Chapter 9) and perform tests of hypothesis (described in Chapter 10). The central limit theorem states that, for large random samples, the shape of the sampling distribution of the sample mean is close to the normal probability distribution. The approximation is more accurate for large samples than for small samples. This is one of the most useful conclusions in statistics. We can reason about the distribution of the sample mean with absolutely no information about the shape of the population distribution from which the sample is taken. In other words, the central limit theorem is true for all distributions.

A formal statement of the central limit theorem follows.

> **CENTRAL LIMIT THEOREM** If all samples of a particular size are selected from any population, the sampling distribution of the sample mean is approximately a normal distribution. This approximation improves with larger samples.

If the population follows a normal probability distribution, then for any sample size the sampling distribution of the sample mean will also be normal. If the population distribution is symmetrical (but not normal), you will see the normal shape of the distribution of the sample mean emerge with samples as small as 10. On the other hand, if you start with a distribution that is skewed or has thick tails, it may require samples of 30 or more to observe the normality feature. This concept is summarized in Chart 8–2

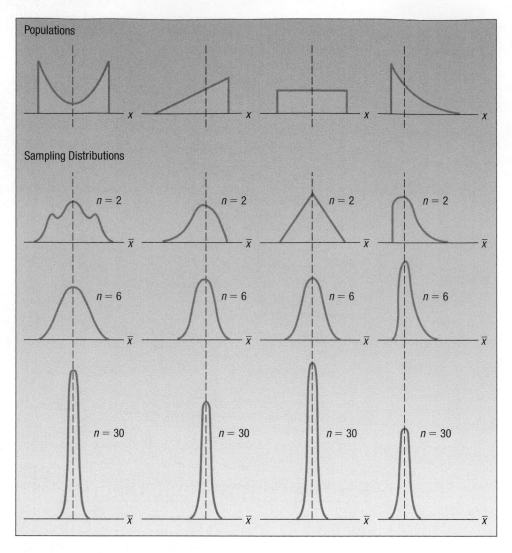

CHART 8–2 Results of the Central Limit Theorem for Several Populations

for various population shapes. Observe the convergence to a normal distribution regardless of the shape of the population distribution.

The idea that the distribution of the sample means from a population that is not normal will converge to normality is illustrated in Charts 8–3, 8–4, and 8–5. We will discuss this example in more detail shortly, but Chart 8–3 is a graph of a frequency distribution that is positively skewed. There are many possible samples of 5 that might be selected from this population. Suppose we randomly select 25 samples of size 5 each from the population portrayed in Chart 8–3 and compute the mean of each sample. These results are shown in Chart 8–4. Notice that the shape of the distribution of sample means has changed from the shape of the original population even though we selected only 25 of the many possible samples. To put it another way, we selected 25 random samples of 5 each from a population that is positively skewed and found the distribution of sample means has changed from the shape of the population. As we take larger samples, that is, $n = 20$ instead of $n = 5$, we will find the distribution of the sample mean will approach the normal distribution. Chart 8–5 shows the results of 25 random samples of 20 observations each from the same population. Observe the clear trend toward the normal probability distribution. This is the point of the central limit theorem. The following example will underscore this condition.

Any sampling distribution of the sample mean will move toward a normal distribution as we increase the sample size.

Example

Ed Spence began his sprocket business 20 years ago. The business has grown over the years and now employs 40 people. Spence Sprockets Inc. faces some major decisions regarding health care for these employees. Before making a final decision on what health care plan to purchase, Ed decides to form a committee of five representative employees. The committee will be asked to study the health care issue carefully and make a recommendation as to what plan best fits the employees' needs. Ed feels the views of newer employees toward health care may differ from those of more experienced employees. If Ed randomly selects this committee, what can he expect in terms of the mean years with Spence Sprockets for those on the committee? How does the shape of the distribution of years of service of all employees (the population) compare with the shape of the sampling distribution of the mean? The years of service (rounded to the nearest year) of the 40 employees currently on the Spence Sprockets Inc. payroll are as follows.

11	4	18	2	1	2	0	2	2	4
3	4	1	2	2	3	3	19	8	3
7	1	0	2	7	0	4	5	1	14
16	8	9	1	1	2	5	10	2	3

Solution

Chart 8–3 shows a histogram for the frequency distribution of the years of service for the population of 40 current employees. This distribution is positively skewed. Why? Because the business has grown in recent years, the distribution shows that 29 of the 40 employees have been with the company less than six years. Also, there are 11 employees who have worked at Spence Sprockets for more than six years. In particular, four employees have been with the company 12 years or more (count the frequencies above 12). So there is a long tail in the distribution of service years to the right, that is, the distribution is positively skewed.

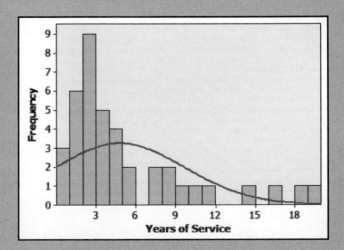

CHART 8–3 Years of Service for Spence Sprockets Inc. Employees

Let's consider the first of Ed Spence's problems. He would like to form a committee of five employees to look into the health care question and suggest what type of health care coverage would be most appropriate for the majority of workers. How should he select the committee? If he selects the committee randomly, what might he expect in terms of mean years of service for those on the committee?

To begin, Ed writes the years of service for each of the 40 employees on pieces of paper and puts them into an old baseball hat. Next, he shuffles the pieces of paper and randomly selects five slips of paper. The years of service for these five employees are 1, 9, 0, 19, and 14 years. Thus, the mean years of service for these five sampled employees is 8.60 years. How does that compare with the population mean? At this point, Ed does not know the population mean, but the number of employees in the population is only 40, so he decides to calculate the mean years of service for *all* his employees. It is 4.8 years, found by adding the years of service for *all* the employees and dividing the total by 40.

$$\mu = \frac{11 + 4 + 18 + \cdots + 2 + 3}{40} = 4.80$$

The difference between the sample mean $(\overline{X})$ and the population mean (μ) is called **sampling error.** In other words, the difference of 3.80 years between the sample mean of 8.60 and the population mean of 4.80 is the sampling error. It is due to chance. Thus, if Ed selected these five employees to constitute the committee, their mean years of service would be larger than the population mean.

What would happen if Ed put the five pieces of paper back into the baseball hat and selected another sample? Would you expect the mean of this second sample to be exactly the same as the previous one? Suppose he selects another sample of five employees and finds the years of service in this sample to be 7, 4, 4, 1, and 3. This sample mean is 3.80 years. The result of selecting 25 samples of five employees and computing the mean for each sample is shown in Table 8–5 and Chart 8–4. There are actually 658,008 possible samples of 5 from the population of 40 employees, found

TABLE 8–5 Twenty-Five Random Samples of Five Employees

Sample	Obs 1	Obs 2	Obs 3	Obs 4	Obs 5	Sum	Mean
A	1	9	0	19	14	43	8.6
B	7	4	4	1	3	19	3.8
C	8	19	8	2	1	38	7.6
D	4	18	2	0	11	35	7.0
E	4	2	4	7	18	35	7.0
F	1	2	0	3	2	8	1.6
G	2	3	2	0	2	9	1.8
H	11	2	9	2	4	28	5.6
I	9	0	4	2	7	22	4.4
J	1	1	1	11	1	15	3.0
K	2	0	0	10	2	14	2.8
L	0	2	3	2	16	23	4.6
M	2	3	1	1	1	8	1.6
N	3	7	3	4	3	20	4.0
O	1	2	3	1	4	11	2.2
P	19	0	1	3	8	31	6.2
Q	5	1	7	14	9	36	7.2
R	5	4	2	3	4	18	3.6
S	14	5	2	2	5	28	5.6
T	2	1	1	4	7	15	3.0
U	3	7	1	2	1	14	2.8
V	0	1	5	1	2	9	1.8
W	0	3	19	4	2	28	5.6
X	4	2	3	4	0	13	2.6
Y	1	1	2	3	2	9	1.8

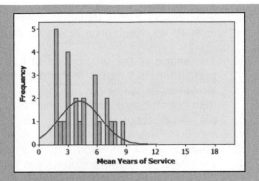

CHART 8–4 Histogram of Mean Years of Service for 25 Samples of Five Employees

by the combination formula (5–9) for 40 things taken 5 at a time. Notice the difference in the shape of the population and the distribution of these sample means. The population of the years of service for employees (Chart 8–3) is positively skewed, but the distribution of these 25 sample means does not reflect the same positive skew. There is also a difference in the range of the sample means versus the range of the population. The population ranged from 0 to 19 years, whereas the sample means range from 1.6 to 8.6 years.

Now let's change the example by increasing the size of each sample from 5 employees to 20. Table 8–6 reports the result of selecting 25 samples of 20 employees each and computing their sample means. These sample means are shown graphically in Chart 8–5. Compare the shape of this distribution to the population

TABLE 8–6 Twenty-Five Random Samples of 20 Employees

				Sample Data				
Sample	Obs 1	Obs 2	Obs 3	–	Obs 19	Obs 20	Sum	Mean
A	3	8	3	–	4	16	79	3.95
B	2	3	8	–	3	1	65	3.25
C	14	5	0	–	19	8	119	5.95
D	9	2	1	–	1	3	87	4.35
E	18	1	2	–	3	14	107	5.35
F	10	4	4	–	2	1	80	4.00
G	5	7	11	–	2	4	131	6.55
H	3	0	2	–	16	5	85	4.25
I	0	0	18	–	2	3	80	4.00
J	2	7	2	–	3	2	81	4.05
K	7	4	5	–	1	2	84	4.20
L	0	3	10	–	0	4	81	4.05
M	4	1	2	–	1	2	88	4.40
N	3	16	1	–	11	1	95	4.75
O	2	19	2	–	2	2	102	5.10
P	2	18	16	–	4	3	100	5.00
Q	3	2	3	–	3	1	102	5.10
R	2	3	1	–	0	2	73	3.65
S	2	14	19	–	0	7	142	7.10
T	0	1	3	–	2	0	61	3.05
U	1	0	1	–	9	3	65	3.25
V	1	9	4	–	2	11	137	6.85
W	8	1	9	–	8	7	107	5.35
X	4	2	0	–	2	5	86	4.30
Y	1	2	1	–	1	18	101	5.05

(Chart 8–3) and to the distribution of sample means where the sample is $n = 5$ (Chart 8–4). You should observe two important features:

1. The shape of the distribution of the sample mean is different from that of the population. In Chart 8–3, the distribution of all employees is positively skewed. However, as we select random samples from this population, the shape of the distribution of the sample mean changes. As we increase the size of the sample, the distribution of the sample mean approaches the normal probability distribution. This illustrates the central limit theorem.
2. There is less dispersion in the sampling distribution of sample means than in the population distribution. In the population, the years of service ranged from 0 to 19 years. When we selected samples of 5, the sample means ranged from 1.6 to 8.6 years, and when we selected samples of 20, the means ranged from 3.05 to 7.10 years.

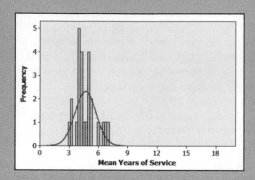

CHART 8–5 Histogram of Mean Years of Service for 25 Samples of 20 Employees

We can also compare the mean of the sample means to the population mean. The mean of the 25 samples of 20 employees reported in Table 8–6 is 4.676 years.

$$\mu_{\bar{X}} = \frac{3.95 + 3.25 + \cdots + 4.30 + 5.05}{25} = 4.676$$

We use the symbol $\mu_{\bar{X}}$ to identify the mean of the distribution of the sample mean. The subscript reminds us that the distribution is of the sample mean. It is read "mu sub X bar." We observe that the mean of the sample means, 4.676 years, is very close to the population mean of 4.80.

What should we conclude from this example? The central limit theorem indicates that, regardless of the shape of the population distribution, the sampling distribution of the sample mean will move toward the normal probability distribution. The larger the number of observations in each sample, the stronger the convergence. The Spence Sprockets Inc. example shows how the central limit theorem works. We began with a positively skewed population (Chart 8–3). Next, we selected 25 random samples of 5 observations, computed the mean of each sample, and finally organized these 25 sample means into a histogram (Chart 8–4). We observe a change in the shape of the sampling distribution of the sample mean from that of the population. The movement is from a positively skewed distribution to a distribution that has the shape of the normal probability distribution.

To further illustrate the effects of the central limit theorem, we increased the number of observations in each sample from 5 to 20. We selected 25 samples of 20 observations each and calculated the mean of each sample. Finally, we organized these sample means into a histogram (Chart 8–5). The shape of the histogram in Chart 8–5 is clearly moving toward the normal probability distribution.

If you go back to Chapter 6 where several binomial distributions with a "success" proportion of .10 are shown in Chart 6–3 in Section 6.5 on page 180, you can see yet another demonstration of the central limit theorem. Observe as n increases from 7 through 12 and 20 up to 40 that the profile of the probability distributions moves closer and closer to a normal probability distribution. Chart 8–5 on page 242 also shows the convergence to normality as n increases. This again reinforces the fact that, as more observations are sampled from any population distribution, the shape of the sampling distribution of the sample mean will get closer and closer to a normal distribution.

The central limit theorem itself (reread the definition in the box on page 237) does not say anything about the dispersion of the sampling distribution of the sample mean or about the comparison of the mean of the sampling distribution of the sample mean to the mean of the population. However, in our Spence Sprockets example, we did observe that there was less dispersion in the distribution of the sample mean than in the population distribution by noting the difference in the range in the population and the range of the sample means. We observe that the mean of the sample means is close to the mean of the population. It can be demonstrated that the mean of the sampling distribution is the population mean (i.e., $\mu_{\bar{X}} = \mu$), and if the standard deviation in the population is σ, the standard deviation of the sample means is $\sigma/\sqrt{n}$, where n is the number of observations in each sample. We refer to $\sigma/\sqrt{n}$ as the **standard error of the mean.** Its longer name is actually the *standard deviation of the sampling distribution of the sample mean*.

LO 8-6 Define the standard error of the mean.

STANDARD ERROR OF THE MEAN	$\sigma_{\bar{X}} = \dfrac{\sigma}{\sqrt{n}}$	**[8–1]**

In this section, we also came to other important conclusions.

1. The mean of the distribution of sample means will be *exactly* equal to the population mean if we are able to select all possible samples of the same size from a given population. That is:

$$\mu = \mu_{\bar{X}}$$

Even if we do not select all samples, we can expect the mean of the distribution of sample means to be close to the population mean.

2. There will be less dispersion in the sampling distribution of the sample mean than in the population. If the standard deviation of the population is σ, the standard deviation of the distribution of sample means is $\sigma/\sqrt{n}$. Note that when we increase the size of the sample, the standard error of the mean decreases.

Self-Review 8–4

Refer to the Spence Sprockets Inc. data on page 239. Select 10 random samples of 5 employees each. Use the methods described earlier in the chapter and the Table of Random Numbers (Appendix B.6) to find the employees to include in the sample. Compute the mean of each sample and plot the sample means on a chart similar to Chart 8–3. What is the mean of your 10 sample means?

Exercises

connect

11. Appendix B.6 is a table of random numbers. Hence, each digit from 0 to 9 has the same likelihood of occurrence. df

  a. Draw a graph showing the population distribution. What is the population mean?

b. Following are the first 10 rows of five digits from Appendix B.6. Assume that these are 10 random samples of five values each. Determine the mean of each sample and plot the means on a chart similar to Chart 8–3. Compare the mean of the sampling distribution of the sample means with the population mean.

0	2	7	1	1
9	4	8	7	3
5	4	9	2	1
7	7	6	4	0
6	1	5	4	5
1	7	1	4	7
1	3	7	4	8
8	7	4	5	5
0	8	9	9	9
7	8	8	0	4

12. Scrapper Elevator Company has 20 sales representatives who sell its product throughout the United States and Canada. The number of units sold last month by each representative is listed below. Assume these sales figures to be the population values.

2	3	2	3	3	4	2	4	3	2	2	7	3	4	5	3	3	3	3	5

  a. Draw a graph showing the population distribution.
  b. Compute the mean of the population.
  c. Select five random samples of 5 each. Compute the mean of each sample. Use the methods described in this chapter and Appendix B.6 to determine the items to be included in the sample.
  d. Compare the mean of the sampling distribution of the sample means to the population mean. Would you expect the two values to be about the same?
  e. Draw a histogram of the sample means. Do you notice a difference in the shape of the distribution of sample means compared to the shape of the population distribution?
13. Consider all of the coins (pennies, nickels, quarters, etc.) in your pocket or purse as a population. Make a frequency table beginning with the current year and counting backward to record the ages (in years) of the coins. For example, if the current year is 2011, then a coin with 2007 stamped on it is 4 years old.
  a. Draw a histogram or other graph showing the population distribution.
  b. Randomly select five coins and record the mean age of the sampled coins. Repeat this sampling process 20 times. Now draw a histogram or other graph showing the distribution of the sample means.
  c. Compare the shapes of the two histograms.
14. Consider the digits in the phone numbers on a randomly selected page of your local phone book a population. Make a frequency table of the final digit of 30 randomly selected phone numbers. For example, if a phone number is 555-9704, record a 4.
  a. Draw a histogram or other graph of this population distribution. Using the uniform distribution, compute the population mean and the population standard deviation.
  b. Also record the sample mean of the final four digits (9704 would lead to a mean of 5). Now draw a histogram or other graph showing the distribution of the sample means.
  c. Compare the shapes of the two histograms.

8.6 Using the Sampling Distribution of the Sample Mean

The previous discussion is important because most business decisions are made on the basis of sample information. Here are some examples.

1. Arm & Hammer Company wants to ensure that its laundry detergent actually contains 100 fluid ounces, as indicated on the label. Historical summaries from

the filling process indicate the mean amount per container is 100 fluid ounces and the standard deviation is 2 fluid ounces. The quality technician in her 10 A.M. check of 40 containers finds the mean amount per container is 99.8 fluid ounces. Should the technician shut down the filling operation?

2. A. C. Nielsen Company provides information to organizations advertising on television. Prior research indicates that adult Americans watch an average of 6.0 hours per day of television. The standard deviation is 1.5 hours. For a sample of 50 adults in the greater Boston area, would it be reasonable that we could randomly select a sample and find that they watch an average of 6.5 hours or more of television per day?

3. Haughton Elevator Company wishes to develop specifications for the number of people who can ride in a new oversized elevator. Suppose the mean weight for an adult is 160 pounds and the standard deviation is 15 pounds. However, the distribution of weights does not follow the normal probability distribution. It is positively skewed. What is the likelihood that for a sample of 30 adults their mean weight is 170 pounds or more?

We can answer the questions in each of these situations using the ideas discussed in the previous section. In each case, we have a population with information about its mean and standard deviation. Using this information and sample size, we can determine the distribution of sample means and compute the probability that a sample mean will fall within a certain range. The sampling distribution will be normally distributed under two conditions:

1. When the samples are taken from populations known to follow the normal distribution. In this case, the size of the sample is not a factor.

2. When the shape of the population distribution is not known or the shape is known to be nonnormal, but our sample contains at least 30 observations. We should point out that the number 30 is a guideline that has evolved over the years. In this case, the central limit theorem guarantees the sampling distribution of the mean follows a normal distribution.

We use formula (7–5) from Section 7.5 in the previous chapter to convert any normal distribution to the standard normal distribution. Using formula (7–5) to compute z values, we can use the standard normal table, Appendix B.1, to find the probability that an observation would fall within a specific range. The formula for finding a z value is:

$$z = \frac{X - \mu}{\sigma}$$

In this formula, X is the value of the random variable, μ is the population mean, and σ the population standard deviation.

LO 8-7 Apply the central limit theorem to find probabilities of selecting possible sample means from a specified population.

However, most business decisions refer to a sample—not just one observation. So we are interested in the distribution of $\overline{X}$, the sample mean, instead of X, the value of one observation. That is the first change we make in formula (7–5). The second is that we use the standard error of the mean of n observations instead of the population standard deviation. That is, we use $\sigma/\sqrt{n}$ in the denominator rather than σ. Therefore, to find the likelihood of a sample mean within a specified range, we first use the following formula to find the corresponding z value. Then we use Appendix B.1 or statistical software to determine the probability.

FINDING THE z VALUE OF $\overline{X}$ WHEN THE POPULATION STANDARD DEVIATION IS KNOWN	$z = \dfrac{\overline{X} - \mu}{\sigma/\sqrt{n}}$	[8–2]

The following example will show the application.

Example

The Quality Assurance Department for Cola, Inc. maintains records regarding the amount of cola in its Jumbo bottle. The actual amount of cola in each bottle is critical, but varies a small amount from one bottle to the next. Cola, Inc. does not wish to underfill the bottles, because it will have a problem with truth in labeling. On the other hand, it cannot overfill each bottle, because it would be giving cola away, hence reducing its profits. Its records indicate that the amount of cola follows the normal probability distribution. The mean amount per bottle is 31.2 ounces and the population standard deviation is 0.4 ounces. At 8 A.M. today the quality technician randomly selected 16 bottles from the filling line. The mean amount of cola contained in the bottles is 31.38 ounces. Is this an unlikely result? Is it likely the process is putting too much soda in the bottles? To put it another way, is the sampling error of 0.18 ounces unusual?

Solution

We can use the results of the previous section to find the likelihood that we could select a sample of 16 (n) bottles from a normal population with a mean of 31.2 (μ) ounces and a population standard deviation of 0.4 (σ) ounces and find the sample mean to be 31.38 ($\overline{X}$) or more. We use formula (8–2) to find the value of z.

$$z = \frac{\overline{X} - \mu}{\sigma/\sqrt{n}} = \frac{31.38 - 31.20}{0.4/\sqrt{16}} = 1.80$$

The numerator of this equation, $\overline{X} - \mu = 31.38 - 31.20 = .18$, is the sampling error. The denominator, $\sigma/\sqrt{n} = 0.4/\sqrt{16} = 0.1$, is the standard error of the sampling distribution of the sample mean. So the z values express the sampling error in standard units—in other words, the standard error.

Next, we compute the likelihood of a z value greater than 1.80. In Appendix B.1, locate the probability corresponding to a z value of 1.80. It is .4641. The likelihood of a z value greater than 1.80 is .0359, found by .5000 − .4641.

What do we conclude? It is unlikely, less than a 4% chance, we could select a sample of 16 observations from a normal population with a mean of 31.2 ounces and a population standard deviation of 0.4 ounces and find the sample mean equal to or greater than 31.38 ounces. We conclude the process is putting too much cola in the bottles. The quality technician should see the production supervisor about reducing the amount of soda in each bottle. This information is summarized in Chart 8–6.

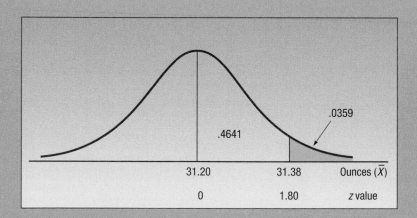

CHART 8–6 Sampling Distribution of the Mean Amount of Cola in a Jumbo Bottle

Self-Review 8–5

Refer to the Cola, Inc. information. Suppose the quality technician selected a sample of 16 Jumbo bottles that averaged 31.08 ounces. What can you conclude about the filling process?

Exercises

connect

15. A normal population has a mean of 60 and a standard deviation of 12. You select a random sample of 9. Compute the probability the sample mean is:
    a. Greater than 63.
    b. Less than 56.
    c. Between 56 and 63.

16. A normal population has a mean of 75 and a standard deviation of 5. You select a sample of 40. Compute the probability the sample mean is:
    a. Less than 74.
    b. Between 74 and 76.
    c. Between 76 and 77.
    d. Greater than 77.

17. In a certain section of Southern California, the distribution of monthly rent for a one-bedroom apartment has a mean of $2,200 and a standard deviation of $250. The distribution of the monthly rent does not follow the normal distribution. In fact, it is positively skewed. What is the probability of selecting a sample of 50 one-bedroom apartments and finding the mean to be at least $1,950 per month?

18. According to an IRS study, it takes a mean of 330 minutes for taxpayers to prepare, copy, and electronically file a 1040 tax form. This distribution of times follows the normal distribution and the standard deviation is 80 minutes. A consumer watchdog agency selects a random sample of 40 taxpayers.
    a. What is the standard error of the mean in this example?
    b. What is the likelihood the sample mean is greater than 320 minutes?
    c. What is the likelihood the sample mean is between 320 and 350 minutes?
    d. What is the likelihood the sample mean is greater than 350 minutes?

Chapter Summary

I. There are many reasons for sampling a population.
   A. The results of a sample may adequately estimate the value of the population parameter, thus saving time and money.
   B. It may be too time consuming to contact all members of the population.
   C. It may be impossible to check or locate all the members of the population.
   D. The cost of studying all the items in the population may be prohibitive.
   E. Often testing destroys the sampled item and it cannot be returned to the population.
II. In an unbiased or probability sample, all members of the population have a chance of being selected for the sample. There are several probability sampling methods.
   A. In a simple random sample, all members of the population have the same chance of being selected for the sample.
   B. In a systematic sample, a random starting point is selected, and then every kth item thereafter is selected for the sample.
   C. In a stratified sample, the population is divided into several groups, called strata, and then a random sample is selected from each stratum.
   D. In cluster sampling, the population is divided into primary units, then samples are drawn from the primary units.

III. The sampling error is the difference between a population parameter and a sample statistic.

IV. The sampling distribution of the sample mean is a probability distribution of all possible sample means of the same sample size.

    A. For a given sample size, the mean of all possible sample means selected from a population is equal to the population mean.

    B. There is less variation in the distribution of the sample mean than in the population distribution.

    C. The standard error of the mean measures the variation in the sampling distribution of the sample mean. The standard error is found by:

$$\sigma_{\overline{X}} = \frac{\sigma}{\sqrt{n}} \qquad\qquad \textbf{[8–1]}$$

    D. If the population follows a normal distribution, the sampling distribution of the sample mean will also follow the normal distribution for samples of any size. Assume the population standard deviation is known. To determine the probability that a sample mean falls in a particular region, use the following formula.

$$z = \frac{\overline{X} - \mu}{\sigma/\sqrt{n}} \qquad\qquad \textbf{[8–2]}$$

Pronunciation Key

SYMBOL	MEANING	PRONUNCIATION
$\mu_{\overline{X}}$	Mean of the sampling distribution of the sample mean	*mu sub X bar*
$\sigma_{\overline{X}}$	Population standard error of the sample mean	*sigma sub X bar*

Chapter Exercises

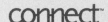

19. The retail stores located in the North Towne Square Mall are:

00	Elder-Beerman	09	Lion Store	18	County Seat
01	Sears	10	Bootleggers	19	Kid Mart
02	Deb Shop	11	Formal Man	20	Lerner
03	Frederick's of Hollywood	12	Leather Ltd.	21	Coach House Gifts
04	Petries	13	B. Dalton Bookseller	22	Spencer Gifts
05	Easy Dreams	14	Pat's Hallmark	23	CPI Photo Finish
06	Summit Stationers	15	Things Remembered	24	Regis Hairstylists
07	E. B. Brown Opticians	16	Pearle Vision Express		
08	Kay-Bee Toy & Hobby	17	Dollar Tree		

    a. If the following random numbers are selected, which retail stores should be contacted for a survey? 11, 65, 86, 62, 06, 10, 12, 77, and 04.

    b. Select a random sample of four retail stores. Use Appendix B.6.

    c. A systematic sampling procedure is to be used. The first store is to be contacted and then every third store. Which stores will be contacted?

20. Medical Mutual Insurance is investigating the cost of a routine office visit to family-practice physicians in the Rochester, New York, area. The following is a list of family-practice physicians in the region. Physicians are to be randomly selected and contacted regarding their charges. The 39 physicians have been coded from 00 to 38. Also noted is whether they are in practice by themselves (S), have a partner (P), or are in a group practice (G).

Number	Physician	Type of Practice	Number	Physician	Type of Practice
00	R. E. Scherbarth, M.D.	S	20	Gregory Yost, M.D.	P
01	Crystal R. Goveia, M.D.	P	21	J. Christian Zona, M.D.	P
02	Mark D. Hillard, M.D.	P	22	Larry Johnson, M.D.	P
03	Jeanine S. Huttner, M.D.	P	23	Sanford Kimmel, M.D.	P
04	Francis Aona, M.D.	P	24	Harry Mayhew, M.D.	S
05	Janet Arrowsmith, M.D.	P	25	Leroy Rodgers, M.D.	S
06	David DeFrance, M.D.	S	26	Thomas Tafelski, M.D.	S
07	Judith Furlong, M.D.	S	27	Mark Zilkoski, M.D.	G
08	Leslie Jackson, M.D.	G	28	Ken Bertka, M.D.	G
09	Paul Langenkamp, M.D.	S	29	Mark DeMichiei, M.D.	G
10	Philip Lepkowski, M.D.	S	30	John Eggert, M.D.	P
11	Wendy Martin, M.D.	S	31	Jeanne Fiorito, M.D.	P
12	Denny Mauricio, M.D.	P	32	Michael Fitzpatrick, M.D.	P
13	Hasmukh Parmar, M.D.	P	33	Charles Holt, D.O.	P
14	Ricardo Pena, M.D.	P	34	Richard Koby, M.D.	P
15	David Reames, M.D.	P	35	John Meier, M.D.	P
16	Ronald Reynolds, M.D.	G	36	Douglas Smucker, M.D.	S
17	Mark Steinmetz, M.D.	G	37	David Weldy, M.D.	P
18	Geza Torok, M.D.	S	38	Cheryl Zaborowski, M.D.	P
19	Mark Young, M.D.	P			

    a. The random numbers obtained from Appendix B.6 are: 31, 94, 43, 36, 03, 24, 17, and 09. Which physicians should be contacted?

    b. Select a random sample of four physicians using the random numbers of Appendix B.6.

    c. A sample is to consist of every fifth physician. The number 04 is selected as the starting point. Which physicians will be contacted?

    d. A sample is to consist of two physicians in solo practice (S), two in partnership (P), and one in group practice (G). Select a sample accordingly. Explain your procedure.

21. A population consists of the following three values: 1, 2, and 3.

    a. List all possible samples of size 2 (including possible repeats) and compute the mean of every sample.

    b. Find the means of the distribution of the sample mean and the population mean. Compare the two values.

    c. Compare the dispersion of the population with that of the sample mean.

    d. Describe the shapes of the two distributions.

22. In the Department of Education at UR University, student records suggest that the population of students spends an average of 5.5 hours per week playing organized sports. The population's standard deviation is 2.2 hours per week. Based on a sample of 121 students, Healthy Lifestyles Incorporated (HLI) would like to apply the central limit theorem to make various estimates.

    a. Compute the standard error of the sample mean.

    b. What is the chance HLI will find a sample mean between 5 and 6 hours?

    c. Calculate the probability that the sample mean will be between 5.3 and 5.7 hours.

    d. How strange would it be to obtain a sample mean greater than 6.5 hours?

23. The manufacturer of eComputers, an economy-priced computer, recently completed the design for a new laptop model. eComputers top management would like some assistance in pricing the new laptop. Two market research firms were contacted and asked to prepare a pricing strategy. Marketing-Gets-Results tested the new eComputers laptop with 50 randomly selected consumers, who indicated they plan to purchase a laptop within the next year. The second marketing research firm, called Marketing-Reaps-Profits, test-marketed the new eComputers laptop with 200 current laptop owners. Which of the marketing research companies' test results will be more useful? Discuss why.

24. Answer the following questions in one or two well-constructed sentences.

    a. What happens to the standard error of the mean if the sample size is increased?

b. What happens to the distribution of the sample means if the sample size is increased?

c. When using the distribution of sample means to estimate the population mean, what is the benefit of using larger sample sizes?

25. There are 25 motels in Goshen, Indiana. The number of rooms in each motel follows:

| 90 | 72 | 75 | 60 | 75 | 72 | 84 | 72 | 88 | 74 | 105 | 115 | 68 | 74 | 80 | 64 | 104 | 82 | 48 | 58 | 60 | 80 | 48 | 58 | 100 |

a. Using a table of random numbers (Appendix B.6), select a random sample of five motels from this population.

b. Obtain a systematic sample by selecting a random starting point among the first five motels and then select every fifth motel.

c. Suppose the last five motels are "cut-rate" motels. Describe how you would select a random sample of three regular motels and two cut-rate motels.

26. As a part of their customer-service program, United Airlines randomly selected 10 passengers from today's 9 A.M. Chicago–Tampa flight. Each sampled passenger is to be interviewed in depth regarding airport facilities, service, and so on. To identify the sample, each passenger was given a number on boarding the aircraft. The numbers started with 001 and ended with 250.

a. Select 10 usable numbers at random using Appendix B.6.

b. The sample of 10 could have been chosen using a systematic sample. Choose the first number using Appendix B.6, and then list the numbers to be interviewed.

c. Evaluate the two methods by giving the advantages and possible disadvantages.

d. In what other way could a random sample be selected from the 250 passengers?

27. Suppose your statistics instructor gave six examinations during the semester. You received the following grades (percent correct): 79, 64, 84, 82, 92, and 77. Instead of averaging the six scores, the instructor indicated he would randomly select two grades and compute the final percent correct based on the two percentages.

a. How many different samples of two test grades are possible?

b. List all possible samples of size two and compute the mean of each.

c. Compute the mean of the sample means and compare it to the population mean.

d. If you were a student, would you like this arrangement? Would the result be different from dropping the lowest score? Write a brief report.

28. At the downtown office of First National Bank, there are five tellers. Last week, the tellers made the following number of errors each: 2, 3, 5, 3, and 5.

a. How many different samples of 2 tellers are possible?

b. List all possible samples of size 2 and compute the mean of each.

c. Compute the mean of the sample means and compare it to the population mean.

29. The Quality Control Department employs five technicians during the day shift. Listed below is the number of times each technician instructed the production foreman to shut down the manufacturing process last week.

Technician	Shutdowns	Technician	Shutdowns
Taylor	4	Rousche	3
Hurley	3	Huang	2
Gupta	5		

a. How many different samples of two technicians are possible from this population?

b. List all possible samples of two observations each and compute the mean of each sample.

c. Compare the mean of the sample means with the population mean.

d. Compare the shape of the population distribution with the shape of the distribution of the sample means.

30. The Appliance Center has six sales representatives at its North Jacksonville outlet. Listed below is the number of refrigerators sold by each last month.

Sales Representative	Number Sold	Sales Representative	Number Sold
Zina Craft	54	Jan Niles	48
Woon Junge	50	Molly Camp	50
Ernie DeBrul	52	Rachel Myak	52

    a. How many samples of size 2 are possible?

    b. Select all possible samples of size 2 and compute the mean number sold.

    c. Organize the sample means into a frequency distribution.

    d. What is the mean of the population? What is the mean of the sample means?

    e. What is the shape of the population distribution?

    f. What is the shape of the distribution of the sample mean?

31. Power+, Inc. produces AA batteries used in remote-controlled toy cars. The mean life of these batteries follows the normal probability distribution with a mean of 35.0 hours and a standard deviation of 5.5 hours. As a part of its quality assurance program, Power+, Inc. tests samples of 25 batteries.

    a. What can you say about the shape of the distribution of the sample mean?

    b. What is the standard error of the distribution of the sample mean?

    c. What proportion of the samples will have a mean useful life of more than 36 hours?

    d. What proportion of the sample will have a mean useful life greater than 34.5 hours?

    e. What proportion of the sample will have a mean useful life between 34.5 and 36.0 hours?

32. CRA CDs Inc. wants the mean lengths of the "cuts" on a CD to be 135 seconds (2 minutes and 15 seconds). This will allow the disk jockeys to have plenty of time for commercials within each 10-minute segment. Assume the distribution of the length of the cuts follows the normal distribution with a population standard deviation of 8 seconds. Suppose we select a sample of 16 cuts from various CDs sold by CRA CDs Inc.

    a. What can we say about the shape of the distribution of the sample mean?

    b. What is the standard error of the mean?

    c. What percent of the sample means will be greater than 140 seconds?

    d. What percent of the sample means will be greater than 128 seconds?

    e. What percent of the sample means will be greater than 128 but less than 140 seconds?

33. Recent studies indicate that the typical 50-year-old woman spends $350 per year for personal-care products. The distribution of the amounts spent follows a normal distribution with a standard deviation of $45 per year. We select a random sample of 40 women. The mean amount spent for those sampled is $335. What is the likelihood of finding a sample mean this large or larger from the specified population?

34. Information from the American Institute of Insurance indicates the mean amount of life insurance per household in the United States is $110,000. This distribution follows the normal distribution with a standard deviation of $40,000.

    a. If we select a random sample of 50 households, what is the standard error of the mean?

    b. What is the expected shape of the distribution of the sample mean?

    c. What is the likelihood of selecting a sample with a mean of at least $112,000?

    d. What is the likelihood of selecting a sample with a mean of more than $100,000?

    e. Find the likelihood of selecting a sample with a mean of more than $100,000 but less than $112,000.

35. The mean age at which men in the United States marry for the first time follows the normal distribution with a mean of 24.8 years. The standard deviation of the distribution is 2.5 years. For a random sample of 60 men, what is the likelihood that the age at which they were married for the first time is less than 25.1 years?

36. A recent study by the Greater Los Angeles Taxi Drivers Association showed that the mean fare charged for service from Hermosa Beach to Los Angeles International Airport is $21 and the standard deviation is $3.50. We select a sample of 15 fares.

    a. What is the likelihood that the sample mean is between $20 and $23?

    b. What must you assume to make the above calculation?

37. Crossett Trucking Company claims that the mean weight of its delivery trucks when they are fully loaded is 6,000 pounds and the standard deviation is 150 pounds. Assume that the population follows the normal distribution. Forty trucks are randomly selected and weighed. Within what limits will 95% of the sample means occur?

38. The mean amount purchased by a typical customer at Churchill's Grocery Store is $23.50, with a standard deviation of $5.00. Assume the distribution of amounts purchased follows the normal distribution. For a sample of 50 customers, answer the following questions.

    a. What is the likelihood the sample mean is at least $25.00?

    b. What is the likelihood the sample mean is greater than $22.50 but less than $25.00?

    c. Within what limits will 90% of the sample means occur?

39. The mean score on a physical fitness test for Division I student-athletes is 947 with a standard deviation of 205. If you select a random sample of 60 of these students, what is the probability the mean is below 900?

40. Suppose we roll a fair die two times.
   a. How many different samples are there?
   b. List each of the possible samples and compute the mean.
   c. On a chart similar to Chart 8–1, compare the distribution of sample means with the distribution of the population.
   d. Compute the mean and the standard deviation of each distribution and compare them.
41. Following is a list of the 50 states with the numbers 0 through 49 assigned to them.

Number	State	Number	State
0	Alabama	25	Montana
1	Alaska	26	Nebraska
2	Arizona	27	Nevada
3	Arkansas	28	New Hampshire
4	California	29	New Jersey
5	Colorado	30	New Mexico
6	Connecticut	31	New York
7	Delaware	32	North Carolina
8	Florida	33	North Dakota
9	Georgia	34	Ohio
10	Hawaii	35	Oklahoma
11	Idaho	36	Oregon
12	Illinois	37	Pennsylvania
13	Indiana	38	Rhode Island
14	Iowa	39	South Carolina
15	Kansas	40	South Dakota
16	Kentucky	41	Tennessee
17	Louisiana	42	Texas
18	Maine	43	Utah
19	Maryland	44	Vermont
20	Massachusetts	45	Virginia
21	Michigan	46	Washington
22	Minnesota	47	West Virginia
23	Mississippi	48	Wisconsin
24	Missouri	49	Wyoming

   a. You wish to select a sample of eight from this list. The selected random numbers are 45, 15, 81, 09, 39, 43, 90, 26, 06, 45, 01, and 42. Which states are included in the sample?
   b. You wish to use a systematic sample of every sixth item and the digit 02 is chosen as the starting point. Which states are included?
42. Human Resource Consulting (HRC) surveyed a random sample of 60 Twin Cities construction companies to find information on the costs of their health care plans. One of the items being tracked is the annual deductible that employees must pay. The Minnesota Department of Labor reports that historically the mean deductible amount per employee is $502 with a standard deviation of $100.
   a. Compute the standard error of the sample mean for HRC.
   b. What is the chance HRC finds a sample mean between $477 and $527?
   c. Calculate the likelihood that the sample mean is between $492 and $512.
   d. What is the probability the sample mean is greater than $550?
43. Over the past decade, the mean number of members of the Information Systems Security Association who have experienced a denial-of-service attack each year is 510, with a standard deviation of 14.28 attacks. Suppose nothing in this environment changes.
   a. What is the likelihood this group will suffer an average of more than 600 attacks in the next 10 years?
   b. Compute the probability the mean number of attacks over the next 10 years is between 500 and 600.
   c. What is the possibility they will experience an average of less than 500 attacks over the next 10 years?

44. An economist uses the price of a gallon of milk as a measure of inflation. She finds that the average price is $3.50 per gallon and the population standard deviation is $0.33. You decide to sample 40 stores, collect their price for a gallon of milk, and compute the mean price for the sample.
    a. What is the standard error of the mean in this experiment?
    b. What is the probability that the sample mean is between $3.46 and $3.54?
    c. What is the probability that the difference between the sample mean and the population mean is less than 0.01?
    d. What is the likelihood the sample mean is greater than $3.60?

45. Nike's annual report says that the average American buys 6.5 pairs of sports shoes per year. Suppose the population standard deviation is 2.1 and that a sample of 81 customers will be examined next year.
    a. What is the standard error of the mean in this experiment?
    b. What is the probability that the sample mean is between 6 and 7 pairs of sports shoes?
    c. What is the probability that the difference between the sample mean and the population mean is less than 0.25 pairs?
    d. What is the likelihood the sample mean is greater than 7 pairs?

Data Set Exercises

(The data for these exercises are available at the text website www.mhhe.com/lindbasic8e).

46. Refer to the Real Estate data, which report information on the homes sold in the Goodyear, Arizona, area last year. Use statistical software to compute the mean and the standard deviation of the selling prices. Assume this to be the population. Select a sample of 10 homes. Compute the mean and the standard deviation of the sample. Determine the likelihood of a sample mean this large or larger from the population.

47. Refer to the Baseball 2010 data, which report information on the 30 Major League Baseball teams for the 2010 season. Over the last decade, the mean attendance per team followed a normal distribution with a mean of 2.25 million per team and a standard deviation of 0.70 million. Use statistical software to compute the mean attendance per team for the 2010 season. Determine the likelihood of a sample mean this large or larger from the population.

48. Refer to the Buena School District bus data. Information provided by manufacturers of school buses suggests the mean maintenance cost per month is $455 per bus. Use statistical software to find the mean and the standard deviation for the Buena buses. Does the Buena data seem to be in line with that reported by the manufacturer? Specifically, what is the probability of the sample mean being less than Buena's, given the manufacturer's data?

Practice Test

Part 1—Objective

1. In a _____ each item in the population has the same chance of being included in the sample.
2. A sample should have at least how many observations? _____ (10, 30, 100, 1,000, no size restriction)
3. When a population is divided into groups based on some characteristic, such as region of the country, the groups are called _____.
4. The difference between a sample mean and the population mean is called the _____.
5. A probability distribution of all possible sample means for a particular sample size is the _____.
6. Suppose a population consisted of 10 individuals and we wished to list all possible samples of size 3. If sampling is without replacement, how many samples are there?
7. What is the name given to the standard deviation of the distribution of sample means? _____
8. The mean of all possible sample means is _____ the population mean. (always larger than, always smaller than, always equal to, not a constant relationship with)
9. If we increase the sample size from 10 to 20, the standard error of the mean will _____. (increase, decrease, stay the same, the result is not predictable)
10. If a population follows the normal distribution, what will be the shape of the distribution of sample means? _____

Part 2—Problem

1. Americans spend a mean of 12.2 minutes per day in the shower. The distribution of time spent in the shower follows the normal distribution with a population standard deviation of 2.3 minutes. What is the likelihood that the mean time in the shower per day for a sample of 12 Americans is 11 minutes or less?

Software Commands

1. The Excel commands to select a simple random sample on page 227 are:
    a. Select the **Data** tab on the top of the menu. Then, on the far right, select **Data Analysis,** then **Sampling** and **OK.**
    b. For **Input Range,** insert *B1:B31*. Since the column is named, click the **Labels** box. Select **Random,** and enter the sample size for the **Number of Samples,** in this case 5. Click on **Output Range** and indicate the place in the spreadsheet where you want the sample information. Note that your sample results will differ from those in the text. Also recall that Excel samples with replacement, so it is possible for a population value to appear more than once in the sample.

Sampling	?	X
Input		OK
Input Range: $B$1:$B$31		Cancel
✓ Labels		Help
Sampling Method		
○ Periodic		
Period:		
● Random		
Number of Samples: 5		
Output options		
● Output Range: $D$1		
○ New Worksheet Ply:		
○ New Workbook		

Chapter 8   Answers to Self-Review

8–1   a. Students selected are Price, Detley, and Molter.
      b. Answers will vary.
      c. Skip it and move to the next random number.

8–2   The students selected are Berry, Francis, Kopp, Poteau, and Swetye.

8–3   a. 10, found by:

$$_5C_2 = \frac{5!}{2!(5-2)!}$$

b.

	Service	Sample Mean
Snow, Tolson	20, 22	21
Snow, Kraft	20, 26	23
Snow, Irwin	20, 24	22
Snow, Jones	20, 28	24
Tolson, Kraft	22, 26	24
Tolson, Irwin	22, 24	23
Tolson, Jones	22, 28	25
Kraft, Irwin	26, 24	25
Kraft, Jones	26, 28	27
Irwin, Jones	24, 28	26

c.

Mean	Number	Probability
21	1	.10
22	1	.10
23	2	.20
24	2	.20
25	2	.20
26	1	.10
27	1	.10
	10	1.00

d. Identical: population mean, μ, is 24, and mean of sample means, $\mu_{\bar{x}}$, is also 24.

e. Sample means range from 21 to 27. Population values go from 20 to 28.

f. Nonnormal.

g. Yes.

8–4 The answers will vary. Here is one solution.

			Sample Number							
	1	**2**	**3**	**4**	**5**	**6**	**7**	**8**	**9**	**10**
	8	2	2	19	3	4	0	4	1	2
	19	1	14	9	2	5	8	2	14	4
	8	3	4	2	4	4	1	14	4	1
	0	3	2	3	1	2	16	1	2	3
	2	1	7	2	19	18	18	16	3	7
Total	37	10	29	35	29	33	43	37	24	17
$\overline{X}$	7.4	2	5.8	7.0	5.8	6.6	8.6	7.4	4.8	3.4

Mean of the 10 sample means is 5.88.

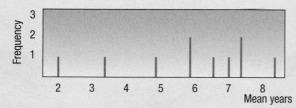

8–5 $z = \dfrac{31.08 - 31.20}{0.4/\sqrt{16}} = -1.20$

Because the sample mean, 31.08, is less than the population mean, 31.20, we want to know if the process is under-filling the bottles. The probability that the mean could be 31.08 ounces or less corresponds to the probability that z is less than -1.20 is $.5000 - .3849 = .1151$. There is more than an 11 percent chance the filling operation will fill bottles with less than 31.08 ounces. The filling process should be checked.

9

Estimation and Confidence Intervals

The American Restaurant Association collected information on the number of meals eaten outside the home per week by young married couples. A survey of 60 couples showed the sample mean number of meals eaten outside the home was 2.76 meals per week, with a standard deviation of 0.75 meals per week. Construct a 99% confidence interval for the population mean. (See Exercise 32 and LO 9-4.)

9.1 Introduction

The previous chapter began our discussion of statistical inference. It introduced both the reasons for, and the methods of, sampling. The reasons for sampling were:

- Contacting the entire population is too time consuming.
- Studying all the items in the population is often too expensive.
- The sample results are usually adequate.
- Certain tests are destructive.
- Checking all the items is physically impossible.

There are several methods of sampling. Simple random sampling is the most widely used method. With this type of sampling, each member of the population has the same chance of being selected to be a part of the sample. Other methods of sampling include systematic sampling, stratified sampling, and cluster sampling.

Chapter 8 assumes information about the population, such as the mean, the standard deviation, or the shape of the population are known. In most business situations, such information is not available. In fact, the purpose of sampling may be to estimate some of these values. For example, you select a sample from a population and use the mean of the sample to estimate the mean of the population.

This chapter considers several important aspects of sampling. We begin by studying **point estimates.** A point estimate is a single value (point) derived from a sample and used to estimate a population value. For example, suppose we select a sample of 50 junior executives and ask how many hours they worked last week. Compute the mean of this sample of 50 and use the value of the sample mean as a point estimate of the unknown population mean. However, a point estimate is a single value. A more informative approach is to present a range of values where we expect the population parameter to occur. Such a range of values is called a **confidence interval.**

Frequently in business we need to determine the size of a sample. How many voters should a polling organization contact to forecast the election outcome? How many products do we need to examine to ensure our quality level? This chapter also develops a strategy for determining the appropriate number of observations in the sample.

9.2 Point Estimate for a Population Mean

A point estimate is a single statistic used to estimate a population parameter. Suppose Best Buy Inc. wants to estimate the mean age of people who purchase LCD HDTV televisions. They select a random sample of 50 recent purchases, determine the age of each buyer, and compute the mean age of the buyers in the sample. The mean of this sample is a point estimate of the population mean.

> **POINT ESTIMATE** The statistic, computed from sample information that estimates a population parameter.

The following examples illustrate point estimates of population means.

1. Tourism is a major source of income for many Caribbean countries, such as Barbados. Suppose the Bureau of Tourism for Barbados wants an estimate of the mean amount spent by tourists visiting the country. It would not be feasible to contact each tourist. Therefore, 500 tourists are randomly selected as they depart the country and asked in detail about their spending while visiting Barbados. The mean amount spent by the sample of 500 tourists is an estimate of the unknown population parameter. That is, we let the sample mean serve as a point estimate of the population mean.

2. Litchfield Home Builders Inc. builds homes in the southeastern region of the United States. One of the major concerns of new buyers is the date when the home will be completed. Recently, Litchfield has been telling customers, "Your home will be completed 45 working days from the date we begin installing drywall." The customer relations department at Litchfield wishes to compare this pledge with recent experience. A sample of 50 homes completed this year revealed that the point estimate of the population mean is 46.7 working days from the start of drywall to the completion of the home. Is it reasonable to conclude that the population mean is still 45 days and that the difference between the sample mean (46.7 days) and the proposed population mean (45 days) is sampling error? In other words, is the sample mean significantly different from the population mean?

3. Recent medical studies indicate that exercise is an important part of a person's overall health. The director of human resources at OCF, a large glass manufacturer, wants an estimate of the number of hours per week employees spend exercising. A sample of 70 employees reveals the mean number of hours of exercise last week is 3.3. This value is a point estimate of the unknown population mean.

    The sample mean, $\overline{X}$, is not the only point estimate of a population parameter. For example, p, a sample proportion, is a point estimate of π, the population proportion; and s, the sample standard deviation, is a point estimate of σ, the population standard deviation.

9.3 Confidence Intervals for a Population Mean

A point estimate, however, tells only part of the story. While we expect the point estimate to be close to the population parameter, we would like to measure how close it really is. A confidence interval serves this purpose. For example, we estimate the mean yearly income for construction workers in the New York–New Jersey area is $85,000. The range of this estimate might be from $81,000 to $89,000. We can describe how confident we are that the population parameter is in the interval. We might say, for instance, that we are 90% confident that the mean yearly income of construction workers in the New York–New Jersey area is between $81,000 and $89,000.

> **CONFIDENCE INTERVAL** A range of values constructed from sample data so that the population parameter is likely to occur within that range at a specified probability. The specified probability is called the *level of confidence.*

To compute a confidence interval for a population mean, we will consider two situations:

*   We use sample data to estimate μ with $\overline{X}$ and the population standard deviation (σ) is known.
*   We use sample data to estimate μ with $\overline{X}$, and the population standard deviation is unknown. In this case, we substitute the sample standard deviation (s) for the population standard deviation (σ).

There are important distinctions in the assumptions between these two situations. We first consider the case where σ is known.

Population Standard Deviation, Known σ

LO 9-3 Compute a confidence interval for the population mean when the population standard deviation is known.

A confidence interval is computed using two statistics: the sample mean, $\overline{X}$, and the standard deviation. From previous chapters, you know that the standard deviation is an important statistic because it measures the dispersion, or width, of a population or sample distribution. In computing a confidence interval, the standard deviation is used to compute the limits of the confidence interval.

To demonstrate the idea of a confidence interval, we start with one simplifying assumption. That assumption is that we know the value of the population standard deviation, σ. Typically, we know the population standard deviation in situations where we have a long history of collected data. Examples are data from monitoring processes that fill soda bottles or cereal boxes, and the results of the SAT Reasoning Test (for college admission). Knowing σ allows us to simplify the development of a confidence interval because we can use the standard normal distribution from Chapter 8.

Recall that the sampling distribution of the sample mean is the distribution of all sample means, $\overline{X}$, of sample size n from a population. The population standard deviation, σ, is known. From this information, and the central limit theorem, we know that the sampling distribution follows the normal probability distribution with a mean of μ and a standard deviation $\sigma/\sqrt{n}$. Also recall that this value is called the standard error.

The results of the central limit theorem allow us to make the following general confidence interval statements using z-statistics:

1. Ninety-five percent of all confidence intervals computed from random samples selected from a population will contain the population mean. These intervals are computed using a z-statistic equal to 1.96.
2. Ninety percent of all confidence intervals computed from random samples selected from a population will contain the population mean. These confidence intervals are computed using a z-statistic equal to 1.65.

These confidence interval statements provide examples of *levels of confidence* and are called a **95% confidence interval** and a **90% confidence interval.** The *95%* and *90%* are the levels of confidence and refer to the percentage of similarly constructed intervals that would include the parameter being estimated—in this case, μ, the population mean.

How are the values of 1.96 and 1.65 obtained? First, let's look for the z value for a 95% confidence interval. The following diagram and Table 9–1 will help explain. Table 9–1 is a reproduction of Appendix B.1, the standard normal table. However, many rows and columns have been eliminated to allow us to better focus on particular rows and columns.

1. First, we divide the confidence level in half, so .9500/2 = .4750.
2. Next, we find the value .4750 in the body of Table 9–1. Note that .4750 is located in the table at the intersection of a row and a column.
3. Locate the corresponding row value in the left margin, which is 1.9, and the column value in the top margin, which is .06. Adding the row and column values gives us a z value of 1.96.
4. Thus, the probability of finding a z value between 0 and 1.96 is .4750.
5. Likewise, because the normal distribution is symmetric, the probability of finding a z value between −1.96 and 0 is also .4750.
6. When we add these two probabilities, the probability that a z value is between −1.96 and 1.96 is .9500.

For the 90% level of confidence, we follow the same steps. First, one-half of the desired confidence interval is .4500. A search of Table 9–1 does not reveal this exact value. However, it is between two values, .4495 and .4505. As in step three, we locate each value in the table. The first, .4495, corresponds to a *z* value of 1.64 and the second, .4505, corresponds to a *z* value of 1.65. To be conservative, we will select the larger of the two *z* values, 1.65, and the exact level of confidence is 90.1%, or 2(0.4505). Next, the probability of finding a *z* value between −1.65 and 0 is .4505, and the probability that a *z* value is between −1.65 and 1.65 is .9010.

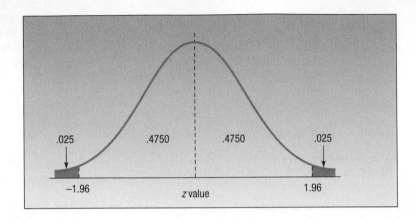

TABLE 9–1 The Standard Normal Table for Selected Values

z	0.00	0.01	0.02	0.03	0.04	0.05	0.06	0.07
⋮	⋮	⋮	⋮	⋮	⋮	⋮	⋮	⋮
1.5	0.4332	0.4345	0.4357	0.4370	0.4382	0.4394	0.4406	0.4418
1.6	0.4452	0.4463	0.4474	0.4484	0.4495	0.4505	0.4515	0.4525
1.7	0.4554	0.4564	0.4573	0.4582	0.4591	0.4599	0.4608	0.4616
1.8	0.4641	0.4649	0.4656	0.4664	0.4671	0.4678	0.4686	0.4693
1.9	0.4713	0.4719	0.4726	0.4732	0.4738	0.4744	0.4750	0.4756
2.0	0.4772	0.4778	0.4783	0.4788	0.4793	0.4798	0.4803	0.4808
2.1	0.4821	0.4826	0.4830	0.4834	0.4838	0.4842	0.4846	0.4850
2.2	0.4861	0.4864	0.4868	0.4871	0.4875	0.4878	0.4881	0.4884

How do we determine a 95% confidence interval? The width of the interval is determined by two factors: (1) the level of confidence, as described in the previous section, and (2) the size of the standard error of the mean. To find the standard error of the mean, recall from the previous chapter (see formula 8–1 on page 243) that the standard error of the mean reports the variation in the distribution of sample means. It is really the standard deviation of the distribution of sample means. The formula is repeated below:

$$\sigma_{\bar{x}} = \frac{\sigma}{\sqrt{n}}$$

where:

$\sigma_{\bar{x}}$ is the symbol for the standard error of the mean. We use a Greek letter because it is a population value, and the subscript $\bar{x}$ reminds us that it refers to a sampling distribution of the sample means.

σ is the population standard deviation.

n is the number of observations in the sample.

The size of the standard error is affected by two values. The first is the standard deviation of the population. The larger the population standard deviation, σ, the larger $\sigma/\sqrt{n}$. If the population is homogeneous, resulting in a small population standard deviation, the standard error will also be small. However, the standard error is also affected by the number of observations in the sample. A large number of observations in the sample will result in a small standard error of estimate, indicating that there is less variability in the sample means.

We can summarize the calculation for a 95% confidence interval using the following formula:

$$\bar{X} \pm 1.96\, \frac{\sigma}{\sqrt{n}}$$

Similarly, a 90.1% confidence interval is computed as follows:

$$\bar{X} \pm 1.65\, \frac{\sigma}{\sqrt{n}}$$

The values 1.96 and 1.65 are z values corresponding to the 95% and the 90.1% confidence intervals, respectively. However, we are not restricted to these values. We can select any confidence level between 0 and 100% and find the corresponding value for z. In general, a confidence interval for the population mean when the population follows the normal distribution and the population standard deviation is known is computed by:

CONFIDENCE INTERVAL FOR A POPULATION MEAN WITH σ KNOWN	$\bar{X} \pm z\, \dfrac{\sigma}{\sqrt{n}}$	[9–1]

To explain these ideas, consider the following example. Del Monte Foods distributes diced peaches in 4-ounce plastic cups. To ensure that each cup contains at least the required amount, Del Monte sets the filling operation to dispense 4.01

ounces of peaches and gel in each cup. Of course, not every cup will contain exactly 4.01 ounces of peaches and gel. Some cups will have more and others less. From historical data, Del Monte knows that 0.04 ounces is the standard deviation of the filling process and that the amount, in ounces, follows the normal probability distribution. The quality control technician selects a sample of 64 cups at the start of each shift, measures the amount in each cup, computes the mean fill amount, and then develops a 95% confidence interval for the population mean. Using the confidence interval, is the process filling the cups to the desired amount? This morning's sample of 64 cups had a sample mean of 4.015 ounces. Based on this information, the 95% confidence interval is:

$$\bar{X} \pm 1.96\, \frac{\sigma}{\sqrt{n}} = 4.015 \pm 1.96\, \frac{0.04}{\sqrt{64}} = 4.015 \pm 0.0098$$

The 95% confidence interval estimates that the population mean is between 4.0052 ounces and 4.0248 ounces of peaches and gel. Recall that the process is set to fill each cup with 4.01 ounces. Because the desired fill amount of 4.01 ounces is in this interval, we conclude that the filling process is achieving the desired results.

In other words, it is reasonable to conclude that the sample mean of 4.015 could have come from a population distribution with a mean of 4.01 ounces.

In this example, we observe that the population mean of 4.01 ounces is in the confidence interval. But this is not always the case. If we selected 100 samples of 64 cups from the population, calculated the sample mean, and developed a confidence interval based on each sample, we would expect to find the population mean in about 95 of the 100 intervals. Or, in contrast, about 5 of the intervals would not contain the population mean. From Chapter 8, this is called sampling error. The following example details repeated sampling from a population.

Example

The American Management Association wishes to have information on the mean income of store managers in the retail industry. A random sample of 49 managers reveals a sample mean of $45,420. The standard deviation of this population is $2,050. The association would like answers to the following questions:

1. What is the population mean?
2. What is a reasonable range of values for the population mean?
3. How do we interpret these results?

Solution

Generally, distributions of salary and income are positively skewed, because a few individuals earn considerably more than others, thus skewing the distribution in the positive direction. Fortunately, the central limit theorem states that the sampling distribution of the mean becomes a normal distribution as sample size increases. In this instance, a sample of 49 store managers is large enough that we can assume that the sampling distribution will follow the normal distribution. Now to answer the questions posed in the example.

1. **What is the population mean?** In this case, we do not know. We do know the sample mean is $45,420. Hence, our best estimate of the unknown population value is the corresponding sample statistic. Thus the sample mean of $45,420 is a *point estimate* of the unknown population mean.
2. **What is a reasonable range of values for the population mean?** The association decides to use the 95% level of confidence. To determine the corresponding confidence interval, we use formula (9–1)

$$\bar{X} \pm z \frac{\sigma}{\sqrt{n}} = \$45,420 \pm 1.96 \frac{\$2,050}{\sqrt{49}} = \$45,420 \pm \$574$$

The confidence interval limits are $44,846 and $45,994. The degree or level of confidence is 95% and the confidence interval is from $44,846 to $45,994. The ± $574 is called the margin of error.

3. **How do we interpret these results?** Suppose we select many samples of 49 store managers, perhaps several hundred. For each sample, we compute the mean and then construct a 95% confidence interval, such as we did in the previous section. We could expect about 95% of these confidence intervals to contain the *population* mean. About 5% of the intervals would not contain the population mean annual income, which is μ. However, a particular confidence interval either contains the population parameter or it does not. The following diagram shows the results of selecting samples from the population of store managers in the retail industry, computing the mean of each and then, using formula (9–1), determining a 95% confidence interval for the population mean. Note that not all intervals include the population mean. Both the endpoints of the fifth sample are less than the population mean. We attribute this to sampling error, and it is the risk we assume when we select the level of confidence.

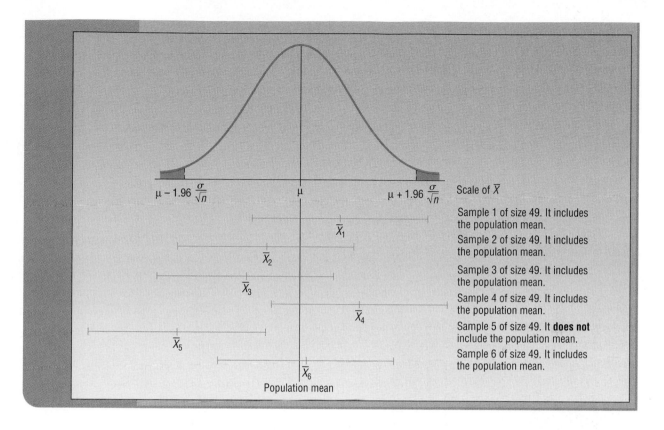

$\mu - 1.96\, \dfrac{\sigma}{\sqrt{n}}$ μ $\mu + 1.96\, \dfrac{\sigma}{\sqrt{n}}$

Scale of $\overline{X}$

Sample 1 of size 49. It includes the population mean.

Sample 2 of size 49. It includes the population mean.

Sample 3 of size 49. It includes the population mean.

Sample 4 of size 49. It includes the population mean.

Sample 5 of size 49. It **does not** include the population mean.

Sample 6 of size 49. It includes the population mean.

$\overline{X}_1$

$\overline{X}_2$

$\overline{X}_3$

$\overline{X}_4$

$\overline{X}_5$

$\overline{X}_6$

Population mean

A Computer Simulation

With the aid of a computer, we can easily create random samples of a desired sample size, *n,* from a population. For each sample of *n* observations with corresponding numerical values, we can calculate the sample mean. With the sample mean, population standard deviation, and confidence level, we can determine the confidence interval for each sample. Then, using all samples and the confidence intervals, we can find the frequency that the population mean is included in the confidence intervals. The following example does just that.

Example

From many years in the automobile leasing business, Town Bank knows that the mean distance driven on an automobile with a four-year lease is 50,000 miles and the standard deviation is 5,000 miles. These are population values. Suppose Town Bank would like to experiment with the idea of sampling to estimate the population mean of 50,000 miles. Town Bank decides to choose a sample size of 30 observations and a 95% confidence interval to estimate the population mean. Using statistical software, 60 random samples with a sample size of 30 are generated and the sample means for each sample computed. Then, using the *n* of 30 and a standard error of 0.913 ($\sigma/\sqrt{n} = 5/\sqrt{30}$), a 95% confidence interval is computed for each sample. Based on this experiment, we want to find the proportion of 95% confidence intervals that include the population mean of 50,000. We expect about 95%, or 57 of the 60 intervals, will include the population mean. To make the calculations easier to understand, we'll conduct the study in thousands of miles, instead of miles.

Solution

The results of the experiment are shown next. In this case, we used Excel. However, Minitab can also be used to simulate the experiment.

	Sample Observations												Sample	95 Percent Confidence Limits	
Sample	1	2	3	4	5	–	–	–	26	27	28	29	30	Mean	Lower Limit	Upper Limit
1	56	47	47	48	58	–	–	–	55	62	48	61	57	51.6	49.811	53.389
2	55	51	52	40	53	–	–	–	47	54	55	55	45	50.77	48.981	52.559
3	42	46	48	46	41	–	–	–	50	52	50	47	45	48.63	46.841	50.419
4	52	49	55	47	49	–	–	–	46	56	49	43	50	49.9	48.111	51.689
5	48	50	53	48	45	–	–	–	46	51	61	49	47	49.03	47.241	50.819
6	49	44	47	46	48	–	–	–	51	44	51	52	43	47.73	45.941	49.519
7	50	53	39	50	46	–	–	–	55	47	43	50	57	50.2	48.411	51.989
8	47	51	49	58	44	–	–	–	49	57	54	48	48	51.17	49.381	52.959
9	51	44	47	56	45	–	–	–	45	51	49	49	52	50.33	48.541	52.119
10	45	44	52	52	56	–	–	–	52	51	52	50	48	50	48.211	51.789
11	43	52	54	46	54	–	–	–	43	46	49	52	52	51.2	49.411	52.989
12	57	53	48	42	55	–	–	–	49	44	46	46	48	49.8	48.011	51.589
13	53	39	47	51	53	–	–	–	42	44	44	55	58	49.6	47.811	51.389
14	56	55	45	43	57	–	–	–	48	51	52	55	47	49.03	47.241	50.819
15	49	50	39	45	44	–	–	–	49	43	44	51	51	49.37	47.581	51.159
16	46	44	55	53	55	–	–	–	44	53	53	43	44	50.13	48.341	51.919
17	64	52	55	55	43	–	–	–	58	46	52	58	55	52.47	50.681	54.259
18	57	51	60	40	53	–	–	–	50	51	53	46	52	50.1	48.311	51.889
19	50	49	51	57	45	–	–	–	53	52	40	45	52	49.6	47.811	51.389
20	45	46	53	57	49	–	–	–	49	43	43	53	48	49.47	47.681	51.259
21	52	45	51	52	45	–	–	–	43	49	49	58	53	50.43	48.641	52.219
22	48	48	52	49	40	–	–	–	50	47	54	51	45	47.53	45.741	49.319
23	48	50	50	53	44	–	–	–	48	57	52	44	39	49.1	47.311	50.889
24	51	51	40	54	52	–	–	–	54	45	50	57	48	50.13	48.341	51.919
25	48	63	41	52	41	–	–	–	48	50	48	44	53	49.33	47.541	51.119
26	47	45	48	59	49	–	–	–	44	47	49	55	42	49.63	47.841	51.419
27	52	45	60	51	52	–	–	–	52	50	54	46	52	49.4	47.611	51.189
28	46	48	46	57	51	–	–	–	51	50	51	41	52	49.33	47.541	51.119
29	46	48	45	42	48	–	–	–	49	43	59	46	50	48.27	46.481	50.059
30	55	48	47	48	48	–	–	–	47	59	54	51	42	50.53	48.741	52.319
31	58	49	56	46	46	–	–	–	44	51	47	51	46	50.77	48.981	52.559
32	53	54	52	58	55	–	–	–	53	52	45	44	51	50	48.211	51.789
33	50	57	56	51	51	–	–	–	58	47	50	56	46	49.7	47.911	51.489
34	61	48	49	53	54	–	–	–	46	46	56	45	54	50.03	48.241	51.819
35	43	42	43	46	49	–	–	–	49	49	56	51	45	49.43	47.641	51.219
36	39	48	48	51	44	–	–	–	54	52	47	50	52	50.07	48.281	51.859
37	48	43	57	42	54	–	–	–	52	50	59	50	52	50.17	48.381	51.959
38	55	43	49	57	45	–	–	–	41	51	51	52	52	49.5	47.711	51.289
39	47	49	58	54	54	–	–	–	50	56	51	56	58	50.37	48.581	52.159
40	47	56	41	50	54	–	–	–	46	56	61	61	45	51.6	49.811	53.389
41	48	47	42	47	62	–	–	–	44	47	49	55	43	49.43	47.641	51.219
42	46	49	43	36	52	–	–	–	45	51	46	51	43	47.67	45.881	49.459
43	44	48	49	48	51	–	–	–	47	52	51	48	49	49.63	47.841	51.419
44	45	52	54	54	49	–	–	–	49	45	53	50	52	49.07	47.281	50.859
45	54	46	54	45	48	–	–	–	55	38	56	50	62	49.53	47.741	51.319
46	48	50	49	52	51	–	–	–	53	57	58	46	50	49.9	48.111	51.689
47	54	55	46	55	50	–	–	–	56	54	50	55	51	50.5	48.711	52.289
48	45	47	47	63	44	–	–	–	45	53	42	53	50	50.1	48.311	51.889
49	47	47	48	54	56	–	–	–	50	48	54	49	51	49.93	48.141	51.719
50	45	61	51	45	54	–	–	–	55	52	47	45	53	51.03	49.241	52.819
51	49	62	43	49	48	–	–	–	49	58	42	58	52	51.07	49.281	52.859
52	54	52	62	43	54	–	–	–	51	57	49	58	55	50.17	48.381	51.959

(continued)

53	46 50 59 56 46	–	–	–	50 51 52 54 53	50.47	48.681	52.259
54	52 50 48 48 58	–	–	–	58 52 43 61 54	51.77	49.981	53.559
55	45 44 46 56 46	–	–	–	43 45 63 48 56	49.37	47.581	51.159
56	60 50 56 51 43	–	–	–	45 43 49 59 54	50.37	48.581	52.159
57	59 56 43 47 52	–	–	–	49 54 50 50 57	49.53	47.741	51.319
58	52 55 48 51 40	–	–	–	53 51 51 52 47	49.77	47.981	51.559
59	53 50 44 53 52	–	–	–	47 50 55 46 51	50.07	48.281	51.859
60	55 54 50 52 43	–	–	–	57 50 48 47 53	52.07	50.281	53.859

To explain, in the first row, the computer software computed 30 random observations based on a distribution with a mean of 50 and a standard deviation of 5. To conserve space, only observations 1 through 5 and 26 through 30 are listed. The first sample's mean is computed and listed as 51.6. In the next columns, the upper and lower limits of the 95% confidence interval for the first sample are shown. The confidence interval calculation for the first sample follows:

$$\bar{X} \pm 1.96 \frac{\sigma}{\sqrt{n}} = 51.6 \pm 1.96 \frac{5}{\sqrt{30}} = 51.6 \pm 1.789$$

This calculation is repeated for all the other samples. The results of the experiment show that 56, or 93.33%, of the sixty 95% confidence intervals include the population mean of 50. Four, or 6.67%, do not include the population mean. The 6.67% is close to the estimate that 5% of the intervals will not include the population mean. The particular intervals are samples 6, 17, 22, and 42. They are highlighted in yellow. This is another example of sampling error, or the possibility that a particular random sample may not be a good representation of the population and that the confidence interval based on the sample does not include the value of the population parameter.

Self-Review 9–1

The Bun-and-Run is a franchise fast-food restaurant located in the Northeast specializing in half-pound hamburgers, fish sandwiches, and chicken sandwiches. Soft drinks and French fries are also available. The Planning Department of Bun-and-Run Inc. reports that the distribution of daily sales for restaurants follows the normal distribution and that the population standard deviation is $3,000. A sample of 40 showed the mean daily sales to be $20,000.
(a) What is the population mean?
(b) What is the best estimate of the population mean? What is this value called?
(c) Develop a 95% confidence interval for the population mean.
(d) Interpret the confidence interval.

Exercises

connect

1. A sample of 49 observations is taken from a normal population with a standard deviation of 10. The sample mean is 55. Determine the 99% confidence interval for the population mean.
2. A sample of 81 observations is taken from a normal population with a standard deviation of 5. The sample mean is 40. Determine the 95% confidence interval for the population mean.
3. A sample of 250 observations is selected from a normal population for which the population standard deviation is known to be 25. The sample mean is 20.
    a. Determine the standard error of the mean.
    b. Explain why we can use formula (9–1) to determine the 95% confidence interval.
    c. Determine the 95% confidence interval for the population mean.

4. Suppose you know σ and you want an 85% confidence level. What value would you use to multiply the standard error of the mean by?

5. A research firm conducted a survey to determine the mean amount steady smokers spend on cigarettes during a week. They found the distribution of amounts spent per week followed the normal distribution with a population standard deviation of $5. A sample of 49 steady smokers revealed that $\overline{X} = \$20$.
   a. What is the point estimate of the population mean? Explain what it indicates.
   b. Using the 95% level of confidence, determine the confidence interval for μ. Explain what it indicates.

6. Refer to the previous exercise. Suppose that 64 smokers (instead of 49) were sampled. Assume the sample mean remained the same.
   a. What is the 95% confidence interval estimate of μ?
   b. Explain why this confidence interval is narrower than the one determined in the previous exercise.

7. Bob Nale is the owner of Nale's Quick Fill. Bob would like to estimate the mean number of gallons of gasoline sold to his customers. Assume the number of gallons sold follows the normal distribution with a population standard deviation of 2.30 gallons. From his records, he selects a random sample of 60 sales and finds the mean number of gallons sold is 8.60.
   a. What is the point estimate of the population mean?
   b. Develop a 99% confidence interval for the population mean.
   c. Interpret the meaning of part (b).

8. Dr. Patton is a professor of English. Recently she counted the number of misspelled words in a group of student essays. She noted the distribution of misspelled words per essay followed the normal distribution with a population standard deviation of 2.44 words per essay. For her 10 A.M. section of 40 students, the mean number of misspelled words was 6.05. Construct a 95% confidence interval for the mean number of misspelled words in the population of student essays.

Population Standard Deviation, σ Unknown

LO 9-4 Compute a confidence interval for the population mean when the population standard deviation is unknown.

In the previous section, we assumed the population standard deviation was known. In the case involving Del Monte 4-ounce cups of peaches, there would likely be a long history of measurements in the filling process. Therefore, it is reasonable to assume the standard deviation of the population is available. However, in most sampling situations the population standard deviation (σ) is not known. Here are some examples where we wish to estimate the population means and it is unlikely we would know the population standard deviations. Suppose each of these studies involves students at West Virginia University.

- The Dean of the Business College wants to estimate the mean number of hours full-time students work at paying jobs each week. He selects a sample of 30 students, contacts each student and asks them how many hours they worked last week. From the sample information, he can calculate the sample mean, but it is not likely he would know or be able to find the *population* standard deviation (σ) required in formula (9–1). He could calculate the standard deviation of the sample and use that as an estimate, but he would not likely know the population standard deviation.

- The Dean of Students wants to estimate the distance the typical commuter student travels to class. She selects a sample of 40 commuter students, contacts each, and determines the one-way distance from each student's home to the center of campus. From the sample data, she calculates the mean travel distance, that is $\overline{X}$. It is unlikely the standard deviation of the population would be known or available, again making formula (9–1) unusable.

- The Director of Student Loans wants to estimate the mean amount owed on student loans at the time of his/her graduation. The director selects a sample of 20 graduating students and contacts each to find the information. From the sample information, the director can estimate the mean amount. However, to develop a confidence interval using formula (9–1), the population standard deviation is necessary. It is not likely this information is available.

Fortunately we can use the sample standard deviation to estimate the population standard deviation. That is, we use *s*, the sample standard deviation, to estimate σ, the population standard deviation. But in doing so, we cannot use formula (9–1). Because we do not know σ, we cannot use the *z* distribution. However, there is a remedy. We use the sample standard deviation and replace the *z* distribution with the *t* distribution.

The *t* distribution is a continuous probability distribution, with many similar characteristics to the *z* distribution. William Gosset, an English brewmaster, was the first to study the *t* distribution.

He was particularly concerned with the exact behavior of the distribution of the following statistic:

$$t = \frac{\bar{X} - \mu}{s/\sqrt{n}}$$

where *s* is an estimate of σ. He was especially worried about the discrepancy between *s* and σ when *s* was calculated from a very small sample. The *t* distribution and the standard normal distribution are shown graphically in Chart 9–1. Note particularly that the *t* distribution is flatter, more spread out, than the standard normal distribution. This is because the standard deviation of the *t* distribution is larger than the standard normal distribution.

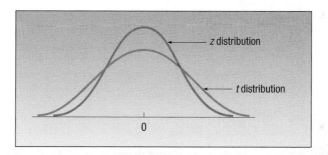

CHART 9–1 The Standard Normal Distribution and Student's *t* Distribution

The following characteristics of the *t* distribution are based on the assumption that the population of interest is normal, or nearly normal.

- It is, like the *z* distribution, a continuous distribution.
- It is, like the *z* distribution, bell-shaped and symmetrical.
- There is not one *t* distribution, but rather a family of *t* distributions. All *t* distributions have a mean of 0, but their standard deviations differ according to the sample size, *n*. There is a *t* distribution for a sample size of 20, another for a sample size of 22, and so on. The standard deviation for a *t* distribution with 5 observations is larger than for a *t* distribution with 20 observations.
- The *t* distribution is more spread out and flatter at the center than the standard normal distribution (see Chart 9–1). As the sample size increases, however, the *t* distribution approaches the standard normal distribution, because the errors in using *s* to estimate σ decrease with larger samples.

Because Student's *t* distribution has a greater spread than the *z* distribution, the value of *t* for a given level of confidence is larger in magnitude than the corresponding *z* value. Chart 9–2 shows the values of *z* for a 95% level of confidence and of *t* for the same level of confidence when the sample size is *n* = 5. How we obtained the actual value of *t* will be explained shortly. For now, observe that for the same level of confidence the *t* distribution is flatter or more spread out than the standard normal distribution.

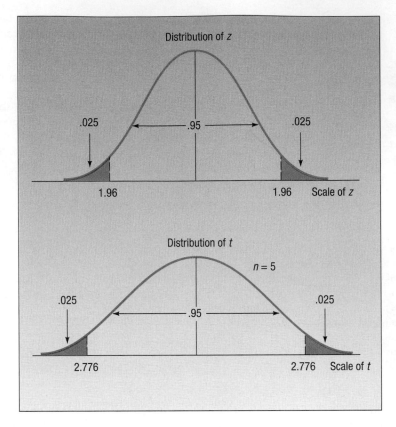

CHART 9–2 Values of z and t for the 95% Level of Confidence

To develop a confidence interval for the population mean using the t distribution, we adjust formula (9–1) as follows.

CONFIDENCE INTERVAL FOR THE POPULATION MEAN, σ UNKNOWN	$\bar{X} \pm t \dfrac{s}{\sqrt{n}}$	**[9–2]**

To determine a confidence interval for the population mean with an unknown standard deviation, we:

1. Assume the sampled population is either normal or approximately normal. This assumption may be questionable for small sample sizes, and becomes more valid with larger sample sizes.
2. Estimate the population standard deviation (σ) with the sample standard deviation (s).
3. Use the t distribution rather than the z distribution.

We should be clear at this point. We base the decision on whether to use the t or the z on whether or not we know σ, the population standard deviation. If we know the population standard deviation, then we use z. If we do not know the population standard deviation, then we must use t. Chart 9–3 summarizes the decision-making process.

The following example will illustrate a confidence interval for a population mean when the population standard deviation is unknown and how to find the appropriate value of t in a table.

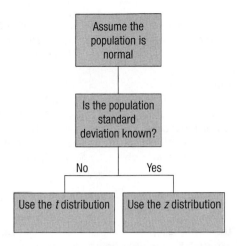

CHART 9–3 Determining When to Use the *z* Distribution or the *t* Distribution

Example

A tire manufacturer wishes to investigate the tread life of its tires. A sample of 10 tires driven 50,000 miles revealed a sample mean of 0.32 inches of tread remaining with a standard deviation of 0.09 inches. Construct a 95% confidence interval for the population mean. Would it be reasonable for the manufacturer to conclude that after 50,000 miles the population mean amount of tread remaining is 0.30 inches?

Solution

To begin, we assume the population distribution is normal. In this case, we don't have a lot of evidence, but the assumption is probably reasonable. We know the sample standard deviation is .09 inches. We use formula (9–2):

$$\overline{X} \pm t \frac{s}{\sqrt{n}}$$

From the information given, $\overline{X} = 0.32$, $s = 0.09$, and $n = 10$. To find the value of t, we use Appendix B.2, a portion of which is reproduced in Table 9–2. Appendix B.2 is also reproduced on the inside back cover of the text. The first step for locating

TABLE 9–2 A Portion of the *t* Distribution

			Confidence Intervals		
	80%	**90%**	**95%**	**98%**	**99%**
			Level of Significance for One-Tailed Test		
df	**0.10**	**0.05**	**0.025**	**0.010**	**0.005**
			Level of Significance for Two-Tailed Test		
	0.20	**0.10**	**0.05**	**0.02**	**0.01**
1	3.078	6.314	12.706	31.821	63.657
2	1.886	2.920	4.303	6.965	9.925
3	1.638	2.353	3.182	4.541	5.841
4	1.533	2.132	2.776	3.747	4.604
5	1.476	2.015	2.571	3.365	4.032
6	1.440	1.943	2.447	3.143	3.707
7	1.415	1.895	2.365	2.998	3.499
8	1.397	1.860	2.306	2.896	3.355
9	1.383	1.833	2.262	2.821	3.250
10	1.372	1.812	2.228	2.764	3.169

t is to move across the columns identified for "Confidence Intervals" to the level of confidence requested. In this case, we want the 95% level of confidence, so we move to the column headed "95%." The column on the left margin is identified as "*df.*" This refers to the number of degrees of freedom. The number of degrees of freedom is the number of observations in the sample minus the number of samples, written $n - 1$. In this case, it is $10 - 1 = 9$. Why did we decide there were 9 degrees of freedom? When sample statistics are being used, it is necessary to determine the number of values that are *free to vary*.

To illustrate the meaning of degrees of freedom: Assume that the mean of four numbers is known to be 5. The four numbers are 7, 4, 1, and 8. The deviations of these numbers from the mean must total 0. The deviations of $+2$, -1, -4, and $+3$ do total 0. If the deviations of $+2$, -1, and -4 are known, then the value of $+3$ is fixed (restricted) in order to satisfy the condition that the sum of the deviations must equal 0. Thus, 1 degree of freedom is lost in a sampling problem involving the standard deviation of the sample because one number (the arithmetic mean) is known. For a 95% level of confidence and 9 degrees of freedom, we select the row with 9 degrees of freedom. The value of *t* is 2.262.

To determine the confidence interval, we substitute the values in formula (9–2).

$$\bar{X} \pm t\frac{s}{\sqrt{n}} = 0.32 \pm 2.262\frac{0.09}{\sqrt{10}} = 0.32 \pm .064$$

The endpoints of the confidence interval are 0.256 and 0.384. How do we interpret this result? If we repeated this study 200 times, calculating the 95% confidence interval with each sample's mean and the standard deviation, 190 of the intervals would include the population mean. Ten of the intervals would not include the population mean. This is the effect of sampling error. A further interpretation is to conclude that the population mean is in this interval. The manufacturer can be reasonably sure (95% confident) that the mean remaining tread depth is between 0.256 and 0.384 inches. Because the value of 0.30 is in this interval, it is possible that the mean of the population is 0.30.

Here is another example to clarify the use of confidence intervals. Suppose an article in your local newspaper reported that the mean time to sell a residential property in the area is 60 days. You select a random sample of 20 homes sold in the last year and find the mean selling time is 65 days. Based on the sample data, you develop a 95% confidence interval for the population mean. You find that the endpoints of the confidence interval are 62 days and 68 days. How do you interpret this result? You can be reasonably confident the population mean is within this range. The value proposed for the population mean, that is, 60 days, is not included in the interval. It is not likely that the population mean is 60 days. The evidence indicates the statement by the local newspaper may not be correct. To put it another way, it seems unreasonable to obtain the sample you did from a population that had a mean selling time of 60 days.

The following example will show additional details for determining and interpreting a confidence interval. We used Minitab to perform the calculations.

Example

The manager of the Inlet Square Mall, near Ft. Myers, Florida, wants to estimate the mean amount spent per shopping visit by customers. A sample of 20 customers reveals the following amounts spent.

$48.16	$42.22	$46.82	$51.45	$23.78	$41.86	$54.86
37.92	52.64	48.59	50.82	46.94	61.83	61.69
49.17	61.46	51.35	52.68	58.84	43.88	

What is the best estimate of the population mean? Determine a 95% confidence interval. Interpret the result. Would it be reasonable to conclude that the population mean is $50? What about $60?

Solution

The mall manager assumes that the population of the amounts spent follows the normal distribution. This is a reasonable assumption in this case. Additionally, the confidence interval technique is quite powerful and tends to commit any errors on the conservative side if the population is not normal.

The population standard deviation is not known. Hence, it is appropriate to use the *t* distribution and formula (9–2) to find the confidence interval. We use the Minitab system to find the mean and standard deviation of this sample. The results are shown below.

↓	C1	C2	C3	C4	C5	C6	C7	C8	C9	C10	C11
	amount										
1	48.16										
2	42.22										
3	46.82										
4	51.45										
5	23.78										
6	41.86										
7	54.86										
8	37.92										
9	52.64										
10	48.59										
11	50.82										
12	46.94										

Descriptive Statistics: amount

Variable	N	N*	Mean	SE Mean	StDev	Minimum	Q1	Median	Q3	Maximum
amount	20	0	49.35	2.02	9.01	23.78	44.62	50.00	54.31	61.83

One-Sample T: amount

Variable	N	Mean	StDev	SE Mean	95% CI
amount	20	49.35	9.01	2.02	(45.13, 53.57)

The mall manager does not know the population mean. The sample mean is the best estimate of that value. From the pictured Minitab output, the mean is $49.35, which is the best estimate, the *point estimate*, of the unknown population mean.

We use formula (9–2) to find the confidence interval. The value of *t* is available from Appendix B.2. There are $n - 1 = 20 - 1 = 19$ degrees of freedom. We move across the row with 19 degrees of freedom to the column for the 95% confidence level. The value at this intersection is 2.093. We substitute these values into formula (9–2) to find the confidence interval.

$$\bar{X} \pm t \frac{s}{\sqrt{n}} = \$49.35 \pm 2.093 \frac{\$9.01}{\sqrt{20}} = \$49.35 \pm \$4.22$$

The endpoints of the confidence interval are $45.13 and $53.57. It is reasonable to conclude that the population mean is in that interval.

The manager of Inlet Square wondered whether the population mean could have been $50 or $60. The value of $50 is within the confidence interval. It is reasonable that the population mean could be $50. The value of $60 is not in the confidence interval. Hence, we conclude that the population mean is unlikely to be $60.

The calculations to construct a confidence interval are also available in Excel. The output follows. Note that the sample mean ($49.35) and the sample standard deviation ($9.01) are the same as those in the Minitab calculations. In the Excel output, the last line also includes the margin of error, which is the amount that is added and subtracted from the sample mean to form the endpoints of the confidence interval. This value is found from

$$t \frac{s}{\sqrt{n}} = 2.093 \frac{\$9.01}{\sqrt{20}} = \$4.22$$

☒ shopping					
	A	**B**	**C**	**D**	**E**
1	**Amount**		**Amount**		
2	48.16				
3	42.22		Mean	49.35	
4	46.82		Standard Error	2.02	
5	51.45		Median	50.00	
6	23.78		Mode	#N/A	
7	41.86		Standard Deviation	9.01	
8	54.86		Sample Variance	81.22	
9	37.92		Kurtosis	2.26	
10	52.64		Skewness	-1.00	
11	48.59		Range	38.05	
12	50.82		Minimum	23.78	
13	46.94		Maximum	61.83	
14	61.83		Sum	986.96	
15	61.69		Count	20.00	
16	49.17		Confidence Level(95.0%)	4.22	
17	61.46				
18	51.35				
19	52.68				
20	58.84				
21	43.88				

Before doing the confidence interval exercises, we would like to point out a useful characteristic of the *t* distribution that will allow us to use the *t* table to quickly find both *z* and *t* values. Earlier in this section, on page 267, we detailed the characteristics of the *t* distribution. The last point indicated that as we increase the sample size the *t* distribution approaches the *z* distribution. In fact, when we reach an infinitely large sample, the *t* distribution is exactly equal to the *z* distribution.

Using the t distribution to find a z value.

To explain, Table 9–3 is a portion of Appendix B.2, with the degrees of freedom between 4 and 99 omitted. To find the appropriate *z* value for a 95% confidence interval, we begin by going to the confidence interval section and selecting the column headed "95%." Move down that column to the last row, which is labeled "∞," or infinite degrees of freedom. The value reported is 1.960, the same value that we found using the standard normal distribution in Appendix B.1. This confirms the convergence of the *t* distribution to the *z* distribution.

What does this mean for us? Instead of searching in the body of the *z* table, we can go to the last row of the *t* table and find the appropriate value to build a confidence interval. An additional benefit is that the values have three decimal places. So, using this table for a 90% confidence interval, go down the column headed "90%" and see the value 1.645, which is a more precise *z* value that can be used for the 90% confidence level. Other *z* values for 98% and 99% confidence intervals are also available with three decimals. **Note that we will use the *t* table, which is summarized in Table 9–3, to find the *z* values with three decimals for all following exercises and problems.**

TABLE 9–3 Student's *t* Distribution

df (degrees of freedom)	Confidence Interval					
	80%	90%	95%	98%	99%	99.9%
	Level of Significance for One-Tailed Test, α					
	0.1	0.05	0.02	0.01	0.001	0.0005
	Level of Significance for Two-Tailed Test, α					
	0.2	0.1	0.05	0.02	0.01	0.001
1	3.078	6.314	12.706	31.821	63.657	636.619
2	1.886	2.920	4.303	6.965	9.925	31.599
3	1.638	2.353	3.182	4.541	5.841	12.924
⋮	⋮	⋮	⋮	⋮	⋮	⋮
100	1.290	1.660	1.984	2.364	2.626	3.390
120	1.289	1.658	1.980	2.358	2.617	3.373
140	1.288	1.656	1.977	2.353	2.611	3.361
160	1.287	1.654	1.975	2.350	2.607	3.352
180	1.286	1.653	1.973	2.347	2.603	3.345
200	1.286	1.653	1.972	2.345	2.601	3.340
∞	1.282	1.645	1.960	2.326	2.576	3.291

Self-Review 9–2

Dottie Kleman is the "Cookie Lady." She bakes and sells cookies at locations in the Philadelphia area. Ms. Kleman is concerned about absenteeism among her workers. The information below reports the number of days absent for a sample of 10 workers during the last two-week pay period.

| 4 | 1 | 2 | 2 | 1 | 2 | 2 | 1 | 0 | 3 |

(a) Determine the mean and the standard deviation of the sample.
(b) What is the population mean? What is the best estimate of that value?
(c) Develop a 95% confidence interval for the population mean. Assume that the population distribution is normal.
(d) Explain why the *t* distribution is used as a part of the confidence interval.
(e) Is it reasonable to conclude that the typical worker does not miss any days during a pay period?

Exercises

connect

9. Use Appendix B.2 to locate the value of *t* under the following conditions.
   a. The sample size is 12 and the level of confidence is 95%.
   b. The sample size is 20 and the level of confidence is 90%.
   c. The sample size is 8 and the level of confidence is 99%.
10. Use Appendix B.2 to locate the value of *t* under the following conditions.
   a. The sample size is 15 and the level of confidence is 95%.
   b. The sample size is 24 and the level of confidence is 98%.
   c. The sample size is 12 and the level of confidence is 90%.
11. The owner of Britten's Egg Farm wants to estimate the mean number of eggs laid per chicken. A sample of 20 chickens shows they laid an average of 20 eggs per month with a standard deviation of 2 eggs per month.
   a. What is the value of the population mean? What is the best estimate of this value?
   b. Explain why we need to use the *t* distribution. What assumption do you need to make?
   c. For a 95% confidence interval, what is the value of *t*?
   d. Develop the 95% confidence interval for the population mean.
   e. Would it be reasonable to conclude that the population mean is 21 eggs? What about 25 eggs?

12. The U.S. Dairy Industry wants to estimate the mean yearly milk consumption. A sample of 16 people reveals the mean yearly consumption to be 60 gallons with a standard deviation of 20 gallons.
   a. What is the value of the population mean? What is the best estimate of this value?
   b. Explain why we need to use the *t* distribution. What assumption do you need to make?
   c. For a 90% confidence interval, what is the value of *t*?
   d. Develop the 90% confidence interval for the population mean.
   e. Would it be reasonable to conclude that the population mean is 63 gallons?

13. Merrill Lynch Securities and Health Care Retirement Inc. are two large employers in downtown Toledo, Ohio. They are considering jointly offering child care for their employees. As a part of the feasibility study, they wish to estimate the mean weekly child-care cost of their employees. A sample of 10 employees who use child care reveals the following amounts spent last week. **(df)**

$107	$92	$97	$95	$105	$101	$91	$99	$95	$104

Develop a 90% confidence interval for the population mean. Interpret the result.

14. The Greater Pittsburgh Area Chamber of Commerce wants to estimate the mean time workers who are employed in the downtown area spend getting to work. A sample of 15 workers reveals the following number of minutes spent traveling. **(df)**

29	38	38	33	38	21	45	34
40	37	37	42	30	29	35	

Develop a 98% confidence interval for the population mean. Interpret the result.

9.4 A Confidence Interval for a Proportion

LO 9-5 Compute a confidence interval for a population proportion.

The material presented so far in this chapter uses the ratio scale of measurement. That is, we use such variables as incomes, weights, distances, and ages. We now want to consider situations such as the following:

- The career services director at Southern Technical Institute reports that 80% of its graduates enter the job market in a position related to their field of study.
- A company representative claims that 45% of Burger King sales are made at the drive-through window.
- A survey of homes in the Chicago area indicated that 85% of the new construction had central air conditioning.
- A recent survey of married men between the ages of 35 and 50 found that 63% felt that both partners should earn a living.

These examples illustrate the nominal scale of measurement. When we measure with a nominal scale, an observation is classified into one of two or more mutually exclusive groups. For example, a graduate of Southern Tech either entered the job market in a position related to his or her field of study or not. A particular Burger King customer either made a purchase at the drive-through window or did not make a purchase at the drive-through window. There are only two possibilities, and the outcome must be classified into one of the two groups.

> **PROPORTION** The fraction, ratio, or percent indicating the part of the sample or the population having a particular trait of interest.

As an example of a proportion, a recent survey indicated that 92 out of 100 people surveyed favored the continued use of daylight savings time in the summer. The sample proportion is 92/100, or .92, or 92%. If we let p represent the sample proportion, X the number of "successes," and n the number of items sampled, we can determine a sample proportion as follows.

SAMPLE PROPORTION	$p = \dfrac{X}{n}$	**[9–3]**

The population proportion is identified by π. Therefore, π refers to the percent of successes in the population. Recall from Chapter 6 that π is the proportion of "successes" in a binomial distribution. This continues our practice of using Greek letters to identify population parameters and Roman letters to identify sample statistics.

To develop a confidence interval for a proportion, we need to meet the following assumptions.

1. The binomial conditions, discussed in Chapter 6, have been met. Briefly, these conditions are:
   a. The sample data is the number of successes in n trials.
   b. There are only two possible outcomes. (We usually label one of the outcomes a "success" and the other a "failure.")
   c. The probability of a success remains the same from one trial to the next.
   d. The trials are independent. This means the outcome on one trial does not affect the outcome on another.
2. The values $n\pi$ and $n(1 - \pi)$ should both be greater than or equal to 5. This condition allows us to invoke the central limit theorem and employ the standard normal distribution, that is, z, to complete a confidence interval.

Developing a point estimate for a population proportion and a confidence interval for a population proportion is similar to doing so for a mean. To illustrate, John Gail is running for Congress from the third district of Nebraska. From a random sample of 100 voters in the district, 60 indicate they plan to vote for him in the upcoming election. The sample proportion is .60, but the population proportion is unknown. That is, we do not know what proportion of voters in the *population* will vote for Mr. Gail. The sample value, .60, is the best estimate we have of the unknown population parameter. So we let p, which is .60, be an estimate of π, which is not known.

To develop a confidence interval for a population proportion, we use:

CONFIDENCE INTERVAL FOR A POPULATION PROPORTION	$p \pm z\sqrt{\dfrac{p(1-p)}{n}}$	**[9–4]**

An example will help to explain the details of determining a confidence interval and interpreting the result.

Example

The union representing the Bottle Blowers of America (BBA) is considering a proposal to merge with the Teamsters Union. According to BBA union bylaws, at least three-fourths of the union membership must approve any merger. A random sample of 2,000 current BBA members reveals 1,600 plan to vote for the merger proposal. What is the estimate of the population proportion? Develop a 95% confidence interval for the population proportion. Basing your decision on this sample information, can you conclude that the necessary proportion of BBA members favor the merger? Why?

Solution

First, calculate the sample proportion from formula (9–3). It is .80, found by

$$p = \frac{X}{n} = \frac{1,600}{2,000} = .80$$

Thus, we estimate that 80% of the population favor the merger proposal. We determine the 95% confidence interval using formula (9–4). The z value corresponding to the 95% level of confidence is 1.96.

$$p \pm z\sqrt{\frac{p(1-p)}{n}} = .80 \pm 1.96\sqrt{\frac{.80(1-.80)}{2,000}} = .80 \pm .018$$

The endpoints of the confidence interval are .782 and .818. The lower endpoint is greater than .75. Hence, we conclude that the merger proposal will likely pass because the interval estimate includes values greater than 75% of the union membership.

To review the interpretation of the confidence interval: If the poll was conducted 100 times with 100 different samples, the confidence intervals constructed from 95 of the samples would contain the true population proportion. In addition, the interpretation of a confidence interval can be very useful in decision making and play a very important role especially on election night. For example, Cliff Obermeyer is running for Congress from the 6th District of New Jersey. Suppose 500 voters are contacted upon leaving the polls and 275 indicate they voted for Mr. Obermeyer. We will assume that the exit poll of 500 voters is a random sample of those voting in the 6th District. That means that 55% of those in the sample voted for Mr. Obermeyer. Based on formula (9–3):

$$p = \frac{X}{n} = \frac{275}{500} = .55$$

Now, to be assured of election, he must earn *more than* 50% of the votes in the population of those voting. At this point, we know a point estimate, which is .55, of the population of voters that will vote for him. But we do not know the percent in the population that will ultimately vote for the candidate. So the question is: Could we take a sample of 500 voters from a population where 50% or less of the voters support Mr. Obermeyer and find that 55% of the sample support him? To put it another way, could the sampling error, which is $p - \pi = .55 - .50 = .05$ be due to chance, or is the population of voters who support Mr. Obermeyer greater than .50. If we develop a confidence interval for the sample proportion and find that .50 is *not* in the interval, then we conclude that the proportion of voters supporting Mr. Obermeyer is greater than .50. What does that mean? Well, it means he should be elected! What if .50 is in the interval? Then we conclude that it is possible that 50% or less of the voters support his candidacy and we cannot conclude that he will be elected based on the sample information. In this case, using the 95% significance level and formula (9–4):

$$p \pm z\sqrt{\frac{p(1-p)}{n}} = .55 \pm 1.96\sqrt{\frac{.55(1-.55)}{500}} = .55 \pm .044$$

So the endpoints of the confidence interval are .55 − .044 = .506 and .55 + .044 = .594. The value of .50 is not in this interval. So we conclude that probably *more than 50%* of the voters support Mr. Obermeyer and that is enough to get him elected.

Is this procedure ever used? Yes! It is exactly the procedure used by television networks, news magazines, and polling organizations on election night.

Self-Review 9–3

A market survey was conducted to estimate the proportion of homemakers who would recognize the brand name of a cleanser based on the shape and the color of the container. Of the 1,400 homemakers sampled, 420 were able to identify the brand by name.
(a) Estimate the value of the population proportion.
(b) Develop a 99% confidence interval for the population proportion.
(c) Interpret your findings.

Exercises

connect

15. The owner of the West End Kwick Fill Gas Station wishes to determine the proportion of customers who use a credit card or debit card to pay at the pump. He surveys 100 customers and finds that 80 paid at the pump.
    a. Estimate the value of the population proportion.
    b. Develop a 95% confidence interval for the population proportion.
    c. Interpret your findings.
16. Ms. Maria Wilson is considering running for mayor of the town of Bear Gulch, Montana. Before completing the petitions, she decides to conduct a survey of voters in Bear Gulch. A sample of 400 voters reveals that 300 would support her in the November election.
    a. Estimate the value of the population proportion.
    b. Develop a 99% confidence interval for the population proportion.
    c. Interpret your findings.
17. The Fox TV network is considering replacing one of its prime-time crime investigation shows with a new family-oriented comedy show. Before a final decision is made, network executives commission a sample of 400 viewers. After viewing the comedy, 250 indicated they would watch the new show and suggested it replace the crime investigation show.
    a. Estimate the value of the population proportion.
    b. Develop a 99% confidence interval for the population proportion.
    c. Interpret your findings.
18. Schadek Silkscreen Printing Inc. purchases plastic cups on which to print logos for sporting events, proms, birthdays, and other special occasions. Zack Schadek, the owner, received a large shipment this morning. To ensure the quality of the shipment, he selected a random sample of 300 cups. He found 15 to be defective.
    a. What is the estimated proportion defective in the population?
    b. Develop a 95% confidence interval for the proportion defective.
    c. Zack has an agreement with his supplier that he is to return lots that are 10% or more defective. Should he return this lot? Explain your decision.

9.5 Choosing an Appropriate Sample Size

When working with confidence intervals, one important variable is sample size. However, in practice, sample size is not a variable. It is a decision we make so that our estimate of a population parameter is a good one. Our decision is based on three variables:

LO 9-6 Calculate the required sample size to estimate a population proportion or population mean.

1. The margin of error the researcher will tolerate.
2. The level of confidence desired, for example, 95%.
3. The variation or dispersion of the population being studied.

The first variable is the *margin of error*. It is designated as *E* and is the amount that is added and subtracted to the sample mean (or sample proportion) to determine the endpoints of the confidence interval. For example, in a study of wages, we may decide that we want to estimate the mean wage of the population with a margin of error of plus or minus $1,000. Or in an opinion poll, we may decide that we want to estimate the population proportion with a margin of error of plus or minus 3.5%. The margin of error is the amount of error we are willing to tolerate in estimating a population parameter. You may wonder why we do not choose small margins of error. There is a trade-off between the margin of error and sample size. A small margin of error will require a larger sample and more money and time to collect the sample. A larger margin of error will permit a smaller sample and result in a wider confidence interval.

The second choice is the *level of confidence.* In working with confidence intervals, we logically choose relatively high levels of confidence such as 95% and 99%. To compute the sample size, we need the *z*-statistic that corresponds to the chosen level of confidence. The 95% level of confidence corresponds to a *z* value of 1.96, and a 90% level of confidence corresponds to a *z* value of 1.645 (using the *t* table). Notice that larger sample sizes (and more time and money to collect the sample) correspond with higher levels of confidence. Also, notice that we use a *z*-statistic.

The third choice to determine the sample size is the *population standard deviation.* If the population is widely dispersed, a large sample is required. On the other hand, if the population is concentrated (homogeneous), the required sample size will be smaller. Often, we do not know the population standard deviation. Here are three suggestions for finding a value for the population standard deviation.

1. **Conduct a pilot study.** This is the most common method. Suppose we want an estimate of the number of hours per week worked by students enrolled in the College of Business at the University of Texas. To test the validity of our questionnaire, we use it on a small sample of students. From this small sample, we compute the standard deviation of the number of hours worked and use this value as the population standard deviation.
2. **Use a comparable study.** Use this approach when there is an estimate of the standard deviation from another study. Suppose we want to estimate the number of hours worked per week by refuse workers. Information from certain state or federal agencies that regularly study the workforce may provide a reliable value to use for the population standard deviation.
3. **Use a range-based approach.** To use this approach, we need to know or have an estimate of the largest and smallest values in the population. Recall from Chapter 3, the Empirical Rule states that virtually all the observations could be expected to be within plus or minus 3 standard deviations of the mean, assuming that the distribution follows the normal distribution. Thus, the distance between the largest and the smallest values is 6 standard deviations. We can estimate the standard deviation as one-sixth of the range. For example, the director of operations at University Bank wants to estimate the number of checks written per month by college students. She believes that the distribution of the number of checks written follows the normal distribution. The minimum and maximum numbers written per month are 2 and 50, so the range is 48, found by $(50 - 2)$. Then 8 checks per month, 48/6, would be the value we would use for the population standard deviation.

Sample Size to Estimate a Population Mean

To estimate a population mean, we can express the interaction among these three factors and the sample size in the following formula. Notice that this formula is the margin of error used to calculate the endpoints of confidence intervals to estimate a population mean!

$$E = z \frac{\sigma}{\sqrt{n}}$$

Solving this equation for n yields the following result.

| SAMPLE SIZE FOR ESTIMATING THE POPULATION MEAN | $n = \left(\dfrac{z\sigma}{E}\right)^2$ | [9–5] |

where:
> n is the size of the sample.
> z is the standard normal value corresponding to the desired level of confidence.
> σ is the population standard deviation.
> E is the maximum allowable error.

Always round sample size up to the next whole number.

The result of this calculation is not always a whole number. When the outcome is not a whole number, the usual practice is to round up *any* fractional result to the next whole number. For example, 201.21 would be rounded up to 202.

Example

A student in public administration wants to determine the mean amount members of city councils in large cities earn per month as remuneration for being a council member. The error in estimating the mean is to be less than $100 with a 95% level of confidence. The student found a report by the Department of Labor that reported a standard deviation of $1,000. What is the required sample size?

Solution

The maximum allowable error, E, is $100. The value of z for a 95% level of confidence is 1.96, and the value of the standard deviation is $1,000. Substituting these values into formula (9–5) gives the required sample size as:

$$n = \left(\frac{z\sigma}{E}\right)^2 = \left(\frac{(1.96)(\$1,000)}{\$100}\right)^2 = (19.6)^2 = 384.16$$

The computed value of 384.16 is rounded up to 385. A sample of 385 is required to meet the specifications. If the student wants to increase the level of confidence, for example to 99%, this will require a larger sample. Using the t table, the z value for a 99% level of confidence is 2.576.

$$n = \left(\frac{z\sigma}{E}\right)^2 = \left(\frac{(2.576)(\$1,000)}{\$100}\right)^2 = (25.76)^2 = 663.58$$

We recommend a sample of 664. Observe how much the change in the confidence level changed the size of the sample. An increase from the 95% to the 99% level of confidence resulted in an increase of 279 observations, or 72% [(664/385) × 100]. This would greatly increase the cost of the study, both in terms of time and money. Hence, the level of confidence should be considered carefully.

Sample Size to Estimate a Population Proportion

To determine the sample size for a proportion, the same three variables need to be specified:

1. The margin of error.
2. The desired level of confidence.
3. The variation or dispersion of the population being studied.

For the binomial distribution, the margin of error is:

$$E = z \sqrt{\frac{\pi(1 - \pi)}{n}}$$

Solving this equation for n yields the following equation

SAMPLE SIZE FOR THE POPULATION PROPORTION

$$n = \pi(1 - \pi)\left(\frac{z}{E}\right)^2$$

[9–6]

where:
  n is the size of the sample.
  z is the standard normal value corresponding to the desired level of confidence.
  π is the population proportion.
  E is the maximum allowable error.

The choices for the z-statistic and the margin of error, E, are the same as the choices for estimating the population mean. However, in this case the population standard deviation for a binomial distribution is represented by $\pi(1 - \pi)$. To find a value of the population proportion, we would find a comparable study or conduct a pilot study. If a reliable value cannot be found, then a value of .50 should be used for π. Note that $\pi(1 - \pi)$ has the largest value using 0.50 and, therefore, without a good estimate of the population proportion, overstates the sample size. This difference will not hurt the estimate of the population proportion.

Example

The study in the previous example also estimates the proportion of cities that have private refuse collectors. The student wants the margin of error to be within .10 of the population proportion, the desired level of confidence is 90%, and no estimate is available for the population proportion. What is the required sample size?

Solution

The estimate of the population proportion is to be within .10, so $E = .10$. The desired level of confidence is .90, which corresponds to a z value of 1.645, using the t table. Because no estimate of the population proportion is available, we use .50. The suggested number of observations is

$$n = (.5)(1 - .5)\left(\frac{1.645}{.10}\right)^2 = 67.65$$

The student needs a random sample of 68 cities.

Self-Review 9–4

The registrar wants to estimate the arithmetic mean grade point average (GPA) of all graduating seniors during the past 10 years. GPAs range between 2.0 and 4.0. The mean GPA is to be estimated within plus or minus .05 of the population mean. Based on prior experience, the population standard deviation is 0.279. Use the 99% level of confidence. Will you assist the college registrar in determining how many transcripts to study?

Exercises

connect™

19. A population is estimated to have a standard deviation of 10. We want to estimate the population mean within 2, with a 95% level of confidence. How large a sample is required?

20. We want to estimate the population mean within 5, with a 99% level of confidence. The population standard deviation is estimated to be 15. How large a sample is required?

21. The estimate of the population proportion is to be within plus or minus .05, with a 95% level of confidence. The best estimate of the population proportion is .15. How large a sample is required?

22. The estimate of the population proportion is to be within plus or minus .10, with a 99% level of confidence. The best estimate of the population proportion is .45. How large a sample is required?

23. A survey is being planned to determine the mean amount of time corporation executives watch television. A pilot survey indicated that the mean time per week is 12 hours, with a standard deviation of 3 hours. It is desired to estimate the mean viewing time within one-quarter hour. The 95% level of confidence is to be used. How many executives should be surveyed?

24. A processor of carrots cuts the green top off each carrot, washes the carrots, and inserts six to a package. Twenty packages are inserted in a box for shipment. To test the weight of the boxes, a few were checked. The mean weight was 20.4 pounds; the standard deviation, 0.5 pounds. How many boxes must the processor sample to be 95% confident that the sample mean does not differ from the population mean by more than 0.2 pounds?

25. Suppose the U.S. president wants an estimate of the proportion of the population who support his current policy toward revisions in the health care system. The president wants the estimate to be within .04 of the true proportion. Assume a 95% level of confidence. The president's political advisors estimated the proportion supporting the current policy to be .60.
   a. How large of a sample is required?
   b. How large of a sample would be necessary if no estimate were available for the proportion supporting current policy?

26. Past surveys reveal that 30% of tourists going to Las Vegas to gamble spend more than $1,000. The Visitor's Bureau of Las Vegas wants to update this percentage.
   a. The new study is to use the 90% confidence level. The estimate is to be within 1% of the population proportion. What is the necessary sample size?
   b. The Bureau feels the sample size determined above is too large. What can be done to reduce the sample? Based on your suggestion, recalculate the sample size.

Chapter Summary

I. A point estimate is a single value (statistic) used to estimate a population value (parameter).

II. A confidence interval is a range of values within which the population parameter is expected to occur.

A. The factors that determine the width of a confidence interval for a mean are:
   1. The number of observations in the sample, n.
   2. The variability in the population, usually estimated by the sample standard deviation, s.
   3. The level of confidence.
      a. To determine the confidence limits when the population standard deviation is known, we use the z distribution. The formula is

$$\overline{X} \pm z \frac{\sigma}{\sqrt{n}} \qquad \text{[9–1]}$$

      b. To determine the confidence limits when the population standard deviation is unknown, we use the t distribution. The formula is

$$\overline{X} \pm t \frac{s}{\sqrt{n}} \qquad \text{[9–2]}$$

III. The major characteristics of the *t* distribution are:
  A. It is a continuous distribution.
  B. It is mound-shaped and symmetrical.
  C. It is flatter, or more spread out, than the standard normal distribution.
  D. There is a family of *t* distributions, depending on the number of degrees of freedom.
IV. A proportion is a ratio, fraction, or percent that indicates the part of the sample or population that has a particular characteristic.
  A. A sample proportion is found by *X*, the number of successes, divided by *n*, the number of observations.
  B. We construct a confidence interval for a sample proportion from the following formula.

$$p \pm z\sqrt{\frac{p(1-p)}{n}} \qquad \textbf{[9–4]}$$

V. We can determine an appropriate sample size for estimating both means and proportions.
  A. There are three factors that determine the sample size when we wish to estimate the mean.
    1. The margin of error, *E*.
    2. The desired level of confidence.
    3. The variation in the population.
    4. The formula to determine the sample size for the mean is

$$n = \left(\frac{z\sigma}{E}\right)^2 \qquad \textbf{[9–5]}$$

  B. There are three factors that determine the sample size when we wish to estimate a proportion.
    1. The margin of error, *E*.
    2. The desired level of confidence.
    3. A value for π to calculate the variation in the population.
    4. The formula to determine the sample size for a proportion is

$$n = \pi(1-\pi)\left(\frac{z}{E}\right)^2 \qquad \textbf{[9–6]}$$

Chapter Exercises

connect

27. A random sample of 85 group leaders, supervisors, and similar personnel at General Motors revealed that, on average, they spent 6.5 years in a particular job before being promoted. The standard deviation of the sample was 1.7 years. Construct a 95% confidence interval.

28. A state meat inspector in Iowa has been given the assignment of estimating the mean net weight of packages of ground chuck labeled "3 pounds." Of course, he realizes that the weights cannot be precisely 3 pounds. A sample of 36 packages reveals the mean weight to be 3.01 pounds, with a standard deviation of 0.03 pounds.
  a. What is the estimated population mean?
  b. Determine a 95% confidence interval for the population mean.

29. As part of their business promotional package, the Milwaukee Chamber of Commerce would like an estimate of the mean cost per month to lease a one-bedroom apartment. A random sample of 40 apartments currently available for lease showed the mean cost per month was $323. The standard deviation of the sample was $25.
  a. Develop a 98% confidence interval for the population mean.
  b. Would it be reasonable to conclude that the population mean is $350 per month?

30. A recent survey of 50 executives who were laid off during a recent recession revealed it took a mean of 26 weeks for them to find another position. The standard deviation of the sample was 6.2 weeks. Construct a 95% confidence interval for the population mean. Is it reasonable that the population mean is 28 weeks? Justify your answer.

31. Marty Rowatti recently assumed the position of director of the YMCA of South Jersey. He would like some current data on how long current members of the YMCA have been members. To investigate, suppose he selects a random sample of 40 current members. The mean length of membership of those included in the sample is 8.32 years and the standard deviation is 3.07 years.
  a. What is the mean of the population?
  b. Develop a 90% confidence interval for the population mean.

c. The previous director, in the summary report she prepared as she retired, indicated the mean length of membership was now "almost 10 years." Does the sample information substantiate this claim? Cite evidence.

32. The American Restaurant Association collected information on the number of meals eaten outside the home per week by young married couples. A survey of 60 couples showed the sample mean number of meals eaten outside the home was 2.76 meals per week, with a standard deviation of 0.75 meals per week. Construct a 99% confidence interval for the population mean.

33. The National Collegiate Athletic Association (NCAA) reported that the mean number of hours spent per week on coaching and recruiting by college football assistant coaches during the season was 70. A random sample of 50 assistant coaches showed the sample mean to be 68.6 hours, with a standard deviation of 8.2 hours.
   a. Using the sample data, construct a 99% confidence interval for the population mean.
   b. Does the 99% confidence interval include the value suggested by the NCAA? Interpret this result.
   c. Suppose you decided to switch from a 99% to a 95% confidence interval. Without performing any calculations, will the interval increase, decrease, or stay the same? Which of the values in the formula will change?

34. The Human Relations Department of Electronics Inc. would like to include a dental plan as part of the benefits package. The question is: How much does a typical employee and his or her family spend per year on dental expenses? A sample of 45 employees reveals the mean amount spent last year was $1,820, with a standard deviation of $660.
   a. Construct a 95% confidence interval for the population mean.
   b. The information from part (a) was given to the president of Electronics Inc. He indicated he could afford $1,700 of dental expenses per employee. Is it possible that the population mean could be $1,700? Justify your answer.

35. A student conducted a study and reported that the 95% confidence interval for the mean ranged from 46 to 54. He was sure that the mean of the sample was 50, that the standard deviation of the sample was 16, and that the sample size was at least 30, but could not remember the exact number. Can you help him out?

36. A recent study by the American Automobile Dealers Association revealed the mean amount of profit per car sold for a sample of 20 dealers was $290, with a standard deviation of $125. Develop a 95% confidence interval for the population mean.

37. A study of 25 graduates of four-year colleges by the American Banker's Association revealed the mean amount owed by a student in student loans was $14,381. The standard deviation of the sample was $1,892. Construct a 90% confidence interval for the population mean. Is it reasonable to conclude that the mean of the population is actually $15,000? Tell why or why not.

38. An important factor in selling a residential property is the number of people who look through the home. A sample of 15 homes recently sold in the Buffalo, New York, area revealed the mean number looking through each home was 24 and the standard deviation of the sample was 5 people. Develop a 98% confidence interval for the population mean.

39. Warren County Telephone Company claims in its annual report that "the typical customer spends $60 per month on local and long-distance service." A sample of 12 subscribers revealed the following amounts spent last month.

$64	$66	$64	$66	$59	$62	$67	$61	$64	$58	$54	$66

   a. What is the point estimate of the population mean?
   b. Develop a 90% confidence interval for the population mean.
   c. Is the company's claim that the "typical customer" spends $60 per month reasonable? Justify your answer.

40. The manufacturer of a new line of ink-jet printers would like to include as part of its advertising the number of pages a user can expect from a print cartridge. A sample of 10 cartridges revealed the following number of pages printed.

2,698	2,028	2,474	2,395	2,372	2,475	1,927	3,006	2,334	2,379

   a. What is the point estimate of the population mean?
   b. Develop a 95% confidence interval for the population mean.

41. Dr. Susan Benner is an industrial psychologist. She is currently studying stress among executives of Internet companies. She developed a questionnaire that she believes measures stress. A score above 80 indicates stress at a dangerous level. A random sample of 15 executives revealed the following stress level scores. (df)

94	78	83	90	78	99	97	90	97	90	93	94	100	75	84

  a. Find the mean stress level for this sample. What is the point estimate of the population mean?
  b. Construct a 95% confidence level for the population mean.
  c. Is it reasonable to conclude that Internet executives have a mean stress level in the dangerous level, according to Dr. Benner's test?

42. As a condition of employment, Fashion Industries applicants must pass a drug test. Of the last 220 applicants, 14 failed the test. Develop a 99% confidence interval for the proportion of applicants that fail the test. Would it be reasonable to conclude that more than 10% of the applicants are now failing the test?

43. Fashion Industries randomly tests its employees throughout the year. Last year in the 400 random tests conducted, 14 employees failed the test. Develop a 99% confidence interval for the proportion of applicants that fail the test. Would it be reasonable to conclude that less than 5% of the employees are not able to pass the random drug test? Explain.

44. During a national debate on changes to health care, a cable news service performs an opinion poll of 500 small-business owners. It shows that 65% of small-business owners do not approve of the changes. Develop a 95% confidence interval for the proportion opposing health care changes. Comment on the result.

45. There are 20,000 eligible voters in York County, South Carolina. A random sample of 500 York County voters revealed 350 plan to vote to return Louella Miller to the state senate. Construct a 99% confidence interval for the proportion of voters in the county who plan to vote for Ms. Miller. From this sample information, can you confirm she will be re-elected?

46. In a poll to estimate presidential popularity, each person in a random sample of 1,000 voters was asked to agree with one of the following statements:
  1. The president is doing a good job.
  2. The president is doing a poor job.
  3. I have no opinion.
  A total of 560 respondents selected the first statement, indicating they thought the president was doing a good job.
  a. Construct a 95% confidence interval for the proportion of respondents who feel the president is doing a good job.
  b. Based on your interval in part (a), is it reasonable to conclude that a majority (more than half) of the population believes the president is doing a good job?

47. It is estimated that 60% of U.S. households subscribe to cable TV. You would like to verify this statement for your class in mass communications. If you want your estimate to be within 5 percentage points, with a 95% level of confidence, how large of a sample is required?

48. You need to estimate the mean number of travel days per year for outside salespeople. The mean of a small pilot study was 150 days, with a standard deviation of 14 days. If you must estimate the population mean within 2 days, how many outside salespeople should you sample? Use the 90% confidence level.

49. You design a survey to determine the mean family income in a rural area of central Florida. The question is, how many families should be sampled? In a pilot sample of 10 families, the standard deviation of the sample was $500. The sponsor of the survey wants you to use the 95% confidence level. The estimate is to be within $100. How many families should be interviewed?

50. *Families USA,* a monthly magazine that discusses issues related to health and health costs, surveyed 20 of its subscribers. It found that the annual health insurance premiums for a family with coverage through an employer averaged $10,979. The standard deviation of the sample was $1,000.
  a. Based on this sample information, develop a 90% confidence interval for the population mean yearly premium.
  b. How large a sample is needed to find the population mean within $250 at 99% confidence?

51. Passenger comfort is influenced by the amount of pressurization in an airline cabin. Higher pressurization permits a closer-to-normal environment and a more relaxed flight. A study by an airline user group recorded the corresponding air pressure on 30 randomly chosen flights. The study revealed a mean equivalent pressure of 8,000 feet with a standard deviation of 300 feet.
    a. Develop a 99% confidence interval for the population mean equivalent pressure.
    b. How large a sample is needed to find the population mean within 25 feet at 95% confidence?

52. A random sample of 25 people employed by the Florida state authority established they earned an average wage (including benefits) of $65.00 per hour. The sample standard deviation was $6.25 per hour.
    a. What is the population mean? What is the best estimate of the population mean?
    b. Develop a 99% confidence interval for the population mean wage (including benefits) for these employees.
    c. How large a sample is needed to assess the population mean with an allowable error of $1.00 at 95% confidence?

53. A film alliance used a random sample of 50 U.S. citizens to estimate that the typical American spent 78 hours watching videos and DVDs last year. The standard deviation of this sample was 9 hours.
    a. Develop a 95% confidence interval for the population mean number of hours spent watching videos and DVDs last year.
    b. How large a sample should be used to be 90% confident the sample mean is within 1.0 hour of the population mean?

54. Dylan Jones kept careful records of the fuel efficiency of his new car. After the first nine times he filled up the tank, he found the mean was 23.4 miles per gallon (mpg) with a sample standard deviation of 0.9 mpg.
    a. Compute the 95% confidence interval for his mpg.
    b. How many times should he fill his gas tank to obtain a margin of error below 0.1 mpg?

55. A survey of 36 randomly selected "iPhone" owners showed that the purchase price has a mean of $416 with a sample standard deviation of $180.
    a. Compute the standard error of the sample mean.
    b. Compute the 95% confidence interval for the mean.
    c. How large a sample is needed to estimate the population mean within $10?

56. You plan to conduct a survey to find what proportion of the workforce has two or more jobs. You decide on the 95% confidence level and state that the estimated proportion must be within 2% of the population proportion. A pilot survey reveals that 5 of the 50 sampled hold two or more jobs. How many in the workforce should be interviewed to meet your requirements?

57. The proportion of public accountants who have changed companies within the last three years is to be estimated within 3%. The 95% level of confidence is to be used. A study conducted several years ago revealed that the percent of public accountants changing companies within three years was 21.
    a. To update this study, the files of how many public accountants should be studied?
    b. How many public accountants should be contacted if no previous estimates of the population proportion are available?

58. As part of an annual review of its accounts, a discount brokerage selects a random sample of 36 customers. Their accounts are reviewed for total account valuation, which showed a mean of $32,000, with a sample standard deviation of $8,200. What is a 90% confidence interval for the mean account valuation of the population of customers?

59. The National Weight Control Registry tries to mine secrets of success from people who have lost at least 30 pounds and kept it off for at least a year. It reports that out of 2,700 registrants, 459 were on low-carbohydrate diets (less than 90 grams a day).
    a. Develop a 95% confidence interval for this fraction.
    b. Is it possible that the population percentage is 18%?
    c. How large a sample is needed to estimate the proportion within 0.5%?

60. Near the time of an election, a cable news service performs an opinion poll of 1,000 probable voters. It shows that the Republican contender has an advantage of 52% to 48%.
    a. Develop a 95% confidence interval for the proportion favoring the Republican candidate.
    b. Estimate the probability that the Democratic candidate is actually leading.
    c. Repeat the above analysis based on a sample of 3,000 probable voters.

61. A sample of 352 subscribers to *Wired* magazine shows the mean time spent using the Internet is 13.4 hours per week, with a sample standard deviation of 6.8 hours. Find the 95% confidence interval for the mean time *Wired* subscribers spend on the Internet.

62. The Tennessee Tourism Institute (TTI) plans to sample information center visitors entering the state to learn the fraction of visitors who plan to camp in the state. Current estimates are that 35% of visitors are campers. How large a sample would you take to estimate at a 95% confidence level the population proportion with an allowable error of 2%?

Data Set Exercises

(The data for these exercises are available at the text website www.mhhe.com/lindbasic8e).

63. Refer to the Real Estate data, which report information on homes sold in the Goodyear, Arizona, area during the last year.
   a. Develop a 95% confidence interval for the mean selling price of the homes.
   b. Develop a 95% confidence interval for the mean distance the home is from the center of the city.
   c. Develop a 95% confidence interval for the proportion of homes with an attached garage.
   d. To report your findings, write a business style memo to Gary Loftus, the president of the Goodyear Chamber of Commerce.

64. Refer to the Baseball 2010 data, which report information on the 30 Major League Baseball teams for the 2010 season.
   a. Develop a 95% confidence interval for the mean number of home runs per team.
   b. Develop a 95% confidence interval for the mean number of errors committed by each team.
   c. Develop a 95% confidence interval for the mean number of stolen bases for each team.

65. Refer to the Buena School District bus data.
   a. Develop a 95% confidence interval for the mean bus maintenance.
   b. Develop a 95% confidence interval for the mean bus miles.
   c. Write a business memo to the state transportation official to report your results.

Practice Test

Part 1—Objective
1. A _____ is a single value computed from sample information used to estimate a population parameter.
2. A _____ is a range of values within which the population parameter is likely to occur.
3. Assuming the same sample size and the same standard deviation, a 90% confidence interval will be _____ a 95% confidence interval. (equal to, wider than, narrower than, can't tell)
4. A _____ shows the fraction of a sample that has a particular characteristic.
5. For a 95% level of confidence, approximately _____ percent of the similarly constructed intervals will include the population parameter being estimated.
6. To construct a confidence interval for a mean, the *z* distribution is used only when the _____ is known. (population mean, population standard deviation, sample size, population size)
7. To develop a confidence interval for a proportion, the four conditions of what probability distribution must be met? _____ (Normal, Poisson, *t* distribution, binomial)
8. As the degrees of freedom increase, the *t* distribution _____. (approaches the binomial distribution, exceeds the normal distribution, approaches the *z* distribution, becomes more positively skewed)
9. The _____ has no effect on the size of the sample. (level of confidence, margin of error, population median, variability in the population)
10. To locate the appropriate *t* value, which is not necessary? (degrees of freedom, level of confidence, population mean)

Part 2—Problems

1. A recent study of 26 Conway, South Carolina, residents revealed they had lived at their current address for a mean of 9.3 years, with a sample standard deviation of 2 years.
   a. What is the population mean?
   b. What is the best estimate of the population mean?
   c. What is the standard error of the mean?
   d. Develop a 90% confidence interval for the population mean.

2. A recent federal report indicated 27% of children ages 2 to 5 ate vegetables at least five times a week. How large a sample is necessary to estimate the true population proportion within 2% with a 98% level of confidence? Be sure to use the evidence in the federal report.

3. The Philadelphia Regional Transport Authority wishes to estimate the proportion of central city workers that use public transportation to get to work. A recent study reported that of 100 workers, 64 used public transportation. Develop a 95% confidence interval.

Software Commands

1. The Minitab commands for the descriptive statistics on page 270 follow. Enter the data in the first column and label this column *Amount*. On the Toolbar, select **Stat, Basic Statistics,** and **Display Descriptive Statistics.** In the dialog box, select *Amount* as the **Variable** and click **OK.**

2. The Minitab commands for the confidence interval for the amount spent at the Inlet Square Mall on page 271 are:
   a. Enter the 20 amounts spent in column *C1* and name the variable *Amount*.
   b. On the Toolbar, select **Stat, Basic Statistics,** and click on **1-Sample t.**
   c. Select **Samples in columns:** and select **Amount** and click **OK.**

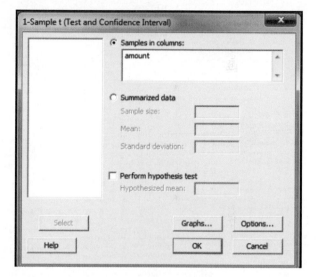

3. The Excel commands for the confidence interval for the amounts spent at the Inlet Square Mall on page 272 are:
   a. Select the **Data** tab on the top menu. Then, on the far right, select **Data Analysis,** and then **Descriptive Statistics,** and click **OK.**
   b. For the **Input Range,** type *A1:A21,* click on **Labels in first row,** type *C1* as the **Output Range,** click on **Summary statistics** and **Confidence Level for Mean,** and then click on **OK.**

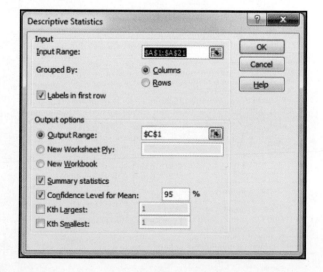

Chapter 9   Answers to Self-Review

9–1 **a.** Unknown. This is the value we wish to estimate.
   b. $20,000, point estimate.
   c. $20,000 \pm 1.96 \dfrac{\$3,000}{\sqrt{40}} = \$20,000 \pm \$930$

   d. The endpoints of the confidence interval are $19,070 and $20,930. About 95% of the intervals similarly constructed would include the population mean.

9–2 **a.** $\bar{X} = \dfrac{18}{10} = 1.8$ $s = \sqrt{\dfrac{11.6}{10-1}} = 1.1353$

   b. The population mean is not known. The best estimate is the sample mean, 1.8 days.

   c. $1.80 \pm 2.262\dfrac{1.1353}{\sqrt{10}} = 1.80 \pm 0.81$

   The endpoints are 0.99 and 2.61.
   d. t is used because the population standard deviation is unknown.

   e. The value of 0 is not in the interval. It is unreasonable to conclude that the mean number of days of work missed is 0 per employee.

9–3 **a.** $p = \dfrac{420}{1,400} = .30$
   b. $.30 \pm 2.576(.0122) = .30 \pm .03$
   c. The interval is between .27 and .33. About 99% of the similarly constructed intervals would include the population proportion.

9–4 $n = \left(\dfrac{2.576(.279)}{.05}\right)^2 = 206.61$
   The sample should be rounded to 207.

One-Sample Tests of Hypothesis

Dole Pineapple Inc. is concerned that the 16-ounce can of sliced pineapple is being overfilled. Assume the standard deviation of the process is .03 ounces. The quality control department took a random sample of 50 cans and found that the arithmetic mean weight was 16.05 ounces. At the 5% level of significance, can we conclude that the mean weight is greater than 16 ounces? Determine the *p*-value. (See Exercise 30 and LO 10-6.)

10.1 Introduction

Chapter 8 began our study of statistical inference. We described how we could select a random sample to estimate the value of a population parameter. For example, we selected a sample of five employees at Spence Sprockets, found the number of years of service for each sampled employee, computed the mean years of service, and used the sample mean to estimate the mean years of service for all employees. In other words, we estimated a population parameter from a sample statistic.

Chapter 9 continued the study of statistical inference by developing a confidence interval. A confidence interval is a range of values within which we expect the population parameter to occur. In this chapter, rather than develop a range of values within which we expect the population parameter to occur, we develop a procedure to test the validity of a statement about a population parameter. Some examples of statements we might want to test are:

- The mean speed of automobiles passing milepost 150 on the West Virginia Turnpike is 68 miles per hour.
- The mean number of miles driven by those leasing a Chevy TrailBlazer for three years is 32,000 miles.
- The mean time an American family lives in a particular single-family dwelling is 11.8 years.
- The mean starting salary for a 2011 college graduate is $50,034, up 3.5% from 2010.
- Thirty-five percent of retirees in the upper Midwest sell their home and move to a warm climate within 1 year of their retirement.
- Eighty percent of those who regularly play the state lotteries never win more than $100 in any one play.

This chapter and several of the following chapters cover statistical hypothesis testing. We begin by defining what we mean by a statistical hypothesis and statistical hypothesis testing. Next, we outline the steps in statistical hypothesis testing. Then we conduct tests of hypothesis for means and proportions. In the last section of the chapter, we describe possible errors due to sampling in hypothesis testing.

10.2 What Is a Hypothesis?

A hypothesis is a statement about a population parameter.

A hypothesis is a statement about a population. Data are then used to check the reasonableness of the statement. To begin, we need to define the word *hypothesis.* In the United States legal system, a person is presumed innocent until proven guilty. A jury hypothesizes that a person charged with a crime is innocent and then reviews the evidence to assess if there is enough evidence to claim that the person is not innocent or guilty as charged. In a similar sense, a patient goes to a physician and reports various symptoms. On the basis of the symptoms, the physician will order certain diagnostic tests, then, according to the symptoms and the test results, determine the treatment to be followed.

In statistical analysis, we make a claim—that is, state a hypothesis—collect data, and then use the data to test the claim. We define a statistical hypothesis as follows.

LO 10-1 Define a hypothesis.

> **HYPOTHESIS** A statement about a population parameter subject to verification.

Statistics in Action

LASIK is a 15-minute surgical procedure that uses a laser to reshape an eye's cornea with the goal of improving eyesight. Research shows that about 5% of all surgeries involve complications such as glare, corneal haze, over-correction or under-correction of vision, and loss of vision. In a statistical sense, the research tests a null hypothesis that the surgery will not improve eyesight with the alternative hypothesis that the surgery will improve eyesight. The sample data of LASIK surgery shows that 5% of all cases result in complications. The 5% represents a Type I error rate. When a person decides to have the surgery, he or she expects to reject the null hypothesis. In 5% of future cases, this expectation will not be met. (Source: *American Academy of Ophthalmology Journal,* Vol. 16, no. 43.)

In most cases, the population is so large that it is not feasible to study all the items, objects, or persons in the population. For example, it would not be possible to contact every systems analyst in the United States to find his or her monthly income. Likewise, the quality assurance department at Cooper Tire cannot check each tire produced to determine whether it will last more than 60,000 miles.

As noted in Chapter 8, an alternative to measuring or interviewing the entire population is to take a sample from the population. We can, therefore, test a statement to determine whether the sample does or does not support the statement concerning the population.

10.3 What Is Hypothesis Testing?

The terms *hypothesis testing* and *testing a hypothesis* are used interchangeably. Hypothesis testing starts with a statement, or assumption, about a population parameter—such as the population mean. This statement is referred to as a *hypothesis.* A hypothesis might be that the mean monthly commission of sales associates in retail electronics stores, such as Best Buy, is $2,000. We cannot contact all these sales associates to ascertain that the mean is in fact $2,000. The cost of locating and interviewing every electronics sales associate in the United States would be exorbitant. To test the validity of the assumption ($\mu = \$2,000$), we must select a sample from the population of all electronics sales associates, calculate sample statistics, and based on certain decision rules reject or fail to reject the hypothesis. A sample mean of $1,000 for the electronics sales associates would certainly cause rejection of the hypothesis. However, suppose the sample mean is $1,995. Can we attribute the $5 difference between $1,995 and the hypothesized $2,000 to sampling error, or is the difference statistically significant?

> **HYPOTHESIS TESTING** A procedure based on sample evidence and probability theory to determine whether the hypothesis is a reasonable statement.

10.4 Five-Step Procedure for Testing a Hypothesis

There is a five-step procedure that systematizes hypothesis testing; when we get to step 5, we are ready to reject or not reject the hypothesis. However, hypothesis testing as used by statisticians does not provide proof that something is true, in the manner in which a mathematician "proves" a statement. It does provide a kind of "proof beyond a reasonable doubt," in the manner of the court system. Hence, there are specific rules of evidence, or procedures, that are followed. The steps are shown in the following diagram. We will discuss in detail each of the steps.

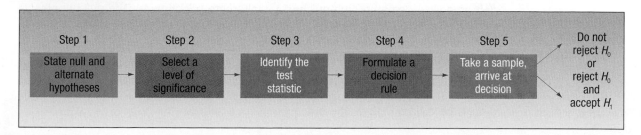

Step 1	Step 2	Step 3	Step 4	Step 5	
State null and alternate hypotheses	Select a level of significance	Identify the test statistic	Formulate a decision rule	Take a sample, arrive at decision	Do not reject H_0 or reject H_0 and accept H_1

Step 1: State the Null Hypothesis (H_0) and the Alternate Hypothesis (H_1)

LO 10-2 Explain the five-step hypothesis-testing procedure.

The first step is to state the hypothesis being tested. It is called the **null hypothesis,** designated H_0, and read "*H sub zero.*" The capital letter *H* stands for hypothesis, and the subscript zero implies "no difference." There is usually a "not" or a "no" term in the null hypothesis, meaning that there is "no change." For example, the null hypothesis is that the mean number of miles driven on the steel-belted tire is not different from 60,000. The null hypothesis would be written H_0: $\mu = 60,000$. Generally speaking, the null hypothesis is developed for the purpose of testing. We either reject or fail to reject the null hypothesis. The null hypothesis is a statement that is not rejected unless our sample data provide convincing evidence that it is false.

We should emphasize that, if the null hypothesis is not rejected on the basis of the sample data, we cannot say that the null hypothesis is true. To put it another way, failing to reject the null hypothesis does not prove that H_0 is true, it means we have *failed to disprove H_0*. To prove without any doubt the null hypothesis is true, the population parameter would have to be known. To actually determine it, we would have to test, survey, or count every item in the population. This is usually not feasible. The alternative is to take a sample from the population.

State the null hypothesis and the alternative hypothesis.

It should also be noted that we often begin the null hypothesis by stating, "There is no *significant* difference between . . . ," or "The mean impact strength of the glass is not *significantly* different from. . . ." When we select a sample from a population, the sample statistic is usually numerically different from the hypothesized population parameter. As an illustration, suppose the hypothesized impact strength of a glass plate is 70 psi, and the mean impact strength of a sample of 12 glass plates is 69.5 psi. We must make a decision about the difference of 0.5 psi. Is it a true difference, that is, a significant difference, or is the difference between the sample statistic (69.5) and the hypothesized population parameter (70.0) due to chance (sampling)? To answer this question, we conduct a test of significance, commonly referred to as a test of hypothesis. To define what is meant by a null hypothesis:

> **NULL HYPOTHESIS** A statement about the value of a population parameter developed for the purpose of testing numerical evidence.

The **alternate hypothesis** describes what you will conclude if you reject the null hypothesis. It is written H_1 and is read "*H sub one.*" It is also referred to as the research hypothesis. The alternate hypothesis is accepted if the sample data provide us with enough statistical evidence that the null hypothesis is false.

> **ALTERNATE HYPOTHESIS** A statement that is accepted if the sample data provide sufficient evidence that the null hypothesis is false.

The following example will help clarify what is meant by the null hypothesis and the alternate hypothesis. A recent article indicated the mean age of U.S. commercial aircraft is 15 years. To conduct a statistical test regarding this statement, the first step is to determine the null and the alternate hypotheses. The null hypothesis represents the current or reported condition. It is written H_0: $\mu = 15$. The alternate hypothesis is that the statement is not true, that is, H_1: $\mu \neq 15$. It is important to remember that no matter how the problem is stated, *the null hypothesis will always contain the equal sign*. The equal sign (=) will never appear in the alternate hypothesis. Why? Because the null hypothesis is the statement being tested, and we need a specific value to include in our calculations. We turn to the alternate hypothesis only if the data suggests the null hypothesis is untrue.

Step 2: Select a Level of Significance

After setting up the null hypothesis and alternate hypothesis, the next step is to state the level of significance.

> **LEVEL OF SIGNIFICANCE** The probability of rejecting the null hypothesis when it is true.

Select a level of significance or risk.

The level of significance is designated α, the Greek letter alpha. It is also sometimes called the level of risk. This may be a more appropriate term because it is the risk you take of rejecting the null hypothesis when it is really true.

There is no one level of significance that is applied to all tests. A decision is made to use the .05 level (often stated as the 5% level), the .01 level, the .10 level, or any other level between 0 and 1. Traditionally, the .05 level is selected for consumer research projects, .01 for quality assurance, and .10 for political polling. You, the researcher, must decide on the level of significance *before* formulating a decision rule and collecting sample data.

To illustrate how it is possible to reject a true hypothesis, suppose a firm manufacturing personal computers uses a large number of printed circuit boards. Suppliers

bid on the boards, and the one with the lowest bid is awarded a sizable contract. Suppose the contract specifies that the computer manufacturer's quality-assurance department will sample all incoming shipments of circuit boards. If more than 6% of the boards sampled are substandard, the shipment will be rejected. The null hypothesis is that the incoming shipment of boards contains 6% or less substandard boards. The alternate hypothesis is that more than 6% of the boards are defective.

A shipment of 4,000 circuit boards was received from Allied Electronics, and the quality assurance department selected a random sample of 50 circuit boards for testing. Of the 50 circuit boards sampled, 4 boards, or 8%, were substandard. The shipment was rejected because it exceeded the maximum of 6% substandard printed circuit boards. If the shipment was actually substandard, then the decision to return the boards to the supplier was correct. However, suppose the 4 substandard printed circuit boards selected in the sample of 50 were the only substandard boards in the shipment of 4,000 boards. Then only $\frac{1}{10}$ of 1% were defective (4/4,000 = .001). In that case, less than 6% of the entire shipment was substandard and rejecting the shipment was an error. In terms of hypothesis testing, we rejected the null hypothesis when we should have failed to reject the null hypothesis. By rejecting a true null hypothesis, we committed a Type I error. The probability of committing a Type I error is α.

> **TYPE I ERROR** Rejecting the null hypothesis, H_0, when it is true.

The probability of committing another type of error, called a Type II error, is designated by the Greek letter beta (β).

> **TYPE II ERROR** Not rejecting the null hypothesis when it is false.

The firm manufacturing personal computers would commit a Type II error if, unknown to the manufacturer, an incoming shipment of printed circuit boards from Allied Electronics contained 15% substandard boards, yet the shipment was accepted. How could this happen? Suppose 2 of the 50 boards in the sample (4%) tested were substandard, and 48 of the 50 were good boards. According to the stated procedure, because the sample contained less than 6% substandard boards, the shipment was accepted. It could be that *by chance* the 48 good boards selected in the sample were the only acceptable ones in the entire shipment consisting of thousands of boards!

LO 10-3 Define Type I and Type II errors.

In retrospect, the researcher cannot study every item or individual in the population. Thus, there is a possibility of two types of error—a Type I error, wherein the null hypothesis is rejected when it should not be rejected, and a Type II error, wherein the null hypothesis is not rejected when it should have been rejected.

We often refer to the probability of these two possible errors as *alpha,* α, and *beta,* β. Alpha (α) is the probability of making a Type I error, and beta (β) is the probability of making a Type II error. The following table summarizes the decisions the researcher could make and the possible consequences.

Null Hypothesis	Researcher	
	Does Not Reject H_0	**Rejects** H_0
H_0 is true	Correct decision	Type I error
H_0 is false	Type II error	Correct decision

Step 3: Select the Test Statistic

There are many test statistics. In this chapter, we use both z and t as the test statistic. In later chapters, we will use such test statistics as F and χ^2, called chi-square.

LO 10-4 Define the term *test statistic* and explain how it is used.

> **TEST STATISTIC** A value, determined from sample information, used to determine whether to reject the null hypothesis.

In hypothesis testing for the mean (μ) when σ is known, the test statistic z is computed by:

$$\text{TESTING A MEAN, } \sigma \text{ KNOWN} \qquad z = \frac{\overline{X} - \mu}{\sigma/\sqrt{n}} \qquad \text{[10–1]}$$

The z value is based on the sampling distribution of $\overline{X}$, which follows the normal distribution with a mean ($\mu_{\overline{x}}$) equal to μ, and a standard deviation $\sigma_{\overline{x}}$, which is equal to $\sigma/\sqrt{n}$. We can thus determine whether the difference between $\overline{X}$ and μ is statistically significant by finding the number of standard deviations $\overline{X}$ is from μ, using formula (10–1).

Step 4: Formulate the Decision Rule

The decision rule states the conditions when H_0 is rejected.

A decision rule is a statement of the specific conditions under which the null hypothesis is rejected and the conditions under which it is not rejected. The region or area of rejection defines the location of all those values that are so large or so small that the probability of their occurrence under a true null hypothesis is rather remote.

Chart 10–1 portrays the rejection region for a test of significance that will be conducted later in the chapter.

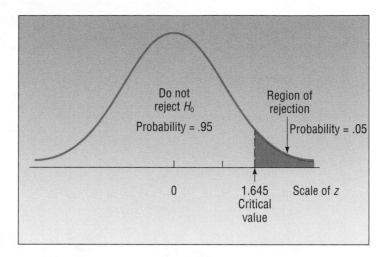

CHART 10–1 Sampling Distribution of the Statistic z, a Right-Tailed Test, .05 Level of Significance

Note in the chart that:

- The area where the null hypothesis is not rejected is to the left of 1.645. We will explain how to get the 1.645 value shortly.
- The area of rejection is to the right of 1.645.
- A one-tailed test is being applied. (This will also be explained later.)
- The .05 level of significance was chosen.
- The sampling distribution of the statistic z follows the normal probability distribution.
- The value 1.645 separates the regions where the null hypothesis is rejected and where it is not rejected.
- The value 1.645 is the **critical value**.

> **CRITICAL VALUE** The dividing point between the region where the null hypothesis is rejected and the region where it is not rejected.

Step 5: Make a Decision

The fifth and final step in hypothesis testing is to compute the test statistic, compare it to the critical value, make a decision to reject or not reject the null hypothesis, and interpret the result. Referring to Chart 10–1, if, based on sample information, z is computed to be 2.34, the null hypothesis is rejected at the .05 level of significance. The decision to reject H_0 was made because 2.34 lies in the region of rejection, that is, beyond 1.645. We would reject the null hypothesis, reasoning that it is highly improbable that a computed z value this large is due to sampling error (chance).

Had the computed value been 1.645 or less, say 0.71, the null hypothesis would not be rejected. It would be reasoned that such a small computed value could be attributed to chance, that is, sampling error.

As noted, only one of two decisions is possible in hypothesis testing—either to reject or not reject the null hypothesis. If the null hypothesis is not rejected, some researchers prefer to say "The sample results do not allow us to reject H_0." Keep in mind, however, that there is always a possibility that the null hypothesis is rejected when it should not be rejected (a Type I error). Also, there is a chance that the null hypothesis is not rejected when it should be rejected (a Type II error).

> **SUMMARY OF THE STEPS IN HYPOTHESIS TESTING**
> 1. Establish the null hypothesis (H_0) and the alternate hypothesis (H_1).
> 2. Select the level of significance, that is, α.
> 3. Select an appropriate test statistic.
> 4. Formulate a decision rule based on steps 1, 2, and 3 above.
> 5. Make a decision regarding the null hypothesis based on the sample information. Interpret the results of the test.

Before actually conducting a test of hypothesis, we describe the difference between a one-tailed test of significance and a two-tailed test.

10.5 One-Tailed and Two-Tailed Tests of Significance

LO 10-5 Distinguish between a one-tailed and a two-tailed test of hypothesis.

Refer to Chart 10–1. It shows a one-tailed test. It is called a one-tailed test because the rejection region is only in one tail of the curve. In this case, it is in the right, or upper, tail of the curve. To illustrate, suppose that the packaging department at General Foods Corporation is concerned that some boxes of Grape Nuts are significantly overweight. The cereal is packaged in 453-gram boxes, so the null hypothesis is H_0: $\mu \le 453$. This is read, "the population mean (μ) is equal to or less than 453." The alternate hypothesis is, therefore, H_1: $\mu > 453$. This is read, "μ is greater than 453." Note that the inequality sign in the alternate hypothesis ($>$) points to the region of rejection in the upper tail. (See Chart 10–1.) Also observe that the null hypothesis includes the equal sign. That is, H_0: $\mu \le 453$. The equality condition always appears in H_0, never in H_1.

Chart 10–2 portrays a situation where the rejection region is in the left (lower) tail of the standard normal distribution. As an illustration, consider the problem of automobile manufacturers, large automobile leasing companies, and other organizations that purchase large quantities of tires. They want the tires to average, say, 60,000 miles of wear under normal usage. They will, therefore, reject a shipment of tires if tests reveal that the mean life of the tires is significantly below 60,000 miles. They gladly accept a shipment if the mean life is greater than 60,000 miles! They are not concerned with this possibility, however. They are concerned only if they have sample evidence to conclude that the tires will average less than 60,000 miles of useful life. Thus, the test is set up to satisfy the concern of the automobile manufacturers that *the mean life of*

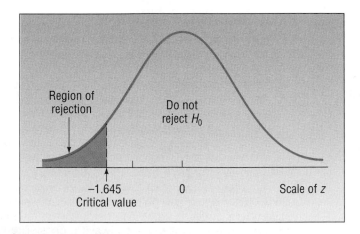

CHART 10–2 Sampling Distribution for the Statistic z, Left-Tailed Test, .05 Level of Significance

Test is one-tailed if H_1 states $\mu >$ or $\mu <$.

If H_1 states a direction, test is one-tailed.

the tires is not less than 60,000 miles. This statement appears in the null hypothesis. The null and alternate hypotheses in this case are written H_0: $\mu \geq 60,000$ and H_1: $\mu < 60,000$.

One way to determine the location of the rejection region is to look at the direction in which the inequality sign in the alternate hypothesis is pointing (either $<$ or $>$). In the tire wear problem, it is pointing to the left, and the rejection region is therefore in the left tail.

In summary, a test is *one-tailed* when the alternate hypothesis, H_1, states a direction, such as:

H_0: The mean income of female stockbrokers is *less than or equal to* $65,000 per year.
H_1: The mean income of female stockbrokers is *greater than* $65,000 per year.

If no direction is specified in the alternate hypothesis, we use a *two-tailed* test. Changing the previous problem to illustrate, we can say:

H_0: The mean income of female stockbrokers is $65,000 per year.
H_1: The mean income of female stockbrokers is *not equal to* $65,000 per year.

If the null hypothesis is rejected and H_1 accepted in the two-tailed case, the mean income could be significantly greater than $65,000 per year or it could be significantly less than $65,000 per year. To accommodate these two possibilities, the 5% area of rejection is divided equally into the two tails of the sampling distribution (2.5% each). Chart 10–3 shows the two areas and the critical values. Note that the total area in the normal distribution is 1.0000, found by .9500 + .0250 + .0250.

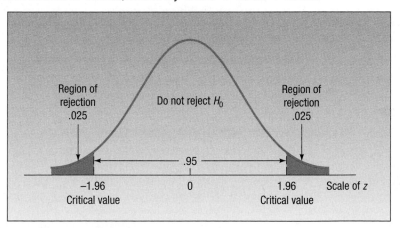

CHART 10–3 Regions of Nonrejection and Rejection for a Two-Tailed Test, .05 Level of Significance

10.6 Testing for a Population Mean: Known Population Standard Deviation

A Two-Tailed Test

An example will show the details of the five-step hypothesis testing procedure and the subsequent decision-making process. We also wish to use a two-tailed test. That is, we are *not* concerned whether the sample results are larger or smaller than the proposed population mean. Rather, we are interested in whether it is *different from* the proposed value for the population mean. We begin, as we did in the previous chapter, with a situation in which we have historical information about the population and in fact know its standard deviation.

Example

LO 10-6 Conduct a test of hypothesis about a population mean.

Jamestown Steel Company manufactures and assembles desks and other office equipment at several plants in western New York state. The weekly production of the Model A325 desk at the Fredonia Plant follows a normal probability distribution with a mean of 200 and a standard deviation of 16. Recently, because of market expansion, new production methods have been introduced and new employees hired. The vice president of manufacturing would like to investigate whether there has been a *change* in the weekly production of the Model A325 desk. Is the mean number of desks produced at the Fredonia Plant *different from* 200 at the .01 significance level?

Solution

In this example, we know two important pieces of information: (1) the population of weekly production follows the normal distribution, and (2) the standard deviation of this normal distribution is 16 desks per week. So it is appropriate to use the *z* statistic for this problem. We use the statistical hypothesis testing procedure to investigate whether the production rate has changed from 200 per week.

Step 1: State the null hypothesis and the alternate hypothesis. The null hypothesis is "The population mean is 200." The alternate hypothesis is "The mean is different from 200" or "The mean is not 200." These two hypotheses are written:

$$H_0: \mu = 200$$

$$H_1: \mu \neq 200$$

This is a *two-tailed test* because the alternate hypothesis does not state a direction. In other words, it does not state whether the mean production is greater than 200 or less than 200. The vice president wants only to find out whether the production rate is different from 200.

Before moving to Step 2 of the hypothesis-testing procedure, we need to emphasize two important points about the null and alternate hypothesis statements. First, notice that the null hypothesis contains the equal sign. Why is this so? Because the value we are actually going to test is always in the null hypothesis. The alternate hypothesis will never contain the equal sign. Second, notice that both the null and the alternate hypothesis contain Greek letters, in this case, the population mean, μ. We always conduct tests of hypothesis that refer to population parameters, never sample statistics. This means you will never see the sample mean, $\overline{X}$, in the null or the alternate hypothesis.

Step 2: Select the level of significance. In the Example description, the significance level selected is .01. This is α, the probability of committing a Type I error, and it is the probability of rejecting a true null hypothesis.

Step 3: Select the test statistic. The test statistic is *z* when the population standard deviation is known. Transforming the production data to standard units (*z* values) permits their use not only in this problem but also in other hypothesis-testing problems. Formula (10–1) for *z* is repeated next with the various letters identified.

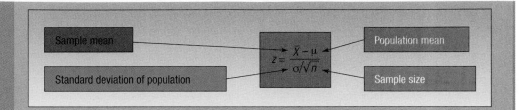

Formula for the test statistic

Step 4: Formulate the decision rule. We formulate the decision rule by first determining the critical values of z. Because this is a two-tailed test, half of .01, or .005, is placed in each tail. The area where H_0 is not rejected, located between the two tails, is therefore .99. Using the Student's t Distribution table in Appendix B.2, move to the top margin called "Level of Significance for Two-Tailed Tests, α," select the column with $\alpha = .01$, and move to the last row, which is labeled ∞, or infinite degrees of freedom. The z value in this cell is 2.576. For your convenience, Appendix B.2, Student's t Distribution, is repeated in the inside back cover. All the facets of this problem are shown in the diagram in Chart 10–4.

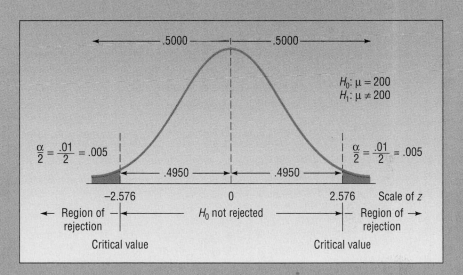

CHART 10–4 Decision Rule for the .01 Significance Level

The decision rule is: if the computed value of z is not between −2.576 and 2.576, reject the null hypothesis. If z falls between −2.576 and 2.576, do not reject the null hypothesis.

Step 5: Make a decision and interpret the result. Take a sample from the population (weekly production), compute z, apply the decision rule, and arrive at a decision to reject H_0 or not to reject H_0. The mean number of desks produced last year (50 weeks, because the plant was shut down 2 weeks for vacation) is 203.5. The standard deviation of the population is 16 desks per week. Computing the z value from formula (10–1):

$$z = \frac{\bar{X} - \mu}{\sigma/\sqrt{n}} = \frac{203.5 - 200}{16/\sqrt{50}} = 1.547$$

Because 1.547 does not fall in the rejection region, H_0 is not rejected. We conclude that the population mean is *not* different from 200. What should we report to the vice president of manufacturing? The sample evidence shows that the new production methods did not change the weekly production rate. The production rate change of 3.5 units per week can reasonably be attributed to sampling error. This information is summarized in the following chart.

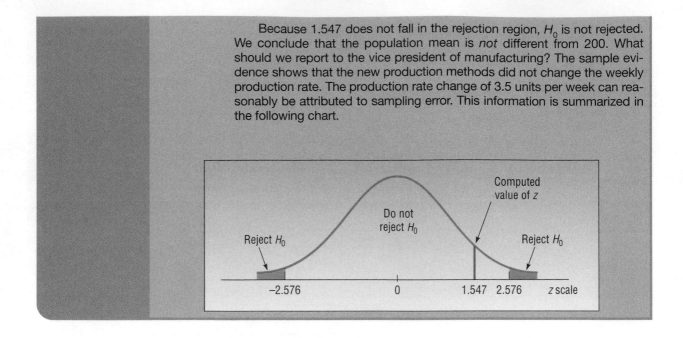

Did we prove that the assembly rate is still 200 per week? Not really. What we did, technically, was *fail to disprove the null hypothesis.* Failing to disprove the hypothesis that the population mean is 200 is not the same thing as proving it to be true. As we suggested in the chapter introduction, the conclusion is analogous to the American judicial system. To explain, suppose a person is accused of a crime but is acquitted by a jury. If a person is acquitted of a crime, the conclusion is that there was not enough evidence to prove the person guilty. The trial did not prove that the individual was innocent, only that there was not enough evidence to prove the defendant guilty. That is what we do in statistical hypothesis testing when we do not reject the null hypothesis. The correct interpretation is that we have failed to disprove the null hypothesis.

We selected the significance level, .01 in this case, before setting up the decision rule and sampling the population. This is the appropriate strategy. The significance level should be set by the investigator, but it should be determined *before* gathering the sample evidence and not changed based on the sample evidence.

Comparing confidence intervals and hypothesis testing.

How does the hypothesis testing procedure just described compare with that of confidence intervals discussed in the previous chapter? When we conducted the test of hypothesis regarding the production of desks, we changed the units from desks per week to a z value. Then we compared the computed value of the test statistic (1.547) to that of the critical values (-2.576 and 2.576). Because the computed value was in the region where the null hypothesis was not rejected, we concluded that the population mean could be 200. To use the confidence interval approach, on the other hand, we would develop a confidence interval, based on formula (9–1). See page 261. The interval would be from 197.671 to 209.329, found by $203.5 \pm 2.576(16/\sqrt{50})$. Note that the proposed population value, 200, is within this interval. Hence, we would conclude that the population mean could reasonably be 200.

In general, H_0 is rejected if the confidence interval does not include the hypothesized value. If the confidence interval includes the hypothesized value, then H_0 is not rejected. So the "do not reject region" for a test of hypothesis is equivalent to the proposed population value occurring in the confidence interval.

Self-Review 10–1

Heinz, a manufacturer of ketchup, uses a particular machine to dispense 16 ounces of its ketchup into containers. From many years of experience with the particular dispensing machine, Heinz knows the amount of product in each container follows a normal distribution with a mean of 16 ounces and a standard deviation of 0.15 ounce. A sample of 50 containers filled last hour revealed the mean amount per container was 16.017 ounces. Does this evidence suggest that the mean amount dispensed is different from 16 ounces? Use the .05 significance level.

(a) State the null hypothesis and the alternate hypothesis.
(b) What is the probability of a Type I error?
(c) Give the formula for the test statistic.
(d) State the decision rule.
(e) Determine the value of the test statistic.
(f) What is your decision regarding the null hypothesis?
(g) Interpret, in a single sentence, the result of the statistical test.

A One-Tailed Test

In the previous Example/Solution, we emphasized that we were concerned only with reporting to the vice president whether there had been a change in the mean number of desks assembled at the Fredonia Plant. We were not concerned with whether the change was an increase or a decrease in the production.

To illustrate a one-tailed test, let's change the problem. Suppose the vice president wants to know whether there has been an *increase* in the number of units assembled. Can we conclude, because of the improved production methods, that the mean number of desks assembled in the last 50 weeks was more than 200? Look at the difference in the way the problem is formulated. In the first case, we wanted to know whether there was a *difference* in the mean number assembled, but now we want to know whether there has been an *increase.* Because we are investigating different questions, we will set our hypotheses differently. The biggest difference occurs in the alternate hypothesis. Before, we stated the alternate hypothesis as "different from"; now we want to state it as "greater than." In symbols:

A two-tailed test:	A one-tailed test:
H_0: $\mu = 200$	H_0: $\mu \le 200$
H_1: $\mu \ne 200$	H_1: $\mu > 200$

The critical values for a one-tailed test are different from a two-tailed test at the same significance level. In the previous Example/Solution, we split the significance level in half and put half in the lower tail and half in the upper tail. In a one-tailed test, we put all the rejection region in one tail. See Chart 10–5.

For the one-tailed test, the critical value of z is 2.326. Using the Student's t Distribution table in Appendix B.2 or inside the back cover, move to the top heading called "Level of Significance for One-Tailed Tests, α," select the column with $\alpha = .01$, and move to the last row, which is labeled ∞, or infinite degrees of freedom. The z value in this cell is 2.326.

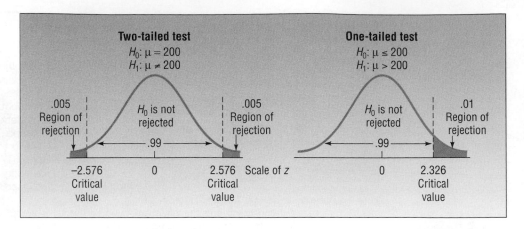

CHART 10–5 Rejection Regions for Two-Tailed and One-Tailed Tests, $\alpha = .01$

10.7 *p*-Value in Hypothesis Testing

LO 10-7 Compute and interpret a *p*-value.

In testing a hypothesis, we compare the test statistic to a critical value. A decision is made to either reject the null hypothesis or not to reject it. So, for example, if the critical value is 1.96 and the computed value of the test statistic is 2.19, the decision is to reject the null hypothesis.

In recent years, spurred by the availability of computer software, additional information is often reported on the strength of the rejection. That is, how confident are we in rejecting the null hypothesis? This approach reports the probability (assuming that the null hypothesis is true) of getting a value of the test statistic at least as extreme as the value actually obtained. This process compares the probability, called the ***p*-value,** with the significance level. If the *p*-value is smaller than the significance level, H_0 is rejected. If it is larger than the significance level, H_0 is not rejected.

> ***p*-VALUE** The probability of observing a sample value as extreme as, or more extreme than, the value observed, given that the null hypothesis is true.

Determining the *p*-value not only results in a decision regarding H_0, but it gives us additional insight into the strength of the decision. A very small *p*-value, such as .0001, indicates that there is little likelihood the H_0 is true. On the other hand, a *p*-value of .2033 means that H_0 is not rejected, and there is little likelihood that it is false.

How do we find the *p*-value? To calculate *p*-values, we will need to use the *z* table (Appendix B.1 and inside the back cover), and, to use this table, we will round *z* test statistics to two decimals. To illustrate how to compute a *p*-value, we will use the example in which we tested the null hypothesis that the mean number of desks produced per week at Fredonia was 200. We did not reject the null hypothesis, because the *z* value of 1.547 fell in the region between -2.576 and 2.576. We agreed not to reject the null hypothesis if the computed value of *z* fell in this region. Rounding 1.547 to 1.55 and using the *z* table, the probability of finding a *z* value of 1.55 or more is .0606, found by $.5000 - .4394$. To put it another way, the probability of obtaining an $\overline{X}$ greater than 203.5 if $\mu = 200$ is .0606. To compute the *p*-value, we need to be concerned with the region less than -1.55 as well as the values greater than 1.55 (because the rejection region is in both tails). The two-tailed *p*-value is .1212, found by 2(.0606). The *p*-value of .1212 is greater than the significance level of .01 decided upon initially, so H_0 is not rejected. The details are shown in the following graph. In general, the area is doubled in a two-sided test. Then the *p*-value can easily be compared with the significance level. The same decision rule is used as in the one-sided test.

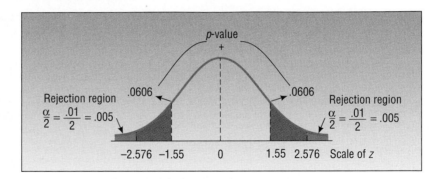

A p-value is a way to express the likelihood that H_0 is false. But how do we interpret a p-value? We have already said that if the p-value is less than the significance level, then we reject H_0; if it is greater than the significance level, then we do not reject H_0. Also, if the p-value is very large, then it is likely that H_0 is true. If the p-value is small, then it is likely that H_0 is not true. The following box will help to interpret p-values.

INTERPRETING THE WEIGHT OF EVIDENCE AGAINST H_0 If the p-value is less than
(a) .10, we have *some* evidence that H_0 is not true.
(b) .05, we have *strong* evidence that H_0 is not true.
(c) .01, we have *very strong* evidence that H_0 is not true.
(d) .001, we have *extremely strong* evidence that H_0 is not true.

Self-Review 10–2 Refer to Self-Review 10–1.
(a) Suppose the next to the last sentence is changed to read: Does this evidence suggest that the mean amount dispensed is *more than* 16 ounces? State the null hypothesis and the alternate hypothesis under these conditions.
(b) What is the decision rule under the new conditions stated in part (a)?
(c) A second sample of 50 filled containers revealed the mean to be 16.040 ounces. What is the value of the test statistic for this sample?
(d) What is your decision regarding the null hypothesis?
(e) Interpret, in a single sentence, the result of the statistical test.
(f) What is the p-value? What is your decision regarding the null hypothesis based on the p-value? Is this the same conclusion reached in part (d)?

Exercises

connect™

For Exercises 1–4, answer the questions: (a) Is this a one- or two-tailed test? (b) What is the decision rule? (c) What is the value of the test statistic? (d) What is your decision regarding H_0? (e) What is the p-value? Interpret it.

1. A sample of 36 observations is selected from a normal population. The sample mean is 49, and the population standard deviation is 5. Conduct the following test of hypothesis using the .05 significance level.

$$H_0: \mu = 50$$
$$H_1: \mu \neq 50$$

2. A sample of 36 observations is selected from a normal population. The sample mean is 12, and the population standard deviation is 3. Conduct the following test of hypothesis using the .01 significance level.

$$H_0: \mu \leq 10$$
$$H_1: \mu > 10$$

3. A sample of 36 observations is selected from a normal population. The sample mean is 21, and the population standard deviation is 5. Conduct the following test of hypothesis using the .05 significance level.

$$H_0: \mu \leq 20$$
$$H_1: \mu > 20$$

4. A sample of 64 observations is selected from a normal population. The sample mean is 215, and the population standard deviation is 15. Conduct the following test of hypothesis using the .025 significance level.

$$H_0: \mu \geq 220$$
$$H_1: \mu < 220$$

For Exercises 5–8: (a) State the null hypothesis and the alternate hypothesis. (b) State the decision rule. (c) Compute the value of the test statistic. (d) What is your decision regarding H_0? (e) What is the *p*-value? Interpret it.

5. The manufacturer of the X-15 steel-belted radial truck tire claims that the mean mileage the tire can be driven before the tread wears out is 60,000 miles. Assume the mileage wear follows the normal distribution and the standard deviation of the distribution is 5,000 miles. Crosset Truck Company bought 48 tires and found that the mean mileage for its trucks is 59,500 miles. Is Crosset's experience different from that claimed by the manufacturer at the .05 significance level?

6. The waiting time for customers at MacBurger Restaurants follows a normal distribution with a population standard deviation of 1 minute. At the Warren Road MacBurger, the quality-assurance department sampled 50 customers and found that the mean waiting time was 2.75 minutes. At the .05 significance level, can we conclude that the mean waiting time is less than 3 minutes?

7. A recent national survey found that high school students watched an average (mean) of 6.8 DVDs per month with a population standard deviation of 0.5 hours. The distribution of times follows the normal distribution. A random sample of 36 college students revealed that the mean number of DVDs watched last month was 6.2. At the .05 significance level, can we conclude that college students watch fewer DVDs a month than high school students?

8. At the time she was hired as a server at the Grumney Family Restaurant, Beth Brigden was told, "You can average $80 a day in tips." Assume the population of daily tips is normally distributed with a standard deviation of $3.24. Over the first 35 days she was employed at the restaurant, the mean daily amount of her tips was $84.85. At the .01 significance level, can Ms. Brigden conclude that her daily tips average more than $80?

10.8 Testing for a Population Mean: Population Standard Deviation Unknown

In the preceding example, we knew σ, the population standard deviation, and that the population followed the normal distribution. In most cases, however, the population standard deviation is unknown. Thus, σ must be based on prior studies or estimated by the sample standard deviation, s. The population standard deviation in the following example is not known, so the sample standard deviation is used to estimate σ.

To find the value of the test statistic, we use the *t* distribution and revise formula [10–1] as follows:

TESTING A MEAN, σ UNKNOWN	$t = \dfrac{\overline{X} - \mu}{s/\sqrt{n}}$	[10–2]

with $n - 1$ degrees of freedom, where:
   $\overline{X}$ is the sample mean.
   μ is the hypothesized population mean.
   s is the sample standard deviation.
   n is the number of observations in the sample.

We encountered this same situation when constructing confidence intervals in the previous chapter. See pages 266–273 in Chapter 9. We summarized this problem in Chart 9–3 on page 269. Under these conditions, the correct statistical procedure is to replace the standard normal distribution with the t distribution. To review, the major characteristics of the t distribution are:

- It is a continuous distribution.
- It is bell-shaped and symmetrical.
- There is a family of t distributions. Each time the degrees of freedom change, a new distribution is created.
- As the number of degrees of freedom increases, the shape of the t distribution approaches that of the standard normal distribution.
- The t distribution is flatter, or more spread out, than the standard normal distribution.

The following example shows the details.

Example

The McFarland Insurance Company Claims Department reports the mean cost to process a claim is $60. An industry comparison showed this amount to be larger than most other insurance companies, so the company instituted cost-cutting measures. To evaluate the effect of the cost-cutting measures, the Supervisor of the Claims Department selected a random sample of 26 claims processed last month and records the cost to process each claim. The sample information is reported in the following.

$45	$49	$62	$40	$43	$61
48	53	67	63	78	64
48	54	51	56	63	69
58	51	58	59	56	57
38	76				

At the .01 significance level, is it reasonable to conclude that the mean cost to process a claim is now less than $60?

Solution

LO 10-6 Conduct a test of hypothesis about a population mean.

We will use the five-step hypothesis testing procedure.

Step 1: State the null hypothesis and the alternate hypothesis. The null hypothesis is that the population mean is at least $60. The alternate hypothesis is that the population mean is less than $60. We can express the null and alternate hypotheses as follows:

$$H_0: \mu \geq \$60$$

$$H_1: \mu < \$60$$

The test is *one*-tailed because we want to determine whether there has been a *reduction* in the cost. The inequality in the alternate hypothesis points to the region of rejection in the left tail of the distribution.

Step 2: Select the level of significance. We decided on the .01 significance level.

Step 3: Select the test statistic. The test statistic in this situation is the t distribution. Why? First it is reasonable to conclude that the distribution of the cost per claim follows the normal distribution. We can confirm this from the histogram in the center of the following Minitab output. Observe the normal distribution superimposed on the frequency distribution.

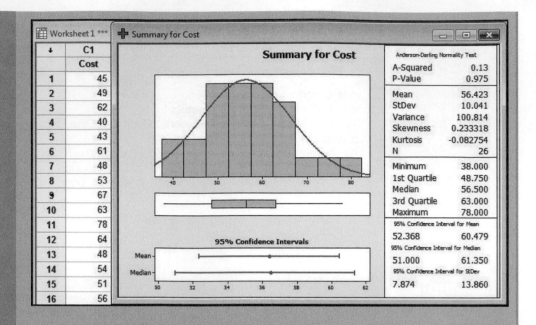

We do not know the standard deviation of the population. So we substitute the sample standard deviation. The value of the test statistic is computed by formula (10–2):

$$t = \frac{\overline{X} - \mu}{s/\sqrt{n}}$$

Step 4: Formulate the decision rule. The critical values of t are given in Appendix B.2, a portion of which is shown in Table 10–1. Appendix B.2 is also repeated in the back inside cover of the text. The far left column of the table is labeled "df" for degrees of freedom. The number of degrees of freedom is the total number of observations in the sample minus the number of populations sampled, written $n - 1$. In this case, the number of observations in the sample is 26, and we sampled 1 population, so there are $26 - 1 = 25$ degrees of freedom. To find the critical value, first locate the row with the appropriate degrees of freedom. This row is shaded in Table 10–1. Next, determine whether the test is one-tailed or two-tailed. In this case, we have a one-tailed test, so find the portion of the table that is labeled "one-tailed." Locate the column with the selected significance level. In this example, the significance level is .01. Move down the column labeled "0.01" until it intersects the row with 25 degrees of freedom. The value is 2.485. Because this is a one-sided test and the rejection region is in the left tail, the critical value is negative. The decision rule is to reject H_0 if the value of t is less than -2.485.

Step 5: Make a decision and interpret the result. From the Minitab output, to the right of the histogram, the mean cost per claim for the sample of 26 observations is $56.42. The standard deviation of this sample is $10.04. We insert these values in formula (10–2) and compute the value of t:

$$t = \frac{\overline{X} - \mu}{s/\sqrt{n}} = \frac{\$56.42 - \$60}{\$10.04/\sqrt{26}} = -1.818$$

TABLE 10–1 A Portion of the *t* Distribution Table

	Confidence Intervals					
	80%	**90%**	**95%**	**98%**	**99%**	**99.9%**
	Level of Significance for One-Tailed Test, α					
df	**0.10**	**0.05**	**0.025**	**0.01**	**0.005**	**0.0005**
	Level of Significance for Two-Tailed Test, α					
	0.20	**0.10**	**0.05**	**0.02**	**0.01**	**0.001**
⋮	⋮	⋮	⋮	⋮	⋮	⋮
21	1.323	1.721	2.080	2.518	2.831	3.819
22	1.321	1.717	2.074	2.508	2.819	3.792
23	1.319	1.714	2.069	2.500	2.807	3.768
24	1.318	1.711	2.064	2.492	2.797	3.745
25	1.316	1.708	2.060	2.485	2.787	3.725
26	1.315	1.706	2.056	2.479	2.779	3.707
27	1.314	1.703	2.052	2.473	2.771	3.690
28	1.313	1.701	2.048	2.467	2.763	3.674
29	1.311	1.699	2.045	2.462	2.756	3.659
30	1.310	1.697	2.042	2.457	2.750	3.646

Because -1.818 lies in the region to the right of the critical value of -2.485, the null hypothesis is not rejected at the .01 significance level. We have not demonstrated that the cost-cutting measures reduced the mean cost per claim to less than \$60. To put it another way, the difference of \$3.58 (\$56.42 − \$60) between the sample mean and the population mean could be due to sampling error. The computed value of *t* is shown in Chart 10–6. It is in the region where the null hypothesis is *not* rejected. The manager should conclude that the cost-cutting measures have not been effective.

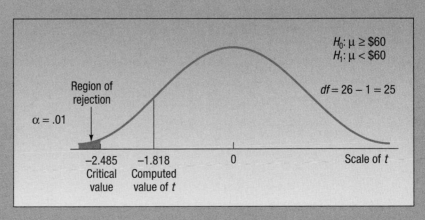

CHART 10–6 Rejection Region, *t* Distribution, .01 Significance Level

In the previous example, the mean and the standard deviation were computed using Minitab. The following example shows the details when the sample mean and sample standard deviation are calculated from sample data.

Example

The Myrtle Beach International Airport's short-term parking lot is close to the ter-minal, so someone meeting an incoming passenger has only a short walk to the baggage claim area, a good place to meet. To decide if the short-term lot has enough parking places, the manager of airport parking needs to know if the mean time in the lot is more than 40 minutes. A sample of 12 recent customers showed they were in the lot the following lengths of time, in minutes.

| 42 | 39 | 42 | 45 | 43 | 40 | 39 | 41 | 40 | 42 | 43 | 42 |

At the .05 significance level, is it reasonable to conclude that the mean time in the lot is more than 40 minutes?

Solution

LO 10-6 Conduct a test of hypothesis about a population mean.

We begin by stating the null hypothesis and the alternate hypothesis. In this case, the question is whether the population mean could be more than 40 minutes. So this is a one-tailed test. We state the two hypotheses as follows:

$$H_0: \mu \leq 40$$
$$H_1: \mu > 40$$

There are 11 degrees of freedom, found by $n - 1 = 12 - 1 = 11$. The critical t value is 1.796, found by referring to Appendix B.2 for a one-tailed test, using $\alpha = .05$ with 11 degrees of freedom. The decision rule is: Reject the null hypothesis if the computed t is greater than 1.796. This information is summarized in Chart 10–7.

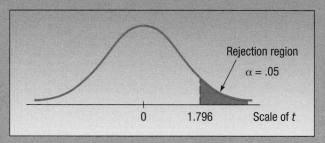

Rejection region
$\alpha = .05$

0   1.796   Scale of t

CHART 10–7 Rejection Region, One-Tailed Test, Student's t Distribution, $\alpha = .05$

We calculate the sample mean using formula (3–2) and the sample standard devi-ation using formula (3–8). The sample mean is 41.5 hours, and the sample standard deviation is 1.784 hours. The details of the calculations are shown in Table 10–2.

TABLE 10–2 Calculations of Sample Mean and Standard Deviation Parking Times

Customer	X, Minutes	$(X - \bar{X})^2$
1	42	0.25
2	39	6.25
3	42	0.25
4	45	12.25
5	43	2.25
6	40	2.25
7	39	6.25
8	41	0.25
9	40	0.25
10	42	0.25
11	43	2.25
12	42	0.25
Total	498	35.00

$$\bar{X} = \frac{\Sigma X}{n} = \frac{498}{12} = 41.5$$

$$s = \sqrt{\frac{\Sigma(X - \bar{X})^2}{n - 1}} = \sqrt{\frac{35}{12 - 1}} = 1.784$$

Now we are ready to compute the value of t, using formula (10-2).

$$t = \frac{\overline{X} - \mu}{s/\sqrt{n}} = \frac{41.5 - 40}{1.784/\sqrt{12}} = 2.913$$

The null hypothesis that the population mean is less than or equal to 40 minutes is rejected, because the computed t value of 2.913 lies in the area to the right of 1.796. We conclude that the time customers spend in the lot is more than 40 minutes.

Self-Review 10–3

The mean life of a battery used in a digital clock is 305 days. The lives of the batteries follow the normal distribution. The battery was recently modified to last longer. A sample of 20 of the modified batteries had a mean life of 311 days with a standard deviation of 12 days. Did the modification increase the mean life of the battery?
(a) State the null hypothesis and the alternate hypothesis.
(b) Show the decision rule graphically. Use the .05 significance level.
(c) Compute the value of t. What is your decision regarding the null hypothesis? Briefly summarize your results.

Exercises

connect™

9. Given the following hypothesis:

$$H_0: \mu \le 10$$
$$H_1: \mu > 10$$

A random sample of 10 observations is selected from a normal population. The sample mean was 12 and the sample standard deviation 3. Using the .05 significance level:
a. State the decision rule.
b. Compute the value of the test statistic.
c. What is your decision regarding the null hypothesis?

10. Given the following hypothesis:

$$H_0: \mu = 400$$
$$H_1: \mu \ne 400$$

A random sample of 12 observations is selected from a normal population. The sample mean was 407 and the sample standard deviation 6. Using the .01 significance level:
a. State the decision rule.
b. Compute the value of the test statistic.
c. What is your decision regarding the null hypothesis?

11. The Rocky Mountain district sales manager of Rath Publishing Inc., a college textbook publishing company, claims that the sales representatives make an average of 40 sales calls per week on professors. Several reps say that this estimate is too low. To investigate, a random sample of 28 sales representatives reveals that the mean number of calls made last week was 42. The standard deviation of the sample is 2.1 calls. Using the .05 significance level, can we conclude that the mean number of calls per salesperson per week is more than 40?

12. The management of White Industries is considering a new method of assembling its golf cart. The present method requires 42.3 minutes, on the average, to assemble a cart. The mean assembly time for a random sample of 24 carts, using the new method, was 40.6 minutes, and the standard deviation of the sample was 2.7 minutes. Using the .10 level of significance, can we conclude that the assembly time using the new method is faster?

13. The mean income per person in the United States is $40,000, and the distribution of incomes follows a normal distribution. A random sample of 10 residents of Wilmington, Delaware, had a mean of $50,000 with a standard deviation of $10,000. At the .05 level of significance, is that enough evidence to conclude that residents of Wilmington, Delaware, have more income than the national average?

14. Most air travelers now use e-tickets. Electronic ticketing allows passengers to not worry about a paper ticket, and it costs the airline companies less to handle than paper ticketing. However, in recent times the airlines have received complaints from passengers regarding their e-tickets, particularly when connecting flights and a change of airlines were

involved. To investigate the problem, an independent watchdog agency contacted a random sample of 20 airports and collected information on the number of complaints the airport had with e-tickets for the month of March. The information is reported below.

| 14 | 14 | 16 | 12 | 12 | 14 | 13 | 16 | 15 | 14 |
| 12 | 15 | 15 | 14 | 13 | 13 | 12 | 13 | 10 | 13 |

At the .05 significance level, can the watchdog agency conclude the mean number of complaints per airport is less than 15 per month?

a. What assumption is necessary before conducting a test of hypothesis?
b. Plot the number of complaints per airport in a frequency distribution or a dot plot. Is it reasonable to conclude that the population follows a normal distribution?
c. Conduct a test of hypothesis and interpret the results.

A Software Solution

The Minitab statistical software system, used in earlier chapters and the previous section, provides an efficient method for conducting a one-sample test of hypothesis for a population mean. The steps to generate the following output are shown in the **Software Commands** section at the end of the chapter.

Worksheet 1 ***									
↓	C1	C2	C3	C4	C5	C6	C7	C8	C9	C10
	Minutes									
1	42									
2	39									
3	42									
4	45									
5	43									
6	40									
7	39									
8	41									
9	40									
10	42									
11	43									
12	42									
13										

```
Session

One-Sample T: Minutes

Test of mu = 40 vs > 40

                                    95% Lower
Variable    N    Mean   StDev  SE Mean    Bound     T      P
Minutes    12  41.500   1.784   0.515    40.575  2.91  0.007
```

An additional feature of most statistical software packages is to report the *p*-value, which gives additional information on the null hypothesis. The *p*-value is the probability of a *t* value as extreme or more extreme than the computed *t* value, given that the null hypothesis is true. Using the Minitab analysis from the previous Parking Lot example, the *p*-value of .007 is the likelihood of a *t* value of 2.91 or larger, given a population mean of 40. Thus, comparing the *p*-value to the significance level tells us whether the null hypothesis was close to being rejected, barely rejected, and so on.

To explain further, refer to the diagram below. The *p*-value of .007 is the brown shaded area and the significance level is the total amber and brown shaded area. Because the *p*-value of .007 is less than the significance level of .05, the null hypothesis is rejected. Had the *p*-value been larger than the significance level—say, .06, .19, or .57—the null hypothesis would not be rejected.

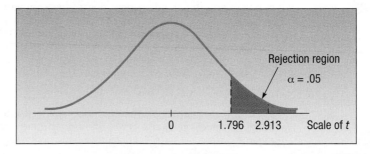

In the preceding example, the alternate hypothesis was one-sided, and the upper (right) tail of the t distribution contained the rejection region. The p-value is the area to the right of 2.913 for a t distribution with 11 degrees of freedom.

What if we were conducting a two-sided test, so that the rejection region is in both the upper and the lower tail? That is, in the Parking Lot example, if H_1 were stated as $\mu \neq 40$, we would have reported the p-value as the area to the right of 2.913 plus the value to the left of -2.913. Both of these values are .007, so the p-value is $.007 + .007 = .014$.

How can we estimate a p-value without a computer? To illustrate, recall that, in the example regarding the length of time at the Parking Lot, we rejected the null hypothesis that $\mu \leq 40$ and accepted the alternate hypothesis that $\mu > 40$. The significance level was .05, so logically the p-value is less than .05. To estimate the p-value more accurately, go to Appendix B.2 and find the row with 11 degrees of freedom. The computed t value of 2.913 is between 2.718 and 3.106. (A portion of Appendix B.2 is reproduced as Table 10–3.) The one-tailed significance level corresponding to 2.718 is .01, and for 3.106 it is .005. Therefore, the p-value is between .005 and .01. The usual practice is to report that the p-value is less than the larger of the two significance levels. So we would report "the p-value is less than .01."

TABLE 10–3 A Portion of Student's t Distribution

	Confidence Intervals					
	80%	90%	95%	98%	99%	99.9%
	Level of Significance for One-Tailed Test, α					
df	0.10	0.05	.0025	0.01	0.005	0.0005
	Level of Significance for Two-Tailed Test, α					
	0.20	0.10	0.05	0.02	0.01	0.001
⋮	⋮	⋮	⋮	⋮	⋮	⋮
9	1.383	1.833	2.262	2.821	3.250	4.781
10	1.372	1.812	2.228	2.764	3.169	4.587
11	1.363	1.796	2.201	2.718	3.106	4.437
12	1.356	1.782	2.179	2.681	3.055	4.318
13	1.350	1.771	2.160	2.650	3.012	4.221
14	1.345	1.761	2.145	2.624	2.977	4.140
15	1.341	1.753	2.131	2.602	2.947	4.073

Self-Review 10–4

A machine is set to fill a small bottle with 9.0 grams of medicine. A sample of eight bottles revealed the following amounts (grams) in each bottle.

9.2	8.7	8.9	8.6	8.8	8.5	8.7	9.0

At the .01 significance level, can we conclude that the mean weight is less than 9.0 grams?
(a) State the null hypothesis and the alternate hypothesis.
(b) How many degrees of freedom are there?
(c) Give the decision rule.
(d) Compute the value of t. What is your decision regarding the null hypothesis?
(e) Estimate the p-value.

Exercises

connect

15. Given the following hypothesis:

$$H_0: \mu \geq 20$$
$$H_1: \mu < 20$$

A random sample of five resulted in the following values: 18, 15, 12, 19, and 21. Assume a normal population. Using the .01 significance level, can we conclude the population mean is less than 20?
   a. State the decision rule.
   b. Compute the value of the test statistic.
   c. What is your decision regarding the null hypothesis?
   d. Estimate the p-value.

16. Given the following hypothesis:

$$H_0: \mu = 100$$
$$H_1: \mu \neq 100$$

A random sample of six resulted in the following values: 118, 105, 112, 119, 105, and 111. Assume a normal population. Using the .05 significance level, can we conclude the mean is different from 100?
   a. State the decision rule.
   b. Compute the value of the test statistic.
   c. What is your decision regarding the null hypothesis?
   d. Estimate the p-value.

17. The amount of water consumed each day by a healthy adult follows a normal distribution with a mean of 1.4 liters. A health campaign promotes the consumption of at least 2.0 liters per day. A sample of 10 adults after the campaign shows the following consumption in liters: (df)

1.5	1.6	1.5	1.4	1.9	1.4	1.3	1.9	1.8	1.7

At the .01 significance level, can we conclude that water consumption has increased? Calculate and interpret the p-value.

18. The liquid chlorine added to swimming pools to combat algae has a relatively short shelf life before it loses its effectiveness. Records indicate that the mean shelf life of a 5-gallon jug of chlorine is 2,160 hours (90 days). As an experiment, Holdlonger was added to the chlorine to find whether it would increase the shelf life. A sample of nine jugs of chlorine had these shelf lives (in hours): (df)

2,159	2,170	2,180	2,179	2,160	2,167	2,171	2,181	2,185

At the .025 level, has Holdlonger increased the shelf life of the chlorine? Estimate the p-value.

19. A Washington, D.C., "think tank" announces the typical teenager sent 50 text messages per day in 2011. To update that estimate, you phone a sample of teenagers and ask them how many text messages they sent the previous day. Their responses were:

51	175	47	49	44	54	145	203	21	59	42	100

At the .05 level, can you conclude that the mean number is greater than 50? Estimate the p-value and describe what it tells you. (df)

20. Hugger Polls contends that an agent conducts a mean of 53 in-depth home surveys every week. A streamlined survey form has been introduced, and Hugger wants to evaluate its effectiveness. The number of in-depth surveys conducted during a week by a random sample of agents are: (df)

53	57	50	55	58	54	60	52	59	62	60	60	51	59	56

At the .05 level of significance, can we conclude that the mean number of interviews conducted by the agents is more than 53 per week? Estimate the p-value.

10.9 Tests Concerning Proportions

In the previous chapter, we discussed confidence intervals for proportions. See Section 9.4 on pages 274–277. We can also conduct a test of hypothesis for a proportion. Recall that a proportion is the ratio of the number of successes to the number of observations. We let X refer to the number of successes and n the number of observations, so the proportion of successes in a fixed number of trials is X/n. Thus, the formula for computing a sample proportion, p, is $p = X/n$. Consider the following potential hypothesis-testing situations.

- Historically, General Motors reports that 70% of leased vehicles are returned with less than 36,000 miles. A recent sample of 200 vehicles returned at the end of their lease showed 158 had less than 36,000 miles. Has the proportion increased?
- The American Association of Retired Persons (AARP) reports that 60% of retired people under the age of 65 would return to work on a full-time basis if a suitable job were available. A sample of 500 retirees under 65 revealed 315 would return to work. Can we conclude that more than 60% would return to work?

LO 10-8 Conduct a test of hypothesis about a population proportion.

- Able Moving and Storage Inc. advises its clients for long-distance residential moves that their household goods will be delivered in 3 to 5 days from the time they are picked up. Able's records show it is successful 90% of the time with this claim. A recent audit revealed it was successful 190 times out of 200. Can the company conclude its success rate has increased?

Some assumptions must be made and conditions met before testing a population proportion. To test a hypothesis about a population proportion, a random sample is chosen from the population. It is assumed that the binomial assumptions discussed in Chapter 6 are met: (1) the sample data collected are the result of counts; (2) the outcome of an experiment is classified into one of two mutually exclusive categories—a "success" or a "failure"; (3) the probability of a success is the same for each trial; and (4) the trials are independent, meaning the outcome of one trial does not affect the outcome of any other trial. The test we will conduct shortly is appropriate when both $n\pi$ and $n(1 - \pi)$ are at least 5. n is the sample size, and π is the population proportion. It takes advantage of the fact that a binomial distribution can be approximated by the normal distribution.

Example

Suppose prior elections in a certain state indicated it is necessary for a candidate for governor to receive at least 80% of the vote in the northern section of the state to be elected. The incumbent governor is interested in assessing his chances of returning to office and plans to conduct a survey of 2,000 registered voters in the northern section of the state. Use the statistical hypothesis-testing procedure to assess the governor's chances of reelection.

Solution

This situation regarding the governor's reelection meets the binomial conditions.

- There are only two possible outcomes. That is, a sampled voter will either vote or not vote for the governor.
- The probability of a success is the same for each trial. In this case, the likelihood a particular sampled voter will support reelection is .80.
- The trials are independent. This means, for example, the likelihood the 23rd voter sampled will support reelection is not affected by what the 24th or 52nd voter does.
- The sample data is the result of counts. We are going to count the number of voters who support reelection in the sample of 2,000.

We use can use a normal approximation to the binomial distribution if both $n\pi$ and $n(1 - \pi)$ exceed 5. In this case, $n = 2,000$ and $\pi = 0.80$. (π is the proportion of the vote in the northern part of the state, or 80%, needed to be elected.) Thus, $n\pi = 2,000(.80) = 1,600$ and $n(1 - \pi) = 2,000(1 - .80) = 400$. Both 1,600 and 400 are greater than 5.

Step 1: **State the null hypothesis and the alternate hypothesis.** The null hypothesis, H_0, is that the population proportion π is .80 or larger. The alternate hypothesis, H_1, is that the proportion is less than .80. From a practical standpoint, the incumbent governor is concerned only when the proportion is less than .80. If it is equal to or greater than .80, he will have no problem; that is, the sample data would indicate he will probably be reelected. These hypotheses are written symbolically as:

$$H_0: \pi \geq .80$$
$$H_1: \pi < .80$$

H_1 states a direction. Thus, as noted previously, the test is one-tailed with the inequality sign pointing to the tail of the distribution containing the region of rejection.

Step 2: **Select the level of significance.** The level of significance is .05. This is the likelihood that a true hypothesis will be rejected.

Step 3: **Select the test statistic.** z is the appropriate statistic, found by:

TEST OF HYPOTHESIS, ONE PROPORTION	$z = \dfrac{p - \pi}{\sqrt{\dfrac{\pi(1 - \pi)}{n}}}$	**[10–3]**

where:
   π is the population proportion.
   p is the sample proportion.
   n is the sample size.

Finding the critical value

Step 4: **Formulate the decision rule.** The critical value or values of z form the dividing point or points between the regions where H_0 is rejected and where it is not rejected. Because the alternate hypothesis states a direction, this is a one-tailed test. The sign of the inequality points to the left, so only the left side of the curve is used. (See Chart 10–8.) The significance level

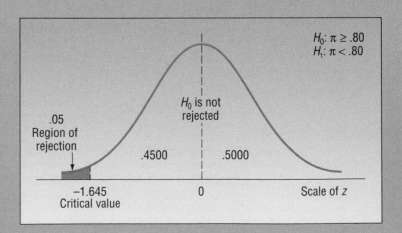

CHART 10–8 Rejection Region for the .05 Level of Significance, One-Tailed Test

was given as .05 in step 2. This probability is in the left tail and determines the region of rejection. The area between zero and the critical value is .4500, found by .5000 − .0500. Referring to Appendix B.2, go to the column indicating a .05 significance level for a one-tailed test, find the row with infinite degrees of freedom, and read the *z-value* of 1.645. The decision rule is, therefore: Reject the null hypothesis and accept the alternate hypothesis if the computed value of *z* falls to the left of −1.645; otherwise do not reject H_0.

Select a sample and make a decision regarding H_0.

Step 5: **Make a decision and interpret the result.** Select a sample and make a decision about H_0. A sample survey of 2,000 potential voters in the northern part of the state revealed that 1,550 planned to vote for the incumbent governor. Is the sample proportion of .775 (found by 1,550/2,000) close enough to .80 to conclude that the difference is due to sampling error? In this case:

p is .775, the proportion in the sample who plan to vote for the governor.
n is 2,000, the number of voters surveyed.
π is .80, the hypothesized population proportion.
z is a normally distributed test statistic when the hypothesis is true and the other assumptions are true.

Using formula (10–3) and computing *z* gives

$$z = \frac{p - \pi}{\sqrt{\dfrac{\pi(1 - \pi)}{n}}} = \frac{\dfrac{1{,}550}{2{,}000} - .80}{\sqrt{\dfrac{.80(1 - .80)}{2{,}000}}} = \frac{.775 - .80}{\sqrt{.00008}} = -2.80$$

The computed value of *z* (−2.80) is in the rejection region, so the null hypothesis is rejected at the .05 level. The difference of 2.5 percentage points between the sample percent (77.5%) and the hypothesized population percent in the northern part of the state necessary to carry the state (80%) is statistically significant. It is unlikely the difference is due to sampling error. To put it another way, the evidence at this point does not support the claim that the incumbent governor will return to the governor's mansion for another four years.

The *p*-value is the probability of finding a *z* value less than −2.80. From Appendix B.1, the probability of a *z* value between zero and −2.80 is .4974. So the *p*-value is .0026, found by .5000 − .4974. The governor cannot be confident of reelection because the *p*-value is less than the significance level.

Self-Review 10–5

A recent insurance industry report indicated that 40% of those persons involved in minor traffic accidents this year have been involved in at least one other traffic accident in the last five years. An advisory group decided to investigate this claim, believing it was too large. A sample of 200 traffic accidents this year showed 74 persons were also involved in another accident within the last five years. Use the .01 significance level.
(a) Can we use *z* as the test statistic? Tell why or why not.
(b) State the null hypothesis and the alternate hypothesis.
(c) Show the decision rule graphically.
(d) Compute the value of *z* and state your decision regarding the null hypothesis.
(e) Determine and interpret the *p*-value.

Exercises

21. The following hypotheses are given.

$$H_0: \pi \leq .70$$
$$H_1: \pi > .70$$

A sample of 100 observations revealed that $p = .75$. At the .05 significance level, can the null hypothesis be rejected?
   a. State the decision rule.
   b. Compute the value of the test statistic.
   c. What is your decision regarding the null hypothesis?

22. The following hypotheses are given.

$$H_0: \pi = .40$$
$$H_1: \pi \neq .40$$

A sample of 120 observations revealed that $p = .30$. At the .05 significance level, can the null hypothesis be rejected?
   a. State the decision rule.
   b. Compute the value of the test statistic.
   c. What is your decision regarding the null hypothesis?

Note: It is recommended that you use the five-step hypothesis-testing procedure in solving the following problems.

23. The National Safety Council reported that 52% of American turnpike drivers are men. A sample of 300 cars traveling southbound on the New Jersey Turnpike yesterday revealed that 170 were driven by men. At the .01 significance level, can we conclude that a larger proportion of men were driving on the New Jersey Turnpike than the national statistics indicate?

24. A recent article in *USA Today* reported that a job awaits only one in three new college graduates. The major reasons given were an overabundance of college graduates and a weak economy. A survey of 200 recent graduates from your school revealed that 80 students had jobs. At the .01 significance level, can we conclude that a larger proportion of students at your school have jobs?

25. Chicken Delight claims that 90% of its orders are delivered within 10 minutes of the time the order is placed. A sample of 100 orders revealed that 82 were delivered within the promised time. At the .10 significance level, can we conclude that less than 90% of the orders are delivered in less than 10 minutes?

26. Research at the University of Toledo indicates that 50% of students change their major area of study after their first year in a program. A random sample of 100 students in the College of Business revealed that 48 had changed their major area of study after their first year of the program. Has there been a significant decrease in the proportion of students who change their major after the first year in this program? Test at the .05 level of significance.

Chapter Summary

I. The objective of hypothesis testing is to verify the validity of a statement about a population parameter.

II. The steps to conduct a test of hypothesis are:
   A. State the null hypothesis (H_0) and the alternate hypothesis (H_1).
   B. Select the level of significance.
      1. The level of significance is the likelihood of rejecting a true null hypothesis.
      2. The most frequently used significance levels are .01, .05, and .10, but any value between 0 and 1.00 is possible.
   C. Select the test statistic.
      1. A test statistic is a value calculated from sample information used to determine whether to reject the null hypothesis.
      2. Two test statistics were considered in this chapter.
         a. The standard normal distribution (the z distribution) is used when the population follows the normal distribution and the population standard deviation is known.
         b. The t distribution is used when the population follows the normal distribution and the population standard deviation is unknown.
         c. The z distribution is used in a test of proportions when both $n\pi$ and $n(1 - \pi)$ are greater than 5.

D. State the decision rule.
   1. The decision rule indicates the condition or conditions when the null hypothesis is rejected.
   2. In a two-tailed test, the rejection region is evenly split between the upper and lower tails.
   3. In a one-tailed test, all of the rejection region is in either the upper or the lower tail.
E. Select a sample, compute the value of the test statistic, make a decision regarding the null hypothesis, and interpret the results.

III. A *p*-value is the probability that the value of the test statistic is as extreme as the value computed, when the null hypothesis is true.

IV. When testing a hypothesis about a population mean:
   A. If the population standard deviation, σ, is known, the test statistic is the standard normal distribution and is determined from:

$$z = \frac{\overline{X} - \mu}{\sigma/\sqrt{n}} \qquad \text{[10–1]}$$

   B. If the population standard deviation is not known, *s* is substituted for σ. The test statistic is the *t* distribution, and its value is determined from:

$$t = \frac{\overline{X} - \mu}{s/\sqrt{n}} \qquad \text{[10–2]}$$

   The major characteristics of the *t* distribution are:
   1. It is a continuous distribution.
   2. It is mound-shaped and symmetrical.
   3. It is flatter, or more spread out, than the standard normal distribution.
   4. There is a family of *t* distributions, depending on the number of degrees of freedom.

V. When testing about a population proportion:
   A. The binomial conditions must be met.
   B. Both $n\pi$ and $n(1 - \pi)$ must be at least 5.
   C. The test statistic is

$$z = \frac{p - \pi}{\sqrt{\dfrac{\pi(1 - \pi)}{n}}} \qquad \text{[10–3]}$$

Pronunciation Key

SYMBOL	MEANING	PRONUNCIATION
H_0	Null hypothesis	*H sub zero*
H_1	Alternate hypothesis	*H sub one*
$\alpha/2$	Two-tailed significance level	*Alpha over 2*

Chapter Exercises

27. According to the local union president, the mean gross income of plumbers in the Salt Lake area follows the normal probability distribution with a mean of $45,000 and a standard deviation of $3,000. A recent investigative reporter for KYAK TV found, for a sample of 120 plumbers, the mean gross income was $45,500. At the .10 significance level, is it reasonable to conclude that the mean income is not equal to $45,000? Determine the *p*-value.

28. Rutter Nursery Company packages its pine bark mulch in 50-pound bags. From a long history, the production department reports that the distribution of the bag weights follows the normal distribution and the standard deviation of this process is 3 pounds per bag. At the end of each day, Jeff Rutter, the production manager, weighs 10 bags and computes the mean weight of the sample. Below are the weights of 10 bags from today's production.

45.6	47.7	47.6	46.3	46.2	47.4	49.2	55.8	47.5	48.5

a. Can Mr. Rutter conclude that the mean weight of the bags is less than 50 pounds? Use the .01 significance level.

b. In a brief report, tell why Mr. Rutter can use the *z* distribution as the test statistic.

c. Compute the *p*-value.

29. A new weight-watching company, Weight Reducers International, advertises that those who join will lose, on the average, 10 pounds the first two weeks with a standard deviation of 2.8 pounds. A random sample of 50 people who joined the new weight reduction program revealed the mean loss to be 9 pounds. At the .05 level of significance, can we conclude that those joining Weight Reducers on average will lose less than 10 pounds? Determine the *p*-value.

30. Dole Pineapple Inc. is concerned that the 16-ounce can of sliced pineapple is being overfilled. Assume the standard deviation of the process is .03 ounces. The quality-control department took a random sample of 50 cans and found that the arithmetic mean weight was 16.05 ounces. At the 5% level of significance, can we conclude that the mean weight is greater than 16 ounces? Determine the *p*-value.

31. According to a recent survey, Americans get a mean of 7 hours of sleep per night. A random sample of 50 students at West Virginia University revealed the mean number of hours slept last night was 6 hours and 48 minutes (6.8 hours). The standard deviation of the sample was 0.9 hours. Is it reasonable to conclude that students at West Virginia sleep less than the typical American? Compute the *p*-value.

32. A statewide real estate sales agency, Farm Associates, specializes in selling farm property in the state of Nebraska. Its records indicate that the mean selling time of farm property is 90 days. Because of recent drought conditions, the agency believes that the mean selling time is now greater than 90 days. A statewide survey of 100 farms sold recently revealed that the mean selling time was 94 days, with a standard deviation of 22 days. At the .10 significance level, has there been an increase in selling time?

33. According to the Census Bureau, 3.13 people reside in the typical American household. A sample of 25 households in Arizona retirement communities showed the mean number of residents per household was 2.86 residents. The standard deviation of this sample was 1.20 residents. At the .05 significance level, is it reasonable to conclude the mean number of residents in the retirement community household is less than 3.13 persons?

34. A recent article in *Vitality* magazine reported that the mean amount of leisure time per week for American men is 40.0 hours. You believe this figure is too large and decide to conduct your own test. In a random sample of 60 men, you find that the mean is 37.8 hours of leisure per week and that the standard deviation of the sample is 12.2 hours. Can you conclude that the information in the article is untrue? Use the .05 significance level. Determine the *p*-value and explain its meaning.

35. According to a study by the Federal Reserve Board, the rate charged on credit card debt is more than 14%. Listed below is the interest rate charged on a sample of 10 credit cards.

14.6	16.7	17.4	17.0	17.8	15.4	13.1	15.8	14.3	14.5

Is it reasonable to conclude the mean rate charged is greater than 14%? Use the .01 significance level.

36. A recent article in *The Wall Street Journal* reported that the home equity loan rate is now less than 6%. A sample of eight small banks in the Midwest revealed the following home equity rates (in percent):

4.8	5.3	6.5	4.8	6.1	5.8	6.2	5.6

At the .01 significance level, can we conclude that the home equity rate for small banks is less than 6%? Estimate the *p*-value.

37. According to the Coffee Research Organization (http://www.coffeeresearch.org) the typical American coffee drinker consumes an average of 3.1 cups per day. A sample of 12 senior citizens revealed they consumed the following amounts of coffee, reported in cups, yesterday.

3.1	3.3	3.5	2.6	2.6	4.3	4.4	3.8	3.1	4.1	3.1	3.2

At the .05 significance level, does this sample data suggest there is a difference between the national average and the sample mean from senior citizens?

38. The postanesthesia care area (recovery room) at St. Luke's Hospital in Maumee, Ohio, was recently enlarged. The hope was that with the enlargement the mean number of patients per day would be more than 25. A random sample of 15 days revealed the following numbers of patients. (df)

25	27	25	26	25	28	28	27	24	26	25	29	25	27	24

At the .01 significance level, can we conclude that the mean number of patients per day is more than 25? Estimate the p-value and interpret it.

39. www.golfsmith.com receives an average of 6.5 returns per day from online shoppers. For a sample of 12 days, it received the following number of returns. (df)

0	4	3	4	9	4	5	9	1	6	7	10

At the .01 significance level, can we conclude the mean number of returns is less than 6.5?

40. During recent seasons, Major League Baseball has been criticized for the length of the games. A report indicated that the average game lasts 3 hours and 30 minutes. A sample of 17 games revealed the following times to completion. (Note that the minutes have been changed to fractions of hours, so that a game that lasted 2 hours and 24 minutes is reported as 2.40 hours.) (df)

2.98	2.40	2.70	2.25	3.23	3.17	2.93	3.18	2.80
2.38	3.75	3.20	3.27	2.52	2.58	4.45	2.45	

Can we conclude that the mean time for a game is less than 3.50 hours? Use the .05 significance level.

41. Watch Corporation of Switzerland claims that its watches on average will neither gain nor lose time during a week. A sample of 18 watches provided the following gains (+) or losses (−) in seconds per week. (df)

−0.38	−0.20	−0.38	−0.32	+0.32	−0.23	+0.30	+0.25	−0.10
−0.37	−0.61	−0.48	−0.47	−0.64	−0.04	−0.20	−0.68	+0.05

Is it reasonable to conclude that the mean gain or loss in time for the watches is 0? Use the .05 significance level. Estimate the p-value.

42. Listed below is the rate of return for one year (reported in percent) for a sample of 12 mutual funds that are classified as taxable money market funds. (df)

4.63	4.15	4.76	4.70	4.65	4.52	4.70	5.06	4.42	4.51	4.24	4.52

Using the .05 significance level, is it reasonable to conclude that the mean rate of return is more than 4.50%?

43. Many grocery stores and large retailers such as Walmart and Kmart have installed self-checkout systems so shoppers can scan their own items and cash out themselves. How do customers like this service and how often do they use it? Listed below is the number of customers using the service for a sample of 15 days at the Walmart on Highway 544 in Surfside, South Carolina. (df)

120	108	120	114	118	91	118	92	104	104
112	97	118	108	117					

Is it reasonable to conclude that the mean number of customers using the self-checkout system is more than 100 per day? Use the .05 significance level.

44. For a recent year, the mean fare to fly from Charlotte, North Carolina, to Seattle, Washington, on a discount ticket was $370. A random sample of round-trip discount fares on this route last month gives: (df)

$421	$386	$390	$430	$410	$350	$370	$380	$399	$365	$391	$375	$381

At the .01 significance level, can we conclude that the mean fare has increased? What is the p-value?

45. The publisher of *Celebrity Living* claims that the mean sales for personality magazines that feature people such as Angelina Jolie or Paris Hilton are 1.5 million copies per week. A sample of 10 comparable titles shows a mean weekly sales last week of 1.3 million copies with a standard deviation of 0.9 million copies. Does this data contradict the publisher's claim? Use the 0.01 significance level.

46. A United Nations report shows the mean family income for Mexican migrants to the United States is $27,000 per year. A FLOC (Farm Labor Organizing Committee) evaluation of 25 Mexican family units reveals a mean to be $30,000 with a sample standard deviation of $10,000. Is this information consistent with the United Nations report? Apply the 0.01 significance level.

47. A coin toss is used to decide which team gets the ball first in most sports. It involves little effort and is believed to give each side the same chance. In 45 Super Bowl games, the National Football Conference has won the coin flip 31 times. Meanwhile, the American Football Conference has won only 14 times. Use the five-step hypothesis-testing procedure at the .01 significance level to test whether this data suggest a fair coin flip.
   a. Why can you employ z as the test statistic?
   b. State the null and alternate hypotheses.
   c. Make a diagram of the decision rule.
   d. Evaluate the test statistic and make the decision.
   e. What is the p-value and what does that imply?

48. According to a study by the American Pet Food Dealers Association, 63% of U.S. households own pets. A report is being prepared for an editorial in the *San Francisco Chronicle*. As part of the editorial, a random sample of 300 households showed 210 own pets. Does this data disagree with the Pet Food Dealers Association data? Use a .05 level of significance.

49. Tina Dennis is the comptroller for Meek Industries. She believes that the current cash-flow problem at Meek is due to the slow collection of accounts receivable. She believes that more than 60% of the accounts are in arrears more than three months. A random sample of 200 accounts showed that 140 were more than three months old. At the .01 significance level, can she conclude that more than 60% of the accounts are in arrears for more than three months?

50. The policy of the Suburban Transit Authority (STA) is to add a bus route if more than 55% of the potential commuters indicate they would use the particular route. A sample of 70 commuters revealed that 42 would use a proposed route from Bowman Park to the downtown area. Does the Bowman-to-downtown route meet the STA criterion? Use the .05 significance level.

51. Past experience at the Crowder Travel Agency indicated that 44% of those persons who wanted the agency to plan a vacation for them wanted to go to Europe. During the most recent busy season, a sampling of 1,000 plans was selected at random from the files. It was found that 480 persons wanted to go to Europe on vacation. Has there been a significant shift upward in the percentage of persons who want to go to Europe? Test at the .05 significance level.

52. Research in the gaming industry showed that 10% of all slot machines in the United States stop working each year. Short's Game Arcade has 60 slot machines and only 3 failed last year. Use the five-step hypothesis-testing procedure at the .05 significance level to test whether this data contradicts the research report.
   a. Why can you employ z as the test statistic?
   b. State the null and alternate hypotheses.
   c. Evaluate the test statistic and make the decision.
   d. What is the p-value and what does that imply?

53. An urban planner claims that, nationally, 20% of all families renting condominiums move during a given year. A random sample of 200 families renting condominiums in the Dallas Metroplex revealed that 56 had moved during the past year. At the .01 significance level, does this evidence suggest that a larger proportion of condominium owners moved in the Dallas area? Determine the p-value.

54. The cost of weddings in the United States has skyrocketed in recent years. As a result, many couples are opting to have their weddings in the Caribbean. A Caribbean vacation resort recently advertised in *Bride Magazine* that the cost of a Caribbean wedding was less than $10,000. Listed below is a total cost in $000 for a sample of eight Caribbean weddings. 🅳🅵

9.7	9.4	11.7	9.0	9.1	10.5	9.1	9.8

At the .05 significance level, is it reasonable to conclude the mean wedding cost is less than $10,000 as advertised?

55. According to an ABC News survey, 40% of Americans do not eat breakfast. A sample of 30 college students found 16 had skipped breakfast that day. Use the .01 significance level to check whether college students are more likely to skip breakfast.

56. After a losing season, there is a great uproar to fire the head football coach. In a random sample of 200 college alumni, 80 favor keeping the coach. Test at the .05 level of significance whether the proportion of alumni who support the coach is less than 50%.

57. During the 1990s, the fatality rate for lung cancer was 80 per 100,000 people. After the turn of the century and the establishment of newer treatments and adjustment in public health advertising, a random sample of 10,000 people exhibits only six deaths due to lung cancer. Test at the .05 significance level whether these data are proof of a reduced fatality rate for lung cancer.

58. The American Water Works Association reports that the per capita water use in a single-family home is 69 gallons per day. Legacy Ranch is a relatively new housing development consisting of 100 homes. The builders installed more efficient water fixtures, such as low-flush toilets, and subsequently conducted a survey of the residences. Thirty-six homes responded, and the sample mean water use per day was 64 gallons with a standard deviation of 8.8 gallons per day. At the .10 level of significance, is that enough evidence to conclude that residents of Legacy Ranch use less water on average?

59. A national grocer's magazine reports the typical shopper spends eight minutes in line waiting to check out. A sample of 24 shoppers at the local Farmer Jack's showed a mean of 7.5 minutes with a standard deviation of 3.2 minutes. Is the waiting time at the local Farmer Jack's less than that reported in the national magazine? Use the .05 significance level.

Data Set Exercises

(The data for these exercises are available at the text website www.mhhe.com/lindbasic8e).

60. Refer to the Real Estate data, which report information on the homes sold in Goodyear, Arizona, last year.
  a. A recent article in the *Arizona Republic* indicated that the mean selling price of the homes in the area is more than $220,000. Can we conclude that the mean selling price in the Goodyear, AZ, area is more than $220,000? Use the .01 significance level. What is the *p*-value?
  b. The same article reported the mean size was more than 2,100 square feet. Can we conclude that the mean size of homes sold in the Goodyear, AZ, area is more than 2,100 square feet? Use the .01 significance level. What is the *p*-value?
  c. Determine the proportion of homes that have an attached garage. At the .05 significance level, can we conclude that more than 60% of the homes sold in the Goodyear, AZ, area had an attached garage? What is the *p*-value?
  d. Determine the proportion of homes that have a pool. At the .05 significance level, can we conclude that more than 60% of the homes sold in the Goodyear, AZ, area had a pool? What is the *p*-value?

61. Refer to the Baseball 2010 data, which report information on the 30 Major League Baseball teams for the 2010 season.
  a. Conduct a test of hypothesis to determine whether the mean payroll of the teams was different from $80.0 million. Use the .05 significance level.
  b. Conduct a test of hypothesis to determine whether the mean attendance was more than 2,000,000 per team.

62. Refer to the Buena School District bus data.
  a. Select the variable for the number of miles traveled last month. Conduct a test of hypothesis to determine whether the mean number of miles traveled is equal to 840. Use the .01 significance level. Find the *p*-value and explain what it means.
  b. Using the maintenance cost variable, conduct a test of hypothesis to determine whether the mean maintenance cost is less than $500 at the .05 significance level. Determine the *p*-value and interpret the result.
  c. Suppose we consider a bus "old" if it is more than eight years old. At the .01 significance level, can we conclude that less than 40% of the buses are old? Report the *p*-value.

Practice Test

Part 1—Objective

1. The _____ is a statement about the value of a population parameter developed for the purpose of testing.
2. We commit a Type II error when we _____ the null hypothesis when it is actually false.
3. The probability of committing a Type I error is equal to the _____.
4. The _____, based on sample information, is used to determine whether to reject the null hypothesis.
5. The _____ value separates the region where the null hypothesis is rejected from the region where it is not rejected.
6. In a _____-tailed test, the significance level is divided equally between the two tails. (one, two, neither)
7. When conducting a test of hypothesis for means (assuming a normal population), we use the standard normal distribution when the population _____ is known.
8. The _____ is the probability of finding a value of the test statistic at least as extreme as the one observed, given that the null hypothesis is true.
9. The _____ conditions are necessary to conduct a test of hypothesis about a proportion.
10. To conduct a test of proportions, the value of $n(\pi)$ and $n(1 - \pi)$ must be at least _____. (1, 5, 30, 1000)

Part 2—Problems

For each of these problems, use the five-step hypothesis-testing procedure.

1. The Park Manager at Fort Fisher State Park in North Carolina believes the typical park visitor spends at least 90 minutes in the park during the summer months. A sample of 18 visitors during the summer months of 2011 revealed the mean time in the park was 96 minutes with a standard deviation of 12 minutes. At the .01 significance level, is it reasonable to conclude that the mean time in the park is greater than 90 minutes?
2. The box fill weight of Frosted Flakes breakfast cereal follows the normal probability distribution with a mean of 9.75 ounces and a standard deviation of 0.27 ounces. A sample of 25 boxes filled this morning showed a mean of 9.85 ounces. Can we conclude that the mean weight is more than 9.75 ounces per box?
3. A recent newspaper article reported that for purchases of more than $500, 67% of young married couples consulted with and sought the approval of their spouse. A sample of 300 young married couples in Chicago revealed 180 consulted with their spouse on their most recent purchase of more than $500. At the .05 significance level, can we conclude that less than 67% of young married couples in Chicago sought the approval of their spouse?

Software Commands

1. The Minitab commands for the histogram and the descriptive statistics on page 306 are:
   a. Enter the 26 sample observations in column *C1* and name the variable *Cost*.
   b. From the menu bar, select **Stat, Basic Statistics,** and **Graphical Summary.** In the dialog box, select **Cost** as the variable and click **OK.**

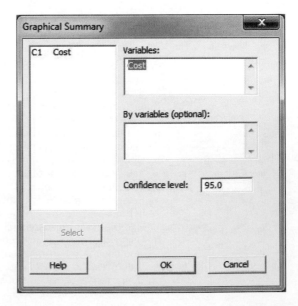

2. The Minitab commands for the one-sample t test on page 310 are:
   a. Enter the sample data into column *C1* and name the variable *Minutes*.
   b. From the menu bar, select **Stat, Basic Statistics,** and **1-Sample t,** and then hit **Enter.**
   c. Select **Minutes** as the variable, select **Perform hypothesized mean,** insert the value *40*. Click **Options.** Under **Alternate,** select **greater than.** Finally, click **OK** twice.

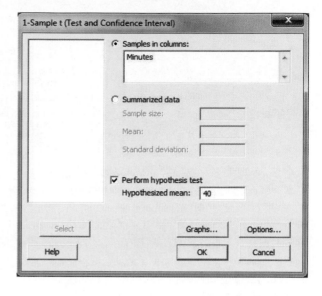

Chapter 10   Answers to Self-Review

10–1 **a.** $H_0: \mu = 16.0; H_1: \mu \neq 16.0$
   b. .05
   c. $z = \dfrac{\overline{X} - \mu}{\sigma/\sqrt{n}}$
   d. Reject H_0 if $z < -1.96$ or $z > 1.96$.
   e. $z = \dfrac{16.017 - 16.0}{0.15/\sqrt{50}} = \dfrac{0.0170}{0.0212} = 0.80$
   f. Do not reject H_0.
   g. We cannot conclude the mean amount dispensed is different from 16.0 ounces.

10–2 **a.** $H_0: \mu \leq 16.0; H_1: \mu > 16.0$
   b. Reject H_0 if $z > 1.645$.
   c. $z = \dfrac{16.040 - 16.0}{0.15/\sqrt{50}} = \dfrac{.0400}{.0212} = 1.89$
   d. Reject H_0.
   e. The mean amount dispensed is more than 16.0 ounces.
   f. p-value $= .5000 - .4706 = .0294$. The p-value is less than α (.05), so H_0 is rejected. It is the same conclusion as in part (d).

10–3 **a.** $H_0: \mu \leq 305; H_1: \mu > 305$
   b. $df = n - 1 = 20 - 1 = 19$
   The decision rule is to reject H_0 if $t > 1.729$.

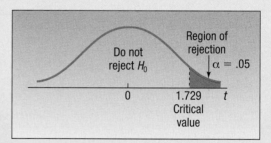

   c. $t = \dfrac{\overline{X} - \mu}{s/\sqrt{n}} = \dfrac{311 - 305}{12/\sqrt{20}} = 2.236$

   Reject H_0 because $2.236 > 1.729$. The modification increased the mean battery life to more than 305 days.

10–4 **a.** $H_0: \mu \geq 9.0; H_1: \mu < 9.0$
   b. 7, found by $n - 1 = 8 - 1 = 7$
   c. Reject H_0 if $t < -2.998$.

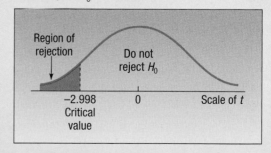

d. $t = -2.494$, found by:

$$s = \sqrt{\frac{0.36}{8-1}} = 0.2268$$

$$\overline{X} = \frac{70.4}{8} = 8.8$$

Then

$$t = \frac{8.8 - 9.0}{0.2268/\sqrt{8}} = -2.494$$

Because -2.494 lies to the right of -2.998, H_0 is not rejected. We have not shown that the mean is less than 9.0.

e. The p-value is between .025 and .010.

10–5 **a.** Yes, because both $n\pi$ and $n(1-\pi)$ exceed 5:
$n\pi = 200(.40) = 80$, and
$n(1-\pi) = 200(.60) = 120$.

b. H_0: $\pi \geq .40$
H_1: $\pi < .40$

c. Reject H_0 if $z < -2.326$.

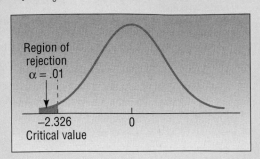

d. $z = -0.87$, found by:

$$z = \frac{.37 - .40}{\sqrt{\dfrac{.40(1-.40)}{200}}} = \frac{-.03}{\sqrt{.0012}} = -0.87$$

Do not reject H_0.

e. The p-value is .1922, found by .5000 − .3078.

Two-Sample Tests of Hypothesis

The Damon family owns a large grape vineyard in western New York along Lake Erie. The grapevines must be sprayed at the beginning of the growing season to protect against various insects and diseases. Two new insecticides have just been marketed, Pernod 5 and Action. When the grapes ripened, 400 of the vines treated with Pernod 5 were checked for infestation, and 400 of the vines treated with Action were checked. Referring to the table in the text, at the .05 significance level, can we conclude that there is a difference in the proportion of vines infested using Pernod 5 as opposed to Action? (See Exercise 9 and LO 11-2.)

11.1 Introduction

Chapter 10 began our study of hypothesis testing. We described the nature of hypothesis testing and conducted tests of a hypothesis in which we compared the results of a single sample to a population value. That is, we selected a single random sample from a population and conducted a test of whether the proposed population value was reasonable. Recall in Chapter 10 that we selected a sample of the number of desks assembled per week at Jamestown Steel Company to determine whether there was a change in the production rate. Similarly, we sampled voters in one area of a particular state to determine whether the population

proportion that would support the governor for reelection was less than .80. In both of these cases, we compared the results of a *single* sample statistic to a population parameter.

In this chapter, we expand the idea of hypothesis testing to two populations. That is, we select random samples from two different populations to determine whether the population means or proportions are equal. Some questions we might want to test are:

1. Is there a difference in the mean value of residential real estate sold by male agents and female agents in south Florida?
2. Were more calls for technical assistance received during the afternoon shift than the morning shift at CraftArt Software last month?
3. In the fast-food industry, is the mean number of days absent for workers under 21 years of age different from the mean number of days absent for workers more than 60 years of age?
4. For examinees who pass the Ohio Certified Public Accounting Examination on the first attempt, is the proportion of The Ohio State University graduates larger than the proportion of University of Cincinnati graduates?

We begin this chapter with the case in which we select random samples from two independent populations and wish to investigate whether these populations have the same mean.

11.2 Two-Sample Tests of Hypothesis: Independent Samples

A city planner in Florida wishes to know whether there is a difference in the mean hourly wage rate of plumbers and electricians in central Florida. A financial accountant wishes to know whether the mean rate of return for high yield mutual funds is different from the mean rate of return on global mutual funds. In each of these cases, there are two independent populations. In the first case, the plumbers represent one population and the electricians the other. In the second case, high-yield mutual funds are one population and global mutual funds the other.

In each of these cases, to investigate the question, we would select a random sample from each population and compute the mean of the two samples. If the two population means are the same, that is, the mean hourly rate is the same for the plumbers and the electricians, we would expect the *difference* between the two sample means to be zero. But what if our sample results yield a difference other than zero? Is that difference due to chance or is it because there is a real

LO 11-1 Test a hypothesis that two independent population means with known population standard deviations are equal.

difference in the hourly earnings? A two-sample test of means will help to answer this question.

We do need to return to the results of Chapter 8. Recall that we showed that a distribution of sample means would tend to approximate the normal distribution. We need to again assume that a distribution of sample means will follow the normal distribution. It can be shown mathematically that the distribution of the differences between sample means for two normal distributions is also normal.

We can illustrate this theory in terms of the city planner in Tampa, Florida. To begin, let's assume some information that is not usually available. Suppose that the population of plumbers has a mean of $30.00 per hour and a standard deviation of $5.00 per hour. The population of electricians has a mean of $29.00 and a standard deviation of $4.50. Now, from this information it is clear that the two population means are not the same. The plumbers actually earn $1.00 per hour more than the electricians. But we cannot expect to uncover this difference each time we sample the two populations.

Suppose we select a random sample of 40 plumbers and a random sample of 35 electricians and compute the mean of each sample. Then, we determine the difference between the sample means. It is this difference between the sample means that holds our interest. If the populations have the same mean, then we would expect the difference between the two sample means to be zero. If there is a difference between the population means, then we expect to find a difference between the sample means.

To understand the theory, we need to take several pairs of samples, compute the mean of each, determine the difference between the sample means, and study the distribution of the differences in the sample means. Because of our study of the distribution of sample means in Chapter 8, we know that the distribution of the sample means follows the normal distribution. If the two distributions of sample means follow the normal distribution, then we can reason that the distribution of their differences will also follow the normal distribution. This is the first hurdle.

The second hurdle refers to the mean of this distribution of differences. If we find the mean of this distribution is zero, that implies that there is no difference in the two populations. On the other hand, if the mean of the distribution of differences is equal to some value other than zero, either positive or negative, then we conclude that the two populations do not have the same mean.

To report some concrete results, let's return to the city planner in Tampa, Florida. Table 11–1 shows the result of selecting 20 different samples of 40 plumbers and 35 electricians, computing the mean of each sample, and finding the difference between the two sample means. In the first case, the sample of 40 plumbers has a mean of $29.80, and for the 35 electricians the mean is $28.76. The difference between the sample means is $1.04. This process was repeated 19 more times. Observe that in 17 of the 20 cases, the differences are positive because the mean of the plumbers is larger than the mean of the electricians. In two cases, the differences are negative because the mean of the electricians is larger than the mean of the plumbers. In one case, the means are equal.

Our final hurdle is that we need to know something about the *variability* of the distribution of differences. To put it another way, what is the standard deviation of this distribution of differences? Statistical theory shows that when we have independent populations, as in this case, the distribution of the differences has a variance (standard deviation squared) equal to the sum of the two individual variances. This means that we can add the variances of the two sampling distributions. To put it another way, the variance of the difference in sample means $(\overline{X}_1 - \overline{X}_2)$ is equal to the sum of the variance for the plumbers and the variance for the electricians.

VARIANCE OF THE DISTRIBUTION OF DIFFERENCES IN MEANS	$\sigma^2_{\overline{X}_1 - \overline{X}_2} = \dfrac{\sigma^2_1}{n_1} + \dfrac{\sigma^2_2}{n_2}$	[11–1]

TABLE 11–1 The Means of Random Samples of Plumbers and Electricians

Sample	Plumbers	Electricians	Difference
1	$29.80	$28.76	$1.04
2	30.32	29.40	0.92
3	30.57	29.94	0.63
4	30.04	28.93	1.11
5	30.09	29.78	0.31
6	30.02	28.66	1.36
7	29.60	29.13	0.47
8	29.63	29.42	0.21
9	30.17	29.29	0.88
10	30.81	29.75	1.06
11	30.09	28.05	2.04
12	29.35	29.07	0.28
13	29.42	28.79	0.63
14	29.78	29.54	0.24
15	29.60	29.60	0.00
16	30.60	30.19	0.41
17	30.79	28.65	2.14
18	29.14	29.95	−0.81
19	29.91	28.75	1.16
20	28.74	29.21	−0.47

The term $\sigma^2_{\bar{X}_1-\bar{X}_2}$ looks complex but need not be difficult to interpret. The σ^2 portion reminds us that it is a variance, and the subscript $\bar{X}_1 - \bar{X}_2$ that it is a distribution of differences in the sample means.

We can put this equation in a more usable form by taking the square root, so that we have the standard deviation of the distribution or "standard error" of the differences. Finally, we standardize the distribution of the differences. The result is the following equation.

$$
\text{TWO-SAMPLE TEST OF MEANS—KNOWN } \sigma \qquad z = \frac{\bar{X}_1 - \bar{X}_2}{\sqrt{\dfrac{\sigma_1^2}{n_1} + \dfrac{\sigma_2^2}{n_2}}} \qquad \text{[11–2]}
$$

Before we present an example, let's review the assumptions necessary for using formula (11–2).

- The two populations follow normal distributions.
- The two samples must be unrelated, that is, independent.
- The standard deviations for both populations must be known.

The following example shows the details of the test of hypothesis for two population means.

Example

Customers at the FoodTown Supermarket have a choice when paying for their groceries. They may check out and pay using the standard cashier-assisted checkout, or they may use the new Fast Lane procedure. In the standard procedure, a FoodTown employee scans each item, puts it on a short conveyor where another employee puts it in a bag and then into the grocery cart. In the Fast Lane procedure, the customer scans each item, bags it, and places the bags in the cart themselves.

The Fast Lane procedure is designed to reduce the time a customer spends in the checkout line.

The Fast Lane facility was recently installed at the Byrne Road FoodTown location. The store manager would like to know if the mean checkout time using the standard checkout method is longer than using the Fast Lane. She gathered the following sample information. The time is measured from when the customer enters the line until their bags are in the cart. Hence the time includes both waiting in line and checking out. What is the p-value?

Customer Type	Sample Mean	Population Standard Deviation	Sample Size
Standard	5.50 minutes	0.40 minutes	50
Fast Lane	5.30 minutes	0.30 minutes	100

Solution

We use the five-step hypothesis-testing procedure to investigate the question.

Step 1: State the null hypothesis and the alternate hypothesis. The null hypothesis is that the mean standard checkout time is less than or equal to the mean Fast Lane checkout time. In other words, the difference of 0.20 minutes between the mean checkout time for the standard method and the mean checkout time for Fast Lane is due to chance. The alternate hypothesis is that the mean checkout time is larger for those using the standard method. We will let μ_S refer to the mean checkout time for the population of standard customers and μ_F the mean checkout time for the Fast Lane customers. The null and alternative hypotheses are:

$$H_0: \mu_S \leq \mu_F$$
$$H_1: \mu_S > \mu_F$$

Step 2: Select the level of significance. The significance level is the probability that we reject the null hypothesis when it is actually true. This likelihood is determined prior to selecting the sample or performing any calculations. The .05 and .01 significance levels are the most common, but other values, such as .02 and .10, are also used. In theory, we may select any value between 0 and 1 for the significance level. In this case, we selected the .01 significance level.

Step 3: Determine the test statistic. In Chapter 10, we used the standard normal distribution (that is, z) and t as test statistics. In this case, we use the z distribution as the test statistic because we assume the two population distributions are both normal and the standard deviations of both populations are known.

Step 4: Formulate a decision rule. The decision rule is based on the null and the alternate hypotheses (i.e., one-tailed or two-tailed test), the level of significance, and the test statistic used. We selected the .01 significance level and the z distribution as the test statistic, and we wish to determine whether the mean checkout time is longer using the standard method. We set the alternate hypothesis to indicate that the mean checkout time is longer for those using the standard method than the Fast Lane method. Hence, the rejection region is in the upper tail of the standard normal distribution (a one-tailed test). To find the critical value, go to Student's t distribution (Appendix B.2). In the table headings, find the row labeled **"Level of Significance for One-Tailed Test"** and select the column for an alpha of .01. Go to the bottom row with infinite degrees of freedom. The z critical value is 2.326. So the decision rule is to reject the null hypothesis if the value of the test statistic exceeds 2.326. Chart 11–1 depicts the decision rule.

Statistics in Action

Do you live to work or work to live? A recent poll of 802 working Americans revealed that, among those who considered their work as a career, the mean number of hours worked per day was 8.7. Among those who considered their work as a job, the mean number of hours worked per day was 7.6.

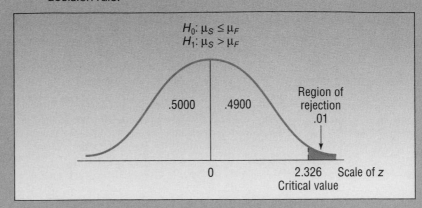

$H_0: \mu_S \leq \mu_F$
$H_1: \mu_S > \mu_F$

.5000   .4900   Region of rejection .01

0   2.326   Scale of z
Critical value

CHART 11–1 Decision Rule for One-Tailed Test at .01 Significance Level

Step 5: Make the decision regarding H_0 and interpret the result. We use formula (11–2) to compute the value of the test statistic.

$$z = \frac{\bar{X}_S - \bar{X}_F}{\sqrt{\frac{\sigma_S^2}{n_S} + \frac{\sigma_F^2}{n_F}}} = \frac{5.5 - 5.3}{\sqrt{\frac{0.40^2}{50} + \frac{0.30^2}{100}}} = \frac{0.2}{0.064031} = 3.123$$

The computed value of 3.123 is larger than the critical value of 2.326. Our decision is to reject the null hypothesis and accept the alternate hypothesis. The difference of .20 minutes between the mean checkout time using the standard method is too large to have occurred by chance. To put it another way, we conclude the Fast Lane method is faster.

What is the p-value for the test statistic? Recall that the p-value is the probability of finding a value of the test statistic this extreme when the null hypothesis is true. To calculate the p-value, we need the probability of a z value larger than 3.123. From Appendix B.1, we cannot find the probability associated with 3.123. The largest value available is 3.09. The area corresponding to 3.09 is .4990. In this case, we can report that the p-value is less than .0010, found by .5000 − .4990. We conclude that there is very little likelihood that the null hypothesis is true!

In summary, the criteria for using formula (11–2) are:

1. *The samples are from independent populations.* This means the checkout time for the Fast Lane customers is unrelated to the checkout time for the other customers. For example, Mr. Smith's checkout time does not affect any other customer's checkout time.
2. *Both populations follow the normal distribution.* In the FoodTown example, this means the population of times in both the standard checkout line and the Fast Lane follow the normal distribution.
3. *Both population standard deviations are known.* In the FoodTown example, the population standard deviation of the Fast Lane times was 0.30 minutes. The standard deviation of the standard checkout times was 0.40 minutes.

Self-Review 11–1

Tom Sevits is the owner of the Appliance Patch. Recently Tom observed a difference in the dollar value of sales between the men and women he employs as sales associates. A sample of 40 days revealed the men sold a mean of $1,400 worth of appliances per day. For a sample of 50 days, the women sold a mean of $1,500 worth of appliances per day. Assume the population standard deviation for men is $200 and for women $250. At the .05 significance level, can Mr. Sevits conclude that the mean amount sold per day is larger for the women?
(a) State the null hypothesis and the alternate hypothesis.
(b) What is the decision rule?
(c) What is the value of the test statistic?
(d) What is your decision regarding the null hypothesis?
(e) What is the p-value?
(f) Interpret the result.

Exercises

connect™

1. A sample of 40 observations is selected from one population with a population standard deviation of 5. The sample mean is 102. A sample of 50 observations is selected from a second population with a population standard deviation of 6. The sample mean is 99. Conduct the following test of hypothesis using the .04 significance level.

$$H_0: \mu_1 = \mu_2$$
$$H_1: \mu_1 \neq \mu_2$$

   a. Is this a one-tailed or a two-tailed test?
   b. State the decision rule.
   c. Compute the value of the test statistic.
   d. What is your decision regarding H_0?
   e. What is the p-value?

2. A sample of 65 observations is selected from one population with a population standard deviation of 0.75. The sample mean is 2.67. A sample of 50 observations is selected from a second population with a population standard deviation of 0.66. The sample mean is 2.59. Conduct the following test of hypothesis using the .08 significance level.

$$H_0: \mu_1 \leq \mu_2$$
$$H_1: \mu_1 > \mu_2$$

   a. Is this a one-tailed or a two-tailed test?
   b. State the decision rule.
   c. Compute the value of the test statistic.
   d. What is your decision regarding H_0?
   e. What is the p-value?

Note: Use the five-step hypothesis-testing procedure to solve the following exercises.

3. Gibbs Baby Food Company wishes to compare the weight gain of infants using its brand versus its competitor's. A sample of 40 babies using the Gibbs products revealed a mean weight gain of 7.6 pounds in the first three months after birth. For the Gibbs brand, the population standard deviation of the sample is 2.3 pounds. A sample of 55 babies using the competitor's brand revealed a mean increase in weight of 8.1 pounds. The population standard deviation is 2.9 pounds. At the .05 significance level, can we conclude that babies using the Gibbs brand gained less weight? Compute the p-value and interpret it.

4. As part of a study of corporate employees, the director of human resources for PNC Inc. wants to compare the distance traveled to work by employees at its office in downtown Cincinnati with the distance for those in downtown Pittsburgh. A sample of 35 Cincinnati employees showed they travel a mean of 370 miles per month. A sample of 40 Pittsburgh employees showed they travel a mean of 380 miles per month. The population standard deviation for the Cincinnati and Pittsburgh employees

are 30 and 26 miles, respectively. At the .05 significance level, is there a difference in the mean number of miles traveled per month between Cincinnati and Pittsburgh employees?

5. Women's height is a suspected factor for difficult deliveries, that is, shorter women are more likely to have Caesarean sections. A medical researcher found in a sample of 45 women who had a normal delivery that their mean height was 61.4 inches. A second sample of 39 women who had a Caesarean section had a mean height of 60.6 inches. Assume that the population of heights of normal deliveries has a population standard deviation of 1.2 inches. Also assume that the heights of the population of women who had Caesarean section births has a standard deviation of 1.1 inches. Are those who had a Caesarean section shorter? Use the .05 significance level. Find the *p*-value and explain what it means.

6. Mary Jo Fitzpatrick is the vice president for Nursing Services at St. Luke's Memorial Hospital. Recently she noticed in the job postings for nurses that those that are unionized seem to offer higher wages. She decided to investigate and gathered the following information.

Group	Mean Wage	Population Standard Deviation	Sample Size
Union	$20.75	$2.25	40
Nonunion	$19.80	$1.90	45

Would it be reasonable for her to conclude that union nurses earn more? Use the .02 significance level. What is the *p*-value?

11.3 Two-Sample Tests about Proportions

In the previous section, we considered a test involving population means. However, we are often interested also in whether two sample proportions come from populations that are equal. Here are several examples.

- The vice president of human resources wishes to know whether there is a difference in the proportion of hourly employees who miss more than five days of work per year at the Atlanta and the Houston plants.
- General Motors is considering a new design for the Chevy Malibu. The design is shown to a group of potential buyers under 30 years of age and another group over 60 years of age. General Motors wishes to know whether there is a difference in the proportion of the two groups who like the new design.
- A consultant to the airline industry is investigating the fear of flying among adults. Specifically, the company wishes to know whether there is a difference in the proportion of men versus women who are fearful of flying.

LO 11-2 Carry out a hypothesis test that two population proportions are equal.

In the above cases, each sampled item or individual can be classified as a "success" or a "failure." That is, in the Chevy Malibu example each potential buyer is classified as "liking the new design" or "not liking the new design." We then compare the proportion in the under 30 group with the proportion in the over 60 group who indicated they liked the new design. Can we conclude that the differences are due to chance? In this study, there is no measurement obtained, only classifying the individuals or objects.

To conduct the test, we assume each sample is large enough that the normal distribution will serve as a good approximation of the binomial distribution. The test statistic follows the standard normal distribution. We compute the value of *z* from the following formula:

TWO-SAMPLE TEST OF PROPORTIONS	$z = \dfrac{p_1 - p_2}{\sqrt{\dfrac{p_c(1 - p_c)}{n_1} + \dfrac{p_c(1 - p_c)}{n_2}}}$	[11–3]

Formula (11–3) is formula (11–2) with the respective sample proportions replacing the sample means and $p_c(1 - p_c)$ replacing the two variances. In addition:

n_1 is the number of observations in the first sample.
n_2 is the number of observations in the second sample.
p_1 is the proportion in the first sample possessing the trait.
p_2 is the proportion in the second sample possessing the trait.
p_c is the pooled proportion possessing the trait in the combined samples. It is called the pooled estimate of the population proportion and is computed from the following formula.

POOLED PROPORTION	$p_c = \dfrac{X_1 + X_2}{n_1 + n_2}$	[11–4]

where:
X_1 is the number possessing the trait in the first sample.
X_2 is the number possessing the trait in the second sample.

The following example will illustrate the two-sample test of proportions.

Example

Manelli Perfume Company recently developed a new fragrance that it plans to market under the name Heavenly. A number of market studies indicate that Heavenly has very good market potential. The Sales Department at Manelli is particularly interested in whether there is a difference in the proportions of younger and older women who would purchase Heavenly if it were marketed. There are two independent populations, a population consisting of the younger women and a population consisting of the older women. Each sampled woman will be asked to smell Heavenly and indicate whether she likes the fragrance well enough to purchase a bottle.

Solution

We will use the usual five-step hypothesis-testing procedure.

Step 1: State H_0 and H_1. In this case, the null hypothesis is: "There is no difference in the proportion of young women and older women who prefer Heavenly." We designate π_1 as the proportion of young women who would purchase Heavenly and π_2 as the proportion of older women who would purchase it. The alternate hypothesis is that the two proportions are not equal.

$$H_0: \pi_1 = \pi_2$$
$$H_1: \pi_1 \neq \pi_2$$

Step 2: Select the level of significance. We choose the .05 significance level in this example.

Step 3: Determine the test statistic. The test statistic follows the standard normal distribution. The value of the test statistic can be computed from formula (11–3).

Step 4: Formulate the decision rule. Recall that the alternate hypothesis from **Step 1** does not state a direction, so this is a two-tailed test. To find the critical value, go to Student's *t* distribution (Appendix B.2). In the table headings, find the row labeled **"Level of Significance for Two-Tailed**

Test" and select the column for an alpha of .05. Go to the bottom row with infinite degrees of freedom. The z critical value is 1.960, so the critical values are -1.960 and 1.960. As before, if the computed test statistic is less than -1.960 or greater than 1.960, the null hypothesis is rejected. This information is summarized in Chart 11–2.

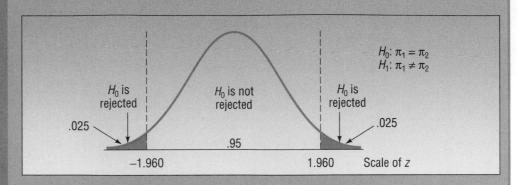

CHART 11–2 Decision Rules for Heavenly Fragrance Test, .05 Significance Level

Step 5: Select a sample and make a decision. A random sample of 100 young women revealed 19 liked the Heavenly fragrance well enough to purchase it. Similarly, a sample of 200 older women revealed 62 liked the fragrance well enough to make a purchase. We let p_1 refer to the young women and p_2 to the older women.

$$p_1 = \frac{X_1}{n_1} = \frac{19}{100} = .19 \qquad p_2 = \frac{X_2}{n_2} = \frac{62}{200} = .31$$

The research question is whether the difference of .12 in the two sample proportions is due to chance or whether there is a difference in the proportion of younger and older women who like the Heavenly fragrance.

   Next, we combine or pool the sample proportions. We use formula (11–4).

$$p_c = \frac{X_1 + X_2}{n_1 + n_2} = \frac{19 + 62}{100 + 200} = \frac{81}{300} = 0.27$$

Note that the pooled proportion is closer to .31 than to .19 because more older women than younger women were sampled.

   We use formula (11–3) to find the value of the test statistic.

$$z = \frac{p_1 - p_2}{\sqrt{\dfrac{p_c(1 - p_c)}{n_1} + \dfrac{p_c(1 - p_c)}{n_2}}} = \frac{.19 - .31}{\sqrt{\dfrac{.27(1 - .27)}{100} + \dfrac{.27(1 - .27)}{200}}} = -2.207$$

The computed value of -2.207 is in the area of rejection; that is, it is to the left of -1.960. Therefore, the null hypothesis is rejected at the .05 significance level. To put it another way, we reject the null hypothesis that the proportion of young women who would purchase Heavenly is equal to the proportion of older women who would purchase Heavenly. It is unlikely that the difference between the two sample proportions is due to chance. To find the p-value, we need to round the z test statistic from -2.207 to -2.21 so that we can use the table Areas under the Normal Curve in Appendix B.1. In the table, find the likelihood, or probability, of a z value less than -2.21 or greater than 2.21. The probability corresponding to 2.21

is .4864, so the likelihood of finding the value of the test statistic to be less than −2.21 or greater than 2.21 is:

$$p\text{-value} = 2(.5000 - .4864) = 2(.0136) = .0272$$

The p-value of .0272 is less than the significance level of .05, so our decision is to reject the null hypothesis. Again, we conclude that there is a difference in the proportion of younger and older women who would purchase Heavenly.

The Minitab system has a procedure to quickly determine the value of the test statistic and compute the p-value. The results follow.

```
Session                                              ─  □  ⌧

Test and CI for Two Proportions

Sample   X    N   Sample p
1       19  100   0.190000
2       62  200   0.310000


Difference = p (1) - p (2)
Estimate for difference:  -0.12
95% CI for difference:  (-0.220102, -0.0198978)
Test for difference = 0 (vs not = 0):  Z = -2.21  P-Value = 0.027

Fisher's exact test: P-Value = 0.028
```

Notice that the Minitab output includes the two sample proportions, the value of z, and the p-value.

Self-Review 11–2 Of 150 adults who tried a new peach-flavored Peppermint Pattie, 87 rated it excellent. Of 200 children sampled, 123 rated it excellent. Using the .10 level of significance, can we conclude that there is a significant difference in the proportion of adults and the proportion of children who rate the new flavor excellent?
(a) State the null hypothesis and the alternate hypothesis.
(b) What is the probability of a Type I error?
(c) Is this a one-tailed or a two-tailed test?
(d) What is the decision rule?
(e) What is the value of the test statistic?
(f) What is your decision regarding the null hypothesis?
(g) What is the p-value? Explain what it means in terms of this problem.

Exercises

connect

7. The null and alternate hypotheses are:

$$H_0: \pi_1 \leq \pi_2$$
$$H_1: \pi_1 > \pi_2$$

A sample of 100 observations from the first population indicated that X_1 is 70. A sample of 150 observations from the second population revealed X_2 to be 90. Use the .05 significance level to test the hypothesis.
a. State the decision rule.
b. Compute the pooled proportion.
c. Compute the value of the test statistic.
d. What is your decision regarding the null hypothesis?

8. The null and alternate hypotheses are:

$$H_0: \pi_1 = \pi_2$$
$$H_1: \pi_1 \neq \pi_2$$

A sample of 200 observations from the first population indicated that X_1 is 170. A sample of 150 observations from the second population revealed X_2 to be 110. Use the .05 significance level to test the hypothesis.

a. State the decision rule.
b. Compute the pooled proportion.
c. Compute the value of the test statistic.
d. What is your decision regarding the null hypothesis?

Note: Use the five-step hypothesis-testing procedure in solving the following exercises.

9. The Damon family owns a large grape vineyard in western New York along Lake Erie. The grapevines must be sprayed at the beginning of the growing season to protect against various insects and diseases. Two new insecticides have just been marketed: Pernod 5 and Action. To test their effectiveness, three long rows were selected and sprayed with Pernod 5, and three others were sprayed with Action. When the grapes ripened, 400 of the vines treated with Pernod 5 were checked for infestation. Likewise, a sample of 400 vines sprayed with Action were checked. The results are:

Insecticide	Number of Vines Checked (sample size)	Number of Infested Vines
Pernod 5	400	24
Action	400	40

At the .05 significance level, can we conclude that there is a difference in the proportion of vines infested using Pernod 5 as opposed to Action?

10. GfK Custom Research North America conducted identical surveys five years apart. One question asked of women was "Are most men basically kind, gentle, and thoughtful?" The earlier survey revealed that, of the 3,000 women surveyed, 2,010 said that they were. The later revealed 1,530 of the 3,000 women surveyed thought that men were kind, gentle, and thoughtful. At the .05 level, can we conclude that women think men are less kind, gentle, and thoughtful in the later survey compared with the earlier one?

11. A nationwide sample of influential Republicans and Democrats was asked as a part of a comprehensive survey whether they favored lowering environmental standards so that high-sulfur coal could be burned in coal-fired power plants. The results were:

	Republicans	Democrats
Number sampled	1,000	800
Number in favor	200	168

At the .02 level of significance, can we conclude that there is a larger proportion of Democrats in favor of lowering the standards? Determine the *p*-value.

12. The research department at the home office of New Hampshire Insurance conducts ongoing research on the causes of automobile accidents, the characteristics of the drivers, and so on. A random sample of 400 policies written on single persons revealed 120 had at least one accident in the previous three-year period. Similarly, a sample of 600 policies written on married persons revealed that 150 had been in at least one accident. At the .05 significance level, is there a significant difference in the proportions of single and married persons having an accident during a three-year period? Determine the *p*-value.

11.4 Comparing Population Means with Unknown Population Standard Deviations

In the previous two sections, we described conditions where the standard normal distribution, that is *z*, is used as the test statistic. In one case, we were working with a variable (calculating the mean) and in the second an attribute (calculating a proportion). In the first case, we wished to compare two sample means from independent populations to determine if they came from the same or equal populations. In that instance, we assumed the population followed the normal probability distribution and that we knew the standard deviation of the population. In many cases, in fact in most cases, we do not know the population standard deviation. We can overcome this problem, as we did in the one sample case in the previous chapter, by substituting the sample standard deviation (s) for the population standard deviation (σ). See formula (10–2) on page 304.

Two-Sample Pooled t-Test

This section describes another method for comparing the sample means of two independent populations to determine if the sampled populations could reasonably have the same mean. The method described does *not* require that we know the standard deviations of the populations. This gives us a great deal more flexibility when investigating the difference in sample means. There are two major differences in this test and the previous test described earlier in this chapter.

1. We assume the sampled populations have equal but unknown standard deviations. Because of this assumption, we combine or "pool" the sample standard deviations.
2. We use the t distribution as the test statistic.

LO 11-3 Conduct a test of a hypothesis that two independent population means are equal, assuming equal but unknown population standard deviations.

The formula for computing the value of the test statistic t is similar to (11–2), but an additional calculation is necessary. The two sample standard deviations are pooled to form a single estimate of the unknown population standard deviation. In essence, we compute a weighted mean of the two sample standard deviations and use this value as an estimate of the unknown population standard deviation. The weights are the degrees of freedom that each sample provides. Why do we need to pool the sample standard deviations? Because we assume that the two populations have equal standard deviations, the best estimate we can make of that value is to combine or pool all the sample information we have about the value of the population standard deviation.

The following formula is used to pool the sample standard deviations. Notice that two factors are involved: the number of observations in each sample and the sample standard deviations themselves.

POOLED VARIANCE	$s_p^2 = \dfrac{(n_1 - 1)s_1^2 + (n_2 - 1)s_2^2}{n_1 + n_2 - 2}$	[11–5]

where:
s_1^2 is the variance (standard deviation squared) of the first sample.
s_2^2 is the variance of the second sample.

The value of t is computed from the following equation.

TWO-SAMPLE TEST OF MEANS—UNKNOWN σ'S	$t = \dfrac{\bar{X}_1 - \bar{X}_2}{\sqrt{s_p^2\left(\dfrac{1}{n_1} + \dfrac{1}{n_2}\right)}}$	[11–6]

where:
$\bar{X}_1$ is the mean of the first sample.
$\bar{X}_2$ is the mean of the second sample.
n_1 is the number of observations in the first sample.
n_2 is the number of observations in the second sample.
s_p^2 is the pooled estimate of the population variance.

The number of degrees of freedom in the test is the total number of items sampled minus the total number of samples. Because there are two samples, there are $n_1 + n_2 - 2$ degrees of freedom.

To summarize, there are three requirements or assumptions for the test.

1. The sampled populations follow the normal distribution.
2. The sampled populations are independent.
3. The standard deviations of the two populations are equal.

The following example/solution explains the details of the test.

Example

Owens Lawn Care Inc. manufactures and assembles lawnmowers that are shipped to dealers throughout the United States and Canada. Two different procedures have been proposed for mounting the engine on the frame of the lawnmower. The question is: Is there a difference in the mean time to mount the engines on the frames of the lawnmowers? The first procedure was developed by longtime Owens employee Herb Welles (designated as procedure 1), and the other procedure was developed by Owens Vice President of Engineering William Atkins (designated as procedure 2). To evaluate the two methods, it was decided to conduct a time and motion study. A sample of five employees was timed using the Welles method and six using the Atkins method. The results, in minutes, are shown below. Is there a difference in the mean mounting times? Use the .10 significance level.

Welles (minutes)	Atkins (minutes)
2	3
4	7
9	5
3	8
2	4
	3

Solution

Following the five steps to test a hypothesis, the null hypothesis states that there is no difference in mean mounting times between the two procedures. The alternate hypothesis indicates that there is a difference.

$$H_0: \mu_1 = \mu_2$$
$$H_1: \mu_1 \neq \mu_2$$

The required assumptions are:

- The observations in the Welles sample are *independent* of the observations in the Atkins sample.
- The two populations follow the normal distribution.
- The two populations have equal but unknown standard deviations.

Is there a difference between the mean assembly times using the Welles and the Atkins methods? The degrees of freedom are equal to the total number of items sampled minus the number of samples. In this case, that is $n_1 + n_2 - 2$. Five assemblers used the Welles method and six the Atkins method. Thus, there are 9 degrees of freedom, found by $5 + 6 - 2$. The critical values of t, from Appendix B.2 for $df = 9$, a two-tailed test, and the .10 significance level, are -1.833 and 1.833. The decision rule is portrayed graphically in Chart 11–3. We do not reject the null hypothesis if the computed value of t falls between -1.833 and 1.833.

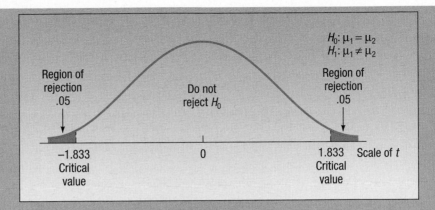

CHART 11–3 Regions of Rejection, Two-Tailed Test, $df = 9$, and .10 Significance Level

We use three steps to compute the value of t.

Step 1: Calculate the sample standard deviations. To compute the sample standard deviations, we use formula (3–9) on page 83. See the details below.

Welles Method		Atkins Method	
X_1	$(X_1 - \bar{X}_1)^2$	X_2	$(X_2 - \bar{X}_2)^2$
2	$(2 - 4)^2 = 4$	3	$(3 - 5)^2 = 4$
4	$(4 - 4)^2 = 0$	7	$(7 - 5)^2 = 4$
9	$(9 - 4)^2 = 25$	5	$(5 - 5)^2 = 0$
3	$(3 - 4)^2 = 1$	8	$(8 - 5)^2 = 9$
2	$(2 - 4)^2 = 4$	4	$(4 - 5)^2 = 1$
20	34	3	$(3 - 5)^2 = 4$
		30	22

$$\bar{X}_1 = \frac{\Sigma X_1}{n_1} = \frac{20}{5} = 4 \qquad\qquad \bar{X}_2 = \frac{\Sigma X_2}{n_2} = \frac{30}{6} = 5$$

$$s_1 = \sqrt{\frac{\Sigma(X_1 - \bar{X}_1)^2}{n_1 - 1}} = \sqrt{\frac{34}{5 - 1}} = 2.9155 \quad s_2 = \sqrt{\frac{\Sigma(X_2 - \bar{X}_2)^2}{n_2 - 1}} = \sqrt{\frac{22}{6 - 1}} = 2.0976$$

Step 2: Pool the sample variances. We use formula (11–5) to pool the sample variances (standard deviations squared).

$$s_p^2 = \frac{(n_1 - 1)s_1^2 + (n_2 - 1)s_2^2}{n_1 + n_2 - 2} = \frac{(5 - 1)(2.9155)^2 + (6 - 1)(2.0976)^2}{5 + 6 - 2} = 6.2222$$

Step 3: Determine the value of t. The mean mounting time for the Welles method is 4.00 minutes, found by $\bar{X}_1 = 20/5$. The mean mounting time for the Atkins method is 5.00 minutes, found by $\bar{X}_2 = 30/6$. We use formula (11–6) to calculate the value of t.

$$t = \frac{\bar{X}_1 - \bar{X}_2}{\sqrt{s_p^2\left(\dfrac{1}{n_1} + \dfrac{1}{n_2}\right)}} = \frac{4.00 - 5.00}{\sqrt{6.2222\left(\dfrac{1}{5} + \dfrac{1}{6}\right)}} = -0.662$$

The decision is not to reject the null hypothesis, because -0.662 falls in the region between -1.833 and 1.833. Our conclusion is that the sample data failed to show a difference between the mean assembly times of the two methods.

We can also estimate the p-value using Appendix B.2. Locate the row with 9 degrees of freedom, and use the two-tailed test column. Find the t value, without regard to the sign, which is closest to our computed value of 0.662. It is 1.383, corresponding to a significance level of .20. Thus, even had we used the 20% significance level, we would not have rejected the null hypothesis of equal means. We can report that the p-value is greater than .20.

Excel has a procedure called "t-Test: Two-Sample Assuming Equal Variances" that will perform the calculations of formulas (11–5) and (11–6) as well as find the sample means and sample variances. The details of the procedure are provided in the Software Commands section at the end of the chapter. The data are input in the first two columns of the Excel spreadsheet. They are labeled "Welles" and "Atkins." The output follows. The value of t, called the "t Stat," is −0.662, and the two-tailed p-value is .525. As we would expect, the p-value is larger than the significance level of .10. The conclusion is not to reject the null hypothesis.

welles and atkins

	A	B	C	D	E	F	G
1	Welles	Atkins		t-Test: Two-Sample Assuming Equal Variances			
2	2	3					
3	4	7			Welles	Atkins	
4	9	5		Mean	4.000	5.000	
5	3	8		Variance	8.500	4.400	
6	2	4		Observations	5.000	6.000	
7		3		Pooled Variance	6.222		
8				Hypothesized Mean Difference	0.000		
9				df	9.000		
10				t Stat	-0.662		
11				P(T<=t) one-tail	0.262		
12				t Critical one-tail	1.833		
13				P(T<=t) two-tail	0.525		
14				t Critical two-tail	2.262		
15							

Self-Review 11–3

The production manager at Bellevue Steel, a manufacturer of wheelchairs, wants to compare the number of defective wheelchairs produced on the day shift with the number on the afternoon shift. A sample of the production from 6 day shifts and 8 afternoon shifts revealed the following number of defects.

Day	5	8	7	6	9	7		
Afternoon	8	10	7	11	9	12	14	9

At the .05 significance level, is there a difference in the mean number of defects per shift?
(a) State the null hypothesis and the alternate hypothesis.
(b) What is the decision rule?
(c) What is the value of the test statistic?
(d) What is your decision regarding the null hypothesis?
(e) What is the p-value?
(f) Interpret the result.
(g) What are the assumptions necessary for this test?

Exercises

connect

For Exercises 13 and 14: (a) state the decision rule, (b) compute the pooled estimate of the population variance, (c) compute the test statistic, (d) state your decision about the null hypothesis, and (e) estimate the p-value.

13. The null and alternate hypotheses are:

$$H_0: \mu_1 = \mu_2$$
$$H_1: \mu_1 \neq \mu_2$$

A random sample of 10 observations from one population revealed a sample mean of 23 and a sample deviation of 4. A random sample of 8 observations from another population revealed a sample mean of 26 and a sample standard deviation of 5. At the .05 significance level, is there a difference between the population means?

14. The null and alternate hypotheses are:

$$H_0: \mu_1 = \mu_2$$
$$H_1: \mu_1 \neq \mu_2$$

A random sample of 15 observations from the first population revealed a sample mean of 350 and a sample standard deviation of 12. A random sample of 17 observations from the second population revealed a sample mean of 342 and a sample standard deviation of 15. At the .10 significance level, is there a difference in the population means?

Note: Use the five-step hypothesis testing procedure for the following exercises.

15. Listed below are the salaries in $000 of the 30 players on the opening-day roster and the disabled list of the 2011 New York Yankees Major League Baseball team.

Player	Salary ($000)	Position
A.J. Burnett	$16,500.0	Pitcher
Alex Rodriguez	32,000.0	Third Baseman
Andruw Jones	1,500.0	Outfielder
Bartolo Colon	900.0	Pitcher
Boone Logan	1,200.0	Pitcher
Brett Gardner	529.5	Outfielder
CC Sabathia	24,285.7	Pitcher
Colin Curtis	420.4	Outfielder
Curtis Granderson	8,250.0	Outfielder
Damaso Marte	4,000.0	Pitcher
David Robertson	460.5	Pitcher
Derek Jeter	14,729.3	Shortstop
Eduardo Nunez	419.3	Shortstop
Eric Chavez	1,500.0	Third Baseman
Francisco Cervelli	455.7	Catcher
Freddy Garcia	1,500.0	Pitcher
Gustavo Molina	455.0	Catcher
Ivan Nova	432.9	Pitcher
Joba Chamberlain	1,400.0	Pitcher
Jorge Posada	13,100.0	Catcher
Luis Ayala	650.0	Pitcher
Mariano Rivera	14,911.7	Pitcher
Mark Teixeira	23,125.0	First Baseman
Nick Swisher	9,100.0	Outfielder
Pedro Feliciano	3,750.0	Pitcher
Phil Hughes	2,700.0	Pitcher
Rafael Soriano	10,000.0	Pitcher
Reegie Corona	414.0	Second Baseman
Robinson Cano	10,000.0	Second Baseman
Russell Martin	$ 4,000.0	Catcher

Sort the players into two groups, pitchers and nonpitchers (position players). Assume equal population variances for the position players and the pitchers. Conduct a test of hypothesis to determine whether the mean salaries between the two groups are the same versus the alternate hypothesis that they are not the same. Use the .01 significance level.

16. A recent study compared the time spent together by single- and dual-earner couples. According to the records kept by the wives during the study, the mean amount of time spent together watching television among the single-earner couples was 61 minutes per day, with a standard deviation of 15.5 minutes. For the dual-earner couples, the mean number of minutes spent watching television was 48.4 minutes, with a standard deviation of 18.1 minutes. At the .01 significance level, can we conclude that the single-earner couples on average spend more time watching television together? There were 15 single-earner and 12 dual-earner couples studied.

17. Ms. Lisa Monnin is the budget director for Nexus Media Inc. She would like to compare the daily travel expenses for the sales staff and the audit staff. She collected the following sample information. (df)

| Sales ($) | 131 | 135 | 146 | 165 | 136 | 142 | |
| Audit ($) | 130 | 102 | 129 | 143 | 149 | 120 | 139 |

At the .10 significance level, can she conclude that the mean daily expenses are greater for the sales staff than the audit staff? What is the *p*-value?

18. The Tampa Bay (Florida) Area Chamber of Commerce wanted to know whether the mean weekly salary of nurses was larger than that of school teachers. To investigate, they collected the following information on the amounts earned last week by a sample of school teachers and nurses. (df)

| School Teachers ($) | 845 | 826 | 827 | 875 | 784 | 809 | 802 | 820 | 829 | 830 | 842 | 832 |
| Nurses ($) | 841 | 890 | 821 | 771 | 850 | 859 | 825 | 829 | | | | |

Is it reasonable to conclude that the mean weekly salary of nurses is higher? Use the .01 significance level. What is the *p*-value?

11.5 Two-Sample Tests of Hypothesis: Dependent Samples

LO 11-4 Explain the difference between dependent and independent samples.

In the Example/Solution beginning on page 338, we tested the difference between the means from two independent samples. We compared the mean time required to mount an engine using the Welles method to the time to mount the engine using the Atkins method. The samples were *independent,* meaning that the sample of assembly times using the Welles method was in no way related to the sample of assembly times using the Atkins method.

There are situations, however, in which the samples are not independent. To put it another way, the samples are *dependent* or *related*. As an example, Nickel Savings and Loan employs two firms, Schadek Appraisals and Bowyer Real Estate, to appraise the value of the real estate properties on which it makes loans. It is important that

these two firms be similar in their appraisal values. To review the consistency of the two appraisal firms, Nickel Savings randomly selects 10 homes and has both Schadek Appraisals and Bowyer Real Estate appraise the value of the selected homes. For each home, there will be a pair of appraisal values. That is, for each home there will be an appraised value from both Schadek Appraisals and Bowyer Real Estate. The appraised values depend on, or are related to, the home selected. This is also referred to as a **paired sample.**

For hypothesis testing, we are interested in the distribution of the *differences* in the appraised value of each home. Hence, there is only one sample. To put it more formally, we are investigating whether the mean of the distribution of differences in the

LO 11-5 Carry out a test of a hypothesis about the mean difference between paired and dependent observations.

appraised values is 0. The sample is made up of the *differences* between the appraised values determined by Schadek Appraisals and the values from Bowyer Real Estate. If the two appraisal firms are reporting similar estimates, then sometimes Schadek Appraisals will be the higher value and sometimes Bowyer Real Estate will have the higher value. However, the mean of the distribution of differences will be 0. On the other hand, if one of the firms consistently reports the larger appraisal values, then the mean of the distribution of the differences will not be 0.

We will use the symbol μ_d to indicate the population mean of the distribution of differences. We assume the distribution of the population of differences follows the normal distribution. The test statistic follows the *t* distribution and we calculate its value from the following formula:

PAIRED *t* TEST	$t = \dfrac{\bar{d}}{s_d/\sqrt{n}}$	[11–7]

There are $n - 1$ degrees of freedom and

$\bar{d}$ is the mean of the difference between the paired or related observations.
s_d is the standard deviation of the differences between the paired or related observations.
n is the number of paired observations.

The standard deviation of the differences is computed by the familiar formula for the standard deviation (see formula 3–9), except *d* is substituted for *X*. The formula is:

$$s_d = \sqrt{\dfrac{\Sigma(d - \bar{d})^2}{n - 1}}$$

The following example illustrates this test.

Example

Recall that Nickel Savings and Loan wishes to compare the two companies it uses to appraise the value of residential homes. Nickel Savings selected a sample of 10 residential properties and scheduled both firms for an appraisal. The results, reported in $000, are:

Home	Schadek	Bowyer
1	235	228
2	210	205
3	231	219
4	242	240
5	205	198
6	230	223
7	231	227
8	210	215
9	225	222
10	249	245

At the .05 significance level, can we conclude there is a difference between the firms' mean appraised home values.

Solution

The first step is to state the null and the alternate hypotheses. In this case, a two-tailed alternative is appropriate because we are interested in determining whether there is a *difference* in the firms' appraised values. We are not interested in showing whether one particular firm appraises property at a higher value than the other. The question is whether the sample differences in the appraised values could have come from a population with a mean of 0. If the population mean of the differences is 0, then we conclude that there is no difference between the two firms' appraised values. The null and alternate hypotheses are:

$$H_0: \mu_d = 0$$
$$H_1: \mu_d \neq 0$$

There are 10 homes appraised by both firms, so $n = 10$, and $df = n - 1 = 10 - 1 = 9$. We have a two-tailed test, and the significance level is .05. To determine the critical value, go to Appendix B.2, move across the row with 9 degrees of freedom to the column for a two-tailed test and the .05 significance level. The value at the intersection is 2.262. This value appears in the box in Table 11–2 on the next page. The decision rule is to reject the null hypothesis if the computed value of t is less than −2.262 or greater than 2.262. Here are the computational details.

Home	Schadek	Bowyer	Difference, d	$(d - \bar{d})$	$(d - \bar{d})^2$
1	235	228	7	2.4	5.76
2	210	205	5	0.4	0.16
3	231	219	12	7.4	54.76
4	242	240	2	−2.6	6.76
5	205	198	7	2.4	5.76
6	230	223	7	2.4	5.76
7	231	227	4	−0.6	0.36
8	210	215	−5	−9.6	92.16
9	225	222	3	−1.6	2.56
10	249	245	4	−0.6	0.36
			46	0	174.40

$$\bar{d} = \frac{\Sigma d}{n} = \frac{46}{10} = 4.60$$

$$s_d = \sqrt{\frac{\Sigma(d - \bar{d})^2}{n - 1}} = \sqrt{\frac{174.4}{10 - 1}} = 4.402$$

Using formula (11–7), the value of the test statistic is 3.305, found by

$$t = \frac{\bar{d}}{s_d/\sqrt{n}} = \frac{4.6}{4.402/\sqrt{10}} = \frac{4.6}{1.3920} = 3.305$$

Because the computed t falls in the rejection region, the null hypothesis is rejected. The population distribution of differences does not have a mean of 0. We conclude that there is a difference between the firms' mean appraised home values. The largest difference of $12,000 is for Home 3. Perhaps that would be an appropriate place to begin a more detailed review.

To find the p-value, we use Appendix B.2 and the section for a two-tailed test. Move along the row with 9 degrees of freedom and find the values of t that are closest to our calculated value. For a .01 significance level, the value of t is 3.250. The computed value is larger than this value, but smaller than the value of 4.781

corresponding to the .001 significance level. Hence, the p-value is less than .01. This information is highlighted in Table 11–2.

TABLE 11–2 A Portion of the t Distribution from Appendix B.2

			Confidence Intervals			
	80%	90%	95%	98%	99%	p-value between 0.01 and 0.001
	Level of Significance for One-Tailed Test					
df	0.10	0.05	0.025	0.01	0.005	
	Level of Significance for Two-Tailed Test					
	0.20	0.10	0.05	0.02	0.01	0.001
1	3.078	6.314	12.706	31.821	63.657	636.619
2	1.886	2.920	4.303	6.965	9.925	31.599
3	1.638	2.353	3.182	4.541	5.841	12.924
Critical t-statistic for 0.05		2.132	2.776	3.747	4.604	8.610
		2.015	2.571	3.365	4.032	6.869
6	1.440	1.943	2.447	3.143	3.707	5.959
7	1.415	1.895	2.365	2.998	3.499	5.408
8	1.397	1.860	2.306	2.896	3.355	5.041
9	1.383	1.833	2.262	2.821	3.250	4.781
10	1.372	1.812	2.228	2.764	3.169	4.587

Excel has a procedure called "t-Test: Paired Two-Sample for Means" that will perform the calculations of formula (11–7). The output from this procedure is given below.

The computed value of t is 3.305, and the two-tailed p-value is .009. Because the p-value is less than .05, we reject the hypothesis that the mean of the distribution of the differences between the appraised values is zero. In fact, this p-value is between .01 and .001. There is a small likelihood that the null hypothesis is true.

▦ paired t test						
◢	A	B	C	D	E	F	G
1	Home	Schadek	Bowyer		t-Test: Paired Two-Sample for Means		
2	1	235	228				
3	2	210	205			Schadek	Bowyer
4	3	231	219		Mean	226.800	222.200
5	4	242	240		Variance	208.844	204.178
6	5	205	198		Observations	10.000	10.000
7	6	230	223		Pearson Correlation	0.953	
8	7	231	227		Hypothesized Mean Difference	0.000	
9	8	210	215		df	9.000	
10	9	225	222		t Stat	3.305	
11	10	249	245		P(T<=t) one-tail	0.005	
12					t Critical one-tail	1.833	
13					P(T<=t) two-tail	0.009	
14					t Critical two-tail	2.262	
15							

11.6 Comparing Dependent and Independent Samples

Beginning students are often confused by the difference between tests for independent samples [formula (11–6)] and tests for dependent samples [formula (11–7)]. How do we tell the difference between dependent and independent samples? There are two types of dependent samples: (1) those characterized by a measurement, an intervention of some type, and then another measurement; and (2) a matching or pairing of the observations. To explain further:

1. The first type of dependent sample is characterized by a measurement followed by an intervention of some kind and then another measurement. This could be called a "before" and "after" study. Two examples will help to clarify. Suppose we want to show that, by placing speakers in the production area and playing soothing music, we are able to increase production. We begin by selecting a sample of workers and measuring their output under the current conditions. The speakers are then installed in the production area, and we again measure the output of the same workers. There are two measurements, before placing the speakers in the production area and after. The intervention is placing speakers in the production area.

    A second example involves an educational firm that offers courses designed to increase test scores and reading ability. Suppose the firm wants to offer a course that will help high school juniors increase their SAT scores. To begin, each student takes the SAT in the junior year in high school. During the summer between the junior and senior year, they participate in the course that gives them tips on taking tests. Finally, during the fall of their senior year in high school, they retake the SAT. Again, the procedure is characterized by a measurement (taking the SAT as a junior), an intervention (the summer workshops), and another measurement (taking the SAT during their senior year).

2. The second type of dependent sample is characterized by matching or pairing observations. The previous Example/Solution regarding Nickel Savings illustrates dependent samples. A property is selected and both firms appraise the same property. As a second example, suppose an industrial psychologist wishes to study the intellectual similarities of newly married couples. She selects a sample of newlyweds. Next, she administers a standard intelligence test to both the man and woman to determine the difference in the scores. Notice the matching that occurred: comparing the scores that are paired or matched by marriage.

Why do we prefer dependent samples to independent samples? By using dependent samples, we are able to reduce the variation in the sampling distribution. To illustrate, we will use the Nickel Savings and Loan example just completed. Suppose we assume that we have two independent samples of real estate property for appraisal and conduct the following test of hypothesis, using formula (11–6). The null and alternate hypotheses are:

$$H_0: \mu_1 = \mu_2$$
$$H_1: \mu_1 \neq \mu_2$$

There are now two independent samples of 10 each. So the number of degrees of freedom is $10 + 10 - 2 = 18$. From Appendix B.2, for the .05 significance level, H_0 is rejected if t is less than -2.101 or greater than 2.101.

We use the same Excel commands as on page 94 in Chapter 3 to find the mean and the standard deviation of the two independent samples. We use the Excel commands on page 358 of this chapter to find the pooled variance and the value of the "t Stat." These values are highlighted in yellow.

Independent t test

	A	B	C	D	E	F	G	H
1	Home	Schadek	Bowyer		t-Test: Two-Sample Assuming Equal Variances			
2	1	235	228					
3	2	210	205			Schadek	Bowyer	
4	3	231	219		Mean	226.800	222.200	
5	4	242	240		Variance	208.844	204.178	
6	5	205	198		Observations	10.000	10.000	
7	6	230	223		Pooled Variance	206.511		
8	7	231	227		Hypothesized Mean Difference	0.000		
9	8	210	215		df	18.000		
10	9	225	222		t Stat	0.716		
11	10	249	245		P(T<=t) one-tail	0.242		
12					t Critical one-tail	1.734		
13	Mean =	226.80	222.20		P(T<=t) two-tail	0.483		
14	S =	14.45	14.29		t Critical two-tail	2.101		
15								

The mean of the appraised value of the 10 properties by Schadek is $226,800, and the standard deviation is $14,500. For Bowyer Real Estate, the mean appraised value is $222,200, and the standard deviation is $14,290. To make the calculations easier, we use $000 instead of $. The value of the pooled estimate of the variance from formula (11–5) is

$$s_p^2 = \frac{(n_1 - 1)s_1^2 + (n_2 - 1)s_2^2}{n_1 + n_2 - 2} = \frac{(10 - 1)(14.45^2) + (10 - 1)(14.29)^2}{10 + 10 - 2} = 206.50$$

From formula (11–6), t is 0.716.

$$t = \frac{\bar{X}_1 - \bar{X}_2}{\sqrt{s_p^2\left(\frac{1}{n_1} + \frac{1}{n_2}\right)}} = \frac{226.8 - 222.2}{\sqrt{206.50\left(\frac{1}{10} + \frac{1}{10}\right)}} = \frac{4.6}{6.4265} = 0.716$$

The computed t (0.716) is less than 2.101, so the null hypothesis is not rejected. We cannot show that there is a difference in the mean appraisal value. That is not the same conclusion that we got before! Why does this happen? The numerator is the same in the paired observations test (4.6). However, the denominator is smaller. In the paired test, the denominator is 1.3920 (see the calculations on page 344). In the case of the independent samples, the denominator is 6.4265. There is more variation or uncertainty. This accounts for the difference in the t values and the difference in the statistical decisions. The denominator measures the standard error of the statistic. When the samples are *not* paired, two kinds of variation are present: differences between the two appraisal firms and the difference in the value of the real estate. Properties numbered 4 and 10 have relatively high values, whereas number 5 is relatively low. These data show how different the values of the property are, but we are really interested in the difference between the two appraisal firms.

In sum, when we can pair or match observations that measure differences for a common variable, a hypothesis test based on dependent samples is more sensitive to detecting a significant difference than a hypothesis test based on independent samples. In the case of comparing the property valuations by Schadek Appraisals and Bowyer Real Estate, the hypothesis test based on dependent samples eliminates the variation between the values of the properties and focuses only on the comparisons in the two appraisals for each property. There is a bit of bad news here. In the dependent samples test, the degrees of freedom are half of what they are if the samples are not paired. For the real estate example, the degrees of freedom drop from 18 to 9 when the observations are paired. However, in most cases, this is a small price to pay for a better test.

Self-Review 11–4   Advertisements by Sylph Fitness Center claim that completing its course will result in losing weight. A random sample of eight recent participants showed the following weights before and after completing the course. At the .01 significance level, can we conclude the students lost weight?

Name	Before	After
Hunter	155	154
Cashman	228	207
Mervine	141	147
Massa	162	157
Creola	211	196
Peterson	164	150
Redding	184	170
Poust	172	165

(a)   State the null hypothesis and the alternate hypothesis.
(b)   What is the critical value of t?
(c)   What is the computed value of t?
(d)   Interpret the result. What is the p-value?
(e)   What assumption needs to be made about the distribution of the differences?

Exercises

connect™

19.   The null and alternate hypotheses are:

$$H_0: \mu_d \leq 0$$
$$H_1: \mu_d > 0$$

The following sample information shows the number of defective units produced on the day shift and the afternoon shift for a sample of four days last month.

	Day			
	1	2	3	4
Day shift	10	12	15	19
Afternoon shift	8	9	12	15

At the .05 significance level, can we conclude there are more defects produced on the afternoon shift?

20.   The null and alternate hypotheses are:

$$H_0: \mu_d = 0$$
$$H_1: \mu_d \neq 0$$

The following paired observations show the number of traffic citations given for speeding by Officer Dhondt and Officer Meredith of the South Carolina Highway Patrol for the last five months.

	Day				
	May	June	July	August	September
Officer Dhondt	30	22	25	19	26
Officer Meredith	26	19	20	15	19

At the .05 significance level, is there a difference in the mean number of citations given by the two officers?

Note: Use the five-step hypothesis-testing procedure to solve the following exercises.

21. The management of Discount Furniture, a chain of discount furniture stores in the Northeast, designed an incentive plan for salespeople. To evaluate this innovative plan, 12 salespeople were selected at random, and their weekly incomes before and after the plan were recorded.

Salesperson	Before	After
Sid Mahone	$320	$340
Carol Quick	290	285
Tom Jackson	421	475
Andy Jones	510	510
Jean Sloan	210	210
Jack Walker	402	500
Peg Mancuso	625	631
Anita Loma	560	560
John Cuso	360	365
Carl Utz	431	431
A. S. Kushner	506	525
Fern Lawton	505	619

Was there a significant increase in the typical salesperson's weekly income due to the innovative incentive plan? Use the .05 significance level. Estimate the *p*-value, and interpret it.

22. The federal government recently granted funds for a special program designed to reduce crime in high-crime areas. A study of the results of the program in eight high-crime areas of Miami, Florida, yielded the following results.

	Number of Crimes by Area							
	A	B	C	D	E	F	G	H
Before	14	7	4	5	17	12	8	9
After	2	7	3	6	8	13	3	5

Has there been a decrease in the number of crimes since the inauguration of the program? Use the .01 significance level. Estimate the *p*-value.

Chapter Summary

I. In comparing two population means, we wish to know whether they could be equal.
   A. We are investigating whether the distribution of the difference between the means could have a mean of 0.
   B. The test statistic follows the standard normal distribution if the population standard deviations are known.
      1. No assumption about the shape of either population is required.
      2. The samples are from independent populations.
      3. The formula to compute the value of *z* is

$$z = \frac{\bar{X}_1 - \bar{X}_2}{\sqrt{\dfrac{\sigma_1^2}{n_1} + \dfrac{\sigma_2^2}{n_2}}}$$

[11–2]

II. We can also test whether two samples came from populations with an equal proportion of successes.

    A. The two sample proportions are pooled using the following formula:

$$p_c = \frac{X_1 + X_2}{n_1 + n_2}$$ [11–4]

    B. We compute the value of the test statistic from the following formula:

$$z = \frac{p_1 - p_2}{\sqrt{\dfrac{p_c(1 - p_c)}{n_1} + \dfrac{p_c(1 - p_c)}{n_2}}}$$ [11–3]

III. The test statistic to compare two means is the t distribution if the population standard deviations are not known.

    A. Both populations must follow the normal distribution.

    B. The populations must have equal standard deviations.

    C. The samples are independent.

    D. Finding the value of t requires two steps.

        1. The first step is to pool the standard deviations according to the following formula:

$$s_p^2 = \frac{(n_1 - 1)s_1^2 + (n_2 - 1)s_2^2}{n_1 + n_2 - 2}$$ [11–5]

        2. The value of t is computed from the following formula:

$$t = \frac{\bar{X}_1 - \bar{X}_2}{\sqrt{s_p^2\left(\dfrac{1}{n_1} + \dfrac{1}{n_2}\right)}}$$ [11–6]

        3. The degrees of freedom for the test are $n_1 + n_2 - 2$.

IV. For dependent samples, we assume the distribution of the paired differences between the populations has a mean of 0.

    A. We first compute the mean and the standard deviation of the sample differences.

    B. The value of the test statistic is computed from the following formula:

$$t = \frac{\bar{d}}{s_d/\sqrt{n}}$$ [11–7]

Pronunciation Key

SYMBOL	MEANING	PRONUNCIATION
p_c	Pooled proportion	p sub c
s_p^2	Pooled sample variance	s sub p squared
$\bar{X}_1$	Mean of the first sample	X bar sub 1
$\bar{X}_2$	Mean of the second sample	X bar sub 2
$\bar{d}$	Mean of the difference between dependent observations	d bar
s_d	Standard deviation of the difference between dependent observations	s sub d

Chapter Exercises

connect

23. A recent study focused on the number of times men and women who live alone buy take-out dinner in a month. Assume that the distributions follow the normal probability distribution. The information is summarized below.

Statistic	Men	Women
Sample mean	24.51	22.69
Population standard deviation	4.48	3.86
Sample size	35	40

At the .01 significance level, is there a difference in the mean number of times men and women order take-out dinners in a month? What is the p-value?

24. Clark Heter is an industrial engineer at Lyons Products. He would like to determine whether there are more units produced on the night shift than on the day shift. Assume the population standard deviation for the number of units produced on the day shift is 21 and is 28 on the night shift. A sample of 54 day-shift workers showed that the mean number of units produced was 345. A sample of 60 night-shift workers showed that the mean number of units produced was 351. At the .05 significance level, is the number of units produced on the night shift larger?

25. Fry Brothers Heating and Air Conditioning Inc. employs Larry Clark and George Murnen to make service calls to repair furnaces and air conditioning units in homes. Tom Fry, the owner, would like to know whether there is a difference in the mean number of service calls they make per day. Assume the population standard deviation for Larry Clark is 1.05 calls per day and 1.23 calls per day for George Murnen. A random sample of 40 days last year showed that Larry Clark made an average of 4.77 calls per day. For a sample of 50 days George Murnen made an average of 5.02 calls per day. At the .05 significance level, is there a difference in the mean number of calls per day between the two employees? What is the p-value?

26. A coffee manufacturer is interested in whether the mean daily consumption of regular-coffee drinkers is less than that of decaffeinated-coffee drinkers. Assume the population standard deviation for those drinking regular coffee is 1.20 cups per day and 1.36 cups per day for those drinking decaffeinated coffee. A random sample of 50 regular-coffee drinkers showed a mean of 4.35 cups per day. A sample of 40 decaffeinated-coffee drinkers showed a mean of 5.84 cups per day. Use the .01 significance level. Compute the p-value.

27. A cell phone company offers two plans to its subscribers. At the time new subscribers sign up, they are asked to provide some demographic information. The mean yearly income for a sample of 40 subscribers to Plan A is $57,000 with a standard deviation of $9,200. For a sample of 30 subscribers to Plan B, the mean income is $61,000 with a standard deviation of $7,100. At the .05 significance level, is it reasonable to conclude the mean income of those selecting Plan B is larger?

28. A computer manufacturer offers a help line that purchasers can call for help 24 hours a day, 7 days a week. Clearing these calls for help in a timely fashion is important to the company's image. After telling the caller that resolution of the problem is important, the caller is asked whether the issue is software or hardware related. The mean time it takes a technician to resolve a software issue is 18 minutes with a standard deviation of 4.2 minutes. This information was obtained from a sample of 35 monitored calls. For a study of 45 hardware issues, the mean time for the technician to resolve the problem was 15.5 minutes with a standard deviation of 3.9 minutes. This information was also obtained from monitored calls. At the .05 significance level, does it take longer to resolve software issues? What is the p-value?

29. Suppose a manufacturer of Ibuprofen, a common headache remedy, recently developed a new formulation of the drug that is claimed to be more effective. To evaluate the new drug, a sample of 200 current users is asked to try it. After a one-month trial, 180 indicated the new drug was more effective in relieving a headache. At the same time, a sample of 300 current Ibuprofen users is given the current drug but told it is the new formulation. From this group, 261 said it was an improvement. At the .05 significance level, can we conclude that the new drug is more effective?

30. Each month the National Association of Purchasing Managers publishes the NAPM index. One of the questions asked on the survey to purchasing agents is: Do you think the economy is contracting? Last month, of the 300 responses, 160 answered yes to the question. This month, 170 of the 290 responses indicated they felt the economy was contracting. At the .05 significance level, can we conclude that a larger proportion of the agents believe the economy is contracting this month?

31. As part of a recent survey among dual-wage-earner couples, an industrial psychologist found that 990 men out of the 1,500 surveyed believed the division of household duties was fair. A sample of 1,600 women found 970 believed the division of household duties was fair. At the .01 significance level, is it reasonable to conclude that the proportion of men who believe the division of household duties is fair is larger? What is the p-value?

32. There are two major cell phone providers in the Colorado Springs, Colorado, area, one called HTC and the other Mountain Communications. We want to investigate whether

there is a difference in the proportion of times a call is successful. During a one-week period, 500 calls were placed at random times throughout the day and night to HTC. 450 of the calls were successful. A similar one-week study with Mountain Communications showed that 352 of 400 calls were successful. At the .01 significance level, is there a difference in the percent of time that cell phone connections are successful?

33. The Consumer Confidence Survey is a monthly review that measures consumer confidence in the U.S. economy. It is based on a typical sample of 5,000 U.S. households. Last month 9.1% of consumers said conditions were "good." In the prior month, only 8.5% held they were "good." Use the five-step hypothesis-testing method at the .05 level of significance to see whether you can determine there is an increase in the share asserting conditions are "good." Find the p-value and explain what it means.

34. A study was conducted to determine if there was a difference in the humor content in British and American trade magazine advertisements. In an independent random sample of 270 American trade magazine advertisements, 56 were humorous. An independent random sample of 203 British trade magazines contained 52 humorous ads. Does this data provide evidence at the .05 significance level that there is a difference in the proportion of humorous ads in British versus American trade magazines?

35. The AP-Petside.com poll contacted 300 married women and 200 married men. All owned pets. One hundred of the women and 36 of the men replied that their pets are better listeners than their spouses. At the .05 significance level, is there a difference between the responses of women and men?

36. The National Basketball Association had 39 black top executives (presidents or vice presidents) among its 388 senior managers. Meanwhile, Major League Baseball had only 11 blacks among its 307 top administrators. Test at the .05 significance level if this reveals the NBA has significantly more black participation in higher levels of management.

37. The manufacturer of an MP3 player wanted to know whether a 10% reduction in price is enough to increase the sales of its product. To investigate, the owner randomly selected eight outlets and sold the MP3 player at the reduced price. At seven randomly selected outlets, the MP3 player was sold at the regular price. Reported below is the number of units sold last month at the sampled outlets. At the .01 significance level, can the manufacturer conclude that the price reduction resulted in an increase in sales?

Regular price	138	121	88	115	141	125	96	
Reduced price	128	134	152	135	114	106	112	120

38. A number of minor automobile accidents occur at various high-risk intersections in Teton County despite traffic lights. The Traffic Department claims that a modification in the type of light will reduce these accidents. The county commissioners have agreed to a proposed experiment. Eight intersections were chosen at random, and the lights at those intersections were modified. The numbers of minor accidents during a six-month period before and after the modifications were:

	Number of Accidents							
	A	B	C	D	E	F	G	H
Before modification	5	7	6	4	8	9	8	10
After modification	3	7	7	0	4	6	8	2

At the .01 significance level, is it reasonable to conclude that the modification reduced the number of traffic accidents?

39. Lester Hollar is vice president for human resources for a large manufacturing company. In recent years, he has noticed an increase in absenteeism that he thinks is related to the general health of the employees. Four years ago, in an attempt to improve the situation, he began a fitness program in which employees exercise during their lunch hour. To evaluate the program, he selected a random sample of eight participants and found the number of days each was absent in the six months before the exercise program began and in the last six months. The results are on the next page. At the .05 significance level, can he conclude that the number of absences has declined? Estimate the p-value.

Employee	Before	After
1	6	5
2	6	2
3	7	1
4	7	3
5	4	3
6	3	6
7	5	3
8	6	7

40. The president of the American Insurance Institute wants to compare the yearly costs of auto insurance offered by two leading companies. He selects a sample of 15 families, some with only a single insured driver, others with several teenage drivers, and pays each family a stipend to contact the two companies and ask for a price quote. To make the data comparable, certain features, such as the deductible amount and limits of liability, are standardized. The sample information is reported below. At the .10 significance level, can we conclude that there is a difference in the amounts quoted?

Family	Southern Car Insurance	American Mutual Insurance
Becker	$2,090	$1,610
Berry	1,683	1,247
Cobb	1,402	2,327
Debuck	1,830	1,367
DuBrul	930	1,461
Eckroate	697	1,789
German	1,741	1,621
Glasson	1,129	1,914
King	1,018	1,956
Kucic	1,881	1,772
Meredith	1,571	1,375
Obeid	874	1,527
Price	1,579	1,767
Phillips	1,577	1,636
Tresize	860	1,188

41. Fairfield Homes is developing two parcels near Pigeon Fork, Tennessee. In order to test different advertising approaches, it uses different media to reach potential buyers. The mean annual family income for 15 people making inquiries at the first development is $150,000, with a standard deviation of $40,000. A corresponding sample of 25 people at the second development had a mean of $180,000, with a standard deviation of $30,000. Assume the population standard deviations are the same. At the .05 significance level, can Fairfield conclude that the population means are different?

42. The following data resulted from a taste test of chocolate bars with and without almonds. 12 people were randomly selected to rate, on a scale of 0 to 5, with 5 as the highest rating, the taste of the bars. If the bar had almonds, it was assigned a code of 1; if no almonds, it was assigned a code of 0. Assume the population standard deviations are the same. At the .05 significance level, do these data show a difference in the taste ratings between chocolate bars with and without almonds?

Rating	With/Without	Rating	With/Without
3	1	1	1
1	1	4	0
0	0	4	0
2	1	2	1
3	1	3	0
1	1	4	0

43. An investigation of the effectiveness of an antibacterial soap in reducing operating room contamination resulted in the accompanying table. The new soap was tested in a sample of eight operating rooms in the greater Seattle area during the last year. (df)

	Operating Room							
	A	B	C	D	E	F	G	H
Before	6.6	6.5	9.0	10.3	11.2	8.1	6.3	11.6
After	6.8	2.4	7.4	8.5	8.1	6.1	3.4	2.0

At the 0.05 significance level, can we conclude the contamination measurements are lower after use of the new soap?

44. The following data on annual rates of return were collected from five stocks listed on the New York Stock Exchange ("the big board") and five stocks listed on NASDAQ. Assume the population standard deviations are the same. At the .10 significance level, can we conclude that the annual rates of return are higher on the big board? (df)

NYSE	NASDAQ
17.16	15.80
17.08	16.28
15.51	16.21
8.43	17.97
25.15	7.77

45. The city of Laguna Beach operates two public parking lots. The one on Ocean Drive can accommodate up to 125 cars and the one on Rio Rancho can accommodate up to 130 cars. City planners are considering both increasing the size of the lots and changing the fee structure. To begin, the Planning Office would like some information on the number of cars in the lots at various times of the day. A junior planner officer is assigned the task of visiting the two lots at random times of the day and evening and counting the number of cars in the lots. The study lasted over a period of one month. Below is the number of cars in the lots for 25 visits of the Ocean Drive lot and 28 visits of the Rio Rancho lot. Assume the population standard deviations are equal. (df)

Ocean Drive

89	115	93	79	113	77	51	75	118	105	106	91	54
63	121	53	81	115	67	53	69	95	121	88	64	

Rio Rancho

128	110	81	126	82	114	93	40	94	45	84	71	74
92	66	69	100	114	113	107	62	77	80	107	90	129
105	124											

Is it reasonable to conclude that there is a difference in the mean number of cars in the two lots? Use the .05 significance level.

46. The amount of income spent on housing is an important component of the cost of living. The total costs of housing for homeowners might include mortgage payments, property taxes, and utility costs (water, heat, electricity). An economist selected a sample of 20 homeowners in New England and then calculated these total housing costs as a percent of monthly income, five years ago and now. The information is reported on the following page. Is it reasonable to conclude the percent is less now than five years ago? (df)

Homeowner	Five Years Ago	Now	Homeowner	Five Years Ago	Now
1	17%	10%	11	35%	32%
2	20	39	12	16	32
3	29	37	13	23	21
4	43	27	14	33	12
5	36	12	15	44	40
6	43	41	16	44	42
7	45	24	17	28	22
8	19	26	18	29	19
9	49	28	19	39	35
10	49	26	20	22	12

47. The CVS Pharmacy located on US 17 in Murrells Inlet has been one of the busiest pharmaceutical retail stores in South Carolina for many years. To try and capture more business in the area, CVS top management opened another store about six miles west on SC 707. After a few months, CVS management decided to compare the business volume at the two stores. One way to measure business volume is to count the number of cars in the store parking lots on random days and times. The results of the survey from the last three months of the year are reported below. To explain, the first observation was on October 2 at 20:52 military time (8:52 p.m.). At that time there were 4 cars in the US 17 lot and 9 cars in the SC 707 lot. At the .05 significance level, is it reasonable to conclude that, based on vehicle counts, the US 17 store has more business volume than the SC 707 store?

Date	Time	Vehicles Count	
		US 17	**SC 707**
Oct 2	20:52	4	9
Oct 11	19:30	5	7
Oct 15	22:08	9	12
Oct 19	11:42	4	5
Oct 25	15:32	10	8
Oct 26	11:02	9	15
Nov 3	11:22	13	7
Nov 5	19:09	20	3
Nov 8	15:10	15	14
Nov 9	13:18	15	11
Nov 15	22:38	13	11
Nov 17	18:46	16	12
Nov 21	15:44	17	8
Nov 22	15:34	15	3
Nov 27	21:42	20	6
Nov 29	9:57	17	13
Nov 30	17:58	5	9
Dec 3	19:54	7	13
Dec 15	18:20	11	6
Dec 16	18:25	14	15
Dec 17	11:08	8	8
Dec 22	21:20	10	3
Dec 24	15:21	4	6
Dec 25	20:21	7	9
Dec 30	14:25	19	4

48. A goal of financial literacy for children is to learn how to manage money wisely. One question is: How much money do children have? A recent study by Schnur Educational

Research Associates revealed the following sample information regarding the monthly allowance that children receive. Is it reasonable to conclude that the mean allowance received by children between 11 and 14 years is more than the allowance received by children between 8 and 10 years? Use the .01 significance level. What is the *p*-value?

8–10 Years	11–14 Years	8–10 Years	11–14 Years
6	19	6	11
13	14	5	8
10	12	7	14
6	8	9	9
14	9	14	20
6	11	12	19
7	9		11
7	8		12
10	8		20

Data Set Exercises

(The data for these exercises are available at the text website www.mhhe.com/lindbasic8e).

49. Refer to the Real Estate data, which report information on the homes sold in Goodyear, Arizona, last year.
   a. At the .05 significance level, can we conclude that there is a difference in the mean selling price of homes with a pool and homes without a pool?
   b. At the .05 significance level, can we conclude that there is a difference in the mean selling price of homes with an attached garage and homes without an attached garage?
   c. At the .05 significance level, can we conclude that there is a difference in the mean selling price of homes in Township 1 and Township 2?
   d. Find the median selling price of the homes. Divide the homes into two groups, those that sold for more than (or equal to) the median price and those that sold for less. Is there a difference in the proportion of homes with a pool that sold at or above the median price versus those that sold for less than the median price? Use the .05 significance level.
   e. Write a summary report on your findings to parts (a), (b), (c), and (d). Address the report to all real estate agents who sell property in Goodyear.
50. Refer to the Baseball 2010 data, which report information on the 30 Major League Baseball teams for the 2010 season.
   a. At the .05 significance level, can we conclude that there is a difference in the mean payroll of teams in the American League versus teams in the National League?
   b. At the .05 significance level, can we conclude that there is a difference in the mean home attendance of teams in the American League versus teams in the National League?
   c. Compute the mean and the standard deviation of the number of wins for the 10 teams with the highest payrolls. Do the same for the 10 teams with the lowest payrolls. At the .05 significance level, is there a difference in the mean number of wins for the two groups?
51. Refer to the Buena School District bus data. Is there a difference in the mean maintenance cost for the diesel versus the gasoline buses? Use the .05 significance level.

Practice Test

Part 1—Objective
1. The hypothesized *difference* between two population means is _____. (0, not equal to 1, 1, at least 1)
2. If the population standard deviations are known for a test of differences of two independent population means, the test statistic is a _____ statistic.
3. When sampled items from two populations are classified as "success" or "failure," the hypothesis test is for differences in population _____.
4. For two independent populations, sample standard deviations are pooled to compute a single estimate of the _____. (population mean, population standard deviation, population proportion, z value)
5. A hypothesis test of differences between two *dependent* populations is based on a single population of mean _____. (differences, populations, standard deviations, t values)
6. The test statistic for a hypothesis test of differences between two dependent populations follows the _____ distribution.
7. Degrees of freedom for a hypothesis test of differences between two dependent populations is _____.
8. For dependent samples, observations are matched or _____.
9. For independent samples, the two samples are different or _____.
10. In a statistics class, for each student the percentage correct on Exam 1 is subtracted from the percentage correct on Exam 2. This is an example of _____ samples.

Part 2—Problems
For each of these problems, use the five-step hypothesis-testing procedure.
1. The city of Myrtle Beach is comparing two taxi companies to see whether they differ in the mean miles traveled per week. The data are summarized in the following table. Using the .05 significance level, is there a difference in the mean miles traveled?

	Yellow Cab	Horse and Buggy Cab
Mean miles	837	797
Standard deviation	30	40
Sample size	14	12

2. Dial Soap Company developed a new soap for men and test marketed the product in two cities. The sample information is reported below. At the .05 significance level, can we conclude there is a difference in the proportion that liked the new soap in the two cities?

City	Liked New Soap	Number Sampled
Erie, PA	128	300
Tustin, CA	149	400

Software Commands

1. The Minitab commands for the two-sample test of proportions on page 335 are:
   a. From the toolbar, select **Stat, Basic Statistics,** and then **2 Proportions.**
   b. In the next dialog box, select **Summarized data,** in the row labeled **First** enter *100* for **Trials** and *19* for **Events.** In the row labeled **Second,** put *200* for **Trials** and *62* for **Events.** Then, click on **Options** and select **Use pooled estimate of p for test,** and click **OK** twice.

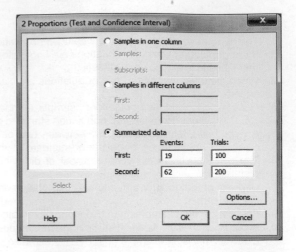

2. The Excel commands for the two-sample *t*-test on page 340 are:
   a. Enter the data into columns A and B (or any other columns) in the spreadsheet. Use the first row of each column to enter the variable name.
   b. Select the **Data** tab on the top menu. Then, on the far right, select **Data Analysis.** Select **t-Test: Two-Sample Assuming Equal Variances,** and then click **OK.**
   c. In the dialog box, indicate that the range of **Variable 1** is from *A1* to *A6* and **Variable 2** from *B1* to *B7,* the **Hypothesized Mean Difference** is *0,* click **Labels, Alpha** is *0.05,* and the **Output Range** is *D1.* Click **OK.**

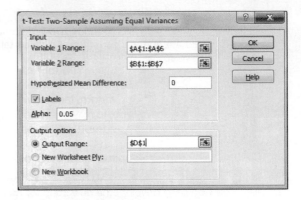

3. The Excel commands for the paired *t*-test on page 345 are:
   a. Enter the data into columns B and C (or any other two columns) in the spreadsheet, with the variable names in the first row.
   b. Select the **Data** tab on the top menu. Then, on the far right, select **Data Analysis.** Select **t-Test: Paired Two Sample for Means,** and then click **OK.**
   c. In the dialog box, indicate that the range of **Variable 1** is from *B1* to *B11* and **Variable 2** from *C1* to *C11,* the **Hypothesized Mean Difference** is *0,* click **Labels, Alpha** is *.05,* and the **Output Range** is *E1.* Click **OK.**

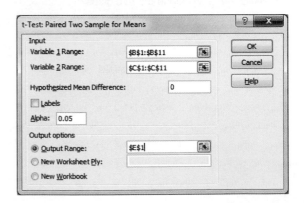

Chapter 11   Answers to Self-Review

11–1 a. $H_0: \mu_W \le \mu_M$
$H_1: \mu_W > \mu_M$
The subscript W refers to the women and M to the men.
b. Reject H_0 if $z > 1.645$.
c. $z = \dfrac{\$1{,}500 - \$1{,}400}{\sqrt{\dfrac{(\$250)^2}{50} + \dfrac{(\$200)^2}{40}}} = 2.11$
d. Reject the null hypothesis.
e. p-value $= .5000 - .4826 = .0174$
f. The mean amount sold per day is larger for women.

11–2 a. $H_0: \pi_1 = \pi_2$
$H_1: \pi_1 \ne \pi_2$
b. .10
c. Two-tailed
d. Reject H_0 if z is less than -1.645 or greater than 1.65.
e. $p_c = \dfrac{87 + 123}{150 + 200} = \dfrac{210}{350} = .60$
$p_1 = \dfrac{87}{150} = .58 \qquad p_2 = \dfrac{123}{200} = .615$
$z = \dfrac{.58 - .615}{\sqrt{\dfrac{.60(.40)}{150} + \dfrac{.60(.40)}{200}}} = -0.66$
f. Do not reject H_0.
g. p-value $= 2(.5000 - .2454) = .5092$
There is no difference in the proportion of adults and children that liked the proposed flavor.

11–3 a. $H_0: \mu_d = \mu_a$
$H_1: \mu_d \ne \mu_a$
b. $df = 6 + 8 - 2 = 12$
Reject H_0 if t is less than -2.179 or t is greater than 2.179.
c. $\bar{X}_1 = \dfrac{42}{6} = 7.00 \quad s_1 = \sqrt{\dfrac{10}{6-1}} = 1.4142$
$\bar{X}_2 = \dfrac{80}{8} = 10.00 \quad s_2 = \sqrt{\dfrac{36}{8-1}} = 2.2678$
$s_p^2 = \dfrac{(6-1)(1.4142)^2 + (8-1)(2.2678)^2}{6 + 8 - 2}$

$= 3.8333$
$t = \dfrac{7.00 - 10.00}{\sqrt{3.8333\left(\dfrac{1}{6} + \dfrac{1}{8}\right)}} = -2.837$

d. Reject H_0 because -2.837 is less than the critical value.
e. The p-value is less than .02.
f. The mean number of defects is not the same on the two shifts.
g. Independent populations, populations follow the normal distribution, populations have equal standard deviations.

11–4 a. $H_0: \mu_d \le 0$, $H_1: \mu_d > 0$.
b. Reject H_0 if $t > 2.998$.
c.

Name	Before	After	d	$(d - \bar{d})$	$(d - \bar{d})^2$
Hunter	155	154	1	−7.875	62.0156
Cashman	228	207	21	12.125	147.0156
Mervine	141	147	−6	−14.875	221.2656
Massa	162	157	5	−3.875	15.0156
Creola	211	196	15	6.125	37.5156
Peterson	164	150	14	5.125	26.2656
Redding	184	170	14	5.125	26.2656
Poust	172	165	7	−1.875	3.5156
			71		538.8750

$\bar{d} = \dfrac{71}{8} = 8.875$

$s_d = \sqrt{\dfrac{538.875}{8-1}} = 8.774$

$t = \dfrac{8.875}{8.774/\sqrt{8}} = 2.861$

d. Do not reject H_0. We cannot conclude that the students lost weight. The p-value is less than .025 but larger than .01.
e. The distribution of the differences must follow a normal distribution.

12

Learning Objectives

When you have completed this chapter, you will be able to:

LO 12-1 List the characteristics of the *F* distribution and locate values in an *F* table.

LO 12-2 Perform a test of hypothesis to determine whether the variances of two populations are equal.

LO 12-3 Describe the ANOVA approach for testing differences in sample means.

LO 12-4 Conduct a test of hypothesis among three or more treatment means and describe the results.

LO 12-5 Organize data into appropriate ANOVA tables for analysis.

LO 12-6 Develop confidence intervals for the differences between treatment means and interpret the results.

Analysis of Variance

A computer manufacturer is about to unveil a new, faster personal computer. The new machine clearly is faster, but initial tests indicate there is more variation in the processing time. The processing time depends on the software, the amount of data to be processed, and the amount of output. A sample of 16 computer runs, covering a range of production jobs, showed that the standard deviation of the processing time was 22 (hundredths of a second) for the new machine and 12 (hundredths of a second) for the current machine. At the .05 significance level, can we conclude that there is more variation in the processing time of the new machine? (See Exercise 16 and LO 12-2.)

12.1 Introduction

In this chapter, we continue our discussion of hypothesis testing. Recall that in Chapters 10 and 11 we examined the general theory of hypothesis testing. We described the case where a sample was selected from the population. We used the z distribution (the standard normal distribution) or the t distribution to determine whether it was reasonable to conclude that the population mean was equal to a specified value. We tested whether two population means are the same. We also conducted both one- and two-sample tests for population proportions, using the standard normal distribution as the distribution of the test statistic. In this chapter, we expand our idea of hypothesis tests. We describe a test for variances and then a test that simultaneously compares several means to determine if they came from equal populations.

12.2 The *F* Distribution

The probability distribution used in this chapter is the F distribution. It was named to honor Sir Ronald Fisher, one of the founders of modern-day statistics. The test statistic for several situations follows this probability distribution. It is used to test whether two samples are from populations having equal variances, and it is also applied when we want to compare several population means simultaneously. The simultaneous comparison of several population means is called **analysis of variance (ANOVA).** In both of these situations, the populations must follow a normal distribution, and the data must be at least interval-scale.

What are the characteristics of the F distribution?

LO 12-1 List the characteristics of the *F* distribution and locate values in an *F* table.

1. **There is a family of *F* distributions.** A particular member of the family is determined by two parameters: the degrees of freedom in the numerator and the degrees of freedom in the denominator. The shape of the distribution is illustrated by the following graph. There is one F distribution for the combination of 29 degrees of freedom in the numerator (df) and 28 degrees of freedom in the denominator. There is another F distribution for 19 degrees in the numerator and 6 degrees of freedom in the denominator. The final distribution shown has 6 degrees of freedom in the numerator and 6 degrees of freedom in the denominator. We will describe the concept of degrees of freedom later in the chapter. Note that the shapes of the distributions change as the degrees of freedom change.

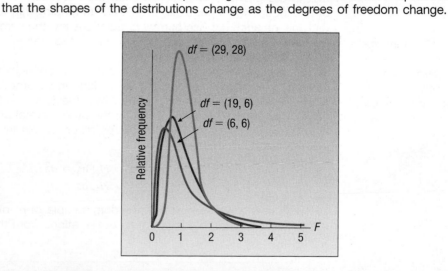

2. **The *F* distribution is continuous.** This means that it can assume an infinite number of values between zero and positive infinity.
3. **The *F* distribution cannot be negative.** The smallest value F can assume is 0.

4. **It is positively skewed.** The long tail of the distribution is to the right-hand side. As the number of degrees of freedom increases in both the numerator and denominator, the distribution approaches a normal distribution.

5. **It is asymptotic.** As the values of X increase, the F distribution approaches the X-axis but never touches it. This is similar to the behavior of the normal probability distribution, described in Chapter 7.

12.3 Comparing Two Population Variances

The first application of the F distribution that we describe occurs when we test the hypothesis that the variance of one normal population equals the variance of another normal population. The following examples will show the use of the test:

- A health services corporation manages two hospitals in Knoxville, Tennessee: St. Mary's North and St. Mary's South. In each hospital, the mean waiting time in the Emergency Department is 42 minutes. The hospital administrator believes that the St. Mary's North Emergency Department has more variation in waiting time than St. Mary's South.

- The mean rate of return on two types of common stock may be the same, but there may be more variation in the rate of return in one than the other. A sample of 10 technology and 10 utility stocks shows the same mean rate of return, but there is likely more variation in the technology stocks.

- A study by the marketing department for a large newspaper found that men and women spent about the same amount of time per day surfing the Net. However, the same report indicated there was nearly twice as much variation in time spent per day among the men than the women.

The F distribution is also used to test assumptions for some statistical tests. Recall that in the previous chapter we used the t test to investigate whether the means of two independent populations differed. To employ that test, we sometimes assume that the variances of two normal populations are the same. See this list of assumptions in Section 11.4 on page 336. The F distribution is used to test if the variances of two normal populations are equal.

LO 12-2 Perform a test of hypothesis to determine whether the variances of two populations are equal.

Regardless of whether we want to determine whether one population has more variation than another population or validate an assumption for a statistical test, we first state the null hypothesis. The null hypothesis is that the variance of one normal population, σ_1^2, equals the variance of the other normal population, σ_2^2. The alternate hypothesis could be that the variances differ. In this instance, the null hypothesis and the alternate hypothesis are:

$$H_0: \sigma_1^2 = \sigma_2^2$$
$$H_1: \sigma_1^2 \neq \sigma_2^2$$

To conduct the test, we select a random sample of n_1 observations from one population, and a random sample of n_2 observations from the second population. The test statistic is defined as follows.

TEST STATISTIC FOR COMPARING TWO VARIANCES	$F = \dfrac{s_1^2}{s_2^2}$	[12–1]

The terms s_1^2 and s_2^2 are the respective sample variances. If the null hypothesis is true, the test statistic follows the F distribution with $n_1 - 1$ and $n_2 - 1$ degrees of freedom. To reduce the size of the table of critical values, the *larger* sample variance is placed in the numerator; hence, the tabled F ratio is always larger than 1.00. Thus, the right-tail critical value is the only one required. The critical value of F for a two-tailed test is found by dividing the significance level in half ($\alpha/2$) and then referring to the appropriate degrees of freedom in Appendix B.4. An example will illustrate.

Example

Lammers Limos offers limousine service from Government Center in downtown Toledo, Ohio, to Metro Airport in Detroit. Sean Lammers, president of the company, is considering two routes. One is via U.S. 25 and the other via I-75. He wants to study the time it takes to drive to the airport using each route and then compare the results. He collected the following sample data, which is reported in minutes. Using the .10 significance level, is there a difference in the variation in the driving times for the two routes?

U.S. Route 25	Interstate 75
52	59
67	60
56	61
45	51
70	56
54	63
64	57
	65

Solution

The mean driving times along the two routes are nearly the same. The mean time is 58.29 minutes for the U.S. 25 route and 59.0 minutes along the I-75 route. However, in evaluating travel times, Mr. Lammers is also concerned about the variation in the travel times. The first step is to compute the two sample variances. We'll use formula (3–9) to compute the sample standard deviations. To obtain the sample variances, we square the standard deviations. Note that we use a subscript of *1* to denote U.S. Route 25 and a subscript of *2* to denote Interstate 75.

U.S. Route 25

$$\bar{X}_1 = \frac{\Sigma X}{n_1} = \frac{408}{7} = 58.29 \qquad s_1 = \sqrt{\frac{\Sigma(X - \bar{X})^2}{n_1 - 1}} = \sqrt{\frac{485.43}{7 - 1}} = 8.9947$$

Interstate 75

$$\bar{X}_2 = \frac{\Sigma X}{n_2} = \frac{472}{8} = 59.00 \qquad s_2 = \sqrt{\frac{\Sigma(X - \bar{X})^2}{n_2 - 1}} = \sqrt{\frac{134}{8 - 1}} = 4.3753$$

There is more variation, as measured by the standard deviation, in the U.S. 25 route than in the I-75 route. This is consistent with his knowledge of the two routes; the U.S. 25 route contains more stoplights, whereas I-75 is a limited-access interstate highway. However, the I-75 route is several miles longer. It is important that the service offered be both timely and consistent, so he decides to conduct a statistical test to determine whether there really is a difference in the variation of the two routes.

We employ the usual five-step hypothesis-testing procedure.

Step 1: We begin by stating the null hypothesis and the alternate hypothesis. The test is two-tailed because we are looking for a difference in the variation of the two routes. We are *not* trying to show that one route has more variation than the other.

$$H_0: \sigma_1^2 = \sigma_2^2$$
$$H_1: \sigma_1^2 \neq \sigma_2^2$$

Step 2: We selected the .10 significance level.

Step 3: The appropriate test statistic follows the F distribution.

Step 4: The critical value is obtained from Appendix B.4, a portion of which is reproduced as Table 12–1. Because we are conducting a two-tailed test, the tabled significance level is .05, found by $\alpha/2 = .10/2 = .05$. There are $n_1 - 1 = 7 - 1 = 6$ degrees of freedom in the numerator, and $n_2 - 1 = 8 - 1 = 7$ degrees of freedom in the denominator. To find the critical value, move horizontally across the top portion of the F table (Table 12–1 or Appendix B.4) for the .05 significance level to 6 degrees of freedom in the numerator. Then move down that column to the critical value opposite 7 degrees of freedom in the denominator. The critical value is 3.87. Thus, the decision rule is: Reject the null hypothesis if the ratio of the sample variances exceeds 3.87.

TABLE 12–1 Critical Values of the F Distribution, $\alpha = .05$

Degrees of Freedom for Denominator	Degrees of Freedom for Numerator			
	5	6	7	8
1	230	234	237	239
2	19.3	19.3	19.4	19.4
3	9.01	8.94	8.89	8.85
4	6.26	6.16	6.09	6.04
5	5.05	4.95	4.88	4.82
6	4.39	4.28	4.21	4.15
7	3.97	3.87	3.79	3.73
8	3.69	3.58	3.50	3.44
9	3.48	3.37	3.29	3.23
10	3.33	3.22	3.14	3.07

Step 5: The final step is to take the ratio of the two sample variances, determine the value of the test statistic, and make a decision regarding the null hypothesis. Note that formula (12–1) refers to the sample *variances* but we calculated the sample *standard deviations*. We need to square the standard deviations to determine the variances.

$$F = \frac{s_1^2}{s_2^2} = \frac{(8.9947)^2}{(4.3753)^2} = 4.23$$

The decision is to reject the null hypothesis, because the computed F value (4.23) is larger than the critical value (3.87). We conclude that there is a difference in the variation of the travel times along the two routes.

As noted, the usual practice is to determine the F ratio by putting the larger of the two sample variances in the numerator. This will force the F ratio to be at least 1.00. This allows us to always use the right tail of the F distribution, thus avoiding the need for more extensive F tables.

A logical question arises: Is it possible to conduct one-tailed tests? For example, suppose in the previous example we suspected that the variance of the times using the U.S. 25 route is *larger* than the variance of the times along the I-75 route. We would state the null and the alternate hypothesis as

$$H_0: \sigma_1^2 \leq \sigma_2^2$$
$$H_1: \sigma_1^2 > \sigma_2^2$$

The test statistic is computed as s_1^2/s_2^2. Notice that we labeled the population with the suspected largest variance as population 1. So s_1^2 appears in the numerator. The F ratio will be larger than 1.00, so we can use the upper tail of the F distribution. Under these conditions, it is not necessary to divide the significance level in half. Because Appendix B.4 gives us only the .05 and .01 significance levels, we are restricted to these levels for one-tailed tests and .10 and .02 for two-tailed tests unless we consult a more complete table or use statistical software to compute the F statistic.

The Excel software system has a procedure to perform a test of variances. Below is the output. The computed value of F is the same as that determined by using formula (12–1).

	A	B	C	D	E	F	G
	Variance Test						
1	**U.S. 25**	**Interstate 75**		**F-Test Two-Sample for Variances**			
2	52	59			**U.S. 25**	**Interstate 75**	
3	67	60		Mean	58.29	59.00	
4	56	61		Variance	80.90	19.14	
5	45	51		Observations	7.00	8.00	
6	70	56		df	6.00	7.00	
7	54	63		F	4.23		
8	64	57		P(F<=f) one-tail	0.04		
9		65		F Critical one-tail	3.87		
10							

Self-Review 12–1 Steele Electric Products Inc. assembles electrical components for cell phones. For the last 10 days, Mark Nagy has averaged 9 rejects, with a standard deviation of 2 rejects per day. Debbie Richmond averaged 8.5 rejects, with a standard deviation of 1.5 rejects, over the same period. At the .05 significance level, can we conclude that there is more variation in the number of rejects per day attributed to Mark?

Exercises

connect

1. What is the critical F value for a sample of six observations in the numerator and four in the denominator? Use a two-tailed test and the .10 significance level.
2. What is the critical F value for a sample of four observations in the numerator and seven in the denominator? Use a one-tailed test and the .01 significance level.

3. The following hypotheses are given.

$$H_0: \sigma_1^2 = \sigma_2^2$$
$$H_1: \sigma_1^2 \neq \sigma_2^2$$

A random sample of eight observations from the first population resulted in a standard deviation of 10. A random sample of six observations from the second population resulted in a standard deviation of 7. At the .02 significance level, is there a difference in the variation of the two populations?

4. The following hypotheses are given.

$$H_0: \sigma_1^2 \leq \sigma_2^2$$
$$H_1: \sigma_1^2 > \sigma_2^2$$

A random sample of five observations from the first population resulted in a standard deviation of 12. A random sample of seven observations from the second population showed a standard deviation of 7. At the .01 significance level, is there more variation in the first population?

5. Arbitron Media Research Inc. conducted a study of the iPod listening habits of men and women. One facet of the study involved the mean listening time. It was discovered that the mean listening time for men was 35 minutes per day. The standard deviation of the sample of the 10 men studied was 10 minutes per day. The mean listening time for the 12 women studied was also 35 minutes, but the standard deviation of the sample was 12 minutes. At the .10 significance level, can we conclude that there is a difference in the variation in the listening times for men and women?

6. A stockbroker at Critical Securities reported that the mean rate of return on a sample of 10 oil stocks was 12.6% with a standard deviation of 3.9%. The mean rate of return on a sample of 8 utility stocks was 10.9% with a standard deviation of 3.5%. At the .05 significance level, can we conclude that there is more variation in the oil stocks?

12.4 ANOVA Assumptions

Another use of the *F* distribution is the analysis of variance (ANOVA) technique in which we compare three or more population means to determine whether they could be equal. To use ANOVA, we assume the following:

1. The populations follow the normal distribution.
2. The populations have equal standard deviations (σ).
3. The populations are independent.

When these conditions are met, *F* is used as the distribution of the test statistic.

Why do we need to study ANOVA? Why can't we just use the test of differences in population means discussed in the previous chapter? We could compare the population means two at a time. The major reason is the unsatisfactory buildup of Type I error. To explain further, suppose we have four different methods (A, B, C, and D) of training new recruits to be firefighters. We randomly assign each of the 40 recruits in this year's class to one of the four methods. At the end of the training program, we administer to the four groups a common test to measure understanding of firefighting techniques. The question is: Is there a difference in the mean test scores among the four groups? An answer to this question will allow us to compare the four training methods.

Using the *t* distribution to compare the four population means, we would have to conduct six different *t* tests. That is, we would need to compare the mean scores for the four methods as follows: A versus B, A versus C, A versus D, B versus C, B versus D, and C versus D. For each *t* test, suppose we choose an $\alpha = .05$. Therefore, the probability of a Type I error, rejecting the null when it is true, is 0.05. The complement is the probability of 0.95 that we do not reject the null when it is true.

Using the *t* distribution leads to a buildup of Type I error.

Because we conduct six separate (independent) tests, the probability that all six decisions are correct is:

$$P(\text{All correct}) = (.95)(.95)(.95)(.95)(.95)(.95) = .735$$

To find the probability of at least one error due to sampling, we subtract this result from 1. Thus, the probability of at least one incorrect decision due to sampling is $1 - .735 = .265$. To summarize, if we conduct six independent tests using the t distribution, the likelihood of rejecting a true null hypothesis because of sampling error is increased from .05 to an unsatisfactory level of .265. ANOVA will allow us to compare the treatment means simultaneously and avoid the buildup of Type I error.

LO 12-3 Describe the ANOVA approach for testing differences in sample means.

ANOVA was first developed for applications in agriculture, and many of the terms related to that context remain. In particular, the term *treatment* is used to identify the different populations being examined. For example, treatment refers to how a plot of ground was treated with a particular type of fertilizer. The following illustration will clarify the term *treatment* and demonstrate an application of ANOVA.

Example

Joyce Kuhlman manages a regional financial center. She wishes to compare the productivity, as measured by the number of customers served, among three employees. Four days are randomly selected and the number of customers served by each employee is recorded. The results are:

Wolfe	White	Korosa
55	66	47
54	76	51
59	67	46
56	71	48

Solution

Is there a difference in the mean number of customers served? Chart 12–1 illustrates how the populations would appear if there were a difference in the treatment means. Note that the populations follow the normal distribution and the variation in each population is the same. However, the means are *not* the same.

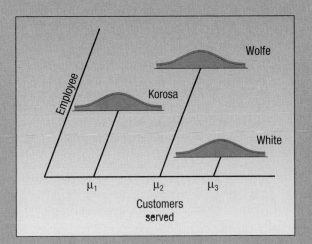

CHART 12–1 Case Where Treatment Means Are Different

Suppose the populations are the same. That is, there is no difference in the (treatment) means. This is shown in Chart 12–2. This would indicate that the population means are the same. Note again that the populations follow the normal distribution and the variation in each of the populations is the same.

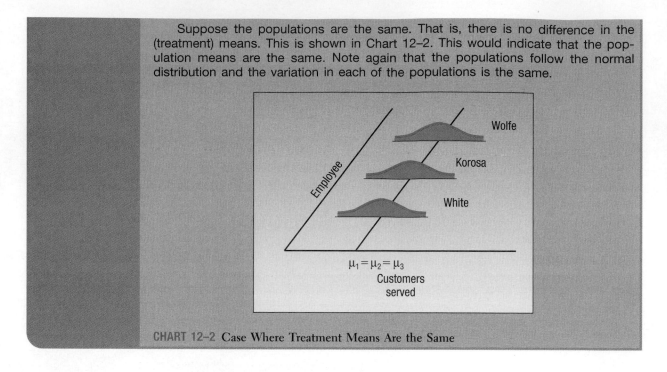

CHART 12–2 Case Where Treatment Means Are the Same

12.5 The ANOVA Test

LO 12-4 Conduct a test of hypothesis among three or more treatment means and describe the results.

How does the ANOVA test work? Recall that we want to determine whether the various sample means came from a single population or populations with different means. We actually compare these sample means through their variances. To explain, on page 366 we listed the assumptions required for ANOVA. One of those assumptions was that the standard deviations of the various normal populations had to be the same. We take advantage of this requirement in the ANOVA test. The underlying strategy is to estimate the population variance (standard deviation squared) two ways and then find the ratio of these two estimates. If this ratio is about 1, then logically the two estimates are the same, and we conclude that the population means are the same. If the ratio is quite different from 1, then we conclude that the population means are not the same. The F distribution serves as a referee by indicating when the ratio of the sample variances is too much greater than 1 to have occurred by chance.

Refer to the financial center example in the previous section. The manager wants to determine whether there is a difference in the mean number of customers served. To begin, find the overall mean of the 12 observations. It is 58, found by $(55 + 54 + \cdots + 48)/12$. Next, for each of the 12 observations find the difference between the particular value and the overall mean. Each of these differences is squared and these squares summed. This term is called the **total variation.**

> **TOTAL VARIATION** The sum of the squared differences between each observation and the overall mean.

In our example, the total variation is 1,082, found by $(55 - 58)^2 + (54 - 58)^2 + \cdots + (48 - 58)^2$.

Next, break this total variation into two components: that which is due to the **treatments** and that which is **random.** To find these two components, determine the mean of each of the treatments. The first source of variation is due to the treatments.

> **TREATMENT VARIATION** The sum of the squared differences between each treatment mean and the grand or overall mean.

In the example, the variation due to the treatments is the sum of the squared differences between the mean number of customers served by each employee and the overall mean. This term is 992. To calculate it, we first find the mean of each of the three treatments. The mean for Wolfe is 56 customers, found by $(55 + 54 + 59 + 56)/4$. The other means are 70 and 48, respectively. The sum of the squares due to the treatments is:

$$(56 - 58)^2 + (56 - 58)^2 + \cdots + (48 - 58)^2 = 4(56 - 58)^2 + 4(70 - 58)^2 + 4(48 - 58)^2$$
$$= 992$$

If there is considerable variation among the treatment means, it is logical that this term will be large. If the treatment means are similar, this term will be a small value. The smallest possible value would be zero. This would occur when all the treatment means are the same.

The other source of variation is referred to as the **random** component, or the error component.

> **RANDOM VARIATION** The sum of the squared differences between each observation and its treatment mean.

In the example, this term is the sum of the squared differences between each value and the mean for that particular employee. The error variation is 90.

$$(55 - 56)^2 + (54 - 56)^2 + \cdots + (48 - 48)^2 = 90$$

We determine the test statistic, which is the ratio of the two estimates of the population variance, from the following equation.

$$F = \frac{\text{Estimate of the population variance based on the differences among the sample means}}{\text{Estimate of the population variance based on the variation within the sample}}$$

Our first estimate of the population variance is based on the treatments, that is, the difference *between* the means. It is $992/2$. Why did we divide by 2? Recall from Chapter 3, to find a sample variance [see formula (3–9)], we divide by the number of observations minus one. In this case, there are three treatments, so we divide by 2. Our first estimate of the population variance is $992/2$.

The variance estimate *within* the treatments is the random variation divided by the total number of observations less the number of treatments—that is, $90/(12 - 3)$. Hence, our second estimate of the population variance is $90/9$. This is actually a generalization of formula (11–5), where we pooled the sample variances from two populations.

The last step is to take the ratio of these two estimates.

$$F = \frac{992/2}{90/9} = 49.6$$

Because this ratio is quite different from 1, we can conclude that the treatment means are not the same. There is a difference in the mean number of customers served by the three employees.

The following is another example, which deals with samples of different sizes.

Example

Recently, airlines cut services, such as meals and snacks during flights, and started charging for luggage. However, they are still concerned about service. A group of four carriers hired Brunner Marketing Research Inc. to survey passengers regarding their level of satisfaction with a recent flight. The survey included questions on ticketing, boarding, in-flight service, baggage handling, pilot communication, and so forth. Twenty-five questions offered a range of possible answers: excellent, good, fair, or poor. A response of excellent was given a score of 4, good a 3, fair a 2, and poor a 1. These responses were then totaled, so the total score was an indication of the satisfaction with the flight. The greater the score, the higher the level of satisfaction with the service. The highest possible score was 100.

Brunner randomly selected and surveyed passengers from the four airlines. Below is the sample information. Is there a difference in the mean satisfaction level among the four airlines? Use the .01 significance level.

Northern	WTA	Pocono	Branson
94	75	70	68
90	68	73	70
85	77	76	72
80	83	78	65
	88	80	74
		68	65
		65	

Solution

We will use the five-step hypothesis-testing procedure.

Step 1: State the null hypothesis and the alternate hypothesis. The null hypothesis is that the mean scores are the same for the four airlines. In the null hypothesis, we use subscripts to denote each airline; 1 corresponds with Northern, 2 with WTA, 3 with Pocono, and 4 with Branson.

$$H_0: \mu_1 = \mu_2 = \mu_3 = \mu_4$$

The alternate hypothesis is that the mean scores are not all the same for the four airlines.

$$H_1: \text{The mean scores are not all equal.}$$

We can also think of the alternate hypothesis as "at least two mean scores are not equal."

If the null hypothesis is not rejected, we conclude that there is no difference in the mean scores for the four airlines. If H_0 is rejected, we conclude that there is a difference in at least one pair of mean scores, but at this point we do not know which pair or how many pairs differ.

Step 2: Select the level of significance. We selected the .01 significance level.

Step 3: Determine the test statistic. The test statistic follows the F distribution.

Step 4: Formulate the decision rule. To determine the decision rule, we need the critical value. The critical value for the F statistic is found in Appendix B.4. The critical values for the .05 significance level are found on the first page and the .01 significance level on the second page. To use this table, we need to know the degrees of freedom in the numerator and the denominator. The degrees of freedom in the numerator equals the number of treatments, designated as k, minus 1. The degrees of freedom in the denominator is the total number of observations, n, minus the number of treatments. For this problem, there are four treatments and a total of 22 observations.

Degrees of freedom in the numerator = $k - 1 = 4 - 1 = 3$

Degrees of freedom in the denominator = $n - k = 22 - 4 = 18$

Refer to Appendix B.4 and the .01 significance level. Move horizontally across the top of the page to 3 degrees of freedom in the numerator. Then move down that column to the row with 18 degrees of freedom. The value at this intersection is 5.09. So the decision rule is to reject H_0 if the computed value of F exceeds 5.09.

LO 12-5 Organize data into appropriate ANOVA tables for analysis.

Step 5: Select the sample, perform the calculations, and make a decision. It is convenient to summarize the calculations of the F statistic in an **ANOVA table.** The format for an ANOVA table is as follows. Statistical software packages also use this format.

ANOVA Table				
Source of Variation	Sum of Squares	Degrees of Freedom	Mean Square	F
Treatments	SST	$k - 1$	$SST/(k - 1) = MST$	MST/MSE
Error	SSE	$n - k$	$SSE/(n - k) = MSE$	
Total	SS total	$n - 1$		

There are three values, or sum of squares, used to compute the test statistic F. You can determine these values by obtaining SS total and SSE, then finding SST by subtraction. The SS total term is the total variation, SST is the variation due to the treatments, and SSE is the variation within the treatments or the random error.

We usually start the process by finding SS total. This is the sum of the squared differences between each observation and the overall mean. The formula for finding SS total is:

$$SS\ total = \Sigma(X - \bar{X}_G)^2 \qquad \textbf{[12–2]}$$

where:

X is each sample observation.
$\bar{X}_G$ is the overall or grand mean.

Next, determine SSE or the sum of the squared errors. This is the sum of the squared differences between each observation and its respective treatment mean. The formula for finding SSE is:

$$SSE = \Sigma(X - \bar{X}_c)^2 \qquad \textbf{[12–3]}$$

where:

$\bar{X}_c$ is the sample mean for treatment c.

The detailed calculations of SS total and SSE for this example follow. To determine the values of SS total and SSE, we start by calculating the overall or grand mean. There are 22 observations and the total is 1,664, so the grand mean is 75.64.

$$\bar{X}_G = \frac{1,664}{22} = 75.64$$

	Northern	WTA	Pocono	Branson	Total
	94	75	70	68	
	90	68	73	70	
	85	77	76	72	
	80	83	78	65	
		88	80	74	
			68	65	
			65		
Column total	349	391	510	414	1,664
n	4	5	7	6	22
Mean	87.25	78.20	72.86	69.00	75.64

Next we find the deviation of each observation from the grand mean, square those deviations, and sum this result for all 22 observations. For example, the first sampled passenger had a score of 94 and the overall or grand mean is 75.64. So $(X - \overline{X}_G) = 94 - 75.64 = 18.36$. For the last passenger, $(X - \overline{X}_G) = 65 - 75.64 = -10.64$. The calculations for all other passengers follow.

Northern	WTA	Pocono	Branson
18.36	−0.64	−5.64	−7.64
14.36	−7.64	−2.64	−5.64
9.36	1.36	0.36	−3.64
4.36	7.36	2.36	−10.64
	12.36	4.36	−1.64
		−7.64	−10.64
		−10.64	

Then square each of these differences and sum all the values. Thus, for the first passenger:

$$(X - \overline{X}_G)^2 = (94 - 75.64)^2 = (18.36)^2 = 337.09$$

Finally, sum all the squared differences as formula (12–2) directs. Our SS total value is 1,485.10.

	Northern	WTA	Pocono	Branson	Total
	337.09	0.41	31.81	58.37	
	206.21	58.37	6.97	31.81	
	87.61	1.85	0.13	13.25	
	19.01	54.17	5.57	113.21	
		152.77	19.01	2.69	SS Total
			58.37	113.21	
			113.21		
Total	649.92	267.57	235.07	332.54	1,485.10

To compute the term SSE, find the deviation between each observation and its treatment mean. In the example, the mean of the first treatment (that is, the passengers on Northern Airlines) is 87.25, found by $\overline{X}_1 = 349/4$. The subscript N refers to Northern Airlines.

The first passenger rated Northern a 94, so $(X - \overline{X}_1) = (94 - 87.25) = 6.75$. The first passenger in the WTA group responded with a total score of 75, so $(X - \overline{X}_2) = (75 - 78.20) = -3.2$. The detail for all the passengers follows.

Northern	WTA	Pocono	Branson
6.75	−3.2	−2.86	−1
2.75	−10.2	0.14	1
−2.25	−1.2	3.14	3
−7.25	4.8	5.14	−4
	9.8	7.14	5
		−4.86	−4
		−7.86	

Each of these values is squared and then summed for all 22 observations. The values are shown in the following table.

	Northern	WTA	Pocono	Branson	Total
	45.5625	10.24	8.18	1	
	7.5625	104.04	0.02	1	
	5.0625	1.44	9.86	9	
	52.5625	23.04	26.42	16	
		96.04	50.98	25	SSE
			23.62	16	
			61.78		
Total	110.7500	234.80	180.86	68	594.41

So the SSE value is 594.41. That is $\Sigma(X - \bar{X}_c)^2 = 594.41$.

Finally, we determine SST, the sum of the squares due to the treatments, by subtraction.

$$SST = SS\ total - SSE \qquad\qquad [12-4]$$

For this example:

$$SST = SS\ total - SSE = 1,485.10 - 594.41 = 890.69$$

To find the computed value of F, work your way across the ANOVA table. The degrees of freedom for the numerator and the denominator are the same as in step 4 on page 370 when we were finding the critical value of F. The term **mean square** is another expression for an estimate of the variance. The mean square for treatments is SST divided by its degrees of freedom. The result is the **mean square for treatments** and is written MST. Compute the **mean square error** in a similar fashion. To be precise, divide SSE by its degrees of freedom. To complete the process and find F, divide MST by MSE.

Insert the particular values of F into an ANOVA table and compute the value of F as follows.

Source of Variation	Sum of Squares	Degrees of Freedom	Mean Square	F
Treatments	890.69	3	296.90	8.99
Error	594.41	18	33.02	
Total	1,485.10	21		

The computed value of F is 8.99, which is greater than the critical value of 5.09, so the null hypothesis is rejected. We conclude the population means are not all equal. The mean scores are not the same for the four airlines. It is likely that the passenger scores are related to the particular airline. At this point, we can only conclude there is a difference in the treatment means. We cannot determine which treatment groups differ or how many treatment groups differ.

As noted in the previous example, the calculations are tedious if the number of observations in each treatment is large. There are many software packages that will perform the calculations and output the results. Following is the Excel output in the form of an ANOVA table for the previous example involving airlines and passenger

Statistics in Action

Have you ever waited in line for a telephone and it seemed like the person using the phone talked on and on? There is evidence that people actually talk longer on public telephones when someone is waiting. In a recent survey, researchers measured the length of time that 56 shoppers in a mall spent on the phone (1) when they were alone, (2) when a person was using the adjacent phone, and (3) when a person was using an adjacent phone and someone was waiting to use the phone. The study, using the one-way ANOVA technique, showed that the mean time using the telephone was significantly less when the person was alone.

ratings. There are some slight differences between the software output and the previous calculations. These differences are due to rounding.

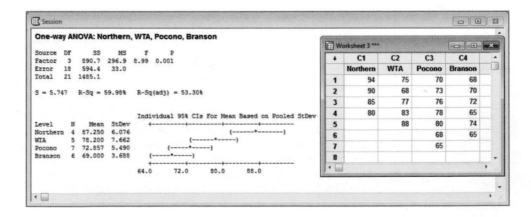

Notice Excel uses the term "Between Groups" for treatments and "Within Groups" for error. However, they have the same meanings. The *p*-value is .0007. This is the probability of finding a value of the test statistic this large or larger when the null hypothesis is true. To put it another way, it is the likelihood of calculating an *F* value larger than 8.99 with 3 degrees of freedom in the numerator and 18 degrees of freedom in the denominator. So when we reject the null hypothesis in this instance, there is a very small likelihood of committing a Type I error!

Following is the Minitab output from the airline passenger ratings example, which is similar to the Excel output. The output is also in the form of an ANOVA table. In addition, Minitab provides information about the differences between means. This is discussed in the next section.

The Minitab system uses the term "Factor" instead of *treatment,* with the same intended meaning.

Self-Review 12–2

Citrus Clean is a new all-purpose cleaner being test-marketed by placing displays in three different locations within various supermarkets. The number of 12-ounce bottles sold from each location within the supermarket is reported below.

Near bread	Near beer	Other cleaners
18	12	26
14	18	28
19	10	30
17	16	32

At the .05 significance level, is there a difference in the mean number of bottles sold at the three locations?
(a) State the null hypothesis and the alternate hypothesis.
(b) What is the decision rule?
(c) Compute the values of SS total, SST, and SSE.
(d) Develop an ANOVA table.
(e) What is your decision regarding the null hypothesis?

Exercises

connect

7. The following is sample information. Test the hypothesis that the treatment means are equal. Use the .05 significance level.

Treatment 1	Treatment 2	Treatment 3
8	3	3
6	2	4
10	4	5
9	3	4

  a. State the null hypothesis and the alternate hypotheses.
  b. What is the decision rule?
  c. Compute SST, SSE, and SS total.
  d. Complete an ANOVA table.
  e. State your decision regarding the null hypothesis.

8. The following is sample information. Test the hypothesis at the .05 significance level that the treatment means are equal.

Treatment 1	Treatment 2	Treatment 3
9	13	10
7	20	9
11	14	15
9	13	14
12		15
10		

  a. State the null hypothesis and the alternate hypotheses.
  b. What is the decision rule?
  c. Compute SST, SSE, and SS total.
  d. Complete an ANOVA table.
  e. State your decision regarding the null hypothesis.

9. A real estate developer is considering investing in a shopping mall on the outskirts of Toledo, Ohio. Three parcels of land are being evaluated. Of particular importance is the income in the area surrounding the proposed mall. A random sample of four families is selected near each proposed mall. Following are the sample results. At the .05 significance level, can the developer conclude there is a difference in the mean income? Use the usual five-step hypothesis testing procedure. (df)

Southwyck Area ($000)	Franklin Park ($000)	Old Orchard ($000)
64	74	75
68	71	80
70	69	76
60	70	78

10. The manager of a computer software company wishes to study the number of hours senior executives spend at their desktop computers. The manager selected a sample of five executives from each of three industries. At the .05 significance level, can she conclude there is a difference in the mean number of hours spent per week by industry? (df)

Banking	Retail	Insurance
12	8	10
10	8	8
10	6	6
12	8	8
10	10	10

12.6 Inferences about Pairs of Treatment Means

Suppose we carry out the ANOVA procedure and make the decision to reject the null hypothesis. This allows us to conclude that all the treatment means are not the same. Sometimes we may be satisfied with this conclusion, but in other instances we may want to know which treatment means differ. This section provides the details for such a test.

Recall that in the Brunner Research example regarding airline passenger ratings, there was a difference in the treatment means. That is, the null hypothesis was rejected and the alternate hypothesis accepted. If the passenger ratings do differ, the question is: Between which groups do the treatment means differ?

LO 12-6 Develop confidence intervals for the differences between treatment means and interpret the results.

Several procedures are available to answer this question. The simplest is through the use of confidence intervals, that is, formula (9–2). From the computer output of the previous example (see the Minitab output on page 374), note that the sample mean score for those passengers rating Northern's service is 87.25, and for those rating Branson's service, the sample mean score is 69.00. Is there enough disparity to justify the conclusion that there is a significant difference in the mean satisfaction scores of the two airlines?

The t distribution, described in Chapters 10 and 11, is used as the basis for this test. Recall that one of the assumptions of ANOVA is that the population variances are the same for all treatments. This common population value is the

mean square error, or MSE, and is determined by SSE/$(n - k)$. A confidence interval for the difference between two populations is found by:

CONFIDENCE INTERVAL FOR THE DIFFERENCE IN TREATMENT MEANS	$(\bar{X}_1 - \bar{X}_2) \pm t \sqrt{MSE\left(\dfrac{1}{n_1} + \dfrac{1}{n_2}\right)}$	**[12–5]**

where:

$\bar{X}_1$ is the mean of the first sample.

$\bar{X}_2$ is the mean of the second sample.

t is obtained from Appendix B.2. The degrees of freedom is equal to $n - k$. MSE is the mean square error term obtained from the ANOVA table [SSE/$(n - k)$].

n_1 is the number of observations in the first sample.

n_2 is the number of observations in the second sample.

How do we decide whether there is a difference in the treatment means? If the confidence interval includes zero, there is *not* a difference between the treatment means. For example, if the left endpoint of the confidence interval has a negative sign and the right endpoint has a positive sign, the interval includes zero and the two means do not differ. So if we develop a confidence interval from formula (12–5) and find the difference in the sample means was 5.00—that is, if $\bar{X}_1 - \bar{X}_2 = 5$ and $t \sqrt{MSE\left(\dfrac{1}{n_1} + \dfrac{1}{n_2}\right)} = 12$—the confidence interval would range from -7.00 up to 17.00. To put it in symbols:

$$(\bar{X}_1 - \bar{X}_2) \pm t \sqrt{MSE\left(\frac{1}{n_1} + \frac{1}{n_2}\right)} = 5.00 \pm 12.00 = -7.00 \text{ up to } 17.00$$

Note that zero is included in this interval. Therefore, we conclude that there is not a significant difference in the selected treatment means.

On the other hand, if the endpoints of the confidence interval have the same sign, this indicates that the treatment means differ. For example, if $\bar{X}_1 - \bar{X}_2 = -0.35$ and $t \sqrt{MSE\left(\dfrac{1}{n_1} + \dfrac{1}{n_2}\right)} = 0.25$, the confidence interval would range from -0.60 up to -0.10. Because -0.60 and -0.10 have the same sign, both negative, zero is not in the interval and we conclude that these treatment means differ.

Using the previous airline example, let us compute the confidence interval for the difference between the mean scores of passengers on Northern (using the subscript, "1") and Branson (using the subscript, "4"). With a 95% level of confidence, the endpoints of the confidence interval are 10.46 and 26.04.

$$(\bar{X}_1 - \bar{X}_4) \pm t \sqrt{MSE\left(\frac{1}{n_1} + \frac{1}{n_4}\right)} = (87.25 - 69.00) \pm 2.101 \sqrt{33.0\left(\frac{1}{4} + \frac{1}{6}\right)}$$

$$= 18.25 \pm 7.79$$

where:

$\bar{X}_1$ is 87.25.

$\bar{X}_4$ is 69.00.

t is 2.101: from Appendix B.2 with $(n - k) = 22 - 4 = 18$ degrees of freedom.

MSE is 33.0: from the ANOVA table with SSE/$(n - k) = 594.4/18$.

n_1 is 4.

n_4 is 6.

The 95% confidence interval ranges from 10.46 up to 26.04. Both endpoints are positive; hence, we can conclude these treatment means differ significantly. That is, passengers on Northern Airlines rated service significantly different from those on Branson Airlines.

Approximate results can also be obtained directly from the Minitab output. Following is the lower portion of the output from page 374. On the left side is the number of observations, the mean, and the standard deviation for each treatment. Seven passengers on Pocono rated the service as 72.857 with a standard deviation of 5.490.

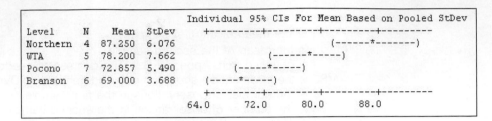

```
                                Individual 95% CIs For Mean Based on Pooled StDev
Level       N    Mean   StDev   +---------+---------+---------+---------
Northern    4   87.250  6.076                              (------*-------)
WTA         5   78.200  7.662                  (------*-----)
Pocono      7   72.857  5.490            (-----*-----)
Branson     6   69.000  3.688     (-----*-----)
                                +---------+---------+---------+---------
                                64.0     72.0      80.0      88.0
```

On the right side of the printout is a confidence interval for each treatment mean. The asterisk (*) indicates the location of the treatment mean and the open parenthesis and close parenthesis, the endpoints of the confidence interval. In those instances where the intervals overlap, the treatment means do not differ. If there is no common area in the confidence intervals, that pair of means differ.

The endpoints of a 95% confidence interval for mean passenger scores for Pocono are about 69 and 77. For Branson, the endpoints of the 95% confidence interval for the mean passenger score are about 64 and 73. There is common area between these points, so we conclude this pair of means does not differ. In other words, there is no significant difference between the mean passenger ratings for Pocono and Branson Airlines. The difference in the mean scores is due to chance.

There are two pairs of means that differ. The mean score of passengers on Northern Airlines is significantly higher than the mean scores of passengers on Pocono Airlines, and the mean scores of passengers on Branson Airlines. There is no common area between these two pairs of confidence intervals.

We should emphasize that this investigation is a step-by-step process. The initial step is to conduct the ANOVA test. Only if the null hypothesis that the treatment means are equal is rejected should any analysis of the individual treatment means be attempted.

Self-Review 12–3

The following data are the semester tuition charges ($000) for a sample of private colleges in various regions of the United States. At the .05 significance level, can we conclude there is a difference in the mean tuition rates for the various regions?

Northeast ($000)	Southeast ($000)	West ($000)
15	13	12
16	14	13
17	15	11
15	13	12
17		11

(a) State the null and the alternate hypotheses.
(b) What is the decision rule?
(c) Develop an ANOVA table. What is the value of the test statistic?
(d) What is your decision regarding the null hypothesis?
(e) Could there be a significant difference between the mean tuition in the Northeast and that of the West? If so, develop a 95% confidence interval for that difference.

Exercises

connect™

11. Given the following sample information, test the hypothesis that the treatment means are equal at the .05 significance level.

Treatment 1	Treatment 2	Treatment 3
8	3	3
11	2	4
10	1	5
	3	4
	2	

a. State the null hypothesis and the alternate hypothesis.
b. What is the decision rule?
c. Compute SST, SSE, and SS total.
d. Complete an ANOVA table.
e. State your decision regarding the null hypothesis.
f. If H_0 is rejected, can we conclude that treatment 1 and treatment 2 differ? Use the 95% level of confidence.

12. Given the following sample information, test the hypothesis that the treatment means are equal at the .05 significance level. (df)

Treatment 1	Treatment 2	Treatment 3
3	9	6
2	6	3
5	5	5
1	6	5
3	8	5
1	5	4
	4	1
	7	5
	6	
	4	

a. State the null hypothesis and the alternate hypothesis.
b. What is the decision rule?
c. Compute SST, SSE, and SS total.
d. Complete an ANOVA table.
e. State your decision regarding the null hypothesis.
f. If H_0 is rejected, can we conclude that treatment 2 and treatment 3 differ? Use the 95% level of confidence.

13. A senior accounting major at Midsouth State University has job offers from four CPA firms. To explore the offers further, she asked a sample of recent trainees how many months each worked for the firm before receiving a raise in salary. The sample information is submitted to Minitab with the following results:

```
Analysis of Variance
Source    DF      SS       MS       F        P
Factor     3    32.33    10.78    2.36    0.133
Error     10    45.67     4.57
Total     13    78.00
```

At the .05 level of significance, is there a difference in the mean number of months before a raise was granted among the four CPA firms?

14. A stock analyst wants to determine whether there is a difference in the mean rate of return for three types of stock: utility, retail, and banking stocks. The following output is obtained:

```
Analysis of Variance
Source     DF        SS        MS       F        P
Factor      2      86.49     43.25    13.09    0.001
Error      13      42.95      3.30
Total      15     129.44
                                     Individual 95% CIs For Mean
                                     Based on Pooled StDev
Level       N      Mean      StDev   ----------+----------+----------+------
Utility     5     17.400     1.916                            (------*------)
Retail      5     11.620     0.356    (------*------)
Banking     6     15.400     2.356                    (------*------)
                                     ----------+----------+----------+------
Pooled StDev = 1.818                      12.0       15.0       18.0
```

a. Using the .05 level of significance, is there a difference in the mean rate of return among the three types of stock?
b. Suppose the null hypothesis is rejected. Can the analyst conclude there is a difference between the mean rates of return for the utility and the retail stocks? Explain.

Chapter Summary

I. The characteristics of the F distribution are:
   A. It is continuous.
   B. Its values cannot be negative.
   C. It is positively skewed.
   D. There is a family of F distributions. Each time the degrees of freedom in either the numerator or the denominator changes, a new distribution is created.
II. The F distribution is used to test whether two population variances are the same.
   A. The sampled populations must follow the normal distribution.
   B. The larger of the two sample variances is placed in the numerator, forcing the ratio to be at least 1.00.
   C. The value of F is computed using the following equation:

$$F = \frac{s_1^2}{s_2^2}$$

[12–1]

III. A one-way ANOVA is used to compare several treatment means.
   A. A treatment is a source of variation.
   B. The assumptions underlying ANOVA are:
      1. The samples are from populations that follow the normal distribution.
      2. The populations have equal standard deviations.
      3. The samples are independent.
   C. The information for finding the value of F is summarized in an ANOVA table.
      1. The formula for SS total, the sum of squares total, is:

$$\text{SS total} = \Sigma(X - \overline{X}_G)^2$$

[12–2]

      2. The formula for SSE, the sum of squares error, is:

$$\text{SSE} = \Sigma(X - \overline{X}_c)^2$$

[12–3]

      3. The formula for the SST, the sum of squares treatment, is found by subtraction.

$$\text{SST} = \text{SS total} - \text{SSE}$$

[12–4]

4. This information is summarized in the following ANOVA table and the value of F determined.

Source of Variation	Sum of Squares	Degrees of Freedom	Mean Square	F
Treatments	SST	$k - 1$	$SST/(k - 1) = MST$	MST/MSE
Error	SSE	$n - k$	$SSE/(n - k) = MSE$	
Total	SS total	$n - 1$		

IV. If a null hypothesis of equal treatment means is rejected, we can identify the pairs of means that differ from the following confidence interval.

$$(\bar{X}_1 - \bar{X}_2) \pm t \sqrt{MSE\left(\frac{1}{n_1} + \frac{1}{n_2}\right)}$$

[12–5]

Pronunciation Key

SYMBOL	MEANING	PRONUNCIATION
SS total	Sum of squares total	*S S total*
SST	Sum of squares treatment	*S S T*
SSE	Sum of squares error	*S S E*
MSE	Mean square error	*M S E*

Chapter Exercises

connect

15. A real estate agent in the coastal area of Georgia wants to compare the variation in the selling price of homes on the oceanfront with those one to three blocks from the ocean. A sample of 21 oceanfront homes sold within the last year revealed the standard deviation of the selling prices was $45,600. A sample of 18 homes, also sold within the last year, that were one to three blocks from the ocean revealed that the standard deviation was $21,330. At the .01 significance level, can we conclude that there is more variation in the selling prices of the oceanfront homes?

16. A computer manufacturer is about to unveil a new, faster personal computer. The new machine clearly is faster, but initial tests indicate there is more variation in the processing time. The processing time depends on the software, the amount of data to be processed, and the amount of output. A sample of 16 computer runs, covering a range of production jobs, showed that the standard deviation of the processing time was 22 (hundredths of a second) for the new machine and 12 (hundredths of a second) for the current machine. At the .05 significance level can we conclude that there is more variation in the processing time of the new machine?

17. There are two Chevrolet dealers in Jamestown, New York. The mean monthly sales at Sharkey Chevy and Dave White Chevrolet are about the same. However, Tom Sharkey, the owner of Sharkey Chevy, believes his sales are more consistent. Below is the number of new cars sold at Sharkey in the last seven months and for the last eight months at Dave White. Do you agree with Mr. Sharkey? Use the .01 significance level.

Sharkey	98	78	54	57	68	64	70	
Dave White	75	81	81	30	82	46	58	101

18. Random samples of five were selected from each of three populations. The sum of squares total was 100. The sum of squares due to the treatments was 40.
   a. Set up the null hypothesis and the alternate hypothesis.
   b. What is the decision rule? Use the .05 significance level.
   c. Complete the ANOVA table. What is the value of F?
   d. What is your decision regarding the null hypothesis?

19. In an ANOVA table, MSE was equal to 10. Random samples of six were selected from each of four populations, where the sum of squares total was 250.
   a. Set up the null hypothesis and the alternate hypothesis.
   b. What is the decision rule? Use the .05 significance level.
   c. Complete the ANOVA table. What is the value of F?
   d. What is your decision regarding the null hypothesis?
20. The following is a partial ANOVA table.

Source	Sum of Squares	df	Mean Square	F
Treatment		2		
Error			20	
Total	500	11		

Complete the table and answer the following questions. Use the .05 significance level.
   a. How many treatments are there?
   b. What is the total sample size?
   c. What is the critical value of F?
   d. Write out the null and alternate hypotheses.
   e. What is your conclusion regarding the null hypothesis?
21. A consumer organization wants to know whether there is a difference in the price of a particular toy at three different types of stores. The price of the toy was checked in a sample of five discount stores, five variety stores, and five department stores. The results are shown below. Use the .05 significance level. (df)

Discount	Variety	Department
$12	$15	$19
13	17	17
14	14	16
12	18	20
15	17	19

22. Jacob Lee is a frequent traveler between Los Angeles and San Francisco. For the past month, he wrote down the flight times on three different airlines. The results are: (df)

Goust	Jet Red	Cloudtran
51	50	52
51	53	55
52	52	60
42	62	64
51	53	61
57	49	49
47	50	49
47	49	
50	58	
60	54	
54	51	
49	49	
48	49	
48	50	

   a. Use the .05 significance level and the five-step hypothesis-testing process to check if there is a difference in the mean flight times among the three airlines.
   b. Develop a 95% confidence interval for the difference in the means between Goust and Cloudtran.

23. The City of Maumee comprises four districts. Police chief Andy North wants to determine whether there is a difference in the mean number of crimes committed among the four districts. He examined the records from six randomly selected days and recorded the number of reported crimes. At the .05 significance level, can Chief North conclude there is a difference in the mean number of crimes among the four districts? (df)

Number of Crimes			
Rec Center	Key Street	Monclova	Whitehouse
13	21	12	16
15	13	14	17
14	18	15	18
15	19	13	15
14	18	12	20
15	19	15	18

24. A study of the effect of television commercials on 12-year-old children measured their attention span, in seconds. The commercials were for clothes, food, and toys. At the .05 significance level, is there a difference in the mean attention span of the children for the various commercials? Are there significant differences between pairs of means? Would you recommend dropping one of the three commercial types? (df)

Clothes	Food	Toys
26	45	60
21	48	51
43	43	43
35	53	54
28	47	63
31	42	53
17	34	48
31	43	58
20	57	47
	47	51
	44	51
	54	

25. When only two treatments are involved, ANOVA and the Student's t test (Chapter 11) result in the same conclusions. Also, $t^2 = F$. As an example, suppose that 14 randomly selected students were divided into two groups, one consisting of 6 students and the other of 8. One group was taught using a combination of lecture and programmed instruction, the other using a combination of lecture and television. At the end of the course, each group was given a 50-item test. The following is a list of the number correct for each of the two groups. (df)

Lecture and Programmed Instruction	Lecture and Television
19	32
17	28
23	31
22	26
17	23
16	24
	27
	25

    a. Using analysis of variance techniques, test H_0 that the two mean test scores are equal; $\alpha = .05$.

    b. Using the *t* test from Chapter 11, compute *t*.

    c. Interpret the results.

26. There are four auto body shops in Bangor, Maine, and all claim to promptly serve customers. To check if there is any difference in service, customers are randomly selected from each repair shop and their waiting times in days are recorded. The output from a statistical software package is:

Summary				
Groups	**Count**	**Sum**	**Average**	**Variance**
Body Shop A	3	15.4	5.133333	0.323333
Body Shop B	4	32	8	1.433333
Body Shop C	5	25.2	5.04	0.748
Body Shop D	4	25.9	6.475	0.595833

ANOVA					
Source of Variation	**SS**	**df**	**MS**	**F**	***p*-value**
Between Groups	23.37321	3	7.791069	9.612506	0.001632
Within Groups	9.726167	12	0.810514		
Total	33.09938	15			

Is there evidence to suggest a difference in the mean waiting times at the four body shops? Use the .05 significance level.

27. The fuel efficiencies for a sample of 27 compact, midsize, and large cars are entered into a statistical software package. Analysis of variance is used to investigate if there is a difference in the mean mileage of the three cars. What do you conclude? Use the .01 significance level.

Summary				
Groups	**Count**	**Sum**	**Average**	**Variance**
Compact	12	268.3	22.35833	9.388106
Midsize	9	172.4	19.15556	7.315278
Large	6	100.5	16.75	7.303

Additional results are shown below.

ANOVA					
Source of Variation	**SS**	**df**	**MS**	**F**	***p*-value**
Between Groups	136.4803	2	68.24014	8.258752	0.001866
Within Groups	198.3064	24	8.262766		
Total	334.7867	26			

28. Three assembly lines are used to produce a certain component for an airliner. To examine the production rate, a random sample of six hourly periods is chosen for each assembly line and the number of components produced during these periods for each line is recorded. The output from a statistical software package is:

Summary				
Groups	**Count**	**Sum**	**Average**	**Variance**
Line A	6	250	41.66667	0.266667
Line B	6	260	43.33333	0.666667
Line C	6	249	41.5	0.7

ANOVA					
Source of Variation	SS	df	MS	F	p-value
Between Groups	12.33333	2	6.166667	11.32653	0.001005
Within Groups	8.166667	15	0.544444		
Total	20.5	17			

a. Use a .01 level of significance to test if there is a difference in the mean production of the three assembly lines.

b. Develop a 99% confidence interval for the difference in the means between Line B and Line C.

29. The postal service groups first-class mail as letters, cards, flats, or parcels. Over a period of three weeks, one item of each kind was sent from a particular postal administrative center. The total time in transit was recorded. A statistical software package was then used to perform the analysis. The results follow.

```
Source    DF        SS       MS       F       P
Factor     3      13.82     4.61    2.72    0.051
Error     68     115.17     1.69
Total     71     128.99

S = 1.301      R-Sq = 10.71%      R-Sq(adj) = 6.77%

                             Individual 95% CIs for Mean Based on
                             Pooled StDev
Level      N     Mean   StDev  ------+---------+---------+---------+---
Letters   18    1.444   1.097  (---------*---------)
Cards     18    1.667   1.455     (---------*---------)
Flats     18    2.444   1.617                 (---------*---------)
Parcels   18    2.389   0.916              (---------*---------)
                             ------+---------+---------+---------+---
                              1.20      1.80      2.40      3.00
```

Use the .05 significance level to test if this evidence suggests a difference in the means for the different types of first-class mail.

30. For your email, you use a filter to block spam from your inbox. The number of items blocked by day of week is recorded and a statistical software system is used to perform the analysis that follows. Here are the results:

```
Source    DF        SS       MS       F       P
Factor     6     1367.8    228.0    5.72    0.000
Error     48     1913.2     39.9
Total     54     3281.0

S = 6.313      R-Sq = 41.69%      R-Sq(adj) = 34.40%

                              Individual 95% CIs for Mean Based on
                              Pooled StDev
Level        N    Mean   StDev  ----+---------+---------+---------+-----
Monday      10   74.000  6.164                       (-----*------)
Tuesday      9   66.111  7.288        (------*------)
Wednesday    7   74.143  2.268                    (-------*-------)
Thursday     8   62.375  5.041   (-------*------)
Friday       8   75.125  4.454                       (------*-------)
Saturday     5   63.200  7.259   (--------*---------)
Sunday       8   72.375  9.164              (-------*------)
                              ----+---------+---------+---------+-----
                               60.0      66.0      72.0      78.0
```

Use the .05 significance level to test if this evidence suggests a difference in the means for the different days of the week.

31. Investors can now make stock trades online for as little as $7 per trade. Some suggest that this will motivate investors to increase the percentage of stocks in their

portfolios. Further, stocks as a percentage of an investor's portfolio may be related to age. To investigate, Dr. Merenick, professor of finance, selected a sample of 64 investors, and determined the percentage of stocks in their portfolios. The sample data is classified by the investors' age and reported below. 🔵

20 up to 35	35 up to 50	50 up to 65	65 or Older
39.2	10.6	29.0	58.9
32.4	64.5	88.2	35.6
50.8	80.0	29.2	26.1
73.6	59.2	81.5	64.8
46.3	65.8	61.4	30.4
40.0	69.5	79.3	71.0
44.8	72.3	73.9	46.1
69.3	78.4	40.8	70.1
45.3	68.6	57.5	91.8
38.8	67.9	55.2	67.2
33.5	40.1	46.9	63.2
34.0	46.7	62.8	59.6
42.7	66.4	62.8	50.2
68.0	71.7	62.5	49.0
42.1	60.1	26.1	
54.4	44.9		
60.2	59.9		
	71.3		

At the .05 significance level, can we conclude that there is a difference in the mean percentage of stocks owned between the various age groups?

32. There are four radio stations in Midland. The stations have different formats (hard rock, classical, country/western, and easy listening), but each is concerned with the number of minutes of music played per hour. From a sample of 10 hours from each station, the following sample means were offered.

$$\bar{X}_1 = 51.32 \qquad \bar{X}_2 = 44.64 \qquad \bar{X}_3 = 47.2 \qquad \bar{X}_4 = 50.85$$

$$\text{SS total} = 650.75$$

a. Determine SST.
b. Determine SSE.
c. Complete an ANOVA table.
d. At the .05 significance level, is there a difference in the treatment means?
e. Is there a difference in the mean amount of music time between station 1 and station 4? Use the .05 significance level.

Data Set Exercises

(The data for these exercises are available at the text website www.mhhe.com/lindbasic8e).

33. Refer to the Real Estate data, which report information on the homes sold in the Goodyear, Arizona, area last year.
   a. At the .02 significance level, is there a difference in the variability of the selling prices of the homes that have a pool versus those that do not have a pool?
   b. At the .02 significance level, is there a difference in the variability of the selling prices of the homes with an attached garage versus those that do not have an attached garage?
   c. At the .05 significance level, is there a difference in the mean selling price of the homes among the five townships?
34. Refer to the Baseball 2010 data, which report information on the 30 Major League Baseball teams for the 2010 season.

a. At the .10 significance level, is there a difference in the variation in team payroll among the American and National League teams?

b. Create a variable that classifies a team's total attendance into three groups: less than 2.0 (million), 2.0 up to 3.0, and 3.0 or more. At the .01 significance level, is there a difference in the mean number of games won among the three groups?

c. Using the same attendance variable developed in part (b), is there a difference in the mean number of home runs hit per team? Use the .01 significance level.

d. Using the same attendance variable developed in part (b), is there a difference in the mean payroll of the three groups? Use the .01 significance level.

35. Refer to the Buena School District bus data.

a. Conduct a test of hypothesis to reveal whether the mean maintenance cost is equal for each of the bus producers. Use the .01 significance level.

b. Conduct a test of hypothesis to determine whether the mean miles traveled is equal for each make of bus. Use the .05 significance level.

c. Develop a 95 percent confidence interval for the disparity in the average maintenance cost between buses made by Bluebird and Thompson.

Practice Test

Part 1—Objective

1. The test statistic for comparing two population variances follows the _____. (*F* distribution, *t* distribution, *z* distribution)
2. The shape of the *F* distribution is _____. (symmetric, positively skewed, negatively skewed, uniform)
3. The *F* statistic is computed as the ratio of two _____.
4. Analysis of Variance (ANOVA) is used to compare two or more _____. (means, proportions, samples sizes, *z* values)
5. The ANOVA test assumes equal _____. (population means, population standard deviations, sample sizes, *z* values)
6. One-way ANOVA partitions total variation into two parts. One is called treatment variation, and the other is _____.
7. In one-way ANOVA, the null hypothesis is that the population means are _____.
8. A mean square is computed as a sum of squares divided by the _____.
9. In one-way ANOVA, differences between treatment means are tested with _____. (confidence intervals, *z* values, significance levels, variances)
10. For a one-way ANOVA, the treatments must be _____. (equal, independent, proportional, none of these)

Part 2—Problems

1. Is the variance of the distance traveled per week by two taxi cab companies operating in the Grand Strand area different? The *Sun News,* the local newspaper, is investigating and obtained the following sample information. Using the .10 significance level, is there a difference in the variance of the miles traveled?

Variable	Yellow Cab	Horse and Buggy Cab
Mean miles	837	797
Standard deviation	30	40
Sample size	14	12

2. The results of a one-way ANOVA are reported below.

ANOVA				
Source of Variation	*SS*	*df*	*MS*	*F*
Between Groups	6.90	2	3.45	5.15
Within Groups	12.04	18	0.67	
Total	19.34	20		

a. How many treatments are in the study?
b. What is the total sample size?
c. What is the critical value of F?
d. Write out the null hypothesis and the alternate hypothesis.
e. What is your decision regarding the null hypothesis?
f. Can we conclude any of the treatment means differ?

Software Commands

1. The Excel commands for the test of variances on page 365 are:
    a. Enter the data for U.S. 25 in column A and for I-75 in column B. Label the two columns.
    b. Select the **Data** tab on the top menu. Then, on the far right, select **Data Analysis**. Select **F-Test: Two-Sample for Variances,** then click **OK.**
    c. The range of the first variable is *A1:A8,* and *B1:B9* for the second. Click on **Labels,** enter *0.05* for **Alpha,** select *D1* for the **Output Range,** and click **OK.**

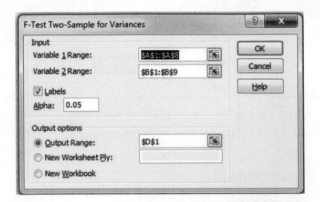

2. The Excel commands for the one-way ANOVA on page 374 are:
    a. Key in data into four columns labeled: *Northern, WTA, Pocono,* and *Branson.*
    b. Select the **Data** tab on the top menu. Then, on the far right, select **Data Analysis.** Select **ANOVA: Single Factor,** then click **OK.**
    c. In the subsequent dialog box, make the input range *A1:D8,* click on **Grouped by Columns,** click on **Labels in first row,** the **Alpha** text box is *.05,* and finally select **Output Range** as *F1* and click **OK.**

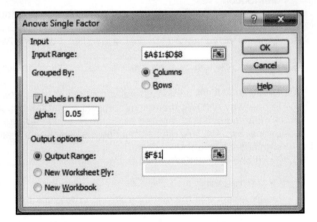

3. The Minitab commands for the one-way ANOVA on page 374 are:
    a. Input the data into four columns and identify the columns as *Northern, WTA, Pocono,* and *Branson.*
    b. Select **Stat, ANOVA,** and **One-way (Unstacked),** select the data in columns C1 to C4, check on **Select** in the lower left, and then click **OK.**

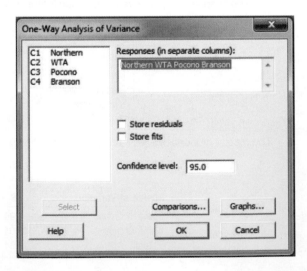

Chapter 12 Answers to Self-Review

12–1 Let Mark's assemblies be population 1, then
$H_0: \sigma_1^2 \leq \sigma_2^2; H_1: \sigma_1^2 > \sigma_2^2; df_1 = 10 - 1 = 9$; and
df_2 also equals 9. H_0 is rejected if $F > 3.18$.

$$F = \frac{(2.0)^2}{(1.5)^2} = 1.78$$

Do not reject H_0.

12–2 a. $H_0: \mu_1 = \mu_2 = \mu_3$
H_1: At least one treatment mean is different.
b. Reject H_0 if $F > 4.26$.

c.
$$\overline{X} = \frac{240}{12} = 20$$
SS total $= (18 - 20)^2 + \cdots + (32 - 20)^2$
$= 578$
SSE $= (18 - 17)^2 + (14 - 17)^2 + \cdots +$
$(32 - 29)^2$
$= 74$
SST $= 578 - 74 = 504$

d.

Source	Sum of Squares	Degrees of Freedom	Mean Square	F
Treatment	504	2	252	30.65
Error	74	9	8.22	
Total	578	11		

e. H_0 is rejected. There is a difference in the mean number of bottles sold at the various locations.

12–3 a. $H_0: \mu_1 = \mu_2 = \mu_3$
H_1: Not all means are equal.
b. H_0 is rejected if $F > 3.98$.
c. $\overline{X}_G = 13.86, \overline{X}_1 = 16, \overline{X}_2 = 13.75, \overline{X}_3 = 11.80$
SS total $= 53.71$
SST $= 44.16$
SSE $= 9.55$

Source	Sum of Squares	df	Mean Square	F
Treatment	44.16	2	22.08	25.43
Error	9.55	11	0.8682	
Total	53.71	13		

d. H_0 is rejected. The treatment means differ.
e. $(16.0 - 11.80) \pm 2.201 \sqrt{0.8682(\frac{1}{5} + \frac{1}{5})} =$
$4.2 \pm 1.30 = 2.90$ and 5.50
These treatment means differ because both endpoints of the confidence interval are of the same sign—positive in this problem.

13

Correlation and Linear Regression

An air travel service samples domestic airline flights to explore the relationship between airfare and distance. The service would like to know if there is a correlation between airfare and flight distance. If there is a correlation, what percentage of the variation in airfare is accounted for by distance? How much does each additional mile add to the fare? (See Exercise 61 and LO 13-2, LO 13-3, and LO 13-7.)

13.1 Introduction

Chapters 2 through 4 presented *descriptive statistics.* We organized raw data into a frequency distribution and computed several measures of location and measures of dispersion to describe the major characteristics of the distribution. In Chapters 5 through 7, we described probability, and from probability statements, we created probability distributions. In Chapter 8, we began the study of *statistical inference,* where we collected a sample to estimate a population parameter such as the population mean or population proportion. In addition, we used the sample data to test a hypothesis about a population mean or a population proportion, the difference between two population means, or the equality of several population means. Each of these tests involved just *one* interval- or ratio-level variable, such as the profit made on a car sale, the income of bank presidents, or the number of patients admitted each month to a particular hospital.

In this chapter, we shift the emphasis to the study of relationships between two interval- or ratio-level variables. In all business fields, identifying and studying relationships between variables can provide information on ways to increase profits, methods to decrease costs, or variables to predict demand. In marketing products, many firms use price reductions through coupons and discount pricing to increase sales. In this example, we are interested in the relationship between two variables: price reductions and sales. To collect the data, a company can test-market a variety of price reduction methods and observe sales. We hope to confirm a relationship that decreasing price leads to increased sales. In economics, you will find many relationships between two variables that are the basis of economics, such as supply and demand and demand and price.

As another familiar example, recall that in Section 4.5 in Chapter 4 we used the Applewood Auto Group data to show the relationship between two variables with a scatter diagram. We plotted the profit for each vehicle sold on the vertical axis and the age of the buyer on the horizontal axis. See the statistical software output on page 114. In that diagram, we observed that as the age of the buyer increased, the profit for each vehicle also increased.

Other examples of relationships between two variables are:

- Does the amount Healthtex spends per month on training its sales force affect its monthly sales?
- Is the number of square feet in a home related to the cost to heat the home in January?
- In a study of fuel efficiency, is there a relationship between miles per gallon and the weight of a car?
- Does the number of hours that students study for an exam influence the exam score?

In this chapter, we carry this idea further. That is, we develop numerical measures to express the relationship between two variables. Is the relationship strong or weak? Is it direct or inverse? In addition, we develop an equation to express the relationship between variables. This will allow us to estimate one variable on the basis of another.

To begin our study of relationships between two variables, we examine the meaning and purpose of **correlation analysis.** We continue by developing an equation that will allow us to estimate the value of one variable based on the value of another. This is called **regression analysis.** We will also evaluate the ability of the equation to accurately make estimations.

Statistics in Action

The space shuttle *Challenger* exploded on January 28, 1986. An investigation of the cause examined four contractors: Rockwell International for the shuttle and engines, Lockheed Martin for ground support, Martin Marietta for the external fuel tanks, and Morton Thiokol for the solid fuel booster rockets. After several months, the investigation blamed the explosion on defective O-rings produced by Morton Thiokol. A study of the contractor's stock *(continued)*

13.2 What Is Correlation Analysis?

When we study the relationship between two interval- or ratio-scale variables, we often start with a scatter diagram. This procedure provides a visual representation of the relationship between the variables. The next step is usually to calculate the correlation coefficient. It provides a quantitative measure of the strength of the relationship between two variables. As an example, the sales manager of Copier Sales of America, which has a large sales force throughout the United States and Canada, wants to determine whether there is a relationship between the number of sales calls made in a month and the number of copiers sold that month. The manager selects a random sample of 10 representatives and determines the number of sales calls each representative made. This information is reported in Table 13–1.

TABLE 13–1 Number of Sales Calls and Copiers Sold for 10 Salespeople

Sales Representative	Number of Sales Calls	Number of Copiers Sold
Tom Keller	20	30
Jeff Hall	40	60
Brian Virost	20	40
Greg Fish	30	60
Susan Welch	10	30
Carlos Ramirez	10	40
Rich Niles	20	40
Mike Kiel	20	50
Mark Reynolds	20	30
Soni Jones	30	70

By reviewing the data, we observe that there does seem to be some relationship between the number of sales calls and the number of units sold. That is, the salespeople who made the most sales calls sold the most units. However, the relationship is not "perfect" or exact. For example, Soni Jones made fewer sales calls than Jeff Hall, but she sold more units.

In addition to the graphical techniques in Chapter 4, we will develop numerical measures to precisely describe the relationship between the two variables, sales calls and copiers sold. This group of statistical techniques is called **correlation analysis.**

> **CORRELATION ANALYSIS** A group of techniques to measure the relationship between two variables.

The basic idea of correlation analysis is to report the relationship between two variables. The usual first step is to plot the data in a **scatter diagram.** An example will show how a scatter diagram is used.

Example

Copier Sales of America sells copiers to businesses of all sizes throughout the United States and Canada. Ms. Marcy Bancer was recently promoted to the position of national sales manager. At the upcoming sales meeting, the sales representatives from all over the country will be in attendance. She would like to impress upon them the importance of making that extra sales call each day. She decides to gather some information on the relationship between the number of sales calls and the number of copiers sold. She selects a random sample of 10 sales representatives and determines the number of sales calls they made last month and the number of copiers they sold. The sample information is reported in Table 13–1. What observations can you make about the relationship between the number of sales calls and the number of copiers sold? Develop a scatter diagram to display the information.

Solution

Based on the information in Table 13–1, Ms. Bancer suspects there is a relationship between the number of sales calls made in a month and the number of copiers sold. Soni Jones sold the most copiers last month, and she was one of three representatives making 30 or more sales calls. On the other hand, Susan Welch and Carlos Ramirez made only 10 sales calls last month. Ms. Welch, along with two others, had the lowest number of copiers sold among the sampled representatives.

The implication is that the number of copiers sold is related to the number of sales calls made. As the number of sales calls increases, it appears the number of copiers sold also increases. We refer to number of sales calls as the **independent variable** and number of copiers sold as the **dependent variable.**

LO 13-1 Define the terms *independent variable* and *dependent variable.*

The independent variable provides the basis for estimation. It is the predictor variable. For example, we would like to predict the expected number of copiers sold if a salesperson makes 20 sales calls. Notice that we choose this value. The independent variable is not a random number.

The dependent variable is the variable that is being predicted or estimated. It can also be described as the result or outcome for a known value of the independent variable. The dependent variable is random. That is, for a given value of the independent variable, there are many possible outcomes for the dependent variable. In this example, notice that five different sales representatives made 20 sales calls. The result or outcome of making 20 sales calls is three different values of the dependent variable.

It is common practice to scale the dependent variable (copiers sold) on the vertical or Y-axis and the independent variable (number of sales calls) on the horizontal or X-axis. To develop the scatter diagram of the Copier Sales of America sales information, we begin with the first sales representative, Tom Keller. Tom made 20 sales calls last month and sold 30 copiers, so $X = 20$ and $Y = 30$. To plot this point, move along the horizontal axis to $X = 20$, then go vertically to $Y = 30$ and place a dot at the intersection. This process is continued until all the paired data are plotted, as shown in Chart 13–1.

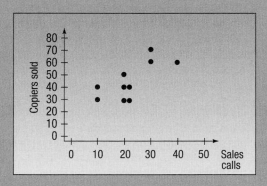

CHART 13–1 Scatter Diagram Showing Sales Calls and Copiers Sold

The scatter diagram shows graphically that the sales representatives who make more calls tend to sell more copiers. It is reasonable for Ms. Bancer, the national sales manager at Copier Sales of America, to tell her salespeople that the more sales calls they make, the more copiers they can expect to sell. Note that while there appears to be a positive relationship between the two variables, all the points do not fall on a straight line. In the following section, you will measure the strength and direction of this relationship between two variables by determining the correlation coefficient.

13.3 The Correlation Coefficient

LO 13-2 Calculate, test, and interpret the relationship between two variables using the correlation coefficient.

Originated by Karl Pearson about 1900, the **correlation coefficient** describes the strength of the relationship between two sets of interval-scaled or ratio-scaled variables. Designated *r*, it is often referred to as *Pearson's r* and as the *Pearson product-moment correlation coefficient*. It can assume any value from −1.00 to +1.00 inclusive. A correlation coefficient of −1.00 or +1.00 indicates *perfect correlation*. For example, a correlation coefficient for the preceding example computed to be +1.00 would indicate that the number of sales calls and the number of copiers sold are perfectly related in a positive linear sense. A computed value of −1.00 reveals that sales calls and the number of copiers sold are perfectly related in an inverse linear sense. How the scatter diagram would appear if the relationship between the two sets of data were linear and perfect is shown in Chart 13–2.

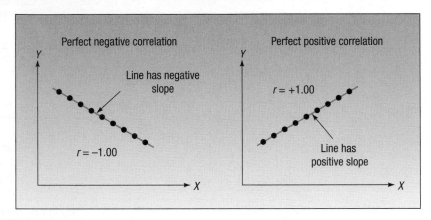

CHART 13–2 Scatter Diagrams Showing Perfect Negative Correlation and Perfect Positive Correlation

If there is absolutely no relationship between the two sets of variables, Pearson's *r* is zero. A correlation coefficient *r* close to 0 (say, .08) shows that the linear relationship is quite weak. The same conclusion is drawn if *r* = −.08. Coefficients of −.91 and +.91 have equal strength; both indicate very strong correlation between the two variables. Thus, *the strength of the correlation does not depend on the direction (either − or +).*

Scatter diagrams for *r* = 0, a weak *r* (say, −.23), and a strong *r* (say, +.87) are shown in Chart 13–3. Note that, if the correlation is weak, there is considerable scatter about a line drawn through the center of the data. For the scatter diagram representing a strong relationship, there is very little scatter about the line. This indicates, in the example shown on the chart, that hours studied is a good predictor of exam score.

The following drawing summarizes the strength and direction of the correlation coefficient.

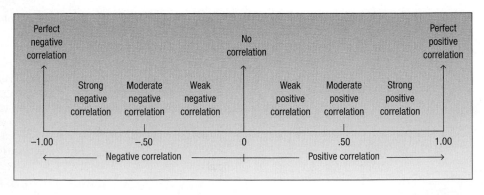

Examples of degrees of correlation

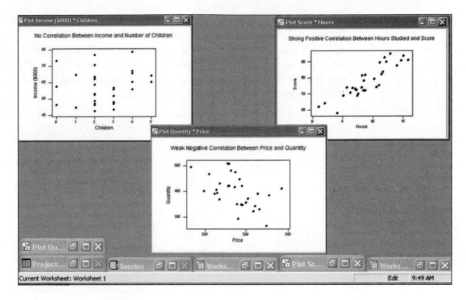

CHART 13–3 Scatter Diagrams Depicting Zero, Weak, and Strong Correlation

CORRELATION COEFFICIENT A measure of the strength of the linear relationship between two variables.

The characteristics of the correlation coefficient are summarized below.

CHARACTERISTICS OF THE CORRELATION COEFFICIENT
1. The sample correlation coefficient is identified by the lowercase letter r.
2. It shows the direction and strength of the linear relationship between two interval- or ratio-scale variables.
3. It ranges from -1 up to and including $+1$.
4. A value near 0 indicates there is little relationship between the variables.
5. A value near 1 indicates a strong direct or positive relationship between the variables.
6. A value near -1 indicates a strong inverse or negative relationship between the variables.

How is the value of the correlation coefficient determined? We will use the Copier Sales of America data, which are reported in Table 13–2, as an example. We begin

TABLE 13–2 Sales Calls and Copiers Sold for 10 Salespeople

Sales Representative	Sales Calls, (X)	Copiers Sold, (Y)
Tom Keller	20	30
Jeff Hall	40	60
Brian Virost	20	40
Greg Fish	30	60
Susan Welch	10	30
Carlos Ramirez	10	40
Rich Niles	20	40
Mike Kiel	20	50
Mark Reynolds	20	30
Soni Jones	30	70
Total	220	450

with a scatter diagram, similar to Chart 13–2. Draw a vertical line through the data values at the mean of the *X*-values and a horizontal line at the mean of the *Y*-values. In Chart 13–4, we've added a vertical line at 22.0 calls ($\overline{X}$ = $\Sigma X/n$ = 220/10 = 22) and a horizontal line at 45.0 copiers ($\overline{Y}$ = $\Sigma Y/n$ = 450/10 = 45.0). These lines pass through the "center" of the data and divide the scatter diagram into four quadrants. Think of moving the origin from (0, 0) to (22, 45).

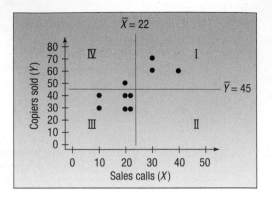

CHART 13–4 Computation of the Correlation Coefficient

Two variables are positively related when the number of copiers sold is above the mean and the number of sales calls is also above the mean. These points appear in the upper-right quadrant (labeled Quadrant I) of Chart 13–4. Similarly, when the number of copiers sold is less than the mean, so is the number of sales calls. These points fall in the lower-left quadrant of Chart 13–4 (labeled Quadrant III). For example, the last person on the list in Table 13–2, Soni Jones, made 30 sales calls and sold 70 copiers. These values are above their respective means, so this point is located in Quadrant I which is in the upper-right quadrant. She made 8 ($X - \overline{X}$ = 30 − 22) more sales calls than the mean and sold 25 ($Y - \overline{Y}$ = 70 − 45) more copiers than the mean. Tom Keller, the first name on the list in Table 13–2, made 20 sales calls and sold 30 copiers. Both of these values are less than their respective mean; hence this point is in the lower-left quadrant. Tom made 2 less sales calls and sold 15 less copiers than the respective means. The deviations from the mean number of sales calls and for the mean number of copiers sold are summarized in Table 13–3 for the 10 sales representatives. The sum of the products of the deviations from the respective means is 900. That is, the term $\Sigma(X - \overline{X})(Y - \overline{Y})$ = 900.

In both the upper-right and the lower-left quadrants, the product of ($X - \overline{X}$)($Y - \overline{Y}$) is positive because both of the factors have the same sign. In our example, this

TABLE 13–3 Deviations from the Mean and Their Products

Sales Representative	Calls, X	Sales, Y	$X - \overline{X}$	$Y - \overline{Y}$	$(X - \overline{X})(Y - \overline{Y})$
Tom Keller	20	30	−2	−15	30
Jeff Hall	40	60	18	15	270
Brian Virost	20	40	−2	−5	10
Greg Fish	30	60	8	15	120
Susan Welch	10	30	−12	−15	180
Carlos Ramirez	10	40	−12	−5	60
Rich Niles	20	40	−2	−5	10
Mike Kiel	20	50	−2	5	−10
Mark Reynolds	20	30	−2	−15	30
Soni Jones	30	70	8	25	200
					900

happens for all sales representatives except Mike Kiel. We can therefore expect the correlation coefficient to have a positive value.

If the two variables are inversely related, one variable will be above the mean and the other below the mean. Most of the points in this case occur in the upper-left and lower-right quadrants, that is, Quadrant II and IV. Now $(X - \overline{X})$ and $(Y - \overline{Y})$ will have opposite signs, so their product is negative. The resulting correlation coefficient is negative.

What happens if there is no linear relationship between the two variables? The points in the scatter diagram will appear in all four quadrants. The negative products of $(X - \overline{X})(Y - \overline{Y})$ offset the positive products, so the sum is near zero. This leads to a correlation coefficient near zero. So, the term $\Sigma(X - \overline{X})(Y - \overline{Y})$ drives the strength as well as the sign of the relationship between the two variables.

The correlation coefficient also needs to be unaffected by the units of the two variables. For example, if we had used hundreds of copiers sold instead of the number sold, the correlation coefficient would be the same. The correlation coefficient is independent of the scale used if we divide the term $\Sigma(X - \overline{X})(Y - \overline{Y})$ by the sample standard deviations. It is also made independent of the sample size and bounded by the values $+1.00$ and -1.00 if we divide by $(n - 1)$.

This reasoning leads to the following formula:

CORRELATION COEFFICIENT	$r = \dfrac{\Sigma(X - \overline{X})(Y - \overline{Y})}{(n - 1)s_x s_y}$	[13–1]

To compute the correlation coefficient, we use the standard deviations of the sample of 10 sales calls and 10 copiers sold. We could use formula (3–9) to calculate the sample standard deviations or we could use a software package. For the specific Excel and Minitab commands, see the **Software Commands** section at the end of Chapter 3. The following is the Excel output. The standard deviation of the number of sales calls is 9.189 and of the number of copiers sold 14.337.

⊞ Calls and Sales							
	A	**B**	**C**	**D**	**E**	**F**	**G**	**H**
1	**Calls**	**Sales**		**Calls**			**Sales**	
2	20	30						
3	40	60		Mean	22.000		Mean	45.000
4	20	40		Standard Error	2.906		Standard Error	4.534
5	30	60		Median	20.000		Median	40.000
6	10	30		Mode	20.000		Mode	30.000
7	10	40		Standard Deviation	9.189		Standard Deviation	14.337
8	20	40		Sample Variance	84.444		Sample Variance	205.556
9	20	50		Kurtosis	0.396		Kurtosis	-1.001
10	20	30		Skewness	0.601		Skewness	0.566
11	30	70		Range	30.000		Range	40.000
12				Minimum	10.000		Minimum	30.000
13				Maximum	40.000		Maximum	70.000
14				Sum	220.000		Sum	450.000
15				Count	10.000		Count	10.000

We now insert these values into formula (13–1) to determine the correlation coefficient:

$$r = \frac{\Sigma(X - \overline{X})(Y - \overline{Y})}{(n - 1)s_x s_y} = \frac{900}{(10 - 1)(9.189)(14.337)} = 0.759$$

How do we interpret a correlation of 0.759? First, it is positive, so we conclude there is a direct relationship between the number of sales calls and the number of copiers sold. This confirms our reasoning based on the scatter diagram,

Chart 13–4. The value of 0.759 is fairly close to 1.00, so we conclude that the association is strong.

We must be careful with the interpretation. The correlation of 0.759 indicates a strong positive association between the variables. Ms. Bancer would be correct to encourage the sales personnel to make that extra sales call, because the number of sales calls made is related to the number of copiers sold. However, does this mean that more sales calls *cause* more sales? No, we have not demonstrated cause and effect here, only that the two variables—sales calls and copiers sold—are related.

If there is a strong relationship (say, .91) between two variables, we are tempted to assume that an increase or decrease in one variable *causes* a change in the other variable. For example, it can be shown that the consumption of Georgia peanuts and the consumption of aspirin have a strong correlation. However, this does not indicate that an increase in the consumption of peanuts *caused* the consumption of aspirin to increase. Likewise, the incomes of professors and the number of inmates in mental institutions have increased proportionately. Further, as the population of donkeys has decreased, there has been an increase in the number of doctoral degrees granted. Relationships such as these are called **spurious correlations.** What we can conclude when we find two variables with a strong correlation is that there is a relationship or association between the two variables, not that a change in one causes a change in the other.

Example

The Applewood Auto Group's marketing department believes younger buyers purchase vehicles on which lower profits are earned and the older buyers purchase vehicles on which higher profits are earned. They would like to use this information as part of an upcoming advertising campaign to try to attract older buyers on which the profits tend to be higher. Develop a scatter diagram depicting the relationship between vehicle profits and age of the buyer. Use statistical software to determine the correlation coefficient. Would this be a useful advertising feature?

Solution

Using the Applewood Auto Group example, the first step is to graph the data using a scatter plot. It is shown in Chart 13–5.

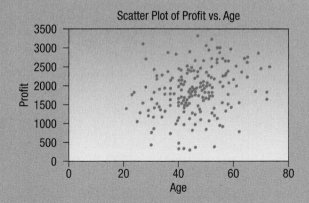

CHART 13–5 Scatter Diagram of Applewood Auto Group Data

The scatter diagram suggests that a positive relationship does exist between age and profit; however, that relationship does not appear strong.

The next step is to calculate the correlation coefficient to evaluate the relative strength of the relationship. Statistical software provides an easy way to calculate the value of the correlation coefficient. The Excel output follows.

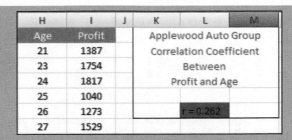

H	I	J	K	L	M
Age	Profit		Applewood Auto Group		
21	1387		Correlation Coefficient		
23	1754		Between		
24	1817		Profit and Age		
25	1040				
26	1273		r = 0.262		
27	1529				

For this data, $r = 0.262$. To evaluate the relationship between a buyer's age and the profit on a car sale:

1. The relationship is positive or direct. Why? Because the sign of the correlation coefficient is positive. This confirms that as the age of the buyer increases, the profit on a car sale also increases.
2. The relationship between the two variables is weak. For a positive relationship, values of the correlation coefficient close to one indicate stronger relationships. In this case, $r = 0.262$. It is closer to zero, and we would observe that the relationship is not very strong.

It is not recommended that Applewood use this information as part of an advertising campaign to attract older more profitable buyers.

Self-Review 13–1

Haverty's Furniture is a family business that has been selling to retail customers in the Chicago area for many years. The company advertises extensively on radio, TV, and the Internet, emphasizing low prices and easy credit terms. The owner would like to review the relationship between sales and the amount spent on advertising. Below is information on sales and advertising expense for the last four months.

Month	Advertising Expense ($ million)	Sales Revenue ($ million)
July	2	7
August	1	3
September	3	8
October	4	10

(a) The owner wants to forecast sales on the basis of advertising expense. Which variable is the dependent variable? Which variable is the independent variable?
(b) Draw a scatter diagram.
(c) Determine the correlation coefficient.
(d) Interpret the strength of the correlation coefficient.

Exercises

connect

1. The following sample observations were randomly selected.

X	4	5	3	6	10
y	4	6	5	7	7

Determine the correlation coefficient and interpret the relationship between X and Y.

2. The following sample observations were randomly selected.

X	5	3	6	3	4	4	6	8
Y	13	15	7	12	13	11	9	5

Determine the correlation coefficient and interpret the relationship between X and Y.

3. Bi-lo Appliance Super-Store has outlets in several large metropolitan areas in New England. The general sales manager aired a commercial for a digital camera on selected local TV stations prior to a sale starting on Saturday and ending Sunday. She obtained the information for Saturday–Sunday digital camera sales at the various outlets and paired it with the number of times the advertisement was shown on the local TV stations. The purpose is to find whether there is any relationship between the number of times the advertisement was aired and digital camera sales. The pairings are:

Location of TV Station	Number of Airings	Saturday–Sunday Sales ($ thousands)
Providence	4	15
Springfield	2	8
New Haven	5	21
Boston	6	24
Hartford	3	17

a. What is the dependent variable?
b. Draw a scatter diagram.
c. Determine the correlation coefficient.
d. Interpret these statistical measures.

4. The production department of Celltronics International wants to explore the relationship between the number of employees who assemble a subassembly and the number produced. As an experiment, two employees were assigned to assemble the subassemblies. They produced 15 during a one-hour period. Then four employees assembled them. They produced 25 during a one-hour period. The complete set of paired observations follows.

Number of Assemblers	One-Hour Production (units)
2	15
4	25
1	10
5	40
3	30

The dependent variable is production; that is, it is assumed that different levels of production result from a different number of employees.
a. Draw a scatter diagram.
b. Based on the scatter diagram, does there appear to be any relationship between the number of assemblers and production? Explain.
c. Compute the correlation coefficient.

5. The city council of Pine Bluffs is considering increasing the number of police in an effort to reduce crime. Before making a final decision, the council asked the chief of police to survey other cities of similar size to determine the relationship between the number of police and the number of crimes reported. The chief gathered the following sample information. 🔵

City	Police	Number of Crimes	City	Police	Number of Crimes
Oxford	15	17	Holgate	17	7
Starksville	17	13	Carey	12	21
Danville	25	5	Whistler	11	19
Athens	27	7	Woodville	22	6

   a. Which variable is the dependent variable and which is the independent variable? Hint: If you were the Chief of Police, which variable would you decide? Which variable is the random variable?
   b. Draw a scatter diagram.
   c. Determine the correlation coefficient.
   d. Interpret the correlation coefficient. Does it surprise you that the correlation coefficient is negative?

6. The owner of Maumee Ford-Mercury-Volvo wants to study the relationship between the age of a car and its selling price. Listed below is a random sample of 12 used cars sold at the dealership during the last year. 🔵

Car	Age (years)	Selling Price ($000)	Car	Age (years)	Selling Price ($000)
1	9	8.1	7	8	7.6
2	7	6.0	8	11	8.0
3	11	3.6	9	10	8.0
4	12	4.0	10	12	6.0
5	8	5.0	11	6	8.6
6	7	10.0	12	6	8.0

   a. Draw a scatter diagram.
   b. Determine the correlation coefficient.
   c. Interpret the correlation coefficient. Does it surprise you that the correlation coefficient is negative?

13.4 Testing the Significance of the Correlation Coefficient

Recall that the sales manager of Copier Sales of America found the correlation between the number of sales calls and the number of copiers sold was 0.759. This indicated a strong positive association between the two variables. However, only 10 salespeople were sampled. Could it be that the correlation in the population is actually 0? This would mean the correlation of 0.759 was due to chance. The population in this example is all the salespeople employed by the firm.

Could the correlation in the population be zero?

Resolving this dilemma requires a statistical test to answer the question: Could there be zero correlation in the population from which the sample was selected? To put it another way, did the computed r come from a population of paired observations with zero correlation? To continue our convention of allowing Greek letters to represent a population parameter, we will let ρ represent the correlation in the population. It is pronounced "rho."

We will continue with the illustration involving sales calls and copiers sold. We employ the same hypothesis testing steps described in Chapter 10. The null hypothesis and the alternate hypothesis are:

H_0: $\rho = 0$ (The correlation in the population is zero.)
H_1: $\rho \neq 0$ (The correlation in the population is different from zero.)

From the way H_1 is stated, we know that the test is two-tailed.
    The formula for t is:

t TEST FOR THE CORRELATION COEFFICIENT	$t = \dfrac{r\sqrt{n-2}}{\sqrt{1-r^2}}$ with $n - 2$ degrees of freedom	**[13–2]**

Using the .05 level of significance, the decision rule in this instance states that if the computed t falls in the range between plus 2.306 and minus 2.306, the null hypothesis is not rejected. To locate the critical value of 2.306, refer to Appendix B.2 for $df = n - 2 = 10 - 2 = 8$. See Chart 13–6.

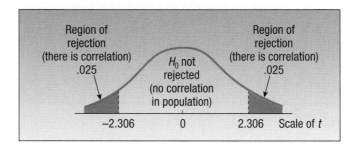

CHART 13–6 Decision Rule for Test of Hypothesis at .05 Significance Level and 8 *df*

Applying formula (13–2) to the example regarding the number of sales calls and units sold:

$$t = \frac{r\sqrt{n-2}}{\sqrt{1-r^2}} = \frac{.759\sqrt{10-2}}{\sqrt{1-.759^2}} = 3.297$$

The computed t is in the rejection region. Thus, H_0 is rejected at the .05 significance level. Hence we conclude the correlation in the population is not zero. From a practical standpoint, it indicates to the sales manager that there is a correlation with respect to the number of sales calls made and the number of copiers sold in the population of salespeople.
    We can also interpret the test of hypothesis in terms of *p*-values. A *p*-value is the likelihood of finding a value of the test statistic more extreme than the one computed, when H_0 is true. To determine the *p*-value, go to the *t* distribution in Appendix B.2 and find the row for 8 degrees of freedom. The value of the test statistic is 3.297, so in the row for 8 degrees of freedom and a two-tailed test, find the value closest to 3.297. For a two-tailed test at the .02 significance level, the critical value is 2.896, and the critical value at the .01 significance level is 3.355. Because 3.297 is between 2.896 and 3.355, we conclude that the *p*-value is between .01 and .02.
    Both Minitab and Excel will report the correlation between two variables. In addition to the correlation, Minitab reports the *p*-value for the test of hypothesis that the correlation in the population between the two variables is 0. The Minitab output is at the top of the following page.

↓	C1	C2	C3	C4	C5	C6	C7	C8
	Calls	Sales						
1	20	30						
2	40	60						
3	20	40						
4	30	60						
5	10	30						
6	10	40						
7	20	40						
8	20	50						
9	20	30						
10	30	70						

Welcome to Minitab, press F1 for help.

Correlations: Calls, Sales

Pearson correlation of Calls and Sales = 0.759
P-Value = 0.011

Example

In the Example on page 399, we found that the correlation coefficient between the profit on the sale of a vehicle by the Applewood Auto Group and the age of the person that purchased the vehicle was 0.262. Because the sign of the correlation coefficient was positive, we concluded there was a direct relationship between the two variables. However, because the amount of correlation was low—that is, near zero—we concluded that an advertising campaign directed toward the older buyers, where there is a large profit, was not warranted. Does this mean we should conclude that there is no relationship between the two variables? Use the .05 significance level.

Solution

To begin to answer the question in the last sentence above, we need to clarify the sample and population issues. Let's assume that the data collected on the 180 vehicles sold by the Applewood Group is a sample from the population of *all* vehicles sold over many years by the Applewood Auto Group. The Greek letter ρ is the correlation coefficient in the population and r the correlation coefficient in the sample.

Our next step is to set up the null hypothesis and the alternate hypothesis. We test the null hypothesis that the correlation coefficient is equal to or less than zero. The alternate hypothesis is that there is positive correlation between the two variables.

H_0: $\rho \leq 0$ (The correlation in the population is zero.)
H_1: $\rho > 0$ (The correlation in the population is positive.)

This is a one-tailed test because we are interested in confirming a positive association between the variables. The test statistic follows the t distribution with $n - 2$ degrees of freedom, so the degrees of freedom is $180 - 2 = 178$. However, 178 degrees of freedom is not in Appendix B.2. The closest value is 180, so we will use that value. Our decision rule is to reject the null hypothesis if the computed value of the test statistic is greater than 1.653.

We use formula (13–2) to find the value of the test statistic.

$$t = \frac{r\sqrt{n-2}}{\sqrt{1-r^2}} = \frac{0.262\sqrt{180-2}}{\sqrt{1-0.262^2}} = 3.622$$

Comparing the value of our test statistic of 3.622 to the critical value of 1.653, we reject the null hypothesis. We conclude that the sample correlation coefficient of 0.262 is too large to have come from a population with no correlation. To put our results another way, there is a positive correlation between profits and age in the population.

This result is confusing and seems contradictory. On one hand, we observed that the correlation coefficient did not indicate a very strong relationship and that the Applewood Auto Group marketing department should not use this information for its promotion and advertising decisions. On the other hand, the hypothesis test indicated that the correlation coefficient is not equal to zero and that a positive relationship between age and profit exists. How can this be? We must be very careful about the interpretation of the hypothesis test results. The conclusion is that the correlation coefficient is not equal to zero and that there is a positive relationship between the amount of profit earned and the age of the buyer. The result of the hypothesis test only shows that a relationship exists. The hypothesis test makes no claims regarding the *strength* of the relationship.

Self-Review 13–2   A sample of 25 mayoral campaigns in medium-sized cities with populations between 50,000 and 250,000 showed that the correlation between the percent of the vote received and the amount spent on the campaign by the candidate was .43. At the .05 significance level, is there a positive association between the variables?

Exercises

7. The following hypotheses are given.

    H_0: $\rho \leq 0$
    H_1: $\rho > 0$

    A random sample of 12 paired observations indicated a correlation of .32. Can we conclude that the correlation in the population is greater than zero? Use the .05 significance level.

8. The following hypotheses are given.

    H_0: $\rho \geq 0$
    H_1: $\rho < 0$

    A random sample of 15 paired observations have a correlation of −.46. Can we conclude that the correlation in the population is less than zero? Use the .05 significance level.

9. Pennsylvania Refining Company is studying the relationship between the pump price of gasoline and the number of gallons sold. For a sample of 20 stations last Tuesday, the correlation was .78. At the .01 significance level, is the correlation in the population greater than zero?

10. A study of 20 worldwide financial institutions showed the correlation between their assets and pretax profit to be .86. At the .05 significance level, can we conclude that there is positive correlation in the population?

11. The Airline Passenger Association studied the relationship between the number of passengers on a particular flight and the cost of the flight. It seems logical that more passengers on the flight will result in more weight and more luggage, which in turn will result in higher fuel costs. For a sample of 15 flights, the correlation between the number of passengers and total fuel cost was .667. Is it reasonable to conclude that there is positive association in the population between the two variables? Use the .01 significance level.

12. The Student Government Association at Middle Carolina University wanted to demonstrate the relationship between the number of beers a student drinks and their blood alcohol content (BAC). A random sample of 18 students participated in a study in which each participating student was randomly assigned a number of 12-ounce cans of beer to drink. Thirty minutes after consuming their assigned number of beers a member of the

local sheriff's office measured their blood alcohol content. The sample information is reported below.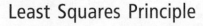

Student	Beers	BAC	Student	Beers	BAC
1	6	0.10	10	3	0.07
2	7	0.09	11	3	0.05
3	7	0.09	12	7	0.08
4	4	0.10	13	1	0.04
5	5	0.10	14	4	0.07
6	3	0.07	15	2	0.06
7	3	0.10	16	7	0.12
8	6	0.12	17	2	0.05
9	6	0.09	18	1	0.02

Use a statistical software package to answer the following questions.

a. Develop a scatter diagram for the number of beers consumed and BAC. Comment on the relationship. Does it appear to be strong or weak? Does it appear to be positive or inverse?

b. Determine the correlation coefficient.

c. At the .01 significance level, is it reasonable to conclude that there is a positive relationship in the population between the number of beers consumed and the BAC? What is the *p*-value?

13.5 Regression Analysis

LO 13-3 Apply regression analysis to estimate the linear relationship between two variables.

In the previous sections of this chapter, we evaluated the direction and the significance of the linear relationship between two variables by finding the correlation coefficient. If the correlation coefficient is significantly different from zero, then the next step is to develop an equation to express the *linear* relationship between the two variables. Using this equation, we will be able to estimate the value of the dependent variable Y based on a selected value of the independent variable X. The technique used to develop the equation and provide the estimates is called **regression analysis.**

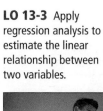

In Table 13–1, we reported the number of sales calls and the number of units sold for a sample of 10 sales representatives employed by Copier Sales of America. Chart 13–1 portrayed this information in a scatter diagram. Recall that we tested the significance of the correlation coefficient (r = 0.759) and concluded that a significant relationship exists between the two variables. Now we want to develop a linear equation that expresses the relationship between the number of sales calls, the independent variable, and the number of units sold, the dependent variable. The equation for the line used to estimate Y on the basis of X is referred to as the **regression equation.**

> **REGRESSION EQUATION** An equation that expresses the linear relationship between two variables.

Least Squares Principle

In regression analysis, our objective is to use the data to position a line that best represents the relationship between the two variables. Our first approach is to use a scatter diagram to visually position the line.

The scatter diagram in Chart 13–1 is reproduced in Chart 13–7, with a line drawn with a ruler through the dots to illustrate that a line would probably fit the data.

However, the line drawn using a straight edge has one disadvantage: Its position is based in part on the judgment of the person drawing the line. The hand-drawn lines in Chart 13–8 represent the judgments of four people. All the lines except line *A* seem to be reasonable. That is, each line is centered among the graphed data. However, each would result in a different estimate of units sold for a particular number of sales calls.

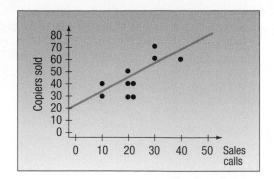

CHART 13–7 Sales Calls and Copiers Sold for 10 Sales Representatives

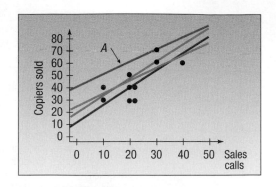

CHART 13–8 Four Lines Superimposed on the Scatter Diagram

However, we would prefer a method that results in a single, best regression line. This method is called the least squares principle. It gives what is commonly referred to as the "best-fitting" line.

> **LEAST SQUARES PRINCIPLE** A mathematical procedure that uses the data to position a line with the objective of minimizing the sum of the squares of the vertical distances between the actual *Y* values and the predicted values of *Y*.

To illustrate this concept, the same data are plotted in the three charts that follow. The dots are the actual values of *Y,* and the asterisks are the predicted values of *Y* for a given value of *X*. The regression line in Chart 13–9 was determined using the least squares method. It is the best-fitting line because the sum of the squares of the vertical deviations about it is at a minimum. The first plotted point ($X = 3$, $Y = 8$) deviates by 2 from the line, found by $10 - 8$. The deviation squared is 4. The squared deviation for the plotted point $X = 4$, $Y = 18$ is 16. The squared deviation for the plotted point $X = 5$, $Y = 16$ is 4. The sum of the squared deviations is 24, found by $4 + 16 + 4$.

Assume that the lines in Charts 13–10 and 13–11 were drawn with a straight edge. The sum of the squared vertical deviations in Chart 13–10 is 44. For Chart 13–11,

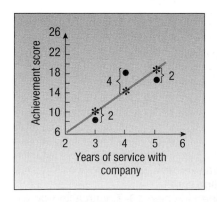

CHART 13–9 The Least Squares Line

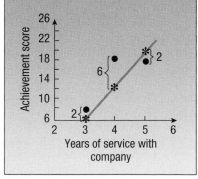

CHART 13–10 Line Drawn with a Straight Edge

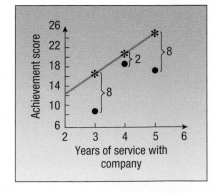

CHART 13–11 Different Line Drawn with a Straight Edge

it is 132. Both sums are greater than the sum for the line in Chart 13–9, found by using the least squares method.

The equation of a line has the form

GENERAL FORM OF LINEAR REGRESSION EQUATION $\hat{Y} = a + bX$ **[13–3]**

where:

$\hat{Y}$, read Y hat, is the estimated value of the Y variable for a selected X value.
a is the Y-intercept. It is the estimated value of Y when X = 0. Another way to put it is: a is the estimated value of Y where the regression line crosses the Y-axis when X is zero.
b is the slope of the line, or the average change in $\hat{Y}$ for each change of one unit (either increase or decrease) in the independent variable X.
X is any value of the independent variable that is selected.

The general form of the linear regression equation is exactly the same form as the equation of any line. a is the Y intercept and b is the slope. The purpose of regression analysis is to calculate the values of a and b to develop a linear equation that best fits the data.

The formulas for a and b are:

SLOPE OF THE REGRESSION LINE $b = r\dfrac{s_y}{s_x}$ **[13–4]**

where:

r is the correlation coefficient.
s_y is the standard deviation of Y (the dependent variable).
s_x is the standard deviation of X (the independent variable).

Y-INTERCEPT $a = \overline{Y} - b\overline{X}$ **[13–5]**

where:

$\overline{Y}$ is the mean of Y (the dependent variable).
$\overline{X}$ is the mean of X (the independent variable).

Example

Recall the example involving Copier Sales of America. The sales manager gathered information on the number of sales calls made and the number of copiers sold for a random sample of 10 sales representatives. As a part of her presentation at the upcoming sales meeting, Ms. Bancer, the sales manager, would like to offer specific information about the relationship between the number of sales calls and the number of copiers sold. Use the least squares method to determine a linear equation to express the relationship between the two variables. What is the expected number of copiers sold by a representative who made 20 calls?

Solution

The first step in determining the regression equation is to find the slope of the least squares regression line. That is, we need the value of b. On page 397, we determined the correlation coefficient r (.759). In the Excel output on the same page, we determined the standard deviation of the independent variable X (9.189) and the standard deviation of the dependent variable Y (14.337). The values are inserted in formula (13–4).

$$b = r\left(\frac{s_y}{s_x}\right) = .759\left(\frac{14.337}{9.189}\right) = 1.1842$$

Next we need to find the value of *a*. To do this, we use the value for *b* that we just calculated as well as the means for the number of sales calls and the number of copiers sold. These means are also available in the Excel printout on page 397. From formula (13–5):

$$a = \bar{Y} - b\bar{X} = 45 - 1.1842(22) = 18.9476$$

LO 13-4 Interpret the regression analysis.

Thus, the regression equation is $\hat{Y} = 18.9476 + 1.1842X$. So if a salesperson makes 20 calls, he or she can expect to sell 42.6316 copiers, found by $\hat{Y} = 18.9476 + 1.1842X = 18.9476 + 1.1842(20)$. The *b* value of 1.1842 indicates that for each additional sales call made the sales representative can expect to increase the number of copiers sold by about 1.2. To put it another way, five additional sales calls in a month will result in about six more copiers being sold, found by 1.1842(5) = 5.921.

The *a* value of 18.9476 is the point where the equation crosses the *Y*-axis. A literal translation is that if no sales calls are made, that is, *X* = 0, 18.9476 copiers will be sold. Note that *X* = 0 is outside the range of values included in the sample and, therefore, should not be used to estimate the number of copiers sold. The sales calls ranged from 10 to 40, so estimates should be limited to that range.

Statistics in Action

In finance, investors are interested in the trade-off between returns and risk. One technique to quantify risk is a regression analysis of a company's stock price (dependent variable) and an average measure of the stock market (independent variable). Often the Standard and Poor's (S&P) 500 Index is used to estimate the market. The regression coefficient, called beta in finance, shows the change in a company's stock price for a one-unit change in the S&P Index. For *(continued)*

Drawing the Regression Line

The least squares equation, $\hat{Y} = 18.9476 + 1.1842X$, can be drawn on the scatter diagram. The first sales representative in the sample is Tom Keller. He made 20 calls. His estimated number of copiers sold is $\hat{Y} = 18.9476 + 1.1842(20) = 42.6316$. The plot *X* = 20 and $\hat{Y} = 42.6316$ is located by moving to 20 on the *X*-axis and then going vertically to 42.6316. The other points on the regression equation can be determined by substituting the particular value of *X* into the regression equation. All the points are connected to give the line. See Chart 13–12.

Sales Representative	Sales Calls (*X*)	Estimated Sales ($\hat{Y}$)	Sales Representative	Sales Calls (*X*)	Estimated Sales ($\hat{Y}$)
Tom Keller	20	42.6316	Carlos Ramirez	10	30.7896
Jeff Hall	40	66.3156	Rich Niles	20	42.6316
Brian Virost	20	42.6316	Mike Kiel	20	42.6316
Greg Fish	30	54.4736	Mark Reynolds	20	42.6316
Susan Welch	10	30.7896	Soni Jones	30	54.4736

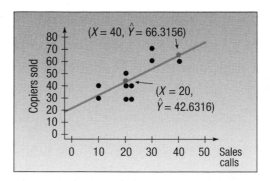

CHART 13–12 The Line of Regression Drawn on the Scatter Diagram

example, if a stock has a beta of 1.5, then when the S&P index increases by 1%, the stock price will increase by 1.5%. The opposite is also true. If the S&P decreases by 1%, the stock price will decrease by 1.5%. If the beta is 1.0, then a 1% change in the index should show a 1% change in a stock price. If the beta is less than 1.0, then a 1% change in the index shows less than a 1% change in the stock price.

The least squares regression line has some interesting and unique features. First, it will always pass through the point $(\bar{X}, \bar{Y})$. To show this is true, we can use the mean number of sales calls to predict the number of copiers sold. In this example, the mean number of sales calls is 22.0, found by $\bar{X} = 220/10$. The mean number of copiers sold is 45.0, found by $\bar{Y} = 450/10 = 45$. If we let $X = 22$ and then use the regression equation to find the estimated value for $\hat{Y}$, the result is:

$$\hat{Y} = 18.9476 + 1.1842(22) = 45$$

The estimated number of copiers sold is exactly equal to the mean number of copiers sold. This simple example shows the regression line will pass through the point represented by the two means. In this case, the regression equation will pass through the point $X = 22$ and $Y = 45$.

Second, as we discussed earlier in this section, there is no other line through the data where the sum of the squared deviations is smaller. To put it another way, the term $\Sigma(Y - \hat{Y})^2$ is smaller for the least squares regression equation than for any other equation. We use Excel to demonstrate this condition.

Residuals

	A	B	C	D	E	F	G	H	I	J
1	Sales	Calls	Sales	Estimated Sales						
2	Representative	(X)	(Y)	$\hat{Y}$	$(Y-\hat{Y})$	$(Y-\hat{Y})^2$	Y^*	$(Y-Y^*)^2$	Y^{**}	$(Y-Y^{**})^2$
3	Tom Keller	20	30	42.6316	-12.6316	159.5573	43	169	40	100
4	Jeff Hall	40	60	66.3156	-6.3156	39.8868	67	49	60	0
5	Brian Virost	20	40	42.6316	-2.6316	6.9253	43	9	40	0
6	Greg Fish	30	60	54.4736	5.5264	30.5411	55	25	50	100
7	Susan Welch	10	30	30.7896	-0.7896	0.6235	31	1	30	0
8	Carlos Ramirez	10	40	30.7896	9.2104	84.8315	31	81	30	100
9	Rich Niles	20	40	42.6316	-2.6316	6.9253	43	9	40	0
10	Mike Kiel	20	50	42.6316	7.3684	54.2933	43	49	40	100
11	Mark Reynolds	20	30	42.6316	-12.6316	159.5573	43	169	40	100
12	Soni Jones	30	70	54.4736	15.5264	241.0691	55	225	50	400
13					0.00	784.2105		786		900
14				Sum of					Least Squares Value	
15				Residuals						

In Columns A, B, and C in the Excel spreadsheet above, we duplicated the sample information on sales and copiers sold from Table 13–1. In column D, we provide the estimated sales values, the $\hat{Y}$ values, as calculated above.

In column E, we calculate the **residuals,** or the error values. This is the difference between the actual values and the predicted values. That is, column E is $(Y - \hat{Y})$. In row 12, the estimate for Soni Jones is

$$\hat{Y} = 18.9476 + 1.1842(30) = 54.4736$$

Soni Jones' actual sales, row 12 column C, is 70. So the residual, or error of estimate, is

$$(Y - \hat{Y}) = (70 - 54.4736) = 15.5264$$

This value reflects the amount the predicted value of sales is "off" from the actual sales value.

Next, in Column F, we square the residuals for each of the sales representatives and total the result. The total is 784.2105.

$$\Sigma(Y - \hat{Y})^2 = 159.5573 + 39.8868 + \cdots + 241.0691 = 784.2105$$

This is the sum of the squared differences or the least squares value. There is no other line through these 10 data points where the sum of the squared differences is smaller.

We can demonstrate the least squares criterion by choosing two arbitrary equations that are close to the least squares equation and determining the sum of the squared differences for these equations. In column G, we use the equation $Y^* = 19 + 1.2X$ to find the predicted value. Notice this equation is very similar to the least squares equation. In Column H, we determine the residuals and square these residuals. For the first sales representative, Tom Keller, row one,

$$Y^* = 19 + 1.2(20) = 43$$

$$(Y - Y^*)^2 = (43 - 30)^2 = 169$$

This procedure is continued for the other nine sales representatives and the squared residuals totaled. The result is 786. This is a larger value (786 versus 784.2105) than the residuals for the least squares line.

In columns I and J on the output, we repeat the above process for yet another equation $Y^{**} = 20 + X$. Again, this equation is similar to the least squares equation. The details for row one are:

$$Y^{**} = 20 + X = 20 + 20 = 40$$

$$(Y - Y^{**})^2 = (30 - 40)^2 = 100$$

This procedure is continued for the other nine sales representatives and the residuals totaled. The result is 900, which is also larger than the least squares values.

What have we shown with the example? The sum of the squared residuals $[\Sigma(Y - \hat{Y})^2]$ for the least squares equation is smaller than for other selected lines. The bottom line is you will not be able to find a line passing through these data points where the sum of the squared residuals is smaller.

Self-Review 13–3

Refer to Self-Review 13–1, where the owner of Haverty's Furniture Company was studying the relationship between sales and the amount spent on advertising. The sales information for the last four months is repeated below.

Month	Advertising Expense ($ million)	Sales Revenue ($ million)
July	2	7
August	1	3
September	3	8
October	4	10

(a) Determine the regression equation.
(b) Interpret the values of a and b.
(c) Estimate sales when $3 million is spent on advertising.

Exercises

connect

13. The following sample observations were randomly selected.

X:	4	5	3	6	10
Y:	4	6	5	7	7

  a. Determine the regression equation.
  b. Determine the value of $\hat{Y}$ when X is 7.

14. The following sample observations were randomly selected.

X:	5	3	6	3	4	4	6	8
Y:	13	15	7	12	13	11	9	5

  a. Determine the regression equation.
  b. Determine the value of $\hat{Y}$ when X is 7.
15. Bradford Electric Illuminating Company is studying the relationship between kilowatt-hours (thousands) used and the number of rooms in a private single-family residence. A random sample of 10 homes yielded the following. df

Number of Rooms	Kilowatt-Hours (thousands)	Number of Rooms	Kilowatt-Hours (thousands)
12	9	8	6
9	7	10	8
14	10	10	10
6	5	5	4
10	8	7	7

  a. Determine the regression equation.
  b. Determine the number of kilowatt-hours, in thousands, for a six-room house.
16. Mr. James McWhinney, president of Daniel-James Financial Services, believes there is a relationship between the number of client contacts and the dollar amount of sales. To document this assertion, Mr. McWhinney gathered the following sample information. The X column indicates the number of client contacts last month, and the Y column shows the value of sales ($ thousands) last month for each client sampled. df

Number of Contacts, X	Sales ($ thousands), Y	Number of Contacts, X	Sales ($ thousands), Y
14	24	23	30
12	14	48	90
20	28	50	85
16	30	55	120
46	80	50	110

  a. Determine the regression equation.
  b. Determine the estimated sales if 40 contacts are made.
17. A recent article in *BusinessWeek* listed the "Best Small Companies." We are interested in the current results of the companies' sales and earnings. A random sample of 12 companies was selected and the sales and earnings, in millions of dollars, are reported below. df

Company	Sales ($ millions)	Earnings ($ millions)	Company	Sales ($ millions)	Earnings ($ millions)
Papa John's International	$89.2	$4.9	Checkmate Electronics	$17.5	$ 2.6
Applied Innovation	18.6	4.4	Royal Grip	11.9	1.7
Integracare	18.2	1.3	M-Wave	19.6	3.5
Wall Data	71.7	8.0	Serving-N-Slide	51.2	8.2
Davidson & Associates	58.6	6.6	Daig	28.6	6.0
Chico's FAS	46.8	4.1	Cobra Golf	69.2	12.8

Let sales be the independent variable and earnings be the dependent variable.
  a. Draw a scatter diagram.
  b. Compute the correlation coefficient.
  c. Determine the regression equation.
  d. For a small company with $50.0 million in sales, estimate the earnings.
18. We are studying mutual bond funds for the purpose of investing in several funds. For this particular study, we want to focus on the assets of a fund and its five-year performance. The question is: Can the five-year rate of return be estimated based on the assets of the

fund? Nine mutual funds were selected at random, and their assets and rates of return are shown below.

Fund	Assets ($ millions)	Return (%)	Fund	Assets ($ millions)	Return (%)
AARP High Quality Bond	$622.2	10.8	MFS Bond A	$494.5	11.6
Babson Bond L	160.4	11.3	Nichols Income	158.3	9.5
Compass Capital Fixed Income	275.7	11.4	T. Rowe Price Short-term	681.0	8.2
Galaxy Bond Retail	433.2	9.1	Thompson Income B	241.3	6.8
Keystone Custodian B-1	437.9	9.2			

    a. Draw a scatter diagram.
    b. Compute the correlation coefficient.
    c. Write a brief report of your findings for parts (b) and (c).
    d. Determine the regression equation. Use assets as the independent variable.
    e. For a fund with $400.0 million in sales, determine the five-year rate of return (in percent).
19. Refer to Exercise 5.
    a. Determine the regression equation.
    b. Estimate the number of crimes for a city with 20 police officers.
    c. Interpret the regression equation.
20. Refer to Exercise 6.
    a. Determine the regression equation.
    b. Estimate the selling price of a 10-year-old car.
    c. Interpret the regression equation.

13.6 Testing the Significance of the Slope

LO 13-5 Evaluate the significance of the slope of the regression equation.

In the prior section, we showed how to find the equation of the regression line that best fits the data. The method for finding the equation is based on the *least squares principle*. The purpose of the regression equation is to quantify a linear relationship between two variables.

The next step is to analyze the regression equation by conducting a test of hypothesis to see if the slope of the regression line is different from zero. Why is this important? If we can show that the slope of the line in the population is different from zero, then we can conclude that using the regression equation adds to our ability to predict or forecast the dependent variable based on the independent variable. If we cannot demonstrate that this slope is different from zero, then we conclude there is no merit to using the independent variable as a predictor. To put it another way, if we cannot show the slope of the line is different from zero, we might as well use the mean of the dependent variable as a predictor, rather than use the regression equation.

Following from the hypothesis-testing procedure in Chapter 10, the null and alternative hypotheses are:

H_0: $\beta = 0$
H_1: $\beta \neq 0$

We use β (the Greek letter beta) to represent the population slope for the regression equation. This is consistent with our policy to identify population parameters by Greek letters. We assumed the information regarding Copier Sales of America, Table 13–2, and the Example for the Applewood Auto Group are samples. Be careful here. Remember, this is a single sample, but when we selected a particular salesperson we identified two pieces of information, how many customers they called on and how many copiers they sold. It is still a single sample, however.

We identified the slope value as *b*. So our computed slope "*b*" is based on a sample and is an estimate of the population's slope, identified as "β." The null hypothesis is that the slope of the regression equation in the population is zero. If this is the case, the regression line is horizontal and there is no relationship between the independent variable, *X*, and the dependent variable, *Y*. In other words, the value of the dependent variable is the same for any value of the independent variable and does not offer us any help in estimating the value of the dependent variable.

What if the null hypothesis is rejected? If the null hypothesis is rejected and the alternate hypothesis accepted, this indicates that the slope of the regression line for the population is not equal to zero. That is, knowing the value of the independent variable allows us to make a better estimate of the dependent variable. To put it another way, a significant relationship exists between the two variables.

Before we test the hypothesis, we use statistical software to determine the needed regression statistics. We continue to use the Copier Sales of America data from Table 13–2 and use Excel to perform the necessary calculations. The following spreadsheet shows three tables to the right of the sample data.

Calls and Sales Regression

	A	B	C	D	E	F	G	H	I	J
1	Sales Representative	Calls	Sales		SUMMARY OUTPUT					
2	Tom Keller	20	30							
3	Jeff Hall	40	60		*Regression Statistics*					
4	Brian Virost	20	40		Multiple R	0.759				
5	Greg Fish	30	60		R Square	0.576				
6	Susan Welch	10	30		Adjusted R Square	0.523				
7	Carlos Ramirez	10	40		Standard Error	9.901				
8	Rich Niles	20	40		Observations	10				
9	Mike Kiel	20	50							
10	Mark Reynolds	20	30		ANOVA					
11	Soni Jones	30	70			*df*	*SS*	*MS*	*F*	*Significance F*
12					Regression	1	1065.789	1065.789	10.872	0.011
13					Residual	8	784.211	98.026		
14					Total	9	1850.000			
15										
16						*Coefficients*	*Standard Error*	*t Stat*	*P-value*	
17					Intercept	18.9474	8.4988	2.2294	0.05635	
18					Calls	1.18421	0.35914	3.29734	0.01090	

1. Starting on the top are the *Regression Statistics*. We will use this information later in the chapter, but notice that the "Multiple R" value is familiar. It is .759, which is the correlation coefficient we calculated in Section 13.2 using formula (13–1).
2. Next is an ANOVA table. This is a useful table for summarizing regression information. We will refer to it later in this chapter and use it extensively in the next chapter when we study multiple regression.
3. At the bottom, highlighted in blue, is the information needed to conduct our test of hypothesis regarding the slope of the line. It includes the value of the slope, which is 1.18421, and the intercept, which is 18.9474. (Note that these values for the slope and the intercept are slightly different from those computed on pages 407 and 408. These small differences are due to rounding.) In the column to the right of the regression coefficient is a column labeled "Standard Error." This is a value similar to the standard error of the mean. Recall that the standard error of the mean reports the variation in the sample means. In a similar fashion, these standard errors report the possible variation in slope and intercept values. The standard error of the slope coefficient is 0.35914.

To test the null hypothesis, we use the *t*-distribution with $(n - 2)$ and the following formula.

$$\text{TEST FOR THE SLOPE} \qquad t = \frac{b - 0}{s_b} \qquad \text{with } n - 2 \text{ degrees of freedom} \qquad [13\text{–}6]$$

where:

    b is the estimate of the regression line's slope calculated from the sample information.

    s_b is the standard error of the slope estimate, also determined from sample information.

Our first step is to set the null and the alternative hypotheses. They are:

$H_0: \beta \le 0$
$H_1: \beta > 0$

Notice that we have a one-tailed test. If we do not reject the null hypothesis, we conclude that the slope of the regression line in the population could be zero. For this reason, the independent variable is of no value in improving our estimate of the dependent variable. In our case, knowing the number of sales calls made by a representative does not help us predict the sales.

If we reject the null hypothesis and accept the alternative, we conclude the slope of the line is greater than zero. Hence, the independent variable is an aid in predicting the dependent variable. Thus, if we know the number of sales calls made by a representative, this will help us forecast that representative's sales. We also know, because we have demonstrated that the slope of the line is greater than zero—that is, positive—that more sales calls will result in the sale of more copiers.

The t-distribution is the test statistic; there are 8 degrees of freedom, found by $n - 2 = 10 - 2$. We use the .05 significance level. From Appendix B.2, the critical value is 1.860. Our decision rule is to reject the null hypothesis if the value computed from formula (13–6) is greater than 1.860. We apply formula (13–6) to find t.

$$t = \frac{b - 0}{s_b} = \frac{1.18421 - 0}{0.35814} = 3.297$$

The computed value of 3.297 exceeds our critical value of 1.860, so we reject the null hypothesis and accept the alternative hypothesis. We conclude that the slope of the line is greater than zero. The independent variable referring to the number of sales calls is useful for obtaining a better estimate of sales.

The table also provides us information on the p-value of this test. This cell is highlighted in purple. So we could select a significance level, say .05, and compare that value with the p-value. In this case, the calculated p-value in the table is .01090, so our decision is to reject the null hypothesis. An important caution is that the p-values reported in the statistical software are usually for a two-*tailed test.*

Before moving on, here is an interesting note. Observe that on page 402, when we conducted a test of hypothesis regarding the correlation coefficient for these same data using formula (13–2), we obtained the same value of the t-statistic, $t = 3.297$. Actually, the two tests are equivalent and will always yield exactly the same values of t and the same p-values.

Self-Review 13–4

Refer to Self-Review 13–1, where the owner of Haverty's Furniture Company studied the relationship between the amount spent on advertising in a month and sales revenue for that month. The amount of sales is the dependent variable, and advertising expense the independent variable. The regression equation in that study was $\hat{Y} = 1.5 + 2.2X$ for a sample of five months. Conduct a test of hypothesis to show there is a positive relationship between advertising and sales. From statistical software, the standard error of the regression coefficient is 0.42. Use the .05 significance level.

Exercises

connect

21. Refer to Exercise 5. The regression equation is $\hat{Y} = 29.29 - 0.96X$, the sample size is 8, and the standard error of the slope is 0.22. Use the .05 significance level. Can we conclude that the slope of the regression line is less than zero?

22. Refer to Exercise 6. The regression equation is $\hat{Y} = 11.18 - 0.49X$, the sample size is 12, and the standard error of the slope is 0.23. Use the .05 significance level. Can we conclude that the slope of the regression line is less than zero?

23. Refer to Exercise 17. The regression equation is $\hat{Y} = 1.85 + .08X$, the sample size is 12, and the standard error of the slope is 0.03. Use the .05 significance level. Can we conclude that the slope of the regression line is *different from zero?*

24. Refer to Exercise 18. The regression equation is $\hat{Y} = 9.9198 - 0.00039X$, the sample size is 9, and the standard error of the slope is 0.0032. Use the .05 significance level. Can we conclude that the slope of the regression line is less than zero?

13.7 Evaluating a Regression Equation's Ability to Predict

The Standard Error of Estimate

LO 13-6 Evaluate a regression equation to predict the dependent variable.

The results of the regression analysis for Copier Sales of America show a significant relationship between "number of sales calls" and "number of copiers sold." By substituting the names of the variables into the equation, it can be written as:

Number of copiers sold = 18.9476 + 1.1842 (Number of sales calls)

This equation can be used to estimate the "number of copiers sold" for any given "number of sales calls" within the range of the data. For example, if the "number of sales calls" is 30, then we can estimate the "number of copiers sold." It is 54.4736, found by 18.9476 + 1.1842(30). The sample data show that two sales representatives, Fish and Jones, each made 30 sales calls. However, they did not sell the same number of copiers, Fish sold 60 copiers and Jones sold 70 copiers. So is the number of sales calls a good predictor of the number of copiers sold?

Perfect prediction, which is finding the *exact outcome,* in economics and business is practically impossible. For example:

- A large electronics firm, with production facilities throughout the United States, has a stock option plan for employees. Suppose that there is a relationship between the employee years with the company and the number of shares owned. This relationship is likely because, as employee years of service increases, the number of shares that an employee earns also increases. If we observe all employees with 20 years of service, they would most likely own different numbers of shares.
- A real estate developer in the southwest United States studied the relationship between the income of buyers and the size, in square feet, of the home they purchased. The developer reasons that as the income of buyers increases, the size of the home purchased will also increase. However, all buyers with an income of $70,000 will not purchase a home of exactly the same size.

What is needed, then, is a measure that describes how precise the prediction of Y is based on X or, conversely, how inaccurate the estimate might be. This measure is called the **standard error of estimate.** The standard error of estimate is symbolized by $s_{y \cdot x}$. The subscript, $y \cdot x$, is interpreted as the standard error of y for a given value of x. It is the same concept as the standard deviation discussed in Chapter 3. The standard deviation measures the dispersion around the mean. The standard error of estimate measures the dispersion about the regression line for a given value of X.

> **STANDARD ERROR OF ESTIMATE** A measure of the dispersion, or scatter, of the observed values around the line of regression for a given value of X.

The standard error of estimate is found using formula (13–7).

| STANDARD ERROR OF ESTIMATE | $s_{y \cdot x} = \sqrt{\dfrac{\Sigma(Y - \hat{Y})^2}{n - 2}}$ | [13–7] |

The calculation of the standard error of estimate requires the sum of the squared differences between each observed value of Y and the predicted value of Y, which is identified as $\hat{Y}$ in the numerator. This calculation is illustrated in the spreadsheet on page 409. See cell F7 in the spreadsheet. It is a very important value. It is the numerator in the calculation of the standard error of the estimate.

$$s_{y \cdot x} = \sqrt{\frac{\Sigma(Y - \hat{Y})^2}{n - 2}} = \sqrt{\frac{784.211}{10 - 2}} = 9.901$$

This calculation can be eliminated by using statistical software such as Excel. The standard error of the estimate is included in Excel's regression analysis and highlighted in yellow on page 413. Its value is 9.901.

If the standard error of estimate is small, this indicates that the data are relatively close to the regression line and the regression equation can be used to predict Y with little error. If the standard error of estimate is large, this indicates that the data are widely scattered around the regression line, and the regression equation will not provide a precise estimate of Y.

The Coefficient of Determination

Using the standard error of the estimate provides a relative measure of a regression equation's ability to predict. We will use it to provide more specific information about a prediction in the next section. In this section, another statistic is explained that will provide a more interpretable measure of a regression equation's ability to predict. It is called the coefficient of determination, or R-square.

> **COEFFICIENT OF DETERMINATION** The proportion of the total variation in the dependent variable Y that is explained, or accounted for, by the variation in the independent variable X.

LO 13-7 Calculate and interpret the coefficient of determination.

The coefficient of determination is easy to compute. It is the correlation coefficient squared. Therefore, the term R-square is also used. With the Copier Sales of America, the correlation coefficient for the relationship between the number of copiers sold and the number of sales calls is 0.759. If we compute $(0.759)^2$, the coefficient of determination is 0.576. See the blue (Multiple R) and green (R-square) highlighted cells in the spreadsheet on page 413. To better interpret the coefficient of determination, convert it to a percentage. Hence, we say that 57.6% of the variation in the number of copiers sold is explained, or accounted for, by the variation in the number of sales calls.

How well can the regression equation predict number of copiers sold with number of sales calls made? If it were possible to make perfect predictions, the coefficient of determination would be 100%. That would mean that the independent variable, number of sales calls, explains or accounts for all the variation in the number of copiers sold. A coefficient of determination of 100% is associated with a correlation coefficient of +1.0 or −1.0. Refer to Chart 13–2 on page 394, which shows that a perfect prediction is associated with a perfect linear relationship where all the data points form a perfect line in a scatter diagram. Our analysis shows that only 57.6% of the variation in copiers sold is explained by the number of sales calls.

Clearly, this data does not form a perfect line. Instead, the data are scattered around the best-fitting, least squares regression line, and there will be error in the predictions. In the next section, the standard error of the estimate is used to provide more specific information regarding the error associated with using the regression equation to make predictions.

Self-Review 13–5

Refer to Self-Review 13–1, where the owner of Haverty's Furniture Company studied the relationship between the amount spent on advertising in a month and sales revenue for that month. The amount of sales is the dependent variable, and advertising expense is the independent variable.
(a) Determine the standard error of estimate.
(b) Determine the coefficient of determination.
(c) Interpret the coefficient of determination.

Exercises

connect™

Note: You may wish to use a software package such as Excel, Minitab, or MegaStat to assist in your calculations.

25. Refer to Exercise 5. Determine the standard error of estimate and the coefficient of determination. Interpret the coefficient of determination.
26. Refer to Exercise 6. Determine the standard error of estimate and the coefficient of determination. Interpret the coefficient of determination.
27. Refer to Exercise 15. Determine the standard error of estimate and the coefficient of determination. Interpret the coefficient of determination.
28. Refer to Exercise 16. Determine the standard error of estimate and the coefficient of determination. Interpret the coefficient of determination.

Relationships among the Correlation Coefficient, the Coefficient of Determination, and the Standard Error of Estimate

In Section 13.7, we described the standard error of estimate. Recall that it measures how close the actual values are to the regression line. When the standard error is small, it indicates that the two variables are closely related. In the calculation of the standard error, the key term is

$$\Sigma(Y - \hat{Y})^2$$

If the value of this term is small, then the standard error will also be small.

The correlation coefficient measures the strength of the linear association between two variables. When the points on the scatter diagram appear close to the line, we note that the correlation coefficient tends to be large. Therefore, the correlation coefficient and the standard error of the estimate are inversely related. As the strength of a linear relationship between two variables increases, the correlation coefficient increases and the standard error of the estimate decreases.

We also noted that the square of the correlation coefficient is the coefficient of determination. The coefficient of determination measures the percentage of the variation in Y that is explained by the variation in X.

A convenient vehicle for showing the relationship among these three measures is an ANOVA table. See the highlighted portion of the spreadsheet on the next page. This table is similar to the analysis of variance table developed in Chapter 12. In that chapter, the total variation was divided into two components: variation due to the *treatments* and that due to *random error*. The concept is similar in regression analysis. The total variation is divided into two components: (1) variation explained by the *regression* (explained by the independent variable) and (2) the *error, or residual*. This is the unexplained variation. These three categories are identified in the first column of the spreadsheet ANOVA table. The column headed "*df*" refers to the degrees of freedom associated with each category. The total number of degrees of freedom is $n - 1$. The number of degrees of freedom in the regression is 1, because there is only one independent variable. The number of degrees of freedom associated with the error term is $n - 2$. The term "SS" located in the middle of the ANOVA table refers to the sum of squares. You should note that the total degrees of freedom is equal to the sum of the regression and residual (error) degrees of freedom, and the total sum of squares is equal to the sum of the regression and residual (error) sum of squares. This is true for any ANOVA table.

Regression Analysis

	B	C	D	E	F	G	H	I	J
1	Calls	Sales		SUMMARY OUTPUT					
2	20	30							
3	40	60		*Regression Statistics*					
4	20	40		Multiple R	0.759				
5	30	60		R Square	0.576				
6	10	30		Adjusted R Square	0.523				
7	10	40		Standard Error	9.901				
8	20	40		Observations	10				
9	20	50							
10	20	30		ANOVA					
11	30	70			*df*	*SS*	*MS*	*F*	*Significance F*
12				Regression	1	1065.789	1065.789	10.872	0.011
13				Residual	8	784.211	98.026		
14				Total	9	1850.000			
15									
16					*Coefficients*	*Standard Error*	*t Stat*	*P-value*	
17				Intercept	18.9474	8.4988	2.2294	0.05635	
18				Calls	1.18421	0.35914	3.29734	0.01090	

The ANOVA sum of squares are computed as follows:

$$\text{Regression Sum of Squares} = \text{SSR} = \Sigma(\hat{Y} - \overline{Y})^2 = 1065.789$$

$$\text{Residual or Error Sum of Squares} = \text{SSE} = \Sigma(Y - \hat{Y})^2 = 784.211$$

$$\text{Total Sum of Squares} = \text{SS total} = \Sigma(Y - \overline{Y})^2 = 1850.00$$

Recall that the coefficient of determination is defined as the percentage of the total variation (SS total) explained by the regression equation (SSR). Using the ANOVA table, the reported value of *R*-square can be validated.

COEFFICIENT OF DETERMINATION
$$r^2 = \frac{\text{SSR}}{\text{SS total}} = 1 - \frac{\text{SSE}}{\text{SS total}} \qquad \textbf{[13–8]}$$

Using the values from the ANOVA table, the coefficient of determination is $1065.789/1850.00 = 0.576$. Therefore, the more variation of the dependent variable (SS total) explained by the independent variable (SSR), the higher the coefficient of determination.

We can also express the coefficient of determination in terms of the error or residual variation:

$$r^2 = 1 - \frac{\text{SSE}}{\text{SS total}} = 1 - \frac{784.211}{1850.00} = 1 - 0.424 = 0.576$$

In this case, the coefficient of determination and the residual or error sum of squares are inversely related. The larger the unexplained or error variation as a percentage of the total variation, the lower is the coefficient of determination. In this case, 42.4% of the total variation in the dependent variable is error or residual variation.

The final observation that relates the correlation coefficient, the coefficient of determination, and the standard error of the estimate is to show the relationship between the standard error of the estimate and SSE. By substituting [SSE Residual or Error Sum of Squares = SSE = $\Sigma(Y - \hat{Y})^2$] into the formula for the standard error of the estimate, we find:

STANDARD ERROR OF ESTIMATE	$s_{y \cdot x} = \sqrt{\dfrac{\text{SSE}}{n - 2}}$	[13–9]

In sum, regression analysis provides two statistics to evaluate the predictive ability of a regression equation, the standard error of the estimate and the coefficient of determination. When reporting the results of a regression analysis, the findings must be clearly explained, especially when using the results to make predictions of the dependent variable. The report must always include a statement regarding the coefficient of determination so that the relative precision of the prediction is known to the reader of the report. Objective reporting of statistical analysis is required so that the readers can make their own decisions.

Exercises

29. Given the following ANOVA table:

Source	DF	SS	MS	F
Regression	1	1000.0	1000.0	26.00
Error	13	500.0	38.46	
Total	14	1500.0		

    a. Determine the coefficient of determination.
    b. Assuming a direct relationship between the variables, what is the correlation coefficient?
    c. Determine the standard error of estimate.
30. On the first statistics exam, the coefficient of determination between the hours studied and the grade earned was 80%. The standard error of estimate was 10. There were 20 students in the class. Develop an ANOVA table for the regression analysis of hours studied as a predictor of the grade earned on the first statistics exam.

13.8 Interval Estimates of Prediction

The standard error of the estimate and the coefficient of determination are two statistics that provide an overall evaluation of the ability of a regression equation to predict a dependent variable. Another way to report the ability of a regression equation to predict is specific to a stated value of the independent variable. For example, we can predict the number of copiers sold (Y) for a selected value of number of sales calls made (X). In fact, we can calculate a confidence interval for the predicted value of the dependent variable for a selected value of the independent variable.

Assumptions Underlying Linear Regression

Before we present the confidence intervals, the assumptions for properly applying linear regression should be reviewed. Chart 13–13 illustrates these assumptions.

1. For each value of X, there are corresponding Y values. These Y values follow the normal distribution.
2. The means of these normal distributions lie on the regression line.

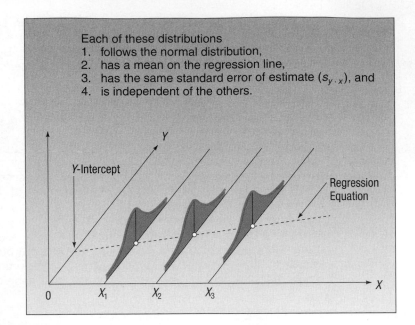

Each of these distributions
1. follows the normal distribution,
2. has a mean on the regression line,
3. has the same standard error of estimate ($s_{y \cdot x}$), and
4. is independent of the others.

CHART 13–13 Regression Assumptions Shown Graphically

3. The standard deviations of these normal distributions are all the same. The best estimate we have of this common standard deviation is the standard error of estimate ($s_{y \cdot x}$).
4. The Y values are statistically independent. This means that in selecting a sample, a particular X does not depend on any other value of X. This assumption is particularly important when data are collected over a period of time. In such situations, the errors for a particular time period are often correlated with those of other time periods.

Recall from Chapter 7 that if the values follow a normal distribution, then the mean plus or minus one standard deviation will encompass 68% of the observations, the mean plus or minus two standard deviations will encompass 95% of the observations, and the mean plus or minus three standard deviations will encompass virtually all of the observations. The same relationship exists between the predicted values $\hat{Y}$ and the standard error of estimate ($s_{y \cdot x}$).

1. $\hat{Y} \pm s_{y \cdot x}$ will include the middle 68% of the observations.
2. $\hat{Y} \pm 2s_{y \cdot x}$ will include the middle 95% of the observations.
3. $\hat{Y} \pm 3s_{y \cdot x}$ will include virtually all the observations.

We can now relate these assumptions to Copier Sales of America, where we studied the relationship between the number of sales calls and the number of copiers sold. Assume that we took a much larger sample than $n = 10$, but that the standard error of estimate was still 9.901. If we drew a parallel line 9.901 units above the regression line and another 9.901 units below the regression line, about 68% of the points would fall between the two lines. Similarly, a line 19.802 [$2s_{y \cdot x} = 2(9.901)$] units above the regression line and another 19.802 units below the regression line should include about 95% of the data values.

As a rough check, refer to column E in the Excel spreadsheet in Section 13.5 on page 409. Three of the 10 deviations exceed one standard error of estimate. That is, the deviations of -12.6319 in row 1, -12.6319 in row 11, and $+15.5264$ in row 12 all exceed the value of 9.901, which is one standard error from the regression line. All of the values are within 19.802 units of the regression line. To put it another way, 7 of the

10 deviations in the sample are within one standard error of the regression line and all are within two—a good result for a relatively small sample.

Constructing Confidence and Prediction Intervals

When using a regression equation, two different predictions can be made for a selected value of the independent variable. The differences are subtle but very important and are related to the assumptions stated in the last section. Recall that for any selected value of the independent variable (X), the dependent variable (Y) is a random variable that is normally distributed with a mean, $\hat{Y}$. Each distribution of Y has a standard deviation equal to the regression analysis' standard error of the estimate.

LO 13-8 Calculate and interpret confidence and prediction intervals.

The first interval estimate is called a **confidence interval.** This is used when the regression equation is used to predict the mean value of Y for a given value of X. For example, we would use a confidence interval to estimate the mean salary of all executives in the retail industry based on their years of experience. To determine the confidence interval for the mean value of Y for a given X, the formula is:

CONFIDENCE INTERVAL FOR THE MEAN OF Y, GIVEN X	$\hat{Y} \pm t(s_{y \cdot x})\sqrt{\dfrac{1}{n} + \dfrac{(X - \bar{X})^2}{\Sigma(X - \bar{X})^2}}$	**[13–10]**

The second interval estimate is called a prediction interval. This is used when the regression equation is used to predict an individual Y ($n = 1$) for a given value of X. For example, we would estimate the salary of a particular retail executive who has 20 years of experience. To determine the prediction interval for an estimate of an individual for a given X, the formula is:

PREDICTION INTERVAL FOR Y, GIVEN X	$\hat{Y} \pm ts_{y \cdot x}\sqrt{1 + \dfrac{1}{n} + \dfrac{(X - \bar{X})^2}{\Sigma(X - \bar{X})^2}}$	**[13–11]**

Example

We return to the Copier Sales of America illustration. Determine a 95% confidence interval for all sales representatives who make 25 calls, and determine a prediction interval for Sheila Baker, a West Coast sales representative who made 25 calls.

Solution

We use formula (13–10) to determine a confidence level. Table 13–4 includes the necessary totals and a repeat of the information of Table 13–2 on page 395.

TABLE 13–4 Calculations Needed for Determining the Confidence Interval and Prediction Interval

Sales Representative	Sales Calls, (X)	Copier Sales, (Y)	$(X - \bar{X})$	$(X - \bar{X})^2$
Tom Keller	20	30	−2	4
Jeff Hall	40	60	18	324
Brian Virost	20	40	−2	4
Greg Fish	30	60	8	64
Susan Welch	10	30	−12	144
Carlos Ramirez	10	40	−12	144
Rich Niles	20	40	−2	4
Mike Kiel	20	50	−2	4
Mark Reynolds	20	30	−2	4
Soni Jones	30	70	8	64
			0	760

The first step is to determine the number of copiers we expect a sales representative to sell if he or she makes 25 calls. It is 48.5526, found by $\hat{Y} = 18.9476 + 1.1842X = 18.9476 + 1.1842(25)$.

To find the t value, we need to first know the number of degrees of freedom. In this case, the degrees of freedom is $n - 2 = 10 - 2 = 8$. We set the confidence level at 95%. To find the value of t, move down the left-hand column of Appendix B.2 to 8 degrees of freedom, then move across to the column with the 95% level of confidence. The value of t is 2.306.

In the previous section, we calculated the standard error of estimate to be 9.901. We let $X = 25$, $\bar{X} = \Sigma X/n = 220/10 = 22$, and from Table 13–4 $\Sigma(X - \bar{X})^2 = 760$. Inserting these values in formula (13–10), the confidence interval is:

$$\text{Confidence Interval} = \hat{Y} \pm ts_{y \cdot x} \sqrt{\frac{1}{n} + \frac{(X - \bar{X})^2}{\Sigma(X - \bar{X})^2}}$$

$$= 48.5526 \pm 2.306(9.901)\sqrt{\frac{1}{10} + \frac{(25 - 22)^2}{760}}$$

$$= 48.5526 \pm 7.6356$$

Thus, the 95% confidence interval for all sales representatives who make 25 calls is from 40.9170 up to 56.1882. To interpret, let's round the values. If a sales representative makes 25 calls, he or she can expect to sell 48.6 copiers. It is likely those sales will range from 40.9 to 56.2 copiers.

Suppose we want to estimate the number of copiers sold by Sheila Baker, who made 25 sales calls. The 95% prediction interval is:

$$\text{Prediction Interval} = \hat{Y} \pm ts_{y \cdot x} \sqrt{1 + \frac{1}{n} + \frac{(X - \bar{X})^2}{\Sigma(X - \bar{X})^2}}$$

$$= 48.5526 \pm 2.306(9.901)\sqrt{1 + \frac{1}{10} + \frac{(25 - 22)^2}{760}}$$

$$= 48.5526 \pm 24.0746$$

Thus, the interval is from 24.478 up to 72.627 copiers. We conclude that the number of copiers sold will be between about 24.5 and 72.6 for a particular sales representative who makes 25 calls. This interval is quite large. It is much larger than the confidence interval for all sales representatives who made 25 calls. It is logical, however, that there should be more variation in the sales estimate for an individual than for a group.

The following Minitab graph shows the relationship between the regression line (in the center), the confidence interval (shown in crimson), and the prediction interval (shown in green). The bands for the prediction interval are always further from the regression line than those for the confidence interval. Also, as the values of X move away from the mean number of calls (22) in either the positive or the negative direction, the confidence interval and prediction interval bands widen. This is caused by the numerator of the right-hand term under the radical in formulas (13–10) and (13–11). That is, as the term $(X - \bar{X})^2$ increases, the widths of the confidence interval and the prediction interval also increase. To put it another way, there is less precision in our estimates as we move away, in either direction, from the mean of the independent variable.

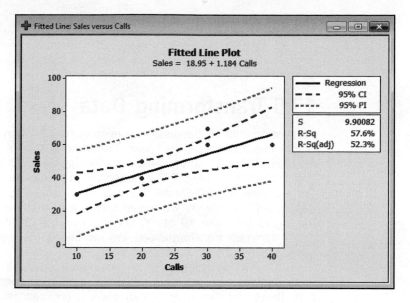

We wish to emphasize again the distinction between a **confidence interval** and a **prediction interval.**

- A confidence interval refers to all cases with a given value of X and is computed by formula (13–10).
- A prediction interval refers to a particular case for a given value of X and is computed using formula (13–11).

The prediction interval will always be wider because of the addition of 1 under the radical in the second equation.

Self-Review 13–6

Refer to the sample data in Self-Review 13–1, where the owner of Haverty's Furniture was studying the relationship between sales and the amount spent on advertising. The sales information for the last four months is repeated below.

Month	Advertising Expense ($ million)	Sales Revenue ($ million)
July	2	7
August	1	3
September	3	8
October	4	10

The regression equation was computed to be $\hat{Y} = 1.5 + 2.2X$, and the standard error 0.9487. Both variables are reported in millions of dollars. Determine the 90% confidence interval for the typical month in which $3 million was spent on advertising.

Exercises

connect

31. Refer to Exercise 13.
  a. Determine the .95 confidence interval for the mean predicted when $X = 7$.
  b. Determine the .95 prediction interval for an individual predicted when $X = 7$.
32. Refer to Exercise 14.
  a. Determine the .95 confidence interval for the mean predicted when $X = 7$.
  b. Determine the .95 prediction interval for an individual predicted when $X = 7$.
33. Refer to Exercise 15.
  a. Determine the .95 confidence interval, in thousands of kilowatt-hours, for the mean of all six-room homes.
  b. Determine the .95 prediction interval, in thousands of kilowatt-hours, for a particular six-room home.

34. Refer to Exercise 16.
    a. Determine the .95 confidence interval, in thousands of dollars, for the mean of all sales personnel who make 40 contacts.
    b. Determine the .95 prediction interval, in thousands of dollars, for a particular salesperson who makes 40 contacts.

13.9 Transforming Data

Regression analysis describes the relationship between two variables. A requirement is that this relationship be linear. The same is true of the correlation coefficient. It measures the strength of a linear relationship between two variables. But what if the relationship is not linear? The remedy is to rescale one or both of the variables so the new relationship is linear. For example, instead of using the actual values of the dependent variable, Y, we would create a new dependent variable by computing the log to the base 10 of Y, Log(Y). This calculation is called a transformation. Other common transformations include taking the square root, the reciprocal, or squaring one or both of the variables.

Thus, two variables could be closely related but their relationship not linear. Be cautious when you are interpreting the correlation coefficient or a regression equation. These statistics may indicate there is no linear relationship, but there could be a relationship of some other nonlinear or curvilinear form. The following example explains the details.

Example

GroceryLand Supermarkets is a regional grocery chain with over 300 stores located in the midwestern United States. The corporate director of marketing for GroceryLand wishes to study the effect of price on the weekly sales of two-liter bottles of their private brand diet cola. The objectives of the study are:

1. To determine whether there is a relationship between selling price and weekly sales. Is this relationship direct or indirect? Is it strong or weak?
2. To determine the effect of price increases or decreases on sales. Can we effectively forecast sales based on the price?

Solution

To begin the project, the marketing director meets with the vice president of sales and other company staff members. They decide that it would be reasonable to price the two-liter bottle of their private brand diet cola from $0.50 up to $2.00. To collect the data needed to analyze the relationship between price and sales, the marketing director selects a random sample of 20 stores and then randomly assigns a selling price for the two-liter bottle of diet cola between $0.50 and $2.00 to each selected store. The director contacts each of the 20 store managers included in the study to tell them the selling price and ask them to report the sales for the product at the end of the week. The results are reported below. For example, store number 17 sold 181 two-liter bottles of diet cola at $0.50 each.

GroceryLand Sales and Price Data			GroceryLand Sales and Price Data		
Store Number	Price	Sales	Store Number	Price	Sales
17	0.50	181	30	0.76	91
121	1.35	33	127	1.79	13
227	0.79	91	266	1.57	22
135	1.71	13	117	1.27	34
6	1.38	34	132	0.96	74
282	1.22	47	120	0.52	164
172	1.03	73	272	0.64	129
296	1.84	11	120	1.05	55
143	1.73	15	194	0.72	107
66	1.62	20	105	0.75	119

To examine the relationship between Price and Sales, we use regression analysis, setting *Price* as the independent variable and *Sales* as the dependent variable. The analysis, will provide important information about the relationship between the variables. The analysis is summarized in the following Minitab output.

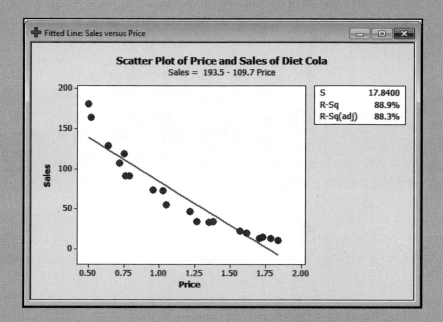

From the output, we can make these conclusions:

1. The relationship between the two variables is inverse or indirect. As the *Price* of the cola increases, the *Sales* of the product decreases. Given basic economic theory of price and demand, this is expected.
2. There is a strong relationship between the two variables. The coefficient of determination is 88.9%. So 88.9% of the variation in *Sales* is accounted for by the variation in *Price*. From the coefficient of determination, we can compute the correlation coefficient as the square root of the coefficient of determination. The correlation coefficient is the square root of 0.889 or 0.943. The sign of the correlation coefficient is negative because sales is inversely related to price. Therefore, the correlation coefficient is -0.943.
3. Before continuing our summary of conclusions, we should look carefully at the scatter diagram and the plot of the regression line. The assumption of a linear relationship is tenuous. If the relationship is linear, the data points should be distributed both above and below the line over the entire range of the independent variable. However, for the highest and lowest prices, the data points are above the regression line. For the selling prices in the middle, most of the data points are below the regression line. So the linear regression equation does not effectively describe the relationship between *Price* and *Sales*. A transformation of the data is needed to create a linear relationship.

By transforming one of the variables, we may be able to change the nonlinear relationship between the variables to a linear relationship. Of the possible choices, the director of marketing decides to transform the dependent variable, *Sales,* by taking the logarithm to the base 10 of each *Sales* value. Note the new variable, *Log-Sales,* in the following analysis. Now, the regression analysis uses *Log-Sales* as the dependent variable and *Price* as the independent variable. This analysis is reported below.

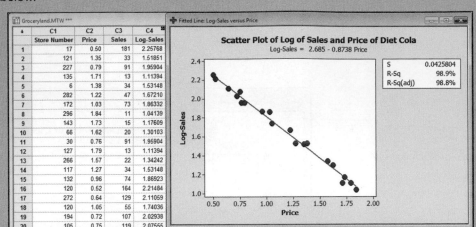

What can we conclude from the regression analysis using the transformation of the dependent variable *Sales?*

1. By transforming the dependent variable, Sales, we increase the coefficient of determination from 0.889 to 0.989. So *Price* explains nearly all of the variation in *Log-Sales.*
2. Compare this result with the scatter diagram before we transformed the dependent variable. The transformed data seem to fit the linear relationship requirement much better. Observe that the data points are both above and below the regression line over the range of *Price.*
3. The regression equation is: $\hat{Y} = 2.685 - 0.8738X$. The sign of the slope value is negative, confirming the inverse association between the variables. We can use the new equation to estimate sales and study the effect of changes in price. For example, if we decided to sell the two-liter bottle of diet cola for $1.25, the predicted *Log-Sales* is:

$$\hat{Y} = 2.685 - 0.8738X = 2.685 - 0.8738(1.25) = 1.593$$

Remember that the regression equation now predicts the log, base10, of *Sales.* Therefore, we must undo the transformation by taking the antilog of 1.593, which is $10^{1.593}$, or 39.174. So, if we price the two-liter diet cola product at $1.25, the predicted weekly sales are 39 bottles. If we increase the price to $2.00, the regression equation would predict a value of .9374. Taking the antilog, $10^{.9374}$, the predicted sales decrease to 8.658, or rounding, 9 two-liter bottles per week. Clearly, as price increases, sales decrease. This relationship will be very helpful to GroceryLand when making pricing decisions for this product.

Exercises

connect

35. Given the following sample observations, develop a scatter diagram, using "X" as the independent variable and "Y" as the dependent variable, and compute the correlation coefficient. Does the relationship between the variables appear to be linear? Try squaring the X-variable and then develop a scatter diagram and determine the correlation coefficient. Summarize your analysis.

X	−8	−16	12	2	18
Y	58	247	153	3	341

36. The Masters, one of the most prestigious golf tournaments on the PGA golf tour, is scheduled in April and played in Augusta, Georgia. In 2011, 48 players received prize money. The 2011 winner, Charl Schwartzel of South Africa, earned a prize of $1,440,000. Adam Scott and Jason Day finished in a tie for second place, each earning $704,000. The data are briefly summarized below. Each player has three corresponding variables: finishing position or rank, score, and prize (in dollars). The complete file is in the data sets labeled as Ex13-36-8e. We want to study the relationship between score and prize. df

Position	Player	Score	Prize
1	Schwartzel	272	$1,440,000
Tied 2	Scott	276	704,000
Tied 2	Day	276	704,000
Tied 4	Ogilvy	278	330,667
Tied 4	Woods	278	330,667
Tied 4	Donald	278	330,667
⋮	⋮	⋮	⋮
Tied 43	Overton	291	28,800
45	Watney	292	26,400
Tied 46	Baddeley	293	24,000
Tied 46	Els	293	24,000
48	Villegas	294	21,920

a. Using *Score* as the independent variable and *Prize* as the dependent variable, develop a scatter diagram. Does the relationship appear to be linear? Does it seem reasonable that as *Score* increases the *Prize* decreases?
b. What percentage of the variation in the dependent variable, *Prize,* is accounted for by the independent variable, *Score?*
c. Calculate a new variable, *Log-Prize*, computing the log to the base 10 of *Prize*. Draw a scatter diagram with *Log-Prize* as the dependent variable and *Score* as the independent variable.
d. Develop a regression equation and compute the coefficient of determination using *Log-Prize* as the dependent variable.
e. Compare the coefficient of determination in parts (b) and (d). What do you conclude?
f. Write out the regression equation developed in part (d). If a player shot a total of 280 for the four rounds, how much would you expect that player to earn?

Chapter Summary

I. A scatter diagram is a graphic tool that portrays the relationship between two variables.
A. The dependent variable is scaled on the *Y*-axis and is the variable being estimated.
B. The independent variable is scaled on the *X*-axis and is the variable used as the predictor.
II. The correlation coefficient measures the strength of the linear association between two variables.
A. Both variables must be at least the interval scale of measurement.
B. The correlation coefficient can range from −1.00 to 1.00.
C. If the correlation between the two variables is 0, there is no association between them.
D. A value of 1.00 indicates perfect positive correlation, and a value of −1.00 indicates perfect negative correlation.

E. A positive sign means there is a direct relationship between the variables, and a negative sign means there is an indirect relationship.

F. It is designated by the letter *r* and found by the following equation:

$$r = \frac{\Sigma(X - \overline{X})(Y - \overline{Y})}{(n - 1)s_x s_y}$$ [13–1]

G. The following equation is used to determine whether the correlation in the population is different from 0.

$$t = \frac{r\sqrt{n - 2}}{\sqrt{1 - r^2}} \quad \text{with } n - 2 \text{ degrees of freedom}$$ [13–2]

III. In regression analysis, we estimate one variable based on another variable.
   A. The variable being estimated is the dependent variable.
   B. The variable used to make the estimate or predict the value is the independent variable.
      1. The relationship between the variables is linear.
      2. Both the independent and the dependent variables must be interval or ratio scale.
      3. The least squares criterion is used to determine the regression equation.

IV. The least squares regression line is of the form $\hat{Y} = a + bX$.
   A. $\hat{Y}$ is the estimated value of *Y* for a selected value of *X*.
   B. *a* is the constant or intercept.
      1. It is the value of $\hat{Y}$ when $X = 0$.
      2. *a* is computed using the following equation.

$$a = \overline{Y} - b\overline{X}$$ [13–5]

   C. *b* is the slope of the fitted line.
      1. It shows the amount of change in $\hat{Y}$ for a change of one unit in *X*.
      2. A positive value for *b* indicates a direct relationship between the two variables. A negative value indicates an inverse relationship.
      3. The sign of *b* and the sign of *r*, the correlation coefficient, are always the same.
      4. *b* is computed using the following equation.

$$b = r\left(\frac{s_y}{s_x}\right)$$ [13–4]

   D. *X* is the value of the independent variable.
V. For a regression equation, the slope is tested for significance.
   A. We test the hypothesis that the slope of the line in the population is 0.
      1. If we do not reject the null hypothesis, we conclude there is no relationship between the two variables.
      2. The test is equivalent to the test for the correlation coefficient.
   B. When testing the null hypothesis about the slope, the test statistic is with $n - 2$ degrees of freedom:

$$t = \frac{b - 0}{s_b}$$ [13–6]

VI. The standard error of estimate measures the variation around the regression line.
   A. It is in the same units as the dependent variable.
   B. It is based on squared deviations from the regression line.
   C. Small values indicate that the points cluster closely about the regression line.
   D. It is computed using the following formula.

$$s_{y \cdot x} = \sqrt{\frac{\Sigma(Y - \hat{Y})^2}{n - 2}}$$ [13–7]

VII. The coefficient of determination is the proportion of the variation of a dependent variable explained by the independent variable.
   A. It ranges from 0 to 1.0.

B. It is the square of the correlation coefficient.
C. It is found from the following formula.

$$r^2 = \frac{\text{SSR}}{\text{SS total}} = 1 - \frac{\text{SSE}}{\text{SS total}} \qquad \textbf{[13–8]}$$

VIII. Inference about linear regression is based on the following assumptions.
   A. For a given value of X, the values of Y are normally distributed about the line of regression.
   B. The standard deviation of each of the normal distributions is the same for all values of X and is estimated by the standard error of estimate.
   C. The deviations from the regression line are independent, with no pattern to the size or direction.
IX. There are two types of interval estimates.
   A. In a confidence interval, the mean value of Y is estimated for a given value of X.
      1. It is computed from the following formula.

$$\hat{Y} \pm t(s_{y \cdot x}) \sqrt{\frac{1}{n} + \frac{(X - \bar{X})^2}{\Sigma(X - \bar{X})^2}} \qquad \textbf{[13–10]}$$

      2. The width of the interval is affected by the level of confidence, the size of the standard error of estimate, and the size of the sample, as well as the value of the independent variable.
   B. In a prediction interval, the individual value of Y is estimated for a given value of X.
      1. It is computed from the following formula.

$$\hat{Y} \pm t s_{y \cdot x} \sqrt{1 + \frac{1}{n} + \frac{(X - \bar{X})^2}{\Sigma(X - \bar{X})^2}} \qquad \textbf{[13–11]}$$

      2. The difference between formulas (13–10) and (13–11) is the 1 under the radical.
         a. The prediction interval will be wider than the confidence interval.
         b. The prediction interval is also based on the level of confidence, the size of the standard error of estimate, the size of the sample, and the value of the independent variable.

Pronunciation Key

SYMBOL	MEANING	PRONUNCIATION
ΣXY	Sum of the products of X and Y	*Sum X Y*
ρ	Correlation coefficient in the population	*Rho*
$\hat{Y}$	Estimated value of Y	*Y hat*
$s_{y \cdot x}$	Standard error of estimate	*s sub y dot x*
r^2	Coefficient of determination	*r square*

Chapter Exercises

connect

37. A regional commuter airline selected a random sample of 25 flights and found that the correlation between the number of passengers and the total weight, in pounds, of luggage stored in the luggage compartment is 0.94. Using the .05 significance level, can we conclude that there is a positive association between the two variables?

38. A sociologist claims that the success of students in college (measured by their GPA) is related to their family's income. For a sample of 20 students, the correlation coefficient is 0.40. Using the 0.01 significance level, can we conclude that there is a positive correlation between the variables?

39. An Environmental Protection Agency study of 12 automobiles revealed a correlation of 0.47 between engine size and emissions. At the .01 significance level, can we conclude that there is a positive association between these variables? What is the *p*-value? Interpret.

40. A suburban hotel derives its gross income from its hotel and restaurant operations. The owners are interested in the relationship between the number of rooms occupied on a nightly basis and the revenue per day in the restaurant. Below is a sample of 25 days (Monday through Thursday) from last year showing the restaurant income and number of rooms occupied. df

Day	Income	Occupied	Day	Income	Occupied
1	$1,452	23	14	$1,425	27
2	1,361	47	15	1,445	34
3	1,426	21	16	1,439	15
4	1,470	39	17	1,348	19
5	1,456	37	18	1,450	38
6	1,430	29	19	1,431	44
7	1,354	23	20	1,446	47
8	1,442	44	21	1,485	43
9	1,394	45	22	1,405	38
10	1,459	16	23	1,461	51
11	1,399	30	24	1,490	61
12	1,458	42	25	1,426	39
13	1,537	54			

Use a statistical software package to answer the following questions.
a. Does the breakfast revenue seem to increase as the number of occupied rooms increases? Draw a scatter diagram to support your conclusion.
b. Determine the correlation coefficient between the two variables. Interpret the value.
c. Is it reasonable to conclude that there is a positive relationship between revenue and occupied rooms? Use the .10 significance level.
d. What percent of the variation in revenue in the restaurant is accounted for by the number of rooms occupied?

41. The table below shows the number of cars (in millions) sold in the United States for various years and the percent of those cars manufactured by GM. df

Year	Cars Sold (millions)	Percent GM	Year	Cars Sold (millions)	Percent GM
1950	6.0	50.2	1985	15.4	40.1
1955	7.8	50.4	1990	13.5	36.0
1960	7.3	44.0	1995	15.5	31.7
1965	10.3	49.9	2000	17.4	28.6
1970	10.1	39.5	2005	16.9	26.9
1975	10.8	43.1	2010	11.6	19.1
1980	11.5	44.0			

Use a statistical software package to answer the following questions.
a. Is the number of cars sold directly or indirectly related to GM's percentage of the market? Draw a scatter diagram to show your conclusion.
b. Determine the correlation coefficient between the two variables. Interpret the value.
c. Is it reasonable to conclude that there is a negative association between the two variables? Use the .01 significance level.
d. How much of the variation in GM's market share is accounted for by the variation in cars sold?

42. For a sample of 32 large U.S. cities, the correlation between the mean number of square feet per office worker and the mean monthly rental rate in the central business district is −.363. At the .05 significance level, can we conclude that there is a negative association in the population between the two variables?

43. The following data from the 2010 NFL football season report the number of points scored and points allowed for each of the 32 NFL teams. df

Team	Points Scored	Points Allowed	Team	Points Scored	Points Allowed
Arizona	289	434	Miami	273	333
Atlanta	414	288	Minnesota	281	348
Baltimore	357	270	New England	518	313
Buffalo	283	425	New Orleans	384	307
Carolina	196	408	NY Giants	394	347
Chicago	334	286	NY Jets	367	304
Cincinnati	322	395	Oakland	410	371
Cleveland	271	332	Philadelphia	439	377
Dallas	394	436	Pittsburgh	375	232
Denver	344	471	San Diego	441	322
Detroit	362	369	San Francisco	305	346
Green Bay	388	240	Seattle	310	407
Houston	390	427	St. Louis	289	328
Indianapolis	435	388	Tampa Bay	341	318
Jacksonville	353	419	Tennessee	356	339
Kansas City	366	326	Washington	302	377

You will want to use statistical software to perform the calculations. Assume that these are sample data.
   a. Determine the correlation coefficient. Are you surprised at the negative association between the variables? Interpret the relationship between "points scored" and "points allowed."
   b. Determine the coefficient of determination. What does the coefficient of determination say about the relationship?
   c. Can we conclude that there is a negative association between "points scored" and "points allowed"? Use the .05 significance level.

44. Meryl's Apparel is an upscale chain of women's clothing stores, located primarily in the southwest United States. Due to recent success, Meryl's top management is planning to expand by locating new stores in other regions of the country. The director of planning has been asked to study the relationship between yearly sales and the store size. As part of the study, the director selects a sample of 25 stores and determines the size of the store in square feet and the sales for last year. The sample data follow. The use of statistical software is suggested. df

Store Size (thousands of square feet)	Sales (millions $)	Store Size (thousands of square feet)	Sales (millions $)
3.7	9.18	0.4	0.55
2.0	4.58	4.2	7.56
5.0	8.22	3.1	2.23
0.7	1.45	2.6	4.49
2.6	6.51	5.2	9.90
2.9	2.82	3.3	8.93
5.2	10.45	3.2	7.60
5.9	9.94	4.9	3.71
3.0	4.43	5.5	5.47
2.4	4.75	2.9	8.22
2.4	7.30	2.2	7.17
0.5	3.33	2.3	4.35
5.0	6.76		

a. Draw a scatter diagram. Use store size as the independent variable. Does there appear to be a relationship between the two variables. Is it positive or negative?

b. Determine the correlation coefficient and the coefficient of determination. Is the relationship strong or weak? Why?

c. At the .05 significance level, can we conclude there is a significant positive correlation?

45. The manufacturer of Cardio Glide exercise equipment wants to study the relationship between the number of months since the glide was purchased and the time, in hours, the equipment was used last week. (df)

Person	Months Owned	Hours Exercised	Person	Months Owned	Hours Exercised
Rupple	12	4	Massa	2	8
Hall	2	10	Sass	8	3
Bennett	6	8	Karl	4	8
Longnecker	9	5	Malrooney	10	2
Phillips	7	5	Veights	5	5

a. Plot the information on a scatter diagram. Let hours of exercise be the dependent variable. Comment on the graph.

b. Determine the correlation coefficient. Interpret.

c. At the .01 significance level, can we conclude that there is a negative association between the variables?

46. The following regression equation was computed from a sample of 20 observations:

$$\hat{Y} = 15 - 5X$$

SSE was found to be 100 and SS total 400.

a. Determine the standard error of estimate.

b. Determine the coefficient of determination.

c. Determine the correlation coefficient. (Caution: Watch the sign!)

47. City planners believe that larger cities are populated by older residents. To investigate the relationship, data on population and median age in 10 large cities were collected. (df)

City	Population (in millions)	Median age
Chicago, IL	2.833	31.5
Dallas, TX	1.233	30.5
Houston, TX	2.144	30.9
Los Angeles, CA	3.849	31.6
New York, NY	8.214	34.2
Philadelphia, PA	1.448	34.2
Phoenix, AZ	1.513	30.7
San Antonio, TX	1.297	31.7
San Diego, CA	1.257	32.5
San Jose, CA	0.930	32.6

a. Plot this data on a scatter diagram with median age as the dependent variable.

b. Find the correlation coefficient.

c. A regression analysis was performed and the resulting regression equation is Median age = 31.4 + 0.272 population. Interpret the meaning of the slope.

d. Estimate the median age for a city of 2.5 million people.

e. Here is a portion of the regression software output. What does it tell you?

```
Predictor        Coef     SE Coef        T        P
Constant      31.3672      0.6158    50.94    0.000
Population     0.2722      0.1901     1.43    0.190
```

f. Using the .10 significance level, test the significance of the slope. Interpret the result. Is there a significant relationship between the two variables?

48. Emily Smith decides to buy a fuel-efficient used car. Here are several vehicles she is considering, with the estimated cost to purchase and the age of the vehicle.

Vehicle	Estimated Cost	Age
Honda Insight	$5,555	8
Toyota Prius	$17,888	3
Toyota Prius	$9,963	6
Toyota Echo	$6,793	5
Honda Civic Hybrid	$10,774	5
Honda Civic Hybrid	$16,310	2
Chevrolet Prizm	$2,475	8
Mazda Protege	$2,808	10
Toyota Corolla	$7,073	9
Acura Integra	$8,978	8
Scion xB	$11,213	2
Scion xA	$9,463	3
Mazda3	$15,055	2
Mini Cooper	$20,705	2

a. Plot this data on a scatter diagram with estimated cost as the dependent variable.
b. Find the correlation coefficient.
c. A regression analysis was performed and the resulting regression equation is Estimated Cost = 18358 − 1534 age. Interpret the meaning of the slope.
d. Estimate the cost of a five-year-old car.
e. Here is a portion of the regression software output. What does it tell you?

```
Predictor        Coef    SE Coef       T        P
Constant        18358       1817    10.10    0.000
Age            -1533.6      306.3    -5.01    0.000
```

f. Using the .10 significance level, test the significance of the slope. Interpret the result. Is there a significant relationship between the two variables?

49. The National Highway Association is studying the relationship between the number of bidders on a highway project and the winning (lowest) bid for the project. Of particular interest is whether the number of bidders increases or decreases the amount of the winning bid.

Project	Number of Bidders, X	Winning Bid ($ millions), Y	Project	Number of Bidders, X	Winning Bid ($ millions), Y
1	9	5.1	9	6	10.3
2	9	8.0	10	6	8.0
3	3	9.7	11	4	8.8
4	10	7.8	12	7	9.4
5	5	7.7	13	7	8.6
6	10	5.5	14	7	8.1
7	7	8.3	15	6	7.8
8	11	5.5			

a. Determine the regression equation. Interpret the equation. Do more bidders tend to increase or decrease the amount of the winning bid?
b. Estimate the amount of the winning bid if there were seven bidders.
c. A new entrance is to be constructed on the Ohio Turnpike. There are seven bidders on the project. Develop a 95% prediction interval for the winning bid.
d. Determine the coefficient of determination. Interpret its value.

50. Mr. William Profit is studying companies going public for the first time. He is particularly interested in the relationship between the size of the offering and the price per share. A sample of 15 companies that recently went public revealed the following information.

Company	Size ($ millions), X	Price per Share, Y	Company	Size ($ millions), X	Price per Share, Y
1	9.0	10.8	9	160.7	11.3
2	94.4	11.3	10	96.5	10.6
3	27.3	11.2	11	83.0	10.5
4	179.2	11.1	12	23.5	10.3
5	71.9	11.1	13	58.7	10.7
6	97.9	11.2	14	93.8	11.0
7	93.5	11.0	15	34.4	10.8
8	70.0	10.7			

a. Determine the regression equation.
b. Conduct a test to determine whether the slope of the regression line is positive.
c. Determine the coefficient of determination. Do you think Mr. Profit should be satisfied with using the size of the offering as the independent variable?

51. Bardi Trucking Co., located in Cleveland, Ohio, makes deliveries in the Great Lakes region, the Southeast, and the Northeast. Jim Bardi, the president, is studying the relationship between the distance a shipment must travel and the length of time, in days, it takes the shipment to arrive at its destination. To investigate, Mr. Bardi selected a random sample of 20 shipments made last month. Shipping distance is the independent variable, and shipping time is the dependent variable. The results are as follows:

Shipment	Distance (miles)	Shipping Time (days)	Shipment	Distance (miles)	Shipping Time (days)
1	656	5	11	862	7
2	853	14	12	679	5
3	646	6	13	835	13
4	783	11	14	607	3
5	610	8	15	665	8
6	841	10	16	647	7
7	785	9	17	685	10
8	639	9	18	720	8
9	762	10	19	652	6
10	762	9	20	828	10

a. Draw a scatter diagram. Based on these data, does it appear that there is a relationship between how many miles a shipment has to go and the time it takes to arrive at its destination?
b. Determine the correlation coefficient. Can we conclude that there is a positive correlation between distance and time? Use the .05 significance level.
c. Determine and interpret the coefficient of determination.
d. Determine the standard error of estimate.
e. Would you recommend using the regression equation to predict shipping time? Why or why not.

52. Super Markets Inc. is considering expanding into the Scottsdale, Arizona, area. You as director of planning, must present an analysis of the proposed expansion to the operating committee of the board of directors. As a part of your proposal, you need to include information on the amount people in the region spend per month for grocery items. You would also like to include information on the relationship between the amount spent for grocery items and income. Your assistant gathered the following sample information.

Household	Amount Spent	Monthly Income
1	$ 555	$4,388
2	489	4,558
⋮	⋮	⋮
39	1,206	9,862
40	1,145	9,883

a. Let the amount spent be the dependent variable and monthly income the independent variable. Create a scatter diagram, using a software package.
b. Determine the regression equation. Interpret the slope value.
c. Determine the correlation coefficient. Can you conclude that it is greater than 0?

53. Below is information on the price per share and the dividend for a sample of 30 companies. 📀

Company	Price per Share	Dividend
1	$20.00	$ 3.14
2	22.01	3.36
⋮	⋮	⋮
29	77.91	17.65
30	80.00	17.36

a. Calculate the regression equation using selling price based on the annual dividend.
b. Test the significance of the slope.
c. Determine the coefficient of determination. Interpret its value.
d. Determine the correlation coefficient. Can you conclude that it is greater than 0 using the .05 significance level?

54. A highway employee performed a regression analysis of the relationship between the number of construction work-zone fatalities and the number of unemployed people in a state. The regression equation is Fatalities = 12.7 + 0.000114 (Unemp). Some additional output is:

```
Predictor          Coef        SE Coef        T        P
Constant         12.726          8.115     1.57    0.134
Unemp        0.00011386     0.00002896     3.93    0.001

Analysis of Variance
Source           DF        SS       MS       F        P
Regression        1     10354    10354   15.46    0.001
Residual Error   18     12054      670
Total            19     22408
```

a. How many states were in the sample?
b. Determine the standard error of estimate.
c. Determine the coefficient of determination.
d. Determine the correlation coefficient.
e. At the .05 significance level, does the evidence suggest there is a positive association between fatalities and the number unemployed?

55. A regression analysis relating the current market value in dollars to the size in square feet of homes in Greene County, Tennessee, follows. The regression equation is: Value = −37,186 + 65.0 Size.

```
Predictor      Coef    SE Coef        T        P
Constant     -37186       4629    -8.03    0.000
Size         64.993      3.047    21.33    0.000

Analysis of Variance
Source           DF           SS             MS         F        P
Regression        1    13548662082    13548662082   454.98    0.000
Residual Error   33      982687392       29778406
Total            34    14531349474
```

a. How many homes were in the sample?
b. Compute the standard error of estimate.
c. Compute the coefficient of determination.
d. Compute the correlation coefficient.
e. At the .05 significance level, does the evidence suggest a positive association between the market value of homes and the size of the home in square feet?

56. The following table shows the mean annual percent return on capital (profitability) and the mean annual percentage sales growth for eight aerospace and defense companies. 🎯

Company	Profitability	Growth
Alliant Techsystems	23.1	8.0
Boeing	13.2	15.6
General Dynamics	24.2	31.2
Honeywell	11.1	2.5
L-3 Communications	10.1	35.4
Northrop Grunmman	10.8	6.0
Rockwell Collins	27.3	8.7
United Technologies	20.1	3.2

a. Compute the correlation coefficient. Conduct a test of hypothesis to determine if it is reasonable to conclude that the population correlation is greater than zero. Use the .05 significance level.
b. Develop the regression equation for profitability based on growth. Can we conclude that the slope of the regression line is negative?
c. Use a software package to determine the residual for each observation. Which company has the largest residual?

57. The following data show the retail price for 12 randomly selected laptop computers along with their corresponding processor speeds in gigahertz. 🎯

Computers	Speed	Price	Computers	Speed	Price
1	2.0	$2,017	7	2.0	$2,197
2	1.6	922	8	1.6	1,387
3	1.6	1,064	9	2.0	2,114
4	1.8	1,942	10	1.6	2,002
5	2.0	2,137	11	1.0	937
6	1.2	1,012	12	1.4	869

a. Develop a linear equation that can be used to describe how the price depends on the processor speed.
b. Based on your regression equation, is there one machine that seems particularly over- or underpriced?
c. Compute the correlation coefficient between the two variables. At the .05 significance level, conduct a test of hypothesis to determine if the population correlation is greater than zero.

58. A consumer buying cooperative tested the effective heating area of 20 different electric space heaters with different wattages. Here are the results. 🎯

Heater	Wattage	Area	Heater	Wattage	Area
1	1,500	205	11	1,250	116
2	750	70	12	500	72
3	1,500	199	13	500	82
4	1,250	151	14	1,500	206
5	1,250	181	15	2,000	245
6	1,250	217	16	1,500	219
7	1,000	94	17	750	63
8	2,000	298	18	1,500	200
9	1,000	135	19	1,250	151
10	1,500	211	20	500	44

a. Compute the correlation between the wattage and heating area. Is there a direct or an indirect relationship?
b. Conduct a test of hypothesis to determine if it is reasonable that the coefficient is greater than zero. Use the .05 significance level.
c. Develop the regression equation for effective heating based on wattage.
d. Which heater looks like the "best buy" based on the size of the residual?

59. A dog trainer is exploring the relationship between the size of the dog (weight in pounds) and its daily food consumption (measured in standard cups). Below is the result of a sample of 18 observations.

Dog	Weight	Consumption	Dog	Weight	Consumption
1	41	3	10	91	5
2	148	8	11	109	6
3	79	5	12	207	10
4	41	4	13	49	3
5	85	5	14	113	6
6	111	6	15	84	5
7	37	3	16	95	5
8	111	6	17	57	4
9	41	3	18	168	9

a. Compute the correlation coefficient. Is it reasonable to conclude that the correlation in the population is greater than zero? Use the .05 significance level.
b. Develop the regression equation for cups based on the dog's weight. How much does each additional cup change the estimated weight of the dog?
c. Is one of the dogs a big undereater or overeater?

60. Waterbury Insurance Company wants to study the relationship between the amount of fire damage and the distance between the burning house and the nearest fire station. This information will be used in setting rates for insurance coverage. For a sample of 30 claims for the last year, the director of the actuarial department determined the distance from the fire station (X) and the amount of fire damage, in thousands of dollars (Y). The MegaStat output is reported below.

```
ANOVA table
Source                  SS      df           MS         F
Regression      1,864.5782      1     1,864.5782     38.83
Residual        1,344.4934     28        48.0176
Total           3,209.0716     29

Regression output
Variables      Coefficients    Std. Error    t(df = 28)
Intercept           12.3601        3.2915         3.755
Distance—X           4.7956        0.7696         6.231
```

Answer the following questions.
a. Write out the regression equation. Is there a direct or indirect relationship between the distance from the fire station and the amount of fire damage?
b. How much damage would you estimate for a fire 5 miles from the nearest fire station?
c. Determine and interpret the coefficient of determination.
d. Determine the correlation coefficient. Interpret its value. How did you determine the sign of the correlation coefficient?
e. Conduct a test of hypothesis to determine if there is a significant relationship between the distance from the fire station and the amount of damage. Use the .01 significance level and a two-tailed test.

61. An air travel service samples domestic airline flights to explore the relationship between airfare and distance. The service would like to know if there is a correlation between airfare and flight distance. If there is a correlation, what percentage of the variation in airfare is accounted for by distance? How much does each additional mile add to the fare? The data follow. (df)

Origin	Destination	Distance	Fare
Detroit, MI	Myrtle Beach, SC	636	$109
Baltimore, MD	Sacramento, CA	2,395	252
Las Vegas, NV	Philadelphia, PA	2,176	221
Sacramento, CA	Seattle, WA	605	151
Atlanta, GA	Orlando, FL	403	138
Boston, MA	Miami, FL	1,258	209
Chicago, IL	Covington, KY	264	254
Columbus, OH	Minneapolis, MN	627	259
Fort Lauderdale, FL	Los Angeles, CA	2,342	215
Chicago, IL	Indianapolis, IN	177	128
Philadelphia, PA	San Francisco, CA	2,521	348
Houston, TX	Raleigh/Durham, NC	1,050	224
Houston, TX	Midland/Odessa, TX	441	175
Cleveland, OH	Dallas/Ft.Worth, TX	1,021	256
Baltimore, MD	Columbus, OH	336	121
Boston, MA	Covington, KY	752	252
Kansas City, MO	San Diego, CA	1,333	206
Milwaukee, WI	Phoenix, AZ	1,460	167
Portland, OR	Washington, DC	2,350	308
Phoenix, AZ	San Jose, CA	621	152
Baltimore, MD	St. Louis, MO	737	175
Houston, TX	Orlando, FL	853	191
Houston, TX	Seattle, WA	1,894	231
Burbank, CA	New York, NY	2,465	251
Atlanta, GA	San Diego, CA	1,891	291
Minneapolis, MN	New York, NY	1,028	260
Atlanta, GA	West Palm Beach, FL	545	123
Kansas City, MO	Seattle, WA	1,489	211
Baltimore, MD	Portland, ME	452	139
New Orleans, LA	Washington, DC	969	243

  a. Draw a scatter diagram with *Distance* as the independent variable and *Fare* as the dependent variable. Is the relationship direct or indirect?
  b. Compute the correlation coefficient. At the .05 significance level, is it reasonable to conclude that the correlation coefficient is greater than zero?
  c. What percentage of the variation in *Fare* is accounted for by *Distance* of a flight?
  d. Determine the regression equation. How much does each additional mile add to the fare? Estimate the fare for a 1,500-mile flight.
  e. A traveler is planning to fly from Atlanta to London Heathrow. The distance is 4,218 miles. She wants to use the regression equation to estimate the fare. Explain why it would not be a good idea to estimate the fare for this international flight with the regression equation.

Data Set Exercises

(The data for these exercises are available at the text website www.mhhe.com/lindbasic8e).

62. Refer to the Real Estate data, which reports information on homes sold in Goodyear, Arizona, last year.
  a. Let selling price be the dependent variable and size of the home the independent variable. Determine the regression equation. Estimate the selling price for a home

with an area of 2,200 square feet. Determine the 95% confidence interval and the 95% prediction interval for the selling price of a home with 2,200 square feet.

b. Let selling price be the dependent variable and distance from the center of the city the independent variable. Determine the regression equation. Estimate the selling price of a home 20 miles from the center of the city. Determine the 95% confidence interval and the 95% prediction interval for homes 20 miles from the center of the city.

c. Can you conclude that the independent variables "distance from the center of the city" and "selling price" are negatively correlated and that the area of the home and the selling price are positively correlated? Use the .05 significance level. Report the *p*-value of the test. Summarize your results in a brief report.

63. Refer to the Baseball 2010 data, which reports information on the 2010 Major League Baseball season. Let the games won be the dependent variable and total team payroll, in millions of dollars, be the independent variable. Determine the regression equation and answer the following questions.

a. Draw a scatter diagram. From the diagram, does there seem to be a direct relationship between the two variables?

b. How many wins would you estimate with a payroll of $100.0 million?

c. How many additional wins will an additional $5 million in payroll bring?

d. At the .05 significance level, can we conclude that the slope of the regression line is positive? Conduct the appropriate test of hypothesis.

e. What percentage of the variation in wins is accounted for by payroll?

f. Determine the correlation between wins and team batting average and between wins and team ERA. Which is stronger? Conduct an appropriate test of hypothesis for each set of variables.

64. Refer to the Buena School bus data. Develop a regression equation that expresses the relationship between age of the bus and maintenance. The age of the bus is the independent variable.

a. Draw a scatter diagram. What does this diagram suggest as to the relationship between the two variables? Is it direct or indirect? Does it appear to be strong or weak?

b. Develop a regression equation. How much does an additional year add to the maintenance cost. What is the estimated maintenance cost for a 10-year-old bus?

c. Conduct a test of hypothesis to determine whether the slope of the regression line is greater than zero. Use the .05 significance level. Interpret your findings from parts (a), (b), and (c) in a brief report.

Practice Test

Part 1—Objective
1. The first step in correlation analysis is to plot the data with a _____.
2. The range of the correlation coefficient is between _____ and _____.
3. In studying the relationship between two variables, if the value of one variable decreases with increases in the other variable, the correlation coefficient is _____. (less than zero, zero, greater than zero)
4. The proportion of variation in the dependent variable that is explained by the variation in the independent variable is measured by the _____.
5. To test the hypothesis that the correlation coefficient is zero, the test statistic follows the _____ distribution.
6. The least squares regression line minimizes the sum of the squared differences between the actual and _____ values of the dependent variable.
7. For a given set of data, the correlation coefficient and the slope of the regression line have the same _____. (values, signs, units, squares)
8. For a regression analysis, a small standard error of the estimate indicates that the coefficient of determination will be _____. (large, small, always 0)
9. In regression analysis, confidence and prediction intervals show the _____ associated with an estimated value of the dependent variable. (error, association, convergence, sample size)
10. A prediction interval is based on an individual value of the _____ variable. (dependent, independent, correlated, estimated)

Part 2—Problems
1. At the end of each calendar year, employees of the G. G. Green Manufacturing Company can purchase company stock. For a sample of employees, the Director of Human Resources investigated the relationship between the number of years of service with the company and the number of shares of company stock owned. The "number of years of service" is used to estimate the "number of shares of stock." Use the following output showing the results of the analysis to answer the questions.

ANOVA Table				
Source	SS	df	MS	F
Regression	152,399.0211	1	152,399.0211	62.67
Residual	55,934.1189	23	2,431.9182	
Total	208,333.1400	24		

Regression Output			
Variables	Coefficients	Std. Error	t (df = 23)
Intercept	197.9229	34.3047	5.770
Years	24.9145	3.1473	7.916

a. How many employees were included in the study?
b. Is "number of shares of stock" or "number of years of service" the dependent variable?
c. Write out the regression equation.
d. Is the relationship between the two variables direct or indirect?
e. Determine the correlation coefficient.
f. How many shares would you expect an employee of 10 years to own?
g. For each additional year of service, how much does "number of shares owned" change?
h. Can we conclude that as years of service increases so do the number of shares of stock owned? Conduct an appropriate test of hypothesis on the slope of the regression line.

Software Commands

1. The Minitab commands for the output showing the correlation coefficient on page 403 are:
   a. Enter the sales representative's name in *C1,* the number of calls in *C2*, and the sales in *C3*.
   b. Select **Stat, Basic Statistics,** and **Correlation.**
   c. Select *Calls* and *Sales* as the variables, click on **Display p-values,** and then click **OK.**

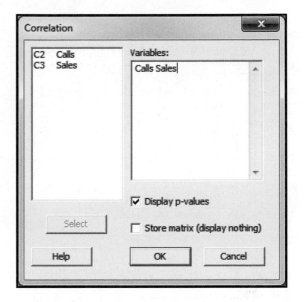

2. The computer commands for the Excel output on page 413 are:
   a. Enter the variable names in row 1 of columns A, B, and C. Enter the data in rows 2 through 11 in the same columns.
   b. Select the **Data** tab on the top of the menu. Then, on the far right, select **Data Analysis.** Select **Regression,** then click **OK.**
   c. For our spreadsheet, we have *Calls* in column B and *Sales* in column C. The **Input Y-Range** is *C1:C11* and the **Input X-Range** is *B1:B11.* Click on **Labels,** select *E1* as the **Output Range,** and click **OK.**

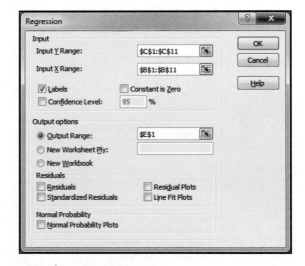

3. The Minitab commands to the confidence intervals and prediction intervals on page 423 are:
   a. Select **Stat, Regression,** and **Fitted line plot.**
   b. In the next dialog box, the **Response (Y)** is Sales and **Predictor (X)** is Calls. Select **Linear** for the type of regression model and then click on **Options.**
   c. In the **Options** dialog box, click on **Display confidence and prediction bands,** use the **95.0 for confidence level,** type an appropriate heading in the **Title** box, then click **OK** and then **OK** again.

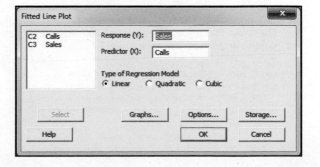

Chapter 13   Answers to Self-Review

13–1 a. Advertising expense is the independent variable, and sales revenue is the dependent variable.

b.

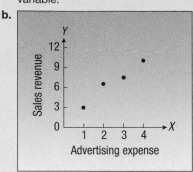

c.

X	Y	$(X - \bar{X})$	$(X - \bar{X})^2$	$(Y - \bar{Y})$	$(Y - \bar{Y})^2$	$(X - \bar{X})(Y - \bar{Y})$
2	7	−0.5	.25	0	0	0
1	3	−1.5	2.25	−4	16	6
3	8	0.5	.25	1	1	0.5
4	10	1.5	2.25	3	9	4.5
10	28		5.00		26	11.0

$$\bar{X} = \frac{10}{4} = 2.5 \qquad \bar{Y} = \frac{28}{4} = 7$$

$$s_x = \sqrt{\frac{5}{3}} = 1.2909944$$

$$s_y = \sqrt{\frac{26}{3}} = 2.9439203$$

$$r = \frac{\Sigma(X - \bar{X})(Y - \bar{Y})}{(n - 1)s_x s_y} = \frac{11}{(4 - 1)(1.2909944)(2.9439203)}$$

$$= 0.9648$$

d. There is a strong correlation between the advertising expense and sales.

13–2 $H_0: \rho \le 0, H_1: \rho > 0.$ H_0 is rejected if $t > 1.714.$

$$t = \frac{.43\sqrt{25 - 2}}{\sqrt{1 - (.43)^2}} = 2.284$$

H_0 is rejected. There is a positive correlation between the percent of the vote received and the amount spent on the campaign.

13–3 a. See the calculations in Self-Review 13–1, part (c).

$$b = \frac{rs_y}{s_x} = \frac{(0.9648)(2.9439)}{1.2910} = 2.2$$

$$a = \frac{28}{4} - 2.2\left(\frac{10}{4}\right) = 7 - 5.5 = 1.5$$

b. The slope is 2.2. This indicates that an increase of \$1 million in advertising will result in an increase of \$2.2 million in sales. The intercept is 1.5. If there was no expenditure for advertising, sales would be \$1.5 million.

c. $\hat{Y} = 1.5 + 2.2(3) = 8.1$

13–4 $H_0: \beta_1 \le 0; H_1: \beta > 0,$ reject H_0 if $t > 3.182.$

$$t = \frac{2.2 - 0}{0.42} = 5.238$$

Reject H_0. The slope of the line is greater than 0.

13–5 a.

Y	$\hat{Y}$	$(Y - \hat{Y})$	$(Y - \hat{Y})^2$
7	5.9	1.1	1.21
3	3.7	−0.7	.49
8	8.1	−0.1	.01
10	10.3	−0.3	.09
			1.80

$$s_{y \cdot x} = \sqrt{\frac{\Sigma(Y - \hat{Y})^2}{n - 2}}$$

$$= \sqrt{\frac{1.80}{4 - 2}} = .9487$$

b. $r^2 = (.9648)^2 = .9308$

c. Ninety-three percent of the variation in sales is accounted for by advertising expense.

13–6 6.58 and 9.62, since $\hat{Y}$ for an X of 3 is 8.1, found by $\hat{Y} = 1.5 + 2.2(3) = 8.1,$ then $\bar{X} = 2.5$ and $\Sigma(X - \bar{X})^2 = 5.$

t from Appendix B.2 for $4 - 2 = 2$ degrees of freedom at the .10 level is 2.920.

$$\hat{Y} \pm t(s_{y \cdot x})\sqrt{\frac{1}{n} + \frac{(X - \bar{X})^2}{\Sigma(X - \bar{X})^2}}$$

$$= 8.1 \pm 2.920(0.9487)\sqrt{\frac{1}{4} + \frac{(3 - 2.5)^2}{5}}$$

$$= 8.1 \pm 2.920(0.9487)(0.5477)$$

$$= 6.58 \text{ and } 9.62 \text{ (in \$ millions)}$$

14

Multiple Regression Analysis

The mortgage department of the Bank of New England is studying data from recent loans. Of particular interest is how such factors as the value of the home being purchased, education level of the head of the household, age of the head of the household, current monthly mortgage payment, and gender of the head of the household relate to the family income. Are the proposed variables effective predictors of the dependent variable family income? (See the Example/Solution in Section 14.8 and LO 14-1.)

Learning Objectives

When you have completed this chapter, you will be able to:

LO 14-1 Describe the relationship between several independent variables and a dependent variable using multiple regression analysis.

LO 14-2 Develop and interpret an ANOVA table.

LO 14-3 Compute and interpret measures of association in multiple regression.

LO 14-4 Conduct a hypothesis test to determine whether a set of regression coefficients differ from zero.

LO 14-5 Conduct a hypothesis test of each regression coefficient.

LO 14-6 Use residual analysis to evaluate the assumptions of multiple regression analysis.

LO 14-7 Evaluate the effects of correlated independent variables.

LO 14-8 Evaluate and use qualitative independent variables.

LO 14-9 Explain stepwise regression.

14.1 Introduction

In Chapter 13, we described the relationship between a pair of interval- or ratio-scaled variables. We began the chapter by studying the correlation coefficient, which measures the strength of the linear relationship between two variables. A coefficient near plus or minus 1.00 ($-.88$ or $.78$, for example) indicates a very strong linear relationship, whereas a value near 0 ($-.12$ or $.18$, for example) means that the relationship is weak. Next we developed a procedure to express the relationship between two variables with a linear equation. We referred to this as a *regression equation.* This equation describes the relationship between the variables.

In multiple linear correlation and regression, we use additional independent variables (denoted $X_1, X_2, \ldots$, and so on) that help us better explain or predict the dependent variable (Y). Almost all of the ideas we saw in simple linear correlation and regression extend to this more general situation. However, the additional independent variables do lead to some new considerations. Multiple regression analysis can be used either as a descriptive or as an inferential technique.

14.2 Multiple Regression Analysis

LO 14-1 Describe the relationship between several independent variables and a dependent variable using multiple regression analysis.

The general descriptive form of a multiple linear equation is shown in formula (14–1). We use k to represent the number of independent variables. So k can be any positive integer.

| GENERAL MULTIPLE REGRESSION EQUATION | $\hat{Y} = a + b_1X_1 + b_2X_2 + b_3X_3 + \cdots + b_kX_k$ | [14–1] |

where:
  a is the intercept, the value of $\hat{Y}$ when all the X's are zero.
  b_j is the amount by which $\hat{Y}$ changes when that particular X_j increases by one unit, with the values of all other independent variables held constant. The subscript j is simply a label that helps to identify each independent variable; it is not used in any calculations. Usually the subscript is an integer value between 1 and k, which is the number of independent variables. However, the subscript can also be a short or abbreviated label. For example, age could be used as a subscript.

In Chapter 13, the regression analysis described and tested the relationship between a dependent variable, $\hat{Y}$, and a single independent variable, X. The relationship between $\hat{Y}$ and X was graphically portrayed by a line. When there are two independent variables, the regression equation is

$$\hat{Y} = a + b_1X_1 + b_2X_2$$

Because there are two independent variables, this relationship is graphically portrayed as a plane and is shown in Chart 14–1. The chart shows the residuals as the difference between the actual Y and the fitted $\hat{Y}$ on the plane. If a multiple regression analysis includes more than two independent variables, we cannot use a graph to illustrate the analysis since graphs are limited to three dimensions.

To illustrate the interpretation of the intercept and the two regression coefficients, suppose the selling price of a home is directly related to the number of rooms and inversely related to its age. We let X_1 refer to the number of rooms, X_2 to the

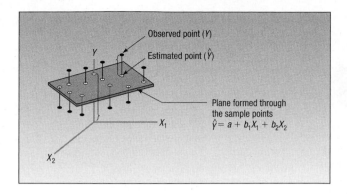

CHART 14–1 Regression Plane with 10 Sample Points

age of the home in years, and Y to the selling price of the home in $000. Suppose the regression equation, calculated using statistical software, is:

$$\hat{Y} = 21.2 + 18.7X_1 - 0.25X_2$$

The intercept, 21.2, indicates that the regression equation (plane) intersects the Y-axis at 21.2. This happens when both the number of rooms and the age of the home are zero. We could say that $21,200 is the average value of a property without a house.

The first regression coefficient, 18.7, indicates that for each increase of 1 room in the size of a home, the selling price will increase by 18.7 ($18,700), *regardless of the age of the home*. The second regression coefficient, −0.25, indicates that for each increase of one year in age, the selling price will decrease by .25 ($250), *regardless of the number of rooms*. As an example, a seven-room home that is 30 years old will sell for $144,600.

$$\hat{Y} = 21.2 + 18.7X_1 - 0.25X_2 = 21.2 + 18.7(7) - .25(30) = 144.6$$

The values for the coefficients in the multiple linear equation are found by using the method of least squares. Recall from the previous chapter that the least squares method makes the sum of the squared differences between the fitted and actual values of Y as small as possible, that is, the term $\Sigma(Y - \hat{Y})^2$ is minimized. The calculations are very tedious, so they are usually performed by a statistical software package, such as Excel or Minitab.

In the following example, we show a multiple regression analysis using three independent variables employing Excel and Minitab. Both packages report a standard set of statistics and reports. However, Minitab also provides advanced regression analysis techniques that we will use later in the chapter.

Example

Salsberry Realty sells homes along the east coast of the United States. One of the questions most frequently asked by prospective buyers is: If we purchase this home, how much can we expect to pay to heat it during the winter? The research department at Salsberry has been asked to develop some guidelines regarding heating costs for single-family homes. Three variables are thought to relate to the heating costs: (1) the mean daily outside temperature, (2) the number of inches of insulation in the attic, and (3) the age in years of the furnace. To investigate, Salsberry's research department selected a random sample of 20 recently sold homes. It determined the cost to heat each home last January, as well as the January outside temperature in the region, the number of inches of insulation in the attic, and the age of the furnace. The sample information is reported in Table 14–1.

TABLE 14–1 Factors in January Heating Cost for a Sample of 20 Homes

Home	Heating Cost ($)	Mean Outside Temperature (°F)	Attic Insulation (inches)	Age of Furnace (years)
1	$250	35	3	6
2	360	29	4	10
3	165	36	7	3
4	43	60	6	9
5	92	65	5	6
6	200	30	5	5
7	355	10	6	7
8	290	7	10	10
9	230	21	9	11
10	120	55	2	5
11	73	54	12	4
12	205	48	5	1
13	400	20	5	15
14	320	39	4	7
15	72	60	8	6
16	272	20	5	8
17	94	58	7	3
18	190	40	8	11
19	235	27	9	8
20	139	30	7	5

The data in Table 14–1 is available in both Excel and Minitab formats at the textbook website, www.mhhe.com/lind8e. The basic instructions for using Excel and Minitab for this data are in the Software Commands section at the end of this chapter.

Determine the multiple regression equation. Which variables are the independent variables? Which variable is the dependent variable? Discuss the regression coefficients. What does it indicate if some coefficients are positive and some coefficients are negative? What is the intercept value? What is the estimated heating cost for a home if the mean outside temperature is 30 degrees, there are 5 inches of insulation in the attic, and the furnace is 10 years old?

Solution

We begin the analysis by defining the dependent and independent variables. The dependent variable is the January heating cost. It is represented by Y. There are three independent variables:

- The mean outside temperature in January, represented by X_1.
- The number of inches of insulation in the attic, represented by X_2.
- The age in years of the furnace, represented by X_3.

Given these definitions, the general form of the multiple regression equation follows. The value $\hat{Y}$ is used to estimate the value of Y.

$$\hat{Y} = a + b_1X_1 + b_2X_2 + b_3X_3$$

Now that we have defined the regression equation, we are ready to use either Excel or Minitab to compute all the statistics needed for the analysis. The outputs from the two software systems are shown on the following page.

To use the regression equation to predict the January heating cost, we need to know the values of the regression coefficients, b_j. These are highlighted in the software reports. Note that the software used the variable names or labels associated with each independent variable. The regression equation intercept, a, is labeled as "constant" in the Minitab output and "intercept" in the Excel output.

Minitab regression results

↓	C1	C2	C3	C4
	Cost	Temp	Insul	Age
1	250	35	3	6
2	360	29	4	10
3	165	36	7	3
4	43	60	6	9
5	92	65	5	6
6	200	30	5	5
7	355	10	6	7
8	290	7	10	10
9	230	21	9	11
10	120	55	2	5
11	73	54	12	4
12	205	48	5	1
13	400	20	5	15
14	320	39	4	7
15	72	60	8	6
16	272	20	5	8
17	94	58	7	3
18	190	40	8	11
19	235	27	9	8
20	139	30	7	5
21				

Regression Analysis: Cost versus Temp, Insul, Age

The regression equation is
Cost = 427 − 4.58 Temp − 14.8 Insul + 6.10 Age

Predictor	Coef	SE Coef	T	P
Constant	427.19	59.60	7.17	0.000
Temp	−4.5827	0.7723	−5.93	0.000
Insul	−14.831	4.754	−3.12	0.007
Age	6.101	4.012	1.52	0.148

S = 51.0486   R-Sq = 80.4%   R-Sq(adj) = 76.7%

Analysis of Variance

Source	DF	SS	MS	F	P
Regression	3	171220	57073	21.90	0.000
Residual Error	16	41695	2606		
Total	19	212916			

Excel regression results

	A	B	C	D	F	G	H	I	J	K	L
1	Cost	Temp	Insul	Age		SUMMARY OUTPUT					
2	250	35	3	6							
3	360	29	4	10		*Regression Statistics*					
4	165	36	7	3		Multiple R	0.897				
5	43	60	6	9		R Square	0.804				
6	92	65	5	6		Adjusted R Square	0.767				
7	200	30	5	5		Standard Error	51.049				
8	355	10	6	7		Observations	20				
9	290	7	10	10							
10	230	21	9	11		ANOVA					
11	120	55	2	5			*df*	*SS*	*MS*	*F*	*Significance F*
12	73	54	12	4		Regression	3	171220.473	57073.491	21.901	0.000
13	205	48	5	1		Residual	16	41695.277	2605.955		
14	400	20	5	15		Total	19	212915.750			
15	320	39	4	7							
16	72	60	8	6			*Coefficients*	*Standard Error*	*t Stat*	*P-value*	
17	272	20	5	8		Intercept	427.194	59.601	7.168	0.000	
18	94	58	7	3		Temp	−4.583	0.772	−5.934	0.000	
19	190	40	8	11		Insul	−14.831	4.754	−3.119	0.007	
20	235	27	9	8		Age	6.101	4.012	1.521	0.148	
21	139	30	7	5							

In this case, the estimated regression equation is:

$$\hat{Y} = 427.194 − 4.583X_1 − 14.831X_2 + 6.101X_3$$

We can now estimate or predict the January heating cost for a home if we know the mean outside temperature, the inches of insulation, and the age of the furnace. For an example home, the mean outside temperature for the month is 30 degrees (X_1), there are 5 inches of insulation in the attic (X_2), and the furnace is 10 years old (X_3). By substituting the values for the independent variables:

$$\hat{Y} = 427.194 − 4.583(30) − 14.831(5) + 6.101(10) = 276.56$$

The estimated January heating cost is $276.56.

The regression coefficients, and their algebraic signs, also provide information about their individual relationships with the January heating cost. The regression coefficient for mean outside temperature is -4.583. The coefficient is negative and shows an inverse relationship between heating cost and temperature. This is not surprising. As the outside temperature increases, the cost to heat the home decreases. The numeric value of the regression coefficient provides more information. If we increase temperature by 1 degree and hold the other two independent variables constant, we can estimate a decrease of $4.583 in monthly heating cost. So if the mean temperature in Boston is 25 degrees and it is 35 degrees in Philadelphia, all other things being the same (insulation and age of furnace), we expect the heating cost would be $45.83 less in Philadelphia.

The attic insulation variable also shows an inverse relationship: the more insulation in the attic, the less the cost to heat the home. So the negative sign for this coefficient is logical. For each additional inch of insulation, we expect the cost to heat the home to decline $14.83 per month, holding the outside temperature and the age of the furnace constant.

The age of the furnace variable shows a direct relationship. With an older furnace, the cost to heat the home increases. Specifically, for each additional year older the furnace is, we expect the cost to increase $6.10 per month.

Self-Review 14–1

There are many restaurants in northeastern South Carolina. They serve beach vacationers in the summer, golfers in the fall and spring, and snowbirds in the winter. Bill and Joyce Tuneall manage several restaurants in the North Jersey area and are considering moving to Myrtle Beach, SC, to open a new restaurant. Before making a final decision, they wish to investigate existing restaurants and what variables seem to be related to profitability. They gather sample information where profit (reported in $000) is the dependent variable and the independent variables are:

X_1 the number of parking spaces near the restaurant.
X_2 the number of hours the restaurant is open per week.
X_3 the distance from the SkyWheel, a landmark in Myrtle Beach.
X_4 the number of servers employed.
X_5 the number of years the current owner has owned the restaurant.

The following is part of the output obtained using statistical software.

Predictor	Coef	SE Coef	T
Constant	2.50	1.50	1.667
X_1	3.00	1.500	2.000
X_2	4.00	3.000	1.333
X_3	-3.00	0.20	-15.00
X_4	0.20	.05	4.00
X_5	1.00	1.50	0.667

(a) What is the amount of profit for a restaurant with 40 parking spaces that is open 72 hours per week, is 10 miles from the SkyWheel, has 20 servers, and has been open 5 years?
(b) Interpret the values of b_2 and b_3 in the multiple regression equation.

Exercises

connect

1. The director of marketing at Reeves Wholesale Products is studying monthly sales. Three independent variables were selected as estimators of sales: regional population, per capita income, and regional unemployment rate. The regression equation was computed to be (in dollars):

$$\hat{Y} = 64{,}100 + 0.394X_1 + 9.6X_2 - 11{,}600X_3$$

    a. What is the full name of the equation?

    b. Interpret the number 64,100.

    c. What are the estimated monthly sales for a particular region with a population of 796,000, per capita income of $6,940, and an unemployment rate of 6.0%?

2. Thompson Photo Works purchased several new, highly sophisticated processing machines. The production department needed some guidance with respect to qualifications needed by an operator. Is age a factor? Is the length of service as an operator (in years) important? In order to explore further the factors needed to estimate performance on the new processing machines, four variables were listed:

$$X_1 = \text{Length of time an employee was in the industry}$$
$$X_2 = \text{Mechanical aptitude test score}$$
$$X_3 = \text{Prior on-the-job rating}$$
$$X_4 = \text{Age}$$

Performance on the new machine is designated Y.

    Thirty employees were selected at random. Data were collected for each, and their performances on the new machines were recorded. A few results are:

Name	Performance on New Machine, Y	Length of Time in Industry, X_1	Mechanical Aptitude Score, X_2	Prior On-the-Job Performance, X_3	Age, X_4
Mike Miraglia	112	12	312	121	52
Sue Trythall	113	2	380	123	27

The equation is:

$$\hat{Y} = 11.6 + 0.4X_1 + 0.286X_2 + 0.112X_3 + 0.002X_4$$

    a. What is this equation called?

    b. How many dependent variables are there? Independent variables?

    c. What is the number 0.286 called?

    d. As age increases by one year, how much does estimated performance on the new machine increase?

    e. Carl Knox applied for a job at Photo Works. He has been in the business for six years, and scored 280 on the mechanical aptitude test. Carl's prior on-the-job performance rating is 97, and he is 35 years old. Estimate Carl's performance on the new machine.

3. A consulting group surveyed General Mills, Inc. employees to research the factors that affect their satisfaction with their quality of life. A special index, called the index of satisfaction, was used to measure satisfaction. Six factors were studied: age at the time of first marriage (X_1), annual income (X_2), number of children living (X_3), value of all assets (X_4), status of health in the form of an index (X_5), and the average number of social activities per week—such as bowling and dancing (X_6). Suppose the multiple regression equation is:

$$\hat{Y} = 16.24 + 0.017X_1 + 0.0028X_2 + 42X_3 + 0.0012X_4 + 0.19X_5 + 26.8X_6$$

    a. What is the estimated index of satisfaction for a person who first married at 18, has an annual income of $26,500, has three children living, has assets of $156,000, has an index of health status of 141, and has 2.5 social activities a week on the average?

    b. Which would add more to satisfaction, an additional income of $10,000 a year or two more social activities a week?

4. Cellulon, a manufacturer of home insulation, wants to develop guidelines for builders and consumers on how the thickness of the insulation in the attic of a home and the outdoor temperature affect natural gas consumption. In the laboratory, it varied the insulation thickness and temperature. A few of the findings are:

Monthly Natural Gas Consumption (cubic feet), Y	Thickness of Insulation (inches), X_1	Outdoor Temperature (°F), X_2
30.3	6	40
26.9	12	40
22.1	8	49

On the basis of the sample results, the regression equation is:

$$\hat{Y} = 62.65 - 1.86X_1 - 0.52X_2$$

a. How much natural gas can homeowners expect to use per month if they install 6 inches of insulation and the outdoor temperature is 40 degrees F?

b. What effect would installing 7 inches of insulation instead of 6 have on the monthly natural gas consumption (assuming the outdoor temperature remains at 40 degrees F)?

c. Why are the regression coefficients b_1 and b_2 negative? Is this logical?

14.3 Evaluating a Multiple Regression Equation

Many statistics and statistical methods are used to evaluate the relationship between a dependent variable and more than one independent variable. Our first step is to express the relationship in terms of a multiple regression equation. The next step follows on the concepts presented in Chapter 13 by using the information in an ANOVA table to evaluate how well the equation fits the data.

The ANOVA Table

LO 14-2 Develop and interpret an ANOVA table.

As in Chapter 13, the statistical analysis of a multiple regression equation is summarized in an ANOVA table. To review, the total variation of the dependent variable, Y, is divided into two components: (1) *regression,* or the variation of Y explained by all the independent variables and (2) *the error or residual,* or unexplained variation of Y. These two categories are identified in the first column of an ANOVA table below. The column headed "*df*" refers to the degrees of freedom associated with each category. The total number of degrees of freedom is $n - 1$. The number of degrees of freedom in the regression is equal to the number of independent variables in the multiple regression equation. We call the regression degrees of freedom k. The number of degrees of freedom associated with the error term is equal to the total degrees of freedom minus the regression degrees of freedom. In multiple regression, the degrees of freedom are $n - (k + 1)$.

Source	df	SS	MS	F
Regression	k	SSR	$MSR = SSR/k$	MSR/MSE
Residual or error	$n - (k + 1)$	SSE	$MSE = SSE/[n - (k + 1)]$	
Total	$n - 1$	SS total		

The term "SS" located in the middle of the ANOVA table refers to the sum of squares. Notice that there is a sum of squares for each source of variation. The sum of squares column shows the amount of variation attributable to each source. The total variation of the dependent variable, Y, is summarized in SS total. This is the numerator of the usual formula to calculate any variation—in other words, the sum of the squared deviations from the mean. It is computed as:

$$\text{Total Sum of Squares} = \text{SS total} = \Sigma(Y - \bar{Y})^2$$

As we have seen, the total sum of squares is the sum of the regression and residual sum of squares. The regression sum of squares is the sum of the squared differences between the estimated or predicted values, $\hat{Y}$, and the overall mean of Y. The regression sum of squares is found by:

$$\text{Regression Sum of Squares} = \text{SSR} = \Sigma(\hat{Y} - \bar{Y})^2$$

The residual sum of squares is the sum of the squared differences between the observed values of the dependent variable, Y, and their corresponding estimated or predicted values, $\hat{Y}$. Notice that this difference is the error of estimating or predicting the dependent variable with the multiple regression equation. It is calculated as:

$$\text{Residual or Error Sum of Squares} = \text{SSE} = \Sigma(Y - \hat{Y})^2$$

We will use the ANOVA table information from the previous example to evaluate the regression equation to estimate January heating costs.

	A	B	C	D	F	G	H	I	J	K	L
1	Cost	Temp	Insul	Age		SUMMARY OUTPUT					
2	250	35	3	6							
3	360	29	4	10		*Regression Statistics*					
4	165	36	7	3		Multiple R	0.897				
5	43	60	6	9		R Square	0.804				
6	92	65	5	6		Adjusted R Square	0.767				
7	200	30	5	5		Standard Error	51.049				
8	355	10	6	7		Observations	20				
9	290	7	10	10							
10	230	21	9	11		ANOVA					
11	120	55	2	5			*df*	*SS*	*MS*	*F*	*Significance F*
12	73	54	12	4		Regression	3	171220.473	57073.491	21.901	0.000
13	205	48	5	1		Residual	16	41695.277	2605.955		
14	400	20	5	15		Total	19	212915.750			
15	320	39	4	7							
16	72	60	8	6			*Coefficients*	*Standard Error*	*t Stat*	*P-value*	
17	272	20	5	8		Intercept	427.194	59.601	7.168	0.000	
18	94	58	7	3		Temp	-4.583	0.772	-5.934	0.000	
19	190	40	8	11		Insul	-14.831	4.754	-3.119	0.007	
20	235	27	9	8		Age	6.101	4.012	1.521	0.148	

Multiple Standard Error of Estimate

LO 14-3 Compute and interpret measures of association in multiple regression.

We begin with the **multiple standard error of estimate.** Recall that the standard error of estimate is comparable to the standard deviation. To explain the details of the standard error of estimate, refer to the first sampled home in row 2 in the Excel spreadsheet above. The actual heating cost for the first observation, Y, is $250, the outside temperature, X_1, is 35 degrees, the depth of insulation, X_2, is 3 inches, and the age of the furnace, X_3, is 6 years. Using the regression equation developed in the previous section, the estimated heating cost for this home is:

$$\hat{Y} = 427.194 - 4.583X_1 - 14.831X_2 + 6.101X_3$$
$$= 427.194 - 4.583(35) - 14.831(3) + 6.101(6)$$
$$= 258.90$$

So we would estimate that a home with a mean January outside temperature of 35 degrees, 3 inches of insulation, and a 6-year-old furnace would cost $258.90 to heat. The actual heating cost was $250, so the residual—which is the difference between the actual value and the estimated value—is $Y - \hat{Y} = 250 - 258.90 = -8.90$. This difference of $8.90 is the random or unexplained error for the first home sampled. Our next step is to square this difference—that is, find $(Y - \hat{Y})^2 = (250 - 258.90)^2 = (-8.90)^2 = 79.21$.

If we repeat this calculation for the other 19 observations and sum all 20 squared differences, the total will be the residual or error sum of squares from the ANOVA table. Using this information, we can calculate the multiple standard error of the estimate as:

| MULTIPLE STANDARD ERROR OF ESTIMATE | $s_{Y.123...k} = \sqrt{\dfrac{\Sigma(Y - \hat{Y})^2}{n - (k + 1)}} = \sqrt{\dfrac{SSR}{n - (k + 1)}}$ | [14–2] |

where:
    Y is the actual observation.
    $\hat{Y}$ is the estimated value computed from the regression equation.
    n is the number of observations in the sample.
    k is the number of independent variables.
    SSR is the Residual Sum of Squares from an ANOVA table.

There is more information in the ANOVA table that can be used to compute the multiple standard error of the estimate. The column headed MS reports the mean squares for the regression and residual sources of variation. These are calculated as the sum of squares divided by the corresponding degrees of freedom. The multiple standard error of the estimate is equal to the square root of the residual MS, which is also called the mean square error or the MSE.

$$s_{Y.123...K} = \sqrt{MSE} = \sqrt{2605.995} = \$51.05$$

How do we interpret the standard error of estimate of 51.05? It is the typical "error" when we use this equation to predict the cost. First, the units are the same as the dependent variable, so the standard error is in dollars, \$51.05. Second, we expect the residuals to be approximately normally distributed, so about 68% of the residuals will be within ±\$51.05 and about 95% within ±2(51.05) or ±\$102.10. As before with similar measures of dispersion, such as the standard error of estimate in Chapter 13, a smaller multiple standard error indicates a better or more effective predictive equation.

Coefficient of Multiple Determination

Next, let's look at the coefficient of multiple determination. Recall from the previous chapter the coefficient of determination is defined as the percent of variation in the dependent variable explained, or accounted for, by the variation in the independent variable. In the multiple regression case, we extend this definition as follows.

> **COEFFICIENT OF MULTIPLE DETERMINATION** The percent of variation in the dependent variable, Y, explained by the variation in the set of independent variables, X_1, X_2, X_3, . . . X_k.

The characteristics of the coefficient of multiple determination are:

1. **It is symbolized by a capital R squared.** In other words, it is written as R^2 because it behaves like the square of a correlation coefficient.
2. **It can range from 0 to 1.** A value near 0 indicates little association between the set of independent variables and the dependent variable. A value near 1 means a strong association.
3. **It cannot assume negative values.** Any number that is squared or raised to the second power cannot be negative.
4. **It is easy to interpret.** Because R^2 is a value between 0 and 1, it is easy to interpret, compare, and understand.

We can calculate the coefficient of determination from the information found in the ANOVA table. We look in the sum of squares column, which is labeled SS in the Excel output, and use the regression sum of squares, SSR, then divide by the total sum of squares, SS total.

COEFFICIENT OF MULTIPLE DETERMINATION	$R^2 = \dfrac{SSR}{SS \text{ total}}$	[14–3]

We can use the residual and total sum of squares from the ANOVA table highlighted in the Excel output on page 451 and compute the coefficient of determination with formula (14-3).

$$R^2 = \frac{SSR}{SS \text{ total}} = \frac{171{,}220.473}{212{,}915.750} = .804$$

How do we interpret this value? We conclude that the independent variables (outside temperature, amount of insulation, and age of furnace) explain, or account for, 80.4% of the variation in heating cost. To put it another way, 19.6% of the variation is due to other sources, such as random error or variables not included in the analysis. Using the ANOVA table, 19.6% is the error sum of squares divided by the total sum of squares. Knowing that the SSR + SSE = SS total, the following relationship is true.

$$1 - R^2 = 1 - \frac{SSR}{SS \text{ total}} = \frac{SSE}{SS \text{ total}} = \frac{41{,}695.277}{212{,}915.750} = .196$$

Adjusted Coefficient of Determination

The coefficient of determination tends to increase as more independent variables are added to a multiple regression model. Each new independent variable causes the predictions to be more accurate. That, in turn, makes SSE smaller and SSR larger. Hence, R^2 increases only because the total number of independent variables increases and not because the added independent variable is necessarily a good predictor of the dependent variable. In fact, if the number of variables, *k,* and the sample size, *n,* are equal, the coefficient of determination is 1.0. In practice, this situation is rare and would also be ethically questionable. To balance the effect that the number of independent variables has on the coefficient of multiple determination, statistical software packages use an *adjusted* coefficient of multiple determination.

ADJUSTED COEFFICIENT OF DETERMINATION	$R^2_{adj} = 1 - \dfrac{\dfrac{SSE}{n-(k+1)}}{\dfrac{SS \text{ total}}{n-1}}$	[14–4]

The error and total sum of squares are divided by their respective degrees of freedom. Notice especially the degrees of freedom for the error sum of squares includes *k,* the number of independent variables. For the cost of heating example, the adjusted coefficient of determination is:

$$R^2_{adj} = 1 - \frac{\dfrac{41{,}695.277}{20-(3+1)}}{\dfrac{212{,}915.750}{20-1}} = 1 - \frac{2{,}605.955}{11{,}206.092} = 1 - .233 = .767$$

If we compare the R^2 (.804) to the adjusted R^2 (0.767), the difference in this case is small.

Self-Review 14–2 Refer to Self-Review 14–1 on the subject of restaurants in Myrtle Beach. The ANOVA portion of the regression output is presented below.

```
Analysis of Variance
Source            DF     SS    MS
Regression         5    100    20
Residual Error    20     40     2
Total             25    140
```

(a) How large was the sample?
(b) How many independent variables are there?
(c) How many dependent variables are there?
(d) Compute the standard error of estimate. About 95% of the residuals will be between what two values?
(e) Determine the coefficient of multiple determination. Interpret this value.
(f) Find the coefficient of multiple determination, adjusted for the degrees of freedom.

Exercises

connect

5. Consider the ANOVA table that follows.

```
Analysis of Variance
Source            DF        SS        MS       F       P
Regression         2    77.907    38.954    4.14    0.021
Residual Error    62   583.693     9.414
Total             64   661.600
```

a. Determine the standard error of estimate. About 95% of the residuals will be between what two values?
b. Determine the coefficient of multiple determination. Interpret this value.
c. Determine the coefficient of multiple determination, adjusted for the degrees of freedom.

6. Consider the ANOVA table that follows.

```
Analysis of Variance
Source            DF        SS        MS       F
Regression         5   3710.00    742.00    12.89
Residual Error    46   2647.38     57.55
Total             51   6357.38
```

a. Determine the standard error of estimate. About 95% of the residuals will be between what two values?
b. Determine the coefficient of multiple determination. Interpret this value.
c. Determine the coefficient of multiple determination, adjusted for the degrees of freedom.

14.4 Inferences in Multiple Linear Regression

Thus far, multiple regression analysis has been viewed only as a way to describe the relationship between a dependent variable and several independent variables. However, the least squares method also has the ability to draw inferences or generalizations about the relationship for an entire population. Recall that when you create confidence intervals or perform hypothesis tests as a part of inferential statistics, you view the data as a random sample taken from some population.

In the multiple regression setting, we assume there is an unknown population regression equation that relates the dependent variable to the k independent variables. This is sometimes called a **model** of the relationship. In symbols, we write:

$$\hat{Y} = \alpha + \beta_1 X_1 + \beta_2 X_2 + \cdots + \beta_k X_k$$

This equation is analogous to formula (14–1) except the coefficients are now reported as Greek letters. We use the Greek letters to denote *population parameters*. Then under a certain set of assumptions, which will be discussed shortly, the computed values of a and b_j are sample statistics. These sample statistics are point estimates of the corresponding population parameters α and β_j. For example, the sample regression coefficient b_2 is a point estimate of the population parameter β_2. The sampling distribution of these point estimates follows the normal probability distribution. These sampling distributions are each centered at their respective parameter values. To put it another way, the means of the sampling distributions are equal to the parameter values to be estimated. Thus, by using the properties of the sampling distributions of these statistics, inferences about the population parameters are possible.

Global Test: Testing the Multiple Regression Model

LO 14-4 Conduct a hypothesis test to determine whether a set of regression coefficients differ from zero.

We can test the ability of the independent variables $X_1, X_2, \ldots, X_k$ to explain the behavior of the dependent variable Y. To put this in question form: Can the dependent variable be estimated without relying on the independent variables? The test used is referred to as the **global test.** Basically, it investigates whether it is possible all the independent variables have zero regression coefficients.

To relate this question to the heating cost example, we will test whether the independent variables (amount of insulation in the attic, mean daily outside temperature, and age of furnace) effectively estimate home heating costs. In testing a hypothesis, we first state the null hypothesis and the alternate hypothesis. In the heating cost example, there are three independent variables. Recall that b_1, b_2, and b_3 are sample regression coefficients. The corresponding coefficients in the population are given the symbols β_1, β_2, and β_3. We now test whether the regression coefficients in the population are all zero. The null hypothesis is:

$$H_0: \beta_1 = \beta_2 = \beta_3 = 0$$

The alternate hypothesis is:

$$H_1: \text{Not all the } \beta_i\text{'s are 0.}$$

If the null hypothesis is true, it implies the regression coefficients are all zero and, logically, none of the independent variables can be used to estimate the dependent variable, heating cost. Should that be the case, we would have to search for some other independent variables—or take a different approach—to predict home heating costs.

To test the null hypothesis that the multiple regression coefficients are all zero, we employ the F distribution introduced in Chapter 12. We will use the .05 level of significance. Recall these characteristics of the F distribution:

1. **There is a family of F distributions.** Each time the degrees of freedom in either the numerator or the denominator changes, a new F distribution is created.
2. **The F distribution cannot be negative.** The smallest possible value is 0.
3. **It is a continuous distribution.** The distribution can assume an infinite number of values between 0 and positive infinity.
4. **It is positively skewed.** The long tail of the distribution is to the right-hand side. As the number of degrees of freedom increases in both the numerator and the denominator, the distribution approaches the normal probability distribution. That is, the distribution will move toward a symmetric distribution.
5. **It is asymptotic.** As the values of X increase, the F curve will approach the horizontal axis, but will never touch it.

The F-statistic to test the global hypothesis follows. As in Chapter 12, it is the ratio of two variances. In this case, the numerator is the regression sum of squares divided by its degrees of freedom, k. The denominator is the residual sum of squares divided by its degrees of freedom, $n - (k + 1)$. The formula follows.

$$\text{GLOBAL TEST} \qquad F = \frac{\text{SSR}/k}{\text{SSE}/[n - (k + 1)]} \qquad \text{[14–5]}$$

Using the ANOVA table, the F-statistic is

$$F = \frac{\text{MSR}}{\text{MSE}} = \frac{\text{SSR}/k}{\text{SSE}/[n - (k + 1)]} = \frac{171{,}220.473/3}{41{,}695.277/[20 - (3 + 1)]} = 21.901$$

Remember that the F-statistic tests the basic null hypothesis that two variances or, in this case, two mean squares are equal. In our global multiple regression hypothesis test, we will reject the null hypothesis, H_0, that all regression coefficients are zero when the regression mean square is larger in comparison to the residual mean square. If this is true, the F-statistic will be relatively large and in the far right tail of the F-distribution, and the p-value will be small, that is, less than our choice of our significance level of 0.05. Thus, we will reject the null hypothesis.

As with other hypothesis-testing methods, the decision rule can be based on either of two methods: (1) comparing the test statistic to a critical value or (2) calculating a p-value based on the test statistic and comparing the p-value to the significance level. The critical value method using the F-statistic requires three pieces of information: (1) the numerator degrees of freedom, (2) the denominator degrees of freedom, and (3) the significance level. The degrees of freedom for the numerator and the denominator are reported in the Excel ANOVA table that follows. The ANOVA output is highlighted in light green. The top number in the column marked "df" is 3, indicating there are 3 degrees of freedom in the numerator. This value corresponds to the number of independent variables. The middle number in the "df" column (16) indicates that there are 16 degrees of freedom in the denominator. The number 16 is found by $n - (k - 1) = 20 - (3 - 1) = 16$.

	A	B	C	D	F	G	H	I	J	K	L
1	Cost	Temp	Insul	Age		SUMMARY OUTPUT					
2	250	35	3	6							
3	360	29	4	10		*Regression Statistics*					
4	165	36	7	3		Multiple R	0.897				
5	43	60	6	9		R Square	0.804				
6	92	65	5	6		Adjusted R Square	0.767				
7	200	30	5	5		Standard Error	51.049				
8	355	10	6	7		Observations	20				
9	290	7	10	10							
10	230	21	9	11		ANOVA					
11	120	55	2	5			*df*	*SS*	*MS*	*F*	*Significance F*
12	73	54	12	4		Regression	3	171220.473	57073.491	21.901	0.000
13	205	48	5	1		Residual	16	41695.277	2605.955		
14	400	20	5	15		Total	19	212915.750			
15	320	39	4	7							
16	72	60	8	6			*Coefficients*	*Standard Error*	*t Stat*	*P-value*	
17	272	20	5	8		Intercept	427.194	59.601	7.168	0.000	
18	94	58	7	3		Temp	-4.583	0.772	-5.934	0.000	
19	190	40	8	11		Insul	-14.831	4.754	-3.119	0.007	
20	235	27	9	8		Age	6.101	4.012	1.521	0.148	
21	139	30	7	5							

regression [Compatibility Mode]

The critical value of F is found in Appendix B.4. Using the table for the .05 significance level, move horizontally to 3 degrees of freedom in the numerator, then down to 16 degrees of freedom in the denominator, and read the critical value. It is 3.24. The region where H_0 is not rejected and the region where H_0 is rejected are shown in the following diagram.

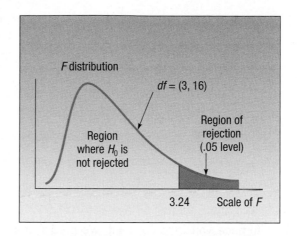

Continuing with the global test, the decision rule is: Do not reject the null hypothesis, H_0, that all the regression coefficients are 0 if the computed value of F is less than or equal to 3.24. If the computed F is greater than 3.24, reject H_0 and accept the alternate hypothesis, H_1.

The computed value of F is 21.90, which is in the rejection region. The null hypothesis that all the multiple regression coefficients are zero is therefore rejected. That is at least one of the independent variables has the ability to explain the variation in the dependent variable (heating cost). We expected this decision. Logically, the outside temperature, the amount of insulation, or age of the furnace have a great bearing on heating costs. The global test assures us that they do.

Testing the null hypothesis can also be based on a p-value, which is reported in the statistical software output for all hypothesis tests. In the case of the F-statistic, the p-value is defined as the probability of observing an F-value as large or larger than the F test statistic, assuming the null hypothesis is true. If the p-value is less than our selected significance level, then reject the null hypothesis. The ANOVA shows the F-statistic's p-value is equal to 0.000. It is clearly less than our significance level of 0.05. Therefore, we reject the global null hypothesis and conclude that at least one of the regression coefficients is not equal to zero.

The decision is the same as when we used the critical value approach. The advantage to using the p-value approach is that the p-value gives us the probability of making a Type I error. The computed p-value is much smaller than our significance level (.000 versus .05). We reject the null hypothesis that all the regression coefficients are 0 and, on the basis of the p-value, there is little likelihood this hypothesis is true.

Evaluating Individual Regression Coefficients

LO 14-5 Conduct a hypothesis test of each regression coefficient.

So far we have shown that at least one, but not necessarily all, of the regression coefficients are not equal to zero and thus useful for predictions. The next step is to test the independent variables *individually* to determine which regression coefficients may be 0 and which are not.

Why is it important to know if any of the β_i's equal 0? If a β could equal 0, it implies that this particular independent variable is of no value in explaining any variation in the dependent value. If there are coefficients for which H_0 cannot be rejected, we may want to eliminate them from the regression equation.

Our strategy is to establish three sets of hypotheses—one for temperature, one for insulation, and one for age of the furnace.

For temperature:	For insulation:	For furnace age:
$H_0: \beta_1 = 0$	$H_0: \beta_2 = 0$	$H_0: \beta_3 = 0$
$H_1: \beta_1 \neq 0$	$H_1: \beta_2 \neq 0$	$H_1: \beta_3 \neq 0$

We will test the hypotheses at the .05 level. Note that these are two-tailed tests.

The test statistic follows Student's *t* distribution with $n - (k + 1)$ degrees of freedom. The number of sample observations is *n*. There are 20 homes in the study, so $n = 20$. The number of independent variables is *k,* which is 3. Thus, there are $n - (k + 1) = 20 - (3 + 1) = 16$ degrees of freedom.

The critical value for *t* is in Appendix B.2. For a two-tailed test with 16 degrees of freedom using the .05 significance level, H_0 is rejected if *t* is less than -2.120 or greater than 2.120.

Refer to the Excel output in the previous section. (See page 456.) The column highlighted in yellow, headed Coefficients, shows the values for the multiple regression equation:

$$\hat{Y} = 427.194 - 4.583X_1 - 14.831X_2 + 6.101X_3$$

Interpreting the term $-4.583X_1$ in the equation: Holding the insulation and age of furnace variables constant, we predict that heating cost will increase about $4.58 for each degree increase in temperature.

The column in the Excel output labeled "Standard Error" shows the standard error of the sample regression coefficients. Recall that Salsberry Realty selected a sample of 20 homes along the East Coast of the United States. If Salsberry Realty selected a second random sample and computed the regression coefficients for that sample, the values would not be exactly the same. If the sampling process was repeated many times, we could construct a sampling distribution for each of these regression coefficients. The column labeled "Standard Error" estimates the variability for each of these regression coefficients. The sampling distributions of the coefficients follow the *t* distribution with $n - (k + 1)$ degrees of freedom. Hence, we are able to test the independent variables individually to determine whether the net regression coefficients differ from zero. The formula is:

TESTING INDIVIDUAL REGRESSION COEFFICIENTS	$t = \dfrac{b_i - 0}{s_{b_i}}$	**[14–6]**

The b_i refers to any one of the regression coefficients, and s_{b_i} refers to the standard deviation of that distribution of the regression coefficient. We include 0 in the equation because the null hypothesis is $\beta_i = 0$.

To illustrate this formula, refer to the test of the regression coefficient for the independent variable temperature. From the computer output on page 456, the regression coefficient for temperature is -4.583. The standard deviation of the sampling distribution of the regression coefficient for the independent variable temperature is 0.772. Inserting these values in formula (14–6):

$$t = \frac{b_1 - 0}{s_{b_1}} = \frac{-4.583 - 0}{0.772} = -5.937$$

The computed value of *t* is -5.937 for temperature (the small difference between the computed value and that shown on the Excel output is due to rounding) and -3.119 for insulation. Both of these *t*-values are in the rejection region to the left of -2.120. Thus, we conclude that the regression coefficients for the temperature and insulation variables are *not* zero. The computed *t* for the age of the furnace is 1.521, so we conclude that could equal 0. The independent variable age of the furnace is not a significant predictor of heating cost. It can be dropped from the analysis.

We can also use *p*-values to test the individual regression coefficients. Again, these are commonly reported in computer software output. The computed *t* ratio for temperature on the Excel output is -5.934 and has a *p*-value of 0.000. Because the *p*-value is less than 0.05, the regression coefficient for the independent variable temperature is not equal to zero and should be included in the equation to predict heating costs. For insulation, the t ratio is -3.119 and has a p-value of 0.007. As with temperature, the p-value is less than 0.05, so we conclude that the insulation regression coefficient is not equal to zero and should be included in the equation to predict heating cost. In contrast to temperature and insulation, the p-value to test the "age of the furnace" regression coefficient is 0.148. It is clearly greater than 0.05, so we conclude that the "age of furnace" regression coefficient could equal 0. Further, as an independent variable it is not a significant predictor of heating cost. Thus, age of furnace should not be included in the equation to predict heating costs.

At this point, we need to develop a strategy for deleting independent variables. In the Salsberry Realty case, there were three independent variables. For the age of furnace variable, we could not conclude that the regression coefficient was different from zero. It is clear that we should drop that variable and rerun the regression equation. Below is the Minitab output where heating cost is the dependent variable and outside temperature and amount of insulation are the independent variables.

	C1	C2	C3
↓	Cost	Temp	Insul
1	250	35	3
2	360	29	4
3	165	36	7
4	43	60	6
5	92	65	5
6	200	30	5
7	355	10	6
8	290	7	10
9	230	21	9
10	120	55	2
11	73	54	12
12	205	48	5
13	400	20	5
14	320	39	4
15	72	60	8
16	272	20	5
17	94	58	7
18	190	40	8
19	235	27	9
20	139	30	7

Regression Analysis: Cost versus Temp, Insul

The regression equation is
Cost = 490 - 5.15 Temp - 14.7 Insul

Predictor	Coef	SE Coef	T	P
Constant	490.29	44.41	11.04	0.000
Temp	-5.1499	0.7019	-7.34	0.000
Insul	-14.718	4.934	-2.98	0.008

S = 52.9824   R-Sq = 77.6%   R-Sq(adj) = 74.9%

Analysis of Variance

Source	DF	SS	MS	F	P
Regression	2	165195	82597	29.42	0.000
Residual Error	17	47721	2807		
Total	19	212916			

Source	DF	Seq SS
Temp	1	140215
Insul	1	24980

Summarizing the results from this new Minitab output:

1. The new regression equation is:

$$\hat{Y} = 490.29 - 5.1499X_1 - 14.718X_2$$

Notice that the regression coefficients for outside temperature (X_1) and amount of insulation (X_2) are similar to but not exactly the same as when we included the independent variable age of the furnace. Compare the above equation to that in the Excel output on page 456. Both of the regression coefficients are negative as in the earlier equation.

2. The details of the global test are as follows:

$$H_0: \beta_1 = \beta_2 = 0$$
$$H_1: \text{Not all of the } \beta_i\text{'s} = 0$$

The F distribution is the test statistic and there are $k = 2$ degrees of freedom in the numerator and $n - (k + 1) = 20 - (2 + 1) = 17$ degrees of freedom in the denominator. Using the .05 significance level and Appendix B.4, the decision rule is to reject H_0 if F is greater than 3.59. We compute the value of F as follows:

$$F = \frac{SSR/k}{SSE/[n - (k + 1)]} = \frac{165,195/2}{47,721/[20 - (2 + 1)]} = 29.42$$

Because the computed value of F (29.42) is greater than the critical value (3.59), the null hypothesis is rejected and the alternate accepted. We conclude that at least one of the regression coefficients is different from 0.

Using the p-value, the F test statistic (29.42) has a p-value (0.000) that is clearly less than 0.05. Therefore, we reject the null hypothesis and accept the alternate. We conclude that at least one of the regression coefficients is different from 0.

3. The next step is to conduct a test of the regression coefficients individually. We want to determine if one or both of the regression coefficients are different from 0. The null and alternate hypotheses for each of the independent variables are:

Outside Temperature   **Insulation**
H_0: $\beta_1 = 0$ H_0: $\beta_2 = 0$
H_1: $\beta_1 \neq 0$ H_1: $\beta_2 \neq 0$

The test statistic is the t distribution with $n - (k + 1) = 20 - (2 + 1) = 17$ degrees of freedom. Using the .05 significance level and Appendix B.2, the decision rule is to reject H_0 if the computed value of t is less than -2.110 or greater than 2.110.

Outside Temperature   **Insulation**

$$t = \frac{b_1 - 0}{s_{b_1}} = \frac{-5.1499 - 0}{0.7019} = -7.34 \quad t = \frac{b_2 - 0}{s_{b_2}} = \frac{-14.718 - 0}{4.934} = -2.98$$

In both tests, we reject H_0 and accept H_1. We conclude that each of the regression coefficients is different from 0. Both outside temperature and amount of insulation are useful variables in explaining the variation in heating costs.

Using p-values, the p-value for the temperature t-statistic is 0.000 and the p-value for the insulation t-statistic is 0.008. Both p-values are less than 0.05, so in both tests we reject the null hypothesis and conclude that each of the regression coefficients is different from 0. Both outside temperature and amount of insulation are useful variables in explaining the variation in heating costs.

In the heating cost example, it was clear which independent variable to delete. However, in some instances which variable to delete may not be as clear-cut. To explain, suppose we develop a multiple regression equation based on five independent variables. We conduct the global test and find that some of the regression coefficients are different from zero. Next, we test the regression coefficients individually and find that three are significant and two are not. The preferred procedure is to drop the single independent variable with the *smallest absolute* t *value* or *largest* p-*value* and rerun the regression equation with the four remaining variables, then, on the new regression equation with four independent variables, conduct the individual tests. If there are still regression coefficients that are not significant, again drop the variable with the smallest absolute t value or the largest, nonsignificant p-value. To describe the process in another way, we should delete only one variable at a time. Each time we delete a variable, we need to rerun the regression equation and check the remaining variables.

This process of selecting variables to include in a regression model can be automated, using Excel, Minitab, MegaStat, or other statistical software. Most of the software systems include methods to sequentially remove and/or add independent variables and at the same time provide estimates of the percentage of variation explained (the R-square term). Two of the common methods are **stepwise regression** and **best subset regression.** It may take a long time, but in the extreme we could compute every regression between the dependent variable and any possible subset of the independent variables.

Unfortunately, on occasion, the software may work "too hard" to find an equation that fits all the quirks of your particular data set. The suggested equation may not represent the relationship in the population. Judgment is needed to choose among the equations presented. Consider whether the results are logical. They should have a simple interpretation and be consistent with your knowledge of the application under study.

Self-Review 14–3

The regression output about eating places in Myrtle Beach is repeated below (see earlier self-reviews).

Predictor	Coef	SE Coef	T	p-value
Constant	2.50	1.50	1.667	–
X_1	3.00	1.500	2.000	0.056
X_2	4.00	3.000	1.333	0.194
X_3	-3.00	0.20	-15.00	0.000
X_4	0.20	.05	4.00	0.000
X_5	1.00	1.50	0.667	0.511

Analysis of Variance

Source	DF	SS	MS	F	p-value
Regression	5	100	20	10	0.000
Residual Error	20	40	2		
Total	25	140			

(a) Perform a global test of hypothesis to check if any of the regression coefficients are different from 0. What do you decide? Use the .05 significance level.
(b) Do an individual test of each independent variable. Which variables would you consider eliminating? Use the .05 significance level.
(c) Outline a plan for possibly removing independent variables.

Exercises

7. Given the following regression output,

Predictor	Coef	SE Coef	T	P
Constant	84.998	1.863	45.61	0.000
X_1	2.391	1.200	1.99	0.051
X_2	-0.4086	0.1717	-2.38	0.020

Analysis of Variance

Source	DF	SS	MS	F	P
Regression	2	77.907	38.954	4.14	0.021
Residual Error	62	583.693	9.414		
Total	64	661.600			

answer the following questions:
a. Write the regression equation.
b. If X_1 is 4 and X_2 is 11, what is the value of the dependent variable?
c. How large is the sample? How many independent variables are there?
d. Conduct a global test of hypothesis to see if any of the set of regression coefficients could be different from 0. Use the .05 significance level. What is your conclusion?
e. Conduct a test of hypothesis for each independent variable. Use the .05 significance level. Which variable would you consider eliminating?
f. Outline a strategy for deleting independent variables in this case.

8. The following regression output was obtained from a study of architectural firms. The dependent variable is the total amount of fees in millions of dollars.

Predictor	Coef	SE Coef	T	p-value
Constant	7.987	2.967	2.69	—
X_1	0.12242	0.03121	3.92	0.000
X_2	−0.12166	0.05353	−2.27	0.028
X_3	−0.06281	0.03901	−1.61	0.114
X_4	0.5235	0.1420	3.69	0.001
X_5	−0.06472	0.03999	−1.62	0.112

Analysis of Variance

Source	DF	SS	MS	F	p-value
Regression	5	3710.00	742.00	12.89	0.000
Residual Error	46	2647.38	57.55		
Total	51	6357.38			

X_1 is the number of architects employed by the company.
X_2 is the number of engineers employed by the company.
X_3 is the number of years involved with health care projects.
X_4 is the number of states in which the firm operates.
X_5 is the percent of the firm's work that is health care–related.

a. Write out the regression equation.
b. How large is the sample? How many independent variables are there?
c. Conduct a global test of hypothesis to see if any of the set of regression coefficients could be different from 0. Use the .05 significance level. What is your conclusion?
d. Conduct a test of hypothesis for each independent variable. Use the .05 significance level. Which variable would you consider eliminating first?
e. Outline a strategy for deleting independent variables in this case.

14.5 Evaluating the Assumptions of Multiple Regression

In the previous section, we described the methods to statistically evaluate the multiple regression equation. The results of the test let us know if at least one of the coefficients was not equal to zero and we described a procedure of evaluating each regression coefficient. We also discussed the decision-making process for including and excluding independent variables in the multiple regression equation.

It is important to know that the validity of the statistical global and individual tests rely on several assumptions. That is, if the assumptions are not true, the results might be biased or misleading. However, strict adherence to the following assumptions is not always possible. Fortunately, the statistical techniques discussed in this chapter work well even when one or more of the assumptions are violated. Even if the values in the multiple regression equation are "off" slightly, our estimates using a multiple regression equation will be closer than any that could be made otherwise. Usually the statistical procedures are robust enough to overcome violations of some assumptions.

In Chapter 13, we listed the necessary assumptions for regression when we considered only a single independent variable. (See Section 13.8 on page 419.) The assumptions for multiple regression are similar.

1. **There is a linear relationship.** That is, there is a straight-line relationship between the dependent variable and the set of independent variables.

2. **The variation in the residuals is the same for both large and small values of $\hat{Y}$.** To put it another way, $(Y - \hat{Y})$ is unrelated to whether $\hat{Y}$ is large or small.
3. **The residuals follow the normal probability distribution.** Recall the residual is the difference between the actual value of Y and the estimated value $\hat{Y}$. So the term $(Y - \hat{Y})$ is computed for every observation in the data set. These residuals should approximately follow a normal probability distribution. In addition, the mean of the residuals is 0.
4. **The independent variables should not be correlated.** That is, we would like to select a set of independent variables that are not themselves correlated.
5. **The residuals are independent.** This means that successive observations of the dependent variable are not correlated. This assumption is often violated when time is involved with the sampled observations.

In this section, we present a brief discussion of each of these assumptions. In addition, we provide methods to validate these assumptions and indicate the consequences if these assumptions cannot be met. For those interested in additional discussion, Kutner, Nachtsheim, Neter, and Li, *Applied Linear Statistical Models,* 5th ed., (McGraw-Hill: 2005), is an excellent reference.

Linear Relationship

Let's begin with the linearity assumption. The idea is that the relationship between the set of independent variables and the dependent variable is linear. If we are considering two independent variables, we can visualize this assumption. The two independent variables and the dependent variable would form a three-dimensional space. The regression equation would then form a plane as shown on page 445. We can evaluate this assumption with scatter diagrams and residual plots.

Using Scatter Diagrams The evaluation of a multiple regression equation should always include a scatter diagram that plots the dependent variable against each independent variable. These graphs help us to visualize the relationships and provide some initial information about the direction (positive or negative), linearity, and strength of the relationship. For example, the scatter diagrams for the home heating example follow. The plots suggest a fairly strong negative, linear relationship between heating cost and temperature, and a weak negative relationship between heating cost and insulation.

LO 14-6 Use residual analysis to evaluate the assumptions of multiple regression analysis.

Using Residual Plots Recall that a residual $(Y - \hat{Y})$ is computed using the multiple regression equation for each observation in a data set. In Chapter 13, we

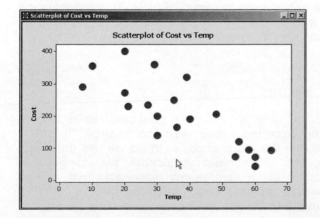

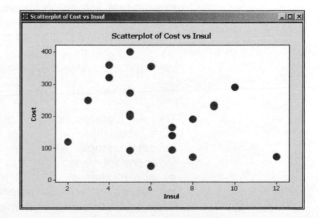

discussed the idea that the best regression line passed through the center of the data in a scatter plot. In this case, you would find a good number of the observations above the regression line (these residuals would have a positive sign), and a good number of the observations below the line (these residuals would have a negative sign). Further, the observations would be scattered above and below the line over the entire range of the independent variable.

The same concept is true for multiple regression, but we cannot graphically portray the multiple regression. However, plots of the residuals can help us evaluate the linearity of the multiple regression equation. To investigate, the residuals are plotted on the vertical axis against the predictor variable, $\hat{Y}$. The graph on the left below shows the residual plots for the home heating cost example. Notice the following:

- The residuals are plotted on the vertical axis and are centered around zero. There are both positive and negative residuals.
- The residual plots show a random distribution of positive and negative values across the entire range of the variable plotted on the horizontal axis.
- The points are scattered and there is no obvious pattern, so there is no reason to doubt the linearity assumption.

This plot supports the assumption of linearity.

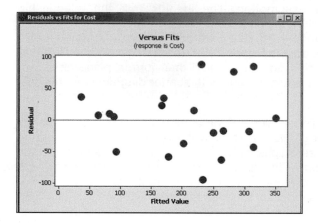 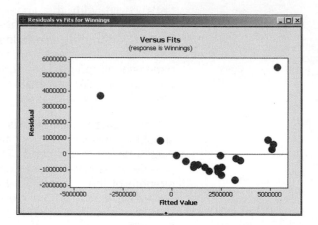

If there is a pattern to the points in the scatter plot, further investigation is necessary. For example, the graph on the right above shows nonrandom residuals. See that the residual plot does *not* show a random distribution of positive and negative values across the entire range of the variable plotted on the horizontal axis. In fact, the graph shows a curvature to the residual plots. This indicates the relationship may not be linear. In this case, we would evaluate different transformations of the equation as discussed in Chapter 13.

Variation in Residuals Same for Large and Small $\hat{Y}$ Values

This requirement indicates that the variation about the predicted values is constant, regardless of whether the predicted values are large or small. To cite a specific example, which may violate the assumption, suppose we use the single independent variable age to explain the variation in income. We suspect that as age increases so does income but it also seems reasonable that as age increases there may be more variation around the regression line. That is, there will likely be more variation in income for a 50-year-old person than for a 35-year-old person. The requirement for constant variation around the regression line is called **homoscedasticity.**

> **HOMOSCEDASTICITY** The variation around the regression equation is the same for all of the values of the independent variables.

To check for homoscedasticity the residuals are plotted against the fitted values of Y. This is the same graph that we used to evaluate the assumption of linearity. (See the graph on the left on the previous page.) Based on the scatter diagram in that software output, it is reasonable to conclude that this assumption has not been violated.

Distribution of Residuals

To be sure that the inferences we make in the global and individual hypotheses tests are valid, we evaluate the distribution of residuals. Ideally, the residuals should follow a normal probability distribution.

To evaluate this assumption, we can organize the residuals into a frequency distribution. The Minitab histogram of the residuals is shown below on the left for the home heating cost example. Although it is difficult to show that the residuals follow a normal distribution with only 20 observations, it does appear the normality assumption is reasonable.

Both Minitab and Excel offer another graph that helps to evaluate the assumption of normally distributed residuals. It is a called a **normal probability plot** and is shown to the right of the histogram. We describe this graph further in Section 15.6 starting on page 511. The normal probability plot supports the assumption of normally distributed residuals if the plotted points are fairly close to a straight line drawn from the lower left to the upper right of the graph.

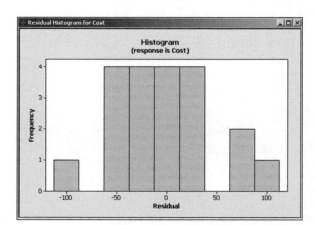
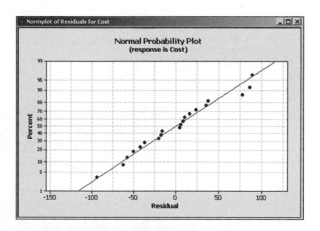

In this case, both graphs support the assumption that the residuals follow the normal probability distribution. Therefore, the inferences that we made based on the global and individual hypothesis tests are supported with the results of this evaluation.

Multicollinearity

LO 14-7 Evaluate the effects of correlated independent variables.

Multicollinearity exists when independent variables are correlated. Correlated independent variables make it difficult to make inferences about the individual regression coefficients and their individual effects on the dependent variable. In practice, it is nearly impossible to select variables that are completely unrelated. To put it another way, it is nearly impossible to create a set of independent variables that are not correlated to some degree. However, a general understanding of the issue of multi-collinearity is important.

First, we should point out that multicollinearity does not affect a multiple regression equation's ability to predict the dependent variable. However, when we are interested in evaluating the relationship between each independent variable and the dependent variable, multicollinearity may show unexpected results.

For example, if we use two highly multicollinear variables, high school GPA and high school class rank, to predict the GPA of incoming college freshmen (dependent variable), we would expect that both independent variables would be positively related to the dependent variable. However, because the independent variables are highly correlated, one of the independent variables may have an unexpected and inexplicable negative sign. In essence, these two independent variables are redundant in that they explain the same variation in the dependent variable.

A second reason for avoiding correlated independent variables is they may lead to erroneous results in the hypothesis tests for the individual independent variables. This is due to the instability of the standard error of estimate. Several clues that indicate problems with multicollinearity include the following:

1. An independent variable known to be an important predictor ends up having a regression coefficient that is not significant.
2. A regression coefficient that should have a positive sign turns out to be negative, or vice versa.
3. When an independent variable is added or removed, there is a drastic change in the values of the remaining regression coefficients.

In our evaluation of a multiple regression equation, an approach to reducing the effects of multicollinearity is to carefully select the independent variables that are included in the regression equation. A general rule is if the correlation between two independent variables is between -0.70 and 0.70, there likely is not a problem using both of the independent variables. A more precise test is to use the **variance inflation factor.** It is usually written *VIF*. The value of *VIF* is found as follows:

VARIANCE INFLATION FACTOR	$VIF = \dfrac{1}{1 - R_j^2}$	[14–7]

The term R_j^2 refers to the coefficient of determination, where the selected *independent variable* is used as a dependent variable and the remaining independent variables are used as independent variables. A *VIF* greater than 10 is considered unsatisfactory, indicating that the independent variable should be removed from the analysis. The following example will explain the details of finding the *VIF*.

Example

Refer to the data in Table 14–1, which relates the heating cost to the independent variables outside temperature, amount of insulation, and age of furnace. Develop a correlation matrix for all the independent variables. Does it appear there is a problem with multicollinearity? Find and interpret the variance inflation factor for each of the independent variables.

Solution

We begin by using the Minitab system to find the correlation matrix for the dependent variable and the three independent variables. A correlation matrix shows the correlations between all pairs of variables. A portion of that output follows:

```
             Cost      Temp     Insul
Temp       −0.812
Insul      −0.257    −0.103
Age         0.537    −0.486    0.064

Cell Contents: Pearson correlation
```

The highlighted area indicates the correlation among the independent variables. Because all of the correlations are between −.70 and .70, we do not suspect problems with multicollinearity. The largest correlation among the independent variables is −0.486 between age and temperature.

To confirm this conclusion, we compute the *VIF* for each of the three independent variables. We will consider the independent variable temperature first. We use Minitab to find the multiple coefficient of determination with temperature as the *dependent variable* and amount of insulation and age of the furnace as independent variables. The relevant Minitab output follows.

```
Regression Analysis: Temp versus Insul, Age

The regression equation is
Temp = 58.0 − 0.51 Insul − 2.51 Age

Predictor      Coef    SE Coef        T        P
Constant      57.99      12.35     4.70    0.000
Insul        −0.509      1.488    −0.34    0.737
Age          −2.509      1.103    −2.27    0.036

S = 16.0311   R−Sq = 24.1%   R−Sq(adj) = 15.2%

Analysis of Variance
Source           DF        SS       MS       F        P
Regression        2    1390.3    695.1    2.70    0.096
Residual Error   17    4368.9    257.0
Total            19    5759.2
```

The coefficient of determination is .241, so inserting this value into the *VIF* formula:

$$VIF = \frac{1}{1 - R_1^2} = \frac{1}{1 - .241} = 1.32$$

The *VIF* value of 1.32 is less than the upper limit of 10. This indicates that the independent variable temperature is not strongly correlated with the other independent variables.

Again, to find the *VIF* for insulation we would develop a regression equation with insulation as the *dependent variable* and temperature and age of furnace as independent variables. For this equation, we would determine the coefficient of determination. This would be the value for R_2^2. We would substitute this value in formula (14-7) and solve for *VIF*.

Fortunately, Minitab will generate the *VIF* values for each of the independent variables. These values are reported in the right-hand column under the heading *VIF* in the following Minitab output. All these values are less than 10. Hence, we conclude there is not a problem with multicollinearity in this example.

```
The regression equation is
Cost = 427 − 4.58 Temp − 14.8 Insul + 6.10 Age

Predictor       Coef    SE Coef        T        P      VIF
Constant      427.19      59.60     7.17    0.000
Temp         −4.5827     0.7723    −5.93    0.000    1.318
Insul       −14.831       4.754    −3.12    0.007    1.011
Age          −6.101       4.012     1.52    0.148    1.310
```

Independent Observations

The fifth assumption about regression and correlation analysis is that successive residuals should be independent. This means that there is not a pattern to the residuals, the residuals are not highly correlated, and there are not long runs of positive or negative residuals. When successive residuals are correlated, we refer to this condition as **autocorrelation.**

Autocorrelation frequently occurs when the data are collected over a period of time. For example, we wish to predict yearly sales of Ages Software Inc. based on the time and the amount spent on advertising. The dependent variable is yearly sales and the independent variables are time and amount spent on advertising. It is likely that for a period of time the actual points will be above the regression plane (remember there are two independent variables) and then for a period of time the points will be below the regression plane. The graph below shows the residuals plotted on the vertical axis and the fitted values $\hat{Y}$ on the horizontal axis. Note the run of residuals above the mean of the residuals, followed by a run below the mean. A scatter plot such as this would indicate possible autocorrelation.

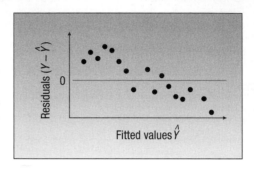

LO 14-8 Evaluate and use qualitative independent variables.

14.6 Qualitative Independent Variables

In the previous example regarding heating cost, the two independent variables outside temperature and insulation were quantitative; that is, numerical in nature. Frequently we wish to use nominal-scale variables—such as gender, whether the home has a swimming pool, or whether the sports team was the home or the visiting team—in our analysis. These are called **qualitative variables** because they describe a particular quality, such as male or female. To use a qualitative variable in regression analysis, we use a scheme of **dummy variables** in which one of the two possible conditions is coded 0 and the other 1.

> **DUMMY VARIABLE** A variable in which there are only two possible outcomes. For analysis, one of the outcomes is coded a 1 and the other a 0.

For example, we might be interested in estimating an executive's salary on the basis of years of job experience and whether he or she graduated from college. "Graduation from college" can take on only one of two conditions: yes or no. Thus, it is considered a qualitative variable.

Suppose in the Salsberry Realty example that the independent variable "garage" is added. For those homes without an attached garage, 0 is used; for homes with an attached garage, a 1 is used. We will refer to the "garage" variable as X_4. The data from Table 14–2 are entered into the Minitab system. Recall that the variable, age of the furnace, is not included in this analysis because we determined that it was not significantly related to heating cost.

Statistics in Action

In recent years, multiple regression has been used in a variety of legal proceedings. It is particularly useful in cases alleging discrimination

(continued)

TABLE 14–2 Home Heating Costs, Temperature, Insulation, and Presence of a Garage for a Sample of 20 Homes

Cost, Y	Temperature, X_1	Insulation, X_2	Garage, X_4
$250	35	3	0
360	29	4	1
165	36	7	0
43	60	6	0
92	65	5	0
200	30	5	0
355	10	6	1
290	7	10	1
230	21	9	0
120	55	2	0
73	54	12	0
205	48	5	1
400	20	5	1
320	39	4	1
72	60	8	0
272	20	5	1
94	58	7	0
190	40	8	1
235	27	9	0
139	30	7	0

by gender or race. As an example, suppose that a woman alleges that Company X's wage rates are unfair to women. To support the claim, the plaintiff produces data showing that, on the average, women earn less than men. In response, Company X argues that its wage rates are based on experience, training, and skill and that its female employees, on the average, are younger and less experienced than the male employees. In fact, the company might further argue that the current situation is actually due to its recent successful efforts to hire more women.

The output from Minitab is:

↓	C1	C2	C3	C5
	Cost	Temp	Insul	Garage
1	250	35	3	0
2	360	29	4	1
3	165	36	7	0
4	43	60	6	0
5	92	65	5	0
6	200	30	5	0
7	355	10	6	1
8	290	7	10	1
9	230	21	9	0
10	120	55	2	0
11	73	54	12	0
12	205	48	5	1
13	400	20	5	1
14	320	39	4	1
15	72	60	8	0
16	272	20	5	1
17	94	58	7	0
18	190	40	8	1
19	235	27	9	0
20	139	30	7	0
21				
22				

TABLE14_1.MTW ***

Session

Regression Analysis: Cost versus Temp, Insul, Garage

The regression equation is
Cost = 394 – 3.96 Temp – 11.3 Insul + 77.4 Garage

Predictor	Coef	SE Coef	T	P	VIF
Constant	393.67	45.00	8.75	0.000	
Temp	–3.9628	0.6527	–6.07	0.000	1.416
Insul	–11.334	4.002	–2.83	0.012	1.077
Garage	77.43	22.78	3.40	0.004	1.438

S = 41.6184   R–Sq = 87.0%   R–Sq(adj) = 84.5%

Analysis of Variance

Source	DF	SS	MS	F	P
Regression	3	185202	61734	35.64	0.000
Residual Error	16	27713	1732		
Total	19	212916			

Source	DF	Seq SS
Temp	1	140215
Insul	1	24980
Garage	1	20008

What is the effect of the garage variable? Should it be included in the analysis? To show the effect of the variable, suppose we have two houses exactly alike next to each other in Buffalo, New York; one has an attached garage, and the other does not. Both homes have 3 inches of insulation, and the mean January temperature in Buffalo is 20 degrees. For the house without an attached garage, a 0 is substituted for X_4 in the regression equation. The estimated heating cost is $280.90, found by:

$$\hat{Y} = 394 - 3.96X_1 - 11.3X_2 + 77.4X_4$$

$$= 394 - 3.96(20) - 11.3(3) + 77.4(0) = 280.90$$

For the house with an attached garage, a 1 is substituted for X_4 in the regression equation. The estimated heating cost is $358.30, found by:

$$\hat{Y} = 394 - 3.96X_1 - 11.3X_2 + 77.4X_4$$

$$= 394 - 3.96(20) - 11.3(3) + 77.4(1) = 358.30$$

The difference between the estimated heating costs is $77.40 ($358.30 − $280.90). Hence, we can expect the cost to heat a house with an attached garage to be $77.40 more than the cost for an equivalent house without a garage.

We have shown the difference between the two types of homes to be $77.40, but is the difference significant? We conduct the following test of hypothesis.

$$H_0: \beta_4 = 0$$

$$H_1: \beta_4 \neq 0$$

The information necessary to answer this question is on the preceding Minitab output. The net regression coefficient for the independent variable garage is 77.43, and the standard deviation of the sampling distribution is 22.78. We identify this as the fourth independent variable, so we use a subscript of 4. Finally, we insert these values in formula (14–6).

$$t = \frac{b_4 - 0}{s_{b_4}} = \frac{77.43 - 0}{22.78} = 3.40$$

There are three independent variables in the analysis, so there are $n - (k + 1) = 20 - (3 + 1) = 16$ degrees of freedom. The critical value from Appendix B.2 is 2.120. The decision rule, using a two-tailed test and the .05 significance level, is to reject H_0 if the computed t is to the left of −2.120 or to the right of 2.120. Because the computed value of 3.40 is to the right of 2.120, the null hypothesis is rejected. We conclude that the regression coefficient is not zero. The independent variable garage should be included in the analysis.

Using the p-value approach, the computed t value of 3.40 has a p-value of 0.004. This value is less than the .05 significance level. Therefore, we reject the null hypothesis. We conclude that the regression coefficient is not zero and the independent variable garage should be included in the analysis.

Is it possible to use a qualitative variable with more than two possible outcomes? Yes, but the coding scheme becomes more complex and will require a series of dummy variables. To explain, suppose a company is studying its sales as they relate to advertising expense by quarter for the last 5 years. Let sales be the dependent variable and advertising expense be the first independent variable, X_1. To include the qualitative information regarding the quarter, we use three additional independent variables. For the variable X_2, the five observations referring to the first quarter of each of the 5 years are coded 1 and the other quarters 0. Similarly, for X_3 the five observations referring to the second quarter are coded 1 and the other quarters 0. For X_4, the five observations referring to the third quarter are coded 1 and the other quarters 0. An observation that does not refer to any of the first three quarters must refer to the fourth quarter, so a distinct independent variable referring to this quarter is not necessary.

Self-Review 14–4

A study by the American Realtors Association investigated the relationship between the commissions earned by sales associates last year and the number of months since the associates earned their real estate licenses. Also of interest in the study is the gender of the sales associate. Below is a portion of the regression output. The dependent variable is commissions, which is reported in $000, and the independent variables are months since the license was earned and gender (female = 1 and male = 0).

```
                        Regression Analysis

                      Regression Statistics
                Multiple R              0.801
                R Square               0.642
                Adjusted R Square      0.600
                Standard Error         3.219
                Observations              20

    ANOVA
                    df         SS          MS         F      p-value
    Regression       2    315.9291    157.9645    15.2468    0.0002
    Residual        17    176.1284     10.36049
    Total           19    492.0575

                Coefficients   Standard Error   t Stat    p-value
    Intercept        15.7625         3.0782      5.121      .0001
    Months            0.4415         0.0839      5.262      .0001
    Gender            3.8598         1.4724      2.621      .0179
```

(a) Write out the regression equation. How much commission would you expect a female agent to make who earned her license 30 months ago?

(b) Do the female agents on the average make more or less than the male agents? How much more?

(c) Conduct a test of hypothesis to determine if the independent variable gender should be included in the analysis. Use the 0.05 significance level. What is your conclusion?

14.7 Stepwise Regression

LO 14-9 Explain stepwise regression.

In our heating cost example (see sample information in Table 14–1 and Table 14–2), we considered four independent variables: the mean outside temperature, the amount of insulation in the home, the age of the furnace, and whether or not there was an attached garage. To obtain the equation, we first ran a global or "all at once" test to determine if any of the regression coefficients were significant. When we found at least one to be significant, we tested the regression coefficients individually to determine which were important. We left out the independent variables that did not have significant regression coefficients and kept the others. By retaining the independent variables with significant coefficients, we found the regression equation that used the fewest independent variables. This made the regression equation easy to interpret and explained as much variation in the dependent variable as possible.

We are now going to describe a technique called **stepwise regression.** This technique is more efficient for building an equation that only includes independent variables with significant regression coefficients.

> **STEPWISE REGRESSION** A step-by-step method to determine a regression equation that begins with a single independent variable and adds or deletes independent variables one by one. Only independent variables with nonzero regression coefficients are included in the regression equation.

In the stepwise method, we develop a sequence of equations. The first equation contains only one independent variable. However, this independent variable is the one from the set of proposed independent variables that explains the most variation in the dependent variable. Stated differently, if we compute all the simple correlations between each independent variable and the dependent variable, the stepwise method first selects the independent variable with the strongest correlation with the dependent variable.

Next, the stepwise method looks at the remaining independent variables and then selects the one that will explain the largest percentage of the variation yet unexplained. We continue this process until all the independent variables with significant regression coefficients are included in the regression equation. The advantages to the stepwise method are:

1. Only independent variables with significant regression coefficients are entered into the equation.
2. The steps involved in building the regression equation are clear.
3. It is efficient in finding the regression equation with only significant regression coefficients.
4. The changes in the multiple standard error of estimate and the coefficient of determination are shown.

The stepwise Minitab output for the heating cost problem follows. Note that the final equation, which is highlighted in blue and reported in column 3, includes the independent variables temperature, garage, and insulation. These are the same independent variables that were included in our equation using the global test and the test for individual independent variables. (See page 469.) The independent variable age, for age of the furnace, is not included because it is not a significant predictor of cost.

Reviewing the steps and interpreting output:

1. The stepwise procedure selects the independent variable temperature first. This variable explains more of the variation in heating cost than any of the other three proposed independent variables. Temperature explains 65.85% of the variation in heating cost. The regression equation is:

$$\hat{Y} = 388.8 - 4.93X_1$$

   There is an inverse relationship between heating cost and temperature. For each degree the temperature increases, heating cost is reduced by $4.93.

2. The next independent variable to enter the regression equation is garage. When this variable is added to the regression equation, the coefficient of determination is increased from 65.85% to 80.46%. That is, by adding garage as an independent variable, we increase the coefficient of determination by 14.61 percentage points. The regression equation after step 2 is:

$$\hat{Y} = 300.3 - 3.56X_1 + 93.0X_4$$

   Usually the regression coefficients will change from one step to the next. In this case, the coefficient for temperature retained its negative sign, but it changed from -4.93 to -3.56. This change is reflective of the added influence of the independent variable garage. Why did the stepwise method select the independent variable garage instead of either insulation or age? The increase in R^2, the coefficient of determination, is larger if garage is included rather than either of the other two variables.

3. At this point, there are two unused variables remaining, insulation and age. Notice on the third step the procedure selects insulation and then stops. This indicates the variable insulation explains more of the remaining variation in heating cost than the age variable does. After the third step, the regression equation is:

$$\hat{Y} = 393.7 - 3.96X_1 + 77.0X_4 - 11.3X_2$$

   At this point, 86.98% of the variation in heating cost is explained by the three independent variables temperature, garage, and insulation. This is the same R^2 value and regression equation we found on page 469 except for rounding differences.

4. Here, the stepwise procedure stops. This means the independent variable age of the furnace does not add significantly to the coefficient of determination.

The stepwise method developed the same regression equation, selected the same independent variables, and found the same coefficient of determination as the global and individual tests described earlier in the chapter. The advantages to the stepwise method is that it is more direct than using a combination of the global and individual procedures.

Other methods of variable selection are available. The stepwise method is also called the **forward selection method** because we begin with no independent variables and add one independent variable to the regression equation at each iteration. There is also the **backward elimination method,** which begins with the entire set of variables and eliminates one independent variable at each iteration.

The methods described so far look at one variable at a time and decide whether to include or eliminate that variable. Another approach is the **best-subset regression.** With this method, we look at the best model using one independent variable, the best model using two independent variables, the best model with three and so on. The criterion is to find the model with the largest R^2 value, regardless of the number of independent variables. Also, each independent variable does not necessarily have a nonzero regression coefficient. Since each independent variable could either be included or not included, there are $2^k - 1$ possible models, where k refers to the number of independent variables. In our heatIng cost example, we considered four independent variables so there are 15 possible regression models, found by $2^4 - 1 = 16 - 1 = 15$. We would examine all regression models using one independent variable, all combinations using two variables, all combinations using three independent variables, and the possibility of using all four independent variables. The advantages to the best-subset method is it may examine combinations of independent variables not considered in the stepwise method. The process is available in Minitab and MegaStat.

Exercises

connect™

9. The production manager of High Point Sofa and Chair, a large furniture manufacturer located in North Carolina, is studying the job performance ratings of a sample of 15 electrical repairmen employed by the company. An aptitude test is required by the human resources department to become an electrical repairman. The production manager was able to get the score for each repairman in the sample. In addition, he determined which of the repairmen were union members (code = 1) and which were not (code = 0). The sample information is reported below.

Worker	Job Performance Score	Aptitude Test Score	Union Membership
Abbott	58	5	0
Anderson	53	4	0
Bender	33	10	0
Bush	97	10	0
Center	36	2	0
Coombs	83	7	0
Eckstine	67	6	0
Gloss	84	9	0
Herd	98	9	1
Householder	45	2	1
Iori	97	8	1
Lindstrom	90	6	1
Mason	96	7	1
Pierse	66	3	1
Rohde	82	6	1

a. Use a statistical software package to develop a multiple regression equation using the job performance score as the dependent variable, and aptitude test score and union membership as independent variables.

    b. Comment on the regression equation. Be sure to include the coefficient of determination and the effect of union membership. Are these two variables effective in explaining the variation in job performance?

    c. Conduct a test of hypothesis to determine if union membership should be included as an independent variable.

10. A real estate developer wishes to study the relationship between the size of home a client will purchase (in square feet) and other variables. Possible independent variables include the family income, family size, whether there is a senior adult parent living with the family (1 for yes, 0 for no), and the total years of education beyond high school for the husband and wife. The sample information is reported below.

Family	Square Feet	Income (000s)	Family Size	Senior Parent	Education
1	2,240	60.8	2	0	4
2	2,380	68.4	2	1	6
3	3,640	104.5	3	0	7
4	3,360	89.3	4	1	0
5	3,080	72.2	4	0	2
6	2,940	114	3	1	10
7	4,480	125.4	6	0	6
8	2,520	83.6	3	0	8
9	4,200	133	5	0	2
10	2,800	95	3	0	6

Develop an appropriate multiple regression equation. Which independent variables would you include in the final regression equation? Use the stepwise method.

14.8 Review of Multiple Regression

We described many topics involving multiple regression in this chapter. In this section of the chapter, we focus on a single example with a solution that reviews the procedure and guides your application of multiple regression analysis.

Example

The Bank of New England is a large financial institution serving the New England states as well as New York and New Jersey. The mortgage department of the Bank of New England is studying data from recent loans. Of particular interest is how such factors as the value of the home being purchased ($000), education level of the head of the household (number of years, beginning with first grade), age of the head of the household, current monthly mortgage payment (in dollars), and gender of the head of the household (male = 1, female = 0) relate to the family income. The mortgage department would like to know whether these variables are effective predictors of family income.

Solution

To begin, consider a random sample of 25 loan applications submitted to the Bank of New England last month. A portion of the sample information is shown in Table 14–3. The entire data set is available at the website (www.mhhe.com/lind8e) and is identified as Bank of New England.

    Next, we develop a correlation matrix. It will show the relationship between each of the independent variables and the dependent variable. This will help identify the independent variables that are more closely related to the dependent variable (family

TABLE 14–3 Information on Sample of 25 Loans by the Bank of New England

Loan	Income ($000)	Value ($000)	Education	Age	Mortgage	Gender
1	100.7	190	14	53	230	1
2	99.0	121	15	49	370	1
3	102.0	161	14	44	397	1
⋮	⋮	⋮	⋮	⋮	⋮	⋮
23	102.3	163	14	46	142	1
24	100.2	150	15	50	343	0
25	96.3	139	14	45	373	0

income.) The correlation matrix will also reveal independent variables that are highly correlated and possibly redundant. The correlation matrix is below.

	Income ($000)	Value ($000)	Education	Age	Mortgage	Gender
Income ($000)	1.0000					
Value ($000)	0.7197	1.0000				
Education	0.1880	0.1437	1.0000			
Age	0.2426	0.2195	0.6209	1.0000		
Mortgage	0.1157	0.3579	-0.2103	-0.0379	1.0000	
Gender	0.4856	0.1841	0.0619	0.1558	-0.1290	1.0000

What can we learn from this correlation matrix?

1. The family income is strongly related to the value of the home. There is also a moderate correlation between the gender of the person seeking the loan and family income. These two correlations are highlighted in yellow in the correlation matrix.
2. The amount of the mortgage has a weak correlation with family income. This correlation is indentified in red.
3. All possible correlations among the independent variables are identified in blue type. Our standard is to look for correlations that exceed an absolute value of .700. Using this standard, none of the independent variables are strongly correlated with each other. This indicates that multicollinearity is not likely.

Next, we compute the multiple regression equation using all the independent variables. The software output follows.

	A	B	C	D	E	F
1	SUMMARY OUTPUT					
2						
3	*Regression Statistics*					
4	Multiple R	0.866				
5	R Square	0.750				
6	Adjusted R Square	0.684				
7	Standard Error	1.478				
8	Observations	25				
9						
10	ANOVA					
11		*df*	*SS*	*MS*	*F*	*P-value*
12	Regression	5	124.3215	24.8643	11.3854	0.0000
13	Residual	19	41.4936	2.1839		
14	Total	24	165.8151			
15						
16		*Coefficients*	*Standard Error*	*t Stat*	*P-value*	
17	Intercept	70.6061	7.4644	9.4591	0.0000	
18	Value ($000)	0.0717	0.0124	5.7686	0.0000	
19	Education	1.6242	0.6031	2.6930	0.0144	
20	Age	-0.1224	0.0781	-1.5661	0.1338	
21	Mortgage	-0.0010	0.0032	-0.3191	0.7531	
22	Gender	1.8066	0.6228	2.9007	0.0092	

The coefficients of determination, that is, both R^2 and adjusted R^2, are reported at the top of the summary output and highlighted in yellow. The R^2 value is 75.0%, so the five independent variables account for three-quarters of the variation in family income. The adjusted R^2 measures the strength of the relationship between the set of independent variables and family income and also accounts for the number of variables in the regression equation. The adjusted R^2 indicates that the five variables account for 68.4% of the variance of family income. Both of these suggest that the proposed independent variables are useful in predicting family income.

The output also includes the regression equation.

$$\hat{Y} = 70.61 + .07(Value) + 1.62(Education) - 0.12(Age)$$
$$- .001(Mortgage) + 1.807(Gender)$$

Be careful in this interpretation. Both income and the value of the home are in thousands of dollars. Here is a summary:

1. An increase of $1,000 dollars in the value of the home suggests an increase of $70 in family income. An increase of one year of education increases income by $1,620, another year older reduces income by $120, and an increase of $1,000 in the mortgage reduces income by $1.
2. If a male is head of the household, the value of family income will increase by $1,807. Remember that "female" was coded 0 and "male" was coded 1, so a male head of household is positively related to home value.
3. The age of the head of household and monthly mortgage payment are inversely related to family income. This is true because the sign of the regression coefficient is negative.

Next we conduct the global hypothesis test. Here we check to see if any of the regression coefficients are different from 0. We use the .05 significance level.

$$H_0: \beta_1 = \beta_2 = \beta_3 = \beta_4 = \beta_5 = 0$$
$$H_1: \text{Not all the } \beta s \text{ are } 0.$$

The p-value from the table (cell F12) is 0.000. Because the p-value is less than the significance level, we reject the null hypothesis and conclude that at least one of the regression coefficients is not equal to zero.

Next we evaluate the individual regression coefficients. Refer to software output p-values to test each regression coefficient. They are reported in cells E18 to E22. The null hypothesis and the alternate hypothesis are:

$$H_0: \beta_i = 0$$
$$H_1: \beta_i \neq 0$$

The subscript i represents any particular independent variable. Again using .05 significance levels, the p-values for the regression coefficients for home value, years of education, and gender are all less than .05. We conclude that these regression coefficients are not equal to zero and are significant predictors of family income. The p-values for age and mortgage amount are greater than the significance level of .05, so we do not reject the null hypotheses for these variables. The regression coefficients are not different from zero and are not related to family income.

Based on the results of testing each of the regression coefficients, we conclude that the variables age and mortgage amount are not effective predictors of family income. Thus, they should be removed from the multiple regression equation. Remember that we must remove one independent variable at a time and redo the analysis to evaluate the overall effect of removing the variable. Our strategy is to remove the variable with the smallest t-statistic or the largest p-value. This variable is mortgage amount. The result of the regression analysis without the mortgage variable follows.

	A	B	C	D	E	F
1	SUMMARY OUTPUT					
2						
3	*Regression Statistics*					
4	Multiple R	0.865				
5	R Square	0.748				
6	Adjusted R Square	0.698				
7	Standard Error	1.444				
8	Observations	25				
9						
10	ANOVA					
11		*df*	*SS*	*MS*	*F*	*P-value*
12	Regression	4	124.0992	31.0248	14.8743	0.0000
13	Residual	20	41.7159	2.0858		
14	Total	24	165.8151			
15						
16		*Coefficients*	*Standard Error*	*t Stat*	*P-value*	
17	Intercept	70.1594	7.1654	9.7915	0.0000	
18	Value ($000)	0.0703	0.0114	6.1734	0.0000	
19	Education	1.6466	0.5854	2.8130	0.0107	
20	Age	-0.1224	0.0764	-1.6025	0.1247	
21	Gender	1.8464	0.5964	3.0959	0.0057	

Observe that the R^2 and adjusted R^2 change very little without the mortgage variable. Also observe that the p-value associated with age is greater than the .05 significance level. So next we remove the age variable and redo the analysis. The regression output with the variables age and mortgage amount removed follows.

	A	B	C	D	E	F
1	SUMMARY OUTPUT					
2						
3	*Regression Statistics*					
4	Multiple R	0.846				
5	R Square	0.716				
6	Adjusted R Square	0.676				
7	Standard Error	1.497				
8	Observations	25				
9						
10	ANOVA					
11		*df*	*SS*	*MS*	*F*	*P-value*
12	Regression	3	118.7429	39.5810	17.6580	0.0000
13	Residual	21	47.0722	2.2415		
14	Total	24	165.8151			
15						
16		*Coefficients*	*Standard Error*	*t Stat*	*P-value*	
17	Intercept	74.5273	6.8696	10.8488	0.0000	
18	Value ($000)	0.0634	0.0109	5.8032	0.0000	
19	Education	1.0158	0.4492	2.2617	0.0344	
20	Gender	1.7697	0.6163	2.8716	0.0091	

From this output, we conclude:

1. The R^2 and adjusted R^2 values have declined but only slightly. Using all five independent variables, the R^2 value was .750. With the two nonsignificant variables removed, the R^2 and adjusted R^2 values are .716 and .676, respectively. We prefer the equation with the fewer number of independent variables. It is easier to interpret.
2. In the ANOVA section, which is reported in rows 10 to 14, we observed that the p-value for the global test is less than .05. Hence, at least one of the regression coefficients is not equal to zero.

3.   Reviewing the significance of the individual coefficients, the *p*-values associated with each of the remaining independent variables are less than .05. We conclude that all the regression coefficients are different from zero. Each independent variable is a useful predictor of family income.

Our final step is to examine the regression assumptions, listed in Section 14.5 beginning on page 462, with our regression model. The first assumption is that there is a linear relationship between each independent variable and the dependent variable. It is not necessary to review the dummy variable Gender, because there are only two possible outcomes. Below are the scatter plots of family income versus home value and family income versus years of education.

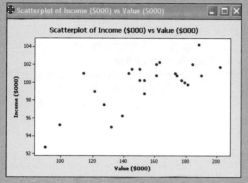
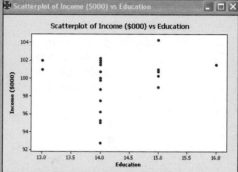

The scatter plot of income versus home value shows a general increasing trend. As the home value increases, so does family income. The points appear to be linear. That is, there is no observable nonlinear pattern in the data. The scatter plot on the right, of income versus years of education, shows that the data are measured to the nearest year and is a discrete variable. Given the measurement method, it is difficult to make an observation that the relationship is linear.

A plot of the residuals is also useful to evaluate the overall assumption of linearity. Recall that a residual is $(Y - \hat{Y})$, the difference between the actual value of the dependent variable (Y) and the predicted value of the dependent variable ($\hat{Y}$). Assuming a linear relationship, the distribution of the residuals should show about an equal proportion of negative residuals (points above the line) and positive residuals (points below the line) centered on zero. There should be no observable pattern to the plots. The graph follows.

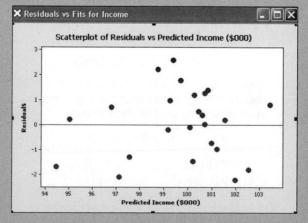

There is no discernable pattern to the plot, so we conclude that the linearity assumption is reasonable.

If the linearity assumption is valid, then the distribution of residuals should follow the normal probability distribution with a mean of zero. To evaluate this assumption, we will use a histogram and a normal probability plot.

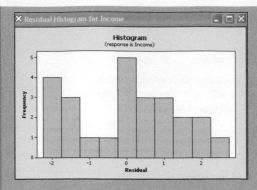
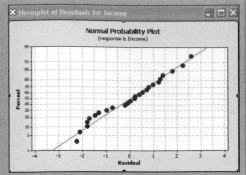

In general, the histogram on the left shows the major characteristics of a normal distribution, that is, a majority of observations in the middle and centered on the mean of zero, with lower frequencies in the tails of the distribution. The normal probability plot on the right is based on a cumulative normal probability distribution. The blue line is the standardized cumulative normal distribution. The red points show the cumulative distribution of the residuals. To confirm the normal distribution of the residuals, the red dots should be close to the blue line. This is true for most of the plot. However, we would note that there are departures and even perhaps a nonlinear pattern in the residuals in the lower part of the graph. As before, we are looking for serious departures from linearity and these are not indicated in these graphs.

The final assumption refers to multicollinearity. This means that the independent variables should not be highly correlated. We suggested a rule of thumb that multicollinearity would be a concern if the correlations among independent variables were close to 0.7 or −0.7. There are no violations of this guideline.

There is a statistical test to more precisely evaluate multicollinearity, the variance inflation factor (VIF). We use Minitab to calculate the VIFs below. The standard is that the VIF should be less than 10. Note that all the VIFs are clearly less than 10, so multicollinearity is not a concern.

```
The regression equation is
Income ($000) = 74.5 + 0.0634 Value ($000) + 1.02 Education + 1.77 Gender

Predictor         Coef     SE Coef       T        P       VIF
Constant        74.527       6.870   10.85    0.000
Value ($000)   0.06336     0.01092    5.80    0.000     1.062
Education       1.0158      0.4492    2.26    0.034     1.030
Gender          1.7697      0.6163    2.87    0.009     1.044
```

To summarize, the multiple regression equation is

$$\hat{Y} = 74.527 + .0634(Value) + 1.0158(Education) + 1.7697(Gender)$$

This equation explains 71.6% of the variation in family income. There are no major departures from the multiple regression assumptions of linearity, normally distributed residuals, and multicollinearity.

Chapter Summary

I. The general form of a multiple regression equation is:

$$\hat{Y} = a + b_1X_1 + b_2X_2 + \cdots + b_kX_k \qquad \text{[14–1]}$$

where a is the Y-intercept when all X's are zero, b_j refers to the sample regression coefficients, and X_j refers to the value of the various independent variables.

    A. There can be any number of independent variables.

    B. The least squares criterion is used to develop the regression equation.

    C. A statistical software package is needed to perform the calculations.

II. An ANOVA table summarizes the multiple regression analysis.

    A. It reports the total amount of the variation in the dependent variable and divides this variation into that explained by the set of independent variables and that not explained.

    B. It reports the degrees of freedom associated with the independent variables, the error variation, and the total variation.

III. There are two measures of the effectiveness of the regression equation.

    A. The multiple standard error of estimate is similar to the standard deviation.

        1. It is measured in the same units as the dependent variable.

        2. It is based on squared deviations from the regression equation.

        3. It ranges from 0 to plus infinity.

        4. It is calculated from the following equation.

$$s_{Y.123...k} = \sqrt{\frac{\Sigma(Y - \hat{Y})^2}{n - (k + 1)}} \qquad \text{[14–2]}$$

    B. The coefficient of multiple determination reports the percent of the variation in the dependent variable explained by the set of independent variables.

        1. It may range from 0 to 1.

        2. It is also based on squared deviations from the regression equation.

        3. It is found by the following equation.

$$R^2 = \frac{\text{SSR}}{\text{SS total}} \qquad \text{[14–3]}$$

        4. When the number of independent variables is large, we adjust the coefficient of determination for the degrees of freedom as follows.

$$R^2_{\text{adj}} = 1 - \frac{\dfrac{\text{SSE}}{n - (k + 1)}}{\dfrac{\text{SS total}}{n - 1}} \qquad \text{[14–4]}$$

IV. A global test is used to investigate whether any of the independent variables have significant regression coefficients.

    A. The null hypothesis is: All the regression coefficients are zero.

    B. The alternate hypothesis is: At least one regression coefficient is not zero.

    C. The test statistic is the F distribution with k (the number of independent variables) degrees of freedom in the numerator and $n - (k + 1)$ degrees of freedom in the denominator, where n is the sample size.

    D. The formula to calculate the value of the test statistic for the global test is:

$$F = \frac{\text{SSR}/k}{\text{SSE}/[n - (k + 1)]} \qquad \text{[14–5]}$$

V. The test for individual variables determines which independent variables have nonzero regression coefficients.

    A. The variables that have zero regression coefficients are usually dropped from the analysis.

    B. The test statistic is the t distribution with $n - (k + 1)$ degrees of freedom.

    C. The formula to calculate the value of the test statistic for the individual test is:

$$t = \frac{b_i - 0}{s_{b_i}} \qquad \text{[14–6]}$$

VI. There are five assumptions to use multiple regression analysis.

    A. The relationship between the dependent variable and the set of independent variables must be linear.

        1. To verify this assumption, develop a scatter diagram and plot the residuals on the vertical axis and the fitted values on the horizontal axis.

        2. If the plots appear random, we conclude the relationship is linear.

    B. The variation is the same for both large and small values of $\hat{Y}$.

        1. Homoscedasticity means the variation is the same for all fitted values of the dependent variable.

2. This condition is checked by developing a scatter diagram with the residuals on the vertical axis and the fitted values on the horizontal axis.

3. If there is no pattern to the plots—that is, they appear random—the residuals meet the homoscedasticity requirement.

C. The residuals follow the normal probability distribution.

1. This condition is checked by developing a histogram and a normal probability plot of the residuals to see if they follow a normal distribution.

2. The mean of the distribution of the residuals is 0.

D. The independent variables are not correlated.

1. A correlation matrix will show all possible correlations among independent variables. Signs of trouble are correlations larger than 0.70 or less than −0.70.

2. Signs of correlated independent variables include when an important predictor variable is found insignificant, when an obvious reversal occurs in signs in one or more of the independent variables, or when a variable is removed from the solution, there is a large change in the regression coefficients.

3. The variance inflation factor is used to identify correlated independent variables.

$$VIF = \frac{1}{1 - R_j^2}$$ [14–7]

E. Each residual is independent of other residuals.

1. Autocorrelation occurs when successive residuals are correlated.

2. When autocorrelation exists, the value of the standard error will be biased and will return poor results for tests of hypothesis regarding the regression coefficients.

VII. Use and interpret qualitative variables in a regression model.

A. A dummy or qualitative independent variable can assume one of two possible outcomes.

1. A value of 1 is assigned to one outcome and 0 the other.

2. Use formula (14–6) to determine if the dummy variable should remain in the equation.

VIII. Stepwise regression is a step-by-step process to find the regression equation.

A. Only independent variables with nonzero regression coefficients enter the equation.

B. Independent variables are added one at a time to the regression equation.

Pronunciation Key

SYMBOL	MEANING	PRONUNCIATION
b_1	Regression coefficient for the first independent variable	b sub 1
b_k	Regression coefficient for any independent variable	b sub k
$s_{Y.123...k}$	Multiple standard error of estimate	s sub Y dot 1, 2, 3 . . . k

Chapter Exercises

connect™

11. A multiple regression equation yields the following partial results.

Source	Sum of Squares	df
Regression	750	4
Error	500	35

a. What is the total sample size?

b. How many independent variables are being considered?

c. Compute the coefficient of determination.

d. Compute the standard error of estimate.

e. Test the hypothesis that none of the regression coefficients is equal to zero. Let $\alpha = .05$.

12. In a multiple regression equation, two independent variables are considered, and the sample size is 25. The regression coefficients and the standard errors are as follows.

$$b_1 = 2.676 \qquad s_{b_1} = 0.56$$

$$b_2 = -0.880 \qquad s_{b_2} = 0.71$$

Conduct a test of hypothesis to determine whether either independent variable has a coefficient equal to zero. Would you consider deleting either variable from the regression equation? Use the .05 significance level.

13. The following output was obtained.

```
Analysis of variance

SOURCE          DF          SS          MS
Regression       5         100          20
Error           20          40           2
Total           25         140

Predictor      Coef       StDev     t-ratio
Constant       3.00        1.50        2.00
   X₁          4.00        3.00        1.33
   X₂          3.00        0.20       15.00
   X₃          0.20        0.05        4.00
   X₄         -2.50        1.00       -2.50
   X₅          3.00        4.00        0.75
```

a. What is the sample size?
b. Compute the value of R^2.
c. Compute the multiple standard error of estimate.
d. Conduct a global test of hypothesis to determine whether any of the regression coefficients are significant. Use the .05 significance level.
e. Test the regression coefficients individually. Would you consider omitting any variable(s)? If so, which one(s)? Use the .05 significance level.

14. In a multiple regression equation, $k = 5$ and $n = 20$, the MSE value is 5.10, and SS total is 519.68. At the .05 significance level, can we conclude that any of the regression coefficients are not equal to 0?

15. The district manager of Jasons, a large discount electronics chain, is investigating why certain stores in her region are performing better than others. She believes that three factors are related to total sales: the number of competitors in the region, the population in the surrounding area, and the amount spent on advertising. From her district, consisting of several hundred stores, she selects a random sample of 30 stores. For each store, she gathered the following information.

Y = total sales last year (in $ thousands)
X_1 = number of competitors in the region
X_2 = population of the region (in millions)
X_3 = advertising expense (in $ thousands)

The sample data were run on Minitab, with the following results.

```
Analysis of variance

SOURCE          DF          SS          MS
Regression       3      3050.00     1016.67
Error           26      2200.00       84.62
Total           29      5250.00

Predictor      Coef       StDev     t-ratio
Constant      14.00        7.00        2.00
   X₁         -1.00        0.70       -1.43
   X₂         30.00        5.20        5.77
   X₃          0.20        0.08        2.50
```

a. What are the estimated sales for the Bryne store, which has four competitors, a regional population of 0.4 (400,000), and an advertising expense of 30 ($30,000)?

b. Compute the R^2 value.

c. Compute the multiple standard error of estimate.

d. Conduct a global test of hypothesis to determine whether any of the regression coefficients are not equal to zero. Use the .05 level of significance.

e. Conduct tests of hypotheses to determine which of the independent variables have significant regression coefficients. Which variables would you consider eliminating? Use the .05 significance level.

16. Suppose that the sales manager of a large automotive parts distributor wants to estimate as early as April the total annual sales of a region. On the basis of regional sales, the total sales for the company can also be estimated. If, based on past experience, it is found that the April estimates of annual sales are reasonably accurate, then in future years the April forecast could be used to revise production schedules and maintain the correct inventory at the retail outlets.

Several factors appear to be related to sales, including the number of retail outlets in the region stocking the company's parts, the number of automobiles in the region registered as of April 1, and the total personal income for the first quarter of the year. Five independent variables were finally selected as being the most important (according to the sales manager). Then the data were gathered for a recent year. The total annual sales for that year for each region were also recorded. Note in the following table that for region 1 there were 1,739 retail outlets stocking the company's automotive parts, there were 9,270,000 registered automobiles in the region as of April 1, and so on. The sales for that year were $37,702,000.

Annual Sales ($ millions), Y	Number of Retail Outlets, X_1	Number of Automobiles Registered (millions), X_2	Personal Income ($ billions), X_3	Average Age of Automobiles (years), X_4	Number of Supervisors, X_5
37.702	1,739	9.27	85.4	3.5	9.0
24.196	1,221	5.86	60.7	5.0	5.0
32.055	1,846	8.81	68.1	4.4	7.0
3.611	120	3.81	20.2	4.0	5.0
17.625	1,096	10.31	33.8	3.5	7.0
45.919	2,290	11.62	95.1	4.1	13.0
29.600	1,687	8.96	69.3	4.1	15.0
8.114	241	6.28	16.3	5.9	11.0
20.116	649	7.77	34.9	5.5	16.0
12.994	1,427	10.92	15.1	4.1	10.0

a. Consider the following correlation matrix. Which single variable has the strongest correlation with the dependent variable? The correlations between the independent variables outlets and income and between cars and outlets are fairly strong. Could this be a problem? What is this condition called?

```
          sales     outlets      cars     income       age
outlets   0.899
cars      0.605     0.775
income    0.964     0.825      0.409
age      -0.323    -0.489     -0.447    -0.349
bosses    0.286     0.183      0.395     0.155     0.291
```

b. The output for all five variables is on the following page. What percent of the variation is explained by the regression equation?

```
The regression equation is
Sales = -19.7 - 0.00063 outlets + 1.74 cars + 0.410 income
        + 2.04 age - 0.034 bosses

        Predictor          Coef      SE Coef          T          P
        Constant        -19.672        5.422      -3.63      0.022
        outlets       -0.000629     0.002638      -0.24      0.823
        cars             1.7399       0.5530       3.15      0.035
        income          0.40994      0.04385       9.35      0.001
        age              2.0357       0.8779       2.32      0.081
        bosses          -0.0344       0.1880      -0.18      0.864

Analysis of Variance
        SOURCE           DF         SS         MS          F          P
        Regression        5    1593.81     318.76     140.36      0.000
        Residual Error    4       9.08       2.27
        Total             9    1602.89
```

c. Conduct a global test of hypothesis to determine whether any of the regression coefficients are not zero. Use the .05 significance level.

d. Conduct a test of hypothesis on each of the independent variables. Would you consider eliminating "outlets" and "bosses"? Use the .05 significance level.

e. The regression has been rerun below with "outlets" and "bosses" eliminated. Compute the coefficient of determination. How much has R^2 changed from the previous analysis?

```
The regression equation is
Sales = -18.9 + 1.61 cars + 0.400 income + 1.96 age

        Predictor          Coef      SE Coef          T          P
        Constant        -18.924        3.636      -5.20      0.002
        cars             1.6129       0.1979       8.15      0.000
        income          0.40031      0.01569      25.52      0.000
        age              1.9637       0.5846       3.36      0.015

Analysis of Variance
        SOURCE           DF         SS         MS          F          P
        Regression        3    1593.66     531.22     345.25      0.000
        Residual Error    6       9.23       1.54
        Total             9    1602.89
```

f. Following is a histogram of the residuals. Does the normality assumption appear reasonable?

```
Histogram of residual  N = 10

Midpoint  Count
   -1.5     1    *
   -1.0     1    *
   -0.5     2    **
   -0.0     2    **
    0.5     2    **
    1.0     1    *
    1.5     1    *
```

g. Following is a plot of the fitted values of Y (i.e., $\hat{Y}$) and the residuals. Do you see any violations of the assumptions?

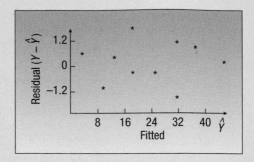

17. The administrator of a new paralegal program at Seagate Technical College wants to estimate the grade point average in the new program. He thought that high school GPA, the
verbal score on the Scholastic Aptitude Test (SAT), and the mathematics score on the
SAT would be good predictors of paralegal GPA. The data on nine students are:

Student	High School GPA	SAT Verbal	SAT Math	Paralegal GPA
1	3.25	480	410	3.21
2	1.80	290	270	1.68
3	2.89	420	410	3.58
4	3.81	500	600	3.92
5	3.13	500	490	3.00
6	2.81	430	460	2.82
7	2.20	320	490	1.65
8	2.14	530	480	2.30
9	2.63	469	440	2.33

a. Consider the following correlation matrix. Which variable has the strongest correlation
with the dependent variable? Some of the correlations among the independent variables are strong. Does this appear to be a problem?

	legal	gpa	verbal
gpa	0.911		
verbal	0.616	0.609	
math	0.487	0.636	0.599

b. Consider the following output. Compute the coefficient of multiple determination.

```
The regression equation is
Legal = -0.411 + 1.20 GPA + 0.00163 Verbal - 0.00194 Math

Predictor            Coef        SE Coef            T          P
Constant          -0.4111        0.7823        -0.53      0.622
GPA                1.2014        0.2955         4.07      0.010
Verbal           0.001629       0.002147         0.76      0.482
Math            -0.001939       0.002074        -0.94      0.393

Analysis of Variance
SOURCE            DF          SS           MS          F          P
Regression         3      4.3595       1.4532      10.33      0.014
Residual Error     5      0.7036       0.1407
Total              8      5.0631

SOURCE      DF    Seq SS
GPA          1    4.2061
Verbal       1    0.0303
Math         1    0.1231
```

c. Conduct a global test of hypothesis from the preceding output. Does it appear that any of the regression coefficients are not equal to zero?

d. Conduct a test of hypothesis on each independent variable. Would you consider eliminating the variables "verbal" and "math"? Let $\alpha = .05$.

e. The analysis has been rerun without "verbal" and "math." See the following output. Compute the coefficient of determination. How much has R^2 changed from the previous analysis?

```
The regression equation is
Legal  =  -0.454  +  1.16  GPA

Predictor          Coef      SE Coef          T          P
Constant        -0.4542       0.5542      -0.82      0.439
GPA              1.1589       0.1977       5.86      0.001

Analysis of Variance
SOURCE          '     DF        SS         MS        F          P
Regression            1     4.2061     4.2061     34.35      0.001
Residual Error        7     0.8570     0.1224
Total                 8     5.0631
```

f. Following is a histogram of the residuals. Does the normality assumption for the residuals seem reasonable?

```
Histogram of residual  N = 9

Midpoint              Count
     -0.4               1   *
     -0.2               3   ***
      0.0               3   ***
      0.2               1   *
      0.4               0
      0.6               1   *
```

g. Following is a plot of the residuals and the $\hat{Y}$ values. Do you see any violation of the assumptions?

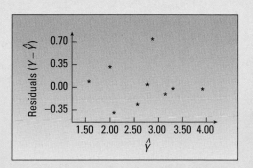

18. Mike Wilde is president of the teachers' union for Otsego School District. In preparing for upcoming negotiations, he would like to investigate the salary structure of classroom teachers in the district. He believes there are three factors that affect a teacher's salary: years of experience, a rating of teaching effectiveness given by the principal, and whether the teacher has a master's degree. A random sample of 20 teachers resulted in the following data.

Salary ($ thousands), Y	Years of Experience, X_1	Principal's Rating, X_2	Master's Degree,* X_3
31.1	8	35	0
33.6	5	43	0
29.3	2	51	1
⋮	⋮	⋮	⋮
30.7	4	62	0
32.8	2	80	1
42.8	8	72	0

*1 = yes, 0 = no.

a. Develop a correlation matrix. Which independent variable has the strongest correlation with the dependent variable? Does it appear there will be any problems with multicollinearity?

b. Determine the regression equation. What salary would you estimate for a teacher with five years' experience, a rating by the principal of 60, and no master's degree?

c. Conduct a global test of hypothesis to determine whether any of the regression coefficients differ from zero. Use the .05 significance level.

d. Conduct a test of hypothesis for the individual regression coefficients. Would you consider deleting any of the independent variables? Use the .05 significance level.

e. If your conclusion in part (d) was to delete one or more independent variables, run the analysis again without those variables.

f. Determine the residuals for the equation of part (e). Use a histogram to verify that the distribution of the residuals is approximately normal.

g. Plot the residuals computed in part (f) in a scatter diagram with the residuals on the Y-axis and the $\hat{Y}$ values on the X-axis. Does the plot reveal any violations of the assumptions of regression?

19. A consumer analyst collected the following data on the screen sizes of popular LCD televisions sold recently at a large retailer: (df)

Manufacturer	Screen	Price
Sharp	46	$1473.00
Samsung	52	2300.00
Samsung	46	1790.00
Sony	40	1250.00
Sharp	42	1546.50
Samsung	46	1922.50
Samsung	40	1372.00
Sharp	37	1149.50
Sharp	46	2000.00
Sony	40	1444.50
Sony	52	2615.00
Samsung	32	747.50
Sharp	37	1314.50
Sharp	32	853.50
Sharp	52	2778.00
Samsung	40	1749.50
Sharp	32	1035.00
Samsung	52	2950.00
Sony	40	1908.50
Sony	52	3103.00
Sony	46	2606.00
Sony	46	2861.00
Sony	52	3434.00

a. Does there appear to be a linear relationship between the screen size and the price?
b. Which variable is the "dependent" variable?
c. Using statistical software, determine the regression equation. Interpret the value of the slope in the regression equation.
d. Include the manufacturer in a multiple linear regression analysis using a "dummy" variable. Does it appear that some manufacturers can command a premium price? *Hint:* You will need to use a set of indicator variables.
e. Test each of the individual coefficients to see if they are significant.
f. Make a plot of the residuals and comment on whether they appear to follow a normal distribution.
g. Plot the residuals versus the fitted values. Do they seem to have the same amount of variation?

20. A regional planner is studying the demographics in a region of a particular state. She has gathered the following data on nine counties.

County	Median Income	Median Age	Coastal
A	$48,157	57.7	1
B	48,568	60.7	1
C	46,816	47.9	1
D	34,876	38.4	0
E	35,478	42.8	0
F	34,465	35.4	0
G	35,026	39.5	0
H	38,599	65.6	0
J	33,315	27.0	0

a. Is there a linear relationship between the median income and median age?
b. Which variable is the "dependent" variable?
c. Use statistical software to determine the regression equation. Interpret the value of the slope in a simple regression equation.
d. Include the aspect that the county is "coastal" or not in a multiple linear regression analysis using a "dummy" variable. Does it appear to be a significant influence on incomes?
e. Test each of the individual coefficients to see if they are significant.
f. Make a plot of the residuals and comment on whether they appear to follow a normal distribution.
g. Plot the residuals versus the fitted values. Do they seem to have the same amount of variation?

21. Great Plains Roofing and Siding Company Inc. sells roofing and siding products to home repair retailers, such as Lowe's and Home Depot, and commercial contractors. The owner is interested in studying the effects of several variables on the value of shingles sold ($000). The marketing manager is arguing that the company should spend more money on advertising, while a market researcher suggests it should focus more on making its brand and product more distinct from its competitors.

The company has divided the United States into 26 marketing districts. In each district, it collected information on the following variables: volume of sales (in thousands of dollars), advertising dollars (in thousands), number of active accounts, number of competing brands, and a rating of district potential.

Sales (000s)	Advertising Dollars (000s)	Number of Accounts	Number of Competitors	Market Potential
79.3	5.5	31	10	8
200.1	2.5	55	8	6
163.2	8.0	67	12	9

(continued)

Sales (000s)	Advertising Dollars (000s)	Number of Accounts	Number of Competitors	Market Potential
200.1	3.0	50	7	16
146.0	3.0	38	8	15
177.7	2.9	71	12	17
⋮	⋮	⋮	⋮	⋮
93.5	4.2	26	8	3
259.0	4.5	75	8	19
331.2	5.6	71	4	9

Conduct a multiple regression analysis to find the best predictors of sales.
a. Draw a scatter diagram comparing sales volume with each of the independent variables. Comment on the results.
b. Develop a correlation matrix. Do you see any problems? Does it appear there are any redundant independent variables?
c. Develop a regression equation. Conduct the global test. Can we conclude that some of the independent variables are useful in explaining the variation in the dependent variable?
d. Conduct a test of each of the independent variables. Are there any that should be dropped?
e. Refine the regression equation so the remaining variables are all significant.
f. Develop a histogram of the residuals and a normal probability plot. Are there any problems?
g. Determine the variance inflation factor for each of the independent variables. Are there any problems?

22. The *Times-Observer* is a daily newspaper in Metro City. Like many city newspapers, the *Times-Observer* is suffering through difficult financial times. The circulation manager is studying other newspapers in similar cities in the United States and Canada. She is particularly interested in what variables relate to the number of subscriptions to the paper. She is able to obtain the following sample information on 25 newspapers in similar cities. The following notation is used: (df)

$$Sub = \text{Number of subscriptions (in thousands)}$$
$$Popul = \text{The metropolitan population (in thousands)}$$
$$Adv = \text{The advertising budget of the paper (in \$ hundreds)}$$
$$Income = \text{The median family income in the metropolitan area (in \$ thousands)}$$

Paper	Sub	Popul	Adv	Income
1	37.95	588.9	13.2	35.1
2	37.66	585.3	13.2	34.7
3	37.55	566.3	19.8	34.8
⋮	⋮	⋮	⋮	⋮
23	38.83	629.6	22.0	35.3
24	38.33	680.0	24.2	34.7
25	40.24	651.2	33.0	35.8

a. Determine the regression equation.
b. Conduct a global test of hypothesis to determine whether any of the regression coefficients are not equal to zero.
c. Conduct a test for the individual coefficients. Would you consider deleting any coefficients?
d. Determine the residuals and plot them against the fitted values. Do you see any problems?
e. Develop a histogram of the residuals. Do you see any problems with the normality assumption?

23. Fred G. Hire is the manager of human resources at Crescent Tool and Die Inc. As part of his yearly report to the CEO, he is required to present an analysis of the salaried employees. Because there are over 1,000 employees, he does not have the staff to gather information on each salaried employee, so he selects a random sample of 30. For each employee, he records monthly salary; service at Crescent, in months; gender (1 = male, 0 = female); and whether the employee has a technical or clerical job. Those working technical jobs are coded 1, and those who are clerical 0. (df)

Sampled Employee	Monthly Salary	Length of Service	Age	Gender	Job
1	$1,769	93	42	1	0
2	1,740	104	33	1	0
3	1,941	104	42	1	1
⋮	⋮	⋮	⋮	⋮	⋮
28	1,791	131	56	0	1
29	2,001	95	30	1	1
30	1,874	98	47	1	0

a. Determine the regression equation, using salary as the dependent variable and the other four variables as independent variables.
b. What is the value of R^2? Comment on this value.
c. Conduct a global test of hypothesis to determine whether any of the independent variables are different from 0.
d. Conduct an individual test to determine whether any of the independent variables can be dropped.
e. Rerun the regression equation, using only the independent variables that are significant. How much more does a man earn per month than a woman? Does it make a difference whether the employee has a technical or a clerical job?

24. Many regions along the coast in North and South Carolina and Georgia have experienced rapid population growth over the last 10 years. It is expected that the growth will continue over the next 10 years. This has motivated many of the large grocery store chains to build new stores in the region. The Kelley's Super Grocery Stores Inc. chain is no exception. The director of planning for Kelley's Super Grocery Stores wants to study adding more stores in this region. He believes there are two main factors that indicate the amount families spend on groceries. The first is their income and the other is the number of people in the family. The director gathered the following sample information. (df)

Family	Food	Income	Size
1	$5.04	$ 73.98	4
2	4.08	54.90	2
3	5.76	94.14	4
⋮	⋮	⋮	⋮
23	4.56	38.16	3
24	5.40	43.74	7
25	4.80	48.42	5

Food and income are reported in thousands of dollars per year, and the variable size refers to the number of people in the household.
a. Develop a correlation matrix. Do you see any problems with multicollinearity?
b. Determine the regression equation. Discuss the regression equation. How much does an additional family member add to the amount spent on food?
c. What is the value of R^2? Can we conclude that this value is greater than 0?
d. Would you consider deleting either of the independent variables?
e. Plot the residuals in a histogram. Is there any problem with the normality assumption?
f. Plot the fitted values against the residuals. Does this plot indicate any problems with homoscedasticity?

25. An investment advisor is studying the relationship between a common stock's price to earnings (P/E) ratio and factors that she thinks would influence it. She has the following data on the earnings per share (EPS) and the dividend percentage (Yield) for a sample of 20 stocks. (df)

Stock	P/E	EPS	Yield
1	20.79	$2.46	1.42
2	3.03	2.69	4.05
3	44.46	−0.28	4.16
⋮	⋮	⋮	⋮
18	30.21	1.71	3.07
19	32.88	0.35	2.21
20	15.19	5.02	3.50

  a. Develop a multiple linear regression with P/E as the dependent variable.
  b. Are either of the two independent variables an effective predictor of P/E?
  c. Interpret the regression coefficients.
  d. Do any of these stocks look particularly undervalued?
  e. Plot the residuals and check the normality assumption. Plot the fitted values against the residuals.
  f. Does there appear to be any problems with homoscedasticity?
  g. Develop a correlation matrix. Do any of the correlations indicate multicollinearity?

26. The Conch Café, located in Gulf Shores, Alabama, features casual lunches with a great view of the Gulf of Mexico. To accommodate the increase in business during the summer vacation season, Fuzzy Conch, the owner, hires a large number of servers as seasonal help. When he interviews a prospective server, he would like to provide data on the amount a server can earn in tips. He believes that the amount of the bill and the number of diners are both related to the amount of the tip. He gathered the following sample information. (df)

Customer	Amount of Tip	Amount of Bill	Number of Diners
1	$7.00	$48.97	5
2	4.50	28.23	4
3	1.00	10.65	1
⋮	⋮	⋮	⋮
28	2.50	26.25	2
29	9.25	56.81	5
30	8.25	50.65	5

  a. Develop a multiple regression equation with the amount of tips as the dependent variable and the amount of the bill and the number of diners as independent variables. Write out the regression equation. How much does another diner add to the amount of the tips?
  b. Conduct a global test of hypothesis to determine if at least one of the independent variables is significant. What is your conclusion?
  c. Conduct an individual test on each of the variables. Should one or the other be deleted?
  d. Use the equation developed in part (c) to determine the coefficient of determination. Interpret the value.
  e. Plot the residuals. Is it reasonable to assume they follow the normal distribution?
  f. Plot the residuals against the fitted values. Is it reasonable to conclude they are random?

27. The president of Blitz Sales Enterprises sells kitchen products through television commercials, often called infomercials. He gathered data from the last 15 weeks of sales to determine the relationship between sales and the number of infomercials. df

Infomercials	Sales ($000s)	Infomercials	Sales ($000s)
20	3.2	22	2.5
15	2.6	15	2.4
25	3.4	25	3.0
10	1.8	16	2.7
18	2.2	12	2.0
18	2.4	20	2.6
15	2.4	25	2.8
12	1.5		

    a. Determine the regression equation. Are the sales predictable from the number of commercials?

    b. Determine the residuals and plot a histogram. Does the normality assumption seem reasonable?

28. The director of special events for Sun City believed that the amount of money spent on fireworks displays on the 4th of July was predictive of attendance at the Fall Festival held in October. She gathered the following data to test her suspicion. df

4th of July ($000)	Fall Festival (000)	4th of July ($000)	Fall Festival (000)
10.6	8.8	9.0	9.5
8.5	6.4	10.0	9.8
12.5	10.8	7.5	6.6
9.0	10.2	10.0	10.1
5.5	6.0	6.0	6.1
12.0	11.1	12.0	11.3
8.0	7.5	10.5	8.8
7.5	8.4		

Determine the regression equation. Is the amount spent on fireworks related to attendance at the Fall Festival?

Data Set Exercises

(The data for these exercises are available at the text website www.mhhe.com/lindbasic8e).

29. Refer to the Real Estate data, which report information on homes sold in Goodyear, Arizona. Use the selling price of the home as the dependent variable and determine the regression equation with number of bedrooms, size of the house, center of the city, and number of bathrooms as independent variables.

    a. Use a statistical software package to determine the multiple regression equation. Discuss each of the variables. For example, are you surprised that the regression coefficient for distance from the center of the city is negative? How much does a garage or a swimming pool add to the selling price of a home?

    b. Determine the value of the Intercept.

    c. Develop a correlation matrix. Which independent variables have strong or weak correlations with the dependent variable? Do you see any problems with multicollinearity?

    d. Conduct the global test on the set of independent variables. Interpret.

    e. Conduct a test of hypothesis on each of the independent variables. Would you consider deleting any of the variables? If so, which ones?

   f. Rerun the analysis until only significant regression coefficients remain in the analysis. Identify these variables.

   g. Develop a histogram of the residuals from the final regression equation developed in part (f). Is it reasonable to conclude that the normality assumption has been met?

   h. Plot the residuals against the fitted values from the final regression equation developed in part (f). Plot the residuals on the vertical axis and the fitted values on the horizontal axis.

30. Refer to the Baseball 2010 data, which report information on the 30 Major League Baseball teams for the 2010 season. Let the number of games won be the dependent variable and the following variables be independent variables: team batting average, number of stolen bases, number of errors committed, team ERA, number of home runs, and whether the team plays in the American or the National League. Add a league code variable using 0 for the National League and 1 for the American League.

   a. Use a statistical software package to determine the multiple regression equation. Discuss each of the variables. For example, are you surprised that the regression coefficient for ERA is negative? Is the number of wins affected by whether the team plays in the National or the American League?

   b. Find the coefficient of determination for this set of independent variables.

   c. Develop a correlation matrix. Which independent variables have strong or weak correlations with the dependent variable? Do you see any problems with multicollinearity?

   d. Conduct a global test on the set of independent variables. Interpret.

   e. Conduct a test of hypothesis on each of the independent variables. Would you consider deleting any of the variables? If so, which ones?

   f. Rerun the analysis until only significant net regression coefficients remain in the analysis. Identify these variables.

   g. Develop a histogram of the residuals from the final regression equation developed in part (f). Is it reasonable to conclude that the normality assumption has been met?

   h. Plot the residuals against the fitted values from the final regression equation developed in part (f). Plot the residuals on the vertical axis and the fitted values on the horizontal axis.

31. Refer to the Buena School District bus data. First, add a variable to change the type of bus (diesel or gasoline) to a qualitative variable. If the bus type is diesel, then set the qualitative variable to 0. If the bus type is gasoline, then set the qualitative variable to 1. Develop a regression equation using statistical software with maintenance as the dependent variable and age, miles, and bus type as the independent variables.

   a. Write out the multiple regression equation analysis. Discuss each of the variables.

   b. Determine the value of R^2. Interpret.

   c. Develop a correlation matrix. Which independent variables have strong or weak correlations with the dependent variable? Do you see any problems with multicollinearity?

   d. Conduct the global test on the set of independent variables. Interpret.

   e. Conduct a test of hypothesis on each of the independent variables. Would you consider deleting any of the variables? If so, which ones?

   f. Rerun the analysis until only significant regression coefficients remain in the analysis. Identify these variables.

   g. Develop a histogram of the residuals from the final regression equation developed in part (f). Is it reasonable to conclude that the normality assumption has been met?

   h. Plot the residuals against the fitted values from the final regression equation developed in part (f) against the fitted values of Y. Plot the residuals on the vertical axis and the fitted values on the horizontal axis.

Practice Test

Part 1—Objective

1. Multiple regression analysis describes the relationship between one dependent variable and two or more _____ .
2. In multiple regression analysis, the regression coefficients are computed using the method of _____ . (residuals, normality, least squares, standardization)
3. In multiple regression analysis, the multiple standard error of the estimate is the square root of the _____ . (mean square error, residual, residual squared, explained variation)

4. The coefficient of multiple determination is the percent of variation in the dependent variable that is explained by the set of _____.
5. The adjusted coefficient of determination compensates for the number of _____. (dependent variables, errors, independent variables)
6. In the Global Test of the regression coefficients, when the hypothesis is rejected, at least one coefficient is _____.
7. The test statistic for the Global Test of regression coefficients is the _____.
8. The test statistic for testing individual regression coefficients is the _____.
9. A scatter plot of the residuals versus the fitted values of the dependent variable evaluates the assumption of _____.
10. Multicollinearity exists when independent variables are _____.
11. The variance inflation factor is used to detect _____.
12. Another term for a qualitative variable is a _____ variable.

Part 2—Problems
1. Given the following ANOVA output:

Source	Sum of Squares	DF	MS
Regression	1050.8	4	262.70
Error	83.8	20	4.19
Total	1134.6	24	

Predictor	Coefficient	St. Dev	t-ratio
Constant	70.06	2.13	32.89
X_1	0.42	0.17	2.47
X_2	0.27	0.21	1.29
X_3	0.75	0.30	2.50
X_4	0.42	0.07	6.00

a. How many independent variables are there in the regression equation?
b. Write out the regression equation.
c. Compute the coefficient of multiple determination.
d. Compute the multiple standard error of estimate.
e. Conduct a hypothesis test to determine if any of the regression coefficients are different from zero.
f. Conduct a hypothesis test on each of the regression coefficients. Can any of them be deleted?

Software Commands

Note: We do not show steps for all the statistical software examples used in this chapter. The following are the first two, which show the basic steps.
1. The Minitab commands for the multiple regression output on page 447 are:
   a. Import the data from the website. The file name is **Tbl14–1.**
   b. Select **Stat, Regression,** and then click on **Regression.**
   c. Select *Cost* as the **Response** variable, and *Temp, Insul,* and *Age* as the **Predictors,** then click on **OK.**

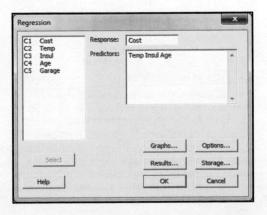

2. The Excel commands to produce the multiple regression output on page 447 are:
   a. Import the data from the website. The file name is **Tbl14.**
   b. Select the **Data** tab on the top menu. Then on the far right, select **Data analysis.** Select **Regression** and click **OK.**
   c. Make the **Input Y Range** *A1:A21,* the **Input X Range** *B1:D21,* check the **Labels** box, the **Output Range** is *G1,* then click **OK.**

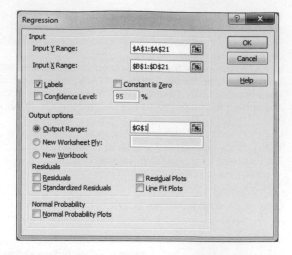

Chapter 14　Answers to Self-Review

14–1 a. $389,500 or 389.5 (in $000); found by

$$2.5 + 3(40) + 4(72) - 3(10) + .2(20) + 1(5)$$
$$= 389.5$$

b. The b_2 of 4 shows profit will go up $4,000 for each extra hour the restaurant is open (if none of the other variables change). The b_3 of -3 implies profit will fall $3,000 for each added mile away from the central area (if none of the other variables change).

14–2 a. The total degrees of freedom $(n - 1)$ is 25. So the sample size is 26.
   b. There are 5 independent variables.
   c. There is only 1 dependent variable (profit).
   d. $S_{Y.12345} = 1.414$, found by $\sqrt{2}$. Ninety-five percent of the residuals will be between -2.828 and 2.828, found by $\pm 2(1.414)$.
   e. $R^2 = .714$, found by 100/140. 71.4% of the deviation in profit is accounted for by these five variables.
   f. $R^2_{adj} = .643$, found by

$$1 - \left[\frac{40}{(26 - (5 + 1))} \right] \Big/ \left[\frac{140}{(26 - 1)} \right]$$

14–3 a. $H_0: \beta_1 = \beta_2 = \beta_3 = \beta_4 = \beta_5 = 0$
   H_1: Not all of the β's are 0.

The decision rule is to reject H_0 if $F > 2.71$. The computed value of F is 10, found by 20/2. So, you reject H_0, which indicates at least one of the regression coefficients is different from zero.

Based on p-values, the decision rule is to reject the null hypothesis if the p-value is less than 0.05. The computed value of F is 10, found by 20/2, and has a p-value of 0.000. Thus, we reject the null hypothesis, which indicates that at least one of the regression coefficients is different from zero.

b. For variable 1: $H_0: \beta_1 = 0$ and $H_1: \beta_1 \neq 0$
The decision rule is: Reject H_0 if $t < -2.086$ or $t > 2.086$. Since 2.000 does not go beyond either of those limits, we fail to reject the null hypothesis. This regression coefficient could be zero. We can consider dropping this variable. By parallel logic, the null hypothesis is rejected for variables 3 and 4.

For variable 1, the decision rule is to reject $H_0: \beta_1 = 0$ if the p-value is less than 0.05. Because the p-value is 0.056, we cannot reject the null hypothesis. This regression coefficient could be zero. Therefore, we can consider dropping this variable. By parallel logic, we reject the null hypothesis for variables 3 and 4.

c. We should consider dropping variables 1, 2, and 5. Variable 5 has the smallest absolute value of t or largest p-value. So delete it first and refigure the regression analysis.

14–4 a. $\hat{Y} = 15.7625 + 0.4415X_1 + 3.8598X_2$
$\hat{Y} = 15.7625 + 0.4415(30) + 3.8598(1)$
$= 32.87$

b. Female agents make $3,860 more than male agents.

c. $H_0: \beta_3 = 0$
$H_1: \beta_3 \neq 0$
$df = 17$, reject H_0 if $t < -2.110$ or $t > 2.110$

$$t = \frac{3.8598 - 0}{1.4724} = 2.621$$

The t-statistic exceeds the critical value of 2.110. Also, the p-value $= 0.0179$ and is less than 0.05. Reject H_0. Gender should be included in the regression equation.

Nonparametric Methods:

Goodness-of-Fit Tests

For many years, TV executives used the guideline that 30% of the audience were watching each of the traditional big three prime-time networks and 10% were watching cable stations on a weekday night. A random sample of 500 viewers in the Tampa–St. Petersburg, Florida, area last Monday night showed that 165 homes were tuned in to the ABC affiliate, 140 to the CBS affiliate, 125 to the NBC affiliate, and the remainder were viewing a cable station. At the .05 significance level, can we conclude that the guideline is still reasonable? (See Exercise 12 and LO 15-2.)

Learning Objectives

When you have completed this chapter, you will be able to:

LO 15-1 Conduct a test of hypothesis comparing an observed set of frequencies to an expected distribution.

LO 15-2 List and explain the characteristics of the chi-square distribution.

LO 15-3 Compute a goodness-of-fit test for unequal expected frequencies.

LO 15-4 Conduct a test of hypothesis to verify that data grouped into a frequency distribution are a sample from a normal population.

LO 15-5 Use graphical and statistical methods to determine whether a set of sample data is from a normal population.

LO 15-6 Perform a chi-square test for independence on a contingency table.

15.1 Introduction

Chapters 9 through 12 discuss data of interval or ratio scale, such as weights of steel ingots, incomes of minorities, and years of employment. We conducted hypothesis tests about a single population mean, two population means, and three or more population means. For these tests, we assume the populations follow the normal probability distribution. However, there are tests available in which no assumption regarding the shape of the population is necessary. These tests are referred to as nonparametric. In this situation, the assumption of a normal population is not necessary.

There are also tests exclusively for data of nominal scale of measurement. Recall from Chapter 1 that nominal data is the "lowest" or most primitive. For this type of measurement, data are classified into categories where there is no natural order. Examples include gender of Congressional representatives, state of birth of students, or brand of peanut butter purchased. In this chapter, we introduce a new test statistic, the chi-square statistic.

15.2 Goodness-of-Fit Test: Equal Expected Frequencies

LO 15-1 Conduct a test of hypothesis comparing an observed set of frequencies to an expected distribution.

The goodness-of-fit test is one of the most commonly used statistical tests. It is particularly useful because it requires only the nominal level of measurement. So we are able to conduct a test of hypothesis on data that has been classified into groups. Our first illustration of this test involves the case when the expected cell frequencies are equal. As the full name implies, the purpose of the goodness-of-fit test is to compare an observed distribution to an expected distribution. An example will describe the hypothesis-testing situation.

Example

Bubba's Fish and Pasta is a chain of restaurants located along the Gulf Coast of Florida. Bubba, the owner, is considering adding steak to his menu. Before doing so, he decides to hire Magnolia Research, LLC, to conduct a survey of adults as to their favorite meal when eating out. Magnolia selected a sample 120 adults and asked each to indicate their favorite meal when dining out. The results are reported in Table 15-1.

TABLE 15–1 Favorite Entrée as Selected by a Sample of 120 Adults

Favorite Entrée	Frequency
Chicken	32
Fish	24
Meat	35
Pasta	29
Total	120

Is it reasonable to conclude there is no preference among the four entrées?

Solution

If there is no difference in the popularity of the four entrées, we would expect the observed frequencies to be equal—or nearly equal. To put it another way, we would expect as many adults to indicate they preferred chicken as fish. Thus, any discrepancy in the observed and expected frequencies is attributed to sampling error or chance.

What is the level of measurement in this problem? Notice that when a person is selected, we can only classify the selected adult as to the entrée preferred. We do not get a reading or a measurement of any kind. The "measurement" or "classification" is based on the selected entrée. In addition, there is no natural order to the favorite entrée.

No one entrée is assumed better than another. Therefore, the nominal scale is appropriate.

If the entrées are equally popular, we would expect 30 adults to select each meal. Why is this so? If there are 120 adults in the sample and four categories, we expect that one-fourth of those surveyed would select each entrée. So 30, found by 120/4, is the expected frequency for each category or cell, assuming there is no preference for any of the entrées. This information is summarized in Table 15–2. An examination of the data indicates meat is the entrée selected most frequently (35 out of 120) and fish is selected least frequently (24 out of 120). Is the difference in the number of times each entrée is selected due to chance, or should we conclude that the entrées are not equally preferred?

TABLE 15–2 Observed and Expected Frequency for Survey of 120 Adults

Favorite Meal	Frequency Observed, f_o	Frequency Expected, f_e
Chicken	32	30
Fish	24	30
Meat	35	30
Pasta	29	30
Total	120	120

To investigate the issue, we use the five-step hypothesis-testing procedure.

Step 1: State the null hypothesis and the alternate hypothesis. The null hypothesis, H_0, is that there is no difference between the set of observed frequencies and the set of expected frequencies. In other words, any difference between the two sets of frequencies is attributed to sampling error. The alternate hypothesis, H_1, is that there is a difference between the observed and expected sets of frequencies. If the null hypothesis is rejected and the alternate hypothesis is accepted, we conclude the preferences are not equally distributed among the four categories (cells).

H_0: There is no difference in the proportion of adults selecting each entrée.

H_1: There is a difference in the proportion of adults selecting each entrée.

Step 2: Select the level of significance. We selected the .05 significance level. The probability is .05 that a true null hypothesis is rejected.

Step 3: Select the test statistic. The test statistic follows the chi-square distribution, designated by χ^2.

CHI-SQUARE TEST STATISTIC
$$\chi^2 = \Sigma \left[\frac{(f_o - f_e)^2}{f_e} \right]$$
[15–1]

with $k - 1$ degrees of freedom, where:

k is the number of categories.
f_o is an observed frequency in a particular category.
f_e is an expected frequency in a particular category.

We will examine the characteristics of the chi-square distribution in more detail shortly.

Step 4: Formulate the decision rule. Recall that the decision rule in hypothesis testing is the value that separates the region where we do not reject H_0 from the region where H_0 is rejected. This number is called the *critical value.* As we will soon see, the chi-square distribution is really a family of distributions. Each distribution has a slightly different shape, depending on the number of degrees of freedom. The number of degrees of freedom is $k - 1$, where k is the number of categories. In this particular problem, there are four categories, the four meal entrées. Because there are four categories, there is $k - 1 = 4 - 1 = 3$ degrees of freedom. As noted, a category is called a *cell,* and there are four cells. The critical value for 3 degrees of freedom and the .05 level of significance is found in Appendix B.3. A portion of that table is shown in Table 15–3. The critical value is 7.815, found by locating 3 degrees of freedom in the left margin and then moving horizontally (to the right) and reading the critical value in the .05 column.

TABLE 15–3 A Portion of the Chi-Square Table

Degrees of Freedom df	Right-Tail Area			
	.10	.05	.02	.01
1	2.706	3.841	5.412	6.635
2	4.605	5.991	7.824	9.210
3	6.251	7.815	9.837	11.345
4	7.779	9.488	11.668	13.277
5	9.236	11.070	13.388	15.086

The decision rule is to reject the null hypothesis if the computed value of chi-square is greater than 7.815. If it is less than or equal to 7.815, we fail to reject the null hypothesis. Chart 15–1 shows the decision rule.

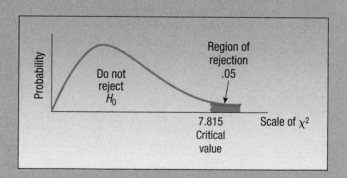

CHART 15–1 Chi-Square Probability Distribution for 3 Degrees of Freedom, Showing the Region of Rejection, .05 Level of Significance

The decision rule indicates that if there are large differences between the observed and expected frequencies, resulting in a computed χ^2 of more than 7.815, the null hypothesis should be rejected. However, if the differences between f_o and f_e are small, the computed χ^2 value will be 7.815 or less, and the null hypothesis should not be rejected. The reasoning is that such small differences between the observed and expected frequencies are probably due to chance.

Step 5: Compute the value of chi-square and make a decision. Of the 120 adults in the sample, 32 indicated their favorite entrée was chicken. The counts were reported in Table 15–1. The calculations for chi-square follow. (Note again that the expected frequencies are the same for each cell.)

Column 1: Determine the differences between each f_o and f_e. That is, $f_o - f_e$. The sum of these differences will always be zero.

Column 2: Square the difference between each observed and expected frequency, that is, $(f_o - f_e)^2$.

Column 3: Divide the result for each observation by the expected frequency, that is, $(f_o - f_e)^2/f_e$. Finally, sum these values. The result is the value of χ^2, which is 2.20.

Favorite Entrée	f_o	f_e	(1) $(f_o - f_e)$	(2) $(f_o - f_e)^2$	(3) $(f_o - f_e)^2/f_e$
Chicken	32	30	2	4	0.133
Fish	24	30	−6	36	1.200
Meat	35	30	5	25	0.833
Pasta	29	30	−1	1	0.033
Total	120	120	0		2.200

The computed χ^2 of 2.200 is not in the rejection region. It is less than the critical value of 7.815. The decision, therefore, is to not reject the null hypothesis. We conclude that the differences between the observed and the expected frequencies could be due to chance. That means there is no preference among the four entrées.

We can use software to compute the value of chi-square. The output of MegaStat follows. The steps are shown in the **Software Commands** section at the end of the chapter. The computed value of chi-square is 2.200, the same value obtained in our earlier calculations. Also note the p-value is .5319, much larger than .05.

```
Goodness-of-Fit Test

    observed      expected      O − E      (O − E)²/E      % of chisq
          32        30.000      2.000          0.133            6.06
          24        30.000     −6.000          1.200           54.55
          35        30.000      5.000          0.833           37.88
          29        30.000     −1.000          0.033            1.52
         120       120.000      0.000          2.200          100.00

        2.20    chi-square
           3    df
       .5319    p-value
```

The chi-square distribution, which is used as the test statistic in this chapter, has the following characteristics.

LO 15-2 List and explain the characteristics of the chi-square distribution.

1. **Chi-square values are never negative.** This is because the difference between f_o and f_e is squared, that is, $(f_o - f_e)^2$.

2. **There is a family of chi-square distributions.** There is a chi-square distribution for 1 degree of freedom, another for 2 degrees of freedom, another for 3 degrees of freedom, and so on. In this type of problem, the number of degrees of freedom is determined by $k - 1$, where k is the number of categories. Therefore, the shape of the chi-square distribution does *not* depend on the size of the sample, but on the number of categories used. For example, if 200 employees

of an airline were classified into one of three categories—flight personnel, ground support, and administrative personnel—there would be $k - 1 = 3 - 1 = 2$ degrees of freedom.

3. **The chi-square distribution is positively skewed.** However, as the number of degrees of freedom increases, the distribution begins to approximate the normal probability distribution. Chart 15–2 shows the distributions for selected degrees of freedom. Notice that for 10 degrees of freedom the curve is approaching a normal distribution.

Shape of χ^2 distribution approaches normal distribution as *df* becomes larger.

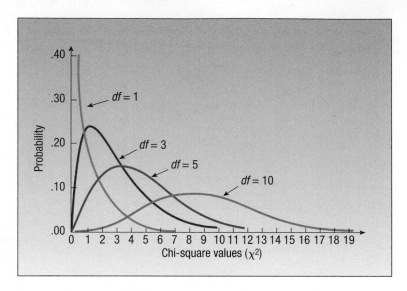

CHART 15–2 Chi-Square Distributions for Selected Degrees of Freedom

---

Self-Review 15–1

The human resources director at Georgetown Paper Inc. is concerned about absenteeism among hourly workers. She decides to sample the company records to determine whether absenteeism is distributed evenly throughout the six-day work week. The hypotheses are:

H_0: Absenteeism is evenly distributed throughout the work week.
H_1: Absenteeism is *not* evenly distributed throughout the work week.

The sample results are:

	Number Absent		**Number Absent**
Monday	12	Thursday	10
Tuesday	9	Friday	9
Wednesday	11	Saturday	9

(a) What are the numbers 12, 9, 11, 10, 9, and 9 called?
(b) How many categories (cells) are there?
(c) What is the *expected* frequency for each day?
(d) How many degrees of freedom are there?
(e) What is the chi-square critical value at the 1% significance level?
(f) Compute the χ^2 test statistic.
(g) What is the decision regarding the null hypothesis?
(h) Specifically, what does this indicate to the human resources director?

Exercises

connect™

1. In a particular chi-square goodness-of-fit test, there are four categories and 200 observations. Use the .05 significance level.
   a. How many degrees of freedom are there?
   b. What is the critical value of chi-square?

2. In a particular chi-square goodness-of-fit test, there are six categories and 500 observations. Use the .01 significance level.
   a. How many degrees of freedom are there?
   b. What is the critical value of chi-square?

3. The null hypothesis and the alternate are:

   H_0: The frequencies are equal.
   H_1: The frequencies are not equal.

   a. State the decision rule, using the .05 significance level.
   b. Compute the value of chi-square.
   c. What is your decision regarding H_0?

Category	f_o
A	10
B	20
C	30

4. The null hypothesis and the alternate are:

   H_0: The frequencies are equal.
   H_1: The frequencies are not equal.

   a. State the decision rule, using the .05 significance level.
   b. Compute the value of chi-square.
   c. What is your decision regarding H_0?

Category	f_o
A	10
B	20
C	30
D	20

5. A six-sided die is rolled 30 times and the numbers 1 through 6 appear as shown in the following frequency distribution. At the .10 significance level, can we conclude that the die is fair?

Outcome	Frequency	Outcome	Frequency
1	3	4	3
2	6	5	9
3	2	6	7

Day	Rounds
Monday	124
Tuesday	74
Wednesday	104
Thursday	98
Friday	120

6. Classic Golf Inc. manages five courses in the Jacksonville, Florida, area. The director of golf wishes to study the number of rounds of golf played per weekday at the five courses. He gathered the following sample information shown to the left. At the .05 significance level, is there a difference in the number of rounds played by day of the week?

7. A group of department store buyers viewed a new line of dresses and gave their opinions of them. The results were: (df)

Opinion	Number of Buyers	Opinion	Number of Buyers
Outstanding	47	Good	39
Excellent	45	Fair	35
Very good	40	Undesirable	34

Because the largest number (47) indicated the new line is outstanding, the head designer thinks that this is a mandate to go into mass production of the dresses. The head sweeper (who somehow became involved in this) believes that there is not a clear mandate and claims that the opinions are evenly distributed among the six categories. He further states that the slight differences among the various counts are probably due to chance. Test the null hypothesis that there is no significant difference among the opinions of the buyers. Test at the .01 level of risk. Follow a formal approach; that is, state the null hypothesis, the alternate hypothesis, and so on.

8. The safety director of Honda USA took samples at random from company records of minor work-related accidents and classified them according to the time the accident took place.

Time	Number of Accidents	Time	Number of Accidents
8 up to 9 A.M.	6	1 up to 2 P.M.	7
9 up to 10 A.M.	6	2 up to 3 P.M.	8
10 up to 11 A.M.	20	3 up to 4 P.M.	19
11 up to 12 P.M.	8	4 up to 5 P.M.	6

Using the goodness-of-fit test and the .01 level of significance, determine whether the accidents are evenly distributed throughout the day. Write a brief explanation of your conclusion.

15.3 Goodness-of-Fit Test: Unequal Expected Frequencies

LO 15-3 Compute a goodness-of-fit test for unequal expected frequencies.

Expected frequencies are not equal in this problem.

The expected frequencies (f_e) in the previous Example/Solution involving preferred entrées were all equal. According to the null hypothesis, it was expected that of the 120 adults in the study, an equal number would select each of the four entrées. So we expect 30 to select chicken, 30 to select fish, and so on. The chi-square test can also be used if the expected frequencies are not equal.

The following Example/Solution illustrates the case of unequal frequencies and also gives a practical use of the chi-square goodness-of-fit test—namely, to find whether a local experience differs from the national experience.

Example

The American Hospital Administrators Association (AHAA) reports the following information concerning the number of times senior citizens are admitted to a hospital during a one-year period. Forty percent are not admitted; 30% are admitted once; 20% are admitted twice, and the remaining 10% are admitted three or more times.

A survey of 150 residents of Bartow Estates, a community devoted to active seniors located in central Florida, revealed 55 residents were not admitted during the last year, 50 were admitted to a hospital once, 32 were admitted twice, and the rest of those in the survey were admitted three or more times. Can we conclude the survey at Bartow Estates is consistent with the information reported by the AHAA? Use the .05 significance level.

Solution

We begin by organizing the above information into Table 15–4. Clearly, we cannot compare percentages given in the study by AHAA to the frequencies reported for the Bartow Estates. However, these percentages can be converted to expected frequencies, f_e. According to AHAA, 40% of the Bartow residents in the survey should not require hospitalization. Thus, if there is no difference between the national experience and those of Bartow Estates, then 40% of the 150 seniors surveyed (60 residents) would not have been hospitalized. Further, 30% of those surveyed were admitted once (45 residents), and so on. The observed frequencies for Bartow residents and the expected frequencies based on the percentages in the national study are given in Table 15–4.

Statistics in Action

Many state governments operate lotteries to help fund education. In many lotteries, numbered balls are mixed and selected by a machine. In a Select Three game, numbered balls are selected randomly from three groups of balls numbered zero through nine. Randomness would predict that the frequency of each number is equal. How would you prove that the selection machine ensured randomness? A chi-square, goodness-of-fit test could be used to prove or disprove randomness.

TABLE 15–4 Summary of Study by AHAA and a Survey of Bartow Estates Residents

Number of Times Admitted	AHAA Percent of Total	Number of Bartow Residents (f_o)	Expected Number of Residents (f_e)
0	40	55	60
1	30	50	45
2	20	32	30
3 or more	10	13	15
Total	100	150	150

The null hypothesis and the alternate hypothesis are:

H_0: There is no difference between the Barstow survey results and the AHAA study of hospital admissions.

H_1: There is a difference between the Barstow survey results and the AHAA study of hospital admissions.

To find the decision rule, we use Appendix B.3 and the .05 significance level. There are four categories, so the degrees of freedom are $df = 4 - 1 = 3$. The critical value is 7.815. Therefore, the decision rule is to reject the null hypothesis if $\chi^2 > 7.815$. The decision rule is portrayed in Chart 15–3.

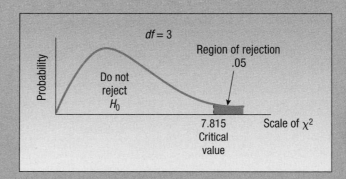

CHART 15–3 Decision Criteria for the Bartow Estates Research Study

Now to compute the chi-square test statistic:

Number of Times Admitted	(f_o)	(f_e)	$f_o - f_e$	$(f_o - f_e)^2/f_e$
0	55	60	−5	0.4167
1	50	45	5	0.5556
2	32	30	2	0.1333
3 or more	13	15	−2	0.2667
Total	150	150	0	1.3723

The computed value of χ^2 (1.3723) lies to the left of 7.815. Thus, we cannot reject the null hypothesis. We conclude that there is no evidence of a difference between the Bartow survey results and the AHAA study of hospital admissions.

15.4 Limitations of Chi-Square

Be careful in applying χ^2 to some problems.

If there is an unusually small expected frequency in a cell, chi-square (if applied) might result in an erroneous conclusion. This can happen because f_e appears in the denominator, and dividing by a very small number makes the quotient quite large! Two generally accepted policies regarding small cell frequencies are:

1. If there are only two cells, the *expected* frequency in each cell should be at least 5. The computation of chi-square would be permissible in the following problem, involving a minimum f_e of 6.

Individual	f_o	f_e
Literate	641	642
Illiterate	7	6

2. For more than two cells, chi-square should *not* be used if more than 20% of the f_e cells have expected frequencies less than 5. According to this policy, it would not be appropriate to use the goodness-of-fit test on the following data. Three of the seven cells, or 43%, have expected frequencies (f_e) of less than 5.

Level of Management	f_o	f_e
Foreman	30	32
Supervisor	110	113
Manager	86	87
Middle management	23	24
Assistant vice president	5	2
Vice president	5	4
Senior vice president	4	1
Total	263	263

To show the reason for the 20% policy, we conducted the goodness-of-fit test on the above data on the levels of management. The MegaStat output follows.

◢	A	B	C	D	E	F	G
1							
2	Goodness of Fit Test						
3							
4		observed	expected	O - E	(O - E)² / E	% of chisq	
5		30	32.000	-2.000	0.125	0.89	
6		110	113.000	-3.000	0.080	0.57	
7		86	87.000	-1.000	0.011	0.08	
8		23	24.000	-1.000	0.042	0.30	
9		5	2.000	3.000	4.500	32.12	
10		5	4.000	1.000	0.250	1.78	
11		4	1.000	3.000	9.000	64.25	
12		263	263.000	0.000	14.008	100.00	
13							
14		14.01	chi-square				
15		6	df				
16		0.0295	p-value				
17							

For this test at the .05 significance level with 6 degrees of freedom, H_0 is rejected if the computed value of chi-square is greater than 12.592. The computed value is 14.01, so we reject the null hypothesis that the observed frequencies represent a random sample from the population of the expected values. Examine the MegaStat output. More than 98% of the computed chi-square value is accounted for by the three vice president categories ([4.500 + .250 + 9.000]/ 14.008 = 0.9815). Logically, too much weight is being given to these categories.

The dilemma can be resolved by combining categories if it is logical to do so. In the above example, we combine the three vice presidential categories, which satisfies the 20% policy.

Level of Management	f_o	f_e
Foreman	30	32
Supervisor	110	113
Manager	86	87
Middle management	23	24
Vice president	14	7
Total	263	263

The computed value of chi-square with the revised categories is 7.26. See the following MegaStat output. This value is less than the critical value of 9.488 for the .05 significance level with 4 degrees of freedom. The null hypothesis is, therefore, not rejected at the .05 significance level. This indicates there is not a significant difference between the observed distribution and the expected distribution.

	A	B	C	D	E	F	G
18	Goodness of Fit Test						
19							
20		observed	expected	O - E	(O - E)² / E	% of chisq	
21		30	32.000	-2.000	0.125	1.72	
22		110	113.000	-3.000	0.080	1.10	
23		86	87.000	-1.000	0.011	0.16	
24		23	24.000	-1.000	0.042	0.57	
25		14	7.000	7.000	7.000	96.45	
26		263	263.000	0.000	7.258	100.00	
27							
28		7.26	chi-square				
29		4	df				
30		.1229	p-value				

Self-Review 15–2

The American Accounting Association classifies accounts receivable as "current," "late," and "not collectible." Industry figures show that 60% of accounts receivable are current, 30% are late, and 10% are not collectible. Massa and Barr, a law firm in Greenville, Ohio, has 500 accounts receivable: 320 are current, 120 are late, and 60 are not collectible. Are these numbers in agreement with the industry distribution? Use the .05 significance level.

Exercises

connect™

Category	f_o
A	30
B	20
C	10

9. The following hypotheses are given:

> H_0: Forty percent of the observations are in category A, 40% are in B, and 20% are in C.
>
> H_1: The distribution of the observations is not as described in H_0.

We took a sample of 60, with the results to the left.
   a. State the decision rule using the .01 significance level.
   b. Compute the value of chi-square.
   c. What is your decision regarding H_0?

10. The chief of security for Mall of the Dakotas was directed to study the problem of missing goods. He selected a sample of 100 boxes that had been tampered with and ascertained that, for 60 of the boxes, the missing pants, shoes, and so on were attributed to shoplifting. For 30 other boxes, employees had stolen the goods, and for the remaining 10 boxes he blamed poor inventory control. In his report to the mall management, can he say that shoplifting is *twice* as likely to be the cause of the loss as compared with either employee theft or poor inventory control and that employee theft and poor inventory control are equally likely? Use the .02 significance level.

11. The bank credit card department of Carolina Bank knows from experience that 5% of its card holders have had some high school, 15% have completed high school, 25% have had some college, and 55% have completed college. Of the 500 card holders whose cards have been called in for failure to pay their charges this month, 50 had some high school, 100 had completed high school, 190 had some college, and 160 had completed college. Can we conclude that the distribution of card holders who do not pay their charges is different from all others? Use the .01 significance level.

12. For many years, TV executives used the guideline that 30% of the audience were watching each of the traditional big three prime-time networks and 10% were watching cable stations on a weekday night. A random sample of 500 viewers in the Tampa–St. Petersburg, Florida, area last Monday night showed that 165 homes were tuned in to the ABC affiliate, 140 to the CBS affiliate, 125 to the NBC affiliate, and the remainder were viewing a cable station. At the .05 significance level, can we conclude that the guideline is still reasonable?

15.5 Testing the Hypothesis that a Distribution of Data Is from a Normal Population

LO 15-4 Conduct a test of hypothesis to verify that data grouped into a frequency distribution are a sample from a normal population.

In Section 15.2 beginning on page 498, we used the goodness-of-fit test to compare an observed set of observations to an expected set of observations. In the Example/Solution regarding Bubba's Fish and Pasta, the observed frequencies are the entrées selected by the sample of 120 adults. We determine the expected frequencies by assuming there is no preference for any of the four entrées, so one-fourth, or 30 adults, are expected to select each entrée. In this section, we compare observed frequencies, grouped into a frequency distribution, with those expected if the sample observations are from a normal population. Why is this test important? In Section 11.4, we assumed the two populations followed the normal distribution when we tested for differences in means. We made the same assumption in Section 12.4 in the ANOVA discussion and in Section 13.6, where we describe the distribution of the residuals in a least squares regression equation. In Section 13.6, we assumed that the distribution of the residuals followed the normal probability distribution.

The following Example/Solution shows the details of using a goodness-of-fit test to investigate the reasonableness of the normality assumption.

Example

Recall in Section 2.3 that we use a frequency distribution to organize the profits from the Applewood Auto Group's sale of 180 vehicles. The frequency distribution is repeated below.

TABLE 15–5 Frequency Distribution of Profits for Vehicles Sold Last Month by Applewood Auto Group

Profit	Frequency
$ 200 up to $ 600	8
600 up to 1,000	11
1,000 up to 1,400	23
1,400 up to 1,800	38
1,800 up to 2,200	45
2,200 up to 2,600	32
2,600 up to 3,000	19
3,000 up to 3,400	4
Total	180

Using statistical software, in Section 3.8 on page 71 in Chapter 3 we determined that the mean profit on a vehicle for the Applewood Auto Group was $1,843.17 and that the standard deviation was $643.63. Is it reasonable to conclude that the profit data is a sample obtained from a normal population? To put it another way, does the profit data follow a normal population? We use the .05 significance level.

Solution

To test for a normal distribution, we need to find the expected frequencies for each class in the distribution, assuming that the expected distribution follows a normal probability distribution. We start with the normal distribution by calculating probabilities for each class. Then we use these probabilities to compute the expected frequencies for each class.

To begin, we need to find the area, or probability, for each of the eight classes in Table 15–5, assuming a normal population with a mean of $1,843.17 and a standard deviation of $643.63. To find this probability, we used formula (7–1). By using this formula, we can convert any normal probability distribution to the standard normal distribution. Formula (7–1) is repeated below.

$$z = \frac{X - \mu}{\sigma}$$

In this case, z is the value of the standard normal distribution, μ is $1,843.17, and σ is $643.63. To illustrate the computation, we select class $200 up to $600 from Table 15–5. We want to determine the expected frequency in this class, assuming the distribution of profits follows a normal distribution. First, we find the z-value corresponding to $200.

$$z = \frac{X - \mu}{\sigma} = \frac{\$200 - \$1843.17}{643.63} = -2.55$$

This indicates that the lower limit of this class is 2.55 standard deviations below the mean. From Appendix B.1, the probability of finding a z-value less than -2.55 is .5000 $-$ .4946 = .0054.

For the upper limit of the $200 up to $600 class:

$$z = \frac{X - \mu}{\sigma} = \frac{\$600 - \$1843.17}{643.63} = -1.93$$

The area to the left of $600 is the probability of a z-value less than -1.93. To find this value, we again use Appendix B.1 and reason that $.5000 - .4732 = .0268$.

Finally, to find the area between $200 and $600:

$$P(\$200 < X < \$600) = P(-2.55 < z < -1.93) = .0268 - .0054 = .0214$$

That is, about 2.14% of the vehicles sold will result in a profit of between $200 and $600.

There is a chance that the profit earned is less than $200. To find this probability:

$$P(X < \$200) = P(z < -2.55) = .5000 - .4946 = .0054$$

We enter these two probabilities in the second and third rows of column 3 in Table 15–6.

TABLE 15–6 Profits at Applewood Auto Group, z Values, Areas under the Normal Distribution, and Expected Frequencies

Profit	z-Values	Area	Found by	Expected Frequency
Under $200	Under -2.55	.0054	0.5000 − 0.4946	0.97
$ 200 up to $ 600	-2.55 up to -1.93	.0214	0.4946 − 0.4732	3.85
600 up to 1,000	-1.93 up to -1.31	.0683	0.4732 − 0.4049	12.29
1,000 up to 1,400	-1.31 up to -0.69	.1500	0.4049 − 0.2549	27.00
1,400 up to 1,800	-0.69 up to -0.07	.2270	0.2549 − 0.0279	40.86
1,800 up to 2,200	-0.07 up to 0.55	.2367	0.0279 + 0.2088	42.61
2,200 up to 2,600	0.55 up to 1.18	.1722	0.3810 − 0.2088	31.00
2,600 up to 3,000	1.18 up to 1.80	.0831	0.4641 − 0.3810	14.96
3,000 up to 3,400	1.80 up to 2.42	.0281	0.4922 − 0.4641	5.06
3,400 or more	2.42 or more	.0078	0.5000 − 0.4922	1.40
Total		1.0000		180.00

Logically, if we sold 180 vehicles we would expect to earn a profit of between $200 and $600 on 3.85 vehicles, found by .0214(180). We would expect to sell 0.97 vehicles with a profit of less than $200, found by 180(.0054). We continue this process for the remaining classes. This information is summarized in Table 15–7. Don't be concerned that we are reporting fractional vehicles.

Before continuing, we should emphasize one of the limitations of tests using chi-square as the test statistic. The second limitation in Section 15.4 on page 506 indicates that if more than 20% of the cells have *expected frequencies* of less than 5, some of the categories should be combined. In Table 15–6, there are three classes in which the expected frequencies are less than 5. Hence, we combine the "Under $200" class with the "$200 up to $600" class and the "$3,400 or more" class with the "$3,000 up to $3,400" class. So the expected frequency in the "Under $600" class is now 4.82, found by 0.97 plus 3.85. We do the same for the "$3,000 and over" class: 5.06 + 1.40 = 6.46. The results are shown in Table 15–7. The computed value of chi-square is 5.220.

Now let's put this information into the formal hypothesis-testing format. The null and alternate hypotheses are:

H_0: The population of profits follows the normal distribution.
H_1: The population of profits does not follow the normal distribution.

To determine the critical value of chi-square, we need to know the degrees of freedom. In this case, there are 8 categories, or classes, so the degrees of freedom is $k - 1 = 8 - 1 = 7$. In addition, the values $1,843.17$, the mean profit, and

TABLE 15–7 Computations of the Chi-Square Statistic

Profit	f_o	f_e	$(f_o - f_e)$	$(f_o - f_e)^2$	$(f_o - f_e)^2/f_e$
Under $600	8	4.82	3.18	10.1124	2.098
$ 600 up to $1,000	11	12.29	−1.29	1.6641	.135
1,000 up to 1,400	23	27.00	−4.00	16.0000	.593
1,400 up to 1,800	38	40.86	−2.86	8.1796	.200
1,800 up to 2,200	45	42.61	2.39	5.7121	.134
2,200 up to 2,600	32	31.00	1.00	1.0000	.032
2,600 up to 3,000	19	14.96	4.04	16.3216	1.091
3,000 and over	4	6.46	−2.46	6.0516	.937
Total	180	180.00	0		5.220

$643.63, the standard deviation of the Applewood Auto Group profits, were computed from a sample. When we estimate population parameters from sample data, we lose a degree of freedom for each estimate. So we lose two more degrees of freedom for estimating the population mean and the population standard deviation. Thus the number of degrees of freedom in this problem is 5, found by $k - 2 - 1 = 8 - 2 - 1 = 5$.

From Appendix B.3, using the .05 significance level, the critical value of chi-square is 11.070. Our decision rule is to reject the null hypothesis if the computed value of chi-square is more than 11.070.

Now to compute the value of chi-square, we use formula (15–1):

$$\chi^2 = \sum \frac{(f_o - f_e)^2}{f_e} = \frac{(8 - 4.82)^2}{4.82} + \cdots + \frac{(4 - 6.46)^2}{6.46} = 5.220$$

The values for each class are shown in the right-hand column of Table 15–7, as well as the column total, which is 5.220. Because the computed value of 5.220 is less than the critical value, we do not reject the null hypothesis. We conclude the evidence does not suggest the distribution of profits is other than normal.

To expand on the calculation of the number of degrees of freedom, if we know the mean and the standard deviation of a population and wish to find whether some sample data conform to a normal, the degrees of freedom is $k - 1$. On the other hand, suppose we have sample data grouped into a frequency distribution, but we do not know the value of the population mean and the population standard deviation. In this case, the degrees of freedom is $k - 2 - 1$. In general, when we use sample statistics to estimate population parameters, we lose a degree of freedom for each parameter we estimate. This is parallel to the situation in Section 14.4 of the chapter on multiple regression where we lost a degree of freedom in the denominator of the F statistic for each independent variable considered.

15.6 Grapical and Statistical Approaches to Confirm Normality

LO 15-5 Use graphical and statistical methods to determine whether a set of sample data is from a normal population.

A disadvantage of the goodness-of-fit test for normality is that a frequency distribution of grouped data is compared to an expected set of normally distributed frequencies. When we organize data into frequency distributions, we know that we lose information about the data. That is, we do not have the raw data. There are several tests that use the raw data rather than data grouped into a frequency distribution. These tests include Kolmogorov-Smirinov, Lilliefors, and Anderson-Darling tests of normality. To complement these statistical tests, graphical methods are available to visually assess the normality of a distribution. We use *p*-values to assess the hypothesis of normality.

We will focus on the Anderson-Darling test of normality. It is based on two steps:

1. We create two cumulative distributions. The first is a cumulative distribution of the raw data. The other is a cumulative normal distribution.
2. We compare the two cumulative distributions by searching for the largest absolute numerical difference between the two distributions. Using a statistical test, if the difference is large, then we reject the null hypothesis that the data are normally distributed.

In addition, we can graph the cumulative distribution of the raw data and the cumulative normal distribution. The graph of the cumulative normal distribution is a straight line. The graph of the raw data will be scattered around the straight line representing the cumulative normal. Using the graph, we can observe that the data are normally distributed if the scatter is relatively close to the straight line that represents the normal cumulative distribution.

To demonstrate the Anderson-Darling test for normality, we will use the Applewood Auto Group profit data shown in Table 2–4. By using graphical methods, we compare the cumulative distribution of the individual profit in Table 2–4 with a cumulative normal distribution. We look for differences between the two graphs. Because we are looking at cumulative distributions, the graphs will increase from left to right. In the following graph, the black dots represent the profit made on each of the 180 vehicles sold by the Applewood Auto Group. The dots are close together and appear to form a curved line. The green line, which is mostly covered by the black dots, represents the cumulative normal distribution. The graph shows that the profit data closely follow the green line and that the distribution of profits follows a normal distribution rather closely.

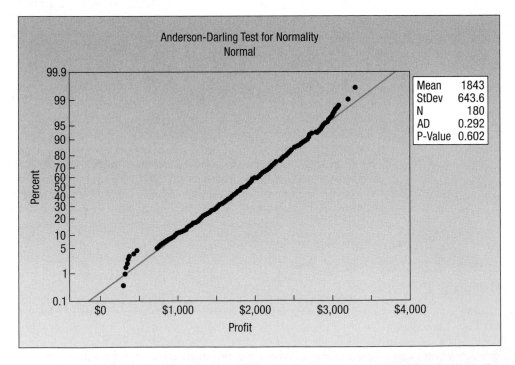

The distribution of profits seems to depart from a normal distribution in the tails, but is this departure sufficient to reject the idea that the profits follow a normal distribution? We can use the Anderson-Darling test to evaluate these differences. For the test, the null and alternate hypotheses are as follows:

H_0: The population of profits follows the normal distribution.
H_1: The population of profits does not follow the normal distribution.

The computational details of the Anderson-Darling test are beyond the scope of this text. However, using computer software, you can see in the table at the top right of the graph that five statistics for the test are summarized. It shows the mean, standard deviation, and sample size. The "AD" is the Anderson-Darling test statistic used to test the null hypothesis. As presented in Chapter 10, every test statistic has a corresponding p-value that is used to make a decision regarding the null hypothesis. We choose 0.05 as the significance level for this test and use the decision rule that if the p-value is greater than the significance level, then we do not reject the null hypothesis. Because the p-value is 0.602, we do not reject the null hypothesis. So in this case, based on our graphical methods and the computed p-value, we make the inference that it is reasonable to assume that profits follow a normal distribution.

Self-Review 15–3

See Self-Review 10–4 on page 311. In that problem, a machine is set to fill a small bottle with 9.0 grams of medicine. A sample of eight bottles revealed the following amounts (grams) in each bottle. We conducted a test of hypothesis regarding the mean. To perform that test, we assumed the sample data followed a normal distribution.

| 9.2 | 8.7 | 8.9 | 8.6 | 8.8 | 8.5 | 8.7 | 9.0 |

Below is a graph showing a cumulative normal distribution and the cumulative frequencies of the weights. Is the normal assumption reasonable? Cite two pieces of evidence to support your decision. Use the .01 significance level.

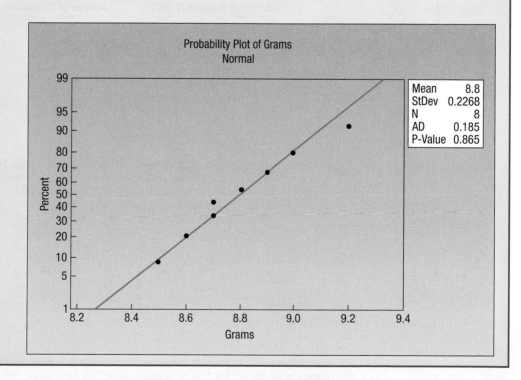

Exercises

13. The IRS is interested in the number of individual tax forms prepared by small accounting firms. They randomly sampled 50 public accounting firms with 10 or fewer employees in the Dallas–Fort Worth area. The following frequency table reports the results of the study. Assume the sample mean is 44.8 clients and the sample standard deviation is 9.37 clients. Is it reasonable to conclude that the sample data are from a population that follows a normal probability distribution? Use the .05 significance level. (df)

Number of Clients	Frequency
20 up to 30	1
30 up to 40	15
40 up to 50	22
50 up to 60	8
60 up to 70	4

14. Advertising expenses are a significant component of the cost of goods sold. Listed below is a frequency distribution showing the advertising expenditures for 60 manufacturing companies located in the Southwest. The mean expense is $52.0 million and the standard deviation is $11.32 million. Is it reasonable to conclude the sample data are from a population that follows a normal probability distribution? Use the .05 significance level. (df)

Advertising Expense ($ Million)	Number of Companies
25 up to 35	5
35 up to 45	10
45 up to 55	21
55 up to 65	16
65 up to 75	8
Total	60

15. The American Diabetes Association recommends a blood glucose reading of less than 130 for those with Type 2 diabetes. Blood glucose measures the amount of sugar in the blood, and Type 2 diabetes often appears in older adults. Below are the readings for February for a recently diagnosed senior citizen. (df)

112	122	116	103	112	96	115	98	106	111
106	124	116	127	116	108	112	112	121	115
124	116	107	118	123	109	109	106		

Is it reasonable to conclude that these readings follow a normal distribution? Use the .05 significance level. Using the following analysis on the next page, test the null hypothesis that the distribution of times is normally distributed. Cite two reasons for your decision.

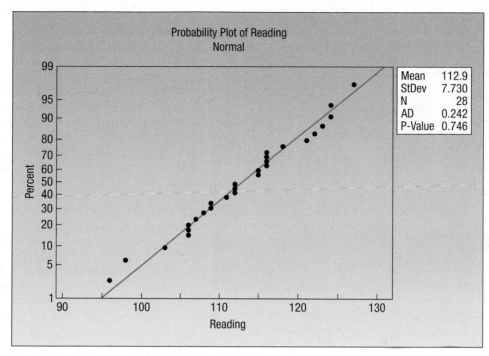

16. Creek Ratz is a popular restaurant located along the coast of northern Florida. They serve a variety of steak and seafood dinners. During the summer beach season, they do not take reservations or accept "call ahead" seating. Management of the restaurant is concerned with the time a patron must wait before being seated for dinner. Listed below is the wait time, in minutes, for the 25 tables seated last Saturday night.

28	39	23	67	37	28	56	40	28	50	51	45	44	65	61
27	24	61	34	44	64	25	24	27	29					

Is it reasonable to conclude that these readings follow a normal distribution? Use the .05 significance level. Using the following analysis, test the null hypothesis that the distribution of times is normally distributed. Cite two reasons for your decision.

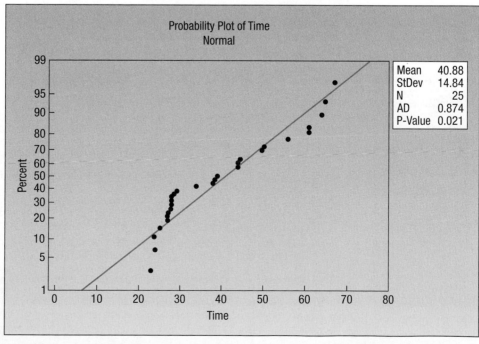

15.7 Contingency Table Analysis

In Section 4.5 in Chapter 4, we discussed bivariate data, where we studied the relationship between two variables. We described a contingency table, which simultaneously summarizes two nominal-scale variables of interest. For example, a sample of students enrolled in the School of Business is classified by gender (male or female) and major (accounting, management, finance, marketing, or quantitative methods). This classification is based on the nominal scale, because there is no natural order to the classifications.

We discussed contingency tables in Section 5.5 in Chapter 5. On page 145, we illustrated the relationship between loyalty to a company and the length of employment and explored whether older employees were likely to be more loyal to the company.

We can use the chi-square statistic to formally test for a relationship between two nominal-scaled variables. To put it another way, is one variable *independent* of the other? Here are some examples where we are interested in testing whether two variables are related.

LO 15-6 Perform a chi-square test for independence on a contingency table.

- Ford Motor Company operates an assembly plant in Dearborn, Michigan. The plant operates three shifts per day, 5 days a week. The quality control manager wishes to compare the quality level on the three shifts. Vehicles are classified by quality level (acceptable, unacceptable) and shift (day, afternoon, night). Is there a difference in the quality level on the three shifts? That is, is the quality of the product related to the shift when it was manufactured? Or is the quality of the product independent of the shift on which it was manufactured?
- A sample of 100 drivers who were stopped for speeding violations was classified by gender and whether or not they were wearing a seat belt. For this sample, is wearing a seatbelt related to gender?
- Does a male released from federal prison make a different adjustment to civilian life if he returns to his hometown or if he goes elsewhere to live? The two variables are adjustment to civilian life and place of residence. Note that both variables are measured on the nominal scale.

Example	The Federal Correction Agency is investigating the last question cited above: Does a male released from federal prison make a different adjustment to civilian life if he returns to his hometown or if he goes elsewhere to live? To put it another way, is there a relationship between adjustment to civilian life and place of residence after release from prison? Use the .01 significance level.
Solution	As before, the first step in hypothesis testing is to state the null and alternate hypotheses.

H_0: There is no relationship between adjustment to civilian life and where the individual lives after being released from prison.

H_1: There is a relationship between adjustment to civilian life and where the individual lives after being released from prison.

The agency's psychologists interviewed 200 randomly selected former prisoners. Using a series of questions, the psychologists classified the adjustment of each individual to civilian life as outstanding, good, fair, or unsatisfactory. The classifications for the 200 former prisoners were tallied as follows. Joseph Camden, for example, returned to his hometown and has shown outstanding adjustment to civilian life. His case is one of the 27 tallies in the upper left box.

Residence after Release from Prison	Adjustment to Civilian Life			
	Outstanding	**Good**	**Fair**	**Unsatisfactory**
Hometown	LHf LHf LHf LHf LHf II	LHf LHf LHf LHf LHf LHf LHf	LHf LHf LHf LHf LHf LHf III	LHf LHf LHf LHf LHf
Not hometown	LHf LHf III	LHf LHf LHf	LHf LHf LHf LHf LHf II	LHf LHf LHf LHf LHf

The tallies in each box, or *cell,* were counted. The counts are given in the following **contingency table.** (See Table 15–8.) In this case, the Federal Correction Agency wondered whether adjustment to civilian life is *contingent on* where the prisoner goes after release from prison.

TABLE 15–8 Adjustment to Civilian Life and Place of Residence

Residence after Release from Prison	Adjustment to Civilian Life				Total
	Outstanding	**Good**	**Fair**	**Unsatisfactory**	
Hometown	27	35	33	25	120
Not hometown	13	15	27	25	80
Total	40	50	60	50	200

Once we know how many rows (2) and columns (4) there are in the contingency table, we can determine the critical value and the decision rule. For a chi-square test of significance where two traits are classified in a contingency table, the degrees of freedom is found by:

$$df = (\text{number of rows} - 1)(\text{number of columns} - 1) = (r - 1)(c - 1)$$

In this problem:

$$df = (r - 1)(c - 1) = (2 - 1)(4 - 1) = 3$$

To find the critical value for 3 degrees of freedom and the .01 level (selected earlier), refer to Appendix B.3. It is 11.345. The decision rule is to reject the null hypothesis if the computed value of χ^2 is greater than 11.345. The decision rule is portrayed graphically in Chart 15–4.

Next we find the computed value of χ^2. The observed frequencies, f_o, are shown in Table 15–8. How are the corresponding expected frequencies, f_e, determined? Note in the "Total" column of Table 15–8 that 120 of the 200 former prisoners (60%) returned to their hometowns. *If there were no relationship* between adjustment and residency after release from prison, we would expect 60% of the 40 ex-prisoners who made outstanding adjustment to civilian life to reside in their hometowns. Thus, the expected frequency f_e for the upper left cell is .60 × 40 = 24. Likewise, if there were no relationship between adjustment and present residence, we would expect 60% of the 50 ex-prisoners (30) who had "good" adjustment to civilian life to reside in their hometowns.

Contingency table consists of count data.

Statistics in Action

A study of 1,000 Americans over the age of 24 showed that 28% never married. Of those, 22% completed college. Twenty-three percent of the 1,000 married and completed college. Can we conclude for the information given that being married is related to completing college? The study indicated that the two variables were related, that the computed value of the chi-square statistic was 9.368, and the *p*-value was .002. Can you duplicate these results?

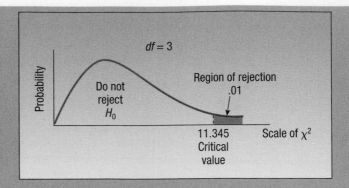

CHART 15–4 Chi-Square Distribution for 3 Degrees of Freedom

Further, notice that 80 of the 200 ex-prisoners studied (40%) did not return to their hometowns to live. Thus, of the 60 considered by the psychologists to have made "fair" adjustment to civilian life, .40 × 60, or 24, would be expected not to return to their hometowns.

The expected frequency for any cell can be determined by

EXPECTED FREQUENCY $f_e = \dfrac{\text{(Row total)(Column total)}}{\text{Grand total}}$ **[15–2]**

From this formula, the expected frequency for the upper left cell (Outstanding and Hometown) in Table 15–8 is:

$$\text{Expected frequency} - \frac{\text{(Row total)(Column total)}}{\text{Grand total}} = \frac{(120)(40)}{200} = 24$$

The observed frequencies, f_o, and the expected frequencies, f_e, for all of the cells in the contingency table are listed in Table 15–9.

TABLE 15–9 Observed and Expected Frequencies

Residence after Release from Prison	Adjustment to Civilian Life									
	Outstanding		Good		Fair		Unsatisfactory		Total	
	f_o	f_e	f_o	f_e	f_o	f_e	f_o	f_e	f_o	f_e
Hometown	27	24	35	30	33	36	25	30	120	120
Not hometown	13	16	15	20	27	24	25	20	80	80
Total	40	40	50	50	60	60	50	50	200	200

Must be equal

$\dfrac{(80)(50)}{200}$

Must be equal

Recall that the computed value of chi-square using formula (15–1) is found by:

$$\chi^2 = \Sigma \left[\frac{(f_o - f_e)^2}{f_e} \right]$$

Starting with the upper left cell:

$$\chi^2 = \frac{(27-24)^2}{24} + \frac{(35-30)^2}{30} + \frac{(33-36)^2}{36} + \frac{(25-30)^2}{30}$$

$$+ \frac{(13-16)^2}{16} + \frac{(15-20)^2}{20} + \frac{(27-24)^2}{24} + \frac{(25-20)^2}{20}$$

$$= 0.375 + 0.833 + 0.250 + 0.833 + 0.563 + 1.250 + 0.375 + 1.250$$

$$= 5.729$$

Because the computed value of chi-square (5.729) lies in the region to the left of 11.345, the null hypothesis is not rejected at the .01 significance level. We conclude there is not enough evidence to prove that a relationship between adjustment to civilian life and where the prisoner resides after being released from prison. For the Federal Correction Agency's advisement program, adjustment to civilian life is not related to where the ex-prisoner lives.

The following output is from the Minitab system.

↓	C1-T	C2	C3	C4	C5	C6
	Residenc	**Outstanding**	**Good**	**Fair**	**Unsatisfactory**	
1	Hometown	27	35	33	25	
2	Not Hometown	13	15	27	25	

Chi-Square Test: Outstanding, Good, Fair, Unsatisfactory

Expected counts are printed below observed counts
Chi-Square contributions are printed below expected counts

```
        Outstanding    Good    Fair  Unsatisfactory  Total
  1              27      35      33              25    120
             24.00   30.00   36.00           30.00
             0.375   0.833   0.250           0.833

  2              13      15      27              25     80
             16.00   20.00   24.00           20.00
             0.563   1.250   0.375           1.250

Total           40      50      60              50    200
```

Chi-Sq = 5.729, DF = 3, P-Value = 0.126

Observe that the value of chi-square is the same as that computed earlier. In addition, the *p*-value is reported, .126. So the probability of finding a value of the test statistic as large or larger is .126 when the null hypothesis is true. The *p*-value also results in the same decision, do not reject the null hypothesis.

Self-Review 15–4

A social scientist sampled 140 people and classified them according to income level and whether or not they played a state lottery in the last month. The sample information is reported below. Is it reasonable to conclude that playing the lottery is related to income level? Use the .05 significance level.

	Income			
	Low	**Middle**	**High**	**Total**
Played	46	28	21	95
Did not play	14	12	19	45
Total	60	40	40	140

(a) What is this table called?
(b) State the null hypothesis and the alternate hypothesis.
(c) What is the decision rule?
(d) Determine the value of chi-square.
(e) Make a decision on the null hypothesis. Interpret the result.

Exercises

connect

17. The director of advertising for the *Carolina Sun Times,* the largest newspaper in the Carolinas, is studying the relationship between the type of community in which a subscriber resides and the section of the newspaper he or she reads first. For a sample of readers, she collected the sample information in the following table.

	National News	Sports	Comics
City	170	124	90
Suburb	120	112	100
Rural	130	90	88

At the .05 significance level, can we conclude there is a relationship between the type of community where the person resides and the section of the paper read first?

18. Four brands of lightbulbs are being considered for use in the final assembly area of the Ford F-150 truck plant in Dearborn, Michigan. The director of purchasing asked for samples of 100 from each manufacturer. The numbers of acceptable and unacceptable bulbs from each manufacturer are shown below. At the .05 significance level, is there a difference in the quality of the bulbs?

	Manufacturer			
	A	B	C	D
Unacceptable	12	8	5	11
Acceptable	88	92	95	89
Total	100	100	100	100

19. The quality control department at Food Town Inc., a grocery chain in upstate New York, conducts a monthly check on the comparison of scanned prices to posted prices. The chart below summarizes the results of a sample of 500 items last month. Company management would like to know whether there is any relationship between error rates on regularly priced items and specially priced items. Use the .01 significance level.

	Regular Price	Advertised Special Price
Undercharge	20	10
Overcharge	15	30
Correct price	200	225

20. The use of cellular phones in automobiles has increased dramatically in the last few years. Of concern to traffic experts, as well as manufacturers of cellular phones, is the effect on accident rates. Is someone who is using a cellular phone more likely to be involved in a traffic accident? What is your conclusion from the following sample information? Use the .05 significance level.

	Had Accident in the Last Year	Did Not Have an Accident in the Last Year
Uses a cell phone	25	300
Does not use a cell phone	50	400

Chapter Summary

I. The characteristics of the chi-square distribution are:
  A. The value of chi-square is never negative.
  B. The chi-square distribution is positively skewed.
  C. There is a family of chi-square distributions.
    1. Each time the degrees of freedom change, a new distribution is formed.
    2. As the degrees of freedom increase, the distribution approaches a normal distribution.
II. A goodness-of-fit test will show whether an observed set of frequencies could have come from a hypothesized population distribution.
  A. The degrees of freedom are $k - 1$, where k is the number of categories.
  B. The formula for computing the value of chi-square is

$$\chi^2 = \Sigma \left[\frac{(f_o - f_e)^2}{f_e} \right] \qquad \text{[15–1]}$$

III. A goodness-of-fit test can also be used to determine whether a sample of observations is from a normal population.
  A. First, find the mean and standard deviation of the sample data.
  B. Group the data into a frequency distribution.
  C. Convert the class limits to z-values.
  D. Find the area or probability between consecutive z-values.
  E. Calculate the chi-square goodness-of-fit statistic based on the observed and expected class frequency.
  F. For each class, find the expected number of observations by multiplying the area or probability by the total number of observations.
  G. If we use the information on the sample mean and the sample standard deviation from the sample data, the degrees of freedom is $k - 3$.
IV. A contingency table is used to test whether two traits or characteristics are related.
  A. Each observation is classified according to two traits.
  B. The expected frequency is determined as follows:

$$f_e = \frac{\text{(Row total)(Column total)}}{\text{Grand total}} \qquad \text{[15–2]}$$

  C. The degrees of freedom are found by:

$$df = (\text{Rows} - 1)(\text{Columns} - 1)$$

  D. The usual hypothesis testing procedure is used.

Pronunciation Key

SYMBOL	MEANING	PRONUNCIATION
χ^2	Probability distribution	*ki square*
f_o	Observed frequency	*f sub oh*
f_e	Expected frequency	*f sub e*

Chapter Exercises

connect

21. Vehicles heading west on Front Street may turn right, left, or go straight ahead at Elm Street. The city traffic engineer believes that half of the vehicles will continue straight through the intersection. Of the remaining half, equal proportions will turn right and left. Two hundred vehicles were observed, with the following results. Can we conclude that the traffic engineer is correct? Use the .10 significance level.

	Straight	Right Turn	Left Turn
Frequency	112	48	40

22. The publisher of a sports magazine plans to offer new subscribers one of three gifts: a sweatshirt with the logo of their favorite team, a coffee cup with the logo of their favorite team, or a pair of earrings also with the logo of their favorite team. In a sample of 500 new subscribers, the number selecting each gift is reported below. At the .05 significance level, is there a preference for the gifts or should we conclude that the gifts are equally well liked?

Gift	Frequency
Sweatshirt	183
Coffee cup	175
Earrings	142

23. In a particular market, there are three commercial television stations, each with its own evening news program from 6:00 to 6:30 P.M. According to a report in this morning's local newspaper, a random sample of 150 viewers last night revealed 53 watched the news on WNAE (channel 5), 64 watched on WRRN (channel 11), and 33 on WSPD (channel 13). At the .05 significance level, is there a difference in the proportion of viewers watching the three channels?

24. There are four entrances to the Government Center Building in downtown Philadelphia. The building maintenance supervisor would like to know if the entrances are equally utilized. To investigate, 400 people were observed entering the building. The number using each entrance is reported below. At the .01 significance level, is there a difference in the use of the four entrances? (df)

Entrance	Frequency
Main Street	140
Broad Street	120
Cherry Street	90
Walnut Street	50
Total	400

25. The owner of a mail-order catalog would like to compare her sales with the geographic distribution of the population. According to the United States Bureau of the Census, 21% of the population lives in the Northeast, 24% in the Midwest, 35% in the South, and 20% in the West. Listed below is a breakdown of a sample of 400 orders randomly selected from those shipped last month. At the .01 significance level, does the distribution of the orders reflect the population? (df)

Region	Frequency
Northeast	68
Midwest	104
South	155
West	73
Total	400

26. Banner Mattress and Furniture Company wishes to study the number of credit applications received per day for the last 300 days. The sample information is reported below.

Number of Credit Applications	Frequency (Number of Days)
0	50
1	77
2	81
3	48
4	31
5 or more	13

To interpret, there were 50 days on which no credit applications were received, 77 days on which only one application was received, and so on. Would it be reasonable to conclude that the population distribution is Poisson with a mean of 2.0? Use the .05 significance level. *Hint:* To find the expected frequencies use the Poisson distribution with a mean of 2.0. Find the probability of exactly one success given a Poisson distribution with a mean of 2.0. Multiply this probability by 300 to find the expected frequency for the number of days in which there was exactly one application. Determine the expected frequency for the other days in a similar manner.

27. Each of the digits in a raffle is thought to have the same chance of occurrence. The table shows the frequency of each digit for consecutive drawings in a California lottery. Perform the chi-square test to see if you reject the hypothesis at the .05 significance level that the digits are from a uniform population.

Digit	Frequency	Digit	Frequency
0	44	5	24
1	32	6	31
2	23	7	27
3	27	8	28
4	23	9	21

28. John Isaac Inc., a designer and installer of industrial signs, employs 60 people. The company recorded the type of the most recent visit to a doctor by each employee. A national assessment conducted in 2010 found that 53% of all physician visits were to primary care physicians, 19% to medical specialists, 17% to surgical specialists, and 11% to emergency departments. Test at the 0.01 significance level if Isaac employees differ significantly from the survey distribution. Here are their results:

Visit Type	Number of Visits
Primary care	29
Medical specialist	11
Surgical specialist	16
Emergency	4

29. The Eckel Manufacturing Company believes that their hourly wages follow a normal probability distribution. To confirm this, 270 employees were sampled, organized into the following frequency distribution. The mean of the distribution is $8.222 and the standard deviation is $1.003. At the .10 significance level, is it reasonable to conclude that the distribution of hourly wages follows a normal distribution?

Hourly Wage	Frequency
$5.50 up to $ 6.50	20
6.50 up to 7.50	24
7.50 up to 8.50	130
8.50 up to 9.50	68
9.50 up to 10.50	28
Total	270

30. The National Cable and Telecommunications Association recently reported that the mean number of HDTVs per household in the United States is 2.30 with a standard deviation

of 1.474 sets. A sample of 100 homes in Boise, Idaho, revealed the following sample information.

Number of HDTVs	Number of Households
0	7
1	27
2	28
3	18
4	10
5 or more	10
Total	100

At the .05 significance level, is it reasonable to conclude that the number of HDTVs per household follows a normal distribution? (Hint: Use limits such as 0.5 up to 1.5, 1.5 up to 2.5, and so on.)

31. Listed below is the enrollment at the 13 state universities in Ohio. Assuming this is sample information, is it reasonable to conclude the enrollments follow a normal distribution. Use the .05 significance level.

College	Enrollment
University of Akron	25,942
Bowling Green State University	18,989
Central State University	1,820
University of Cincinnati	36,415
Cleveland State University	15,664
Kent State University	34,056
Miami University	17,161
Ohio State University	59,091
Ohio University	20,437
Shawnee State University	4,300
University of Toledo	20,775
Wright State University	18,786
Youngstown State University	14,682

32. The Apollo space program lasted from 1967 until 1972 and included 13 missions. The missions lasted from as little as 7 hours to as long as 301 hours. The duration of the flights is listed below. Assuming this is sample information, is it reasonable to conclude these flight times follow the normal distribution? Use statistical software and the .05 significance level.

9	195	241	301	216	260	7	244	192	147	10	295	142

33. A survey by *Houston Chronicle* investigated the public's attitude toward the federal deficit. Each sampled citizen was classified as to whether they felt the government should reduce the deficit, increase the deficit, or if they had no opinion. The sample results of the study by gender are reported below.

Gender	Reduce the Deficit	Increase the Deficit	No Opinion
Female	244	194	68
Male	305	114	25

At the .05 significance level, is it reasonable to conclude that gender is independent of a person's position on the deficit?

34. A study regarding the relationship between age and the amount of pressure sales personnel feel in relation to their jobs revealed the following sample information. At the .01 significance level, is there a relationship between job pressure and age? 🌐

Age (years)	Degree of Job Pressure		
	Low	Medium	High
Less than 25	20	18	22
25 up to 40	50	46	44
40 up to 60	58	63	59
60 and older	34	43	43

35. The claims department at Wise Insurance Company believes that younger drivers have more accidents and, therefore, should be charged higher insurance rates. Investigating a sample of 1,200 Wise policyholders revealed the following breakdown on whether a claim had been filed in the last three years and the age of the policyholder. Is it reasonable to conclude that there is a relationship between the age of the policyholder and whether or not the person filed a claim? Use the .05 significance level. 🌐

Age Group	No Claim	Claim
16 up to 25	170	74
25 up to 40	240	58
40 up to 55	400	44
55 or older	190	24
Total	1,000	200

36. A sample of employees at a large chemical plant was asked to indicate a preference for one of three pension plans. The results are given in the following table. Does it seem that there is a relationship between the pension plan selected and the job classification of the employees? Use the .01 significance level. 🌐

Job Class	Pension Plan		
	Plan A	Plan B	Plan C
Supervisor	10	13	29
Clerical	19	80	19
Labor	81	57	22

37. Did you ever purchase a bag of M&M's candies and wonder about the distribution of colors? For peanut M&M's, 12% are brown, 15% yellow, 12% red, 23% blue, 23% orange, and 15% green. A 6-oz. bag purchased at the Book Store at Coastal Carolina University had 12 blue, 14 brown, 13 yellow, 14 red, 7 orange, and 12 green. Is it reasonable to conclude that the actual distribution agrees with the expected distribution? Use the .05 significance level. Conduct your own trial. Be sure to share with your instructor. 🌐

Data Set Exercises

(The data for these exercises are available at the text website www.mhhe.com/lindbasic8e).

38. Refer to the Real Estate data, which report information on homes sold in the Goodyear, Arizona, area last year.
  a. Select the variable selling price and use the graphical method to determine whether the assumption that the prices follow a normal distribution is reasonable. Use the .05 significance level.
  b. Develop a contingency table that shows whether a home has a pool and the township in which the house is located. Is there an association between the variables pool and township? Use the .05 significance level.
  c. Develop a contingency table that shows whether a home has an attached garage and the township in which the home is located. Is there an association between the variables attached garage and township? Use the .05 significance level.

39. Refer to the Baseball 2010 data, which report information on the 30 Major League Baseball teams for the 2010 season.
  a. Set up a variable that divides the teams into two groups, those that had a winning season and those that did not. There are 162 games in the season, so define a winning season as having won 81 or more games. Next, find the median team payroll and divide the teams into two payroll groups. Let the 15 teams with the largest payrolls be in one group and the 15 teams with the smallest payrolls be in the other. At the .05 significance level, is there a relationship between payrolls and winning?
  b. Use a statistical software program to determine whether the variables payroll and attendance follow a normal distribution. Use the .05 significance level.

40. Refer to the Buena School District bus data.
  a. Find the median maintenance cost and the median age of the buses. Organize the data into a two-by-two contingency table, with buses above and below the median of each variable. Determine whether the age of the bus is related to the amount of the maintenance cost. Use the .05 significance level.
  b. Is there a relationship between the maintenance cost and the manufacturer of the bus? Use the breakdown in part (a) for the buses above and below the median maintenance cost and the bus manufacturers to create a contingency table. Use the .05 significance level.
  c. Use statistical software and the .05 significance level to determine whether it is reasonable to assume that the distributions of age of the bus, maintenance cost, and miles traveled last month follow a normal distribution.

Practice Test

Part 1—Objective

1. The _____ level of measurement is required for the chi-square goodness-of-fit test.
2. To use the chi-square distribution as the test statistic, what should we assume about the population distribution? _____. (It is normally distributed; it meets the binomial conditions; or no assumption is necessary about the population distribution)
3. Which of the following is *not* a characteristic of the chi-square distribution? _____ (positively skewed, based on degrees of freedom, can have negative chi-square values)
4. In a contingency table, how many variables are summarized? _____ (two, four, fifty)
5. For a contingency table with 4 columns and 3 rows, there are _____ degrees of freedom.
6. In a contingency table, we test the null hypothesis that the variables are _____. (independent, dependent, mutually exclusive, normally distributed)
7. A sample of 100 undergraduate business students is classified by five majors. For a goodness-of-fit test, there are _____ degrees of freedom.
8. The sum of the observed and expected frequencies _____. (are the same, must be more than 30, can assume negative values, must be at least 5%)
9. In a goodness-of-fit test with 200 observations and 4 degrees of freedom, the critical value of chi-square, assuming the .05 significance level, is _____.
10. The shape of the chi-square distribution is based on the _____. (shape of the population, degrees of freedom, level of significance, level of measurement)

Part 2—Problems

1. A recent census report indicated 65% of families have both a mother and father, 20% have only a mother, 10% have only a father, and 5% have no mother or father. A random sample of 200 children from a rural school district revealed the following:

Mother and Father	Mother Only	Father Only	No Mother or Father	Total
120	40	30	10	200

   Is there sufficient evidence to conclude that the proportion of families with a father and/or a mother in the particular rural school district differs from the proportions reported in the recent census? Use the .05 significance level.

2. A book publisher wants to investigate the type of books selected for recreational reading by men and women. A random sample provided the following information.

	Type of Book			
Gender	Mystery	Romance	Self-Help	Total
Men	250	100	190	540
Women	130	170	200	500

   At the .05 significance level, should we conclude that gender is related to the type of book selected?

Software Commands

1. The MegaStat commands to create the chi-square goodness-of-fit test on page 501 are:
    a. Enter the information from Table 15–2 into a worksheet as shown.
    b. Select **MegaStat, Chi-Square/Crosstabs,** and **Goodness of Fit Test** and hit **Enter.**
    c. In the dialog box, select *B1:B4* as the **Observed values,** *C1:C4* as the **Expected values,** and enter *0* as the **Number of parameters estimated from the data.** Click **OK.**

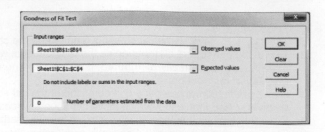

2. The MegaStat commands to create the chi-square goodness-of-fit tests on pages 506 and 507 are the same except for the number of items in the observed and expected frequency columns. Only one dialog box is shown.
    a. Enter the Levels of Management information shown on page 506.
    b. Select **MegaStat, Chi-Square/Crosstabs,** and **Goodness of Fit Test** and hit **Enter.**
    c. In the dialog box, select *B1:B7* as the **Observed values,** *C1:C7* as the **Expected values,** and enter *0* as the **Number of parameters estimated from the data.** Click **OK.**

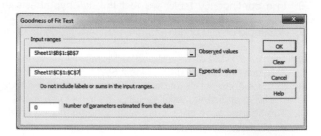

3. The Minitab commands for the normality test on page 512 are:
    a. Enter the data from the Applewood Auto Group.
    b. Select **Stat, Basic Statistics,** and **Normality Test.**
    c. Select the variable **Profit,** check **None** for **Percentile Lines,** and select **Anderson-Darling** as **the Test for Normality.**

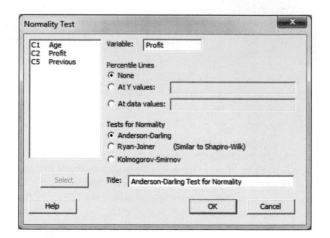

4. The Minitab commands for the chi-square analysis on page 519 are:
    a. Enter the names of the variables in the first row and the data in the next two rows.
    b. Select **Stat, Table,** and then click on **Chi-Square Test** and hit **Enter.**
    c. In the dialog box, select the columns labeled *Outstanding to Unsatisfactory* and click **OK.**

Chapter 15   Answers to Self-Review

15–1 a. Observed frequencies.

  b. Six (six days of the week).

  c. 10. Total observed frequencies $\div$ 6 = 60/6 = 10.

  d. 5; $k - 1 = 6 - 1 = 5$.

  e. 15.086 (from the chi-square table in Appendix B.3).

  f.
$$\chi^2 = \Sigma\left[\frac{(f_o - f_e)^2}{f_e}\right] = \frac{(12 - 10)^2}{10} + \cdots + \frac{(9 - 10)^2}{10} = 0.8$$

  g. Do not reject H_0.

  h. Absenteeism is distributed evenly throughout the week. The observed differences are due to sampling variation.

15–2 H_0: $P_C = .60$, $P_L = .30$, and $P_U = .10$.
H_1: Distribution is not as above.
Reject H_0 if $\chi^2 > 5.991$.

Category	f_o	f_e	$\dfrac{(f_o - f_e)^2}{f_e}$
Current	320	300	1.33
Late	120	150	6.00
Uncollectible	60	50	2.00
	500	500	9.33

Reject H_0. The accounts receivable data does not reflect the national average.

15–3 The p-value is 0.865, which is larger than .01, the significance level, so the null hypothesis is not rejected. It is reasonable to conclude that the population distribution is normal.

15–4 a. Contingency table

  b. H_0: There is no relationship between income and whether the person played the lottery.
  H_1: There is a relationship between income and whether the person played the lottery.

  c. Reject H_0 if χ^2 is greater than 5.991.

  d.
$$\chi^2 = \frac{(46 - 40.71)^2}{40.71} + \frac{(28 - 27.14)^2}{27.14} + \frac{(21 - 27.14)^2}{27.14}$$
$$+ \frac{(14 - 19.29)^2}{19.29} + \frac{(12 - 12.86)^2}{12.86} + \frac{(19 - 12.86)^2}{12.86}$$
$$= 6.544$$

  e. Reject H_0. There is a relationship between income level and playing the lottery.

Appendixes

Appendix A: Data Sets

A.1 Data Set 1—Goodyear, Arizona, Real Estate Sales Data

Variables

x_1 = Selling price in $000
x_2 = Number of bedrooms
x_3 = Size of the home in square feet
x_4 = Pool (1 = yes, 0 = no)
x_5 = Distance from the center of the city in miles
x_6 = Township
x_7 = Garage attached (1 = yes, 0 = no)
x_8 = Number of bathrooms

105 homes sold

x_1	x_2	x_3	x_4	x_5	x_6	x_7	x_8
263.1	4	2,300	0	17	5	1	2.0
182.4	4	2,100	1	19	4	0	2.0
242.1	3	2,300	1	12	3	0	2.0
213.6	2	2,200	1	16	2	0	2.5
139.9	2	2,100	1	28	1	0	1.5
245.4	2	2,100	0	12	1	1	2.0
327.2	6	2,500	1	15	3	1	2.0
271.8	2	2,100	1	9	2	1	2.5
221.1	3	2,300	0	18	1	0	1.5
266.6	4	2,400	1	13	4	1	2.0
292.4	4	2,100	1	14	3	1	2.0
209.0	2	1,700	1	8	4	1	1.5
270.8	6	2,500	1	7	4	1	2.0
246.1	4	2,100	1	18	3	1	2.0
194.4	2	2,300	1	11	3	0	2.0
281.3	3	2,100	1	16	2	1	2.0
172.7	4	2,200	0	16	3	0	2.0
207.5	5	2,300	0	21	4	0	2.5
198.9	3	2,200	0	10	4	1	2.0
209.3	6	1,900	0	15	4	1	2.0
252.3	4	2,600	1	8	4	1	2.0
192.9	4	1,900	0	14	2	1	2.5
209.3	5	2,100	1	20	5	0	1.5
345.3	8	2,600	1	9	4	1	2.0
326.3	6	2,100	1	11	5	1	3.0
173.1	2	2,200	0	21	5	1	1.5
187.0	2	1,900	1	26	4	0	2.0
257.2	2	2,100	1	9	4	1	2.0
233.0	3	2,200	1	14	3	1	1.5
180.4	2	2,000	1	11	5	0	2.0
234.0	2	1,700	1	19	3	1	2.0
207.1	2	2,000	1	11	5	1	2.0
247.7	5	2,400	1	16	2	1	2.0
166.2	3	2,000	0	16	2	1	2.0
177.1	2	1,900	1	10	5	1	2.0

(continued)

Appendix A

A.1 Data Set 1—Goodyear, Arizona, Real Estate Sales Data (*continued*)

X_1	X_2	X_3	X_4	X_5	X_6	X_7	X_8
182.7	4	2,000	0	14	4	0	2.5
216.0	4	2,300	1	19	2	0	2.0
312.1	6	2,600	1	7	5	1	2.5
199.8	3	2,100	1	19	3	1	2.0
273.2	5	2,200	1	16	2	1	3.0
206.0	3	2,100	0	9	3	0	1.5
232.2	3	1,900	0	16	1	1	1.5
198.3	4	2,100	0	19	1	1	1.5
205.1	3	2,000	0	20	4	0	2.0
175.6	4	2,300	0	24	4	1	2.0
307.8	3	2,400	0	21	2	1	3.0
269.2	5	2,200	1	8	5	1	3.0
224.8	3	2,200	1	17	1	1	2.5
171.6	3	2,000	0	16	4	0	2.0
216.8	3	2,200	1	15	1	1	2.0
192.6	6	2,200	0	14	1	0	2.0
236.4	5	2,200	1	20	3	1	2.0
172.4	3	2,200	1	23	3	0	2.0
251.4	3	1,900	1	12	2	1	2.0
246.0	6	2,300	1	7	3	1	3.0
147.4	6	1,700	0	12	1	0	2.0
176.0	4	2,200	1	15	1	1	2.0
228.4	3	2,300	1	17	5	1	1.5
166.5	3	1,600	0	19	3	0	2.5
189.4	4	2,200	1	24	1	1	2.0
312.1	7	2,400	1	13	3	1	3.0
289.8	6	2,000	1	21	3	1	3.0
269.9	5	2,200	0	11	4	1	2.5
154.3	2	2,000	1	13	2	0	2.0
222.1	2	2,100	1	9	5	1	2.0
209.7	5	2,200	0	13	2	1	2.0
190.9	3	2,200	0	18	3	1	2.0
254.3	4	2,500	0	15	3	1	2.0
207.5	3	2,100	0	10	2	0	2.0
209.7	4	2,200	0	19	2	1	2.0
294.0	2	2,100	1	13	2	1	2.5
176.3	2	2,000	0	17	3	0	2.0
294.3	7	2,400	1	8	4	1	2.0
224.0	3	1,900	0	6	1	1	2.0
125.0	2	1,900	1	18	4	0	1.5
236.8	4	2,600	0	17	5	1	2.0
164.1	4	2,300	1	19	4	0	2.0
217.8	3	2,500	1	12	3	0	2.0
192.2	2	2,400	1	16	2	0	2.5
125.9	2	2,400	1	28	1	0	1.5

Appendix A

A.1 Data Set 1—Goodyear, Arizona, Real Estate Sales Data (*concluded*)

X_1	X_2	X_3	X_4	X_5	X_6	X_7	X_8
220.9	2	2,300	0	12	1	1	2.0
294.5	6	2,700	1	15	3	1	2.0
244.6	2	2,300	1	9	2	1	2.5
199.0	3	2,500	0	18	1	0	1.5
240.0	4	2,600	1	13	4	1	2.0
263.2	4	2,300	1	14	3	1	2.0
188.1	2	1,900	1	8	4	1	1.5
243.7	6	2,700	1	7	4	1	2.0
221.5	4	2,300	1	18	3	1	2.0
175.0	2	2,500	1	11	3	0	2.0
253.2	3	2,300	1	16	2	1	2.0
155.4	4	2,400	0	16	3	0	2.0
186.7	5	2,500	0	21	4	0	2.5
179.0	3	2,400	0	10	4	1	2.0
188.3	6	2,100	0	15	4	1	2.0
227.1	4	2,900	1	8	4	1	2.0
173.6	4	2,100	0	14	2	1	2.5
188.3	5	2,300	1	20	5	0	1.5
310.8	8	2,900	1	9	4	1	2.0
293.7	6	2,400	1	11	5	1	3.0
179.0	3	2,400	1	8	4	1	2.0
188.3	6	2,100	0	14	2	1	2.5
227.1	4	2,900	1	20	5	0	1.5
173.6	4	2,100	1	9	4	1	2.0
188.3	5	2,300	1	11	5	1	3.0

Appendix A

A.2 Data Set 2—Baseball Statistics, 2010 Season

Variables

x_1 = Team

x_2 = League (American = 1, National = 0)

x_3 = Built (year stadium was built)

x_4 = Size (stadium capacity)

x_5 = Payroll (team total, $ millions)

x_6 = Wins

x_7 = Attendance (total for team in millions)

x_8 = BA (team batting average)

x_9 = ERA (team earned run average)

x_{10} = HR (team home runs)

x_{11} = Errors (team errors)

x_{12} = SB (team stolen bases)

x_{13} = Year

x_{14} = Average player salary ($)

Team, x_1	League, x_2	Built, x_3	Size, x_4	Payroll, x_5	Wins, x_6	Attendance, x_7	BA, x_8	ERA, x_9	HR, x_{10}	Errors, x_{11}	SB, x_{12}	Year, x_{13}	Average Player Salary, x_{14}
Arizona Diamondbacks	NL	1998	49,033	60.7	65	2.06	0.250	4.81	180	102	86	1989	$ 512,930
Atlanta Braves	NL	1996	50,091	84.4	91	2.51	0.258	3.56	139	126	63	1990	578,930
Baltimore Orioles	AL	1992	48,876	81.6	66	1.73	0.259	4.59	133	105	76	1991	891,188
Boston Red Sox	AL	1912	39,928	162.7	89	3.05	0.268	4.20	211	111	68	1992	1,084,408
Chicago Cubs	NL	1914	41,118	146.9	75	3.06	0.257	4.18	149	126	55	1993	1,120,254
Chicago White Sox	AL	1991	40,615	108.3	88	2.19	0.268	4.09	177	103	160	1994	1,188,679
Cincinnati Reds	NL	2003	42,059	72.4	91	2.06	0.272	4.01	188	72	93	1995	1,071,029
Cleveland Indians	AL	1994	43,345	61.2	69	1.39	0.248	4.30	128	110	91	1996	1,176,967
Colorado Rockies	NL	1995	50,445	84.2	83	2.88	0.263	4.14	173	101	99	1997	1,383,578
Detroit Tigers	AL	2000	41,782	122.9	81	2.46	0.268	4.30	152	109	69	1998	1,441,406
Florida Marlins	NL	1987	36,331	55.6	80	1.54	0.254	4.08	152	123	92	1999	1,720,050
Houston Astros	NL	2000	40,950	92.4	76	2.33	0.247	4.09	108	103	100	2000	1,988,034
Kansas City Royals	AL	1973	40,793	72.3	67	1.62	0.274	4.97	121	121	115	2001	2,264,403
Los Angeles Angels	AL	1966	45,050	105.0	80	3.25	0.248	4.04	155	113	104	2002	2,383,235
Los Angeles Dodgers	NL	1962	56,000	94.9	80	3.56	0.252	4.01	120	98	92	2003	2,555,476
Milwaukee Brewers	NL	2001	42,200	81.1	77	2.78	0.262	4.58	182	101	81	2004	2,486,609
Minnesota Twins	AL	2010	40,000	97.6	94	3.22	0.273	3.95	142	78	68	2005	2,632,655
New York Mets	NL	2009	45,000	132.7	79	2.56	0.249	3.70	128	87	130	2006	2,866,544
New York Yankees	AL	2009	52,325	206.3	95	3.77	0.267	4.06	201	69	103	2007	2,944,556
Oakland Athletics	AL	1966	34,077	51.7	81	1.42	0.256	3.56	109	99	156	2008	3,154,845
Philadelphia Phillies	NL	2004	43,647	141.9	97	3.65	0.260	3.67	166	83	108	2009	3,240,206
Pittsburgh Pirates	NL	2001	38,496	34.9	57	1.61	0.242	5.00	126	127	87	2010	3,297,828
San Diego Padres	NL	2004	42,445	37.8	90	2.13	0.246	3.39	132	72	124		
San Francisco Giants	NL	2000	41,503	97.8	92	3.04	0.257	3.36	162	73	55		
Seattle Mariners	AL	1999	47,116	98.4	61	2.09	0.236	3.93	101	110	142		
St. Louis Cardinals	NL	2006	49,660	93.5	86	3.30	0.263	3.57	150	99	79		
Tampa Bay Rays	AL	1990	36,048	71.9	96	1.84	0.247	3.78	160	85	172		
Texas Rangers	AL	1994	49,115	55.3	90	2.51	0.276	3.93	162	105	123		
Toronto Blue Jays	AL	1989	50,516	62.7	85	1.63	0.248	4.22	257	92	58		
Washington Nationals	NL	2008	41,888	61.4	69	1.83	0.250	4.13	149	127	110		

Appendix A

A.3 Data Set 3—Buena School District Bus Data

Variables

x_1 = Bus number
x_2 = Maintenance cost ($)
x_3 = Age
x_4 = Miles
x_5 = Bus type (diesel or gasoline)
x_6 = Bus manufacturer (Bluebird, Keiser, Thompson)
x_7 = Passengers

Bus Number, x_1	Maintenance Cost, x_2	Age, x_3	Miles, x_4	Bus Type, x_5	Bus Manufacturer, x_6	Passengers, x_7
135	329	7	853	Diesel	Bluebird	55
120	503	10	883	Diesel	Keiser	42
200	505	10	822	Diesel	Bluebird	55
40	466	10	865	Gasoline	Bluebird	55
427	359	7	751	Gasoline	Keiser	55
759	546	8	870	Diesel	Keiser	55
10	427	5	780	Gasoline	Keiser	14
880	474	9	857	Gasoline	Keiser	55
481	382	3	818	Gasoline	Keiser	6
387	422	8	869	Gasoline	Bluebird	55
326	433	9	848	Diesel	Bluebird	55
861	474	10	845	Gasoline	Bluebird	55
122	558	10	885	Gasoline	Bluebird	55
156	561	12	838	Diesel	Thompson	55
887	357	8	760	Diesel	Bluebird	6
686	329	3	741	Diesel	Bluebird	55
490	497	10	859	Gasoline	Bluebird	55
370	459	8	826	Gasoline	Keiser	55
464	355	3	806	Gasoline	Bluebird	55
875	489	9	858	Diesel	Bluebird	55
883	436	2	785	Gasoline	Bluebird	55
57	455	7	828	Diesel	Bluebird	55
482	514	11	980	Gasoline	Bluebird	55
704	503	8	857	Diesel	Bluebird	55
989	380	9	803	Diesel	Keiser	55
731	432	6	819	Diesel	Bluebird	42
75	478	6	821	Diesel	Bluebird	55
162	406	3	798	Gasoline	Keiser	55
732	471	9	815	Diesel	Keiser	42
751	444	2	757	Diesel	Keiser	14
600	493	10	1008	Diesel	Bluebird	55
948	452	9	831	Diesel	Keiser	42
358	461	6	849	Diesel	Bluebird	55
833	496	8	839	Diesel	Thompson	55
692	469	8	812	Diesel	Bluebird	55

Appendix A

A.3 Data Set 3—Buena School District Bus Data (*concluded*)

Bus Number, x_1	Maintenance Cost, x_2	Age, x_3	Miles, x_4	Bus Type, x_5	Bus Manufacturer, x_6	Passengers, x_7
61	442	9	809	Diesel	Keiser	55
9	414	4	864	Gasoline	Keiser	55
314	459	11	859	Diesel	Thompson	6
396	457	2	815	Diesel	Thompson	55
365	462	6	799	Diesel	Keiser	55
398	570	9	844	Diesel	Thompson	14
43	439	9	832	Gasoline	Bluebird	55
500	369	5	842	Gasoline	Bluebird	55
279	390	2	792	Diesel	Bluebird	55
693	469	9	775	Gasoline	Keiser	55
884	381	9	882	Diesel	Bluebird	55
977	501	7	874	Diesel	Bluebird	55
38	432	6	837	Gasoline	Keiser	14
725	392	5	774	Diesel	Bluebird	55
982	441	1	823	Diesel	Bluebird	55
724	448	8	790	Diesel	Keiser	42
603	468	4	800	Diesel	Keiser	14
168	467	7	827	Gasoline	Thompson	55
45	478	6	830	Diesel	Keiser	55
754	515	14	895	Diesel	Keiser	14
39	411	6	804	Gasoline	Bluebird	55
671	504	8	866	Gasoline	Thompson	55
418	504	9	842	Diesel	Bluebird	55
984	392	8	851	Diesel	Bluebird	55
953	423	10	835	Diesel	Bluebird	55
507	410	7	866	Diesel	Bluebird	55
540	529	4	846	Gasoline	Bluebird	55
695	477	2	802	Diesel	Bluebird	55
193	540	11	847	Diesel	Thompson	55
321	450	6	856	Diesel	Bluebird	6
918	390	5	799	Diesel	Bluebird	55
101	424	4	827	Diesel	Bluebird	55
714	433	7	817	Diesel	Bluebird	42
678	428	7	842	Diesel	Keiser	55
768	494	7	815	Diesel	Bluebird	42
29	396	6	784	Gasoline	Bluebird	55
554	458	4	817	Diesel	Bluebird	14
767	493	6	816	Diesel	Keiser	55
699	475	9	816	Gasoline	Bluebird	55
954	476	10	827	Diesel	Bluebird	42
705	403	4	806	Diesel	Keiser	42
660	337	6	819	Gasoline	Bluebird	55
520	492	10	836	Diesel	Bluebird	55
814	426	4	757	Diesel	Bluebird	55
353	449	4	817	Gasoline	Keiser	55

Appendix A

A.4 Data Set 4—Applewood Auto Group

x_1 = **Age**—the age of the buyer at the time of the purchase
x_2 = **Profit**—the amount earned by the dealership on the sale of each vehicle
x_3 = **Location**—the dealership where the vehicle was purchased
x_4 = **Vehicle type**—SUV, sedan, compact, hybrid, or truck
x_5 = **Previous**—the number of vehicles previously purchased at any of the four Applewood dealerships by the customer

Age x_1	Profit x_2	Location x_3	Vehicle-Type x_4	Previous x_5	Age x_1	Profit x_2	Location x_3	Vehicle-Type x_4	Previous x_5
21	$1,387	Tionesta	Sedan	0	40	$1,485	Sheffield	Compact	0
23	1,754	Sheffield	SUV	1	40	1,509	Kane	SUV	2
24	1,817	Sheffield	Hybrid	1	40	1,638	Sheffield	Sedan	0
25	1,040	Sheffield	Compact	0	40	1,961	Sheffield	Sedan	1
26	1,273	Kane	Sedan	1	40	2,127	Olean	Truck	0
27	1,529	Sheffield	Sedan	1	40	2,430	Tionesta	Sedan	1
27	3,082	Kane	Truck	0	41	1,704	Sheffield	Sedan	1
28	1,951	Kane	SUV	1	41	1,876	Kane	Sedan	2
28	2,692	Tionesta	Compact	0	41	2,010	Tionesta	Sedan	1
29	1,206	Sheffield	Sedan	0	41	2,165	Tionesta	SUV	0
29	1,342	Kane	Sedan	2	41	2,231	Tionesta	SUV	2
30	443	Kane	Sedan	3	41	2,389	Kane	Truck	1
30	754	Olean	Sedan	2	42	335	Olean	SUV	1
30	1,621	Sheffield	Truck	1	42	963	Kane	Sedan	0
31	870	Tionesta	Sedan	1	42	1,298	Tionesta	Sedan	1
31	1,174	Kane	Truck	0	42	1,410	Kane	SUV	2
31	1,412	Sheffield	Sedan	1	42	1,553	Tionesta	Compact	0
31	1,809	Tionesta	Sedan	1	42	1,648	Olean	SUV	0
31	2,415	Kane	Sedan	0	42	2,071	Kane	SUV	0
32	1,546	Sheffield	Truck	3	42	2,116	Kane	Compact	2
32	2,148	Tionesta	SUV	2	43	1,500	Tionesta	Sedan	0
32	2,207	Sheffield	Compact	0	43	1,549	Kane	SUV	2
32	2,252	Tionesta	SUV	0	43	2,348	Tionesta	Sedan	0
33	1,428	Kane	SUV	2	43	2,498	Tionesta	SUV	1
33	1,889	Olean	SUV	1	44	294	Kane	SUV	1
34	1,166	Olean	Sedan	1	44	1,115	Kane	Truck	0
34	1,320	Tionesta	Sedan	1	44	1,124	Tionesta	Compact	2
34	2,265	Olean	Sedan	0	44	1,532	Tionesta	SUV	3
35	1,323	Olean	Sedan	2	44	1,688	Kane	Sedan	4
35	1,760	Kane	Sedan	1	44	1,822	Kane	SUV	0
35	1,919	Tionesta	SUV	1	44	1,897	Sheffield	Compact	0
36	2,357	Kane	SUV	2	44	2,445	Kane	SUV	0
36	2,866	Kane	Sedan	1	44	2,886	Olean	SUV	1
37	732	Olean	SUV	1	45	820	Kane	Compact	1
37	1,464	Olean	Sedan	3	45	1,266	Olean	Sedan	0
37	1,626	Tionesta	Compact	4	45	1,741	Olean	Compact	2
37	1,762	Olean	SUV	1	45	1,772	Olean	Compact	1
37	1,915	Tionesta	SUV	2	45	1,932	Tionesta	Sedan	1
37	2,119	Kane	Hybrid	1	45	2,350	Sheffield	Compact	0
38	1,766	Sheffield	SUV	0	45	2,422	Kane	Sedan	1
38	2,201	Sheffield	Hybrid	2	45	2,446	Olean	Compact	1
39	996	Kane	Compact	2	46	369	Olean	Sedan	1
39	2,813	Tionesta	SUV	0	46	978	Kane	Sedan	1
40	323	Kane	Sedan	0	46	1,238	Sheffield	Compact	1
40	352	Sheffield	Compact	0	46	1,818	Kane	SUV	0
40	482	Olean	Sedan	1	46	1,824	Olean	Truck	0
40	1,144	Tionesta	Truck	0	46	1,907	Olean	Sedan	0

Appendix A

A.4 Data Set 4—Applewood Auto Group (*concluded*)

Age x_1	Profit x_2	Location x_3	Vehicle-Type x_4	Previous x_5	Age x_1	Profit x_2	Location x_3	Vehicle-Type x_4	Previous x_5
46	$1,938	Kane	Sedan	0	53	$1,401	Tionesta	Sedan	2
46	1,940	Kane	Truck	3	53	2,175	Olean	Sedan	1
46	2,197	Sheffield	Sedan	1	54	1,118	Sheffield	Compact	1
46	2,646	Tionesta	Sedan	2	54	2,584	Olean	Compact	2
47	1,461	Kane	Sedan	0	54	2,666	Tionesta	Truck	0
47	1,731	Tionesta	Compact	0	54	2,991	Tionesta	Sedan	0
47	2,230	Tionesta	Sedan	1	55	934	Sheffield	Truck	1
47	2,341	Sheffield	SUV	1	55	2,063	Kane	SUV	1
47	3,292	Olean	Sedan	2	55	2,083	Sheffield	Sedan	1
48	1,108	Sheffield	Sedan	1	55	2,856	Olean	Hybrid	1
48	1,295	Sheffield	SUV	1	55	2,989	Tionesta	Compact	1
48	1,344	Sheffield	SUV	0	56	910	Sheffield	SUV	0
48	1,906	Kane	Sedan	1	56	1,536	Kane	Sedan	0
48	1,952	Tionesta	Compact	1	56	1,957	Sheffield	SUV	1
48	2,070	Kane	SUV	1	56	2,240	Olean	Sedan	0
48	2,454	Kane	Sedan	1	56	2,695	Kane	Sedan	2
49	1,606	Olean	Compact	0	57	1,325	Olean	Sedan	1
49	1,680	Kane	SUV	3	57	2,250	Sheffield	Sedan	2
49	1,827	Tionesta	Truck	3	57	2,279	Sheffield	Hybrid	1
49	1,915	Tionesta	SUV	1	57	2,626	Sheffield	Sedan	2
49	2,084	Tionesta	Sedan	0	58	1,501	Sheffield	Hybrid	1
49	2,639	Sheffield	SUV	0	58	1,752	Kane	Sedan	3
50	842	Kane	SUV	0	58	2,058	Kane	SUV	1
50	1,963	Sheffield	Sedan	1	58	2,370	Tionesta	Compact	0
50	2,059	Sheffield	Sedan	1	58	2,637	Sheffield	SUV	1
50	2,338	Tionesta	SUV	0	59	1,426	Sheffield	Sedan	0
50	3,043	Kane	Sedan	0	59	2,944	Olean	SUV	2
51	1,059	Kane	SUV	1	60	2,147	Olean	Sedan	2
51	1,674	Sheffield	Sedan	1	61	1,973	Kane	SUV	3
51	1,807	Tionesta	Sedan	1	61	2,502	Olean	Sedan	0
51	2,056	Sheffield	Hybrid	0	62	783	Sheffield	Hybrid	1
51	2,236	Tionesta	SUV	2	62	1,538	Olean	Truck	1
51	2,928	Kane	SUV	0	63	2,339	Olean	Compact	1
52	1,269	Tionesta	Sedan	1	64	2,700	Kane	Truck	0
52	1,717	Sheffield	SUV	3	65	2,222	Kane	Truck	1
52	1,797	Kane	Sedan	1	65	2,597	Sheffield	Truck	0
52	1,955	Olean	Hybrid	2	65	2,742	Tionesta	SUV	2
52	2,199	Tionesta	SUV	0	68	1,837	Sheffield	Sedan	1
52	2,482	Olean	Compact	0	69	2,842	Kane	SUV	0
52	2,701	Sheffield	SUV	0	70	2,434	Olean	Sedan	4
52	3,210	Olean	Truck	4	72	1,640	Olean	Sedan	1
53	377	Olean	SUV	1	72	1,821	Tionesta	SUV	1
53	1,220	Olean	Sedan	0	73	2,487	Olean	Compact	4

Appendix B: Tables

B.1 Areas under the Normal Curve

Example:
If $z = 1.96$, then
$P(0 \text{ to } z) = 0.4750$.

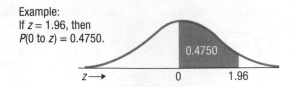

0.4750

$z \longrightarrow$ 0   1.96

z	0.00	0.01	0.02	0.03	0.04	0.05	0.06	0.07	0.08	0.09
0.0	0.0000	0.0040	0.0080	0.0120	0.0160	0.0199	0.0239	0.0279	0.0319	0.0359
0.1	0.0398	0.0438	0.0478	0.0517	0.0557	0.0596	0.0636	0.0675	0.0714	0.0753
0.2	0.0793	0.0832	0.0871	0.0910	0.0948	0.0987	0.1026	0.1064	0.1103	0.1141
0.3	0.1179	0.1217	0.1255	0.1293	0.1331	0.1368	0.1406	0.1443	0.1480	0.1517
0.4	0.1554	0.1591	0.1628	0.1664	0.1700	0.1736	0.1772	0.1808	0.1844	0.1879
0.5	0.1915	0.1950	0.1985	0.2019	0.2054	0.2088	0.2123	0.2157	0.2190	0.2224
0.6	0.2257	0.2291	0.2324	0.2357	0.2389	0.2422	0.2454	0.2486	0.2517	0.2549
0.7	0.2580	0.2611	0.2642	0.2673	0.2704	0.2734	0.2764	0.2794	0.2823	0.2852
0.8	0.2881	0.2910	0.2939	0.2967	0.2995	0.3023	0.3051	0.3078	0.3106	0.3133
0.9	0.3159	0.3186	0.3212	0.3238	0.3264	0.3289	0.3315	0.3340	0.3365	0.3389
1.0	0.3413	0.3438	0.3461	0.3485	0.3508	0.3531	0.3554	0.3577	0.3599	0.3621
1.1	0.3643	0.3665	0.3686	0.3708	0.3729	0.3749	0.3770	0.3790	0.3810	0.3830
1.2	0.3849	0.3869	0.3888	0.3907	0.3925	0.3944	0.3962	0.3980	0.3997	0.4015
1.3	0.4032	0.4049	0.4066	0.4082	0.4099	0.4115	0.4131	0.4147	0.4162	0.4177
1.4	0.4192	0.4207	0.4222	0.4236	0.4251	0.4265	0.4279	0.4292	0.4306	0.4319
1.5	0.4332	0.4345	0.4357	0.4370	0.4382	0.4394	0.4406	0.4418	0.4429	0.4441
1.6	0.4452	0.4463	0.4474	0.4484	0.4495	0.4505	0.4515	0.4525	0.4535	0.4545
1.7	0.4554	0.4564	0.4573	0.4582	0.4591	0.4599	0.4608	0.4616	0.4625	0.4633
1.8	0.4641	0.4649	0.4656	0.4664	0.4671	0.4678	0.4686	0.4693	0.4699	0.4706
1.9	0.4713	0.4719	0.4726	0.4732	0.4738	0.4744	0.4750	0.4756	0.4761	0.4767
2.0	0.4772	0.4778	0.4783	0.4788	0.4793	0.4798	0.4803	0.4808	0.4812	0.4817
2.1	0.4821	0.4826	0.4830	0.4834	0.4838	0.4842	0.4846	0.4850	0.4854	0.4857
2.2	0.4861	0.4864	0.4868	0.4871	0.4875	0.4878	0.4881	0.4884	0.4887	0.4890
2.3	0.4893	0.4896	0.4898	0.4901	0.4904	0.4906	0.4909	0.4911	0.4913	0.4916
2.4	0.4918	0.4920	0.4922	0.4925	0.4927	0.4929	0.4931	0.4932	0.4934	0.4936
2.5	0.4938	0.4940	0.4941	0.4943	0.4945	0.4946	0.4948	0.4949	0.4951	0.4952
2.6	0.4953	0.4955	0.4956	0.4957	0.4959	0.4960	0.4961	0.4962	0.4963	0.4964
2.7	0.4965	0.4966	0.4967	0.4968	0.4969	0.4970	0.4971	0.4972	0.4973	0.4974
2.8	0.4974	0.4975	0.4976	0.4977	0.4977	0.4978	0.4979	0.4979	0.4980	0.4981
2.9	0.4981	0.4982	0.4982	0.4983	0.4984	0.4984	0.4985	0.4985	0.4986	0.4986
3.0	0.4987	0.4987	0.4987	0.4988	0.4988	0.4989	0.4989	0.4989	0.4990	0.4990

Appendix B

B.2 Student's *t* Distribution

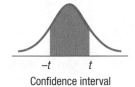
Confidence interval

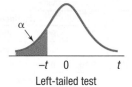
Left-tailed test

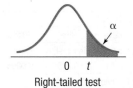
Right-tailed test

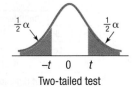
Two-tailed test

	Confidence Intervals, *c*							Confidence Intervals, *c*					
	80%	90%	95%	98%	99%	99.9%		80%	90%	95%	98%	99%	99.9%
	Level of Significance for One-Tailed Test, α							Level of Significance for One-Tailed Test, α					
df	0.10	0.05	0.025	0.01	0.005	0.0005	*df*	0.10	0.05	0.025	0.01	0.005	0.0005
	Level of Significance for Two-Tailed Test, α							Level of Significance for Two-Tailed Test, α					
	0.20	0.10	0.05	0.02	0.01	0.001		0.20	0.10	0.05	0.02	0.01	0.001
1	3.078	6.314	12.706	31.821	63.657	636.619	36	1.306	1.688	2.028	2.434	2.719	3.582
2	1.886	2.920	4.303	6.965	9.925	31.599	37	1.305	1.687	2.026	2.431	2.715	3.574
3	1.638	2.353	3.182	4.541	5.841	12.924	38	1.304	1.686	2.024	2.429	2.712	3.566
4	1.533	2.132	2.776	3.747	4.604	8.610	39	1.304	1.685	2.023	2.426	2.708	3.558
5	1.476	2.015	2.571	3.365	4.032	6.869	40	1.303	1.684	2.021	2.423	2.704	3.551
6	1.440	1.943	2.447	3.143	3.707	5.959	41	1.303	1.683	2.020	2.421	2.701	3.544
7	1.415	1.895	2.365	2.998	3.499	5.408	42	1.302	1.682	2.018	2.418	2.698	3.538
8	1.397	1.860	2.306	2.896	3.355	5.041	43	1.302	1.681	2.017	2.416	2.695	3.532
9	1.383	1.833	2.262	2.821	3.250	4.781	44	1.301	1.680	2.015	2.414	2.692	3.526
10	1.372	1.812	2.228	2.764	3.169	4.587	45	1.301	1.679	2.014	2.412	2.690	3.520
11	1.363	1.796	2.201	2.718	3.106	4.437	46	1.300	1.679	2.013	2.410	2.687	3.515
12	1.356	1.782	2.179	2.681	3.055	4.318	47	1.300	1.678	2.012	2.408	2.685	3.510
13	1.350	1.771	2.160	2.650	3.012	4.221	48	1.299	1.677	2.011	2.407	2.682	3.505
14	1.345	1.761	2.145	2.624	2.977	4.140	49	1.299	1.677	2.010	2.405	2.680	3.500
15	1.341	1.753	2.131	2.602	2.947	4.073	50	1.299	1.676	2.009	2.403	2.678	3.496
16	1.337	1.746	2.120	2.583	2.921	4.015	51	1.298	1.675	2.008	2.402	2.676	3.492
17	1.333	1.740	2.110	2.567	2.898	3.965	52	1.298	1.675	2.007	2.400	2.674	3.488
18	1.330	1.734	2.101	2.552	2.878	3.922	53	1.298	1.674	2.006	2.399	2.672	3.484
19	1.328	1.729	2.093	2.539	2.861	3.883	54	1.297	1.674	2.005	2.397	2.670	3.480
20	1.325	1.725	2.086	2.528	2.845	3.850	55	1.297	1.673	2.004	2.396	2.668	3.476
21	1.323	1.721	2.080	2.518	2.831	3.819	56	1.297	1.673	2.003	2.395	2.667	3.473
22	1.321	1.717	2.074	2.508	2.819	3.792	57	1.297	1.672	2.002	2.394	2.665	3.470
23	1.319	1.714	2.069	2.500	2.807	3.768	58	1.296	1.672	2.002	2.392	2.663	3.466
24	1.318	1.711	2.064	2.492	2.797	3.745	59	1.296	1.671	2.001	2.391	2.662	3.463
25	1.316	1.708	2.060	2.485	2.787	3.725	60	1.296	1.671	2.000	2.390	2.660	3.460
26	1.315	1.706	2.056	2.479	2.779	3.707	61	1.296	1.670	2.000	2.389	2.659	3.457
27	1.314	1.703	2.052	2.473	2.771	3.690	62	1.295	1.670	1.999	2.388	2.657	3.454
28	1.313	1.701	2.048	2.467	2.763	3.674	63	1.295	1.669	1.998	2.387	2.656	3.452
29	1.311	1.699	2.045	2.462	2.756	3.659	64	1.295	1.669	1.998	2.386	2.655	3.449
30	1.310	1.697	2.042	2.457	2.750	3.646	65	1.295	1.669	1.997	2.385	2.654	3.447
31	1.309	1.696	2.040	2.453	2.744	3.633	66	1.295	1.668	1.997	2.384	2.652	3.444
32	1.309	1.694	2.037	2.449	2.738	3.622	67	1.294	1.668	1.996	2.383	2.651	3.442
33	1.308	1.692	2.035	2.445	2.733	3.611	68	1.294	1.668	1.995	2.382	2.650	3.439
34	1.307	1.691	2.032	2.441	2.728	3.601	69	1.294	1.667	1.995	2.382	2.649	3.437
35	1.306	1.690	2.030	2.438	2.724	3.591	70	1.294	1.667	1.994	2.381	2.648	3.435

(continued)

Appendix B

B.2 Student's *t* Distribution (*concluded*)

	Confidence Intervals, *c*							Confidence Intervals, *c*					
	80%	90%	95%	98%	99%	99.9%		80%	90%	95%	98%	99%	99.9%
	Level of Significance for One-Tailed Test, α							Level of Significance for One-Tailed Test, α					
df	0.10	0.05	0.025	0.01	0.005	0.0005	*df*	0.10	0.05	0.025	0.01	0.005	0.0005
	Level of Significance for Two-Tailed Test, α							Level of Significance for Two-Tailed Test, α					
	0.20	0.10	0.05	0.02	0.01	0.001		0.20	0.10	0.05	0.02	0.01	0.001
71	1.294	1.667	1.994	2.380	2.647	3.433	89	1.291	1.662	1.987	2.369	2.632	3.403
72	1.293	1.666	1.993	2.379	2.646	3.431	90	1.291	1.662	1.987	2.368	2.632	3.402
73	1.293	1.666	1.993	2.379	2.645	3.429							
74	1.293	1.666	1.993	2.378	2.644	3.427	91	1.291	1.662	1.986	2.368	2.631	3.401
75	1.293	1.665	1.992	2.377	2.643	3.425	92	1.291	1.662	1.986	2.368	2.630	3.399
							93	1.291	1.661	1.986	2.367	2.630	3.398
76	1.293	1.665	1.992	2.376	2.642	3.423	94	1.291	1.661	1.986	2.367	2.629	3.397
77	1.293	1.665	1.991	2.376	2.641	3.421	95	1.291	1.661	1.985	2.366	2.629	3.396
78	1.292	1.665	1.991	2.375	2.640	3.420							
79	1.292	1.664	1.990	2.374	2.640	3.418	96	1.290	1.661	1.985	2.366	2.628	3.395
80	1.292	1.664	1.990	2.374	2.639	3.416	97	1.290	1.661	1.985	2.365	2.627	3.394
							98	1.290	1.661	1.984	2.365	2.627	3.393
81	1.292	1.664	1.990	2.373	2.638	3.415	99	1.290	1.660	1.984	2.365	2.626	3.392
82	1.292	1.664	1.989	2.373	2.637	3.413	100	1.290	1.660	1.984	2.364	2.626	3.390
83	1.292	1.663	1.989	2.372	2.636	3.412							
84	1.292	1.663	1.989	2.372	2.636	3.410	120	1.289	1.658	1.980	2.358	2.617	3.373
85	1.292	1.663	1.988	2.371	2.635	3.409	140	1.288	1.656	1.977	2.353	2.611	3.361
							160	1.287	1.654	1.975	2.350	2.607	3.352
86	1.291	1.663	1.988	2.370	2.634	3.407	180	1.286	1.653	1.973	2.347	2.603	3.345
87	1.291	1.663	1.988	2.370	2.634	3.406	200	1.286	1.653	1.972	2.345	2.601	3.340
88	1.291	1.662	1.987	2.369	2.633	3.405	∞	1.282	1.645	1.960	2.326	2.576	3.291

Appendix B

B.3 Critical Values of Chi-Square

This table contains the values of χ^2 that correspond to a specific right-tail area and specific degrees of freedom.

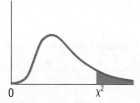

Example: With 17 *df* and a .02 area in the upper tail, $\chi^2 = 30.995$

Degrees of Freedom, df	Right-Tail Area			
	0.10	0.05	0.02	0.01
1	2.706	3.841	5.412	6.635
2	4.605	5.991	7.824	9.210
3	6.251	7.815	9.837	11.345
4	7.779	9.488	11.668	13.277
5	9.236	11.070	13.388	15.086
6	10.645	12.592	15.033	16.812
7	12.017	14.067	16.622	18.475
8	13.362	15.507	18.168	20.090
9	14.684	16.919	19.679	21.666
10	15.987	18.307	21.161	23.209
11	17.275	19.675	22.618	24.725
12	18.549	21.026	24.054	26.217
13	19.812	22.362	25.472	27.688
14	21.064	23.685	26.873	29.141
15	22.307	24.996	28.259	30.578
16	23.542	26.296	29.633	32.000
17	24.769	27.587	30.995	33.409
18	25.989	28.869	32.346	34.805
19	27.204	30.144	33.687	36.191
20	28.412	31.410	35.020	37.566
21	29.615	32.671	36.343	38.932
22	30.813	33.924	37.659	40.289
23	32.007	35.172	38.968	41.638
24	33.196	36.415	40.270	42.980
25	34.382	37.652	41.566	44.314
26	35.563	38.885	42.856	45.642
27	36.741	40.113	44.140	46.963
28	37.916	41.337	45.419	48.278
29	39.087	42.557	46.693	49.588
30	40.256	43.773	47.962	50.892

Appendix B

B.4 Critical Values of the *F* Distribution at a 5 Percent Level of Significance

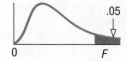

		Degrees of Freedom for the Numerator														
		1	2	3	4	5	6	7	8	9	10	12	15	20	24	30	40
Degrees of Freedom for the Denominator	1	161	200	216	225	230	234	237	239	241	242	244	246	248	249	250	251
	2	18.5	19.0	19.2	19.2	19.3	19.3	19.4	19.4	19.4	19.4	19.4	19.4	19.4	19.5	19.5	19.5
	3	10.1	9.55	9.28	9.12	9.01	8.94	8.89	8.85	8.81	8.79	8.74	8.70	8.66	8.64	8.62	8.59
	4	7.71	6.94	6.59	6.39	6.26	6.16	6.09	6.04	6.00	5.96	5.91	5.86	5.80	5.77	5.75	5.72
	5	6.61	5.79	5.41	5.19	5.05	4.95	4.88	4.82	4.77	4.74	4.68	4.62	4.56	4.53	4.50	4.46
	6	5.99	5.14	4.76	4.53	4.39	4.28	4.21	4.15	4.10	4.06	4.00	3.94	3.87	3.84	3.81	3.77
	7	5.59	4.74	4.35	4.12	3.97	3.87	3.79	3.73	3.68	3.64	3.57	3.51	3.44	3.41	3.38	3.34
	8	5.32	4.46	4.07	3.84	3.69	3.58	3.50	3.44	3.39	3.35	3.28	3.22	3.15	3.12	3.08	3.04
	9	5.12	4.26	3.86	3.63	3.48	3.37	3.29	3.23	3.18	3.14	3.07	3.01	2.94	2.90	2.86	2.83
	10	4.96	4.10	3.71	3.48	3.33	3.22	3.14	3.07	3.02	2.98	2.91	2.85	2.77	2.74	2.70	2.66
	11	4.84	3.98	3.59	3.36	3.20	3.09	3.01	2.95	2.90	2.85	2.79	2.72	2.65	2.61	2.57	2.53
	12	4.75	3.89	3.49	3.26	3.11	3.00	2.91	2.85	2.80	2.75	2.69	2.62	2.54	2.51	2.47	2.43
	13	4.67	3.81	3.41	3.18	3.03	2.92	2.83	2.77	2.71	2.67	2.60	2.53	2.46	2.42	2.38	2.34
	14	4.60	3.74	3.34	3.11	2.96	2.85	2.76	2.70	2.65	2.60	2.53	2.46	2.39	2.35	2.31	2.27
	15	4.54	3.68	3.29	3.06	2.90	2.79	2.71	2.64	2.59	2.54	2.48	2.40	2.33	2.29	2.25	2.20
	16	4.49	3.63	3.24	3.01	2.85	2.74	2.66	2.59	2.54	2.49	2.42	2.35	2.28	2.24	2.19	2.15
	17	4.45	3.59	3.20	2.96	2.81	2.70	2.61	2.55	2.49	2.45	2.38	2.31	2.23	2.19	2.15	2.10
	18	4.41	3.55	3.16	2.93	2.77	2.66	2.58	2.51	2.46	2.41	2.34	2.27	2.19	2.15	2.11	2.06
	19	4.38	3.52	3.13	2.90	2.74	2.63	2.54	2.48	2.42	2.38	2.31	2.23	2.16	2.11	2.07	2.03
	20	4.35	3.49	3.10	2.87	2.71	2.60	2.51	2.45	2.39	2.35	2.28	2.20	2.12	2.08	2.04	1.99
	21	4.32	3.47	3.07	2.84	2.68	2.57	2.49	2.42	2.37	2.32	2.25	2.18	2.10	2.05	2.01	1.96
	22	4.30	3.44	3.05	2.82	2.66	2.55	2.46	2.40	2.34	2.30	2.23	2.15	2.07	2.03	1.98	1.94
	23	4.28	3.42	3.03	2.80	2.64	2.53	2.44	2.37	2.32	2.27	2.20	2.13	2.05	2.01	1.96	1.91
	24	4.26	3.40	3.01	2.78	2.62	2.51	2.42	2.36	2.30	2.25	2.18	2.11	2.03	1.98	1.94	1.89
	25	4.24	3.39	2.99	2.76	2.60	2.49	2.40	2.34	2.28	2.24	2.16	2.09	2.01	1.96	1.92	1.87
	30	4.17	3.32	2.92	2.69	2.53	2.42	2.33	2.27	2.21	2.16	2.09	2.01	1.93	1.89	1.84	1.79
	40	4.08	3.23	2.84	2.61	2.45	2.34	2.25	2.18	2.12	2.08	2.00	1.92	1.84	1.79	1.74	1.69
	60	4.00	3.15	2.76	2.53	2.37	2.25	2.17	2.10	2.04	1.99	1.92	1.84	1.75	1.70	1.65	1.59
	120	3.92	3.07	2.68	2.45	2.29	2.18	2.09	2.02	1.96	1.91	1.83	1.75	1.66	1.61	1.55	1.50
	∞	3.84	3.00	2.60	2.37	2.21	2.10	2.01	1.94	1.88	1.83	1.75	1.67	1.57	1.52	1.46	1.39

Appendix B

B.4 Critical Values of the *F* Distribution at a 1 Percent Level of Significance (*concluded*)

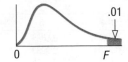

		Degrees of Freedom for the Numerator														
	1	**2**	**3**	**4**	**5**	**6**	**7**	**8**	**9**	**10**	**12**	**15**	**20**	**24**	**30**	**40**
1	4052	5000	5403	5625	5764	5859	5928	5981	6022	6056	6106	6157	6209	6235	6261	6287
2	98.5	99.0	99.2	99.2	99.3	99.3	99.4	99.4	99.4	99.4	99.4	99.4	99.4	99.5	99.5	99.5
3	34.1	30.8	29.5	28.7	28.2	27.9	27.7	27.5	27.3	27.2	27.1	26.9	26.7	26.6	26.5	26.4
4	21.2	18.0	16.7	16.0	15.5	15.2	15.0	14.8	14.7	14.5	14.4	14.2	14.0	13.9	13.8	13.7
5	16.3	13.3	12.1	11.4	11.0	10.7	10.5	10.3	10.2	10.1	9.89	9.72	9.55	9.47	9.38	9.29
6	13.7	10.9	9.78	9.15	8.75	8.47	8.26	8.10	7.98	7.87	7.72	7.56	7.40	7.31	7.23	7.14
7	12.2	9.55	8.45	7.85	7.46	7.19	6.99	6.84	6.72	6.62	6.47	6.31	6.16	6.07	5.99	5.91
8	11.3	8.65	7.59	7.01	6.63	6.37	6.18	6.03	5.91	5.81	5.67	5.52	5.36	5.28	5.20	5.12
9	10.6	8.02	6.99	6.42	6.06	5.80	5.61	5.47	5.35	5.26	5.11	4.96	4.81	4.73	4.65	4.57
10	10.0	7.56	6.55	5.99	5.64	5.39	5.20	5.06	4.94	4.85	4.71	4.56	4.41	4.33	4.25	4.17
11	9.65	7.21	6.22	5.67	5.32	5.07	4.89	4.74	4.63	4.54	4.40	4.25	4.10	4.02	3.94	3.86
12	9.33	6.93	5.95	5.41	5.06	4.82	4.64	4.50	4.39	4.30	4.16	4.01	3.86	3.78	3.70	3.62
13	9.07	6.70	5.74	5.21	4.86	4.62	4.44	4.30	4.19	4.10	3.96	3.82	3.66	3.59	3.51	3.43
14	8.86	6.51	5.56	5.04	4.69	4.46	4.28	4.14	4.03	3.94	3.80	3.66	3.51	3.43	3.35	3.27
15	8.68	6.36	5.42	4.89	4.56	4.32	4.14	4.00	3.89	3.80	3.67	3.52	3.37	3.29	3.21	3.13
16	8.53	6.23	5.29	4.77	4.44	4.20	4.03	3.89	3.78	3.69	3.55	3.41	3.26	3.18	3.10	3.02
17	8.40	6.11	5.18	4.67	4.34	4.10	3.93	3.79	3.68	3.59	3.46	3.31	3.16	3.08	3.00	2.92
18	8.29	6.01	5.09	4.58	4.25	4.01	3.84	3.71	3.60	3.51	3.37	3.23	3.08	3.00	2.92	2.84
19	8.18	5.93	5.01	4.50	4.17	3.94	3.77	3.63	3.52	3.43	3.30	3.15	3.00	2.92	2.84	2.76
20	8.10	5.85	4.94	4.43	4.10	3.87	3.70	3.56	3.46	3.37	3.23	3.09	2.94	2.86	2.78	2.69
21	8.02	5.78	4.87	4.37	4.04	3.81	3.64	3.51	3.40	3.31	3.17	3.03	2.88	2.80	2.72	2.64
22	7.95	5.72	4.82	4.31	3.99	3.76	3.59	3.45	3.35	3.26	3.12	2.98	2.83	2.75	2.67	2.58
23	7.88	5.66	4.76	4.26	3.94	3.71	3.54	3.41	3.30	3.21	3.07	2.93	2.78	2.70	2.62	2.54
24	7.82	5.61	4.72	4.22	3.90	3.67	3.50	3.36	3.26	3.17	3.03	2.89	2.74	2.66	2.58	2.49
25	7.77	5.57	4.68	4.18	3.85	3.63	3.46	3.32	3.22	3.13	2.99	2.85	2.70	2.62	2.54	2.45
30	7.56	5.39	4.51	4.02	3.70	3.47	3.30	3.17	3.07	2.98	2.84	2.70	2.55	2.47	2.39	2.30
40	7.31	5.18	4.31	3.83	3.51	3.29	3.12	2.99	2.89	2.80	2.66	2.52	2.37	2.29	2.20	2.11
60	7.08	4.98	4.13	3.65	3.34	3.12	2.95	2.82	2.72	2.63	2.50	2.35	2.20	2.12	2.03	1.94
120	6.85	4.79	3.95	3.48	3.17	2.96	2.79	2.66	2.56	2.47	2.34	2.19	2.03	1.95	1.86	1.76
∞	6.63	4.61	3.78	3.32	3.02	2.80	2.64	2.51	2.41	2.32	2.18	2.04	1.88	1.79	1.70	1.59

Degrees of Freedom for the Denominator

Appendix B

B.5 Poisson Distribution

x	μ 0.1	0.2	0.3	0.4	0.5	0.6	0.7	0.8	0.9
0	0.9048	0.8187	0.7408	0.6703	0.6065	0.5488	0.4966	0.4493	0.4066
1	0.0905	0.1637	0.2222	0.2681	0.3033	0.3293	0.3476	0.3595	0.3659
2	0.0045	0.0164	0.0333	0.0536	0.0758	0.0988	0.1217	0.1438	0.1647
3	0.0002	0.0011	0.0033	0.0072	0.0126	0.0198	0.0284	0.0383	0.0494
4	0.0000	0.0001	0.0003	0.0007	0.0016	0.0030	0.0050	0.0077	0.0111
5	0.0000	0.0000	0.0000	0.0001	0.0002	0.0004	0.0007	0.0012	0.0020
6	0.0000	0.0000	0.0000	0.0000	0.0000	0.0000	0.0001	0.0002	0.0003
7	0.0000	0.0000	0.0000	0.0000	0.0000	0.0000	0.0000	0.0000	0.0000

x	μ 1.0	2.0	3.0	4.0	5.0	6.0	7.0	8.0	9.0
0	0.3679	0.1353	0.0498	0.0183	0.0067	0.0025	0.0009	0.0003	0.0001
1	0.3679	0.2707	0.1494	0.0733	0.0337	0.0149	0.0064	0.0027	0.0011
2	0.1839	0.2707	0.2240	0.1465	0.0842	0.0446	0.0223	0.0107	0.0050
3	0.0613	0.1804	0.2240	0.1954	0.1404	0.0892	0.0521	0.0286	0.0150
4	0.0153	0.0902	0.1680	0.1954	0.1755	0.1339	0.0912	0.0573	0.0337
5	0.0031	0.0361	0.1008	0.1563	0.1755	0.1606	0.1277	0.0916	0.0607
6	0.0005	0.0120	0.0504	0.1042	0.1462	0.1606	0.1490	0.1221	0.0911
7	0.0001	0.0034	0.0216	0.0595	0.1044	0.1377	0.1490	0.1396	0.1171
8	0.0000	0.0009	0.0081	0.0298	0.0653	0.1033	0.1304	0.1396	0.1318
9	0.0000	0.0002	0.0027	0.0132	0.0363	0.0688	0.1014	0.1241	0.1318
10	0.0000	0.0000	0.0008	0.0053	0.0181	0.0413	0.0710	0.0993	0.1186
11	0.0000	0.0000	0.0002	0.0019	0.0082	0.0225	0.0452	0.0722	0.0970
12	0.0000	0.0000	0.0001	0.0006	0.0034	0.0113	0.0263	0.0481	0.0728
13	0.0000	0.0000	0.0000	0.0002	0.0013	0.0052	0.0142	0.0296	0.0504
14	0.0000	0.0000	0.0000	0.0001	0.0005	0.0022	0.0071	0.0169	0.0324
15	0.0000	0.0000	0.0000	0.0000	0.0002	0.0009	0.0033	0.0090	0.0194
16	0.0000	0.0000	0.0000	0.0000	0.0000	0.0003	0.0014	0.0045	0.0109
17	0.0000	0.0000	0.0000	0.0000	0.0000	0.0001	0.0006	0.0021	0.0058
18	0.0000	0.0000	0.0000	0.0000	0.0000	0.0000	0.0002	0.0009	0.0029
19	0.0000	0.0000	0.0000	0.0000	0.0000	0.0000	0.0001	0.0004	0.0014
20	0.0000	0.0000	0.0000	0.0000	0.0000	0.0000	0.0000	0.0002	0.0006
21	0.0000	0.0000	0.0000	0.0000	0.0000	0.0000	0.0000	0.0001	0.0003
22	0.0000	0.0000	0.0000	0.0000	0.0000	0.0000	0.0000	0.0000	0.0001

02711	08182	75997	79866	58095	83319	80295	79741	74599	84379
94873	90935	31684	63952	09865	14491	99518	93394	34691	14985
54921	78680	06635	98689	17306	25170	65928	87709	30533	89736
77640	97636	37397	93379	56454	59818	45827	74164	71666	46977
61545	00835	93251	87203	36759	49197	85967	01704	19634	21898
17147	19519	22497	16857	42426	84822	92598	49186	88247	39967
13748	04742	92460	85801	53444	65626	58710	55406	17173	69776
87455	14813	50373	28037	91182	32786	65261	11173	34376	36408
08999	57409	91185	10200	61411	23392	47797	56377	71635	08601
78804	81333	53809	32471	46034	36306	22498	19239	85428	55721
82173	26921	28472	98958	07960	66124	89731	95069	18625	92405
97594	25168	89178	68190	05043	17407	48201	83917	11413	72920
73881	67176	93504	42636	38233	16154	96451	57925	29667	30859
46071	22912	90326	42453	88108	72064	58601	32357	90610	32921
44492	19686	12495	93135	95185	77799	52441	88272	22024	80631
31864	72170	37722	55794	14636	05148	54505	50113	21119	25228
51574	90692	43339	65689	76539	27909	05467	21727	51141	72949
35350	76132	92925	92124	92634	35681	43690	89136	35599	84138
46943	36502	01172	46045	46991	33804	80006	35542	61056	75666
22665	87226	33304	57975	03985	21566	65796	72915	81466	89205
39437	97957	11838	10433	21564	51570	73558	27495	34533	57808
77082	47784	40098	97962	89845	28392	78187	06112	08169	11261
24544	25649	43370	28007	06779	72402	62632	53956	24709	06978
27503	15558	37738	24849	70722	71859	83736	06016	94397	12529
24590	24545	06435	52758	45685	90151	46516	49644	92686	84870
48155	86226	40359	28723	15364	69125	12609	57171	86857	31702
20226	53752	90648	24362	83314	00014	19207	69413	97016	86290
70178	73444	38790	53626	93780	18629	68766	24371	74639	30782
10169	41465	51935	05711	09799	79077	88159	33437	68519	03040
81084	03701	28598	70013	63794	53169	97054	60303	23259	96196
69202	20777	21727	81511	51887	16175	53746	46516	70339	62727
80561	95787	89426	93325	86412	57479	54194	52153	19197	81877
08199	26703	95128	48599	09333	12584	24374	31232	61782	44032
98883	28220	39358	53720	80161	83371	15181	11131	12219	55920
84568	69286	76054	21615	80883	36797	82845	39139	90900	18172
04269	35173	95745	53893	86022	77722	52498	84193	22448	22571
10538	13124	36099	13140	37706	44562	57179	44693	67877	01549
77843	24955	25900	63843	95029	93859	93634	20205	66294	41218
12034	94636	49455	76362	83532	31062	69903	91186	65768	55949
10524	72829	47641	93315	80875	28090	97728	52560	34937	79548
68935	76632	46984	61772	92786	22651	07086	89754	44143	97687
89450	65665	29190	43709	11172	34481	95977	47535	25658	73898
90696	20451	24211	97310	60446	73530	62865	96574	13829	72226
49006	32047	93086	00112	20470	17136	28255	86328	07293	38809
74591	87025	52368	59416	34417	70557	86746	55809	53628	12000
06315	17012	77103	00968	07235	10728	42189	33292	51487	64443
62386	09184	62092	46617	99419	64230	95034	85481	07857	42510
86848	82122	04028	36959	87827	12813	08627	80699	13345	51695
65643	69480	46598	04501	40403	91408	32343	48130	49303	90689
11084	46534	78957	77353	39578	77868	22970	84349	09184	70603

Appendix B

B.7 Wilcoxon *T* Values

				2α			
	.15	.10	.05	.04	.03	.02	.01
				α			
n	.075	.050	.025	.020	.015	.010	.005
4	0						
5	1	0					
6	2	2	0	0			
7	4	3	2	1	0	0	
8	7	5	3	3	2	1	0
9	9	8	5	5	4	3	1
10	12	10	8	7	6	5	3
11	16	13	10	9	8	7	5
12	19	17	13	12	11	9	7
13	24	21	17	16	14	12	9
14	28	25	21	19	18	15	12
15	33	30	25	23	21	19	15
16	39	35	29	28	26	23	19
17	45	41	34	33	30	27	23
18	51	47	40	38	35	32	27
19	58	53	46	43	41	37	32
20	65	60	52	50	47	43	37
21	73	67	58	56	53	49	42
22	81	75	65	63	59	55	48
23	89	83	73	70	66	62	54
24	98	91	81	78	74	69	61
25	108	100	89	86	82	76	68
26	118	110	98	94	90	84	75
27	128	119	107	103	99	92	83
28	138	130	116	112	108	101	91
29	150	140	126	122	117	110	100
30	161	151	137	132	127	120	109
31	173	163	147	143	137	130	118
32	186	175	159	154	148	140	128
33	199	187	170	165	159	151	138
34	212	200	182	177	171	162	148
35	226	213	195	189	182	173	159
40	302	286	264	257	249	238	220
50	487	466	434	425	413	397	373
60	718	690	648	636	620	600	567
70	995	960	907	891	872	846	805
80	1,318	1,276	1,211	1,192	1,168	1,136	1,086
90	1,688	1,638	1,560	1,537	1,509	1,471	1,410
100	2,105	2,045	1,955	1,928	1,894	1,850	1,779

Appendix B

B.8 Factors for Control Charts

Number of Items in Sample, n	Chart for Averages	Chart for Ranges		
	Factors for Control Limits	Factors for Central Line	Factors for Control Limits	
	A_2	d_2	D_3	D_4
2	1.880	1.128	0	3.267
3	1.023	1.693	0	2.575
4	.729	2.059	0	2.282
5	.577	2.326	0	2.115
6	.483	2.534	0	2.004
7	.419	2.704	.076	1.924
8	.373	2.847	.136	1.864
9	.337	2.970	.184	1.816
10	.308	3.078	.223	1.777
11	.285	3.173	.256	1.744
12	.266	3.258	.284	1.716
13	.249	3.336	.308	1.692
14	.235	3.407	.329	1.671
15	.223	3.472	.348	1.652

SOURCE: Adapted from American Society for Testing and Materials, *Manual on Quality Control of Materials,* 1951, Table B2, p. 115. For a more detailed table and explanation, see J. Duncan Acheson, *Quality Control and Industrial Statistics,* 3d ed. (Homewood, IL: Richard D. Irwin, 1974), Table M, p. 927.

Appendix B

B.9 Binomial Probability Distribution

$n = 1$
Probability

x	0.05	0.10	0.20	0.30	0.40	0.50	0.60	0.70	0.80	0.90	0.95
0	0.950	0.900	0.800	0.700	0.600	0.500	0.400	0.300	0.200	0.100	0.050
1	0.050	0.100	0.200	0.300	0.400	0.500	0.600	0.700	0.800	0.900	0.950

$n = 2$
Probability

x	0.05	0.10	0.20	0.30	0.40	0.50	0.60	0.70	0.80	0.90	0.95
0	0.903	0.810	0.640	0.490	0.360	0.250	0.160	0.090	0.040	0.010	0.003
1	0.095	0.180	0.320	0.420	0.480	0.500	0.480	0.420	0.320	0.180	0.095
2	0.003	0.010	0.040	0.090	0.160	0.250	0.360	0.490	0.640	0.810	0.903

$n = 3$
Probability

x	0.05	0.10	0.20	0.30	0.40	0.50	0.60	0.70	0.80	0.90	0.95
0	0.857	0.729	0.512	0.343	0.216	0.125	0.064	0.027	0.008	0.001	0.000
1	0.135	0.243	0.384	0.441	0.432	0.375	0.288	0.189	0.096	0.027	0.007
2	0.007	0.027	0.096	0.189	0.288	0.375	0.432	0.441	0.384	0.243	0.135
3	0.000	0.001	0.008	0.027	0.064	0.125	0.216	0.343	0.512	0.729	0.857

$n = 4$
Probability

x	0.05	0.10	0.20	0.30	0.40	0.50	0.60	0.70	0.80	0.90	0.95
0	0.815	0.656	0.410	0.240	0.130	0.063	0.026	0.008	0.002	0.000	0.000
1	0.171	0.292	0.410	0.412	0.346	0.250	0.154	0.076	0.026	0.004	0.000
2	0.014	0.049	0.154	0.265	0.346	0.375	0.346	0.265	0.154	0.049	0.014
3	0.000	0.004	0.026	0.076	0.154	0.250	0.346	0.412	0.410	0.292	0.171
4	0.000	0.000	0.002	0.008	0.026	0.063	0.130	0.240	0.410	0.656	0.815

$n = 5$
Probability

x	0.05	0.10	0.20	0.30	0.40	0.50	0.60	0.70	0.80	0.90	0.95
0	0.774	0.590	0.328	0.168	0.078	0.031	0.010	0.002	0.000	0.000	0.000
1	0.204	0.328	0.410	0.360	0.259	0.156	0.077	0.028	0.006	0.000	0.000
2	0.021	0.073	0.205	0.309	0.346	0.313	0.230	0.132	0.051	0.008	0.001
3	0.001	0.008	0.051	0.132	0.230	0.313	0.346	0.309	0.205	0.073	0.021
4	0.000	0.000	0.006	0.028	0.077	0.156	0.259	0.360	0.410	0.328	0.204
5	0.000	0.000	0.000	0.002	0.010	0.031	0.078	0.168	0.328	0.590	0.774

B.9 Binomial Probability Distribution (*continued*)

n = 6

Probability

x	0.05	0.10	0.20	0.30	0.40	0.50	0.60	0.70	0.80	0.90	0.95
0	0.735	0.531	0.262	0.118	0.047	0.016	0.004	0.001	0.000	0.000	0.000
1	0.232	0.354	0.393	0.303	0.187	0.094	0.037	0.010	0.002	0.000	0.000
2	0.031	0.098	0.246	0.324	0.311	0.234	0.138	0.060	0.015	0.001	0.000
3	0.002	0.015	0.082	0.185	0.276	0.313	0.276	0.185	0.082	0.015	0.002
4	0.000	0.001	0.015	0.060	0.138	0.234	0.311	0.324	0.246	0.098	0.031
5	0.000	0.000	0.002	0.010	0.037	0.094	0.187	0.303	0.393	0.354	0.232
6	0.000	0.000	0.000	0.001	0.004	0.016	0.047	0.118	0.262	0.531	0.735

n = 7

Probability

x	0.05	0.10	0.20	0.30	0.40	0.50	0.60	0.70	0.80	0.90	0.95
0	0.698	0.478	0.210	0.082	0.028	0.008	0.002	0.000	0.000	0.000	0.000
1	0.257	0.372	0.367	0.247	0.131	0.055	0.017	0.004	0.000	0.000	0.000
2	0.041	0.124	0.275	0.318	0.261	0.164	0.077	0.025	0.004	0.000	0.000
3	0.004	0.023	0.115	0.227	0.290	0.273	0.194	0.097	0.029	0.003	0.000
4	0.000	0.003	0.029	0.097	0.194	0.273	0.290	0.227	0.115	0.023	0.004
5	0.000	0.000	0.004	0.025	0.077	0.164	0.261	0.318	0.275	0.124	0.041
6	0.000	0.000	0.000	0.004	0.017	0.055	0.131	0.247	0.367	0.372	0.257
7	0.000	0.000	0.000	0.000	0.002	0.008	0.028	0.082	0.210	0.478	0.698

n = 8

Probability

x	0.05	0.10	0.20	0.30	0.40	0.50	0.60	0.70	0.80	0.90	0.95
0	0.663	0.430	0.168	0.058	0.017	0.004	0.001	0.000	0.000	0.000	0.000
1	0.279	0.383	0.336	0.198	0.090	0.031	0.008	0.001	0.000	0.000	0.000
2	0.051	0.149	0.294	0.296	0.209	0.109	0.041	0.010	0.001	0.000	0.000
3	0.005	0.033	0.147	0.254	0.279	0.219	0.124	0.047	0.009	0.000	0.000
4	0.000	0.005	0.046	0.136	0.232	0.273	0.232	0.136	0.046	0.005	0.000
5	0.000	0.000	0.009	0.047	0.124	0.219	0.279	0.254	0.147	0.033	0.005
6	0.000	0.000	0.001	0.010	0.041	0.109	0.209	0.296	0.294	0.149	0.051
7	0.000	0.000	0.000	0.001	0.008	0.031	0.090	0.198	0.336	0.383	0.279
8	0.000	0.000	0.000	0.000	0.001	0.004	0.017	0.058	0.168	0.430	0.663

(*continued*)

Appendix B

B.9 Binomial Probability Distribution (*continued*)

$n = 9$

x	\multicolumn{11}{c}{Probability}
	0.05	0.10	0.20	0.30	0.40	0.50	0.60	0.70	0.80	0.90	0.95
0	0.630	0.387	0.134	0.040	0.010	0.002	0.000	0.000	0.000	0.000	0.000
1	0.299	0.387	0.302	0.156	0.060	0.018	0.004	0.000	0.000	0.000	0.000
2	0.063	0.172	0.302	0.267	0.161	0.070	0.021	0.004	0.000	0.000	0.000
3	0.008	0.045	0.176	0.267	0.251	0.164	0.074	0.021	0.003	0.000	0.000
4	0.001	0.007	0.066	0.172	0.251	0.246	0.167	0.074	0.017	0.001	0.000
5	0.000	0.001	0.017	0.074	0.167	0.246	0.251	0.172	0.066	0.007	0.001
6	0.000	0.000	0.003	0.021	0.074	0.164	0.251	0.267	0.176	0.045	0.008
7	0.000	0.000	0.000	0.004	0.021	0.070	0.161	0.267	0.302	0.172	0.063
8	0.000	0.000	0.000	0.000	0.004	0.018	0.060	0.156	0.302	0.387	0.299
9	0.000	0.000	0.000	0.000	0.000	0.002	0.010	0.040	0.134	0.387	0.630

$n = 10$

x	\multicolumn{11}{c}{Probability}
	0.05	0.10	0.20	0.30	0.40	0.50	0.60	0.70	0.80	0.90	0.95
0	0.599	0.349	0.107	0.028	0.006	0.001	0.000	0.000	0.000	0.000	0.000
1	0.315	0.387	0.268	0.121	0.040	0.010	0.002	0.000	0.000	0.000	0.000
2	0.075	0.194	0.302	0.233	0.121	0.044	0.011	0.001	0.000	0.000	0.000
3	0.010	0.057	0.201	0.267	0.215	0.117	0.042	0.009	0.001	0.000	0.000
4	0.001	0.011	0.088	0.200	0.251	0.205	0.111	0.037	0.006	0.000	0.000
5	0.000	0.001	0.026	0.103	0.201	0.246	0.201	0.103	0.026	0.001	0.000
6	0.000	0.000	0.006	0.037	0.111	0.205	0.251	0.200	0.088	0.011	0.001
7	0.000	0.000	0.001	0.009	0.042	0.117	0.215	0.267	0.201	0.057	0.010
8	0.000	0.000	0.000	0.001	0.011	0.044	0.121	0.233	0.302	0.194	0.075
9	0.000	0.000	0.000	0.000	0.002	0.010	0.040	0.121	0.268	0.387	0.315
10	0.000	0.000	0.000	0.000	0.000	0.001	0.006	0.028	0.107	0.349	0.599

$n = 11$

x	\multicolumn{11}{c}{Probability}
	0.05	0.10	0.20	0.30	0.40	0.50	0.60	0.70	0.80	0.90	0.95
0	0.569	0.314	0.086	0.020	0.004	0.000	0.000	0.000	0.000	0.000	0.000
1	0.329	0.384	0.236	0.093	0.027	0.005	0.001	0.000	0.000	0.000	0.000
2	0.087	0.213	0.295	0.200	0.089	0.027	0.005	0.001	0.000	0.000	0.000
3	0.014	0.071	0.221	0.257	0.177	0.081	0.023	0.004	0.000	0.000	0.000
4	0.001	0.016	0.111	0.220	0.236	0.161	0.070	0.017	0.002	0.000	0.000
5	0.000	0.002	0.039	0.132	0.221	0.226	0.147	0.057	0.010	0.000	0.000
6	0.000	0.000	0.010	0.057	0.147	0.226	0.221	0.132	0.039	0.002	0.000
7	0.000	0.000	0.002	0.017	0.070	0.161	0.236	0.220	0.111	0.016	0.001
8	0.000	0.000	0.000	0.004	0.023	0.081	0.177	0.257	0.221	0.071	0.014
9	0.000	0.000	0.000	0.001	0.005	0.027	0.089	0.200	0.295	0.213	0.087
10	0.000	0.000	0.000	0.000	0.001	0.005	0.027	0.093	0.236	0.384	0.329
11	0.000	0.000	0.000	0.000	0.000	0.000	0.004	0.020	0.086	0.314	0.569

B.9 Binomial Probability Distribution (*continued*)

n = 12

Probability

x	0.05	0.10	0.20	0.30	0.40	0.50	0.60	0.70	0.80	0.90	0.95
0	0.540	0.282	0.069	0.014	0.002	0.000	0.000	0.000	0.000	0.000	0.000
1	0.341	0.377	0.206	0.071	0.017	0.003	0.000	0.000	0.000	0.000	0.000
2	0.099	0.230	0.283	0.168	0.064	0.016	0.002	0.000	0.000	0.000	0.000
3	0.017	0.085	0.236	0.240	0.142	0.054	0.012	0.001	0.000	0.000	0.000
4	0.002	0.021	0.133	0.231	0.213	0.121	0.042	0.008	0.001	0.000	0.000
5	0.000	0.004	0.053	0.158	0.227	0.193	0.101	0.029	0.003	0.000	0.000
6	0.000	0.000	0.016	0.079	0.177	0.226	0.177	0.079	0.016	0.000	0.000
7	0.000	0.000	0.003	0.029	0.101	0.193	0.227	0.158	0.053	0.004	0.000
8	0.000	0.000	0.001	0.008	0.042	0.121	0.213	0.231	0.133	0.021	0.002
9	0.000	0.000	0.000	0.001	0.012	0.054	0.142	0.240	0.236	0.085	0.017
10	0.000	0.000	0.000	0.000	0.002	0.016	0.064	0.168	0.283	0.230	0.099
11	0.000	0.000	0.000	0.000	0.000	0.003	0.017	0.071	0.206	0.377	0.341
12	0.000	0.000	0.000	0.000	0.000	0.000	0.002	0.014	0.069	0.282	0.540

n = 13

Probability

x	0.05	0.10	0.20	0.30	0.40	0.50	0.60	0.70	0.80	0.90	0.95
0	0.513	0.254	0.055	0.010	0.001	0.000	0.000	0.000	0.000	0.000	0.000
1	0.351	0.367	0.179	0.054	0.011	0.002	0.000	0.000	0.000	0.000	0.000
2	0.111	0.245	0.268	0.139	0.045	0.010	0.001	0.000	0.000	0.000	0.000
3	0.021	0.100	0.246	0.218	0.111	0.035	0.006	0.001	0.000	0.000	0.000
4	0.003	0.028	0.154	0.234	0.184	0.087	0.024	0.003	0.000	0.000	0.000
5	0.000	0.006	0.069	0.180	0.221	0.157	0.066	0.014	0.001	0.000	0.000
6	0.000	0.001	0.023	0.103	0.197	0.209	0.131	0.044	0.006	0.000	0.000
7	0.000	0.000	0.006	0.044	0.131	0.209	0.197	0.103	0.023	0.001	0.000
8	0.000	0.000	0.001	0.014	0.066	0.157	0.221	0.180	0.069	0.006	0.000
9	0.000	0.000	0.000	0.003	0.024	0.087	0.184	0.234	0.154	0.028	0.003
10	0.000	0.000	0.000	0.001	0.006	0.035	0.111	0.218	0.246	0.100	0.021
11	0.000	0.000	0.000	0.000	0.001	0.010	0.045	0.139	0.268	0.245	0.111
12	0.000	0.000	0.000	0.000	0.000	0.002	0.011	0.054	0.179	0.367	0.351
13	0.000	0.000	0.000	0.000	0.000	0.000	0.001	0.010	0.055	0.254	0.513

(*continued*)

Appendix B

B.9 Binomial Probability Distribution (*concluded*)

$n = 14$

Probability

x	0.05	0.10	0.20	0.30	0.40	0.50	0.60	0.70	0.80	0.90	0.95
0	0.488	0.229	0.044	0.007	0.001	0.000	0.000	0.000	0.000	0.000	0.000
1	0.359	0.356	0.154	0.041	0.007	0.001	0.000	0.000	0.000	0.000	0.000
2	0.123	0.257	0.250	0.113	0.032	0.006	0.001	0.000	0.000	0.000	0.000
3	0.026	0.114	0.250	0.194	0.085	0.022	0.003	0.000	0.000	0.000	0.000
4	0.004	0.035	0.172	0.229	0.155	0.061	0.014	0.001	0.000	0.000	0.000
5	0.000	0.008	0.086	0.196	0.207	0.122	0.041	0.007	0.000	0.000	0.000
6	0.000	0.001	0.032	0.126	0.207	0.183	0.092	0.023	0.002	0.000	0.000
7	0.000	0.000	0.009	0.062	0.157	0.209	0.157	0.062	0.009	0.000	0.000
8	0.000	0.000	0.002	0.023	0.092	0.183	0.207	0.126	0.032	0.001	0.000
9	0.000	0.000	0.000	0.007	0.041	0.122	0.207	0.196	0.086	0.008	0.000
10	0.000	0.000	0.000	0.001	0.014	0.061	0.155	0.229	0.172	0.035	0.004
11	0.000	0.000	0.000	0.000	0.003	0.022	0.085	0.194	0.250	0.114	0.026
12	0.000	0.000	0.000	0.000	0.001	0.006	0.032	0.113	0.250	0.257	0.123
13	0.000	0.000	0.000	0.000	0.000	0.001	0.007	0.041	0.154	0.356	0.359
14	0.000	0.000	0.000	0.000	0.000	0.000	0.001	0.007	0.044	0.229	0.488

$n = 15$

Probability

x	0.05	0.10	0.20	0.30	0.40	0.50	0.60	0.70	0.80	0.90	0.95
0	0.463	0.206	0.035	0.005	0.000	0.000	0.000	0.000	0.000	0.000	0.000
1	0.366	0.343	0.132	0.031	0.005	0.000	0.000	0.000	0.000	0.000	0.000
2	0.135	0.267	0.231	0.092	0.022	0.003	0.000	0.000	0.000	0.000	0.000
3	0.031	0.129	0.250	0.170	0.063	0.014	0.002	0.000	0.000	0.000	0.000
4	0.005	0.043	0.188	0.219	0.127	0.042	0.007	0.001	0.000	0.000	0.000
5	0.001	0.010	0.103	0.206	0.186	0.092	0.024	0.003	0.000	0.000	0.000
6	0.000	0.002	0.043	0.147	0.207	0.153	0.061	0.012	0.001	0.000	0.000
7	0.000	0.000	0.014	0.081	0.177	0.196	0.118	0.035	0.003	0.000	0.000
8	0.000	0.000	0.003	0.035	0.118	0.196	0.177	0.081	0.014	0.000	0.000
9	0.000	0.000	0.001	0.012	0.061	0.153	0.207	0.147	0.043	0.002	0.000
10	0.000	0.000	0.000	0.003	0.024	0.092	0.186	0.206	0.103	0.010	0.001
11	0.000	0.000	0.000	0.001	0.007	0.042	0.127	0.219	0.188	0.043	0.005
12	0.000	0.000	0.000	0.000	0.002	0.014	0.063	0.170	0.250	0.129	0.031
13	0.000	0.000	0.000	0.000	0.000	0.003	0.022	0.092	0.231	0.267	0.135
14	0.000	0.000	0.000	0.000	0.000	0.000	0.005	0.031	0.132	0.343	0.366
15	0.000	0.000	0.000	0.000	0.000	0.000	0.000	0.005	0.035	0.206	0.463

Appendix C: Answers

Answers to Odd-Numbered Chapter Exercises

CHAPTER 1
1. **a.** Interval
   b. Ratio
   c. Nominal
   d. Nominal
   e. Ordinal
   f. Ratio
3. Answers will vary.
5. Qualitative data is not numerical, whereas quantitative data is numerical. Examples will vary by student.
7. A discrete variable may assume only certain values. A continuous variable may assume an infinite number of values within a given range. The number of traffic citations issued each day during February in Garden City Beach, South Carolina, is a discrete variable. The weight of commercial trucks passing the weigh station at milepost 195 on Interstate 95 in North Carolina is a continuous variable.
9. **a.** Ordinal
   b. Interval
   c. The newer system provides information on the distance between exits.
11. If you were using this store as typical of all Barnes & Noble stores, then it would be sample data. However, if you were considering it as the only store of interest, then the data would represent the population.
13.

	Discrete Variable	Continuous Variable
Qualitative	b. Gender d. Soft drink preference	
Quantitative	f. SAT scores g. Student rank in class h. Rating of a finance professor i. Number of home computers	a. Salary c. Sales volume of MP3 players e. Temperature

	Discrete	Continuous
Nominal	b. Gender	
Ordinal	d. Soft drink preference g. Student rank in class h. Rating of a finance professor	
Interval	f. SAT scores	e. Temperature
Ratio	i. Number of home computers	a. Salary c. Sales volume of MP3 players

15. According to the sample information, 120/300 or 40% would accept a job transfer.
17. **a.** Total sales increased by 106,041, found by 1,255,337 − 1,149,296, which is a 9.2% increase.

b. Market shares are:

	2010	2009
General Motors	22.9%	22.0%
Ford Motor	19.9%	16.2%
Chrysler	11.3%	12.7%
Toyota	15.8%	19.7%
American Honda	11.8%	12.4%
Nissan NA	10.6%	9.4%
Hyundai	5.1%	4.8%
Mazda	2.6%	2.8%

Ford has gained 3.7% and Toyota lost 3.9% of their market shares.
c. Percentage changes are:

General Motors	increase of 13.7%
Ford Motor	increase of 34.3%
Chrysler	decrease of 3.2%
Toyota	decrease of 12.4%
American Honda	increase of 3.9%
Nissan NA	increase of 22.8%
Hyundai	increase of 17.0%
Mazda	increase of 2.9%

Ford and Nissan had increases of more than 20%. General Motors and Hyundai had increases of more than 10%. Meanwhile, Toyota had a decrease of over 10%.
19. Earnings increased each year over the previous year until a large peak in 2008. Then there was a rather large drop in 2009. Earnings increased again in 2010.
21. **a.** League is a qualitative variable; the others are quantitative.
   b. League is a nominal-level variable; the others are ratio-level variables.

CHAPTER 2
1. 25% market share.
3.

Season	Frequency	Relative Frequency
Winter	100	.10
Spring	300	.30
Summer	400	.40
Fall	200	.20
	1,000	1.00

5. **a.** A frequency table.

Color	Frequency	Relative Frequency
Bright White	130	0.10
Metallic Black	104	0.08
Magnetic Lime	325	0.25
Tangerine Orange	455	0.35
Fusion Red	286	0.22
Total	1,300	1.00

b.

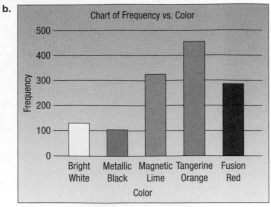

c.

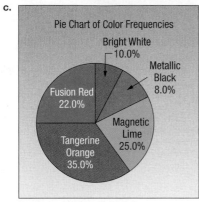

d. 350,000 orange, 250,000 lime, 220,000 red, 100,000 white, and 80,000 black, found by multiplying relative frequency by 1,000,000 production.

7. $2^5 = 32$, $2^6 = 64$, therefore, 6 classes

9. $2^7 = 128$, $2^8 = 256$, suggests 8 classes

$i \geq \dfrac{\$567 - \$235}{8} = 41$ Class intervals of 45 or 50 would be acceptable.

11. **a.** $2^4 = 16$ Suggests 5 classes.

  b. $i \geq \dfrac{31 - 25}{5} = 1.2$ Use interval of 1.5.

  c. 24

  d.

Units	f	Relative Frequency
24.0 up to 25.5	2	0.125
25.5 up to 27.0	4	0.250
27.0 up to 28.5	8	0.500
28.5 up to 30.0	0	0.000
30.0 up to 31.5	2	0.125
Total	16	1.000

  e. The largest concentration is in the 27.0 up to 28.5 class (8).

13. **a.**

Number of Visits	f
0 up to 3	9
3 up to 6	21
6 up to 9	13
9 up to 12	4
12 up to 15	3
15 up to 18	1
Total	51

b. The largest group of shoppers (21) shop at the BiLo Supermarket 3, 4, or 5 times during a month period. Some customers visit the store only 1 time during the month, but others shop as many as 15 times.

c.

Number of Visits	Percent of Total
0 up to 3	17.65
3 up to 6	41.18
6 up to 9	25.49
9 up to 12	7.84
12 up to 15	5.88
15 up to 18	1.96
Total	100.00

15. **a.** Histogram
  b. 100
  c. 5
  d. 28
  e. 0.28
  f. 12.5
  g. 13

17. **a.** 50
  b. 1.5 thousand miles, or 1,500 miles.
  c.

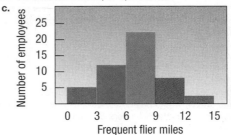

  d. $X = 1.5$, $Y = 5$
  e.

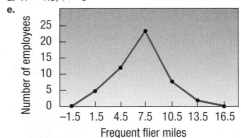

  f. For the 50 employees, about half traveled between 6,000 and 9,000 miles. Five employees traveled less than 3,000 miles, and 2 traveled more than 12,000 miles.

19. **a.** 40
  b. 5
  c. 11 or 12
  d. About $20/hr
  e. About $9/hr
  f. About 75%

21. **a.** 5
  b.

Frequent Flier Miles	f	CF
0 up to 3	5	5
3 up to 6	12	17
6 up to 9	23	40
9 up to 12	8	48
12 up to 15	2	50

c.

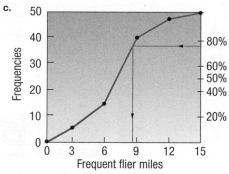

d. About 8.7 thousand miles

23. **a.** A qualitative variable uses either the nominal or ordinal scale of measurement. It is usually the result of counts. Quantitative variables are either discrete or continuous. There is a natural order to the results for a quantitative variable. Quantitative variables can use either the interval or ratio scale of measurement.
   b. Both types of variables can be used for samples and populations.

25. **a.** Frequency table
   b.

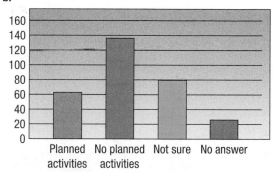

   c.

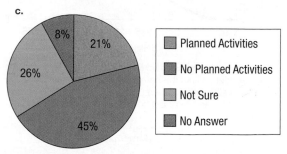

   d. A pie chart would be better because it clearly shows that nearly half of the customers prefer no planned activities.

27. $2^6 = 64$ and $2^7 = 128$, suggest 7 classes

29. **a.** 5, because $2^4 = 16 < 25$ and $2^5 = 32 > 25$
   b. $i \geq \dfrac{48 - 16}{5} = 6.4$ Use interval of 7.
   c. 15
   d.

Class		Frequency
15 up to 22	|||	3
22 up to 29	JHÍ III	8
29 up to 36	JHÍ II	7
36 up to 43	JHÍ	5
43 up to 50	II	2
		25

   e. It is fairly symmetric, with most of the values between 22 and 36.

31. **a.** $2^5 = 32$, $2^6 = 64$, 6 classes recommended.
   b. $i = \dfrac{10 - 1}{6} = 1.5$, use an interval of 2.
   c. 0
   d.

Class	Frequency
0 up to 2	1
2 up to 4	5
4 up to 6	12
6 up to 8	17
8 up to 10	8

   e. The distribution is fairly symmetric or bell-shaped with a large peak in the middle of the two classes of 4 up to 8.

33.

Class	Frequency
0 up to 200	19
200 up to 400	1
400 up to 600	4
600 up to 800	1
800 up to 1000	2

This distribution is positively skewed with a large "tail" to the right or positive values. Notice that the top 7 tunes account for 4,342 plays out of a total of 5,968 or about 73% of all plays.

35. **a.** 56   **c.** 55
   b. 10 (found by $60 - 50$)   **d.** 17

37. **a.** $30.50, found by ($265 − $82)/6
   b. $35
   c.

$ 70 up to $105	4
105 up to 140	17
140 up to 175	14
175 up to 210	2
210 up to 245	6
245 up to 280	1

   d. The purchases range from a low of about $70 to a high of about $280. The concentration is in the $105 up to $140 and $140 up to $175 classes.

39.

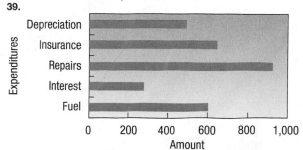

41.

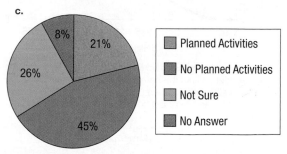

SC Income	Percent	Cumulative
Wages	73	73
Dividends	11	84
IRA	8	92
Pensions	3	95
Social Security	2	97
Other	3	100

By far the largest part of income in South Carolina is wages. Almost three-fourths of the adjusted gross income comes from wages. Dividends and IRAs each contribute roughly another 10%.

43. a. Since $2^6 = 64 < 70 < 128 = 2^7$, 7 classes are recommended. The interval should be at least $(1,002.2 - 3.3)/7 = 142.7$. Use 150 as a convenient value.

Frequency Distribution	
0 up to 150	28
150 up to 300	19
300 up to 450	15
450 up to 600	2
600 up to 750	4
750 up to 1050	1
Total	70

b.

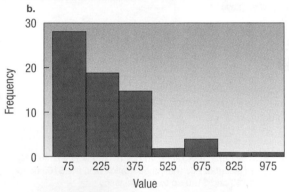

45. a. Pie chart
b. 215, found by 0.43×500
c. Seventy-eight percent are in either a house of worship (43%) or outdoors (35%).

47. a.

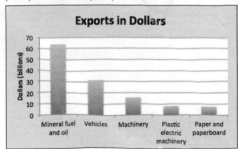

b. 0.42; $(63.9 + 31.6)/224.9$
c. 0.75; $(63.9 + 31.6)/127.0$

49.

Color	Frequency
Brown	130
Yellow	98
Red	96
Blue	52
Orange	35
Green	33
	444

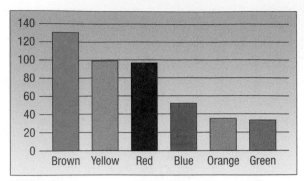

Brown, yellow, and red M&M's make up almost 75 percent. The other 25 percent are blue, orange, and green.

51. $i \geq \dfrac{345.3 - 125.0}{7} = 31.47$ Use interval of 35.

Selling Price	f	CF
110 up to 145	3	3
145 up to 180	19	22
180 up to 215	31	53
215 up to 250	25	78
250 up to 285	14	92
285 up to 320	10	102
320 up to 355	3	105

a. Most homes (53%) are in the 180 up to 250 range.
b. $127.5 (110 + 17.5)$; $337.5 (320 + 17.5)$
c.

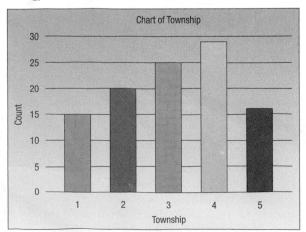

About 42 homes sold for less than 200.
About 55% of the homes sold for less than 220.
So 45% sold for more.
Less than 1% of the homes sold for less than 125.

d.

Townships 3 and 4 have more sales than the average and Townships 1 and 5 have somewhat less than the average.

53. Since $2^6 = 64 < 80 < 128 = 2^7$, use 7 classes. The interval should be at least $(1008 - 741)/7 = 38.14$ miles. Use 40. The resulting frequency distribution is:

Class	f
730 up to 770	5
770 up to 810	17
810 up to 850	37
850 up to 890	18
890 up to 930	1
930 up to 970	0
970 up to 1010	2

a. The typical amount driven is 830 miles. The range is from 730 up to 1010 miles.
b. The distribution is "bell shaped" around 830. However, there are two outliers up around 1000 miles.
c.

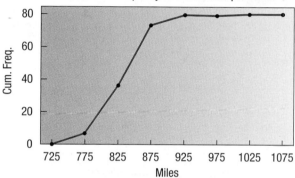

Cumulative Frequency of Miles Driven per Month

Forty percent of the buses were driven fewer than 820 miles.
Fifty-nine buses were driven less than 850 miles.

d.

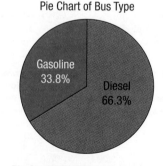

Pie Chart of Bus Type

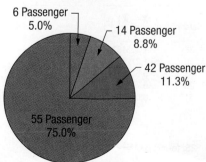

Pie Chart of Seats

The first chart shows that about two-thirds of the buses are diesel. The second diagram shows that nearly three fourths of the buses have 55 seats.

CHAPTER 3

1. $\mu = 5.4$, found by 27/5
3. **a.** $\bar{X} = 7.0$, found by 28/4
   b. $(5 - 7) + (9 - 7) + (4 - 7) + (10 - 7) = 0$
5. $\bar{X} = 14.58$, found by 43.74/3
7. **a.** 15.4, found by 154/10
   b. Population parameter, since it includes all the salespeople at Midtown Ford
9. **a.** \$54.55, found by \$1,091/20
   b. A sample statistic—assuming that the power company serves more than 20 customers
11. $\bar{X} = \dfrac{\Sigma X}{n}$ so
   $\Sigma X = \bar{X} \cdot n = (\$5430)(30) = \$162,900$
13. \$22.91, found by $\dfrac{300(\$20) + 400(\$25) + 400(\$23)}{300 + 400 + 400}$
15. \$17.75, found by (\$400 + \$750 + \$2,400)/200
17. **a.** No mode
   b. The given value would be the mode.
   c. 3 and 4 bimodal
19. **a.** Mean = 3.33
   b. Median = 5
   c. Mode = 5
21. **a.** Median = 2.9
   b. Mode = 2.9
23. $\bar{X} = \dfrac{647}{11} = 58.82$
   Median = 58, Mode = 58
   Any of the three measures would be satisfactory.
25. **a.** $\bar{X} = \dfrac{90.4}{12} = 7.53$
   b. Median = 7.45. There are several modes: 6.5, 7.3, 7.8, and 8.7.
   c. $\bar{X} = \dfrac{33.8}{4} = 8.45,$
   Median = 8.7
   About 1 percentage point higher in Winter
27. **a.** 7, found by $10 - 3$.
   b. 6, found by 30/5.
   c. 2.4, found by 12/5.
   d. The difference between the highest number sold (10) and the smallest number sold (3) is 7. On average, the number of HDTVs sold deviates by 2.4 from the mean of 6.
29. **a.** 30, found by $54 - 24$.
   b. 38, found by 380/10.
   c. 7.2, found by 72/10.
   d. The difference of 54 and 24 is 30. On average, the number of minutes required to install a door deviates 7.2 minutes from the mean of 38 minutes.
31.

State	Mean	Median	Range
California	33.10	34.0	32
Iowa	24.50	25.0	19

The mean and median ratings were higher for California, but there was also more variation in California.
33. **a.** 5
   b. 4.4, found by
   $$\dfrac{(8 - 5)^2 + (3 - 5)^2 + (7 - 5)^2 + (3 - 5)^2 + (4 - 5)^2}{5}$$
35. **a.** \$2.77
   b. 1.26, found by
   $$\dfrac{\substack{(2.68 - 2.77)^2 + (1.03 - 2.77)^2 + (2.26 - 2.77)^2 \\ + (4.30 - 2.77)^2 + (3.58 - 2.77)^2}}{5}$$

37. a. Range: 7.3, found by $11.6 - 4.3$. Arithmetic mean: 6.94, found by 34.7/5. Variance: 6.5944, found by 32.972/5. Standard deviation: 2.568, found by $\sqrt{6.5944}$.

b. Dennis has a higher mean return $(11.76 > 6.94)$. However, Dennis has greater spread in its returns on equity $(16.89 > 6.59)$.

39. a. $\bar{X} = 4$

$$s^2 = \frac{(7-4)^2 + \cdots + (3-4)^2}{5-1} = \frac{22}{5-1} = 5.5$$

b. $s = 2.3452$

41. a. $\bar{X} = 38$

$$s^2 = \frac{(28-38)^2 + \cdots + (42-38)^2}{10-1} = 82.667$$

$$s^2 = \frac{744}{10-1} = 82.667$$

b. $s = 9.0921$

43. a. $\bar{X} = \dfrac{951}{10} = 95.1$

$$s^2 = \frac{(101-95.1)^2 + \cdots + (88-95.1)^2}{10-1}$$

$$= \frac{1,112.9}{9} = 123.66$$

b. $s = \sqrt{123.66} = 11.12$

45. About 69%, found by $1 - 1/(1.8)^2$

47. a. About 95%
b. 47.5%, 2.5%

49. a. Mean = 5, found by $(6+4+3+7+5)/5$. Median is 5, found by rearranging the values and selecting the middle value.

b. Population, because all partners were included

c. $\Sigma(X - \mu) = (6-5) + (4-5) + (3-5) + (7-5) + (5-5) = 0$

51. $\bar{X} = \dfrac{545}{16} = 34.06$

Median = 37.50

53. The mean is 35.675, found by 1427/40. The median is 36, found by sorting the data and averaging the 20th and 21st observations.

55. $\bar{X}_w = \dfrac{\$5.00(270) + \$6.50(300) + \$8.00(100)}{270 + 300 + 100} = \$6.12$

57. $\bar{X}_w = \dfrac{[15,300(4.5) + 10,400(3.0) + 150,600(10.2)]}{176,300} = 9.28$

59.
a. 55, found by $72 - 17$
b. 14.4, found by 144/10, where $\bar{X} = 43.2$
c. 17.6245

61. a. There were 13 flights, so all items are considered.

b. $\mu = \dfrac{2,259}{13} = 173.77$

Median = 195

c. Range = $301 - 7 = 294$

$$s = \sqrt{\frac{133,846}{13}} = 101.47$$

63. a. The mean is $717.20, found by $17,930/25. The median is $717.00 and there are two modes, $710 and $722.

b. The range is $90, found by $771 - $681, and the standard deviation is $24.87, found by the square root of 14,850/24.

c. From $667.46 up to $766.94, found by $717.20 $\pm 2(\$24.87)$.

65. a. Mean = 9.1, found by 273/30. Median is 9, found by averaging the 15th and 16th values.

b. Range = 14, found by $18 - 4$. Standard deviation = 3.566, found by the square root of (368.7/29).

67. a. The mean team payroll is $91,016,667, rounded to $91.0 million. The median is $84,300,000, rounded to $84.3 million. Since the distribution is positively skewed, the median is a better measure of location.

b. The range is $171,400,000, or $171.4 million. The standard deviation is $38,254,935, or $38.3 million. Using the data rounded to the nearest $0.1 million, 75% of the team payrolls are between $14.4 million and $167.6 million.

c. The AL mean and standard deviation are $96,992,857, or $98.0 million, and $43,724,812, or $43.7 million. The NL mean and standard deviation are $85,787,500, or $85.8 million, and $33,314,739, or $33.3 million. The AL team payroll has a larger mean and more dispersion.

CHAPTER 4

1. a. Dot plot **b.** 15
c. 1, 7 **d.** 2 and 3

3. Median = 53, found by $(11+1)(\frac{1}{2})$ ∴ 6th value in from lowest
$Q_1 = 49$, found by $(11+1)(\frac{1}{4})$ ∴ 3rd value in from lowest
$Q_3 = 55$, found by $(11+1)(\frac{3}{4})$ ∴ 9th value in from lowest

5. a. $Q_1 = 33.25$, $Q_3 = 50.25$
b. $D_2 = 27.8$, $D_8 = 52.6$
c. $P_{67} = 47$

7. a. 350
b. $Q_1 = 175$, $Q_3 = 930$
c. $930 - 175 = 755$
d. Less than 0, or more than about 2,060
e. There are no outliers.
f. The distribution is positively skewed.

9.

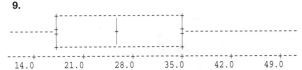

The distribution is somewhat positively skewed. Note that the dashed line above 35 is longer than below 18.

11. a. The mean is 30.8, found by 154/5. The median is 31.0, and the standard deviation is 3.96, found by

$$s = \sqrt{\frac{62.8}{4}} = 3.96$$

b. -0.15, found by $\dfrac{3(30.8 - 31.0)}{3.96}$

c.

Salary	$\left(\dfrac{X - \bar{X}}{s}\right)$	$\left(\dfrac{X - \bar{X}}{s}\right)^3$
36	1.313131	2.264250504
26	-1.212121	-1.780894343
33	0.555556	0.171467764
28	-0.707071	-0.353499282
31	0.050505	0.000128826
		0.301453469

0.125, found by $[5/(4 \times 3)] \times 0.301$

13. a. The mean is 21.93, found by 328.9/15. The median is 15.8, and the standard deviation is 21.18, found by

$$s = \sqrt{\frac{6283}{14}} = 21.18$$

b. 0.868, found by [3(21.93 − 15.8)]/21.18
c. 2.444, found by [15/(14 × 13)] × 29.658

15.

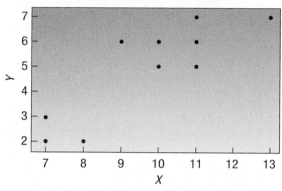

Scatter Diagram of *Y* versus *X*

There is a positive relationship between the variables.

17. a. Both variables are nominal scale.
b. Contingency table
c. Men are about twice as likely to order a dessert. From the table, 32% of the men ordered dessert, but only 15% of the women.

19. a. Dot plot
b. 15
c. 5

21. a. $L_{50} = (20 + 1)\frac{50}{100} = 10.50$

Median $= \frac{83.7 + 85.6}{2} = 84.65$

$L_{25} = (21)(.25) = 5.25$
$Q_1 = 66.6 + .25(72.9 − 66.6) = 68.175$
$L_{75} = 21(.75) = 15.75$
$Q_3 = 87.1 + .75(90.2 − 87.1) = 89.425$

b. $L_{26} = 21(.26) = 5.46$
$P_{26} = 66.6 + .46(72.9 − 66.6) = 69.498$
$L_{83} = 21(.83) = 17.43$
$P_{83} = 93.3 + .43(98.6 − 93.3) = 95.579$

c.

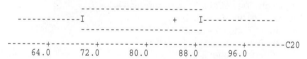

23. a. $Q_1 = 26.25$, $Q_3 = 35.75$, Median = 31.50

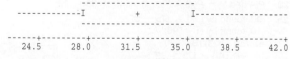

b. $Q_1 = 33.25$, $Q_3 = 38.75$, Median = 37.50

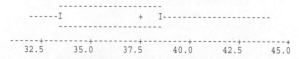

c. The median time for public transportation is about 6 minutes less. There is more variation in public

transportation. The difference between Q_1 and Q_3 is 9.5 minutes for public transportation and 5.5 minutes for private transportation.

25. The distribution is positively skewed. The first quartile is about $20 and the third quartile is about $90. There is one outlier located at $255. The median is about $50.

27. a.

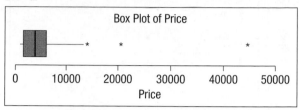

Median is 3733. First quartile is 1478. Third quartile is 6141. So prices over 13,135.5, found by 6141 + 1.5 (6141 − 1478), are outliers. There are three (13,925, 20,413, and 44,312).

b.

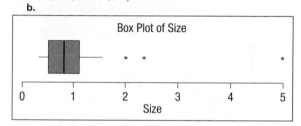

Median is 0.84. First quartile is 0.515. Third quartile is 1.12. So sizes over 2.0275, found by 1.12 + 1.5 (1.12 − 0.515), are outliers. There are three (2.03, 2.35, and 5.03).

c.

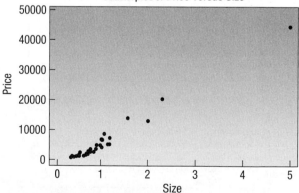

There is a direct association between them. The first observation is larger on both scales.

d.

Shape\Cut	Average	Good	Ideal	Premium	Ultra Ideal	All
Emerald	0	0	1	0	0	1
Marquise	0	2	0	1	0	3
Oval	0	0	0	1	0	1
Princess	1	0	2	2	0	5
Round	1	3	3	13	3	23
Total	2	5	6	17	3	33

The majority of the diamonds are round (23). Premium cut is most common (17). The Round Premium combination occurs most often (13).

29. $sk = 0.065$ or $sk = \dfrac{3(7.7143 - 8.0)}{3.9036} = -0.22$

31.

Scatterplot of Accidents versus Age

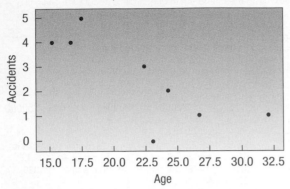

As age increases, the number of accidents decreases.

33. **a.** 139,340,000
   b. 5.4% unemployed, found by (7523/139,340)100
   c. Men $=$ 5.64%
   Women $=$ 5.12%

35. **a.**

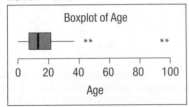

There are five outliers. There is a group of three around 50 years (Angels, Athletics, and Dodgers) and a group of two close to 100 years old (Cubs and Red Sox).

b.

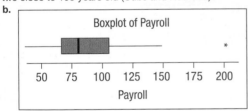

Using equation 4–1 (if using Excel, see software commands) and rounding to the nearest $0.1 million, the first quartile is $61.4 million, the third quartile is $105.8 million. The distribution is positively skewed, with the New York Yankees a definite outlier.

c.

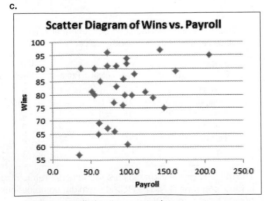

Higher payrolls lead to more wins.

d.

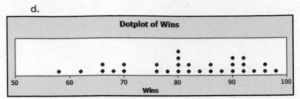

The distribution is fairly uniform between 57 and 97.

CHAPTER 5

1.

	Person	
Outcome	1	2
1	A	A
2	A	F
3	F	A
4	F	F

3. **a.** .176, found by $\dfrac{6}{34}$ **b.** Empirical

5. **a.** Empirical
   b. Classical
   c. Classical
   d. Empirical, based on seismological data

7. **a.** The survey of 40 people about environmental issues
   b. 26 or more respond yes, for example.
   c. $10/40 = .25$
   d. Empirical
   e. The events are not equally likely, but they are mutually exclusive.

9. **a.** Answers will vary. Here are some possibilities:
   123, 124, 125, 999
   b. $(1/10)^3$
   c. Classical

11. $P(A \text{ or } B) = P(A) + P(B) = .30 + .20 = .50$
   $P(\text{neither}) = 1 - .50 = .50$.

13. **a.** $102/200 = .51$
   b. .49, found by $61/200 + 37/200 = .305 + .185$.
   Special rule of addition.

15. $P(\text{above } C) = .25 + .50 = .75$

17. $P(A \text{ or } B) = P(A) + P(B) - P(A \text{ and } B)$
   $= .20 + .30 - .15 = .35$

19. When two events are mutually exclusive, it means that if one occurs, the other event cannot occur. Therefore, the probability of their joint occurrence is zero.

21. **a.** $P(P \text{ and } F) = 0.20$
   b. $P(P \text{ and } D) = 0.30$
   c. No
   d. Joint probability
   e. $P(P \text{ or } D \text{ or } F) = 1 - P(P \text{ and } D \text{ and } F)$
   $= 1 - .10 = .90$

23. $P(A \text{ and } B) = P(A) \times P(B|A) = .40 \times .30 = .12$

25. .90, found by $(.80 + .60) - .5$.
   .10, found by $(1 - .90)$.

27. **a.** $P(A_1) = 3/10 = .30$
   b. $P(B_1|A_2) = 1/3 = .33$
   c. $P(B_2 \text{ and } A_3) = 1/10 = .10$

29. **a.** A contingency table
   b. .27, found by $300/500 \times 135/300$
   c. The tree diagram would appear as:

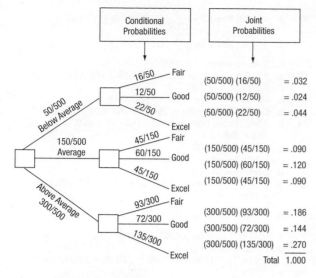

	Conditional Probabilities		Joint Probabilities

50/500 Below Average

- 16/50 → Fair — (50/500) (16/50) = .032
- 12/50 → Good — (50/500) (12/50) = .024
- 22/50 → Excel — (50/500) (22/50) = .044

150/500 Average

- 45/150 → Fair — (150/500) (45/150) = .090
- 60/150 → Good — (150/500) (60/150) = .120
- 45/150 → Excel — (150/500) (45/150) = .090

300/500 Above Average

- 93/300 → Fair — (300/500) (93/300) = .186
- 72/300 → Good — (300/500) (72/300) = .144
- 135/300 → Excel — (300/500) (135/300) = .270

Total 1.000

31.   **a.** Contingency table
     b. 0.842, found by 32/38
     c. Independence requires that $P(A \mid B) = P(A)$. One possibility is: $P(\text{Good} \mid 20 \text{ up to } 30 \text{ yards}) = P(\text{Good})$. Does $12/12 = 32/38$? No, the two variables are not independent.
     d. 0.895, found by $12/38 + 32/38 - 10/38$
     e. 0.026, found by 1/38

33.   **a.** 78,960,960
     b. 840, found by (7)(6)(5)(4). That is 7!/3!
     c. 10, found by 5!/3!2!

35. 210, found by (10)(9)(8)(7)/(4)(3)(2)

37. 120, found by 5!

39. 10,897,286,400, found by
     $_{15}P_{10} = (15)(14)(13)(12)(11)(10)(9)(8)(7)(6)$

41.   **a.** Asking teenagers to compare their reactions to a newly developed soft drink.
     b. Answers will vary. One possibility is more than half of the respondents like it.

43. Subjective

45.   **a.** 4/9, found by $(2/3) \cdot (2/3)$.
     b. 3/4, because $(3/4) \cdot (2/3) = 0.5$.

47.   **a.** .8145, found by $(.95)^4$
     b. Special rule of multiplication
     c. $P(A \text{ and } B \text{ and } C \text{ and } D) = P(A) \times P(B) \times P(C) \times P(D)$

49.   **a.** .08, found by $.80 \times .10$
     b. No; 90% of females attended college, 78% of males
     c.

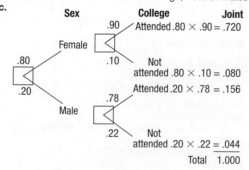

Sex	College	Joint

Female .80
- .90 Attended $.80 \times .90 = .720$
- .10 Not attended $.80 \times .10 = .080$

Male .20
- .78 Attended $.20 \times .78 = .156$
- .22 Not attended $.20 \times .22 = .044$

Total 1.000

     d. Yes, because all the possible outcomes are shown on the tree diagram.

51.   **a.** 0.57, found by 57/100
     b. 0.97, found by $(57/100) + (40/100)$
     c. Yes, because an employee cannot be both.
     d. 0.03, found by $1 - 0.97$

53.   **a.** 1/2, found by $(2/3)(3/4)$
     b. 1/12, found by $(1/3)(1/4)$
     c. 11/12, found by $1 - 1/12$

55.   **a.** 0.9039, found by $(0.98)^5$
     b. 0.0961, found by $1 - 0.9039$

57.   **a.** 0.0333, found by $(4/10)(3/9)(2/8)$
     b. 0.1667, found by $(6/10)(5/9)(4/8)$
     c. 0.8333, found by $1 - 0.1667$
     d. Dependent

59.   **a.** 0.3818, found by $(9/12)(8/11)(7/10)$
     b. 0.6182, found by $1 - 0.3818$

61.   **a.** $P(S) \cdot P(R \mid S) = .60(.85) = 0.51$
     b. $P(S) \cdot P(PR \mid S) = .60(1 - .85) = 0.09$

63.   **a.** $P(\text{not perfect}) = P(\text{bad sector}) + P(\text{defective})$

$$= \frac{112}{1,000} + \frac{31}{1,000} = .143$$

     b. $P(\text{defective} \mid \text{not perfect}) = \dfrac{.031}{.143} = .217$

65.   **a.** $P(P \text{ or } D) = (1/50)(9/10) + (49/50)(1/10) = 0.116$
     b. $P(\text{No}) = (49/50)(9/10) = 0.882$
     c. $P(\text{No on 3}) = (0.882)^3 = 0.686$
     d. $P(\text{at least one prize}) = 1 - 0.686 = 0.314$

67. Yes, 256 is found by 2^8.

69. .9744, found by $1 - (.40)^4$

71.   **a.** .185, found by $(.15)(.95) + (.05)(.85)$
     b. .0075, found by $(.15)(.05)$

73.   **a.** $P(F \text{ and } >60) = .25$, found by solving with the general rule of multiplication:
        $P(F) \cdot P(>60 \mid F) = (.5)(.5)$
     b. 0
     c. .3333, found by 1/3

75. $26^4 = 456,976$

77. 0.512, found by $(0.8)^3$

79. .525, found by $1 - (.78)^3$

81.   **a.**

Winning Season	Attendance			
	Low	Moderate	High	Total
No	6	5	3	14
Yes	3	7	6	16
Total	9	12	9	30

     1. 0.5333, found by 16/30
     2. 0.6333, found by $16/30 + 9/30 - 6/30 = 19/30$
     3. 0.6777, found by 6/9
     4. 0.1000, found by 3/30

     b.

	Losing Season	Winning Season	Total
New	7	8	15
Old	7	8	15
Total	14	16	30

     1. 0.5333, found by 16/30
     2. 0.2667, found by 8/30
     3. 0.7667, found by $16/30 + 15/30 - 8/30$

CHAPTER 6

1. Mean = 1.3, variance = .81, found by:

$$\mu = 0(.20) + 1(.40) + 2(.30) + 3(.10) = 1.3$$

$$\sigma^2 = (0 - 1.3)^2(.2) + (1 - 1.3)^2(.4)$$
$$+ (2 - 1.3)^2(.3) + (3 - 1.3)^2(.1)$$
$$= .81$$

3. Mean = 14.5, variance = 27.25, found by:

$$\mu = 5(.1) + 10(.3) + 15(.2) + 20(.4) = 14.5$$

$$\sigma^2 = (5 - 14.5)^2(.1) + (10 - 14.5)^2(.3)$$
$$+ (15 - 14.5)^2(.2) + (20 - 14.5)^2(.4)$$
$$= 27.25$$

5. a.

Calls, x	Frequency	$P(x)$	$xP(x)$	$(x - \mu)^2 P(x)$
0	8	.16	0	.4624
1	10	.20	.20	.0980
2	22	.44	.88	.0396
3	9	.18	.54	.3042
4	1	.02	.08	.1058
	50		1.70	1.0100

b. Discrete distribution, because only certain outcomes are possible.

c. $\mu = \Sigma x \cdot P(x) = 1.70$

d. $\sigma = \sqrt{1.01} = 1.005$

7.

Amount	$P(x)$	$xP(x)$	$(x - \mu)^2 P(x)$
10	.50	5	60.50
25	.40	10	6.40
50	.08	4	67.28
100	.02	2	124.82
		21	259.00

a. $\mu = \Sigma xP(x) = 21$

b. $\sigma^2 = \Sigma(x - \mu)^2 P(x) = 259$

$\sigma = \sqrt{259} = 16.093$

9. a. $P(2) = \dfrac{4!}{2!(4 - 2)!} (.25)^2(.75)^{4-2} = .2109$

b. $P(3) = \dfrac{4!}{3!(4 - 3)!} (.25)^3(.75)^{4-3} = .0469$

11. a.

X	$P(X)$
0	.064
1	.288
2	.432
3	.216

b. $\mu = 1.8$

$\sigma^2 = 0.72$

$\sigma = \sqrt{0.72} = .8485$

13. a. .2668, found by $P(2) = \dfrac{9!}{(9 - 2)!2!} (.3)^2(.7)^7$

b. .1715, found by $P(4) = \dfrac{9!}{(9 - 4)!4!} (.3)^4(.7)^5$

c. .0404, found by $P(0) = \dfrac{9!}{(9 - 0)!0!} (.3)^0(.7)^9$

15. a. .2824, found by $P(0) = \dfrac{12!}{(12 - 0)!0!} (.10)^0(.9)^{12}$

b. .3765, found by $P(1) = \dfrac{12!}{(12 - 1)!1!} (.10)^1(.9)^{11}$

c. .2301, found by $P(2) = \dfrac{12!}{(12 - 2)!2!} (.10)^2(.9)^{10}$

d. $\mu = 1.2$, found by 12(.10)

$\sigma = 1.0392$, found by $\sqrt{1.08}$

17. a. 0.1858, found by $\dfrac{15!}{2!13!} (0.23)^2(0.77)^{13}$

b. 0.1416, found by $\dfrac{15!}{5!10!} (0.23)^5(0.77)^{10}$

c. 3.45, found by (0.23)(15)

19. a. 0.296, found by using Appendix B.9 with n of 8, π of 0.30, and x of 2

b. $P(x \le 2) = 0.058 + 0.198 + 0.296 = 0.552$

c. 0.448, found by $P(x \ge 3) = 1 - P(x \le 2) = 1 - 0.552$

21. a. 0.387, found from Appendix B.9 with n of 9, π of 0.90, and x of 9

b. $P(X < 5) = 0.001$

c. 0.992, found by $1 - 0.008$

d. 0.947, found by $1 - 0.053$

23. a. $\mu = 10.5$, found by 15(0.7) and $\sigma = \sqrt{15(0.7)(0.3)} = 1.7748$

b. 0.2061, found by $\dfrac{15!}{10!5!} (0.7)^{10}(0.3)^5$

c. 0.4247, found by 0.2061 + 0.2186

d. 0.5154, found by
0.2186 + 0.1700 + 0.0916 + 0.0305 + 0.0047

25. a. .6703

b. .3297

27. a. .0613

b. .0803

29. $\mu = 6$

$P(X \ge 5) = 1 - (.0025 + .0149 + .0446 + .0892 + .1339)$
$= .7149$

31. A random variable is a quantitative or qualitative outcome that results from a chance experiment. A probability distribution also includes the likelihood of each possible outcome.

33. $\mu = \$1,000(.25) + \$2,000(.60) + \$5,000(.15) = \$2,200$

$\sigma^2 = (1,000 - 2,200)^2 .25 + (\$2,000 - \$2,200)^2 .60 + (5,000 - 2,200)^2 .15$
$= 1,560,000$

35. $\mu = 12(.25) + \cdots + 15(.1) = 13.2$

$\sigma^2 = (12 - 13.2)^2 .25 + \cdots + (15 - 13.2)^2 .10 = 0.86$

$\sigma = \sqrt{0.86} = .927$

37. a. $\mu = 10(.35) = 3.5$

b. $P(X = 4) = {}_{10}C_4 (.35)^4 (.65)^6 = 210(.0150)(.0754) = .2375$

c. $P(X \ge 4) = {}_{10}C_x (.35)^X (.65)^{10-X}$
$= .2375 + .1536 + \cdots + .0000 = .4862$

39. a. 6, found by 0.4×15

b. 0.0245, found by $\dfrac{15!}{10!5!} (0.4)^{10}(0.6)^5$

c. 0.0338, found by
0.0245 + 0.0074 + 0.0016 + 0.0003 + 0.0000

d. 0.0093, found by 0.0338 − 0.0245

41. a. $\mu = 20(0.075) = 1.5$

$\sigma = \sqrt{20(0.075)(0.925)} = 1.1779$

b. 0.2103, found by $\dfrac{20!}{0!20!} (0.075)^0(0.925)^{20}$

c. 0.7897, found by 1 − 0.2103

43. a. 0.1311, found by $\dfrac{16!}{4!12!} (0.15)^4(0.85)^{12}$

b. 2.4, found by (0.15)(16)

c. 0.2100, found by
1 − 0.0743 − 0.2097 − 0.2775 − 0.2285

45. 0.279

47. $\mu = 4.0$, from Appendix B.5

a. .0183

b. .1954

c. .6289

d. .5665

49. a. 0.1733, found by $\dfrac{(3.1)^4 e^{-3.1}}{4!}$

b. 0.0450, found by $\dfrac{(3.1)^0 e^{-3.1}}{0!}$

c. 0.9550, found by $1 - 0.0450$

51. $\mu = n\pi = 23\left(\dfrac{2}{113}\right) = .407$

$P(2) = \dfrac{(.407)^2 e^{-.407}}{2!} = 0.0551$

$P(0) = \dfrac{(.407)^0 e^{-.407}}{0!} = 0.6656$

53. a. $\mu = n\pi = 15(.67) = 10.05$

$\sigma = \sqrt{n\pi(1-\pi)} = \sqrt{15(.67)(.33)} = 1.8211$

b. $P(8) = {}_{15}C_8(.67)^8(.33)^7 = 6435(.0406)(.000426) = .1114$

c. $P(x \ge 8) = .1114 + .1759 + \cdots + .0025 = .9163$

55. The mean number of home runs per game is 1.89835, found by $4613/(15 \times 162)$.

a. $P(0) = \dfrac{1.89835^0 \, e^{-1.89835}}{0!} = 0.14982$

b. $P(2) = \dfrac{1.89835^2 \, e^{-1.89835}}{2!} = 0.26995$

c. $P(X >= 4) = 0.1250 = 1 - (0.1498 + 0.2844 + 0.2700 + 0.1708)$

CHAPTER 7

1. a. $b = 10, a = 6$

b. $\mu = \dfrac{6 + 10}{2} = 8$

c. $\sigma = \sqrt{\dfrac{(10-6)^2}{12}} = 1.1547$

d. $\text{Area} = \dfrac{1}{(10-6)} \cdot \dfrac{(10-6)}{1} = 1$

e. $P(X > 7) = \dfrac{1}{(10-6)} \cdot \dfrac{10-7}{1} = \dfrac{3}{4} = .75$

f. $P(7 \le x \le 9) = \dfrac{1}{(10-6)} \cdot \dfrac{(9-7)}{1} = \dfrac{2}{4} = .50$

3. a. 0.30, found by $(30 - 27)/(30 - 20)$
b. 0.40, found by $(24 - 20)/(30 - 20)$

5. a. $a = 0.5, b = 3.00$

b. $\mu = \dfrac{0.5 + 3.00}{2} = 1.75$

$\sigma = \sqrt{\dfrac{(3.00 - .50)^2}{12}} = .72$

c. $P(x < 1) = \dfrac{1}{(3.0 - 0.5)} \cdot \dfrac{1 - .5}{1} = \dfrac{.5}{2.5} = 0.2$

d. 0, found by $\dfrac{1}{(3.0 - 0.5)} \dfrac{(1.0 - 1.0)}{1}$

e. $P(x > 1.5) = \dfrac{1}{(3.0 - 0.5)} \cdot \dfrac{3.0 - 1.5}{1} = \dfrac{1.5}{2.5} = 0.6$

7. The actual shape of a normal distribution depends on its mean and standard deviation. Thus, there is a normal distribution, and an accompanying normal curve, for a mean of 7 and a standard deviation of 2. There is another normal curve for a mean of $25,000 and a standard deviation of $1,742, and so on.

9. a. 490 and 510, found by $500 \pm 1(10)$
b. 480 and 520, found by $500 \pm 2(10)$
c. 470 and 530, found by $500 \pm 3(10)$

11. $Z_{Rob} = \dfrac{\$50,000 - \$60,000}{\$5,000} = -2$

$Z_{Rachel} = \dfrac{\$50,000 - \$35,000}{\$8,000} = 1.875$

Adjusting for their industries, Rob is well below average and Rachel well above.

13. a. 1.25, found by $z = \dfrac{25 - 20}{4.0} = 1.25$

b. 0.3944, found in Appendix B.1

c. 0.3085, found by $z = \dfrac{18 - 20}{2.5} = -0.5$

Find 0.1915 in Appendix B.1 for $z = -0.5$, then $0.5000 - 0.1915 = 0.3085$

15. a. 0.3413, found by $z = \dfrac{\$24 - \$20.50}{\$3.50} = 1.00$,

then find 0.3413 in Appendix B.1 for $z = 1$
b. 0.1587, found by $0.5000 - 0.3413 = 0.1587$

c. 0.3336, found by $z = \dfrac{\$19.00 - \$20.50}{\$3.50} = -0.43$

Find 0.1664 in Appendix B.1, for $z = -0.43$, then $0.5000 - 0.1664 = 0.3336$

17. a. 0.8276: First find $z = -1.5$, found by $(44 - 50)/4$ and $z = 1.25 = (55 - 50)/4$. The area between -1.5 and 0 is 0.4332 and the area between 0 and 1.25 is 0.3944, both from Appendix B.1. Then adding the two areas we find that $0.4332 + 0.3944 = 0.8276$.

b. 0.1056, found by $0.5000 - .3944$, where $z = 1.25$
c. 0.2029: Recall that the area for $z = 1.25$ is 0.3944, and the area for $z = 0.5$, found by $(52 - 50)/4$, is 0.1915. Then subtract $0.3944 - 0.1915$ and find 0.2029.

19. a. 0.4052, where $z = [(3100 - 3000)/410] = 0.24$; leads to $0.5 - 0.0948 = 0.4052$.

b. 0.2940; the z value for $3,500 is 1.22, found by $[(3500 - 3000)/410]$, and the corresponding area is 0.3888. Leads to $0.3888 - 0.0948 = 0.2940$

c. 0.8552; the z value for $2,250 is -1.83, found by $[(2250 - 3000)/410]$, and the corresponding area is 0.4664. Then, $0.4664 + 0.3888 = 0.8552$

21. a. 0.0764, found by $z = (20 - 15)/3.5 = 1.43$, then $0.5000 - 0.4236 = 0.0764$

b. 0.9236, found by $0.5000 + 0.4236$, where $z = 1.43$
c. 0.1185, found by $z = (12 - 15)/3.5 = -0.86$. The area under the curve is 0.3051, then $z = (10 - 15)/3.5 = -1.43$. The area is 0.4236. Finally, $0.4236 - 0.3051 = 0.1185$.

23. $X = 56.60$, found by adding 0.5000 (the area left of the mean) and then finding a z value that forces 45% of the data to fall inside the curve. Solving for X: $1.65 = (X - 50)/4 = 56.60$.

25. $1,630, found by $\$2,100 - 1.88(\$250)$

27. a. 214.8 hours: Find a z value where 0.4900 of area is between 0 and z. That value is $z = 2.33$. Then solve for X: $2.33 = (X - 195)/8.5$, so $X = 214.8$ hours.
b. 270.2 hours: Find a z value where 0.4900 of area is between 0 and $(-z)$. That value is $z = -2.33$. Then solve for X: $-2.33 = (X - 290)/8.5$, so $X = 270.2$ hours.

29. 41.7%, found by $12 + 1.65(18)$

31. a. $\mu = \dfrac{11.96 + 12.05}{2} = 12.005$

b. $\sigma = \sqrt{\dfrac{(12.05 - 11.96)^2}{12}} = .0260$

c. $P(X < 12) = \dfrac{1}{(12.05 - 11.96)} \dfrac{12.00 - 11.96}{1} = \dfrac{.04}{.09} = .44$

d. $P(X > 11.98) = \dfrac{1}{(12.05 - 11.96)} \left(\dfrac{12.05 - 11.98}{1}\right)$
$= \dfrac{.07}{.09} = .78$

e. All cans have more than 11.00 ounces, so the probability is 100%.

33. a. $\mu = \dfrac{4 + 10}{2} = 7$

b. $\sigma = \sqrt{\dfrac{(10 - 4)^2}{12}} = 1.732$

c. $P(X < 6) = \dfrac{1}{(10 - 4)} \cdot \left(\dfrac{6 - 4}{1}\right) = \dfrac{2}{6} = .33$

d. $P(X > 5) = \dfrac{1}{(10 - 4)} \cdot \left(\dfrac{10 - 5}{1}\right) = \dfrac{5}{6} = .83$

35. a. −0.4 for net sales, found by $(170 - 180)/25$. 2.92 for employees, found by $(1{,}850 - 1{,}500)/120$.

b. Net sales are 0.4 standard deviations below the mean. Employees is 2.92 standard deviations above the mean.

c. 65.54 percent of the aluminum fabricators have greater net sales compared with Clarion, found by $0.1554 + 0.5000$. Only 0.18% have more employees than Clarion, found by $0.5000 - 0.4982$.

37. a. 0.5000, because $z = \dfrac{30 - 490}{90} = -5.11$

b. 0.2514, found by $0.5000 - 0.2486$

c. 0.6374, found by $0.2486 + 0.3888$

d. 0.3450, found by $0.3888 - 0.0438$

39. a. 0.3015, found by $0.5000 - 0.1985$

b. 0.2579, found by $0.4564 - 0.1985$

c. 0.0011, found by $0.5000 - 0.4989$

d. 1,818, found by $1{,}280 + 1.28(420)$

41. a. 90.82%: First find $z = 1.33$, found by $(40 - 34)/4.5$. The area between 0 and 1.33 is 0.4082. Then add 0.5000 and 0.4082 and find 0.9082 or 90.82%.

b. 78.23%: First find $z = -0.78$ found by $(25 - 29)/5.1$. The area between 0 and (−0.78) is 0.2823. Then add 0.5000 and 0.2823 and find 0.7823 or 78.23%.

c. 44.5 hours/week for women: Find a z value where 0.4900 of the area is between 0 and z. That value is 2.33. Then solve for X: $2.33 = (X - 34)/4.5$, so $X = 44.5$ hours/week. 40.9 hours/week for men: $2.33 = (X - 29)/5.1$, so $X = 40.9$ hours/week.

43. About 4,099 units, found by solving for X. $1.65 = (X - 4{,}000)/60$

45. a. 15.39%, found by $(8 - 10.3)/2.25 = -1.02$, then $0.5000 - 0.3461 = 0.1539$.

b. 17.31%, found by:
$z = (12 - 10.3)/2.25 = 0.76$. Area is 0.2764.
$z = (14 - 10.3)/2.25 = 1.64$. Area is 0.4495.
The area between 12 and 14 is 0.1731, found by $0.4495 - 0.2764$.

c. Yes, but it is rather remote. Reasoning: On 99.73% of the days, returns are between 3.55 and 17.05, found by $10.3 \pm 3(2.25)$. Thus, the chance of less than 3.55 returns is rather remote.

47. a. 21.19% found by $z = (9.00 - 9.20)/0.25 = -0.80$, so $0.5000 - 0.2881 = 0.2119$

b. Increase the mean. $z = (9.00 - 9.25)/0.25 = -1.00$, $P = 0.5000 - 0.3413 = 0.1587$.
Reduce the standard deviation. $z = (9.00 - 9.20)/0.15 = -1.33$; $P = 0.5000 - 0.4082 = 0.0918$.
Reducing the standard deviation is better because a smaller percent of the hams will be below the limit.

49. a. $z = (60 - 52)/5 = 1.60$, so $0.5000 - 0.4452 = 0.0548$

b. Let $z = 0.67$, so $0.67 = (X - 52)/5$ and $X = 55.35$, set mileage at 55,350

c. $z = (45 - 52)/5 = -1.40$, so $0.5000 - 0.4192 = 0.0808$

51. $\dfrac{470 - \mu}{\sigma} = 0.25 \qquad \dfrac{500 - \mu}{\sigma} = 1.28 \qquad \sigma = 29{,}126$ and $\mu = 462{,}718$

53. a. $1.65 = (45 - \mu)/5 \qquad \mu = 36.75$

b. $1.65 = (45 - \mu)/10 \qquad \mu = 28.5$

c. $z = (30 - 28.5)/10 = 0.15$, then $0.5000 + 0.0596 = 0.5596$

55. a. Estimate is 2.043, rounding up to 3; $z = (3.5 - 2.436)/0.713 = 1.49$; leads to $0.5000 - 0.4319 = 0.0681$. 2.043 teams is $(30)(0.0681)$, rounding up to 3. There were actually 3 teams that exceeded 3.5 million. Estimate is fairly accurate.

b. Estimate is 25.7, or 26 teams. $z = (50 - 91.020)/38.258 = -1.07$; leads to $0.3577 + 0.5000 = 0.8577$. 25.7 teams is $0.8577(30)$. There were actually 28 teams that exceeded $50 million in payroll. Estimate is fairly accurate.

CHAPTER 8

1. a. 303 Louisiana, 5155 S. Main, 3501 Monroe, 2652 W. Central

b. Answers will vary.

c. 630 Dixie Hwy, 835 S. McCord Rd, 4624 Woodville Rd

d. Answers will vary.

3. a. Bob Schmidt Chevrolet
Great Lakes Ford Nissan
Grogan Towne Chrysler
Southside Lincoln Mercury
Rouen Chrysler Jeep Eagle

b. Answers will vary.

c. Yark Automotive
Thayer Chevrolet Toyota
Franklin Park Lincoln Mercury
Mathews Ford Oregon Inc.
Valiton Chrysler

5. a.

Sample	Values	Sum	Mean
1	12, 12	24	12
2	12, 14	26	13
3	12, 16	28	14
4	12, 14	26	13
5	12, 16	28	14
6	14, 16	30	15

b. $\mu_{\bar{x}} = (12 + 13 + 14 + 13 + 14 + 15)/6 = 13.5$
$\mu = (12 + 12 + 14 + 16)/4 = 13.5$

c. More dispersion with population data compared to the sample means. The sample means vary from 12 to 15, whereas the population varies from 12 to 16.

7. a.

Sample	Values	Sum	Mean
1	12, 12, 14	38	12.66
2	12, 12, 15	39	13.00
3	12, 12, 20	44	14.66
4	14, 15, 20	49	16.33
5	12, 14, 15	41	13.66
6	12, 14, 15	41	13.66
7	12, 15, 20	47	15.66
8	12, 15, 20	47	15.66
9	12, 14, 20	46	15.33
10	12, 14, 20	46	15.33

b. $\mu_{\bar{x}} = \dfrac{(12.66 + \cdots + 15.33 + 15.33)}{10} = 14.6$
$\mu = (12 + 12 + 14 + 15 + 20)/5 = 14.6$

c. The dispersion of the population is greater than that of the sample means. The sample means vary from 12.66 to 16.33, whereas the population varies from 12 to 20.

9. a. 20, found by $_6C_3$

b.

Sample	Cases	Sum	Mean
Ruud, Wu, Sass	3, 6, 3	12	4.00
Ruud, Sass, Flores	3, 3, 3	9	3.00
⋮	⋮	⋮	⋮
Sass, Flores, Schueller	3, 3, 1	7	2.33

c. $\mu_{\bar{x}} = 2.67$, found by $\frac{53.33}{20}$.

$\mu = 2.67$, found by $(3 + 6 + 3 + 3 + 0 + 1)/6$. They are equal.

d.

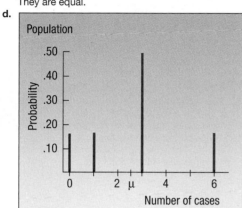

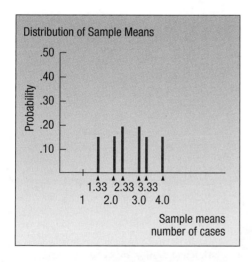

Sample Mean	Number of Means	Probability
1.33	3	.1500
2.00	3	.1500
2.33	4	.2000
3.00	4	.2000
3.33	3	.1500
4.00	3	.1500
	20	1.0000

The population has more dispersion than the sample means. The sample means vary from 1.33 to 4.0. The population varies from 0 to 6.

11. a.

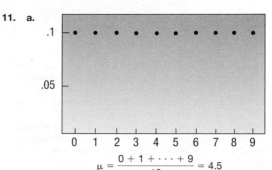

$$\mu = \frac{0 + 1 + \cdots + 9}{10} = 4.5$$

b.

Sample	Sum	$\bar{X}$	Sample	Sum	$\bar{X}$
1	11	2.2	6	20	4.0
2	31	6.2	7	23	4.6
3	21	4.2	8	29	5.8
4	24	4.8	9	35	7.0
5	21	4.2	10	27	5.4

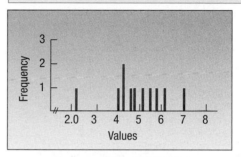

The mean of the 10 sample means is 4.84, which is close to the population mean of 4.5. The sample means range from 2.2 to 7.0, whereas the population values range from 0 to 9. From the above graph, the sample means tend to cluster between 4 and 5.

13. a.–c. Answers will vary depending on the coins in your possession.

15. a. $z = \dfrac{63 - 60}{12/\sqrt{9}} = 0.75$

$P = .2266$, found by $.5000 - .2734$

b. $z = \dfrac{56 - 60}{12/\sqrt{9}} = -1.00$

$P = .1587$, found by $.5000 - .3413$

c. $P = .6147$, found by $0.3413 + 0.2734$

17. $z = \dfrac{1,950 - 2,200}{250/\sqrt{50}} = -7.07$ $P = 1$, or virtually certain

19. a. Formal Man, Summit Stationers, Bootleggers, Leather Ltd, Petries

b. Answers may vary.

c. Elder-Beerman, Frederick's of Hollywood, Summit Stationers, Lion Store, Leather Ltd., Things Remembered, County Seat, Coach House Gifts, Regis Hairstylists

21. a.

Samples	Mean	Deviation from Mean	Square of Deviation
1, 1	1.0	−1.0	1.0
1, 2	1.5	−0.5	0.25
1, 3	2.0	0.0	0.0
2, 1	1.5	−0.5	0.25
2, 2	2.0	0.0	0.0
2, 3	2.5	0.5	0.25
3, 1	2.0	0.0	0.0
3, 2	2.5	0.5	0.25
3, 3	3.0	1.0	1.0

b. Mean of sample means is $(1.0 + 1.5 + 2.0 + \cdots + 3.0)/9 = 18/9 = 2.0$. The population mean is $(1 + 2 + 3)/3 = 6/3 = 2$. They are the same value.

c. Variance of sample means is $(1.0 + 0.25 + 0.0 + \cdots + 1.0)/9 = 3/9 = 1/3$. Variance of the population values is $(1 + 0 + 1)/3 = 2/3$. The variance of the population is twice as large as that of the sample means.

d. Sample means follow a triangular shape peaking at 2. The population is uniform between 1 and 3.

23. Larger samples provide narrower estimates of a population mean. So the company with 200 sampled customers can provide more precise estimates. In addition, they are selected consumers who are familiar with laptop computers and may be better able to evaluate the new computer.

25. **a.** We selected 60, 104, 75, 72, and 48. Answers will vary.

b. We selected the third observation. So the sample consists of 75, 72, 68, 82, 48. Answers will vary.

c. Number the first 20 motels from 00 to 19. Randomly select three numbers. Then number the last five numbers 20 to 24. Randomly select two numbers from that group.

27. **a.** 15, found by $_6C_2$

b.

Sample	Value	Sum	Mean
1	79, 64	143	71.5
2	79, 84	163	81.5
⋮	⋮	⋮	⋮
15	92, 77	169	84.5
			1,195.0

c. $\mu_{\bar{x}} = 79.67$, found by $1{,}195/15$.
$\mu = 79.67$, found by $478/6$.
They are equal.

d. No. The student is not graded on all available information. He/she is as likely to get a lower grade based on the sample as a higher grade.

29. **a.** 10, found by $_5C_2$

b.

Number of Shutdowns	Mean	Number of Shutdowns	Mean
4, 3	3.5	3, 3	3.0
4, 5	4.5	3, 2	2.5
4, 3	3.5	5, 3	4.0
4, 2	3.0	5, 2	3.5
3, 5	4.0	3, 2	2.5

Sample Mean	Frequency	Probability
2.5	2	.20
3.0	2	.20
3.5	3	.30
4.0	2	.20
4.5	1	.10
	10	1.00

c. $\mu_{\bar{x}} = (3.5 + 4.5 + \cdots + 2.5)/10 = 3.4$
$\mu = (4 + 3 + 5 + 3 + 2)/5 = 3.4$
The two means are equal.

d. The population values are relatively uniform in shape. The distribution of sample means tends toward normality.

31. **a.** The distribution will be normal.

b. $\sigma_{\bar{x}} = \dfrac{5.5}{\sqrt{25}} = 1.1$

c. $z = \dfrac{36 - 35}{5.5/\sqrt{25}} = 0.91$
$P = 0.1814$, found by $0.5000 - 0.3186$

d. $z = \dfrac{34.5 - 35}{5.5/\sqrt{25}} = -0.45$
$P = 0.6736$, found by $0.5000 + 0.1736$

e. 0.4922, found by $0.3186 + 0.1736$

33. $z = \dfrac{\$335 - \$350}{\$45/\sqrt{40}} = -2.11$
$P = 0.9826$, found by $0.5000 + 0.4826$

35. $z = \dfrac{25.1 - 24.8}{2.5/\sqrt{60}} = 0.93$
$P = 0.8238$, found by $0.5000 + 0.3238$

37. Between 5,954 and 6,046, found by $6{,}000 \pm 1.96\,(150/\sqrt{40})$

39. $z = \dfrac{900 - 947}{205/\sqrt{60}} = -1.78$
$P = 0.0375$, found by $0.5000 - 0.4625$

41. **a.** Alaska, Connecticut, Georgia, Kansas, Nebraska, South Carolina, Virginia, Utah

b. Arizona, Florida, Iowa, Massachusetts, Nebraska, North Carolina, Rhode Island, Vermont

43. **a.** $z = \dfrac{600 - 510}{14.28/\sqrt{10}} = 19.9$, $P = 0.00$, or virtually never

b. $z = \dfrac{500 - 510}{14.28/\sqrt{10}} = -2.21$,
$P = 0.4864 + 0.5000 = 0.9864$

c. $z = \dfrac{500 - 510}{14.28/\sqrt{10}} = -2.21$,
$P = 0.5000 - 0.4864 = 0.0136$

45. **a.** $\sigma_{\bar{x}} = \dfrac{2.1}{\sqrt{81}} = 0.23$

b. $z = \dfrac{7.0 - 6.5}{2.1/\sqrt{81}} = 2.14$, $z = \dfrac{6.0 - 6.5}{2.1/\sqrt{81}} = -2.14$,
$P = .4838 + .4838 = .9676$

c. $z = \dfrac{6.75 - 6.5}{2.1/\sqrt{81}} = 1.07$, $z = \dfrac{6.25 - 6.5}{2.1/\sqrt{81}} = -1.07$,
$P = .3577 + .3577 = .7154$

d. .0162 found by $.5000 - .4838$

47. Mean 2010 attendance is 2.436 million. Likelihood of a sample mean this large or larger is 0.0721, found by $0.5000 - 0.4279$. The z value is 1.46.

CHAPTER 9

1. 51.32 and 58.68, found by $55 \pm 2.576(10/\sqrt{49})$

3. **a.** 1.581, found by $\sigma_{\bar{x}} = 25/\sqrt{250}$

b. The population is normally distributed and the population variance is known.

c. 16.901 and 23.099, found by 20 ± 3.099

5. **a.** $20. It is our best estimate of the population mean.

b. $18.60 and $21.40, found by $\$20 \pm 1.96(\$5/\sqrt{49})$. About 95% of the intervals similarly constructed will include the population mean.

7. **a.** 8.60 gallons.

b. 7.84 and 9.36, found by $8.60 \pm 2.576(2.30/\sqrt{60})$

c. If 100 such intervals were determined, the population mean would be included in about 99 intervals.

9. **a.** 2.201

b. 1.729

c. 3.499

11. **a.** The population mean is unknown, but the best estimate is 20, the sample mean.
   b. Use the t distribution since the standard deviation is unknown. However, assume the population is normally distributed.
   c. 2.093
   d. Between 19.06 and 20.94, found by $20 \pm 2.093(2/\sqrt{20})$
   e. Neither value is reasonable, because they are not inside the interval.

13. Between 95.39 and 101.81, found by $98.6 \pm 1.833(5.54/\sqrt{10})$

15. **a.** 0.8, found by 80/100
   b. Between 0.72 and 0.88, found by
   $$0.8 \pm 1.96\left(\sqrt{\frac{0.8(1-0.8)}{100}}\right)$$
   c. We are reasonably sure the population proportion is between 72% and 88%.

17. **a.** 0.625, found by 250/400
   b. Between 0.563 and 0.687, found by
   $$0.625 \pm 2.576\left(\sqrt{\frac{0.625(1-0.625)}{400}}\right)$$
   c. We are reasonably sure the population proportion is between 56% and 69%.

19. 97, found by $n = \left(\dfrac{1.96 \times 10}{2}\right)^2 = 96.04$

21. 196, found by $n = 0.15(0.85)\left(\dfrac{1.96}{0.05}\right)^2 = 195.9216$

23. 554, found by $n = \left(\dfrac{1.96 \times 3}{0.25}\right)^2 = 553.19$

25. **a.** 577, found by $n = 0.60(0.40)\left(\dfrac{1.96}{0.04}\right)^2 = 576.24$
   b. 601, found by $n = 0.50(0.50)\left(\dfrac{1.96}{0.04}\right)^2 = 600.25$

27. 6.13 years to 6.87 years, found by $6.5 \pm 1.989(1.7/\sqrt{85})$

29. **a.** Between $313.41 and 332.59, found by
   $$323 \pm 2.426\left(\frac{25}{\sqrt{40}}\right).$$
   b. $350 is not reasonable, because it is outside of the confidence interval.

31. **a.** The population mean is unknown.
   b. Between 7.50 and 9.14, found by $8.32 \pm 1.685(3.07/\sqrt{40})$
   c. 10 is not reasonable because it is outside the confidence interval.

33. **a.** 65.49 up to 71.71 hours, found by $68.6 \pm 2.680(8.2/\sqrt{50})$
   b. The value suggested by the NCAA is included in the confidence interval. Therefore, it is reasonable.
   c. Changing the confidence interval to 95 would reduce the width of the interval. The value of 2.680 would change to 2.010.

35. 61, found by $1.96(16/\sqrt{n}) = 4$

37. Between $13,734 up to $15,028, found by $14,381 \pm 1.711(1,892/\sqrt{25})$. 15,000 is reasonable because it is inside the confidence interval.

39. **a.** $62.583, found by $751/12
   b. Between $60.54 and $64.63, found by $62.583 \pm 1.796(3.94/\sqrt{12})$
   c. $60 is not reasonable, because it is outside of the confidence interval.

41. **a.** 89.4667, found by 1,342/15
   b. Between 84.99 and 93.94, found by $89.4667 \pm 2.145(8.08/\sqrt{15})$
   c. Yes, because even the lower limit of the confidence interval is above 80.

43. The confidence interval is between 0.011 and 0.059, found by $0.035 \pm 2.576\left(\sqrt{\dfrac{0.035(1-0.035)}{400}}\right)$. It would not be reasonable to conclude that fewer than 5% of the employees are now failing the test, because 0.05 is inside the confidence interval.

45. Between .65 and .75, found by $.7 \pm 2.576\sqrt{(.7)(.3)/500}$. Yes, she will be reelected. She will receive more than 50% of the vote.

47. 369, found by $n = 0.60(1-0.60)(1.96/0.05)^2$

49. 97, found by $[(1.96 \times 500)/100]^2$

51. **a.** Between 7,849 and 8,151, found by $8,000 \pm 2.756(300/\sqrt{30})$
   b. 554, found by $n = \left(\dfrac{(1.96)(300)}{25}\right)^2$

53. **a.** Between 75.44 and 80.56, found by $78 \pm 2.010(9/\sqrt{50})$
   b. 220, found by $n = \left(\dfrac{(1.645)(9)}{1.0}\right)^2$

55. **a.** 30, found by $180/\sqrt{36}$
   b. $355.10 and $476.90, found by $416 \pm 2.030\left(\dfrac{\$180}{\sqrt{36}}\right)$
   c. About 1,245, found by $\left(\dfrac{1.96(180)}{10}\right)^2$

57. **a.** 708.13, rounded up to 709, found by $0.21(1-0.21)(1.96/0.03)^2$
   b. 1,068, found by $0.50(0.50)(1.96/0.03)^2$

59. **a.** Between 0.156 and 0.184, found by
   $$0.17 \pm 1.96\sqrt{\frac{(0.17)(1-0.17)}{2700}}$$
   b. Yes, because 18% is inside the confidence interval.
   c. 21,682; found by $0.17(1-0.17)[1.96/0.005]^2$

61. Between 12.69 and 14.11, found by $13.4 \pm 1.96(6.8/\sqrt{352})$

63. **a.** For selling price: 211.99 up to 230.22, found by $221.1 \pm (1.983)(47.11/\sqrt{105}) = 221.1 \pm 9.12$
   b. For distance: 13.685 up to 15.572, found by $14.629 \pm (1.983)(4.874/\sqrt{105}) = 14.629 \pm 0.943$
   c. For garage: 0.5867 up to 0.7657, found by $0.6762 \pm (1.96)\sqrt{\dfrac{0.6762(1-0.6762)}{105}} = 0.6762 \pm 0.0895$
   d. Answers may vary.

65. **a.** Between $438.34 and 462.24, found by $450.29 \pm 1.99\left(\dfrac{53.69}{\sqrt{80}}\right)$
   b. Between 820.72 and 839.50, found by $830.11 \pm 1.99\left(\dfrac{42.19}{\sqrt{80}}\right)$
   c. Answers will vary.

CHAPTER 10

1. **a.** Two-tailed
   b. Reject H_0 when z does not fall in the region between -1.96 and 1.96.
   c. -1.2, found by $z = (49-50)/(5/\sqrt{36}) = -1.2$
   d. Fail to reject H_0.
   e. $p = .2302$, found by $2(.5000 - .3849)$. A 23.02% chance of finding a z value this large when H_0 is true.

3. **a.** One-tailed
   b. Reject H_0 when $z > 1.645$.
   c. 1.2, found by $z = (21-20)/(5/\sqrt{36}) = 1.2$
   d. Fail to reject H_0 at the .05 significance level
   e. $p = .1151$, found by $.5000 - .3849$. An 11.51% chance of finding a z value this large or larger when the null hypothesis is true.

5. a. $H_0: \mu = 60{,}000 \qquad H_1: \mu \neq 60{,}000$

b. Reject H_0 if $z < -1.96$ or $z > 1.96$.

c. -0.69, found by:

$$z = \frac{59{,}500 - 60{,}000}{(5{,}000/\sqrt{48})} = -0.69$$

d. Do not reject H_0.

e. $p = .4902$, found by $2(.5000 - .2549)$. Crosset's experience is not different from that claimed by the manufacturer. If H_0 is true, the probability of finding a value more extreme than this is .4902.

7. a. $H_0: \mu \geq 6.8 \qquad H_1: \mu < 6.8$

b. Reject H_0 if $z < -1.645$

c. $z = \dfrac{6.2 - 6.8}{0.5/\sqrt{36}} = -7.2$

d. H_0 is rejected.

e. $p = 0$. The mean number of DVDs watched is less than 6.8 per month. If H_0 is true, there is virtually no chance of getting a statistic this small.

9. a. Reject H_0 when $t > 1.833$.

b. $t = \dfrac{12 - 10}{(3/\sqrt{10})} = 2.108$

c. Reject H_0. The mean is greater than 10.

11. $H_0: \mu \leq 40 \qquad H_1: \mu > 40$

Reject H_0 if $t > 1.703$.

$$t = \frac{42 - 40}{(2.1/\sqrt{28})} = 5.040$$

Reject H_0 and conclude that the mean number of calls is greater than 40 per week.

13. $H_0: \mu \leq 40{,}000 \qquad H_1: \mu > 40{,}000$

Reject H_0 if $t > 1.833$.

$$t = \frac{50{,}000 - 40{,}000}{10{,}000/\sqrt{10}} = 3.16$$

Reject H_0 and conclude that the mean income in Wilmington is greater than $40,000.

15. a. Reject H_0 if $t < -3.747$.

b. $\overline{X} = 17$ and $s = \sqrt{\dfrac{50}{5-1}} = 3.536$

$$t = \frac{17 - 20}{(3.536/\sqrt{5})} = -1.90$$

c. Do not reject H_0. We cannot conclude the population mean is less than 20.

d. Between .05 and .10, about .065

17. $H_0: \mu \leq 1.4 \qquad H_1: \mu > 1.4$

Reject H_0 if $t > 2.821$.

$$t = \frac{1.6 - 1.4}{0.216/\sqrt{10}} = 2.93$$

Reject H_0 and conclude that the drug has increased the amount of water consumption. The p-value is between 0.01 and 0.005.
There is a slight probability (between one chance in 100 and one chance in 200) this rise could have arisen by chance.

19. $H_0: \mu \leq 50 \qquad H_1: \mu > 50$

Reject H_0 if $t > 1.796$.

$$t = \frac{82.5 - 50}{59.5/\sqrt{12}} = 1.89$$

Reject H_0 and conclude that the mean number of text messages is greater than 50. The p-value is less than 0.05. There is a slight probability (less than one chance in 20) this could happen by chance.

21. a. H_0 is rejected if $z > 1.645$.

b. 1.09, found by $z = (0.75 - 0.70)/\sqrt{(0.70 \times 0.30)/100}$

c. H_0 is not rejected.

23. a. $H_0: \pi \leq 0.52 \qquad H_1: \pi > 0.52$

b. H_0 is rejected if $z > 2.326$.

c. 1.62, found by $z = (.5667 - .52)/\sqrt{(0.52 \times 0.48)/300}$

d. H_0 is not rejected. We cannot conclude that the proportion of men driving on the Ohio Turnpike is larger than 0.52.

25. a. $H_0: \pi \geq 0.90 \qquad H_1: \pi < 0.90$

b. H_0 is rejected if $z < -1.282$.

c. -2.67, found by $z = (0.82 - 0.90)/\sqrt{(0.90 \times 0.10)/100}$

d. H_0 is rejected. Fewer than 90% of the customers receive their orders in less than 10 minutes.

27. $H_0: \mu = \$45{,}000 \qquad H_1: \mu \neq \$45{,}000$

Reject H_0 if $z < -1.645$ or $z > 1.645$.

$$z = \frac{45{,}500 - 45{,}000}{\$3{,}000/\sqrt{120}} = 1.83$$

Reject H_0. We can conclude that the mean salary is not $45,000. p-value 0.0672, found by $2(0.5000 - 0.4664)$.

29. $H_0: \mu \geq 10 \qquad H_1: \mu < 10$

Reject H_0 if $z < -1.645$.

$$z = \frac{9.0 - 10.0}{2.8/\sqrt{50}} = -2.53$$

Reject H_0. The mean weight loss is less than 10 pounds.
p-value $= 0.5000 - 0.4943 = 0.0057$

31. $H_0: \mu \geq 7.0 \qquad H_1: \mu < 7.0$

Assuming a 5% significance level, reject H_0 if $t < -1.677$.

$$t = \frac{6.8 - 7.0}{0.9/\sqrt{50}} = -1.57$$

Do not reject H_0. West Virginia students are not sleeping less than 6 hours. p-value is between .05 and .10.

33. $H_0: \mu \geq 3.13 \qquad H_1: \mu < 3.13$

Reject H_0 if $t < -1.711$

$$t = \frac{2.86 - 3.13}{1.20/\sqrt{25}} = -1.13$$

We fail to reject H_0 and conclude that the mean number of residents is not necessarily less than 3.13.

35. $H_0: \mu \leq 14 \qquad H_1: \mu > 14$

Reject H_0 if $t > 2.821$.
$\overline{X} = 15.66 \qquad s = 1.544$

$$t = \frac{15.66 - 14.00}{1.544/\sqrt{10}} = 3.400$$

Reject H_0. The average rate is greater than 14%.

37. $H_0: \mu = 3.1 \qquad H_1: \mu \neq 3.1$ Assume a normal population.

Reject H_0 if $t < -2.201$ or $t > 2.201$.

$$\overline{X} = \frac{41.1}{12} = 3.425$$

$$s = \sqrt{\frac{4.0625}{12 - 1}} = .6077$$

$$t = \frac{3.425 - 3.1}{.6077/\sqrt{12}} = 1.853$$

Do not reject H_0. Cannot show a difference between senior citizens and the national average. p-value is about 0.09.

39. $H_0: \mu \geq 6.5 \qquad H_1: \mu < 6.5$ Assume a normal population.

Reject H_0 if $t < -2.718$.
$\overline{X} = 5.1667 \qquad s = 3.1575$

$$t = \frac{5.1667 - 6.5}{3.1575/\sqrt{12}} = -1.463$$

Do not reject H_0. The p-value is greater than 0.05.

41. $H_0: \mu = 0 \qquad H_1: \mu \neq 0$

Reject H_0 if $t < -2.110$ or $t > 2.110$.

$\overline{X} = -0.2322 \qquad s = 0.3120$

$$t = \frac{-0.2322 - 0}{0.3120/\sqrt{18}} = -3.158$$

Reject H_0. The mean gain or loss does not equal 0.
The p-value is less than 0.01, but greater than 0.001.

43. $H_0: \mu \le 100 \qquad H_1: \mu > 100$ Assume a normal population.
Reject H_0 if $t > 1.761$.

$$\overline{X} = \frac{1,641}{15} = 109.4$$

$$s = \sqrt{\frac{1,389.6}{15 - 1}} = 9.9628$$

$$t = \frac{109.4 - 100}{9.9628/\sqrt{15}} = 3.654$$

Reject H_0. The mean number with the scanner is greater
than 100. p-value is 0.001.

45. $H_0: \mu = 1.5 \qquad H_1: \mu \ne 1.5$
Reject H_0 if $t > 3.250$ or $t < -3.250$.

$$t = \frac{1.3 - 1.5}{0.9/\sqrt{10}} = -0.703$$

Do not reject H_0.

47. a. This is a binomial situation with both the mean number of
successes and failures equal to 22.5, found by 0.5×45.
   b. $H_0: \pi = 0.50 \qquad H_1: \pi \ne 0.50$
   c.

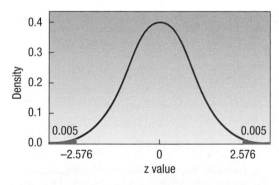

Distribution Plot
Normal, Mean = 0, StDev = 1

Reject H_0 if z is not between -2.576 and 2.576.

   d. $z = \dfrac{\left(\dfrac{31}{45}\right) - 0.50}{\sqrt{0.50(1 - 0.50)/45}} = 2.534$ We do not reject the

null hypothesis. These data do not prove the coin flip is
biased.
   e. The p-value is 0.0114, found by $2 \times (0.5000 - 0.4943)$.
A value this extreme will happen about once out of fifty
times with a fair coin.

49. $H_0: \pi \le 0.60 \qquad H_1: \pi > 0.60$
H_0 is rejected if $z > 2.326$.

$$z = \frac{.70 - .60}{\sqrt{\dfrac{.60(.40)}{200}}} = 2.89$$

H_0 is rejected. Ms. Dennis is correct. More than 60% of the
accounts are more than three months old.

51. $H_0: \pi \le 0.44 \qquad H_1: \pi > 0.44$
H_0 is rejected if $z > 1.645$.

$$z = \frac{0.480 - 0.44}{\sqrt{(0.44 \times 0.56)/1,000}} = 2.55$$

H_0 is rejected. We conclude that there has been an increase
in the proportion of people wanting to go to Europe.

53. $H_0: \pi \le 0.20 \qquad H_1: \pi > 0.20$
H_0 is rejected if $z > 2.326$

$$z = \frac{(56/200) - 0.20}{\sqrt{(0.20 \times 0.80)/200}} = 2.83$$

H_0 is rejected. More than 20% of the owners move during a
particular year. p-value $= 0.5000 - 0.4977 = 0.0023$.

55. $H_0: \pi \le 0.40 \qquad H_1: \pi > 0.40$
Reject H_0 if z is greater than 2.326.

$$z = \frac{(16/30) - 0.40}{\sqrt{[0.40(1 - 0.40)/30]}} = 1.49$$

Do not reject the null hypothesis. These data do not show
that college students are more likely to skip breakfast.

57. $H_0: \pi \ge 0.0008 \qquad H_1: \pi < 0.0008$
H_0 is rejected if $z < -1.645$.

$$z = \frac{0.0006 - 0.0008}{\sqrt{\dfrac{0.0008(0.9992)}{10,000}}} = -0.707 \quad H_0 \text{ is not rejected.}$$

These data do not prove there is a reduced fatality rate.

59. $H_0: \mu \ge 8 \qquad H_1: \mu < 8$
Reject H_0 if $t < -1.714$.

$$t = \frac{7.5 - 8}{3.2/\sqrt{24}} = -0.77$$

Do not reject the null hypothesis. The time is not less.

61. a. $H_0: \mu = 80 \qquad H_1: \mu \ne 80$
Reject H_0 if t is not between -2.045 and 2.045.
$t = \dfrac{91.02 - 80}{38.26/\sqrt{30}} = 1.578$ Do not reject the null.
The mean payroll could be $80.0 million.
   b. $H_0: \mu \le 2,000,000 \qquad H_1: \mu > 2,000,000$
Reject H_0 if t is > 1.699.
$$t = \frac{2,436,000 - 2,000,000}{713,000/\sqrt{30}} = 3.349$$
Reject the null. The mean attendance was more
than 2,000,000.

CHAPTER 11

1. a. Two-tailed test
   b. Reject H_0 if $z < -2.05$ or $z > 2.05$
   c. $z = \dfrac{102 - 99}{\sqrt{\dfrac{5^2}{40} + \dfrac{6^2}{50}}} = 2.59$
   d. Reject H_0
   e. p-value $= .0096$, found by $2(.5000 - .4952)$
3. Step 1 $H_0: \mu_1 \ge \mu_2 \qquad H_1: \mu_1 < \mu_2$
   Step 2 The .05 significance level was chosen.
   Step 3 Reject H_0 if $z < -1.645$.
   Step 4 -0.94, found by:

$$z = \frac{7.6 - 8.1}{\sqrt{\dfrac{(2.3)^2}{40} + \dfrac{(2.9)^2}{55}}} = -0.94$$

   Step 5 Do not reject H_0. Babies using the Gibbs brand did
not gain less weight. p-value $= .1736$, found by
$.5000 - .3264$.
5. $H_0: \mu_1 \le \mu_2 \qquad H_1: \mu_1 > \mu_2$
If $z > 1.645$, reject H_0.

$$z = \frac{61.4 - 60.6}{\sqrt{\dfrac{(1.2)^2}{45} + \dfrac{(1.1)^2}{39}}} = 3.187$$

Reject the null. It is reasonable to conclude that those who had a Caesarean section are shorter.
The p-value is virtually zero. That much of a difference could almost never be due to sampling error.

7. a. H_0 is rejected if $z > 1.645$.
   b. 0.64, found by $p_c = \dfrac{70 + 90}{100 + 150}$
   c. 1.61, found by
   $$z = \frac{0.70 - 0.60}{\sqrt{[(0.64 \times 0.36)/100] + [(0.64 \times 0.36)/150]}}$$
   d. H_0 is not rejected.

9. a. $H_0: \pi_1 = \pi_2$ $H_1: \pi_1 \neq \pi_2$
   b. H_0 is rejected if $z < -1.96$ or $z > 1.96$.
   c. $p_c = \dfrac{24 + 40}{400 + 400} = 0.08$
   d. -2.09, found by
   $$z = \frac{0.06 - 0.10}{\sqrt{[(0.08 \times 0.92)/400] + [(0.08 \times 0.92)/400]}}$$
   e. H_0 is rejected. The proportion infested is not the same in the two fields.

11. $H_0: \pi_d \leq \pi_r$ $H_1: \pi_d > \pi_r$
   H_0 is rejected if $z > 2.05$.
   $$p_c = \frac{168 + 200}{800 + 1{,}000} = 0.2044$$
   $$z = \frac{0.21 - 0.20}{\sqrt{\dfrac{(0.2044)(0.7956)}{800} + \dfrac{(0.2044)(0.7956)}{1{,}000}}} = 0.52$$
   H_0 is not rejected. We cannot conclude that a larger proportion of Democrats favor lowering the standards. p-value = 0.3015.

13. a. Reject H_0 if $t > 2.120$ or $t < -2.120$.
   $df = 10 + 8 - 2 = 16$
   b. $s_p^2 = \dfrac{(10 - 1)(4)^2 + (8 - 1)(5)^2}{10 + 8 - 2} = 19.9375$
   c. $t = \dfrac{23 - 26}{\sqrt{19.9375\left(\dfrac{1}{10} + \dfrac{1}{8}\right)}} = -1.416$
   d. Do not reject H_0.
   e. p-value is greater than 0.10 and less than 0.20.

15. $H_0: \mu_1 = \mu_2$ $H_1: \mu_1 \neq \mu_2$
   $df = n_1 + n_2 - 2 = 16 + 14 - 2 = 28$
   Reject H_0 if $t > 2.376$ or $t < -2.376$.
   $$s_p^2 = \frac{(16 - 1)(9380.646)^2 + (14 - 1)(7547.931)^2}{16 + 14 - 2} = 73{,}591{,}939.53$$
   $$t = \frac{5906 - 7500}{\sqrt{73{,}791{,}939.53\left(\dfrac{1}{16} + \dfrac{1}{14}\right)}} = -0.5075$$
   Do not reject H_0. The data do not suggest any statistical difference between the average salaries of pitchers versus position players.

17. $H_0: \mu_s \leq \mu_a$ $H_1: \mu_s > \mu_a$
   $df = 6 + 7 - 2 = 11$
   Reject H_0 if $t > 1.363$.
   $$s_p^2 = \frac{(6 - 1)(12.2)^2 + (7 - 1)(15.8)^2}{6 + 7 - 2} = 203.82$$
   $$t = \frac{142.5 - 130.3}{\sqrt{203.82\left(\dfrac{1}{6} + \dfrac{1}{7}\right)}} = 1.536$$
   Reject H_0. The mean daily expenses are greater for the sales staff. The p-value is between 0.05 and 0.10.

19. a. Reject H_0 if $t > 2.353$.
   b. $\bar{d} = \dfrac{12}{4} = 3.00$ $s_d = \sqrt{\dfrac{2}{3}} = 0.816$
   c. $t = \dfrac{3.00}{0.816/\sqrt{4}} = 7.35$
   d. Reject H_0. There are more defective parts produced on the day shift.
   e. p-value is less than 0.005, but greater than 0.0005.

21. $H_0: \mu_d \leq 0$ $H_1: \mu_d > 0$
   $\bar{d} = 25.917$
   $s_d = 40.791$
   Reject H_0 if $t > 1.796$.
   $$t = \frac{25.917}{40.791/\sqrt{12}} = 2.20$$
   Reject H_0. The incentive plan resulted in an increase in weekly income. The p-value is about .025.

23. $H_0: \mu_m = \mu_w$ $H_1: \mu_m \neq \mu_w$
   Reject H_0 if $z > 2.576$ or $t < -2.576$.
   $$z = \frac{24.51 - 22.69}{\sqrt{\left(\dfrac{4.48^2}{35} + \dfrac{3.86^2}{40}\right)}} = 1.871$$
   Do not reject H_0. The p-value is 0.0614, found by $2(0.5000 - 0.4693)$.

25. $H_0: \mu_1 = \mu_2$; $H_1: \mu_1 \neq \mu_2$
   Reject H_0 if $z < -1.96$ or $z > 1.96$.
   $$z = \frac{4.77 - 5.02}{\sqrt{\dfrac{(1.05)^2}{40} + \dfrac{(1.23)^2}{50}}} = -1.04$$
   H_0. is not rejected. There is no difference in the mean number of calls. p-value = $2(0.5000 - 0.3508) = 0.2984$.

27. $H_0: \mu_B \leq \mu_A$ $H_1: \mu_B > \mu_A$.
   $df = n_B + n_A - 2 = 30 + 40 - 2 = 68$
   Reject H_0 if $t > 1.668$
   $$s_p^2 = \frac{(30 - 1)(7100)^2 + (40 - 1)(9200)^2}{30 + 40 - 2} = 70{,}041{,}911.76$$
   $$t = \frac{61{,}000 - 57{,}000}{\sqrt{70{,}041{,}911.76\left(\dfrac{1}{30} + \dfrac{1}{40}\right)}} = 1.979$$
   Reject H_0. The mean income of Plan B subscribers is greater than that of Plan A subscribers. The p-value is between 0.025 and 0.010.

29. $H_0: \pi_1 \leq \pi_2$ $H_1: \pi_1 > \pi_2$
   Reject H_0 if $z > 1.645$.
   $$p_c = \frac{180 + 261}{200 + 300} = 0.882$$
   $$z = \frac{0.90 - 0.87}{\sqrt{\dfrac{0.882(0.118)}{200} + \dfrac{0.882(0.118)}{300}}} = 1.019$$
   H_0 is not rejected. There is no difference in the proportions that found relief with the new and the old drugs.

31. $H_0: \pi_1 \leq \pi_2$ $H_1: \pi_1 > \pi_2$
   If $z > 2.326$, reject H_0.
   $$p_c = \frac{990 + 970}{1{,}500 + 1{,}600} = 0.63$$
   $$z = \frac{.6600 - .60625}{\sqrt{\dfrac{.63(.37)}{1{,}500} + \dfrac{.63(.37)}{1{,}600}}} = 3.10$$
   Reject the null hypothesis. We can conclude the proportion of men who believe the division is fair is greater. The p-value is less than 0.001.

33. $H_0: \pi_1 \leq \pi_2$ $H_1: \pi_1 > \pi_2$ H_0 is rejected if $z > 1.645$.

$$p_c = \frac{.091 + .085}{2} = .088$$

$$z = \frac{0.091 - 0.085}{\sqrt{\dfrac{(0.088)(0.912)}{5000} + \dfrac{(0.088)(0.912)}{5000}}} = 1.059$$

H_0 is not rejected. There has not been an increase in the proportion calling conditions "good." The p-value is 0.1446, found by $0.5000 - 0.3554$. The increase in the percentages will happen by chance in one out of every seven cases.

35. $H_0: \pi_1 = \pi_2$ $H_1: \pi_1 \neq \pi_2$

H_0 is rejected if z is not between -1.96 and 1.96.

$$p_c = \frac{100 + 36}{300 + 200} = .272$$

$$z = \frac{\dfrac{100}{300} - \dfrac{36}{200}}{\sqrt{\dfrac{(0.272)(0.728)}{300} + \dfrac{(0.272)(0.728)}{200}}} = 3.775$$

H_0 is rejected. There is a difference in the replies of the sexes.

37. $H_0: \mu_1 \leq \mu_2$ $H_1: \mu_1 > \mu_2$ Reject H_0 if $t > 2.650$.

$\overline{X}_1 = 125.125$ $s_1 = 15.094$
$\overline{X}_2 = 117.714$ $s_2 = 19.914$

$$s_p^2 = \frac{(8-1)(15.094)^2 + (7-1)(19.914)^2}{8+7-2} = 305.708$$

$$t = \frac{125.125 - 117.714}{\sqrt{305.708\left(\dfrac{1}{8} + \dfrac{1}{7}\right)}} = 0.819$$

H_0 is not rejected. There is no difference in the mean number sold at the regular price and the mean number sold at the reduced price.

39. $H_0: \mu_d \leq 0$ $H_1: \mu_d > 0$ Reject H_0 if $t > 1.895$.
$\overline{d} = 1.75$ $s_d = 2.9155$

$$t = \frac{1.75}{2.9155/\sqrt{8}} = 1.698$$

Do not reject H_0. There is no difference in the mean number of absences. The p-value is greater than 0.05 but less than .10.

41. $H_0: \mu_1 = \mu_2$ $H_1: \mu_1 \neq \mu_2$

Reject H_0 if $t < -2.024$ or $t > 2.204$.

$$s_p^2 = \frac{(15-1)(40)^2 + (25-1)(30)^2}{15+25-2} = 1157.89$$

$$t = \frac{150 - 180}{\sqrt{1157.89\left(\dfrac{1}{15} + \dfrac{1}{25}\right)}} = -2.699$$

Reject the null hypothesis. The population means are different.

43. $H_0: \mu_d \leq 0$ $H_1: \mu_d > 0$
Reject H_0 if $t > 1.895$.
$\overline{d} = 3.11$ $s_d = 2.91$

$$t = \frac{3.11}{2.91/\sqrt{8}} = 3.02$$

Reject H_0. The mean is lower.

45. $H_0: \mu_O = \mu_R$ $H_1: \mu_O \neq \mu_R$
$df = 25 + 28 - 2 = 51$
Reject H_0 if $t < -2.008$ or $t > 2.008$.
$\overline{X}_O = 86.24$, $s_O = 23.43$
$\overline{X}_R = 92.04$, $s_R = 24.12$

$$s_p^2 = \frac{(25-1)(23.43)^2 + (28-1)(24.12)^2}{25+28-2} = 566.335$$

$$t = \frac{86.24 - 92.04}{\sqrt{566.335\left(\dfrac{1}{25} + \dfrac{1}{28}\right)}} = -0.886$$

Do not reject H_0. There is no difference in the mean number of cars in the two lots.

47. Defining $d = $ (Count at US 17 $-$ Count at SC 707)
$H_0: \mu_d \leq 0$ $H_1: \mu_d > 0$ $df = n - 1 = 25 - 1 = 24$
Reject H_0 if $t > 1.711$.

$$\overline{d} = 2.8; \quad S_d = 6.589$$

$$t = \frac{2.8}{6.589/\sqrt{25}} = 2.125$$

Reject H_0; p-value = 0.022. Based on automobile counts, the US 17 store has more business volume than the SC 707 store.

49. a. $\mu_1 = $ without pool $\mu_2 = $ with pool
$H_0: \mu_1 = \mu_2$ $H_1: \mu_1 \neq \mu_2$
Reject H_0 if $t > 1.983$ or $t < -1.983$.
$\overline{X}_1 = 202.8$ $s_1 = 33.7$ $n_1 = 38$
$\overline{X}_2 = 231.5$ $s_2 = 50.46$ $n_2 = 67$

$$s_p^2 = \frac{(38-1)(33.7)^2 + (67-1)(50.46)^2}{38+67-2} = 2{,}041.05$$

$$t = \frac{202.8 - 231.5}{\sqrt{2{,}041.05\left(\dfrac{1}{38} + \dfrac{1}{67}\right)}} = -3.12$$

Reject H_0. There is a difference in mean selling price for homes with and without a pool.

b. $\mu_1 = $ without attached garage $\mu_2 = $ with garage
$H_0: \mu_1 = \mu_2$ $H_1: \mu_1 \neq \mu_2$
Reject H_0 if $t > 1.983$ or $t < -1.983$.
$\alpha = 0.05$ $df = 34 + 71 - 2 = 103$
$\overline{X}_1 = 185.45$ $s_1 = 28.00$
$\overline{X}_2 = 238.18$ $s_2 = 44.88$

$$s_p^2 = \frac{(34-1)(28.00)^2 + (71-1)(44.88)^2}{103} = 1{,}620.07$$

$$t = \frac{185.45 - 238.18}{\sqrt{1{,}620.07\left(\dfrac{1}{34} + \dfrac{1}{71}\right)}} = -6.28$$

Reject H_0. There is a difference in mean selling price for homes with and without an attached garage.

c. $H_0: \mu_1 = \mu_2$ $H_1: \mu_1 \neq \mu_2$
Reject H_0 if $t > 2.036$ or $t < -2.036$.
$\overline{X}_1 = 196.91$ $s_1 = 35.78$ $n_1 = 15$
$\overline{X}_2 = 227.45$ $s_2 = 44.19$ $n_2 = 20$

$$s_p^2 = \frac{(15-1)(35.78)^2 + (20-1)(44.19)^2}{15+20-2} = 1{,}667.43$$

$$t = \frac{196.91 - 227.45}{\sqrt{1{,}667.43\left(\dfrac{1}{15} + \dfrac{1}{20}\right)}} = -2.19$$

Reject H_0. There is a difference in mean selling price for homes in Township 1 and Township 2.

d. $H_0: \pi_1 = \pi_2$ $H_1: \pi_1 \neq \pi_2$
If z is not between -1.96 and 1.96, reject H_0.

$$p_c = \frac{24 + 43}{52 + 53} = 0.64$$

$$z = \frac{0.462 - 0.811}{\sqrt{0.64 \times 0.36/52 + 0.64 \times 0.36/53}} = -3.73$$

Reject the null hypothesis. There is a difference.

51. $H_0: \mu_1 = \mu_2$ $H_1: \mu_1 \neq \mu_2$
If t is not between -1.991 and 1.991, reject H_0.

$$s_p^2 = \frac{(53-1)(52.9)^2 + (27-1)(55.1)^2}{53+27-2} = 2878$$

$$t = \frac{454.8 - 441.5}{\sqrt{2878\left(\dfrac{1}{53} + \dfrac{1}{27}\right)}} = 1.05$$

Do not reject H_0. There may be no difference in the mean maintenance cost for the two types of buses.

CHAPTER 12

1. 9.01, from Appendix B.4
3. Reject H_0 if $F > 10.5$, where degrees of freedom in the numerator are 7 and 5 in the denominator. Computed $F = 2.04$, found by:

$$F = \frac{s_1^2}{s_2^2} = \frac{(10)^2}{(7)^2} = 2.04$$

Do not reject H_0. There is no difference in the variations of the two populations.

5. H_0: $\sigma_1^2 = \sigma_2^2$ H_1: $\sigma_1^2 \neq \sigma_2^2$
Reject H_0 where $F > 3.10$. (3.10 is about halfway between 3.14 and 3.07.) Computed $F = 1.44$, found by:

$$F = \frac{(12)^2}{(10)^2} = 1.44$$

Do not reject H_0. There is no difference in the variations of the two populations.

7. a. H_0: $\mu_1 = \mu_2 = \mu_3$; H_1: Treatment means are not all the same.
   b. Reject H_0 if $F > 4.26$.

c & d.

Source	SS	df	MS	F
Treatment	62.17	2	31.08	21.94
Error	12.75	9	1.42	
Total	74.92	11		

   e. Reject H_0. The treatment means are not all the same.

9. H_0: $\mu_1 = \mu_2 = \mu_3$; H_1: Treatment means are not all the same. Reject H_0 if $F > 4.26$.

Source	SS	df	MS	F
Treatment	276.50	2	138.25	14.18
Error	87.75	9	9.75	

Reject H_0. The treatment means are not all the same.

11. a. H_0: $\mu_1 = \mu_2 = \mu_3$; H_1: Not all means are the same.
    b. Reject H_0 if $F > 4.26$.
    c. SST = 107.20, SSE = 9.47, SS total = 116.67.
    d.

Source	SS	df	MS	F
Treatment	107.20	2	53.600	50.96
Error	9.47	9	1.052	
Total	116.67	11		

   e. Since $50.96 > 4.26$, H_0 is rejected. At least one of the means differs.
   f. $(\overline{X}_1 - \overline{X}_2) \pm t\sqrt{MSE(1/n_1 + 1/n_2)}$
   = $(9.667 - 2.20) \pm 2.262 \sqrt{1.052(1/3 + 1/5)}$
   = 7.467 ± 1.69
   = $[5.777, 9.157]$
   Yes, we can conclude that treatments 1 and 2 have different means.

13. H_0: $\mu_1 = \mu_2 = \mu_3 = \mu_4$; H_1: Not all means are equal. H_0 is rejected if $F > 3.71$.

Source	SS	df	MS	F
Treatment	32.33	3	10.77	2.36
Error	45.67	10	4.567	
Total	78.00	13		

Because 2.36 is less than 3.71, H_0 is not rejected. There is no difference in the mean number of weeks.

15. H_0: $\sigma_1^2 \leq \sigma_2^2$; H_1: $\sigma_1^2 > \sigma_2^2$. $df_1 = 21 - 1 = 20$; $df_2 = 18 - 1 = 17$. H_0 is rejected if $F > 3.16$.

$$F = \frac{(45,600)^2}{(21,330)^2} = 4.57$$

Reject H_0. There is more variation in the selling price of oceanfront homes.

17. Sharkey: $n = 7$ $s_s = 14.79$
    White: $n = 8$ $s_w = 22.95$
    H_0: $\sigma_w^2 \leq \sigma_s^2$; H_1: $\sigma_w^2 > \sigma_s^2$. $df_s = 7 - 1 = 6$; $df_w = 8 - 1 = 7$. Reject H_0 if $F > 8.26$.

$$F = \frac{(22.95)^2}{(14.79)^2} = 2.41$$

Cannot reject H_0. There is no difference in the variation of the monthly sales.

19. a. H_0: $\mu_1 = \mu_2 = \mu_3 = \mu_4$
       H_1: Treatment means are not all equal.
    b. $\alpha = .05$ Reject H_0 if $F > 3.10$.
    c.

Source	SS	df	MS	F
Treatment	50	$4 - 1 = 3$	50/3	1.67
Error	200	$24 - 4 = 20$	10	
Total	250	$24 - 1 = 23$		

    d. Do not reject H_0.

21. H_0: $\mu_1 = \mu_2 = \mu_3$; H_1: Not all treatment means are equal. H_0 is rejected if $F > 3.89$.

Source	SS	df	MS	F
Treatment	63.33	2	31.667	13.38
Error	28.40	12	2.367	
Total	91.73	14		

H_0 is rejected. There is a difference in the treatment means.

23. H_0: $\mu_1 = \mu_2 = \mu_3 = \mu_4$; H_1: Not all means are equal. H_0 is rejected if $F > 3.10$.

Source	SS	df	MS	F
Factor	87.79	3	29.26	9.12
Error	64.17	20	3.21	
Total	151.96	23		

Because the computed F of $9.12 > 3.10$, the null hypothesis of no difference is rejected at the .05 level.

25. a. H_0: $\mu_1 = \mu_2$; H_1: $\mu_1 \neq \mu_2$. Critical value of $F = 4.75$.

Source	SS	df	MS	F
Treatment	219.43	1	219.43	23.10
Error	114.00	12	9.5	
Total	333.43	13		

   b. $t = \dfrac{19 - 27}{\sqrt{9.5\left(\dfrac{1}{6} + \dfrac{1}{8}\right)}} = -4.806$

   Then $t^2 = F$. That is $(-4.806)^2 = 23.10$.
   c. H_0 is rejected. There is a difference in the mean scores.

27. The null hypothesis is rejected because the F statistic (8.26) is greater than the critical value (5.61) at the .01 significance level. The p-value (.0019) is also less than the significance level. The mean gasoline mileages are not the same.

29. H_0: $\mu_1 = \mu_2 = \mu_3 = \mu_4$. H_1: At least one mean is different. Reject H_0 if $F > 2.7395$. Since 2.72 is less than 2.7395, H_0 is

not rejected. You can also see this conclusion from the p-value of 0.051, which is greater than 0.05. There is no difference in the means for the different types of first-class mail.

31. $H_0: \mu_1 = \mu_2 = \mu_3 = \mu_4$; H_1: The treatment means are not equal. Reject H_0: if $F > 2.76$.

Source	df	SS	MS	F
Treatment	3	1,552	517	1.84
Error	60	16,846	281	
Total	63	18,399		

Because the computed F of $1.84 < 2.76$, do not reject the null hypothesis of no difference at the 0.05 level. The mean proportions of stock investment could be the same for all age groups.

33. a. $H_0: \sigma_{np}^2 = \sigma_p^2$ $H_1: \sigma_{np}^2 \neq \sigma_p^2$

Reject H_0 if $F > 2.05$ (estimated).
$df_1 = 67 - 1 = 66$; $df_2 = 38 - 1 = 37$

$$F = \frac{(50.57)^2}{(33.71)^2} = 2.25$$

Reject H_0. There is a difference in the variance of the two selling prices.

b. $H_0: \sigma_g^2 = \sigma_{ng}^2$; $H_1: \sigma_g^2 \neq \sigma_{ng}^2$.

Reject H_0 if $F > 2.21$ (estimated).

$$F = \frac{(44.88)^2}{(28.00)^2} = 2.57$$

Reject H_0. There is a difference in the variance of the two selling prices.

c.

Source	SS	df	MS	F
Township	13,263	4	3,316	1.52
Error	217,505	100	2,175	
Total	230,768	104		

$H_0: \mu_1 = \mu_2 = \mu_3 = \mu_4 = \mu_5$; H_1: Not all treatment means are equal. Reject H_0 if $F > 2.46$.
Do not reject H_0. There is no difference in the mean selling prices in the five townships.

35. a. $H_0: \mu_1 = \mu_2 = \mu_3$ H_1: Not all treatment means are equal. Reject H_0 if $F > 4.89$.

Source	SS	df	MS	F
Treatment	28,996	2	14,498	5.62
Error	198,696	77	2,580	
Total	227,692	79		

Reject H_0. The mean maintenance costs are different.
b. $H_0: \mu_1 = \mu_2 = \mu_3$ H_1: Not all treatment means are equal. Reject H_0 if $F > 3.12$.

Source	SS	df	MS	F
Treatment	5,095	2	2,547	1.45
Error	135,513	77	1,760	
Total	140,608	79		

Do not reject H_0. The mean miles traveled are not different.

c. $(441.81 - 506.75) \pm 1.991 \sqrt{2580\left(\dfrac{1}{47} + \dfrac{1}{8}\right)}$

This reduces to -64.94 ± 38.68, so the difference is between -103.62 and -26.26. To put it another way, Bluebird is less costly than Thompson by an amount between \$26.26 and \$103.62.

CHAPTER 13

1. $\Sigma(X - \overline{X})(Y - \overline{Y}) = 10.6$, $s_x = 2.7019$, $s_y = 1.3038$

$$r = \frac{10.6}{(5 - 1)(2.7019)(1.3038)} = 0.7522$$

3. a. Sales.
b.

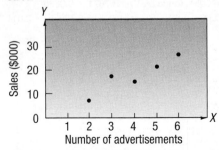

c. $\Sigma(X - \overline{X})(Y - \overline{Y}) = 36$, $n = 5$, $s_x = 1.5811$, $s_y = 6.1237$

$$r = \frac{36}{(5 - 1)(1.5811)(6.1237)} = 0.9295$$

d. There is a strong positive association between the variables.

5. a. Police is the independent variable, and crime is the dependent variable.
b.

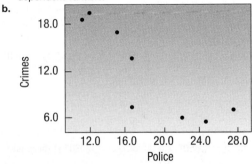

c. $n = 8$, $\Sigma(X - \overline{X})(Y - \overline{Y}) = -231.75$, $s_x = 5.8737$, $s_y = 6.4462$

$$r = \frac{-231.75}{(8 - 1)(5.8737)(6.4462)} = -0.8744$$

d. Strong inverse relationship. As the number of police increases, the crime decreases.

7. Reject H_0 if $t > 1.812$.

$$t = \frac{.32\sqrt{12 - 2}}{\sqrt{1 - (.32)^2}} = 1.068$$

Do not reject H_0.

9. $H_0: \rho \leq 0$; $H_1: \rho > 0$. Reject H_0 if $t > 2.552$. $df = 18$.

$$t = \frac{.78\sqrt{20 - 2}}{\sqrt{1 - (.78)^2}} = 5.288$$

Reject H_0. There is a positive correlation between gallons sold and the pump price.

11. $H_0: \rho \leq 0$ $H_1: \rho > 0$
Reject H_0 if $t > 2.650$.

$$t = \frac{0.667\sqrt{15 - 2}}{\sqrt{1 - 0.667^2}} = 3.228$$

Reject H_0. There is a positive correlation between the number of passengers and plane weight.

13. a. $\hat{Y} = 3.7778 + 0.3630X$

$$b = 0.7522\left(\frac{1.3038}{2.7019}\right) = 0.3630$$

$$a = 5.8 - 0.3630(5.6) = 3.7671$$

b. 6.3081, found by $\hat{Y} = 3.7671 + 0.3630(7)$

15. a. $\Sigma(X - \bar{X})(Y - \bar{Y}) = 44.6$, $s_x = 2.726$, $s_y = 2.011$

$$r = \frac{44.6}{(10 - 1)(2.726)(2.011)} = .904$$

$$b = .904\left(\frac{2.011}{2.726}\right) = 0.667$$

$$a = 7.4 - .677(9.1) = 1.333$$

b. $\hat{Y} = 1.333 + .667(6) = 5.335$

17. a.

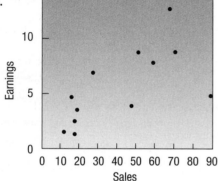

b. $\Sigma(X - \bar{X})(Y - \bar{Y}) = 629.64$, $s_x = 26.17$, $s_y = 3.248$

$$r = \frac{629.64}{(12 - 1)(26.17)(3.248)} = .6734$$

c. $b = .6734\left(\frac{3.248}{26.170}\right) = 0.0836$

$$a = \frac{64.1}{12} - 0.0836\left(\frac{501.10}{12}\right) = 1.8507$$

d. $\hat{Y} = 1.8507 + 0.0836(50.0) = 6.0307$ ($ millions)

19. a. $b = -.8744\left(\frac{6.4462}{5.8737}\right) = -0.9596$

$$a = \frac{95}{8} - (-0.9596)\left(\frac{146}{8}\right) = 29.3877$$

b. 10.1957, found by $29.3877 - 0.9596(20)$

c. For each policeman added, crime goes down by almost one.

21. $H_0: \beta \geq 0$ $H_1: \beta < 0$ $df = n - 2 = 8 - 2 = 6$
Reject H_0 if $t < -1.943$.

$$t = -0.96/0.22 = -4.364$$

Reject H_0 and conclude the slope is less than zero.

23. $H_0: \beta = 0$ $H_1: \beta \neq 0$ $df = n - 2 = 12 - 2 = 10$
Reject H_0 if t not between -2.228 and 2.228

$$t = 0.08/0.03 = 2.667$$

Reject H_0 and conclude the slope is different from zero.

25. The standard error of estimate is 3.379, found by $\sqrt{\frac{68.4877}{8 - 2}}$.

The coefficient of determination is 0.76, found by $(-0.874)^2$. Seventy-six percent of the variation in crimes can be explained by the variation in police.

27. The standard error of estimate is 0.913, found by $\sqrt{\frac{6.667}{10 - 2}}$.

The coefficient of determination is 0.82, found by 29.733/36.4.
Eighty-two percent of the variation in kilowatt hours can be explained by the variation in the number of rooms.

29. a. $r^2 = \frac{1000}{1500} = .6667$

b. $r = \sqrt{.6667} = .8165$

c. $s_{y.x} = \sqrt{\frac{500}{13}} = 6.2017$

31. a. $6.308 \pm (3.182)(.993)\sqrt{.2 + \frac{(7 - 5.6)^2}{29.2}}$

$= 6.308 \pm 1.633$
$= [4.675, 7.941]$

b. $6.308 \pm (3.182)(.993)\sqrt{1 + 1/5 + .0671}$
$= [2.751, 9.865]$

33. a. 4.2939, 6.3721
b. 2.9854, 7.6806

35. No, relationship is nonlinear. Correlation coefficient is 0.298. The correlation is 0.298 Yes, transformed relationship is linear. Correlation coefficient is 0.99.

37. $H_0: \rho \leq 0$; $H_1: \rho > 0$. Reject H_0 if $t > 1.714$.

$$t = \frac{.94\sqrt{25 - 2}}{\sqrt{1 - (.94)^2}} = 13.213$$

Reject H_0. There is a positive correlation between passengers and weight of luggage.

39. $H_0: \rho \leq 0$; $H_1: \rho > 0$. Reject H_0 if $t > 2.764$.

$$t = \frac{.47\sqrt{12 - 2}}{\sqrt{1 - (.47)^2}} = 1.684$$

Do not reject H_0. There is not a positive correlation between engine size and performance. p-value is greater than .05, but less than .10.

41. a.

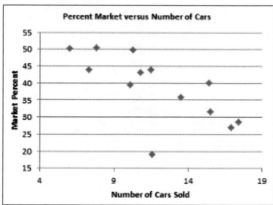

The sales volume is inversely related to their market share.

b. $\bar{X} = \frac{154.1}{13} = 11.854$ $\bar{Y} = \frac{503.5}{13} = 38.7308$

$$s_x = \sqrt{\frac{163.032}{12}} = 3.686 \qquad s_y = \sqrt{\frac{1154.41}{12}} = 9.808$$

$$r = \frac{-299.792}{(13 - 1)(3.686)(9.808)} = -0.691$$

c. $H_0: \rho \geq 0$ $H_1: \rho < 0$
Reject H_0 if $t < -2.718$.

$$df = 11 \qquad t = \frac{-0.691\sqrt{13 - 2}}{\sqrt{1 - (-0.691)^2}} = -3.17$$

Reject H_0. There is a negative correlation between cars sold and market share.

d. 47.7%, found by $(-0.691)^2$, of the variation in market share is accounted for by variation in cars sold.

43. a. $r = -0.241$
b. $R^2 = (-0.241)^2 = 0.0581$; relationship is very weak

c. H_0: $\rho \geq 0$; H_1: $\rho < 0$. Reject H_0 if $t < -1.697$

$$t = \frac{-0.241\sqrt{32 - 2}}{\sqrt{1 - (-0.241)^2}} = -1.36$$

Do not reject H_0. There is not enough evidence to suggest that points scored and points allowed per game are negatively or inversely related.

45. a.

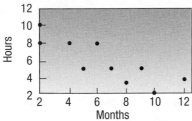

There is an inverse relationship between the variables. As the months owned increase, the number of hours exercised decreases.

b. $r = -0.827$

c. H_0: $\rho \geq 0$; H_1: $\rho < 0$. Reject H_0 if $t < -2.896$.

$$t = \frac{-0.827\sqrt{10 - 2}}{\sqrt{1 - (-0.827)^2}} = -4.16$$

Reject H_0. There is a negative association between months owned and hours exercised.

47. a. Median age and population are directly related.

b. $r = \dfrac{11.93418}{(10 - 1)(2.207)(1.330)} = 0.452$

c. The slope of 0.272 indicates that for each increase of 1 million in the population, the median age increases on average by 0.272 years.

d. The median age is 32.08 years, found by $31.4 + 0.272(2.5)$.

e. The p-value (0.190) for the population variable is greater than, say, 0.05. A test for significance of that coefficient would fail to be rejected. In other words, it is possible the population coefficient is zero.

f. H_0: $\rho = 0$ H_1: $\rho \neq 0$ Reject H_0 if t is not between -2.306 and 2.306.

$$df = 8 \qquad t = \frac{0.452\sqrt{10 - 2}}{\sqrt{1 - (0.452)^2}} = 1.433$$

Do not reject H_0.
There may be no relationship between age and population.

49. a. $b = -0.4667$, $a = 11.2358$

b. $\hat{Y} = 11.2358 - 0.4667(7.0) = 7.9689$

c. $7.9689 \pm (2.160)(1.114)\sqrt{1 + \dfrac{1}{15} + \dfrac{(7 - 7.1333)^2}{73.7333}}$

$= 7.9689 \pm 2.4854$

$= [5.4835, 10.4543]$

d. $r^2 = 0.499$. Nearly 50% of the variation in the amount of the bid is explained by the number of bidders.

51. a.

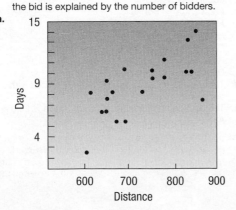

There appears to be a relationship between the two variables. As the distance increases, so does the shipping time.

b. $r = 2.004$

H_0: $\rho \leq 0$; H_1: $\rho > 0$. Reject H_0 If $t > 1.734$.

$$t = \frac{0.692\sqrt{20 - 2}}{\sqrt{1 - (0.692)^2}} = 4.067$$

H_0 is rejected. There is a positive association between shipping distance and shipping time.

c. $r^2 = 0.479$. Nearly half of the variation in shipping time is explained by shipping distance.

d. $s_{y \cdot x} = 2.004$

53. a. $b = 2.41$

$a = 26.8$

The regression equation is: Price $= 26.8 + 2.41 \times$ Dividend. For each additional dollar of dividend, the price increases by \$2.41.

b. $r^2 = \dfrac{5{,}057.6}{7{,}682.7} = 0.658$ Thus, 65.8% of the variation in price is explained by the dividend.

c. $r = \sqrt{.658} = 0.811$ H_0: $\rho \leq 0$ H_1: $\rho > 0$

At the 5% level, reject H_0 when $t > 1.701$.

$$t = \frac{0.811\sqrt{30 - 2}}{\sqrt{1 - (0.811)^2}} = 7.34$$

Thus, H_0 is rejected. The population correlation is positive.

55. a. 35

b. $s_{y \cdot x} = \sqrt{29{,}778{,}406} = 5{,}456.96$

c. $r^2 = \dfrac{13{,}548{,}662{,}082}{14{,}531{,}349{,}474} = 0.932$

d. $r = \sqrt{0.932} = 0.966$

e. H_0: $\rho \leq 0$, H_1: $\rho > 0$; reject H_0 if $t > 1.692$.

$$t = \frac{.966\sqrt{35 - 2}}{\sqrt{1 - (.966)^2}} = 21.46$$

Reject H_0. There is a direct relationship between size of the house and its market value.

57. a. The regression equation is Price $= -773 + 1{,}408$ Speed.

b. The second laptop (1.6, 922) with a residual of -557.60, is priced \$557.60 below the predicted price. That is a noticeable "bargain."

c. The correlation of Speed and Price is 0.835.

H_0: $\rho \leq 0$ H_1: $\rho > 0$ Reject H_0 if $t > 1.8125$.

$$t = \frac{0.835\sqrt{12 - 2}}{\sqrt{1 - (0.835)^2}} = 4.799$$

Reject H_0. It is reasonable to say the population correlation is positive.

59. a. $r = .987$, H_0: $\rho \leq 0$, H_1: $\rho > 0$. Reject H_0 if $t > 1.746$.

$$t = \frac{.987\sqrt{18 - 2}}{\sqrt{1 - (.987)^2}} = 24.564$$

b. $\hat{Y} = -29.7 + 22.93X$; an additional cup increases the dog's weight by almost 23 pounds.

c. Dog number 4 is an overeater.

61. a.

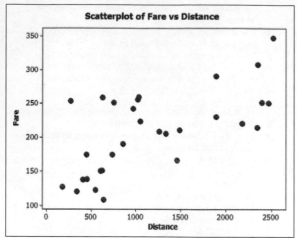

The relationship is direct. Fares increase for longer flights.
b. The correlation of *Distance* and *Fare* is 0.656.

$$H_0: \rho \le 0 \qquad H_1: \rho > 0$$

Reject H_0 if $t > 1.701$ $df = 28$

$$t = \frac{0.656\sqrt{30 - 2}}{\sqrt{1 - (0.656)^2}} = 4.599$$

Reject H_0. There is a significant positive correlation between fares and distances.
c. 43%, found by $(0.656)^2$, of the variation in fares is explained by the variation in distance.
d. The regression equation is *Fare* = 147.08 + 0.05265 *Distance*. Each additional mile adds $0.05265 to the fare. A 1,500-mile flight would cost $226.06, found by $147.08 + 0.05265(1500).
e. A flight of 4,218 miles is outside the range of the sampled data. So the regression equation may not be useful.

63. a. There does seem to be a direct relationship between the variables.

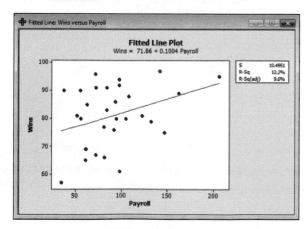

b. $(71.86 + .1004\,(100)) = 81.90$ wins
c. $(.1004 \times 5) = .5020$ wins
d. $H_0: \beta \le 0$; $H_1: \beta > 0$. $df = n - 2 = 30 - 2 = 28$
Reject H_0 if $t > 1.701$. $t = 0.1004/0.05094 = 1.97$
Reject H_0 and conclude the slope is positive.
e. 0.1218, or 12.18%, found by 427.86/3512.00

f. The correlation between wins and batting average is 0.461; the correlation between wins and ERA is −0.681. The relationship between wins and ERA is stronger. For batting average: $H_0: \rho \le 0$; $H_1: \rho > 0$.
Reject H_0 if $t > 1.701$.

$$t = \frac{0.461\sqrt{30 - 2}}{\sqrt{1 - (0.461)^2}} = 2.749$$

Rejected H_0. Team wins and team batting average are positively related.
    For ERA, $H_0: \rho \ge 0$; $H_1: \rho < 0$.
    Reject H_0 if $t < -1.701$.

$$t = \frac{-0.681\sqrt{30 - 2}}{\sqrt{1 - (-0.681)^2}} = -4.921$$

Rejected H_0. Team wins and ERA are inversely related.

CHAPTER 14

1. a. Multiple regression equation
   b. The *Y*-intercept
   c. $\hat{Y} = 64{,}100 + 0.394(796{,}000) + 9.6(6{,}940)$
       $- 11{,}600(6.0) = \$374{,}748$
3. a. 497.736, found by
       $\hat{Y} = 16.24 + 0.017(18)$
         $+ 0.0028(26{,}500) + 42(3)$
         $+ 0.0012(156{,}000)$
         $+ 0.19(141) + 26.8(2.5)$
   b. Two more social activities. Income added only 28 to the index; social activities added 53.6.

5. a. $s_{Y \cdot 12} = \sqrt{\dfrac{SSE}{n - (k + 1)}} = \sqrt{\dfrac{583.693}{65 - (2 + 1)}}$
       $= \sqrt{9.414} = 3.068$
    95% of the residuals will be between ± 6.136, found by 2(3.068).
   b. $R^2 = \dfrac{SSR}{SS\ total} = \dfrac{77.907}{661.6} = .118$
    The independent variables explain 11.8% of the variation.

   c. $R^2_{adj} = 1 - \dfrac{\dfrac{SSE}{n - (k + 1)}}{\dfrac{SS\ total}{n - 1}} = 1 - \dfrac{\dfrac{583.693}{65 - (2 + 1)}}{\dfrac{661.6}{65 - 1}}$

                $= 1 - \dfrac{9.414}{10.3375} = 1 - .911 = .089$

7. a. $\hat{Y} = 84.998 + 2.391X_1 - 0.4086X_2$
   b. 90.0674, found by $\hat{Y} = 84.998 + 2.391(4) - 0.4086(11)$
   c. $n = 65$ and $k = 2$
   d. $H_0: \beta_1 = \beta_2 = 0$ H_1: Not all β's are 0
       Reject H_0 if $F > 3.15$.
       $F = 4.14$, reject H_0. Not all net regression coefficients equal zero.
   e. For X_1 For X_2
       $H_0: \beta_1 = 0$ $H_0: \beta_2 = 0$
       $H_1: \beta_1 \ne 0$ $H_1: \beta_2 \ne 0$
       $t = 1.99$ $t = -2.38$
       Reject H_0 if $t > 2.0$ or $t < -2.0$.
       Delete variable 1 and keep 2.
   f. The regression analysis should be repeated with only X_2 as the independent variable.
9. a. The regression equation is: Performance = 29.3 + 5.22 Aptitude + 22.1 Union

Predictor	Coef	SE Coef	T	P
Constant	29.28	12.77	2.29	0.041
Aptitude	5.222	1.702	3.07	0.010
Union	22.135	8.852	2.50	0.028

```
S = 16.9166 R-Sq = 53.3% R-Sq (adj) = 45.5%
Analysis of Variance
Source          DF      SS      MS      F      P
Regression       2   3919.3  1959.6   6.85  0.010
Residual Error  12   3434.0   286.2
Total           14   7353.3
```

b. These variables are effective in predicting performance. They explain 45.5% of the variation in performance. In particular, union membership increases the typical performance by 22.1.

c. $H_0: \beta_2 = 0 \qquad H_1: \beta_2 \neq 0$

Reject H_0 if $t < -2.179$ or $t > 2.179$.

Since 2.50 is greater than 2.179, we reject the null hypothesis and conclude that union membership is significant and should be included.

11. a. $n = 40$

b. 4

c. $R^2 = \dfrac{750}{1250} = .60$

d. $s_{y \cdot 1234} = \sqrt{500/35} = 3.7796$

e. $H_0: \beta_1 = \beta_2 = \beta_3 = \beta_4 = 0$

H_1: Not all the βs equal zero.

H_0 is rejected if $F > 2.65$.

$$F = \dfrac{750/4}{500/35} = 13.125$$

H_0 is rejected. At least one β_i does not equal zero.

13. a. $n = 26$

b. $R^2 = 100/140 = .7143$

c. 1.4142, found by $\sqrt{2}$

d. $H_0: \beta_1 = \beta_2 = \beta_3 = \beta_4 = \beta_5 = 0$

H_1: Not all the βs are 0.

H_0 is rejected if $F > 2.71$.

Computed $F = 10.0$. Reject H_0. At least one regression coefficient is not zero.

e. H_0 is rejected in each case if $t < -2.086$ or $t > 2.086$. X_1 and X_5 should be dropped.

15. a. $28,000

b. $R^2 = \dfrac{SSR}{SS\ total} = \dfrac{3,050}{5,250} = .5809$

c. 9.199, found by $\sqrt{84.62}$

d. H_0 is rejected if $F > 2.97$ (approximately)

$$\text{Computed } F = \dfrac{1,016.67}{84.62} = 12.01$$

H_0 is rejected. At least one regression coefficient is not zero.

e. If computed t is to the left of -2.056 or to the right of 2.056, the null hypothesis in each of these cases is rejected. Computed t for X_2 and X_3 exceed the critical value. Thus, "population" and "advertising expenses" should be retained and "number of competitors," X_1, dropped.

17. a. The strongest correlation is between GPA and legal. No problem with multicollinearity.

b. $R^2 = \dfrac{4.3595}{5.0631} = .8610$

c. H_0 is rejected if $F > 5.41$.

$$F = \dfrac{1.4532}{0.1407} = 10.328$$

At least one coefficient is not zero.

d. Any H_0 is rejected if $t < -2.571$ or $t > 2.571$. It appears that only GPA is significant. Verbal and math could be eliminated.

e. $R^2 = \dfrac{4.2061}{5.0631} = .8307$

R^2 has only been reduced .0303.

f. The residuals appear slightly skewed (positive), but acceptable.

g. There does not seem to be a problem with the plot.

19. a. The correlation of Screen and Price is 0.893. So there does appear to be a linear relationship between the two.

b. Price is the "dependent" variable.

c. The regression equation is Price = -2484 + 101 Screen. For each inch increase in screen size, the price increases $101 on average.

d. Using "dummy" indicator variables for Sharp and Sony, the regression equation is Price = -2308 + 94.1 Screen + 15 Manufacturer Sharp + 381 Manufacturer Sony. Sharp can obtain on average $15 more than Samsung and Sony can collect an additional benefit of $381 more than Samsung.

e. Here is some of the output.

```
Predictor            Coef  SE Coef      T      P
Constant          -2308.2    492.0  -4.69  0.000
Screen              94.12    10.83   8.69  0.000
Manufacturer_Sharp   15.1    171.6   0.09  0.931
Manufacturer_Sony   381.4    168.8   2.26  0.036
```

The p-value for Sharp is relatively large. A test of their coefficient would not be rejected. That means they may not have any real advantage over Samsung. On the other hand, the p-value for the Sony coefficient is quite small. That indicates that it did not happen by chance and there is some real advantage to Sony over Samsung.

f. A histogram of the residuals indicates they follow a normal distribution.

g. The residual variation may be increasing for larger fitted values.

21. a.

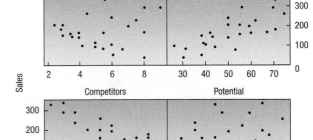

Scatter Diagram of Sales vs. Advertising, Accounts, Competitors, Potential

Sales seem to fall with the number of competitors and rise with the number of accounts and potential.

b. Pearson correlations

	Sales	Advertising	Accounts	Competitors
Advertising	0.159			
Accounts	0.783	0.173		
Competitors	-0.833	-0.038	-0.324	
Potential	0.407	-0.071	0.468	-0.202

The number of accounts and the market potential are moderately correlated.

c. The regression equation is:

Sales = 178 + 1.81 Advertising + 3.32 Accounts − 21.2 Competitors + 0.325 Potential

Predictor	Coef	SE Coef	T	P
Constant	178.32	12.96	13.76	0.000
Advertising	1.807	1.081	1.67	0.109
Accounts	3.3178	0.1629	20.37	0.000
Competitors	−21.1850	0.7879	−26.89	0.000
Potential	0.3245	0.4678	0.69	0.495

S = 9.60441   R-Sq = 98.9%   R-Sq(adj) = 98.7%

Analysis of Variance

Source	DF	SS	MS	F	P
Regression	4	176777	44194	479.10	0.000
Residual Error	21	1937	92		
Total	25	178714			

The computed F value is quite large. So we can reject the null hypothesis that all of the regression coefficients are zero. We conclude that some of the independent variables are effective in explaining sales.

d. Market potential and advertising have large p-values (0.495 and 0.109, respectively). You would probably drop them.

e. If you omit potential, the regression equation is:

Sales = 180 + 1.68 Advertising + 3.37 Accounts − 21.2 Competitors

Predictor	Coef	SE Coef	T	P
Constant	179.84	12.62	14.25	0.000
Advertising	1.677	1.052	1.59	0.125
Accounts	3.3694	0.1432	23.52	0.000
Competitors	−21.2165	0.7773	−27.30	0.000

Now advertising is not significant. That would also lead you to cut out the advertising variable and report that the polished regression equation is:

Sales = 187 + 3.41 Accounts − 21.2 Competitors

Predictor	Coef	SE Coef	T	P
Constant	186.69	12.26	15.23	0.000
Accounts	3.4081	0.1458	23.37	0.000
Competitors	−21.1930	0.8028	−26.40	0.000

f.

Histogram of the Residuals
(response is Sales)

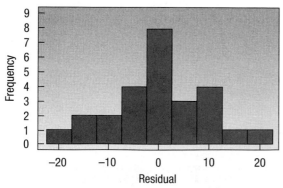

The histogram looks to be normal. There are no problems shown in this plot.

g. The variance inflation factor for both variables is 1.1. They are less than 10. There are no troubles as this value indicates the independent variables are not strongly correlated with each other.

23. The computer output is:

Predictor	Coef	StDev	t-ratio	p
Constant	651.9	345.3	1.89	0.071
Service	13.422	5.125	2.62	0.015
Age	−6.710	6.349	−1.06	0.301
Gender	205.65	90.27	2.28	0.032
Job	−33.45	89.55	−0.37	0.712

Analysis of Variance

SOURCE	DF	SS	MS	F	p
Regression	4	1066830	266708	4.77	0.005
Error	25	1398651	55946		
Total	29	2465481			

a. $\hat{Y} = 651.9 + 13.422X_1 − 6.710X_2 + 205.65X_3 − 33.45X_4$

b. $R^2 = .433$, which is somewhat low for this type of study.

c. $H_0: \beta_1 = \beta_2 = \beta_3 = \beta_4 = 0$; H_1: not all βs equal zero. Reject H_0 if $F > 2.76$.

$$F = \frac{1{,}066{,}830/4}{1{,}398{,}651/25} = 4.77$$

H_0 is rejected. Not all the β_i's equal 0.

d. Using the .05 significance level, reject the hypothesis that the regression coefficient is 0 if $t < −2.060$ or $t > 2.060$. Service and gender should remain in the analyses; age and job should be dropped.

e. Following is the computer output using the independent variables service and gender.

Predictor	Coef	StDev	t-ratio	p
Constant	784.2	316.8	2.48	0.020
Service	9.021	3.106	2.90	0.007
Gender	224.41	87.35	2.57	0.016

Analysis of Variance

SOURCE	DF	SS	MS	F	p
Regression	2	998779	499389	9.19	0.001
Error	27	1466703	54322		
Total	29	2465481			

A man earns $224 more per month than a woman. The difference between technical and clerical jobs is not significant.

25. **a.** $\hat{Y} = 29.913 − 5.324X_1 + 1.449X_2$

b. EPS is ($t = −3.26$, p-value $= .005$). Yield is not ($t = 0.81$, p-value $= .431$).

c. An increase of 1 in EPS results in a decline of 5.324 in P/E. When yield increases by one, P/E increases by 1.449.

d. Stock number 2 is undervalued.

e. Below is a residual plot. It does *not* appear to follow the normal distribution.

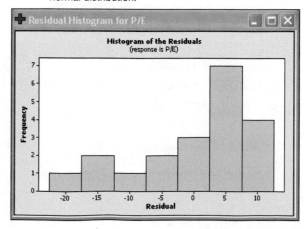

f. There does not seem to be a problem with the plot of the residuals versus the fitted values.

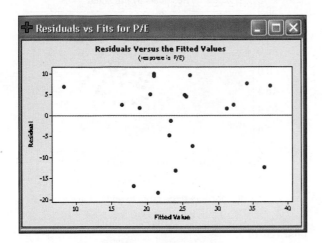

g. The correlation between yield and EPS is not a problem. No problem with multicollinearity.

	P/E	EPS
EPS	−0.602	
Yield	.054	.162

27. a. The regression equation is
Sales (000) = 1.02 + 0.0829 Infomercials

```
Predictor        Coef    SE Coef      T       P
Constant        1.0188   0.3105    3.28   0.006
Infomercials    0.08291  0.01680   4.94   0.000

Analysis of Variance
Source          DF    SS       MS       F       P
Regression       1  2.3214   2.3214   24.36   0.000
Residual Error  13  1.2386   0.0953
Total           14  3.5600
```

The global test demonstrates there is a relationship between sales and the number of infomercials.

b.

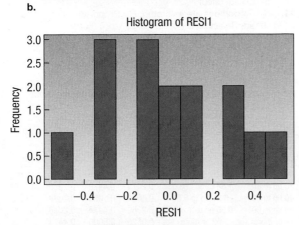

Histogram of RESI1

The residuals appear to follow the normal distribution.

29. The computer output is as follows:

```
Predictor       Coef      SE Coef        T       P
Constant        38.71      39.02       .99    .324
Bedrooms         7.118      2.551      2.79   0.006
Size             0.03800    0.01468    2.59   0.011
Pool            18.321      6.999      2.62   0.010
Distance        −0.9295     0.7279    −1.28   0.205
Garage          35.810      7.638      4.69   0.000
Baths           23.315      9.025      2.58   0.011

S = 33.21  R-Sq = 53.2%  R-Sq (adj) = 50.3%

Analysis of Variance
SOURCE          DF     SS      MS      F      P
Regression       6  122676   20446  18.54  0.000
Residual Error  98  108092    1103
Total          104  230768
```

a. Each additional bedroom adds about $7,000 to the selling price, each additional square foot adds $38, a pool adds $18,300 to the value, an attached garage increases the value by $35,800, and each mile the home is from the center of the city reduces the selling price by $929.

b. The R-square value is 0.532.

c. The correlation matrix is as follows:

	Price	Bedrooms	Size	Pool	Distance	Garage
Bedrooms	0.467					
Size	0.371	0.383				
Pool	0.294	0.005	0.201			
Distance	−0.347	−0.153	−0.117	−0.139		
Garage	0.526	0.234	0.083	0.114	−0.359	
Baths	0.382	0.329	0.024	0.055	−0.195	0.221

The independent variable *garage* has the strongest correlation with price. Distance is inversely related, as expected, and there does not seem to be a problem with correlation among the independent variables.

d. The results of the global test suggest that some of the independent variables have net regression coefficients different from zero.

e. We can delete *distance*.

f. The new regression output follows.

```
Predictor       Coef      SE Coef        T       P
Constant        17.01      35.24       .48    .630
Bedrooms         7.169      2.559      2.80   0.006
Size             0.03919    0.01470   −2.67   0.009
Pool            19.110      6.994      2.73   0.007
Garage          38.847      7.281      5.34   0.000
Baths           24.624      8.995      2.74   0.007

S = 33.32  R-Sq = 52.4%  R-Sq(adj) = 50.0%

Analysis of Variance
SOURCE          DF     SS      MS      F      P
Regression       5  120877   24175  21.78  0.000
Residual Error  99  109890    1110
Total          104  230768
```

In reviewing the *p*-values for the various regression coefficients, all are less than .05. We leave all the independent variables.

g. & h. Analysis of the residuals, not shown, indicates the normality assumption is reasonable. In addition, there is no pattern to the plots of the residuals and the fitted values of *Y*.

31. a. The regression equation is

$$\text{Maintenance} = 102 + 5.94\ \text{Age} + 0.374\ \text{Miles} - 11.8\ \text{GasolineIndicator}$$

Each additional year of age adds $5.94 to upkeep cost. Every extra mile adds $0.374 to maintenance total. Gasoline buses are cheaper to maintain than diesel by $11.80 per year.

b. The coefficient of determination is 0.286, found by 65135/227692. Twenty-nine percent of the variation in maintenance cost is explained by these variables.

c. The correlation matrix is:

	Maintenance	Age	Miles
Age	0.465		
Miles	0.450	0.522	
GasolineIndicato	−0.118	−0.068	0.025

Age and Miles both have moderately strong correlations with maintenance cost. The highest correlation among the independent variables is 0.522 between Age and Miles. That is smaller than 0.70 so multicollinearity may not be a problem.

d.

```
Analysis of Variance
Source           DF      SS      MS      F      P
Regression        3   65135   21712  10.15  0.000
Residual Error   76  162558    2139
Total            79  227692
```

The p-value is zero. Reject the null hypothesis of all coefficients being zero and say at least one is important.

e.

```
Predictor              Coef SE Coef       T      P
Constant              102.3   112.9    0.91  0.368
Age                   5.939   2.227    2.67  0.009
Miles                0.3740  0.1450    2.58  0.012
GasolineIndicator    −11.80   10.99   −1.07  0.286
```

The p-value of the gasoline indicator is bigger than 0.10. Consider deleting it.

f. The condensed regression equation is

$$\text{Maintenance} = 106 + 6.17\ \text{Age} + 0.363\ \text{Miles}$$

g.

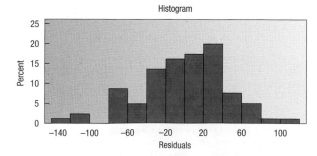

Histogram

The normality conjecture appears realistic.

h.

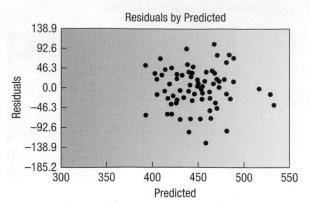

Residuals by Predicted

This plot appears to be random and to have a constant variance.

CHAPTER 15

1. a. 3
   b. 7.815
3. a. Reject H_0 if $\chi^2 > 5.991$
   b. $\chi^2 = \dfrac{(10 - 20)^2}{20} + \dfrac{(20 - 20)^2}{20} + \dfrac{(30 - 20)^2}{20} = 10.0$
   c. Reject H_0. The proportions are not equal.
5. H_0: The outcomes are the same; H_1: The outcomes are not the same. Reject H_0 if $\chi^2 > 9.236$.

$$\chi^2 = \frac{(3 - 5)^2}{5} + \cdots + \frac{(7 - 5)^2}{5} = 7.60$$

Do not reject H_0. Cannot reject H_0 since outcomes are the same.
7. H_0: There is no difference in the proportions. H_1: There is a difference in the proportions. Reject H_0 if $\chi^2 > 15.086$.

$$\chi^2 = \frac{(47 - 40)^2}{40} + \cdots + \frac{(34 - 40)^2}{40} = 3.400$$

Do not reject H_0. There is no difference in the proportions.
9. a. Reject H_0 if $\chi^2 > 9.210$.
   b. $\chi^2 = \dfrac{(30 - 24)^2}{24} + \dfrac{(20 - 24)^2}{24} + \dfrac{(10 - 12)^2}{12} = 2.50$
   c. Do not reject H_0.
11. H_0: Proportions are as stated; H_1: Proportions are not as stated. Reject H_0 if $\chi^2 > 11.345$.

$$\chi^2 = \frac{(50 - 25)^2}{25} + \cdots + \frac{(160 - 275)^2}{275} = 115.22$$

Reject H_0. The proportions are not as stated.
13. H_0: The population of clients follows a normal distribution. H_1: The population of clients does not follow a normal distribution.
Reject the null if chi-square is greater than 5.991.

Number of Clients	z-values	Area	Found by	f_e
Under 30	Under −1.58	0.0571	0.5000 − 0.4429	2.855
30 up to 40	−1.58 up to −0.51	0.2479	0.4429 − 0.1950	12.395
40 up to 50	−0.51 up to 0.55	0.4038	0.1950 + 0.2088	20.19
50 up to 60	0.55 up to 1.62	0.2386	0.4474 − 0.2088	11.93
60 or more	1.62 or more	0.0526	0.5000 − 0.4474	2.63

The first and last class both have expected frequencies smaller than 5. They are combined with adjacent classes.

Number of Clients	Area	f_e	f_o	$f_e - f_o$	$(f_o - f_e)^2$	$[(f_o - f_e)^2]/f_e$
Under 40	0.3050	15.25	16	−0.75	0.5625	0.0369
40 up to 50	0.4038	20.19	22	−1.81	3.2761	0.1623
50 or more	0.2912	14.56	12	2.56	6.5536	0.4501
Total	1.0000	50.00	50	0		0.6493

Since 0.6493 is not greater than 5.991, we fail to reject the null hypothesis. These data could be from a normal distribution.

15. The p-value of 0.746 is greater than 0.05 and the plotted values are close to the line. Thus it is reasonable to say the readings are normally distributed.

17. H_0: There is no relationship between community size and section read. H_1: There is a relationship. Reject H_0 if $\chi^2 > 9.488$.

$$\chi^2 = \frac{(170 - 157.50)^2}{157.50} + \cdots + \frac{(88 - 83.62)^2}{83.62} = 7.340$$

Do not reject H_0. There is no relationship between community size and section read.

19. H_0: No relationship between error rates and item type. H_1: There is a relationship between error rates and item type. Reject H_0 if $\chi^2 > 9.21$.

$$\chi^2 = \frac{(20 - 14.1)^2}{14.1} + \cdots + \frac{(225 - 225.25)^2}{225.25} = 8.033$$

Do not reject H_0. There is not a relationship between error rates and item type.

21. H_0: $\pi_s = 0.50$, $\pi_r = \pi_e = 0.25$
H_1: Distribution is not as given above.
$df = 2$. Reject H_0 if $\chi^2 > 4.605$.

Turn	f_o	f_e	$f_o - f_e$	$(f_o - f_e)^2/f_e$
Straight	112	100	12	1.44
Right	48	50	−2	0.08
Left	40	50	−10	2.00
Total	200	200		3.52

H_0 is not rejected. The proportions are as given in the null hypothesis.

23. H_0: There is no preference with respect to TV stations. H_1: There is a preference with respect to TV stations. $df = 3 - 1 = 2$. H_0 is rejected if $\chi^2 > 5.991$.

TV Station	f_o	f_e	$f_o - f_e$	$(f_o - f_e)^2$	$(f_o - f_e)^2/f_e$
WNAE	53	50	3	9	0.18
WRRN	64	50	14	196	3.92
WSPD	33	50	−17	289	5.78
	150	150	0		9.88

H_0 is rejected. There is a preference for TV stations.

25. H_0: $\pi_n = 0.21$, $\pi_m = 0.24$, $\pi_s = 0.35$, $\pi_w = 0.20$
H_1: The distribution is not as given.
Reject H_0 if $\chi^2 > 11.345$.

Region	f_o	f_e	$f_o - f_e$	$(f_o - f_e)^2/f_e$
Northeast	68	84	−16	3.0476
Midwest	104	96	8	0.6667
South	155	140	15	1.6071
West	73	80	−7	0.6125
Total	400	400	0	5.9339

H_0 is not rejected. The distribution of order destinations reflects the population.

27. H_0: The proportions are the same.
H_1: The proportions are not the same.
Reject H_0 if $\chi^2 > 16.919$.

f_o	f_e	$f_o - f_e$	$(f_o - f_e)^2$	$(f_o - f_e)^2/f_e$
44	28	16	256	9.143
32	28	4	16	0.571
23	28	−5	25	0.893
27	28	−1	1	0.036
23	28	−5	25	0.893
24	28	−4	16	0.571
31	28	3	9	0.321
27	28	−1	1	0.036
28	28	0	0	0.000
21	28	−7	49	1.750
				14.214

Do not reject H_0. The digits are evenly distributed.

29. H_0: The population of wages follows a normal distribution.
H_1: The population of hourly wages does not follow a normal distribution.
Reject the null if chi-square is greater than 7.779.

Wage	z-values	Area	Found by	f_e	f_o	$f_e - f_o$	$(f_o - f_e)^2$	$[(f_o - f_e)^2]/f_e$
Under $6.50	Under −1.72	0.0427	0.5000 − 0.4573	11.529	20	−8.471	71.7578	6.2241
6.50 up to 7.50	−1.72 up to −0.72	0.1931	0.4573 − 0.2642	52.137	24	28.137	791.6908	15.1848
7.50 up to 8.50	−0.72 up to 0.28	0.3745	0.2642 + 0.1103	101.115	130	−28.885	834.3432	8.2514
8.50 up to 9.50	0.28 up to 1.27	0.2877	0.3980 − 0.1103	77.679	68	9.679	93.6830	1.2060
9.50 or more	1.27 or more	0.1020	0.5000 − 0.3980	27.54	28	−0.46	0.2116	0.0077
Total		1.0000		270	270	0		30.874

Since 30.874 is greater than 7.779, we reject the null hypothesis; wages do not follow a normal distribution.

31.

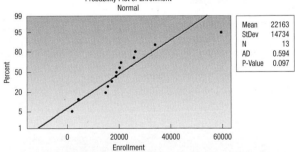

The p-value (0.097) is greater than 0.05. Do not reject the null hypothesis. The data could be normally distributed.

33. H_0: Gender and attitude toward the deficit are not related.
H_1: Gender and attitude toward the deficit are related.
Reject H_0 if $\chi^2 > 5.991$.

$$\chi^2 = \frac{(244 - 292.41)^2}{292.41} + \frac{(194 - 164.05)^2}{164.05}$$
$$+ \frac{(68 - 49.53)^2}{49.53} + \frac{(305 - 256.59)^2}{256.59}$$
$$+ \frac{(114 - 143.95)^2}{143.95} + \frac{(25 - 43.47)^2}{43.47} = 43.578$$

Since $43.578 > 5.991$, you reject H_0. A person's position on the deficit is influenced by his or her gender.

35. H_0: Whether a claim is filed and age are not related.
H_1: Whether a claim is filed and age are related.
Reject H_0 if $\chi^2 > 7.815$.

$$\chi^2 = \frac{(170 - 203.33)^2}{203.33} + \cdots + \frac{(24 - 35.67)^2}{35.67} = 53.639$$

Reject H_0. Age is related to whether a claim is filed.

37. H_0: $\pi_{BL} = \pi_O = .23$, $\pi_Y = \pi_G = .15$, $\pi_{BR} = \pi_R = .12$. H_1: The proportions are not as given. Reject H_0 if $\chi^2 > 15.086$.

Color	f_o	f_e	$(f_o - f_e)^2/f_e$
Blue	12	16.56	1.256
Brown	14	8.64	3.325
Yellow	13	10.80	0.448
Red	14	8.64	3.325
Orange	7	16.56	5.519
Green	12	10.80	0.133
Total	72		14.006

Do not reject H_0. The color distribution agrees with the manufacturer's information.

39. a. H_0: Payroll and winning are not related.
H_1: Payroll and winning are related.
Reject H_0 if $\chi^2 > 3.84$.

	Payroll		
Winning	Lower Half	Top Half	Total
No	8	6	14
Yes	7	9	16
Total	15	15	

$$\chi^2 = \frac{(8-7)^2}{7} + \frac{(6-7)^2}{7} + \frac{(7-8)^2}{8} + \frac{(9-8)^2}{8} = 0.5357$$

Do not reject H_0. Conclude that payroll and winning may not be related.

b.

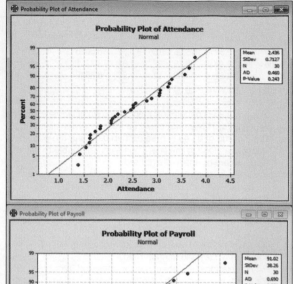

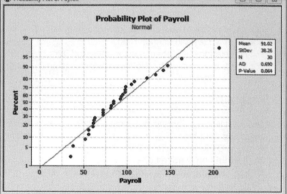

The attendance p-value is 0.243, which is greater than 0.05. Do not reject the null hypothesis. Attendance could be normally distributed. The payroll p-value is 0.064, which is greater than 0.05. Do not reject the null hypothesis. Payroll could be normally distributed.

Appendix C

Solutions to Practice Tests

PRACTICE TEST—CHAPTER 1
Part I
1. Statistics
2. Descriptive statistics
3. Statistical inference
4. Sample
5. Population
6. Nominal
7. Ratio
8. Ordinal
9. Interval
10. Discrete
11. Nominal
12. Nominal

Part II
1. a. 11.1
   b. About 3 to 1
   c. 65
2. a. Ordinal
   b. 67.7%

PRACTICE TEST—CHAPTER 2
Part I
1. Frequency table
2. Frequency distribution
3. Bar chart
4. Pie chart
5. Histogram or frequency polygon
6. 7
7. Class interval
8. Midpoint
9. Total number of observations
10. Upper class limits

Part II
1. a. $30
   b. 105
   c. 52
   d. .19
   e. $165
   f. $120, $330
   g.

Selling Price of Homes in Warren, PA

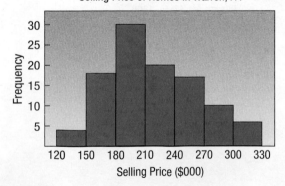

Selling Price of Homes in Warren, PA

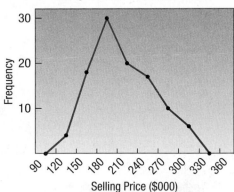

PRACTICE TEST—CHAPTER 3
Part I
1. Parameter
2. Statistic
3. Zero
4. Median
5. 50%
6. Mode
7. Range
8. Variance
9. Variance
10. Never
11. Median
12. Normal rule or empirical rule

Part II
1. a. $\bar{X} = \dfrac{560}{8} = 70$
   b. Median = 71.5
   c. Range = $80 - 52 = 28$
   d. $s = \sqrt{\dfrac{610.0}{8 - 1}} = 9.335$

2. $\bar{X}_w = \dfrac{200(\$36) + 300(\$40) + 500(\$50)}{200 + 300 + 500} = \$44.20$

3. $-0.88 \pm 2(1.41)$
   -0.88 ± 2.82
   $-3.70, 1.94$

PRACTICE TEST—CHAPTER 4
Part I
1. Dot plot
2. Box plot
3. Scatter diagram
4. Contingency table
5. Quartile
6. Percentile
7. Skewness
8. First quartile
9. Inter quartile range

585

Part II

1. a.

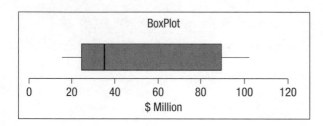

DotPlot

$ Million

b. $L_{50} = (11 + 1)\dfrac{50}{100} = 6$

median = 35

c. $L_{25} = (11 + 1)\dfrac{25}{100} = 3$

$Q_1 = 23$

d. $L_{75} = (11 + 1)\dfrac{75}{100} = 9$

$Q_3 = 91$

BoxPlot

$ Million

2. a. $P(H) = \dfrac{144}{449} = 0.32$

b. $P(H \mid < 30) = \dfrac{21}{89} = 0.24$

c. $P(H \mid > 60) = \dfrac{75}{203} = 0.37.$ Age is related to high blood pressure, because $P(H \mid > 60)$ is greater than $P(H \mid < 30)$.

PRACTICE TEST—CHAPTER 5
Part I

1. Probability
2. Experiment
3. Event
4. Relative frequency
5. Subjective
6. Classical
7. Mutually exclusive
8. Exhaustive
9. Mutually exclusive
10. Complement rule
11. Joint probability
12. Independent

Part II

1. a. $P(\text{Both}) = P(B_1) \cdot P(B_2 \mid B_1)$

$= \left(\dfrac{5}{20}\right)\left(\dfrac{4}{19}\right) = .0526$

b. $P(\text{at least 1}) = 1 - P(\text{neither})$

$= 1 - \left(\dfrac{15}{20}\right)\left(\dfrac{14}{19}\right) = 1 - .5526 = .4474$

2. $P(\text{At least 1}) = P(\text{Jogs}) + P(\text{Bike}) - P(\text{Both})$

$= .30 + .20 - 12 = .38$

3. $X = 5! = 120$

PRACTICE TEST—CHAPTER 6
Part I

1. Probability distribution
2. Probability
3. One
4. Mean
5. Two
6. Never
7. Equal
8. π
9. .075
10. .183

Part II

1. a. Binomial

b. $P(x = 1) = {}_{16}C_1(.15)^1(.85)^{15} = (16)(.15)(.0874) = .210$

c. $P(x \geq 1) = 1 - P(x = 0) = 1 - {}_{16}C_0(.15)^0(.85)^{16} = .9257$

2. a. Poisson

b. $P(x = 3) = \dfrac{3^3 e^{-3}}{3!} = \dfrac{27}{(6)(20.0855)} = .224$

c. $P(x = 0) = \dfrac{3^0 e^{-3}}{0!} = .050$

d. $P(x \geq 1) = 1 - P(x = 0) = 1 - .050 = .950$

3.

Exemptions x	Probability $P(x)$	$X \cdot P(x)$	$(x-2.2)^2 \cdot P(x)$
1	0.2	0.2	0.288
2	0.5	1	0.02
3	0.2	0.6	0.128
4	0.1	0.4	0.324
		2.2	0.76

a. $\mu = 1(.2) + 2(.5) + 3(.2) + 4(.1) = 2.2$

b. $\sigma^2 = (1 - 2.2)^2(.2) + \cdots + (4 - 2.2)^2(.1) = 0.76$

PRACTICE TEST—CHAPTER 7
Part I

1. One
2. Infinite
3. Discrete
4. Always equal
5. Infinite
6. One
7. Any of these values
8. .2764
9. .9396
10. .0450

Part II

1. a. $z = \dfrac{2000 - 1600}{850} = .47$

$P(0 \leq z < .47) = .1808$

b. $z = \dfrac{900 - 1600}{850} = -0.82$

$P(-0.82 \leq z \leq .47) = .2939 + .1808 = .4747$

c. $z = \dfrac{1800 - 1600}{850} = 0.24$

$P(0.24 \leq z \leq .47) = .1808 - .0948 = -.0860$

d. $1.65 = \dfrac{X - 1600}{850}$

$X = 1600 + 1.65(850) = \$3002.50$

PRACTICE TEST—CHAPTER 8
Part I
1. Random sample
2. No size restriction
3. Strata
4. Sampling error
5. Sampling distribution of sample means
6. 120
7. Standard error of the mean
8. Always equal
9. Decrease
10. Normal distribution

Part II
1. $z = \dfrac{11 - 12.2}{2.3/\sqrt{12}} = -1.81$

   $P(z < -1.81) = .5000 - .4649 = .0351$

PRACTICE TEST—CHAPTER 9
Part I
1. Point estimate
2. Confidence interval
3. Narrower
4. Proportion
5. 95
6. Standard deviation
7. Binomial
8. z distribution
9. Population median
10. Population mean

Part II
1. **a.** Unknown
   b. 9.3 years
   c. $s_{\bar{x}} = \dfrac{2.0}{\sqrt{26}} = 0.392$
   d. $9.3 \pm (1.708)\dfrac{2.0}{\sqrt{26}}$

   9.3 ± 0.67
   $(8.63, 9.97)$

2. $n = (.27)(.73)\left(\dfrac{2.326}{.02}\right)^2 = 2.666$

3. $.64 \pm 1.96\sqrt{\dfrac{.64(.36)}{100}}$

   $.64 \pm .094$
   $[.546, .734]$

PRACTICE TEST—CHAPTER 10
Part I
1. Null hypothesis
2. Accept
3. Significant level
4. Test statistic
5. Critical value
6. Two
7. Standard deviation (or variance)
8. p-value
9. Binomial
10. Five

Part II
1. $H_0{:}\mu \le 90$, $H_1{:}\mu > 90$
   $df = 18 - 1 = 17$
   Reject H_0 if $t > 2.567$
   $t = \dfrac{96 - 90}{12/\sqrt{18}} = 2.121$

Do not reject H_0. We cannot conclude that the mean time in the park is more than 90 minutes.
2. $H_0{:}\mu \le 9.75$ $H_1{:}\mu > 9.75$
   Reject H_0 if $z > 1.645$
   note σ is known, so z is used and we assume a .05 significance level.
   $z = \dfrac{9.85 - 9.75}{0.27/\sqrt{25}} = 1.852$
   Reject H_0. The mean weight is more than 9.75 ounces.
3. $H_0{:}\pi \ge 0.67$, $H_1{:}\pi < 0.67$
   Reject H_0 if $z < -1.645$.
   $z = \dfrac{\dfrac{180}{300} - 0.67}{\sqrt{\dfrac{0.67(1 - 0.67)}{300}}} = -2.578$
   Reject H_0. Less than .67 of the couples seek their mate's approval.

PRACTICE TEST—CHAPTER 11
Part I
1. Zero
2. z
3. Proportions
4. Population standard deviation
5. Difference
6. t distribution
7. $n - 2$
8. Paired
9. Independent
10. Dependent sample

Part II
1. $H_0{:}\mu_y = \mu_h$; $H_1{:}\mu_y \ne \mu_h$
   $df = 14 + 12 - 2 = 24$
   Reject H_0 if $t < -2.064$ or $t > 2.064$
   $s_p^2 = \dfrac{(14 - 1)30^2 + (12 - 1)(40)^2}{14 + 12 - 2} = 1220.83$
   $t = \dfrac{837 - 797}{\sqrt{1220.83\left(\dfrac{1}{14} + \dfrac{1}{12}\right)}} = \dfrac{40.0}{13.7455} = 2.910$

   Reject H_0. There is a difference in the mean miles traveled.
2. $H_0{:}\pi_E = \pi_T$ $H_1{:}\pi_E \ne \pi_T$
   Reject H_0 if $z < -1.96$ or $z > 1.96$
   $P_C = \dfrac{128 + 149}{300 + 400} = \dfrac{277}{700} = .396$
   $z = \dfrac{\dfrac{128}{300} - \dfrac{149}{400}}{\sqrt{\dfrac{.396(1 - .396)}{300} + \dfrac{.396(1 - .396)}{400}}} = \dfrac{.054}{.037} = 1.459$

   Do not reject H_0. There is no difference on the proportion that liked the soap in the two cities.

PRACTICE TEST—CHAPTER 12
Part I
1. F distribution
2. Positively skewed
3. Variances
4. Means
5. Population standard deviations
6. Error or Residual
7. Equal
8. Degrees of freedom
9. Variances
10. Independent

Part II

1. $H_0: \sigma_h^2 = \sigma_y^2$; $H_1: \sigma_h^2 \neq \sigma_y^2$

   $df_y = 12 - 1 = 11$ $df_h = 14 - 1 = 13$

   Reject H_0 if $F > 2.635$.

   $F = \dfrac{(40)^2}{(30)^2} = 1.78$

   Do not reject H_0. Cannot conclude there is a difference in the variation of the miles traveled.

2. **a.** 3
   b. 21
   c. 3.55
   d. $H_0: \mu_1 = \mu_2 = \mu_3$
      H_1: not all treatment means are the same
   e. Reject H_0
   f. The treatment means are not the same.

PRACTICE TEST—CHAPTER 13
Part I

1. Scatter diagram
2. −1 and 1
3. Less than zero
4. Coefficient of determination
5. t
6. Predicted or fitted
7. Sign
8. Larger
9. Error
10. Independent

Part II

1. **a.** 25
   b. Shares of stock
   c. $\hat{Y} = 197.9229 + 24.9145X$
   d. Direct

   e. $r = \sqrt{\dfrac{152{,}399.0211}{208{,}333.1400}} = 0.855$

   f. $\hat{Y} = 197.9229 + 24.9145(10) = 447.0679$, or 447

   g. Increase almost 25
   h. $H_0: \beta \leq 0$
      $H_1: \beta > 0$
      Reject H_0 if $t > 1.71$
      $t = \dfrac{24.9145}{3.1473} = 7.916$

      Reject H_0. There is a positive relationship between years and shares.

PRACTICE TEST—CHAPTER 14
Part I

1. Independent variables
2. Least squares
3. Mean square error
4. Independent variables
5. Independent variable
6. Different from zero
7. F distribution
8. t distribution
9. Linearity
10. Correlated
11. Multicollinearity
12. Dummy variable

Part II

1. **a.** Four
   b. $\hat{Y} = 70.06 + 0.42x_1 + 0.27x_2 + 0.75x_3 + 0.42x_4$
   c. $R^2 = \dfrac{1050.8}{1134.6} = 0.926$
   d. $s_{y.1234} = \sqrt{4.19} = 2.05$
   e. $H_0: \beta_1 = \beta_2 = \beta_3 = \beta_4 = 0$
      H_1: not all $\beta_i = 0$
      Reject H_0 if $F > 2.87$.
      $F = \dfrac{262.70}{4.19} = 62.70$
      Reject H_0. Not all the regression coefficients equal zero.
   d. $H_0: \beta_i = 0$, $H_1: \beta_i \neq 0$
      Reject H_0 if $t < -2.086$ or $t > 2.086$.

$\beta_1 = 0$	$\beta_2 = 0$	$\beta_3 = 0$	$\beta_4 = 0$
$\beta_1 \neq 0$	$\beta_2 \neq 0$	$\beta_3 \neq 0$	$\beta_4 \neq 0$
$t = 2.47$	$t = 1.29$	$t = 2.50$	$t = 6.00$
Reject H_0	Do not reject H_0	Reject H_0	Reject H_0

Conclusion. Drop variable 2 and retain the others.

PRACTICE TEST—CHAPTER 15
Part I

1. Nominal
2. No assumption
3. Can have negative values
4. 2
5. 6
6. Independent
7. 4
8. The same
9. 9.488
10. Degrees of freedom

Part II

1. H_0: There is no difference between the school district and census data.
   H_1: There is a difference between the school district and census data.
   Reject H_0 if $\chi^2 > 7.815$.
   $\chi^2 = \dfrac{(120 - 130)^2}{130} + \dfrac{(40 - 40)^2}{40} + \dfrac{(30 - 20)^2}{20} + \dfrac{(10 - 10)^2}{10} = 5.77$
   Do not reject H_0. There is no difference between the census and school district data.

2. H_0: Gender and book type are independent.
   H_1: Gender and book type are related.
   Reject H_0 if $\chi^2 > 5.991$.
   $\chi^2 = \dfrac{(250 - 197.31)^2}{197.31} + \cdots + \dfrac{(200 - 187.5)^2}{187.5} = 54.842$
   Reject H_0. Men and women read different types of books.

Photo Credits

Chapter 1
Page 1: Barnes & Noble, Inc.;
Page 2: John A. Rizzo / Getty Images;
Page 5: Image Source / Picture Quest;
Page 9: Rachel Epstein / The Image Works

Chapter 2
Page 21: Courtesy Merrill Lynch; Cover
photo by Kara Phelps; Page 22: Justin
Sullivan / Getty Images; Page 23:
Photodisc / Getty Images

Chapter 3
Page 59: Andy Lyons / Getty Images;
Page 60: Digital Vision / Getty Images;
Page 62: Bloomberg via Getty Images;
Page 76: Spencer Grant / Photoedit

Chapter 4
Page 97: Randy Faris / Corbis;
Page 100: Somos / Veer / Getty Images;
Page 102: Ryan McVay / Getty Images;
Page 113: Steve Mason / Getty Images

Chapter 5
Page 126: Karin Slade / Getty Images;
Page 127: Robert Galbraith / Reuters /
Landov; Page 135: Teri Stratford;
Page 138: Tony Arruga / Corbis

Chapter 6
Page 165: JGI / Jamie Grill / Getty Images;
Page 171: Thinkstock / JupiterImages;
Page 174: Kent Gilbert / AP Photo

Chapter 7
Page 196: Barry Austin Photography /
Photodisc / Getty Images; Page 197:
C. Sherburne / PhotoLink / Getty Images;
Page 213: JupiterImages / Getty Images

Chapter 8
Page 223: JB Reed / Landov;
Page 225: David Epperson / Getty Images

Chapter 9
Page 256: Jack Hollingsworth / Photodisc /
Getty Images; Page 258: © Corbis;
All Rights Reserved; Page 261: Del Monte
Corporation; Page 271: PhotoLink / Getty
Images; Page 274: Rich Pedroncelli /
AP Photo

Chapter 10
Page 289: Photo Source Hawaii / Alamy;
Page 290: Russell Illig / Getty Images;
Page 293: Jim Stern / Bloomberg via Getty
Images; Page 298: Robert Nicholas / Getty
Images; Page 301: Gene J. Puskar /
AP Photo

Chapter 11
Page 325: Charles O'Rear / Corbis;
Page 326: Joe Raedle / Getty Images;
Page 329: NCR Corporation;
Page 333: Mick Broughton / Alamy;
Page 342: Photodisc / Getty Images

Chapter 12
Page 360: George Nikitin / AP Photo;
Page 362: The McGraw-Hill Companies,
Inc. / John Flournoy, photographer;
Page 363: Daniel Acker / Bloomberg
News / Getty Images

Chapter 13
Page 390: Charles O'Rear / Corbis;
Page 391: Friend Giving Samples by Sue
R. Day; Page 405: Thinkstock / Superstock

Chapter 14
Page 443: Keith Brofsky / Getty Images

Chapter 15
Page 497: Najiah Feanny/Corbis;
Page 499: © Ian Dagnall / Alamy;
Page 509: Steve Mason / Getty Images;
Page 516: Scott Olson / Getty Images

Index

CHAPTER 3

• Population mean

$$\mu = \frac{\Sigma X}{N}$$ [3–1]

• Sample mean, raw data

$$\bar{X} = \frac{\Sigma X}{n}$$ [3–2]

• Weighted mean

$$\bar{X}_w = \frac{w_1 X_1 + w_2 X_2 + \cdots + w_n X_n}{w_1 + w_2 + \cdots + w_n}$$ [3–3]

• Range

Range = Maximum value − Minimum value   [3–4]

• Mean deviation

$$MD = \frac{\Sigma |X - \bar{X}|}{n}$$ [3–5]

• Population variance

$$\sigma^2 = \frac{\Sigma (X - \mu)^2}{N}$$ [3–6]

• Population standard deviation

$$\sigma = \sqrt{\frac{\Sigma (X - \mu)^2}{N}}$$ [3–7]

• Sample variance

$$s^2 = \frac{\Sigma (X - \bar{X})^2}{n - 1}$$ [3–8]

• Sample standard deviation

$$s = \sqrt{\frac{\Sigma (X - \bar{X})^2}{n - 1}}$$ [3–9]

CHAPTER 4

• Location of a percentile

$$L_p = (n + 1)\frac{P}{100}$$ [4–1]

• Pearson's coefficient of skewness

$$sk = \frac{3(\bar{X} - \text{Median})}{s}$$ [4–2]

• Software coefficient of skewness

$$sk = \frac{n}{(n - 1)(n - 2)}\left[\Sigma\left(\frac{X - \bar{X}}{s}\right)^3\right]$$ [4–3]

CHAPTER 5

• Special rule of addition

$$P(A \text{ or } B) = P(A) + P(B)$$ [5–2]

• Complement rule

$$P(A) = 1 - P(\sim A)$$ [5–3]

• General rule of addition

$$P(A \text{ or } B) = P(A) + P(B) - P(A \text{ and } B)$$ [5–4]

• Special rule of multiplication

$$P(A \text{ and } B) = P(A)P(B)$$ [5–5]

• General rule of multiplication

$$P(A \text{ and } B) = P(A)P(B|A)$$ [5–6]

• Multiplication formula

Total outcomes = $(m)(n)$ [5–7]

• Number of permutations

$$_nP_r = \frac{n!}{(n - r)!}$$ [5–8]

• Number of combinations

$$_nC_r = \frac{n!}{r!(n - r)!}$$ [5–9]

CHAPTER 6

• Mean of a probability distribution

$$\mu = \Sigma[xP(x)]$$ [6–1]

• Variance of a probability distribution

$$\sigma^2 = \Sigma[(x - \mu)^2 P(x)]$$ [6–2]

• Binomial probability distribution

$$P(x) = {}_nC_x\,\pi^x(1 - \pi)^{n - x}$$ [6–3]

• Mean of a binomial distribution

$$\mu = n\pi$$ [6–4]

• Variance of a binomial distribution

$$\sigma^2 = n\pi(1 - \pi)$$ [6–5]

• Poisson probability distribution

$$P(x) = \frac{\mu^x e^{-\mu}}{x!}$$ [6–6]

• Mean of a Poisson distribution

$$\mu = n\pi$$ [6–7]

CHAPTER 7

• Mean of a uniform distribution

$$\mu = \frac{a + b}{2}$$ [7–1]

• Standard deviation of a uniform distribution

$$\sigma = \sqrt{\frac{(b - a)^2}{12}}$$ [7–2]

• Uniform probability distribution

$$P(x) = \frac{1}{b - a}$$ [7–3]

if $a \le x \le b$ and 0 elsewhere

• Normal probability distribution

$$P(x) = \frac{1}{\sigma\sqrt{2\pi}}\,e^{-\left[\frac{(x - \mu)^2}{2\sigma^2}\right]}$$ [7–4]

• Standard normal value

$$z = \frac{X - \mu}{\sigma}$$ [7–5]

CHAPTER 8

• Standard error of mean

$$\sigma_{\bar{X}} = \frac{\sigma}{\sqrt{n}}$$ [8–1]

• z-value, μ and σ known

$$z = \frac{\bar{X} - \mu}{\sigma/\sqrt{n}}$$ [8–2]

CHAPTER 9

• Confidence interval for μ, with σ known

$$\bar{X} \pm z\frac{\sigma}{\sqrt{n}}$$ [9–1]

• Confidence interval for μ, σ unknown

$$\bar{X} \pm t\frac{s}{\sqrt{n}}$$ [9–2]

• Sample proportion

$$p = \frac{X}{n}$$ [9–3]

• Confidence interval for proportion

$$p \pm z\sqrt{\frac{p(1 - p)}{n}}$$ [9–4]

- Sample size for estimating mean

$$n = \left(\frac{z\sigma}{E}\right)^2 \qquad \text{[9–5]}$$

- Sample size for a proportion

$$n = \pi(1 - \pi)\left(\frac{z}{E}\right)^2 \qquad \text{[9–6]}$$

CHAPTER 10
- Testing a mean, σ known

$$z = \frac{\bar{X} - \mu}{\sigma/\sqrt{n}} \qquad \text{[10–1]}$$

- Testing a mean, σ unknown

$$t = \frac{\bar{X} - \mu}{s/\sqrt{n}} \qquad \text{[10–2]}$$

- Test of hypothesis, one proportion

$$z = \frac{p - \pi}{\sqrt{\dfrac{\pi(1 - \pi)}{n}}} \qquad \text{[10–3]}$$

CHAPTER 11
- Variance of the distribution of difference in means

$$\sigma^2_{\bar{X}_1 - \bar{X}_2} = \frac{\sigma_1^2}{n_1} + \frac{\sigma_2^2}{n_2} \qquad \text{[11–1]}$$

- Two-sample test of means, known σ

$$z = \frac{\bar{X}_1 - \bar{X}_2}{\sqrt{\dfrac{\sigma_1^2}{n_1} + \dfrac{\sigma_2^2}{n_2}}} \qquad \text{[11–2]}$$

- Two-sample test of proportions

$$z = \frac{p_1 - p_2}{\sqrt{\dfrac{p_c(1 - p_c)}{n_1} + \dfrac{p_c(1 - p_c)}{n_2}}} \qquad \text{[11–3]}$$

- Pooled proportion

$$p_c = \frac{X_1 + X_2}{n_1 + n_2} \qquad \text{[11–4]}$$

- Pooled variance

$$s_p^2 = \frac{(n_1 - 1) s_1^2 + (n_2 - 1) s_2^2}{n_1 + n_2 - 2} \qquad \text{[11–5]}$$

- Two-sample test of means, unknown but equal σ

$$t = \frac{\bar{X}_1 - \bar{X}_2}{\sqrt{s_p^2\left(\dfrac{1}{n_1} + \dfrac{1}{n_2}\right)}} \qquad \text{[11–6]}$$

- Paired t test

$$t = \frac{\bar{d}}{s_d/\sqrt{n}} \qquad \text{[11–7]}$$

CHAPTER 12
- Test for comparing two variances

$$F = \frac{s_1^2}{s_2^2} \qquad \text{[12–1]}$$

- Sum of squares, total

$$\text{SS total} = \Sigma(X - \bar{X}_G)^2 \qquad \text{[12–2]}$$

- Sum of squares, error

$$\text{SSE} = \Sigma(X - \bar{X}_c)^2 \qquad \text{[12–3]}$$

- Sum of squares, treatments

$$\text{SST} = \text{SS total} - \text{SSE} \qquad \text{[12–4]}$$

- Confidence interval for differences in treatment means

$$(\bar{X}_1 - \bar{X}_2) \pm t \sqrt{\text{MSE}\left(\frac{1}{n_1} + \frac{1}{n_2}\right)} \qquad \text{[12–5]}$$

CHAPTER 13
- Correlation coefficient

$$r = \frac{\Sigma(X - \bar{X})(Y - \bar{Y})}{(n - 1) s_x s_y} \qquad \text{[13–1]}$$

- Test for significant correlation

$$t = \frac{r\sqrt{n - 2}}{\sqrt{1 - r^2}} \qquad \text{[13–2]}$$

- Linear regression equation

$$\hat{Y} = a + bX \qquad \text{[13–3]}$$

- Slope of the regression line

$$b = r\frac{s_y}{s_x} \qquad \text{[13–4]}$$

- Intercept of the regression line

$$a = \bar{Y} - b\bar{X} \qquad \text{[13–5]}$$

- Test for a zero slope

$$t = \frac{b - 0}{s_b} \qquad \text{[13–6]}$$

- Standard error of estimate

$$s_{y \cdot x} = \sqrt{\frac{\Sigma(Y - \hat{Y})^2}{n - 2}} \qquad \text{[13–7]}$$

- Coefficient of determination

$$r^2 = \frac{\text{SSR}}{\text{SS total}} = 1 - \frac{\text{SSE}}{\text{SS total}} \qquad \text{[13–8]}$$

- Standard error of estimate

$$s_{y \cdot x} = \sqrt{\frac{\text{SSE}}{n - 2}} \qquad \text{[13–9]}$$

- Confidence interval

$$\hat{Y} \pm t(s_{y \cdot x}) \sqrt{\frac{1}{n} + \frac{(X - \bar{X})^2}{\Sigma(X - \bar{X})^2}} \qquad \text{[13–10]}$$

- Prediction interval

$$\hat{Y} \pm t(s_{y \cdot x}) \sqrt{1 + \frac{1}{n} + \frac{(X - \bar{X})^2}{\Sigma(X - \bar{X})^2}} \qquad \text{[13–11]}$$

CHAPTER 14
- Multiple regression equation

$$\hat{Y} = a + b_1X_1 + b_2X_2 + \cdots + b_kX_k \qquad \text{[14–1]}$$

- Multiple standard error of estimate

$$s_{Y \cdot 123 \ldots k} = \sqrt{\frac{\Sigma(Y - \hat{Y})^2}{n - (k + 1)}} \qquad \text{[14–2]}$$

- Coefficient of multiple determination

$$R^2 = \frac{\text{SSR}}{\text{SS total}} \qquad \text{[14–3]}$$

- Adjusted coefficient of determination

$$R_{adj}^2 = 1 - \frac{\dfrac{\text{SSE}}{n - (k + 1)}}{\dfrac{\text{SS total}}{n - 1}} \qquad \text{[14–4]}$$

- Global test of hypothesis

$$F = \frac{\text{SSR}/k}{\text{SSE}/[n - (k + 1)]} \qquad \text{[14–5]}$$

- Testing for a particular regression coefficient

$$t = \frac{b_i - 0}{s_{b_i}} \qquad \text{[14–6]}$$

- Variance inflation factor

$$VIF = \frac{1}{1 - R_j^2} \qquad \text{[14–7]}$$

CHAPTER 15
- Chi-square test statistic

$$\chi^2 = \Sigma\left[\frac{(f_o - f_e)^2}{f_e}\right] \qquad \text{[15–1]}$$

- Expected frequency

$$f_e = \frac{(\text{Row total})(\text{Column total})}{\text{Grand total}} \qquad \text{[15–2]}$$